INTELLIGENCE COMMUNITY
LEGAL REFERENCE BOOK

D1527760

OFFICE OF THE DIRECTOR OF NATIONAL INTELLIGENCE
OFFICE OF GENERAL COUNSEL

WINTER 2012

For sale by the Superintendent of Documents, U.S. Government Printing Office
Internet: bookstore.gpo.gov Phone: toll free (866) 512-1800; DC area (202) 512-1800
Fax: (202) 512-2104 Mail: Stop IDCC, Washington, DC 20402-0001

ISBN 978-0-16-090176-8

INTRODUCTION

On behalf of the Director of National Intelligence, I am pleased to make available the updated Winter 2012 Intelligence Community Legal Reference Book. We have expanded and updated the Reference Book to reflect legal developments since the previous edition was published in 2009 and in response to comments received from the Intelligence Community to that edition. Additionally, we are pleased to announce there will be an online version coming soon, which will offer a searchable version of the book and additional reference materials. We encourage you to use the resource once available at www.dni.gov/ogc.

The Intelligence Community draws much of its authority and guidance from the body of law contained in this collection. We hope this proves to be a useful resource to professionals across the federal government.

This new edition is the result of many hours of hard work. I would like to extend my thanks to those across the Community who assisted the Office of General Counsel in recommending and preparing the authorities contained herein. I hope you find this book a valuable addition to your library and a useful tool as you carry out your vital mission.

Robert S. Litt
General Counsel
Winter 2012

ABOUT THIS BOOK

The documents presented in this book have been updated to incorporate all amendments made since the Summer 2009 version through January 3, 2012, at which point the documents were, where possible, verified against the United States Code maintained by The Library of Congress and Westlaw. The text of these documents should be cited as "as amended."

All documents in this book are UNCLASSIFIED.

This compilation was a significant effort and required many judgments concerning what text to include and how to organize the book. We welcome your thoughts for improving future versions.

TABLE OF CONTENTS

* Selected provisions of these documents are presented in this book.

THE CONSTITUTION OF THE UNITED STATES OF AMERICA

PREAMBLE

We the People of the United States, in Order to form a more perfect Union, establish Justice, insure domestic Tranquillity, provide for the common defense, promote the general Welfare, and secure the Blessings of Liberty to ourselves and our Posterity, do ordain and establish this Constitution for the United States of America.

ARTICLE. I.

SECTION 1.

All legislative Powers herein granted shall be vested in a Congress of the United States, which shall consist of a Senate and House of Representatives.

SECTION 2.

The House of Representatives shall be composed of Members chosen every second Year by the People of the several States, and the Electors in each State shall have the Qualifications requisite for Electors of the most numerous Branch of the State Legislature.

No Person shall be a Representative who shall not have attained to the age of twenty five Years, and been seven Years a Citizen of the United States, and who shall not, when elected, be an Inhabitant of that State in which he shall be chosen.

Representatives and direct Taxes shall be apportioned among the several States which may be included within this Union, according to their respective Numbers, which shall be determined by adding to the whole Number of free Persons, including those bound to Service for a Term of Years, and excluding Indians not taxed, three fifths of all other Persons. The actual Enumeration shall be made within three Years after the first Meeting of the Congress of the United States, and within every subsequent Term of ten Years, in such Manner as they shall by Law direct. The Number of Representatives shall not exceed one for every thirty Thousand, but each State shall have at Least one Representative; and until such enumeration shall be made, the State of New Hampshire shall be entitled to chuse three, Massachusetts eight, Rhode-Island and Providence Plantations one, Connecticut five, New-York six, New Jersey four, Pennsylvania eight, Delaware one, Maryland six, Virginia ten, North Carolina five, South Carolina five, and Georgia three.

When vacancies happen in the Representation from any State, the Executive Authority thereof shall issue Writs of Election to fill such Vacancies.

The House of Representatives shall chuse their Speaker and other Officers; and shall have the sole Power of Impeachment.

SECTION 3.

The Senate of the United States shall be composed of two Senators from each State, chosen by the Legislature thereof, for six Years; and each Senator shall have one Vote.

Immediately after they shall be assembled in Consequence of the first Election, they shall be divided as equally as may be into three Classes. The Seats of the Senators of the first Class shall be vacated at the Expiration of the second Year, of the second Class at the Expiration of the fourth Year, and of the third Class at the Expiration of the sixth Year, so that one third may be chosen every second Year; and if Vacancies happen by Resignation, or otherwise, during the Recess of the Legislature of any State, the Executive thereof may make temporary Appointments until the next Meeting of the Legislature, which shall then fill such Vacancies.

No Person shall be a Senator who shall not have attained to the Age of thirty Years, and been nine Years a Citizen of the United States, and who shall not, when elected, be an Inhabitant of that State for which he shall be chosen.

The Vice President of the United States shall be President of the Senate but shall have no Vote, unless they be equally divided.

The Senate shall chuse their other Officers, and also a President pro tempore, in the Absence of the Vice President, or when he shall exercise the Office of President of the United States.

The Senate shall have the sole Power to try all Impeachments. When sitting for that Purpose, they shall be on Oath or Affirmation. When the President of the United States is tried the Chief Justice shall preside: And no Person shall be convicted without the Concurrence of two thirds of the Members present.

Judgment in Cases of Impeachment shall not extend further than to removal from Office, and disqualification to hold and enjoy any Office of honor, Trust or Profit under the United States: but the Party convicted shall nevertheless be liable and subject to Indictment, Trial, Judgment and Punishment, according to Law.

SECTION 4.

The Times, Places and Manner of holding Elections for Senators and Representatives, shall be prescribed in each State by the Legislature thereof; but the Congress may at any time by Law make or alter such Regulations, except as to the Places of chusing Senators.

The Congress shall assemble at least once in every Year, and such Meeting shall be on the first Monday in December, unless they shall by Law appoint a different Day.

SECTION 5.

Each House shall be the Judge of the Elections, Returns and Qualifications of its own Members, and a Majority of each shall constitute a Quorum to do Business; but a smaller Number may adjourn from day to day, and may be authorized to compel the Attendance of absent Members, in such Manner, and under such Penalties as each House may provide.

Each House may determine the Rules of its Proceedings, punish its Members for disorderly Behaviour, and, with the Concurrence of two thirds, expel a Member.

Each House shall keep a Journal of its Proceedings, and from time to time publish the same, excepting such Parts as may in their Judgment require Secrecy; and the Yeas and Nays of the Members of either House on any question shall, at the Desire of one fifth of those Present, be entered on the Journal.

Neither House, during the Session of Congress, shall, without the Consent of the other, adjourn for more than three days, nor to any other Place than that in which the two Houses shall be sitting.

SECTION 6.

The Senators and Representatives shall receive a Compensation for their Services, to be ascertained by Law, and paid out of the Treasury of the United States. They shall in all Cases, except Treason, Felony and Breach of the Peace, be privileged from Arrest during their Attendance at the Session of their respective Houses, and in going to and returning from the same; and for any Speech or Debate in either House, they shall not be questioned in any other Place.

No Senator or Representative shall, during the Time for which he was elected, be appointed to any civil Office under the Authority of the United States, which shall have been created, or the Emoluments whereof shall have been encreased during such time; and no Person holding any Office under the United States, shall be a Member of either House during his Continuance in Office.

SECTION 7.

All Bills for raising Revenue shall originate in the House of Representatives; but the Senate may propose or concur with amendments as on other Bills.

Every Bill which shall have passed the House of Representatives and the Senate, shall, before it become a law, be presented to the President of the United States: If he approve he shall sign it, but if not he shall return it, with his Objections to that House in which it shall have originated, who shall enter the Objections at large on their Journal, and proceed to reconsider it. If after such Reconsideration two thirds of that House shall agree to pass the Bill, it shall be sent, together with the Objections, to the other House, by which it shall likewise be reconsidered, and if approved by two thirds of that House, it shall become a Law. But in all such Cases the Votes of both Houses shall be determined by Yeas and Nays, and the Names of the Persons voting for and against the Bill shall be entered on the Journal of each House respectively. If any Bill shall not be returned by the President within ten Days (Sundays excepted) after it shall have been presented to him, the Same shall be a Law, in like Manner as if he had signed it, unless the Congress by their Adjournment prevent its Return, in which Case it shall not be a Law

Every Order, Resolution, or Vote to which the Concurrence of the Senate and House of Representatives may be necessary (except on a question of Adjournment) shall be presented to the President of the United States; and before the Same shall take Effect, shall be approved by him, or being disapproved by him, shall be repassed by two thirds of the Senate and House of Representatives, according to the Rules and Limitations prescribed in the Case of a Bill.

SECTION 8.

The Congress shall have Power To lay and collect Taxes, Duties, Imposts and Excises, to pay the Debts and provide for the common Defence and general Welfare of the United States; but all Duties, Imposts and Excises shall be uniform throughout the United States;

To borrow Money on the credit of the United States;

To regulate Commerce with foreign Nations, and among the several States, and with the Indian Tribes;

To establish an uniform Rule of Naturalization, and uniform Laws on the subject of Bankruptcies throughout the United States;

To coin Money, regulate the Value thereof, and of foreign Coin, and fix the Standard of Weights and Measures;

To provide for the Punishment of counterfeiting the Securities and current Coin of the United States;

To establish Post Offices and post Roads;

To promote the Progress of Science and useful Arts, by securing for limited Times to Authors and Inventors the exclusive Right to their respective Writings and Discoveries;

To constitute Tribunals inferior to the supreme Court;

To define and punish Piracies and Felonies committed on the high Seas, and Offences against the Law of Nations;

To declare War, grant Letters of Marque and Reprisal, and make Rules concerning Captures on Land and Water;

To raise and support Armies, but no Appropriation of Money to that Use shall be for a longer Term than two Years;

To provide and maintain a Navy;

To make Rules for the Government and Regulation of the land and naval Forces;

To provide for calling forth the Militia to execute the Laws of the Union, suppress Insurrections and repeal Invasions;

To provide for organizing, arming, and disciplining, the Militia, and for governing such Part of them as may be employed in the Service of the United States, reserving to the States respectively, the Appointment of the Officers, and the Authority of training the Militia according to the discipline prescribed by Congress;

To exercise exclusive Legislation in all Cases whatsoever, over such District (not exceeding ten Miles square) as may, by Cession of Particular States, and the Acceptance of Congress, become the Seat of the Government of the United States, and to exercise like Authority over all Places purchased by the Consent of the Legislature of the State in which the Same shall be, for the Erection of Forts, Magazines, Arsenals, dock-Yards and other needful Buildings;—And

To make all Laws which shall be necessary and proper for carrying into Execution the foregoing Powers and all other Powers vested by this Constitution in the Government of the United States, or in any Department or Officer thereof.

SECTION 9.

The Migration or Importation of such Persons as any of the States now existing shall think proper to admit, shall not be prohibited by the Congress prior to the Year one thousand eight hundred and eight, but a Tax or duty may be imposed on such Importation, not exceeding ten dollars for each Person.

The Privilege of the Writ of Habeas Corpus shall not be suspended, unless when in Cases or Rebellion or Invasion the public Safety may require it.

No Bill of Attainder or ex post facto Law shall be passed.

No Capitation, or other direct, Tax shall be laid, unless in Proportion to the Census of Enumeration herein before directed to be taken.

No Tax or Duty shall be laid on Articles exported from any State.

No Preference shall be given by any Regulation of Commerce or Revenue to the Ports of one State over those of another: nor shall Vessels bound to, or from, one State, be obliged to enter, clear or pay Duties in another.

No Money shall be drawn from the Treasury, but in Consequence of Appropriations made by Law; and a regular Statement and Account of the Receipts and Expenditures of all public Money shall be published from time to time.

No Title of Nobility shall be granted by the United States: And no Person holding any Office of Profit or Trust under them, shall, without the Consent of the Congress, accept of any present, Emolument, Office, or Title, of any kind whatever, from any King, Prince or foreign State.

SECTION 10.

No State shall enter into any Treaty, Alliance, or Confederation; grant Letters of Marque and Reprisal; coin Money; emit Bills of Credit; make any Thing but gold and silver Coin a Tender in Payment of Debts; pass any Bill of Attainder, ex post facto Law, or Law impairing the Obligation of Contracts, or grant any Title of Nobility.

No State shall, without the Consent of the Congress, lay any Imposts or Duties on Imports or Exports, except what may be absolutely necessary for executing it's inspection Laws: and the net Produce of all Duties and Imposts, laid by any State on Imports or Exports, shall be for the Use of the Treasury of the United States; and all such Laws shall be subject to the Revision and Controul of the Congress.

No State shall, without the Consent of Congress, lay any Duty of Tonnage, keep Troops, or Ships of War in time of Peace, enter into any Agreement or Compact with another State, or with a foreign Power, or engage in War, unless actually invaded, or in such imminent Danger as will not admit of delay.

ARTICLE. II.

SECTION 1.

The executive Power shall be vested in a President of the United States of America. He shall hold his Office during the Term of four Years, and, together with the Vice President, chosen for the same Term, be elected, as follows:

Each State shall appoint, in such Manner as the Legislature thereof may direct, a Number of Electors, equal to the whole Number of Senators and Representatives to which the State may be entitled in the Congress: but no Senator or Representative, or Person holding an Office of Trust or Profit under the United States, shall be appointed an Elector.

The Electors shall meet in their respective States, and vote by Ballot for two Persons, of whom one at least shall not be an Inhabitant of the same State with themselves. And they shall make a List of all the Persons voted for, and of the Number of Votes for each; which List they shall sign and certify, and transmit sealed to the Seat of the Government of the United States, directed to the President of the Senate. The President of the Senate shall, in the Presence of the Senate and House of Representatives, open all the Certificates, and the Votes shall then be counted. The Person having the greatest Number of Votes shall be the President, if such Number be a Majority of the whole Number of Electors appointed; and if there be more than one who have such Majority, and have an equal Number of Votes, then the House of Representatives shall immediately chuse by Ballot one of them for President; and if no Person have a Majority, then from the five highest on the List the said House shall in like Manner chuse the President. But in chusing the President, the Votes shall be taken by States, the Representatives from each State having one Vote; a quorum for this Purpose shall consist of a Member or Members from two thirds of the States, and a Majority of all the States shall be necessary to a Choice. In every Case, after the Choice of the President, the Person having the greatest Number of Votes of the Electors shall be the Vice President. But if there should remain two or more who have equal Votes, the Senate shall chuse from them by Ballot the Vice President.

The Congress may determine the Time of chusing the Electors, and the Day on which they shall give their Votes; which Day shall be the same throughout the United States.

No Person except a natural born Citizen, or a Citizen of the United States, at the time of the Adoption of this Constitution, shall be eligible to the Office of President; neither shall any person be eligible to that Office who shall not have attained to the Age of thirty five Years, and been fourteen Years a Resident within the United States.

In Case of the Removal of the President from Office, or of his Death, Resignation, or Inability to discharge the Powers and Duties of the said Office, the Same shall devolve on the Vice President, and the Congress may by Law provide for the Case of Removal, Death, Resignation or Inability, both of the President and Vice President, declaring what Officer shall then act as President, and such Officer shall act accordingly, until the Disability be removed, or a President shall be elected.

The President shall, at stated Times, receive for his Services, a Compensation, which shall neither be encreased nor diminished during the Period for which he shall have been elected, and he shall not receive within that Period any other Emolument from the United States, or any of them.

Before he enter on the Execution of his Office, he shall take the following Oath or Affirmation:—"I do solemnly swear (or affirm) that I will faithfully execute the Office of President of the United States, and will to the best of my Ability, preserve, protect and defend the Constitution of the United States."

SECTION 2.
The President shall be Commander in Chief of the Army and Navy of the United States, and of the Militia of the several States, when called into the actual Service

of the United States; he may require the Opinion, in writing, of the principal Officer in each of the executive Departments, upon any Subject relating to the Duties of their respective Offices, and he shall have Power to Grant Reprieves and Pardons for Offences against the United States, except in Cases of Impeachment.

He shall have Power, by and with the Advice and Consent of the Senate, to make Treaties, provided two thirds of the Senators present concur; and he shall nominate, and by and with the Advice and Consent of the Senate, shall appoint Ambassadors, other public Ministers and Consuls, Judges of the supreme Court, and all other Officers of the United States, whose Appointments are not herein otherwise provided for, and which shall be established by Law: but the Congress may by Law vest the Appointment of such inferior Officers, as they think proper, in the President alone, in the Courts of Law, or in the Heads of Departments.

The President shall have Power to fill up all Vacancies that may happen during the Recess of the Senate, by granting Commissions which shall expire at the End of their next Session.

SECTION 3.

He shall from time to time give to the Congress Information on the State of the Union, and recommend to their Consideration such Measures as he shall judge necessary and expedient; he may, on extraordinary Occasions, convene both Houses, or either of them, and in Case of Disagreement between them, with Respect to the Time of Adjournment, he may adjourn them to such Time as he shall think proper; he shall receive Ambassadors and other public Ministers; he shall take Care that the Laws be faithfully executed, and shall Commission all the Officers of the United States.

SECTION 4.

The President, Vice President and all Civil Officers of the United States, shall be removed from Office on Impeachment for and Conviction of, Treason, Bribery, or other high Crimes and Misdemeanors.

ARTICLE. III.

SECTION 1.

The judicial Power of the United States, shall be vested in one supreme Court, and in such inferior Courts as the Congress may from time to time ordain and establish. The Judges, both of the supreme and inferior Courts, shall hold their Offices during good Behaviour, and shall, at stated Times, receive for their Services, a Compensation, which shall not be diminished during their Continuance in Office.

SECTION 2.

The judicial Power shall extend to all Cases, in Law and Equity, arising under this Constitution, the Laws of the United States, and Treaties made, or which shall be made, under their Authority;—to all Cases affecting Ambassadors, other public ministers and Consuls;—to all Cases of admiralty and maritime Jurisdiction;—to Controversies to which the United States shall be a Party;—to Controversies between two or more States;—between a State and Citizens of another State;—between Citizens of different States;—between Citizens of the same State claiming Lands under Grants of different States, and between a State, or the Citizens thereof, and foreign States, Citizens or Subjects.

In all Cases affecting Ambassadors, other public Ministers and Consuls, and those in which a State shall be Party, the supreme Court shall have original Jurisdiction. In all the other Cases before mentioned, the supreme Court shall have appellate Jurisdiction, both as to Law and Fact, with such Exceptions, and under such Regulations as the Congress shall make.

The Trial of all Crimes, except in Cases of Impeachment, shall be by Jury; and such Trial shall be held in the State where the said Crimes shall have been committed; but when not committed within any State, the Trial shall be at such Place or Places as the Congress may by Law have directed.

SECTION 3.

Treason against the United States, shall consist only in levying War against them, or in adhering to their Enemies, giving them Aid and Comfort. No Person shall be convicted of Treason unless on the Testimony of two Witnesses to the same overt Act, or on Confession in open Court.

The Congress shall have Power to declare the Punishment of Treason, but no Attainder of Treason shall work Corruption of Blood, or Forfeiture except during the Life of the Person attainted.

ARTICLE. IV.

SECTION 1.

Full Faith and Credit shall be given in each State to the public Acts, Records, and judicial Proceedings of every other State. And the Congress may by general Laws prescribe the Manner in which such Acts, Records and Proceedings shall be proved, and the Effect thereof.

SECTION 2.

The Citizens of each State shall be entitled to all Privileges and Immunities of Citizens in the several States.

A Person charged in any State with Treason, Felony, or other Crime, who shall flee from Justice, and be found in another State, shall on Demand of the executive Authority of the State from which he fled, be delivered up, to be removed to the State having Jurisdiction of the Crime.

No Person held to Service or Labour in one State, under the Laws thereof, escaping into another, shall, in Consequence of any Law or Regulation therein, be discharged from such Service or Labour, but shall be delivered up on Claim of the Party to whom such Service or Labour may be due.

SECTION 3.

New States may be admitted by the Congress into this Union; but no new State shall be formed or erected within the Jurisdiction of any other State; nor any State be formed by the Junction of two or more States, or Parts of States, without the Consent of the Legislatures of the States concerned as well as of the Congress.

The Congress shall have Power to dispose of and make all needful Rules and Regulations respecting the Territory or other Property belonging to the United States; and nothing in this Constitution shall be so construed as to Prejudice any Claims of the United States, or of any particular State.

SECTION 4.

The United States shall guarantee to every State in this Union a Republican Form of Government, and shall protect each of them against Invasion; and on Application of the Legislature, or of the Executive (when the Legislature cannot be convened) against domestic Violence.

ARTICLE. V.

The Congress, whenever two thirds of both Houses shall deem it necessary, shall propose Amendments to this Constitution, or, on the Application of the Legislatures of two thirds of the several States, shall call a Convention for proposing Amendments, which, in either Case, shall be valid to all Intents and Purposes, as Part of this Constitution, when ratified by the Legislatures of three fourths of the several States, or by Conventions in three fourths thereof, as the one or the other Mode of Ratification may be proposed by the Congress;

Provided that no Amendment which may be made prior to the Year One thousand eight hundred and eight shall in any Manner affect the first and fourth Clauses in the Ninth Section of the first Article; and that no State, without its Consent, shall be deprived of its equal Suffrage in the Senate.

ARTICLE. VI.

All Debts contracted and Engagements entered into, before the Adoption of this Constitution, shall be as valid against the United States under this Constitution, as under the Confederation.

This Constitution, and the Laws of the United States which shall be made in Pursuance thereof; and all Treaties made, or which shall be made, under the Authority of the United States, shall be the supreme Law of the Land; and the Judges in every State shall be bound thereby, any Thing in the Constitution or Laws of any state to the Contrary notwithstanding.

The Senators and Representatives before mentioned, and the Members of the several State Legislatures, and all executive and judicial Officers, both of the United States and of the several States, shall be bound by Oath or Affirmation, to support this Constitution; but no religious Test shall ever be required as a Qualification to any Office or public Trust under the United States.

ARTICLE. VII.

The Ratification of the Conventions of nine States, shall be sufficient for the Establishment of this Constitution between the States so ratifying the same.

AMENDMENT I.

Congress shall make no law respecting an establishment of religion, or prohibiting the free exercise thereof; or abridging the freedom of speech, or of the press; or the right of the people peaceably to assemble, and to petition the Government for a redress of grievances.

AMENDMENT II.

A well regulated Militia, being necessary to the security of a free State, the right of the people to keep and bear Arms, shall not be infringed.

AMENDMENT III.

No Soldier shall, in time of peace be quartered in any house, without the consent of the Owner, nor in time of war, but in a manner to be prescribed by law.

AMENDMENT IV.

The right of the people to be secure in their persons, houses, papers, and effects, against unreasonable searches and seizures, shall not be violated, and no Warrants shall issue, but upon probable cause, supported by Oath or affirmation, and particularly describing the place to be searched, and the persons or things to be seized.

AMENDMENT V.

No person shall be held to answer for a capital, or otherwise infamous crime, unless on a presentment or indictment of a Grand Jury, except in cases arising in the land or naval forces, or in the Militia, when in actual service in time of War or public danger; nor shall any person be subject for the same offence to be twice put in jeopardy of life or limb; nor shall be compelled in any criminal case to be a witness against himself, nor be deprived of life, liberty, or property, without due process of law; nor shall private property be taken for public use, without just compensation.

AMENDMENT VI.

In all criminal prosecutions, the accused shall enjoy the right to a speedy and public trial, by an impartial jury of the State and district wherein the crime shall have been committed, which district shall have been previously ascertained by law, and to be informed of the nature and cause of the accusation; to be confronted with the witnesses against him; to have compulsory process for obtaining witnesses in his favor, and to have the Assistance of Counsel for his defence.

AMENDMENT VII.

In Suits at common law, where the value in controversy shall exceed twenty dollars, the right of trial by jury shall be preserved, and no fact tried by a jury, shall be otherwise re-examined in any Court of the United States, than according to the rules of the common law.

AMENDMENT VIII.

Excessive bail shall not be required, nor excessive fines imposed, nor cruel and unusual punishments inflicted.

AMENDMENT IX.

The enumeration in the Constitution, of certain rights, shall not be construed to deny or disparage others retained by the people.

AMENDMENT X.

The powers not delegated to the United States by the Constitution, nor prohibited by it to the States, are reserved to the States respectively, or to the people.

AMENDMENT XI.

The Judicial power of the United States shall not be construed to extend to any suit in law or equity, commenced or prosecuted against one of the United States by Citizens of another State, or by Citizens or Subjects of any Foreign State.

AMENDMENT XII.

The Electors shall meet in their respective states and vote by ballot for President and Vice-President, one of whom, at least, shall not be an inhabitant of the same state with themselves; they shall name in their ballots the person voted for as President, and in distinct ballots the person voted for as Vice- President, and they shall make distinct lists of all persons voted for as President, and of all persons voted for as Vice-President, and of the number of votes for each, which lists they shall sign and certify, and transmit sealed to the seat of the government of the United States, directed to the President of the Senate;—The President of the Senate shall, in the presence of the Senate and House of Representatives, open all the certificates and the votes shall then be counted;—The person having the greatest Number of votes for President, shall be the President, if such number be a majority of the whole number of Electors appointed; and if no person have such majority, then from the persons having the highest numbers not exceeding three on the list of those voted for as President, the House of Representatives shall choose immediately, by ballot, the President. But in choosing the President, the votes shall be taken by states, the representation from each state having one vote; a quorum for this purpose shall consist of a member or members from two-thirds of the states, and a majority of all the states shall be necessary to a choice. And if the House of Representatives shall not choose a President whenever the right of choice shall devolve upon them, before the fourth day of March next following, then the Vice- President shall act as President, as in the case of the death or other constitutional disability of the President—The person having the greatest number of votes as Vice-President, shall be the Vice-President, if such number be a majority of the whole number of Electors appointed, and if no person have a majority, then from the two highest numbers on the list, the Senate shall choose the Vice-President; a quorum for the purpose shall consist of two-thirds of the whole number of Senators, and a majority of the whole number shall be necessary to a choice. But no person constitutionally ineligible to the office of President shall be eligible to that of Vice-President of the United States.

AMENDMENT XIII.

SECTION. 1. Neither slavery nor involuntary servitude, except as a punishment for crime whereof the party shall have been duly convicted, shall exist within the United States, or any place subject to their jurisdiction.

SECTION. 2. Congress shall have power to enforce this article by appropriate legislation.

AMENDMENT XIV.

SECTION. 1. All persons born or naturalized in the United States and subject to the jurisdiction thereof, are citizens of the United States and of the State wherein they reside. No State shall make or enforce any law which shall abridge the privileges or immunities of citizens of the United States; nor shall any State deprive any person of life, liberty, or property, without due process of law; nor deny to any person within its jurisdiction the equal protection of the laws.

SECTION. 2. Representatives shall be apportioned among the several States according to their respective numbers, counting the whole number of persons in each State, excluding Indians not taxed. But when the right to vote at any election for the choice of electors for President and Vice President of the United States, Representatives in Congress, the Executive and Judicial officers of a State, or the members of the Legislature thereof, is denied to any of the male inhabitants of such State, being twenty-one years of age, and citizens of the United States, or in any way abridged, except for participation in rebellion, or other crime, the basis of representation therein shall be reduced in the proportion which the number of such male citizens shall bear to the whole number of male citizens twenty-one years of age in such State.

SECTION. 3. No person shall be a Senator or Representative in Congress, or elector of President and Vice President, or hold any office, civil or military, under the United States, or under any State, who, having previously taken an oath, as a member of Congress, or as an officer of the United States, or as a member of any State legislature, or as an executive or judicial officer of any State, to support the Constitution of the United States, shall have engaged in insurrection or rebellion against the same, or given aid or comfort to the enemies thereof. But Congress may by a vote of two-thirds of each House, remove such disability.

SECTION. 4. The validity of the public debt of the United States, authorized by law, including debts incurred for payment of pensions and bounties for services in suppressing insurrection or rebellion, shall not be questioned. But neither the United States nor any State shall assume or pay any debt or obligation incurred in aid of insurrection or rebellion against the United States, or any claim for the loss or emancipation of any slave; but all such debts, obligations and claims shall be held illegal and void.

SECTION. 5. The Congress shall have power to enforce, by appropriate legislation, the provisions of this article.

AMENDMENT XV.

SECTION. 1. The right of citizens of the United States to vote shall not be denied or abridged by the United States or by any State on account of race, color, or previous condition of servitude.

SECTION. 2. The Congress shall have power to enforce this article by appropriate legislation.

AMENDMENT XVI.

The Congress shall have power to lay and collect taxes on incomes, from whatever source derived, without apportionment among the several States, and without regard to any census or enumeration.

AMENDMENT XVII.

The Senate of the United States shall be composed of two Senators from each State, elected by the people thereof, for six years; and each Senator shall have one vote. The electors in each State shall have the qualifications requisite for electors of the most numerous branch of the State legislatures.

When vacancies happen in the representation of any State in the Senate, the executive authority of such State shall issue writs of election to fill such vacancies: Provided, That the legislature of any State may empower the executive thereof to make temporary appointments until the people fill the vacancies by election as the legislature may direct.

This amendment shall not be so construed as to affect the election or term of any Senator chosen before it becomes valid as part of the Constitution.

AMENDMENT XVIII.

SECTION. 1. After one year from the ratification of this article the manufacture, sale, or transportation of intoxicating liquors within, the importation thereof into, or the exportation thereof from the United States and all territory subject to the jurisdiction thereof for beverage purposes is hereby prohibited.

SECTION. 2. The Congress and the several States shall have concurrent power to enforce this article by appropriate legislation.

SECTION. 3. This article shall be inoperative unless it shall have been ratified as an amendment to the Constitution by the legislatures of the several States, as provided in the Constitution, within seven years from the date of the submission hereof to the States by the Congress.

AMENDMENT XIX.

The right of citizens of the United States to vote shall not be denied or abridged by the United States or by any State on account of sex. Congress shall have power to enforce this article by appropriate legislation.

AMENDMENT XX.

SECTION. 1. The terms of the President and Vice President shall end at noon on the 20th day of January, and the terms of Senators and Representatives at noon on the 3d day of January, of the years in which such terms would have ended if this article had not been ratified; and the terms of their successors shall then begin.

SECTION. 2. The Congress shall assemble at least once in every year, and such meeting shall begin at noon on the 3d day of January, unless they shall by law appoint a different day.

SECTION. 3. If, at the time fixed for the beginning of the term of the President, the President elect shall have died, the Vice President elect shall become President. If a President shall not have been chosen before the time fixed for the beginning of his term, or if the President elect shall have failed to qualify, then the Vice President elect shall act as President until a President shall have qualified; and the Congress may by law provide for the case wherein neither a President elect nor a Vice President elect shall have qualified, declaring who shall then act as President, or the manner in which one who is to act shall be selected, and such person shall act accordingly until a President or Vice President shall have qualified.

SECTION. 4. The Congress may by law provide for the case of the death of any of the persons from whom the House of Representatives may choose a President whenever the right of choice shall have devolved upon them, and for the case of the death of any of the persons from whom the Senate may choose a Vice President whenever the right of choice shall have devolved upon them.

SECTION. 5. Sections 1 and 2 shall take effect on the 15th day of October following the ratification of this article.

SECTION. 6. This article shall be inoperative unless it shall have been ratified as an amendment to the Constitution by the legislatures of three-fourths of the several States within seven years from the date of its submission.

AMENDMENT XXI.

SECTION. 1. The eighteenth article of amendment to the Constitution of the United States is hereby repealed.

SECTION. 2. The transportation or importation into any State, Territory, or possession of the United States for delivery or use therein of intoxicating liquors, in violation of the laws thereof, is hereby prohibited.

SECTION. 3. This article shall be inoperative unless it shall have been ratified as an amendment to the Constitution by conventions in the several States, as provided in the Constitution, within seven years from the date of the submission hereof to the States by the Congress.

AMENDMENT XXII.

SECTION. 1. No person shall be elected to the office of the President more than twice, and no person who has held the office of President, or acted as President, for more than two years of a term to which some other person was elected President shall be elected to the office of the President more than once. But this Article shall not apply to any person holding the office of President, when this Article was proposed by the Congress, and shall not prevent any person who may be holding the office of President, or acting as President, during the term within which this Article becomes operative from holding the office of President or acting as President during the remainder of such term.

SECTION. 2. This article shall be inoperative unless it shall have been ratified as an amendment to the Constitution by the legislatures of three-fourths of the several States within seven years from the date of its submission to the States by the Congress.

AMENDMENT XXIII.

SECTION. 1. The District constituting the seat of Government of the United States shall appoint in such manner as the Congress may direct: A number of electors of President and Vice President equal to the whole number of Senators and Representatives in Congress to which the District would be entitled if it were a State, but in no event more than the least populous State; they shall be in addition to those appointed by the States, but they shall be considered, for the purposes of the election of President and Vice President, to be electors appointed by a State; and they shall meet in the District and perform such duties as provided by the twelfth article of amendment.

SECTION. 2. The Congress shall have power to enforce this article by appropriate legislation.

AMENDMENT XXIV.

SECTION. 1. The right of citizens of the United States to vote in any primary or other election for President or Vice President, for electors for President or Vice President, or for Senator or Representative in Congress, shall not be denied or abridged by the United States or any State by reason of failure to pay any poll tax or other tax.

SECTION. 2. The Congress shall have power to enforce this article by appropriate legislation.

AMENDMENT XXV.

SECTION. 1. In case of the removal of the President from office or of his death or resignation, the Vice President shall become President.

SECTION. 2. Whenever there is a vacancy in the office of the Vice President, the President shall nominate a Vice President who shall take office upon confirmation by a majority vote of both Houses of Congress.

SECTION. 3. Whenever the President transmits to the President pro tempore of the Senate and the Speaker of the House of Representatives has written declaration that he is unable to discharge the powers and duties of his office, and until he transmits to them a written declaration to the contrary, such powers and duties shall be discharged by the Vice President as Acting President.

SECTION. 4. Whenever the Vice President and a majority of either the principal officers of the executive departments or of such other body as Congress may by law provide, transmit to the President pro tempore of the Senate and the Speaker of the House of Representatives their written declaration that the President is unable to discharge the powers and duties of his office, the Vice President shall immediately assume the powers and duties of the office as Acting President.

Thereafter, when the President transmits to the President pro tempore of the Senate and the Speaker of the House of Representatives has written declaration that no inability exists, he shall resume the powers and duties of his office unless the Vice President and a majority of either the principal officers of the executive department or of such other body as Congress may by law provide, transmit within four days to the President pro tempore of the Senate and the Speaker of the House of Representatives their written declaration that the President is unable to discharge the powers and duties of his office. Thereupon Congress shall decide the issue, assembling within forty-eight hours for that purpose if not in session. If the Congress, within twenty-one days after receipt of the latter written declaration, or, if Congress is not in session, within twenty-one days after Congress is required to assemble, determines by two-thirds vote of both Houses that the President is unable to discharge the powers and duties of his office, the Vice President shall continue to discharge the same as Acting President; otherwise, the President shall resume the powers and duties of his office.

AMENDMENT **XXVI.**

SECTION. 1. The right of citizens of the United States, who are eighteen years of age or older, to vote shall not be denied or abridged by the United States or by any State on account of age.

Section. 2. The Congress shall have power to enforce this article by appropriate legislation.

AMENDMENT **XXVII.**

No law varying the compensation for the services of the Senators and Representatives shall take effect, until an election of Representatives shall have intervened.

NATIONAL SECURITY ACT OF 1947

(Public Law 235 of July 26, 1947; 61 STAT. 496)

AN ACT To promote the national security by providing for a Secretary of Defense; for a National Military Establishment; for a Department of the Army, a Department of the Navy, and a Department of the Air Force; and for the coordination of the activities of the National Military Establishment with other departments and agencies of the Government concerned with the national security.

Be it enacted by the Senate and House of Representatives of the United States of America in Congress assembled,

SHORT TITLE

That this Act may be cited as the "National Security Act of 1947".

TABLE OF CONTENTS

TITLE VII—PROTECTION OF OPERATIONAL FILES

TITLE XI—OTHER PROVISIONS

DECLARATION OF POLICY

SEC. 2. [50 U.S.C. §401]

In enacting this legislation, it is the intent of Congress to provide a comprehensive program for the future security of the United States; to provide for the establishment of integrated policies and procedures for the departments, agencies, and functions of the Government relating to the national security; to provide a Department of Defense, including the three military Departments of the Army, the Navy (including naval aviation and the United States Marine Corps), and the Air Force under the direction, authority, and control of the Secretary of Defense; to provide that each military department shall be separately organized under its own Secretary and shall function under the direction, authority, and control of the Secretary of Defense; to provide for their unified direction under civilian control of the Secretary of Defense but not to merge these departments or services; to provide for the establishment of unified or specified combatant commands, and a clear and direct line of command to such commands; to eliminate unnecessary duplication in the Department of Defense, and particularly in the field of research and engineering by vesting its overall direction and control in the Secretary of Defense; to provide more effective, efficient, and economical administration in the Department of Defense; to provide for the unified strategic direction of the combatant forces, for their operation under unified command, and for their integration into an efficient team of land, naval, and air forces but not to establish a single Chief of Staff over the armed forces nor an overall armed forces general staff.

DEFINITIONS

SEC. 3. [50 U.S.C. §401a]

As used in this Act:

(1) The term "intelligence" includes foreign intelligence and counterintelligence.

(2) The term "foreign intelligence" means information relating to the capabilities, intentions, or activities of foreign governments or elements thereof, foreign organizations, or foreign persons, or international terrorist activities.

(3) The term "counterintelligence" means information gathered and activities conducted to protect against espionage, other intelligence activities, sabotage, or assassinations conducted by or on behalf of foreign governments or elements thereof, foreign organizations, or foreign persons, or international terrorist activities.

(4) The term "intelligence community" includes the following:

> (A) The Office of the Director of National Intelligence.
> (B) The Central Intelligence Agency.
> (C) The National Security Agency.
> (D) The Defense Intelligence Agency.
> (E) The National Geospatial-Intelligence Agency.
> (F) The National Reconnaissance Office.
> (G) Other offices within the Department of Defense for the collection of specialized national intelligence through reconnaissance programs.
> (H) The intelligence elements of the Army, the Navy, the Air Force, the Marine Corps, the Coast Guard, the Federal Bureau of Investigation, the Drug Enforcement Administration, and the Department of Energy.
> (I) The Bureau of Intelligence and Research of the Department of State.
> (J) The Office of Intelligence and Analysis of the Department of the Treasury.
> (K) The Office of Intelligence and Analysis of the Department of Homeland Security.
> (L) Such other elements of any department or agency as may be designated by the President, or designated jointly by the Director of National Intelligence and the head of the department or agency concerned, as an element of the intelligence community.

(5) The terms "national intelligence" and "intelligence related to national security" refer to all intelligence, regardless of the source from which derived and including information gathered within or outside the United States, that—

> (A) pertains, as determined consistent with any guidance issued by the President, to more than one United States Government agency; and
> (B) that involves—
>> (i) threats to the United States, its people, property, or interests;
>> (ii) the development, proliferation, or use of weapons of mass destruction; or
>> (iii) any other matter bearing on United States national or homeland security.

(6) The term "National Intelligence Program" refers to all programs, projects, and activities of the intelligence community, as well as any other programs of the intelligence community designated jointly by the Director of National Intelligence and the head of a United States department or agency or by the President. Such term does not include programs, projects, or activities of the

military departments to acquire intelligence solely for the planning and conduct of tactical military operations by United States Armed Forces.

(7) The term "congressional intelligence committees" means—

> (A) the Select Committee on Intelligence of the Senate; and
> (B) the Permanent Select Committee on Intelligence of the House of Representatives.

TITLE I—COORDINATION FOR NATIONAL SECURITY

NATIONAL SECURITY COUNCIL

SEC. 101. [50 U.S.C. §402]

(a) There is here established a council to be known as the National Security Council (thereinafter in this section referred to as the "Council"). The President of the United States shall preside over meetings of the Council: *Provided,* That in his absence he may designate a member of the Council to preside in his place. The function of the Council shall be to advise the President with respect to the integration of domestic, foreign, and military policies relating to the national security so as to enable the military services and the other departments and agencies of the Government to cooperate more effectively in matters involving the national security.

The Council shall be composed of—

> (1) the President;
> (2) the Vice President;
> (3) the Secretary of State;
> (4) the Secretary of Defense;
> (5) the Secretary of Energy;
> (6) the Director for Mutual Security;
> (7) the Chairman of the National Security Resources Board; and
> (8) the Secretaries and Under Secretaries of other executive departments and of the military departments, the Chairman of the Munitions Board, and the Chairman of the Research and Development Board, when appointed by the President by and with the advice and consent of the Senate, to serve at his pleasure.

(b) In addition to performing such other functions as the President may direct, for the purpose of more effectively coordinating the policies and functions of the departments and agencies of the Government relating to the national security, it shall, subject to the direction of the President, be the duty of the Council—

> (1) to assess and appraise the objectives, commitments, and risks of the United States in relation to our actual and potential military power, in the

interest of national security, for the purpose of making recommendations to the President in connection therewith; and

(2) to consider policies on matters of common interest to the departments and agencies of the Government concerned with the national security, and to make recommendations to the President in connection therewith.

(c) The Council shall have a staff to be headed by a civilian executive secretary who shall be appointed by the President. The executive secretary, subject to the direction of the Council, is authorized, subject to the civil-service laws and the Classification Act of 1923, as amended, to appoint and fix the compensation of such personnel as may be necessary to perform such duties as may be prescribed by the Council in connection with the performance of its functions.

(d) The Council shall, from time to time, make such recommendations, and such other reports to the President as it deems appropriate or as the President may require.

(e) The Chairman (or in his absence the Vice Chairman) of the Joint Chiefs of Staff may, in his role as principal military adviser to the National Security Council and subject to the direction of the President, attend and participate in meetings of the National Security Council.

(f) The Director of National Drug Control Policy may, in the role of the Director as principal adviser to the National Security Council on national drug control policy, and subject to the direction of the President, attend and participate in meetings of the National Security Council.

(g) The President shall establish within the National Security Council a board to be known as the "Board for Low Intensity Conflict". The principal function of the board shall be to coordinate the policies of the United States for low intensity conflict.

(h)(1) There is established within the National Security Council a committee to be known as the Committee on Foreign Intelligence (in this subsection referred to as the "Committee").

(2) The Committee shall be composed of the following:

(A) The Director of National Intelligence.

(B) The Secretary of State.

(C) The Secretary of Defense.

(D) The Assistant to the President for National Security Affairs, who shall serve as the chairperson of the Committee.

(E) Such other members as the President may designate.

(3) The function of the Committee shall be to assist the Council in its activities by—

(A) identifying the intelligence required to address the national security interests of the United States as specified by the President;

(B) establishing priorities (including funding priorities) among the programs, projects, and activities that address such interests and requirements; and

(C) establishing policies relating to the conduct of intelligence activities of the United States, including appropriate roles and missions for the elements of the intelligence community and appropriate targets of intelligence collection activities.

(4) In carrying out its function, the Committee shall—

(A) conduct an annual review of the national security interests of the United States;

(B) identify on an annual basis, and at such other times as the Council may require, the intelligence required to meet such interests and establish an order of priority for the collection and analysis of such intelligence; and

(C) conduct an annual review of the elements of the intelligence community in order to determine the success of such elements in collecting, analyzing, and disseminating the intelligence identified under subparagraph (B).

(5) The Committee shall submit each year to the Council and to the Director of National Intelligence a comprehensive report on its activities during the preceding year, including its activities under paragraphs (3) and (4).

(i)(1) There is established within the National Security Council a committee to be known as the Committee on Transnational Threats (in this subsection referred to as the "Committee").

(2) The Committee shall include the following members:

(A) The Director of National Intelligence.

(B) The Secretary of State.

(C) The Secretary of Defense.

(D) The Attorney General.

(E) The Assistant to the President for National Security Affairs, who shall serve as the chairperson of the Committee.

(F) Such other members as the President may designate.

(3) The function of the Committee shall be to coordinate and direct the activities of the United States Government relating to combating transnational threats.

(4) In carrying out its function, the Committee shall—

(A) identify transnational threats;

(B) develop strategies to enable the United States Government to respond to transnational threats identified under subparagraph (A);

(C) monitor implementation of such strategies;

(D) make recommendations as to appropriate responses to specific transnational threats;

(E) assist in the resolution of operational and policy differences among Federal departments and agencies in their responses to transnational threats;

(F) develop policies and procedures to ensure the effective sharing of information about transnational threats among Federal departments and agencies, including law enforcement agencies and the elements of the intelligence community; and

(G) develop guidelines to enhance and improve the coordination of activities of Federal law enforcement agencies and elements of the intelligence community outside the United States with respect to transnational threats.

(5) For purposes of this subsection, the term "transnational threat" means the following:

(A) Any transnational activity (including international terrorism, narcotics trafficking, the proliferation of weapons of mass destruction and the delivery systems for such weapons, and organized crime) that threatens the national security of the United States.

(B) Any individual or group that engages in an activity referred to in subparagraph (A).

(j) The Director of National Intelligence (or, in the Director's absence, the Principal Deputy Director of National Intelligence) may, in the performance of the Director's duties under this Act and subject to the direction of the President, attend and participate in meetings of the National Security Council.

(k) It is the sense of the Congress that there should be within the staff of the National Security Council a Special Adviser to the President on International Religious Freedom, whose position should be comparable to that of a director within the Executive Office of the President. The Special Adviser should serve as a resource for executive branch officials, compiling and maintaining information on the facts and circumstances of violations of religious freedom (as defined in section 3 of the International Religious Freedom Act of 1998), and making policy recommendations. The Special Adviser should serve as liaison with the Ambassador at Large for International Religious Freedom, the United States Commission on International Religious Freedom, Congress and, as advisable, religious nongovernmental organizations.

(l) PARTICIPATION OF COORDINATOR FOR THE PREVENTION OF WEAPONS OF MASS DESTRUCTION PROLIFERATION AND TERRORISM.—The United States Coordinator for the Prevention of Weapons of Mass Destruction Proliferation and Terrorism (or, in the Coordinator's absence, the Deputy United States Coordinator) may, in the performance of the Coordinator's duty as principal advisor to the President on all matters relating to the prevention of weapons of mass destruction proliferation and terrorism, and, subject to the direction of the President, attend and participate in meetings of the National Security Council and the Homeland Security Council.

JOINT INTELLIGENCE COMMUNITY COUNCIL

SEC. 101A. [50 U.S.C. §402-1]

(a) JOINT INTELLIGENCE COMMUNITY COUNCIL.—There is a Joint Intelligence Community Council.

(b) MEMBERSHIP.—The Joint Intelligence Community Council shall consist of the following:

(1) The Director of National Intelligence, who shall chair the Council.

(2) The Secretary of State.

(3) The Secretary of the Treasury.

(4) The Secretary of Defense.

(5) The Attorney General.

(6) The Secretary of Energy.

(7) The Secretary of Homeland Security.

(8) Such other officers of the United States Government as the President may designate from time to time.

(c) FUNCTIONS.—The Joint Intelligence Community Council shall assist the Director of National Intelligence in developing and implementing a joint, unified national intelligence effort to protect national security by—

(1) advising the Director on establishing requirements, developing budgets, financial management, and monitoring and evaluating the performance of the intelligence community, and on such other matters as the Director may request; and

(2) ensuring the timely execution of programs, policies, and directives established or developed by the Director.

(d) MEETINGS.—The Director of National Intelligence shall convene regular meetings of the Joint Intelligence Community Council.

(e) ADVICE AND OPINIONS OF MEMBERS OTHER THAN CHAIRMAN.—

(1) A member of the Joint Intelligence Community Council (other than the Chairman) may submit to the Chairman advice or an opinion in disagreement with, or advice or an opinion in addition to, the advice presented by the Director of National Intelligence to the President or the National Security Council, in the role of the Chairman as Chairman of the Joint Intelligence Community Council. If a member submits such advice or opinion, the Chairman shall present the advice or opinion of such member at the same time the Chairman presents the advice of the

Chairman to the President or the National Security Council, as the case may be.

(2) The Chairman shall establish procedures to ensure that the presentation of the advice of the Chairman to the President or the National Security Council is not unduly delayed by reason of the submission of the individual advice or opinion of another member of the Council.

(f) RECOMMENDATIONS TO CONGRESS.—Any member of the Joint Intelligence Community Council may make such recommendations to Congress relating to the intelligence community as such member considers appropriate.

DIRECTOR OF NATIONAL INTELLIGENCE

SEC. 102. [50 U.S.C. §403]
(a) DIRECTOR OF NATIONAL INTELLIGENCE.—

(1) There is a Director of National Intelligence who shall be appointed by the President, by and with the advice and consent of the Senate. Any individual nominated for appointment as Director of National Intelligence shall have extensive national security expertise.

(2) The Director of National Intelligence shall not be located within the Executive Office of the President.

(b) PRINCIPAL RESPONSIBILITY.—Subject to the authority, direction, and control of the President, the Director of National Intelligence shall—

(1) serve as head of the intelligence community;

(2) act as the principal adviser to the President, to the National Security Council, and the Homeland Security Council for intelligence matters related to the national security; and

(3) consistent with section 1018 of the National Security Intelligence Reform Act of 2004, oversee and direct the implementation of the National Intelligence Program.

(c) PROHIBITION ON DUAL SERVICE.—The individual serving in the position of Director of National Intelligence shall not, while so serving, also serve as the Director of the Central Intelligence Agency or as the head of any other element of the intelligence community.

RESPONSIBILITIES AND AUTHORITIES OF
THE DIRECTOR OF NATIONAL INTELLIGENCE

SEC. 102A. [50 U.S.C. §403-1]
(a) PROVISION OF INTELLIGENCE.—

(1) The Director of National Intelligence shall be responsible for ensuring that national intelligence is provided—

(A) to the President;

(B) to the heads of departments and agencies of the executive branch;

(C) to the Chairman of the Joint Chiefs of Staff and senior military commanders;

(D) to the Senate and House of Representatives and the committees thereof; and

(E) to such other persons as the Director of National Intelligence determines to be appropriate.

(2) Such national intelligence should be timely, objective, independent of political considerations, and based upon all sources available to the intelligence community and other appropriate entities.

(b) ACCESS TO INTELLIGENCE.—Unless otherwise directed by the President, the Director of National Intelligence shall have access to all national intelligence and intelligence related to the national security which is collected by any Federal department, agency, or other entity, except as otherwise provided by law or, as appropriate, under guidelines agreed upon by the Attorney General and the Director of National Intelligence.

(c) BUDGET AUTHORITIES.—

(1) With respect to budget requests and appropriations for the National Intelligence Program, the Director of National Intelligence shall—

(A) based on intelligence priorities set by the President, provide to the heads of departments containing agencies or organizations within the intelligence community, and to the heads of such agencies and organizations, guidance for developing the National Intelligence Program budget pertaining to such agencies and organizations;

(B) based on budget proposals provided to the Director of National Intelligence by the heads of agencies and organizations within the intelligence community and the heads of their respective departments and, as appropriate, after obtaining the advice of the Joint Intelligence Community Council, develop and determine an annual consolidated National Intelligence Program budget; and

(C) present such consolidated National Intelligence Program budget, together with any comments from the heads of departments containing agencies or organizations within the intelligence community, to the President for approval.

(2) In addition to the information provided under paragraph (1)(B), the heads of agencies and organizations within the intelligence community shall provide the Director of National Intelligence such other information

as the Director shall request for the purpose of determining the annual consolidated National Intelligence Program budget under that paragraph.

(3)(A) The Director of National Intelligence shall participate in the development by the Secretary of Defense of the annual budget for the Military Intelligence Program or any successor program or programs.

    (B) The Director of National Intelligence shall provide guidance for the development of the annual budget for each element of the intelligence community that is not within the National Intelligence Program.

(4) The Director of National Intelligence shall ensure the effective execution of the annual budget for intelligence and intelligence-related activities.

(5)(A) The Director of National Intelligence shall be responsible for managing appropriations for the National Intelligence Program by directing the allotment or allocation of such appropriations through the heads of the departments containing agencies or organizations within the intelligence community and the Director of the Central Intelligence Agency, with prior notice (including the provision of appropriate supporting information) to the head of the department containing an agency or organization receiving any such allocation or allotment or the Director of the Central Intelligence Agency.

    (B) Notwithstanding any other provision of law, pursuant to relevant appropriations Acts for the National Intelligence Program, the Director of the Office of Management and Budget shall exercise the authority of the Director of the Office of Management and Budget to apportion funds, at the exclusive direction of the Director of National Intelligence, for allocation to the elements of the intelligence community through the relevant host executive departments and the Central Intelligence Agency. Department comptrollers or appropriate budget execution officers shall allot, allocate, reprogram, or transfer funds appropriated for the National Intelligence Program in an expeditious manner.

    (C) The Director of National Intelligence shall monitor the implementation and execution of the National Intelligence Program by the heads of the elements of the intelligence community that manage programs and activities that are part of the National Intelligence Program, which may include audits and evaluations.

(6) Apportionment and allotment of funds under this subsection shall be subject to chapter 13 and section 1517 of title 31, United States Code,

and the Congressional Budget and Impoundment Control Act of 1974 (2 U.S.C. §621 et seq.).

(7)(A) The Director of National Intelligence shall provide a semi-annual report, beginning April 1, 2005, and ending April 1, 2007, to the President and the Congress regarding implementation of this section.

(B) The Director of National Intelligence shall report to the President and the Congress not later than 15 days after learning of any instance in which a departmental comptroller acts in a manner inconsistent with the law (including permanent statutes, authorization Acts, and appropriations Acts), or the direction of the Director of National Intelligence, in carrying out the National Intelligence Program.

(d) ROLE OF DIRECTOR OF NATIONAL INTELLIGENCE IN TRANSFER AND REPROGRAMMING OF FUNDS.—

(1)(A) No funds made available under the National Intelligence Program may be transferred or reprogrammed without the prior approval of the Director of National Intelligence, except in accordance with procedures prescribed by the Director of National Intelligence.

(B) The Secretary of Defense shall consult with the Director of National Intelligence before transferring or reprogramming funds made available under the Military Intelligence Program or any successor program or programs.

(2) Subject to the succeeding provisions of this subsection, the Director of National Intelligence may transfer or reprogram funds appropriated for a program within the National Intelligence Program—

(A) to another such program;

(B) to other departments or agencies of the United States Government for the development and fielding of systems of common concern related to the collection, processing, analysis, exploitation, and dissemination of intelligence information; or

(C) to a program funded by appropriations not within the National Intelligence Program to address critical gaps in intelligence information sharing or access capabilities.

(3) The Director of National Intelligence may only transfer or reprogram funds referred to in paragraph (1)(A)—

(A) with the approval of the Director of the Office of Management and Budget; and

(B) after consultation with the heads of departments containing agencies or organizations within the intelligence community to the extent such agencies or organizations are affected, and, in the case of the Central Intelligence Agency, after consultation with the Director of the Central Intelligence Agency.

(4) The amounts available for transfer or reprogramming in the National Intelligence Program in any given fiscal year, and the terms and conditions governing such transfers and reprogrammings, are subject to the provisions of annual appropriations Acts and this subsection.

(5)(A) A transfer or reprogramming of funds may be made under this subsection only if—

(i) the funds are being transferred to an activity that is a higher priority intelligence activity;

(ii) the transfer or reprogramming supports an emergent need, improves program effectiveness, or increases efficiency;

(iii) the transfer or reprogramming does not involve a transfer or reprogramming of funds to a Reserve for Contingencies of the Director of National Intelligence or the Reserve for Contingencies of the Central Intelligence Agency;

(iv) the transfer or reprogramming results in a cumulative transfer or reprogramming of funds out of any department or agency, as appropriate, funded in the National Intelligence Program in a single fiscal year—

(I) that is less than $150,000,000, and

(II) that is less than 5 percent of amounts available to a department or agency under the National Intelligence Program; and

(v) the transfer or reprogramming does not terminate an acquisition program.

(B) A transfer or reprogramming may be made without regard to a limitation set forth in clause (iv) or (v) of subparagraph (A) if the transfer has the concurrence of the head of the department involved or the Director of the Central Intelligence Agency (in the case of the Central Intelligence Agency). The authority to provide such concurrence may only be delegated by the head of the department involved or the Director of the Central Intelligence Agency (in the case of the Central Intelligence Agency)to the deputy of such officer.

(6) Funds transferred or reprogrammed under this subsection shall remain available for the same period as the appropriations account to which transferred or reprogrammed.

(7) Any transfer or reprogramming of funds under this subsection shall be carried out in accordance with existing procedures applicable to

reprogramming notifications for the appropriate congressional committees. Any proposed transfer or reprogramming for which notice is given to the appropriate congressional committees shall be accompanied by a report explaining the nature of the proposed transfer or reprogramming and how it satisfies the requirements of this subsection. In addition, the congressional intelligence committees shall be promptly notified of any transfer or reprogramming of funds made pursuant to this subsection in any case in which the transfer or reprogramming would not have otherwise required reprogramming notification under procedures in effect as of the date of the enactment of this subsection.

(e) TRANSFER OF PERSONNEL.—

(1)(A) In addition to any other authorities available under law for such purposes, in the first twelve months after establishment of a new national intelligence center, the Director of National Intelligence, with the approval of the Director of the Office of Management and Budget and in consultation with the congressional committees of jurisdiction referred to in subparagraph (B), may transfer not more than 100 personnel authorized for elements of the intelligence community to such center.

(B) The Director of National Intelligence shall promptly provide notice of any transfer of personnel made pursuant to this paragraph to—

(i) the congressional intelligence committees;

(ii) the Committees on Appropriations of the Senate and the House of Representatives;

(iii) in the case of the transfer of personnel to or from the Department of Defense, the Committees on Armed Services of the Senate and the House of Representatives; and

(iv) in the case of the transfer of personnel to or from the Department of Justice, to the Committees on the Judiciary of the Senate and the House of Representatives.

(C) The Director shall include in any notice under subparagraph (B) an explanation of the nature of the transfer and how it satisfies the requirements of this subsection.

(2)(A) The Director of National Intelligence, with the approval of the Director of the Office of Management and Budget and in accordance with procedures to be developed by the Director of National Intelligence and the heads of the departments and agencies concerned, may transfer personnel authorized for an element of the intelligence community to another such element for a period of not more than 2 years.

(B) A transfer of personnel may be made under this paragraph only if—

(i) the personnel are being transferred to an activity that is a higher priority intelligence activity; and

(ii) the transfer supports an emergent need, improves program effectiveness, or increases efficiency.

(C) The Director of National Intelligence shall promptly provide notice of any transfer of personnel made pursuant to this paragraph to—

(i) the congressional intelligence committees;

(ii) in the case of the transfer of personnel to or from the Department of Defense, the Committees on Armed Services of the Senate and the House of Representatives; and

(iii) in the case of the transfer of personnel to or from the Department of Justice, to the Committees on the Judiciary of the Senate and the House of Representatives.

(D) The Director shall include in any notice under subparagraph (C) an explanation of the nature of the transfer and how it satisfies the requirements of this paragraph.

(3)(A) In addition to the number of full-time equivalent positions authorized for the Office of the Director of National Intelligence for a fiscal year, there is authorized for such Office for each fiscal year an additional 100 full-time equivalent positions that may be used only for the purposes described in subparagraph (B).

(B) Except as provided in subparagraph (C), the Director of National Intelligence may use a full-time equivalent position authorized under subparagraph (A) only for the purpose of providing a temporary transfer of personnel made in accordance with paragraph (2) to an element of the intelligence community to enable such element to increase the total number of personnel authorized for such element, on a temporary basis—

(i) during a period in which a permanent employee of such element is absent to participate in critical language training; or

(ii) to accept a permanent employee of another element of the intelligence community to provide language-capable services.

(C) Paragraph (2)(B) shall not apply with respect to a transfer of personnel made under subparagraph (B).

(D) For each of the fiscal years 2010, 2011, and 2012, the Director of National Intelligence shall submit to the congressional intelligence committees an annual report on the use of authorities under this paragraph. Each such report shall include a description of—

(i) the number of transfers of personnel made by the Director pursuant to subparagraph (B), disaggregated by each element of the intelligence community;

(ii) the critical language needs that were fulfilled or partially fulfilled through the use of such transfers; and

(iii) the cost to carry out subparagraph (B).

(4) It is the sense of Congress that—

(A) the nature of the national security threats facing the United States will continue to challenge the intelligence community to respond rapidly and flexibly to bring analytic resources to bear against emerging and unforeseen requirements;

(B) both the Office of the Director of National Intelligence and any analytic centers determined to be necessary should be fully and properly supported with appropriate levels of personnel resources and that the President's yearly budget requests adequately support those needs; and

(C) the President should utilize all legal and administrative discretion to ensure that the Director of National Intelligence and all other elements of the intelligence community have the necessary resources and procedures to respond promptly and effectively to emerging and unforeseen national security challenges.

(f) TASKING AND OTHER AUTHORITIES.—

(1)(A) The Director of National Intelligence shall—

(i) establish objectives, priorities, and guidance for the intelligence community to ensure timely and effective collection, processing, analysis, and dissemination (including access by users to collected data consistent with applicable law and, as appropriate, the guidelines referred to in subsection (b) and analytic products generated by or within the intelligence community) of national intelligence;

(ii) determine requirements and priorities for, and manage and direct the tasking of, collection, analysis, production, and dissemination of national intelligence by elements of the intelligence community, including—

(I) approving requirements (including those requirements responding to needs provided by consumers) for collection and analysis; and

(II) resolving conflicts in collection requirements and in the tasking of national collection assets of the elements of the intelligence community; and

(iii) provide advisory tasking to intelligence elements of those agencies and departments not within the National Intelligence Program.

(B) The authority of the Director of National Intelligence under subparagraph (A) shall not apply—

(i) insofar as the President so directs;

(ii) with respect to clause (ii) of subparagraph (A), insofar as the Secretary of Defense exercises tasking authority under plans or arrangements agreed upon by the Secretary of Defense and the Director of National Intelligence; or

(iii) to the direct dissemination of information to State government and local government officials and private sector entities pursuant to sections 201 and 892 of the Homeland Security Act of 2002 (6 U.S.C. §121, 482).

(2) The Director of National Intelligence shall oversee the National Counterterrorism Center and may establish such other national intelligence centers as the Director determines necessary.

(3)(A) The Director of National Intelligence shall prescribe, in consultation with the heads of other agencies or elements of the intelligence community, and the heads of their respective departments, personnel policies and programs applicable to the intelligence community that—

(i) encourage and facilitate assignments and details of personnel to national intelligence centers, and between elements of the intelligence community;

(ii) set standards for education, training, and career development of personnel of the intelligence community;

(iii) encourage and facilitate the recruitment and retention by the intelligence community of highly qualified individuals for the effective conduct of intelligence activities;

(iv) ensure that the personnel of the intelligence community are sufficiently diverse for purposes of the collection and analysis of intelligence through the recruitment and training of women, minorities, and individuals with diverse ethnic, cultural, and linguistic backgrounds;

(v) make service in more than one element of the intelligence community a condition of promotion to such positions within the intelligence community as the Director shall specify; and

(vi) ensure the effective management of intelligence community personnel who are responsible for intelligence community-wide matters.

(B) Policies prescribed under subparagraph (A) shall not be inconsistent with the personnel policies otherwise applicable to members of the uniformed services.

(4) The Director of National Intelligence shall ensure compliance with the Constitution and laws of the United States by the Central Intelligence Agency and shall ensure such compliance by other elements of the intelligence community through the host executive departments that manage the programs and activities that are part of the National Intelligence Program.

(5) The Director of National Intelligence shall ensure the elimination of waste and unnecessary duplication within the intelligence community.

(6) The Director of National Intelligence shall establish requirements and priorities for foreign intelligence information to be collected under the Foreign Intelligence Surveillance Act of 1978 (50 U.S.C. §1801 et seq.), and provide assistance to the Attorney General to ensure that information derived from electronic surveillance or physical searches under that Act is disseminated so it may be used efficiently and effectively for national intelligence purposes, except that the Director shall have no authority to direct or undertake electronic surveillance or physical search operations pursuant to that Act unless authorized by statute or Executive order.

(7)(A) The Director of National Intelligence shall, if the Director determines it is necessary, or may, if requested by a congressional intelligence committee, conduct an accountability review of an element of the intelligence community or the personnel of such element in relation to a failure or deficiency within the intelligence community.

(B)The Director of National Intelligence, in consultation with the Attorney General, shall establish guidelines and procedures for conducting an accountability review under subparagraph (A).

(C)(i) The Director of National Intelligence shall provide the findings of an accountability review conducted under subparagraph (A) and the Director's recommendations for corrective or punitive action, if any, to the head of the applicable element of the intelligence community. Such recommendations may include a recommendation for dismissal of personnel.

(ii)If the head of such element does not implement a recommendation made by the Director under clause (i), the head of such element shall submit to the congressional intelligence committees a notice of the determination not to implement the recommendation, including the reasons for the determination.

(D) The requirements of this paragraph shall not be construed to limit any authority of the Director of National Intelligence under subsection (m) or with respect to supervision of the Central Intelligence Agency.

(8) The Director of National Intelligence shall perform such other functions as the President may direct.

(9) Nothing in this title shall be construed as affecting the role of the Department of Justice or the Attorney General under the Foreign Intelligence Surveillance Act of 1978.

(g) INTELLIGENCE INFORMATION SHARING.—

(1) The Director of National Intelligence shall have principal authority to ensure maximum availability of and access to intelligence information within the intelligence community consistent with national security requirements. The Director of National Intelligence shall—

(A) establish uniform security standards and procedures;

(B) establish common information technology standards, protocols, and interfaces;

(C) ensure development of information technology systems that include multi-level security and intelligence integration capabilities;

(D) establish policies and procedures to resolve conflicts between the need to share intelligence information and the need to protect intelligence sources and methods;

(E) develop an enterprise architecture for the intelligence community and ensure that elements of the intelligence community comply with such architecture; and

(F) have procurement approval authority over all enterprise architecture-related information technology items funded in the National Intelligence Program.

(2) The President shall ensure that the Director of National Intelligence has all necessary support and authorities to fully and effectively implement paragraph (1).

(3) Except as otherwise directed by the President or with the specific written agreement of the head of the department or agency in question, a Federal agency or official shall not be considered to have met any obligation to provide any information, report, assessment, or other material (including unevaluated intelligence information) to that department or agency solely by virtue of having provided that information, report, assessment, or other material to the Director of National Intelligence or the National Counterterrorism Center.

(4) Not later than February 1 of each year, the Director of National Intelligence shall submit to the President and to the Congress an annual report that identifies any statute, regulation, policy, or practice that the Director believes impedes the ability of the Director to fully and effectively implement paragraph (1).

(h) ANALYSIS.—To ensure the most accurate analysis of intelligence is derived from all sources to support national security needs, the Director of National Intelligence shall—

(1) implement policies and procedures—

(A) to encourage sound analytic methods and tradecraft throughout the elements of the intelligence community;

(B) to ensure that analysis is based upon all sources available; and

(C) to ensure that the elements of the intelligence community regularly conduct competitive analysis of analytic products, whether such products are produced by or disseminated to such elements;

(2) ensure that resource allocation for intelligence analysis is appropriately proportional to resource allocation for intelligence collection systems and operations in order to maximize analysis of all collected data;

(3) ensure that differences in analytic judgment are fully considered and brought to the attention of policymakers; and

(4) ensure that sufficient relationships are established between intelligence collectors and analysts to facilitate greater understanding of the needs of analysts.

(i) PROTECTION OF INTELLIGENCE SOURCES AND METHODS.—

(1) The Director of National Intelligence shall protect intelligence sources and methods from unauthorized disclosure.

(2) Consistent with paragraph (1), in order to maximize the dissemination of intelligence, the Director of National Intelligence shall

establish and implement guidelines for the intelligence community for the following purposes:

(A) Classification of information under applicable law, Executive orders, or other Presidential directives.

(B) Access to and dissemination of intelligence, both in final form and in the form when initially gathered.

(C) Preparation of intelligence products in such a way that source information is removed to allow for dissemination at the lowest level of classification possible or in unclassified form to the extent practicable.

(3) The Director may only delegate a duty or authority given the Director under this subsection to the Principal Deputy Director of National Intelligence.

(j) UNIFORM PROCEDURES FOR SENSITIVE COMPARTMENTED INFORMATION.—The Director of National Intelligence, subject to the direction of the President, shall—

(1) establish uniform standards and procedures for the grant of access to sensitive compartmented information to any officer or employee of any agency or department of the United States and to employees of contractors of those agencies or departments;

(2) ensure the consistent implementation of those standards and procedures throughout such agencies and departments;

(3) ensure that security clearances granted by individual elements of the intelligence community are recognized by all elements of the intelligence community, and under contracts entered into by those agencies; and

(4) ensure that the process for investigation and adjudication of an application for access to sensitive compartmented information is performed in the most expeditious manner possible consistent with applicable standards for national security.

(k) COORDINATION WITH FOREIGN GOVERNMENTS.—Under the direction of the President and in a manner consistent with section 207 of the Foreign Service Act of 1980 (22 U.S.C. §3927), the Director of National Intelligence shall oversee the coordination of the relationships between elements of the intelligence community and the intelligence or security services of foreign governments or international organizations on all matters involving intelligence related to the national security or involving intelligence acquired through clandestine means.

(l) ENHANCED PERSONNEL MANAGEMENT.—

(1)(A) The Director of National Intelligence shall, under regulations prescribed by the Director, provide incentives for personnel of elements of the intelligence community to serve—

(i) on the staff of the Director of National Intelligence;

(ii) on the staff of the national intelligence centers;

(iii) on the staff of the National Counterterrorism Center; and

(iv) in other positions in support of the intelligence community management functions of the Director.

(B) Incentives under subparagraph (A) may include financial incentives, bonuses, and such other awards and incentives as the Director considers appropriate.

(2)(A) Notwithstanding any other provision of law, the personnel of an element of the intelligence community who are assigned or detailed under paragraph (1)(A) to service under the Director of National Intelligence shall be promoted at rates equivalent to or better than personnel of such element who are not so assigned or detailed.

(B) The Director may prescribe regulations to carry out this paragraph.

(3)(A) The Director of National Intelligence shall prescribe mechanisms to facilitate the rotation of personnel of the intelligence community through various elements of the intelligence community in the course of their careers in order to facilitate the widest possible understanding by such personnel of the variety of intelligence requirements, methods, users, and capabilities.

(B) The mechanisms prescribed under subparagraph (A) may include the following:

(i) The establishment of special occupational categories involving service, over the course of a career, in more than one element of the intelligence community.

(ii) The provision of rewards for service in positions undertaking analysis and planning of operations involving two or more elements of the intelligence community.

(iii) The establishment of requirements for education, training, service, and evaluation for service involving more than one element of the intelligence community.

(C) It is the sense of Congress that the mechanisms prescribed under this subsection should, to the extent practical, seek to duplicate for civilian personnel within the intelligence community the joint officer management policies established by chapter 38 of title 10, United States Code, and the other amendments made by title IV of the Goldwater-Nichols Department of Defense Reorganization Act of 1986 (Public Law 99-433).

(4)(A) Except as provided in subparagraph (B) and subparagraph (D), this subsection shall not apply with respect to personnel of the elements of the intelligence community who are members of the uniformed services.

(B) Mechanisms that establish requirements for education and training pursuant to paragraph (3)(B)(iii) may apply with respect to members of the uniformed services who are assigned to an element of the intelligence community funded through the National Intelligence Program, but such mechanisms shall not be inconsistent with personnel policies and education and training requirements otherwise applicable to members of the uniformed services.

(C) The personnel policies and programs developed and implemented under this subsection with respect to law enforcement officers (as that term is defined in section 5541(3) of title 5, United States Code) shall not affect the ability of law enforcement entities to conduct operations or, through the applicable chain of command, to control the activities of such law enforcement officers.

(D) Assignment to the Office of the Director of National Intelligence of commissioned officers of the Armed Forces shall be considered a joint-duty assignment for purposes of the joint officer management policies prescribed by chapter 38 of title 10, United States Code, and other provisions of that title.

(m) ADDITIONAL AUTHORITY WITH RESPECT TO PERSONNEL.—

(1) In addition to the authorities under subsection (f)(3), the Director of National Intelligence may exercise with respect to the personnel of the Office of the Director of National Intelligence any authority of the Director of the Central Intelligence Agency with respect to the personnel of the Central Intelligence Agency under the Central Intelligence Agency Act of 1949 (50 U.S.C. §403a et seq.), and other applicable provisions of law, as of the date of the enactment of this subsection to the same extent, and subject to the same conditions and limitations, that the Director of the Central Intelligence Agency may exercise such authority with respect to personnel of the Central Intelligence Agency.

(2) Employees and applicants for employment of the Office of the Director of National Intelligence shall have the same rights and protections under the Office of the Director of National Intelligence as employees of the Central Intelligence Agency have under the Central Intelligence Agency Act of 1949, and other applicable provisions of law, as of the date of the enactment of this subsection.

(n) ACQUISITION AND OTHER AUTHORITIES.—

(1) In carrying out the responsibilities and authorities under this section, the Director of National Intelligence may exercise the acquisition and

appropriations authorities referred to in the Central Intelligence Agency Act of 1949 (50 U.S.C. §403a et seq.) other than the authorities referred to in section 8(b) of that Act (50 U.S.C. §403j(b)).

(2) For the purpose of the exercise of any authority referred to in paragraph (1), a reference to the head of an agency shall be deemed to be a reference to the Director of National Intelligence or the Principal Deputy Director of National Intelligence.

(3)(A) Any determination or decision to be made under an authority referred to in paragraph (1) by the head of an agency may be made with respect to individual purchases and contracts or with respect to classes of purchases or contracts, and shall be final.

(B) Except as provided in subparagraph (C), the Director of National Intelligence or the Principal Deputy Director of National Intelligence may, in such official's discretion, delegate to any officer or other official of the Office of the Director of National Intelligence any authority to make a determination or decision as the head of the agency under an authority referred to in paragraph (1).

(C) The limitations and conditions set forth in section 3(d) of the Central Intelligence Agency Act of 1949 (50 U.S.C. §403c(d)) shall apply to the exercise by the Director of National Intelligence of an authority referred to in paragraph (1).

(D) Each determination or decision required by an authority referred to in the second sentence of section 3(d) of the Central Intelligence Agency Act of 1949 shall be based upon written findings made by the official making such determination or decision, which findings shall be final and shall be available within the Office of the Director of National Intelligence for a period of at least six years following the date of such determination or decision.

(4)(A) In addition to the authority referred to in paragraph (1), the Director of National Intelligence may authorize the head of an element of the intelligence community to exercise an acquisition authority referred to in section 3 or 8(a) of the Central Intelligence Agency Act of 1949 (50 U.S.C. 403c and 403j(a)) for an acquisition by such element that is more than 50 percent funded under the National Intelligence Program.

(B) The head of an element of the intelligence community may not exercise an authority referred to in subparagraph (A) until—

(i) the head of such element (without delegation) submits

to the Director of National Intelligence a written request that includes—

(I) a description of such authority requested to be exercised;

(II) an explanation of the need for such authority, including an explanation of the reasons that other authorities are insufficient; and

(III) a certification that the mission of such element would be—

(aa) impaired if such authority is not exercised; or

(bb) significantly and measurably enhanced if such authority is exercised; and

(ii) the Director of National Intelligence issues a written authorization that includes—

(I) a description of the authority referred to in subparagraph (A) that is authorized to be exercised; and

(II) a justification to support the exercise of such authority.

(C) A request and authorization to exercise an authority referred to in subparagraph (A) may be made with respect to an individual acquisition or with respect to a specific class of acquisitions described in the request and authorization referred to in subparagraph (B).

(D)(i) A request from a head of an element of the intelligence community located within one of the departments described in clause (ii) to exercise an authority referred to in subparagraph (A) shall be submitted to the Director of National Intelligence in accordance with any procedures established by the head of such department.

(ii) The departments described in this clause are the Department of Defense, the Department of Energy, the Department of Homeland Security, the Department of Justice, the Department of State, and the Department of the Treasury.

(E)(i) The head of an element of the intelligence community may not be authorized to utilize an authority referred to in subparagraph (A) for a class of acquisitions for a period of more than 3 years, except that the Director of National Intelligence (without delegation) may authorize the use of such an authority for not more than 6 years.

 (ii) Each authorization to utilize an authority referred to in subparagraph (A) may be extended in accordance with the requirements of subparagraph (B) for successive periods of not more than 3 years, except that the Director of National Intelligence (without delegation) may authorize an extension period of not more than 6 years.

(F) Subject to clauses (i) and (ii) of subparagraph (E), the Director of National Intelligence may only delegate the authority of the Director under subparagraphs (A) through (E) to the Principal Deputy Director of National Intelligence or a Deputy Director of National Intelligence.

(G) The Director of National Intelligence shall submit—

 (i) to the congressional intelligence committees a notification of an authorization to exercise an authority referred to in subparagraph (A) or an extension of such authorization that includes the written authorization referred to in subparagraph (B)(ii); and

 (ii) to the Director of the Office of Management and Budget a notification of an authorization to exercise an authority referred to in subparagraph (A) for an acquisition or class of acquisitions that will exceed $50,000,000 annually.

(H) Requests and authorizations to exercise an authority referred to in subparagraph (A) shall remain available within the Office of the Director of National Intelligence for a period of at least 6 years following the date of such request or authorization.

(I) Nothing in this paragraph may be construed to alter or otherwise limit the authority of the Central Intelligence Agency to independently exercise an authority under section 3 or 8(a) of the Central Intelligence Agency Act of 1949 (50 U.S.C. 403c and 403j(a)).

(o) CONSIDERATION OF VIEWS OF ELEMENTS OF INTELLIGENCE COMMUNITY.— In carrying out the duties and responsibilities under this section, the Director of National Intelligence shall take into account the views of a head of a department containing an element of the intelligence community and of the Director of the Central Intelligence Agency.

(p) RESPONSIBILITY OF DIRECTOR OF NATIONAL INTELLIGENCE REGARDING NATIONAL INTELLIGENCE PROGRAM BUDGET CONCERNING THE DEPARTMENT OF DEFENSE.—Subject to the direction of the President, the Director of National

Intelligence shall, after consultation with the Secretary of Defense, ensure that the National Intelligence Program budgets for the elements of the intelligence community that are within the Department of Defense are adequate to satisfy the national intelligence needs of the Department of Defense, including the needs of the Chairman of the Joint Chiefs of Staff and the commanders of the unified and specified commands, and wherever such elements are performing Government-wide functions, the needs of other Federal departments and agencies.

(q) ACQUISITIONS OF MAJOR SYSTEMS.—

    (1) For each intelligence program within the National Intelligence Program for the acquisition of a major system, the Director of National Intelligence shall—

        (A) require the development and implementation of a program management plan that includes cost, schedule, and performance goals and program milestone criteria, except that with respect to Department of Defense programs the Director shall consult with the Secretary of Defense;

        (B) serve as exclusive milestone decision authority, except that with respect to Department of Defense programs the Director shall serve as milestone decision authority jointly with the Secretary of Defense or the designee of the Secretary; and

        (C) periodically—

            (i) review and assess the progress made toward the achievement of the goals and milestones established in such plan; and

            (ii) submit to Congress a report on the results of such review and assessment.

    (2) If the Director of National Intelligence and the Secretary of Defense are unable to reach an agreement on a milestone decision under paragraph (1)(B), the President shall resolve the conflict.

    (3) Nothing in this subsection may be construed to limit the authority of the Director of National Intelligence to delegate to any other official any authority to perform the responsibilities of the Director under this subsection.

    (4) In this subsection:

        (A) The term "intelligence program", with respect to the acquisition of a major system, means a program that—

            (i) is carried out to acquire such major system for an element of the intelligence community; and

            (ii) is funded in whole out of amounts available for the National Intelligence Program.

(B) The term "major system" has the meaning given such term in section 4(9) of the Federal Property and Administrative Services Act of 1949 (41 U.S.C. §403(9)).

(r) PERFORMANCE OF COMMON SERVICES.—The Director of National Intelligence shall, in consultation with the heads of departments and agencies of the United States Government containing elements within the intelligence community and with the Director of the Central Intelligence Agency, coordinate the performance by the elements of the intelligence community within the National Intelligence Program of such services as are of common concern to the intelligence community, which services the Director of National Intelligence determines can be more efficiently accomplished in a consolidated manner.

(s) PAY AUTHORITY FOR CRITICAL POSITIONS.—(1) Notwithstanding any pay limitation established under any other provision of law applicable to employees in elements of the intelligence community, the Director of National Intelligence may, in coordination with the Director of the Office of Personnel Management and the Director of the Office of Management and Budget, grant authority to the head of a department or agency to fix the rate of basic pay for one or more positions within the intelligence community at a rate in excess of any applicable limitation, subject to the provisions of this subsection. The exercise of authority so granted is at the discretion of the head of the department or agency employing the individual in a position covered by such authority, subject to the provisions of this subsection and any conditions established by the Director of National Intelligence when granting such authority.

(2) Authority under this subsection may be granted or exercised only –
　　　(A) with respect to a position that requires an extremely high level of expertise and is critical to successful accomplishment of an important mission; and
　　　(B) to the extent necessary to recruit or retain an individual exceptionally well qualified for the position.

(3) The head of a department or agency may not fix a rate of basic pay under this subsection at a rate greater than the rate payable for level II of the Executive Schedule under section 5313 of title 5, United States Code, except upon written approval of the Director of National Intelligence or as otherwise authorized by law.

(4) The head of a department or agency may not fix a rate of basic pay under this subsection at a rate greater than the rate payable for level I of the Executive Schedule under section 5312 of title 5, United States Code, except upon written approval of the President in response to a request by the Director of National Intelligence or as otherwise authorized by law.

(5) Any grant of authority under this subsection for a position shall terminate at the discretion of the Director of National Intelligence.

(6)(A) The Director of National Intelligence shall notify the congressional intelligence committees not later than 30 days after the date on which the Director grants authority to the head of a department or agency under this subsection.

    (B) The head of a department or agency to which the Director of National Intelligence grants authority under this subsection shall notify the congressional intelligence committees and the Director of the exercise of such authority not later than 30 days after the date on which such head exercises such authority.

(t) AWARD OF RANK TO MEMBERS OF THE SENIOR NATIONAL INTELLIGENCE SERVICE. – (1) The President, based on the recommendation of the Director of National Intelligence, may award a rank to a member of the Senior National Intelligence Service or other intelligence community senior civilian officer not already covered by such a rank award program in the same manner in which a career appointee of an agency may be awarded a rank under section 4507 of title 5, United States Code.

    (2) The President may establish procedures to award a rank under paragraph (1) to a member of the Senior National Intelligence Service or a senior civilian officer of the intelligence community whose identity as such a member or officer is classified information (as defined in section 606(1)).

(u) CONFLICT OF INTEREST REGULATIONS.—(1) The Director of National Intelligence, in consultation with the Director of the Office of Government Ethics, shall issue regulations prohibiting an officer or employee of an element of the intelligence community from engaging in outside employment if such employment creates a conflict of interest or appearance thereof.

    (2) The Director of National Intelligence shall annually submit to the congressional intelligence committees a report describing all outside employment for officers and employees of elements of the intelligence community that was authorized by the head of an element of the intelligence community during the preceding calendar year. Such report shall be submitted each year on the date provided in section 507.

(v) AUTHORITY TO ESTABLISH POSITIONS IN EXCEPTED SERVICE.—(1) The Director of National Intelligence, with the concurrence of the head of the covered department concerned and in consultation with the Director of the Office of Personnel Management, may—

    (A) convert competitive service positions, and the incumbents of such positions, within an element of the intelligence community in such department, to excepted service positions as the Director of National Intelligence determines necessary to carry out the intelligence functions of such element; and

(B) establish new positions in the excepted service within an element of the intelligence community in such department, if the Director of National Intelligence determines such positions are necessary to carry out the intelligence functions of such element.

(2) An incumbent occupying a position on the date of the enactment of the Intelligence Authorization Act for Fiscal Year 2012 selected to be converted to the excepted service under this section shall have the right to refuse such conversion. Once such individual no longer occupies the position, the position may be converted to the excepted service.

(3) In this subsection, the term "covered department" means the Department of Energy, the Department of Homeland Security, the Department of State, or the Department of the Treasury.

(w) NUCLEAR PROLIFERATION ASSESSMENT STATEMENTS INTELLIGENCE COMMUNITY ADDENDUM.—The Director of National Intelligence, in consultation with the heads of the appropriate elements of the intelligence community and the Secretary of State, shall provide to the President, the congressional intelligence committees, the Committee on Foreign Affairs of the House of Representatives, and the Committee on Foreign Relations of the Senate an addendum to each Nuclear Proliferation Assessment Statement accompanying a civilian nuclear cooperation agreement, containing a comprehensive analysis of the country's export control system with respect to nuclear-related matters, including interactions with other countries of proliferation concern and the actual or suspected nuclear, dual-use, or missile-related transfers to such countries.

OFFICE OF THE DIRECTOR OF NATIONAL INTELLIGENCE

SEC. 103. [50 U.S.C. §403-3]

(a) OFFICE OF DIRECTOR OF NATIONAL INTELLIGENCE.—There is an Office of the Director of National Intelligence.

(b) FUNCTION.—The function of the Office of the Director of National Intelligence is to assist the Director of National Intelligence in carrying out the duties and responsibilities of the Director under this Act and other applicable provisions of law, and to carry out such other duties as may be prescribed by the President or by law.

(c) COMPOSITION.—The Office of the Director of National Intelligence is composed of the following:

(1) The Director of National Intelligence.

(2) The Principal Deputy Director of National Intelligence.

(3) Any Deputy Director of National Intelligence appointed under section 103A.

(4) The National Intelligence Council.

(5) The General Counsel.

(6) The Civil Liberties Protection Officer.

(7) The Director of Science and Technology.

(8) The National Counterintelligence Executive (including the Office of the National Counterintelligence Executive).

(9) The Chief Information Officer of the Intelligence Community.

(10) The Inspector General of the Intelligence Community.

(11) The Director of the National Counterterrorism Center.

(12) The Director of the National Counter Proliferation Center.

(13) The Chief Financial Officer of the Intelligence Community.

(14) Such other offices and officials as may be established by law or the Director may establish or designate in the Office, including national intelligence centers.

(d) STAFF.—

(1) To assist the Director of National Intelligence in fulfilling the duties and responsibilities of the Director, the Director shall employ and utilize in the Office of the Director of National Intelligence a professional staff having an expertise in matters relating to such duties and responsibilities, and may establish permanent positions and appropriate rates of pay with respect to that staff.

(2) The staff of the Office of the Director of National Intelligence under paragraph (1) shall include the staff of the Office of the Deputy Director of Central Intelligence for Community Management that is transferred to the Office of the Director of National Intelligence under section 1091 of the National Security Intelligence Reform Act of 2004.

(e) TEMPORARY FILLING OF VACANCIES.—With respect to filling temporarily a vacancy in an office within the Office of the Director of National Intelligence (other than that of the Director of National Intelligence), section 3345(a)(3) of title 5, United States Code, may be applied—

(1) in the matter preceding subparagraph (A), by substituting 'an element of the intelligence community, as that term is defined in section 3(4) of the National Security Act of 1947 (50 U.S.C. 401a(4)),' for 'such Executive agency'; and

(2) in subparagraph (A), by substituting 'the intelligence community' for 'such agency'.

(f) LOCATION OF THE OFFICE OF THE DIRECTOR OF NATIONAL INTELLIGENCE.—The headquarters of the Office of the Director of National Intelligence may be located in the Washington metropolitan region, as that term is defined in section 8301 of title 40, United States Code.

DEPUTY DIRECTORS OF NATIONAL INTELLIGENCE

SEC. 103A. [50 U.S.C. §403-3a]

(a) PRINCIPAL DEPUTY DIRECTOR OF NATIONAL INTELLIGENCE.—

(1) There is a Principal Deputy Director of National Intelligence who shall be appointed by the President, by and with the advice and consent of the Senate.

(2) In the event of a vacancy in the position of Principal Deputy Director of National Intelligence, the Director of National Intelligence shall recommend to the President an individual for appointment as Principal Deputy Director of National Intelligence.

(3) Any individual nominated for appointment as Principal Deputy Director of National Intelligence shall have extensive national security experience and management expertise.

(4) The individual serving as Principal Deputy Director of National Intelligence shall not, while so serving, serve in any capacity in any other element of the intelligence community.

(5) The Principal Deputy Director of National Intelligence shall assist the Director of National Intelligence in carrying out the duties and responsibilities of the Director.

(6) The Principal Deputy Director of National Intelligence shall act for, and exercise the powers of, the Director of National Intelligence during the absence or disability of the Director of National Intelligence or during a vacancy in the position of Director of National Intelligence.

(b) DEPUTY DIRECTORS OF NATIONAL INTELLIGENCE.—

(1) There may be not more than four Deputy Directors of National Intelligence who shall be appointed by the Director of National Intelligence.

(2) Each Deputy Director of National Intelligence appointed under this subsection shall have such duties, responsibilities, and authorities as the Director of National Intelligence may assign or are specified by law.

(c) MILITARY STATUS OF DIRECTOR OF NATIONAL INTELLIGENCE AND PRINCIPAL DEPUTY DIRECTOR OF NATIONAL INTELLIGENCE.—

(1) Not more than one of the individuals serving in the positions specified in paragraph (2) may be a commissioned officer of the Armed Forces in active status.

(2) The positions referred to in this paragraph are the following:

(A) The Director of National Intelligence.

(B) The Principal Deputy Director of National Intelligence.

(3) It is the sense of Congress that, under ordinary circumstances, it is desirable that one of the individuals serving in the positions specified in paragraph (2)—

> (A) be a commissioned officer of the Armed Forces, in active status; or
>
> (B) have, by training or experience, an appreciation of military intelligence activities and requirements.

(4) A commissioned officer of the Armed Forces, while serving in a position specified in paragraph (2)—

> (A) shall not be subject to supervision or control by the Secretary of Defense or by any officer or employee of the Department of Defense;
>
> (B) shall not exercise, by reason of the officer's status as a commissioned officer, any supervision or control with respect to any of the military or civilian personnel of the Department of Defense except as otherwise authorized by law; and
>
> (C) shall not be counted against the numbers and percentages of commissioned officers of the rank and grade of such officer authorized for the military department of that officer.

(5) Except as provided in subparagraph (A) or (B) of paragraph (4), the appointment of an officer of the Armed Forces to a position specified in paragraph (2) shall not affect the status, position, rank, or grade of such officer in the Armed Forces, or any emolument, perquisite, right, privilege, or benefit incident to or arising out of such status, position, rank, or grade.

(6) A commissioned officer of the Armed Forces on active duty who is appointed to a position specified in paragraph (2), while serving in such position and while remaining on active duty, shall continue to receive military pay and allowances and shall not receive the pay prescribed for such position. Funds from which such pay and allowances are paid shall be reimbursed from funds available to the Director of National Intelligence.

NATIONAL INTELLIGENCE COUNCIL

SEC. 103B. [50 U.S.C. §403–3b]

(a) NATIONAL INTELLIGENCE COUNCIL.—There is a National Intelligence Council.

(b) COMPOSITION.—

> (1) The National Intelligence Council shall be composed of senior analysts within the intelligence community and substantive experts from

the public and private sector, who shall be appointed by, report to, and serve at the pleasure of, the Director of National Intelligence.

(2) The Director shall prescribe appropriate security requirements for personnel appointed from the private sector as a condition of service on the Council, or as contractors of the Council or employees of such contractors, to ensure the protection of intelligence sources and methods while avoiding, wherever possible, unduly intrusive requirements which the Director considers to be unnecessary for this purpose.

(c) DUTIES AND RESPONSIBILITIES.—

(1) The National Intelligence Council shall—

(A) produce national intelligence estimates for the United States Government, including alternative views held by elements of the intelligence community and other information as specified in paragraph (2);

(B) evaluate community-wide collection and production of intelligence by the intelligence community and the requirements and resources of such collection and production; and

(C) otherwise assist the Director of National Intelligence in carrying out the responsibilities of the Director under section 102A.

(2) The Director of National Intelligence shall ensure that the Council satisfies the needs of policymakers and other consumers of intelligence.

(d) SERVICES AS SENIOR INTELLIGENCE ADVISERS.—Within their respective areas of expertise and under the direction of the Director of National Intelligence, the members of the National Intelligence Council shall constitute the senior intelligence advisers of the intelligence community for purposes of representing the views of the intelligence community within the United States Government.

(e) AUTHORITY TO CONTRACT.—Subject to the direction and control of the Director of National Intelligence, the National Intelligence Council may carry out its responsibilities under this section by contract, including contracts for substantive experts necessary to assist the Council with particular assessments under this section.

(f) STAFF.—The Director of National Intelligence shall make available to the National Intelligence Council such staff as may be necessary to permit the Council to carry out its responsibilities under this section.

(g) AVAILABILITY OF COUNCIL AND STAFF.—

(1) The Director of National Intelligence shall take appropriate measures to ensure that the National Intelligence Council and its staff satisfy the needs of policymaking officials and other consumers of intelligence.

(2) The Council shall be readily accessible to policymaking officials and other appropriate individuals not otherwise associated with the intelligence community.

(h) SUPPORT.—The heads of the elements of the intelligence community shall, as appropriate, furnish such support to the National Intelligence Council, including the preparation of intelligence analyses, as may be required by the Director of National Intelligence.

(i) NATIONAL INTELLIGENCE COUNCIL PRODUCT.—For purposes of this section, the term "National Intelligence Council product" includes a National Intelligence Estimate and any other intelligence community assessment that sets forth the judgment of the intelligence community as a whole on a matter covered by such product.

GENERAL COUNSEL

SEC. 103C. [50 U.S.C. §403-3c]

(a) GENERAL COUNSEL.—There is a General Counsel of the Office of the Director of National Intelligence who shall be appointed by the President, by and with the advice and consent of the Senate.

(b) PROHIBITION ON DUAL SERVICE AS GENERAL COUNSEL OF ANOTHER AGENCY.—The individual serving in the position of General Counsel may not, while so serving, also serve as the General Counsel of any other department, agency, or element of the United States Government.

(c) SCOPE OF POSITION.—The General Counsel is the chief legal officer of the Office of the Director of National Intelligence.

(d) FUNCTIONS.—The General Counsel shall perform such functions as the Director of National Intelligence may prescribe.

CIVIL LIBERTIES PROTECTION OFFICER

SEC. 103D. [50 U.S.C. §403-3d]

(a) CIVIL LIBERTIES PROTECTION OFFICER.—

(1) Within the Office of the Director of National Intelligence, there is a Civil Liberties Protection Officer who shall be appointed by the Director of National Intelligence.

(2) The Civil Liberties Protection Officer shall report directly to the Director of National Intelligence.

(b) DUTIES.—The Civil Liberties Protection Officer shall—

(1) ensure that the protection of civil liberties and privacy is appropriately incorporated in the policies and procedures developed for and implemented by the Office of the Director of National Intelligence and the elements of the intelligence community within the National Intelligence Program;

(2) oversee compliance by the Office and the Director of National Intelligence with requirements under the Constitution and all laws,

regulations, Executive orders, and implementing guidelines relating to civil liberties and privacy;

(3) review and assess complaints and other information indicating possible abuses of civil liberties and privacy in the administration of the programs and operations of the Office and the Director of National Intelligence and, as appropriate, investigate any such complaint or information;

(4) ensure that the use of technologies sustain, and do not erode, privacy protections relating to the use, collection, and disclosure of personal information;

(5) ensure that personal information contained in a system of records subject to section 552a of title 5, United States Code (popularly referred to as the Privacy Act'), is handled in full compliance with fair information practices as set out in that section;

(6) conduct privacy impact assessments when appropriate or as required by law; and

(7) perform such other duties as may be prescribed by the Director of National Intelligence or specified by law.

(c) USE OF AGENCY INSPECTORS GENERAL.—When appropriate, the Civil Liberties Protection Officer may refer complaints to the Office of Inspector General having responsibility for the affected element of the department or agency of the intelligence community to conduct an investigation under paragraph (3) of subsection (b).

DIRECTOR OF SCIENCE AND TECHNOLOGY

SEC. 103E. [50 U.S.C. §403-3e]

(a) DIRECTOR OF SCIENCE AND TECHNOLOGY.—There is a Director of Science and Technology within the Office of the Director of National Intelligence who shall be appointed by the Director of National Intelligence.

(b) REQUIREMENT RELATING TO APPOINTMENT.—An individual appointed as Director of Science and Technology shall have a professional background and experience appropriate for the duties of the Director of Science and Technology.

(c) DUTIES.—The Director of Science and Technology shall—

(1) act as the chief representative of the Director of National Intelligence for science and technology;

(2) chair the Director of National Intelligence Science and Technology Committee under subsection (d);

(3) assist the Director in formulating a long-term strategy for scientific advances in the field of intelligence;

(4) assist the Director on the science and technology elements of the budget of the Office of the Director of National Intelligence; and

(5) perform other such duties as may be prescribed by the Director of National Intelligence or specified by law.

(d) DIRECTOR OF NATIONAL INTELLIGENCE SCIENCE AND TECHNOLOGY COMMITTEE.—

(1) There is within the Office of the Director of Science and Technology a Director of National Intelligence Science and Technology Committee.

(2) The Committee shall be composed of the principal science officers of the National Intelligence Program.

(3) The Committee shall—

(A) coordinate advances in research and development related to intelligence; and

(B) perform such other functions as the Director of Science and Technology shall prescribe.

NATIONAL COUNTERINTELLIGENCE EXECUTIVE

SEC. 103F. [50 U.S.C. §403-3f]

(a) NATIONAL COUNTERINTELLIGENCE EXECUTIVE.—The National Counterintelligence Executive under section 902 of the Counterintelligence Enhancement Act of 2002 (title IX of Public Law 107-306; 50 U.S.C. §402b et seq.) is a component of the Office of the Director of National Intelligence.

(b) DUTIES.—The National Counterintelligence Executive shall perform the duties provided in the Counterintelligence Enhancement Act of 2002 and such other duties as may be prescribed by the Director of National Intelligence or specified by law.

CHIEF INFORMATION OFFICER

SEC. 103G. [50 U.S.C. §403-3g]

(a) CHIEF INFORMATION OFFICER.—To assist the Director of National Intelligence in carrying out the responsibilities of the Director under this Act and other applicable provisions of law, there shall be within the Office of the Director of National Intelligence a Chief Information Officer of the Intelligence Community who shall be appointed by the President.

(b) DUTIES AND RESPONSIBILITIES.—Subject to the direction of the Director of National Intelligence, the Chief Information Officer of the Intelligence Community shall—

(1) manage activities relating to the information technology infrastructure and enterprise architecture requirements of the intelligence community;

(2) have procurement approval authority over all information technology items related to the enterprise architectures of all intelligence community components;

(3) direct and manage all information technology-related procurement for the intelligence community; and

(4) ensure that all expenditures for information technology and research and development activities are consistent with the intelligence community enterprise architecture and the strategy of the Director for such architecture.

(c) PROHIBITION ON SIMULTANEOUS SERVICE AS OTHER CHIEF INFORMATION OFFICER.—An individual serving in the position of Chief Information Officer of the Intelligence Community may not, while so serving, serve as the chief information officer of any other department or agency, or component thereof, of the United States Government.

INSPECTOR GENERAL OF THE INTELLIGENCE COMMUNITY

Sec. 103H. [50 USC 403-3h.] (a) OFFICE OF INSPECTOR GENERAL OF THE INTELLIGENCE COMMUNITY.—There is within the Office of the Director of National Intelligence an Office of the Inspector General of the Intelligence Community.

(b) PURPOSE.—The purpose of the Office of the Inspector General of the Intelligence Community is—

(1) to create an objective and effective office, appropriately accountable to Congress, to initiate and conduct independent investigations, inspections, audits, and reviews on programs and activities within the responsibility and authority of the Director of National Intelligence;

(2) to provide leadership and coordination and recommend policies for activities designed—

(A) to promote economy, efficiency, and effectiveness in the administration and implementation of such programs and activities; and

(B) to prevent and detect fraud and abuse in such programs and activities;

(3) to provide a means for keeping the Director of National Intelligence fully and currently informed about—

(A) problems and deficiencies relating to the administration of programs and activities within the responsibility and authority of the Director of National Intelligence; and

(B) the necessity for, and the progress of, corrective actions; and

(4) in the manner prescribed by this section, to ensure that the congressional intelligence committees are kept similarly informed of—

(A) significant problems and deficiencies relating to programs and activities within the responsibility and authority of the Director of National Intelligence; and

(B) the necessity for, and the progress of, corrective actions.

(c) INSPECTOR GENERAL OF THE INTELLIGENCE COMMUNITY.—

(1) There is an Inspector General of the Intelligence Community, who shall be the head of the Office of the Inspector General of the Intelligence Community, who shall be appointed by the President, by and with the advice and consent of the Senate.

(2) The nomination of an individual for appointment as Inspector General shall be made—

(A) without regard to political affiliation;

(B) on the basis of integrity, compliance with security standards of the intelligence community, and prior experience in the field of intelligence or national security; and

(C) on the basis of demonstrated ability in accounting, financial analysis, law, management analysis, public administration, or investigations.

(3) The Inspector General shall report directly to and be under the general supervision of the Director of National Intelligence.

(4) The Inspector General may be removed from office only by the President. The President shall communicate in writing to the congressional intelligence committees the reasons for the removal not later than 30 days prior to the effective date of such removal. Nothing in this paragraph shall be construed to prohibit a personnel action otherwise authorized by law, other than transfer or removal.

(d) ASSISTANT INSPECTORS GENERAL.—

Subject to the policies of the Director of National Intelligence, the Inspector General of the Intelligence Community shall—

(1) appoint an Assistant Inspector General for Audit who shall have the responsibility for supervising the performance of auditing activities relating to programs and activities within the responsibility and authority of the Director;

(2) appoint an Assistant Inspector General for Investigations who shall have the responsibility for supervising the performance of investigative activities relating to such programs and activities; and

(3) appoint other Assistant Inspectors General that, in the judgment of the Inspector General, are necessary to carry out the duties of the Inspector General.

(e) DUTIES AND RESPONSIBILITIES.—It shall be the duty and responsibility of the Inspector General of the Intelligence Community—

(1) to provide policy direction for, and to plan, conduct, supervise, and coordinate independently, the investigations, inspections, audits, and reviews relating to programs and activities within the responsibility and authority of the Director of National Intelligence;

(2) to keep the Director of National Intelligence fully and currently informed concerning violations of law and regulations, fraud, and other serious problems, abuses, and deficiencies relating to the programs and activities within the responsibility and authority of the Director, to recommend corrective action concerning such problems, and to report on the progress made in implementing such corrective action;

(3) to take due regard for the protection of intelligence sources and methods in the preparation of all reports issued by the Inspector General, and, to the extent consistent with the purpose and objective of such reports, take such measures as may be appropriate to minimize the disclosure of intelligence sources and methods described in such reports; and

(4) in the execution of the duties and responsibilities under this section, to comply with generally accepted government auditing.

(f) LIMITATIONS ON ACTIVITIES.—(1) The Director of National Intelligence may prohibit the Inspector General of the Intelligence Community from initiating, carrying out, or completing any investigation, inspection, audit, or review if the Director determines that such prohibition is necessary to protect vital national security interests of the United States.

(2) Not later than seven days after the date on which the Director exercises the authority under paragraph (1), the Director shall submit to the congressional intelligence committees an appropriately classified statement of the reasons for the exercise of such authority.

(3) The Director shall advise the Inspector General at the time a statement under paragraph (2) is submitted, and, to the extent consistent with the protection of intelligence sources and methods, provide the Inspector General with a copy of such statement.

(4) The Inspector General may submit to the congressional intelligence committees any comments on the statement of which the Inspector General has notice under paragraph (3) that the Inspector General considers appropriate.

(g) AUTHORITIES.—(1) The Inspector General of the Intelligence Community shall have direct and prompt access to the Director of National Intelligence when necessary for any purpose pertaining to the performance of the duties of the Inspector General.

(2)(A) The Inspector General shall, subject to the limitations in subsection (f), make such investigations and reports relating to the administration of the programs and activities within the authorities and responsibilities of the Director as are, in the judgment of the Inspector General, necessary or desirable.

(B) The Inspector General shall have access to any employee, or any employee of a contractor, of any element of the intelligence community needed for the performance of the duties of the Inspector General.

(C) The Inspector General shall have direct access to all records, reports, audits, reviews, documents, papers, recommendations, or other materials that relate to the programs and activities with respect to which the Inspector General has responsibilities under this section.

(D) The level of classification or compartmentation of information shall not, in and of itself, provide a sufficient rationale for denying the Inspector General access to any materials under subparagraph (C).

(E) The Director, or on the recommendation of the Director, another appropriate official of the intelligence community, shall take appropriate administrative actions against an employee, or an employee of a contractor, of an element of the intelligence community that fails to cooperate with the Inspector General. Such administrative action may include loss of employment or the termination of an existing contractual relationship.

(3) The Inspector General is authorized to receive and investigate, pursuant to subsection (h), complaints or information from any person concerning the existence of an activity within the authorities and responsibilities of the Director of National Intelligence constituting a violation of laws, rules, or regulations, or mismanagement, gross waste of funds, abuse of authority, or a substantial and specific danger to the public health and safety. Once such complaint or information has been received from an employee of the intelligence community—

(A) the Inspector General shall not disclose the identity of the employee without the consent of the employee, unless the Inspector General determines that such disclosure is unavoidable during the course of the investigation or the disclosure is made to an official of the Department of Justice responsible for determining whether a prosecution should be undertaken; and

(B) no action constituting a reprisal, or threat of reprisal, for making such complaint or disclosing such information to the Inspector General may be taken by any employee in a position to take such actions, unless the complaint was made or the information was disclosed with the knowledge that it was false or with willful disregard for its truth or falsity.

(4) The Inspector General shall have the authority to administer to or take from any person an oath, affirmation, or affidavit, whenever necessary in the performance of the duties of the Inspector General, which oath, affirmation, or affidavit when administered or taken by or before an employee of the Office of the Inspector General of the Intelligence Community designated by the Inspector General shall have the same force and effect as if administered or taken by, or before, an officer having a seal.

(5)(A) Except as provided in subparagraph (B), the Inspector General is authorized to require by subpoena the production of all information, documents, reports, answers, records, accounts, papers, and other data in any medium (including electronically stored information, as well as any tangible thing) and documentary evidence necessary in the performance of the duties and responsibilities of the Inspector General.

(B) In the case of departments, agencies, and other elements of the United States Government, the Inspector General shall obtain information, documents, reports, answers, records, accounts, papers, and other data and evidence for the purpose specified in subparagraph (A) using procedures other than by subpoenas.

(C) The Inspector General may not issue a subpoena for, or on behalf of, any component of the Office of the Director of National Intelligence or any element of the intelligence community, including the Office of the Director of National Intelligence.

(D) In the case of contumacy or refusal to obey a subpoena issued under this paragraph, the subpoena shall be enforceable by order of any appropriate district court of the United States.

(6) The Inspector General may obtain services as authorized by section 3109 of title 5, United States Code, at rates for individuals not to exceed the daily equivalent of the maximum annual rate of basic pay payable for grade GS-15 of the General Schedule under section 5332 of title 5, United States Code.

(7) The Inspector General may, to the extent and in such amounts as may be provided in appropriations, enter into contracts and other arrangements for audits, studies, analyses, and other services with public agencies and with private persons, and to make such payments as may be necessary to carry out the provisions of this section.

(h) COORDINATION AMONG INSPECTORS GENERAL.—(1)(A) In the event of a matter within the jurisdiction of the Inspector General of the Intelligence Community that may be subject to an investigation, inspection, audit, or review by both the Inspector General of the Intelligence Community and an inspector general with oversight responsibility for an element of the intelligence community, the Inspector General of the Intelligence Community and such other inspector general shall expeditiously resolve the question of which inspector general shall conduct such investigation, inspection, audit, or review to avoid unnecessary duplication of the activities of the inspectors general.

> (B) In attempting to resolve a question under subparagraph (A), the inspectors general concerned may request the assistance of the Intelligence Community Inspectors General Forum established under paragraph (2). In the event of a dispute between an inspector general within a department or agency of the United States Government and the Inspector General of the Intelligence Community that has not been resolved with the assistance of such Forum, the inspectors general shall submit the question to the Director of National Intelligence and the head of the affected department or agency for resolution.

(2)(A) There is established the Intelligence Community Inspectors General Forum, which shall consist of all statutory or administrative inspectors general with oversight responsibility for an element of the intelligence community.

> (B) The Inspector General of the Intelligence Community shall serve as the Chair of the Forum established under subparagraph (A). The Forum shall have no administrative authority over any inspector general, but shall serve as a mechanism for informing its members of the work of individual members of the Forum that may be of common interest and discussing questions about jurisdiction or access to employees, employees of contract personnel, records, audits, reviews, documents, recommendations, or other materials that may involve or be of assistance to more than one of its members.

> (3) The inspector general conducting an investigation, inspection, audit, or review covered by paragraph (1) shall submit the results of such investigation, inspection, audit, or review to any other inspector general, including the Inspector General of the Intelligence Community, with jurisdiction to conduct such investigation, inspection, audit, or review who did not conduct such investigation, inspection, audit, or review.

(i) COUNSEL TO THE INSPECTOR GENERAL.—(1) The Inspector General of the Intelligence Community shall—

> (A) appoint a Counsel to the Inspector General who shall report to the Inspector General; or
>
> (B) obtain the services of a counsel appointed by and directly reporting to another inspector general or the Council of the

Inspectors General on Integrity and Efficiency on a reimbursable basis.

(2) The counsel appointed or obtained under paragraph (1) shall perform such functions as the Inspector General may prescribe.

(j) STAFF AND OTHER SUPPORT.—(1) The Director of National Intelligence shall provide the Inspector General of the Intelligence Community with appropriate and adequate office space at central and field office locations, together with such equipment, office supplies, maintenance services, and communications facilities and services as may be necessary for the operation of such offices.

(2)(A) Subject to applicable law and the policies of the Director of National Intelligence, the Inspector General shall select, appoint, and employ such officers and employees as may be necessary to carry out the functions, powers, and duties of the Inspector General. The Inspector General shall ensure that any officer or employee so selected, appointed, or employed has security clearances appropriate for the assigned duties of such officer or employee.

(B) In making selections under subparagraph (A), the Inspector General shall ensure that such officers and employees have the requisite training and experience to enable the Inspector General to carry out the duties of the Inspector General effectively.

(C) In meeting the requirements of this paragraph, the Inspector General shall create within the Office of the Inspector General of the Intelligence Community a career cadre of sufficient size to provide appropriate continuity and objectivity needed for the effective performance of the duties of the Inspector General.

(3) Consistent with budgetary and personnel resources allocated by the Director of National Intelligence, the Inspector General has final approval of—

(A) the selection of internal and external candidates for employment with the Office of the Inspector General; and

(B) all other personnel decisions concerning personnel permanently assigned to the Office of the Inspector General, including selection and appointment to the Senior Intelligence Service, but excluding all security-based determinations that are not within the authority of a head of a component of the Office of the Director of National Intelligence.

(4)(A) Subject to the concurrence of the Director of National Intelligence, the Inspector General may request such information or assistance as may be necessary for carrying out the duties and responsibilities of the Inspector General from any department, agency, or other element of the United States Government.

(B) Upon request of the Inspector General for information or assistance under subparagraph (A), the head of the department, agency, or element concerned shall, insofar as is practicable and not in contravention of any existing statutory restriction or regulation of the department, agency, or element, furnish to the Inspector General, such information or assistance.

(C) The Inspector General of the Intelligence Community may, upon reasonable notice to the head of any element of the intelligence community and in coordination with that element's inspector general pursuant to subsection (h), conduct, as authorized by this section, an investigation, inspection, audit, or review of such element and may enter into any place occupied by such element for purposes of the performance of the duties of the Inspector General.

(k) REPORTS.—(1)(A) The Inspector General of the Intelligence Community shall, not later than January 31 and July 31 of each year, prepare and submit to the Director of National Intelligence a classified, and, as appropriate, unclassified semiannual report summarizing the activities of the Office of the Inspector General of the Intelligence Community during the immediately preceding 6-month period ending December 31 (of the preceding year) and June 30, respectively. The Inspector General of the Intelligence Community shall provide any portion of the report involving a component of a department of the United States Government to the head of that department simultaneously with submission of the report to the Director of National Intelligence.

(B) Each report under this paragraph shall include, at a minimum, the following:

(i) A list of the title or subject of each investigation, inspection, audit, or review conducted during the period covered by such report.

(ii) A description of significant problems, abuses, and deficiencies relating to the administration of programs and activities of the intelligence community within the responsibility and authority of the Director of National Intelligence, and in the relationships between elements of the intelligence community, identified by the Inspector General during the period covered by such report.

(iii) A description of the recommendations for corrective action made by the Inspector General during the period covered by such report with respect to significant problems, abuses, or deficiencies identified in clause (ii).

(iv) A statement of whether or not corrective action has

been completed on each significant recommendation described in previous semiannual reports, and, in a case where corrective action has been completed, a description of such corrective action.

(v) A certification of whether or not the Inspector General has had full and direct access to all information relevant to the performance of the functions of the Inspector General.

(vi) A description of the exercise of the subpoena authority under subsection (g)(5) by the Inspector General during the period covered by such report.

(vii) Such recommendations as the Inspector General considers appropriate for legislation to promote economy, efficiency, and effectiveness in the administration and implementation of programs and activities within the responsibility and authority of the Director of National Intelligence, and to detect and eliminate fraud and abuse in such programs and activities.

(C) Not later than 30 days after the date of receipt of a report under subparagraph (A), the Director shall transmit the report to the congressional intelligence committees together with any comments the Director considers appropriate. The Director shall transmit to the committees of the Senate and of the House of Representatives with jurisdiction over a department of the United States Government any portion of the report involving a component of such department simultaneously with submission of the report to the congressional intelligence committees.

(2)(A) The Inspector General shall report immediately to the Director whenever the Inspector General becomes aware of particularly serious or flagrant problems, abuses, or deficiencies relating to programs and activities within the responsibility and authority of the Director of National Intelligence.

(B) The Director shall transmit to the congressional intelligence committees each report under subparagraph (A) within 7 calendar days of receipt of such report, together with such comments as the Director considers appropriate. The Director shall transmit to the committees of the Senate and of the House of Representatives with jurisdiction over a department of the United States Government any portion of each report under subparagraph (A) that involves a problem, abuse, or deficiency related to a component of such department simultaneously with transmission of the report to the congressional intelligence committees.

(3)(A) In the event that—

(i) the Inspector General is unable to resolve any differences with the Director affecting the execution of the duties or responsibilities of the Inspector General;

(ii) an investigation, inspection, audit, or review carried out by the Inspector General focuses on any current or former intelligence community official who—

(I) holds or held a position in an element of the intelligence community that is subject to appointment by the President, whether or not by and with the advice and consent of the Senate, including such a position held on an acting basis;

(II) holds or held a position in an element of the intelligence community, including a position held on an acting basis, that is appointed by the Director of National Intelligence; or

(III) holds or held a position as head of an element of the intelligence community or a position covered by subsection (b) or (c) of section 106;

(iii) a matter requires a report by the Inspector General to the Department of Justice on possible criminal conduct by a current or former official described in clause (ii);

(iv) the Inspector General receives notice from the Department of Justice declining or approving prosecution of possible criminal conduct of any current or former official described in clause (ii); or

(v) the Inspector General, after exhausting all possible alternatives, is unable to obtain significant documentary information in the course of an investigation, inspection, audit, or review, the Inspector General shall immediately notify, and submit a report to, the congressional intelligence committees on such matter.

(B) The Inspector General shall submit to the committees of the Senate and of the House of Representatives with jurisdiction over a department of the United States Government any portion of each report under subparagraph (A) that involves an investigation, inspection, audit, or review carried out by the Inspector General focused on any current or former official of a component of such department simultaneously with submission of the report to the congressional intelligence committees.

(4) The Director shall submit to the congressional intelligence committees any report or findings and recommendations of an investigation, inspection, audit, or review conducted by the office which has been requested by the Chairman or Vice Chairman or ranking minority member of either committee.

(5)(A) An employee of an element of the intelligence community, an employee assigned or detailed to an element of the intelligence community, or an employee of a contractor to the intelligence community who intends to report to Congress a complaint or information with respect to an urgent concern may report such complaint or information to the Inspector General.

(B) Not later than the end of the 14-calendar-day period beginning on the date of receipt from an employee of a complaint or information under subparagraph (A), the Inspector General shall determine whether the complaint or information appears credible. Upon making such a determination, the Inspector General shall transmit to the Director a notice of that determination, together with the complaint or information.

(C) Upon receipt of a transmittal from the Inspector General under subparagraph (B), the Director shall, within 7 calendar days of such receipt, forward such transmittal to the congressional intelligence committees, together with any comments the Director considers appropriate.

(D)(i) If the Inspector General does not find credible under subparagraph (B) a complaint or information submitted under subparagraph (A), or does not transmit the complaint or information to the Director in accurate form under subparagraph (B), the employee (subject to clause (ii)) may submit the complaint or information to Congress by contacting either or both of the congressional intelligence committees directly.

(ii) An employee may contact the congressional intelligence committees directly as described in clause (i) only if the employee—

(I) before making such a contact, furnishes to the Director, through the Inspector General, a statement of the employee's complaint or information and notice of the employee's intent to contact the congressional intelligence committees directly; and

(II) obtains and follows from the Director, through the Inspector General, direction on how to contact the congressional intelligence committees in accordance with appropriate security practices.

(iii) A member or employee of one of the congressional intelligence committees who receives a complaint or information under this subparagraph does so in that member or employee's official capacity as a member or employee of such committee.

(E) The Inspector General shall notify an employee who reports a complaint or information to the Inspector General under this paragraph of each action taken under this paragraph with respect to the complaint or information. Such notice shall be provided not later than 3 days after any such action is taken.

(F) An action taken by the Director or the Inspector General under this paragraph shall not be subject to judicial review.

(G) In this paragraph, the term "urgent concern" means any of the following:

(i) A serious or flagrant problem, abuse, violation of law or Executive order, or deficiency relating to the funding, administration, or operation of an intelligence activity within the responsibility and authority of the Director of National Intelligence involving classified information, but does not include differences of opinions concerning public policy matters.

(ii) A false statement to Congress, or a willful withholding from Congress, on an issue of material fact relating to the funding, administration, or operation of an intelligence activity.

(iii) An action, including a personnel action described in section 2302(a)(2)(A) of title 5, United States Code, constituting reprisal or threat of reprisal prohibited under subsection (g)(3)(B) of this section in response to an employee's reporting an urgent concern in accordance with this paragraph.

(H) Nothing in this section shall be construed to limit the protections afforded to an employee under section 17(d) of the Central Intelligence Agency Act of 1949 (50 U.S.C. 403q(d)) or section 8H of the Inspector General Act of 1978 (5 U.S.C. App.).

(6) In accordance with section 535 of title 28, United States

Code, the Inspector General shall expeditiously report to the Attorney General any information, allegation, or complaint received by the Inspector General relating to violations of Federal criminal law that involves a program or operation of an element of the intelligence community, or in the relationships between the elements of the intelligence community, consistent with such guidelines as may be issued by the Attorney General pursuant to subsection (b)(2) of such section. A copy of each such report shall be furnished to the Director.

(l) CONSTRUCTION OF DUTIES REGARDING ELEMENTS OF INTELLIGENCE COMMUNITY.—Except as resolved pursuant to subsection (h), the performance by the Inspector General of the Intelligence Community of any duty, responsibility, or function regarding an element of the intelligence community shall not be construed to modify or affect the duties and responsibilities of any other inspector general having duties and responsibilities relating to such element.

(m) SEPARATE BUDGET ACCOUNT.—The Director of National Intelligence shall, in accordance with procedures issued by the Director in consultation with the congressional intelligence committees, include in the National Intelligence Program budget a separate account for the Office of the Inspector General of the Intelligence Community.

(n) BUDGET.—(1) For each fiscal year, the Inspector General of the Intelligence Community shall transmit a budget estimate and request to the Director of National Intelligence that specifies for such fiscal year—

(A) the aggregate amount requested for the operations of the Inspector General;

(B) the amount requested for all training requirements of the Inspector General, including a certification from the Inspector General that the amount requested is sufficient to fund all training requirements for the Office of the Inspector General; and

(C) the amount requested to support the Council of the Inspectors General on Integrity and Efficiency, including a justification for such amount.

(2) In transmitting a proposed budget to the President for a fiscal year, the Director of National Intelligence shall include for such fiscal year—

(A) the aggregate amount requested for the Inspector General of the Intelligence Community;

(B) the amount requested for Inspector General training;

(C) the amount requested to support the Council of the Inspectors General on Integrity and Efficiency; and

(D) the comments of the Inspector General, if any, with respect to such proposed budget.

(3) The Director of National Intelligence shall submit to the congressional intelligence committees, the Committee on Appropriations of the Senate, and the Committee on Appropriations of the House of Representatives for each fiscal year—

(A) a separate statement of the budget estimate transmitted pursuant to paragraph (1);

(B) the amount requested by the Director for the Inspector General pursuant to paragraph (2)(A);

(C) the amount requested by the Director for the training of personnel of the Office of the Inspector General pursuant to paragraph (2)(B);

(D) the amount requested by the Director for support for the Council of the Inspectors General on Integrity and Efficiency pursuant to paragraph (2)(C); and

(E) the comments of the Inspector General under paragraph (2)(D), if any, on the amounts requested pursuant to paragraph (2), including whether such amounts would substantially inhibit the Inspector General from performing the duties of the Office of the Inspector General.

(o) INFORMATION ON WEBSITE.—(1) The Director of National Intelligence shall establish and maintain on the homepage of the publicly accessible website of the Office of the Director of National Intelligence information relating to the Office of the Inspector General of the Intelligence Community including methods to contact the Inspector General.

(2) The information referred to in paragraph (1) shall be obvious and facilitate accessibility to the information related to the Office of the Inspector General of the Intelligence Community.

CHIEF FINANCIAL OFFICER OF THE INTELLIGENCE COMMUNITY

Sec. 103I. [50 USC 403-3i.] (a) CHIEF FINANCIAL OFFICER OF THE INTELLIGENCE COMMUNITY.—To assist the Director of National Intelligence in carrying out the responsibilities of the Director under this Act and other applicable provisions of law, there is within the Office of the Director of National Intelligence a Chief Financial Officer of the Intelligence Community who shall be appointed by the Director.

(b) DUTIES AND RESPONSIBILITIES.—Subject to the direction of the Director of National Intelligence, the Chief Financial Officer of the Intelligence Community shall—

(1) serve as the principal advisor to the Director of National Intelligence and the Principal Deputy Director of National Intelligence on the

management and allocation of intelligence community budgetary resources;

(2) participate in overseeing a comprehensive and integrated strategic process for resource management within the intelligence community;

(3) ensure that the strategic plan of the Director of National Intelligence—

(A) is based on budgetary constraints as specified in the Future Year Intelligence Plans and Long-term Budget Projections required under section 506G; and

(B) contains specific goals and objectives to support a performance-based budget;

(4) prior to the obligation or expenditure of funds for the acquisition of any major system pursuant to a Milestone A or Milestone B decision, receive verification from appropriate authorities that the national requirements for meeting the strategic plan of the Director have been established, and that such requirements are prioritized based on budgetary constraints as specified in the Future Year Intelligence Plans and the Long-term Budget Projections for such major system required under section 506G;

(5) ensure that the collection architectures of the Director are based on budgetary constraints as specified in the Future Year Intelligence Plans and the Long-term Budget Projections required under section 506G;

(6) coordinate or approve representations made to Congress by the intelligence community regarding National Intelligence Program budgetary resources;

(7) participate in key mission requirements, acquisitions, or architectural boards formed within or by the Office of the Director of National Intelligence; and

(8) perform such other duties as may be prescribed by the Director of National Intelligence.

(c) OTHER LAW.—The Chief Financial Officer of the Intelligence Community shall serve as the Chief Financial Officer of the intelligence community and, to the extent applicable, shall have the duties, responsibilities, and authorities specified in chapter 9 of title 31, United States Code.

(d) PROHIBITION ON SIMULTANEOUS SERVICE AS OTHER CHIEF FINANCIAL OFFICER.—An individual serving in the position of Chief Financial Officer of the Intelligence Community may not, while so serving, serve as the chief financial officer of any other department or agency, or component thereof, of the United States Government.

(e) DEFINITIONS.—In this section:

(1) The term "major system" has the meaning given that term in section 506A(e).

(2) The term "Milestone A" has the meaning given that term in section 506G(f).

(3) The term "Milestone B" has the meaning given that term in section 506C(e).

CENTRAL INTELLIGENCE AGENCY

SEC. 104. [50 U.S.C. §403-4]

(a) CENTRAL INTELLIGENCE AGENCY.—There is a Central Intelligence Agency.

(b) FUNCTION.—The function of the Central Intelligence Agency is to assist the Director of the Central Intelligence Agency in carrying out the responsibilities specified in section 104A(c).

DIRECTOR OF THE CENTRAL INTELLIGENCE AGENCY

SEC. 104A. [50 U.S.C. §403-4a]

(a) DIRECTOR OF CENTRAL INTELLIGENCE AGENCY.—There is a Director of the Central Intelligence Agency who shall be appointed by the President, by and with the advice and consent of the Senate.

(b) SUPERVISION.—The Director of the Central Intelligence Agency shall report to the Director of National Intelligence regarding the activities of the Central Intelligence Agency.

(c) DUTIES.—The Director of the Central Intelligence Agency shall—

(1) serve as the head of the Central Intelligence Agency; and

(2) carry out the responsibilities specified in subsection (d).

(d) RESPONSIBILITIES.—The Director of the Central Intelligence Agency shall—

(1) collect intelligence through human sources and by other appropriate means, except that the Director of the Central Intelligence Agency shall have no police, subpoena, or law enforcement powers or internal security functions;

(2) correlate and evaluate intelligence related to the national security and provide appropriate dissemination of such intelligence;

(3) provide overall direction for and coordination of the collection of national intelligence outside the United States through human sources by elements of the intelligence community authorized to undertake such collection and, in coordination with other departments, agencies, or elements of the United States Government which are authorized to undertake such collection, ensure that the most effective use is made of resources and that appropriate account is taken of the risks to the United States and those involved in such collection; and

(4) perform such other functions and duties related to intelligence affecting the national security as the President or the Director of National Intelligence may direct.

(e) TERMINATION OF EMPLOYMENT OF CIA EMPLOYEES.—

(1) Notwithstanding the provisions of any other law, the Director of the Central Intelligence Agency may, in the discretion of the Director, terminate the employment of any officer or employee of the Central Intelligence Agency whenever the Director deems the termination of employment of such officer or employee necessary or advisable in the interests of the United States.

(2) Any termination of employment of an officer or employee under paragraph (1) shall not affect the right of the officer or employee to seek or accept employment in any other department, agency, or element of the United States Government if declared eligible for such employment by the Office of Personnel Management.

(f) COORDINATION WITH FOREIGN GOVERNMENTS.—Under the direction of the Director of National Intelligence and in a manner consistent with section 207 of the Foreign Service Act of 1980 (22 U.S.C. §3927), the Director of the Central Intelligence Agency shall coordinate the relationships between elements of the intelligence community and the intelligence or security services of foreign governments or international organizations on all matters involving intelligence related to the national security or involving intelligence acquired through clandestine means.

(g) FOREIGN LANGUAGE PROFICIENCY FOR CERTAIN SENIOR LEVEL POSITIONS IN CENTRAL INTELLIGENCE AGENCY.—

(1) Except as provided pursuant to paragraph (2), an individual in the Directorate of Intelligence career service or the National Clandestine Service career service may not be appointed or promoted to a position in the Senior Intelligence Service in the Directorate of Intelligence or the National Clandestine Service of the Central Intelligence Agency unless the Director of the Central Intelligence Agency determines that the individual has been certified as having a professional speaking and reading proficiency in a foreign language, such proficiency being at least level 3 on the Interagency Language Roundtable Language Skills Level or commensurate proficiency level using such other indicator of proficiency as the Director of the Central Intelligence Agency considers appropriate.

(2) The Director of the Central Intelligence Agency may, in the discretion of the Director, waive the application of paragraph (1) to any position, category of positions, or occupation otherwise covered by that paragraph if the Director determines that foreign language proficiency is not necessary for the successful performance of the duties and responsibilities of such position, category of positions, or occupation.

DEPUTY DIRECTOR OF THE CENTRAL INTELLIGENCE AGENCY

Sec. 104B. [50 USC 403-4c.] (a) DEPUTY
DIRECTOR OF THE CENTRAL INTELLIGENCE AGENCY.—There is a Deputy
Director of the Central Intelligence Agency who shall be appointed by the
President.

(b) DUTIES.—The Deputy Director of the Central Intelligence Agency shall—(1)
assist the Director of the Central Intelligence Agency in carrying out the duties
and responsibilities of the Director of the Central Intelligence Agency; and
> (2) during the absence or disability of the Director of the Central
> Intelligence Agency, or during a vacancy in the position of Director of
> the Central Intelligence Agency, act for and exercise the powers of the
> Director of the Central Intelligence Agency.

RESPONSIBILITIES OF THE SECRETARY OF DEFENSE
PERTAINING TO THE NATIONAL INTELLIGENCE PROGRAM

SEC. 105. [50 U.S.C. §403–5]
(a) IN GENERAL.—Consistent with the sections 102 and 102A, the Secretary of
Defense, in consultation with the Director of National Intelligence, shall—
> (1) ensure that the budgets of the elements of the intelligence community
> within the Department of Defense are adequate to satisfy the overall
> intelligence needs of the Department of Defense, including the needs of
> the Chairman of the Joint Chiefs of Staff and the commanders of the
> unified and specified commands and, wherever such elements are
> performing government wide functions, the needs of other departments
> and agencies;
> (2) ensure appropriate implementation of the policies and resource
> decisions of the Director by elements of the Department of Defense
> within the National Intelligence Program;
> (3) ensure that the tactical intelligence activities of the Department of
> Defense complement and are compatible with intelligence activities
> under the National Intelligence Program;
> (4) ensure that the elements of the intelligence community within the
> Department of Defense are responsive and timely with respect to
> satisfying the needs of operational military forces;
> (5) eliminate waste and unnecessary duplication among the intelligence
> activities of the Department of Defense; and
> (6) ensure that intelligence activities of the Department of Defense are
> conducted jointly where appropriate.

(b) RESPONSIBILITY FOR THE PERFORMANCE OF SPECIFIC FUNCTIONS.—
Consistent with sections 102 and 102A of this Act, the Secretary of Defense shall
ensure—

> (1) through the National Security Agency (except as otherwise directed
> by the President or the National Security Council), the continued
> operation of an effective unified organization for the conduct of signals
> intelligence activities and shall ensure that the product is disseminated in
> a timely manner to authorized recipients;
>
> (2) through the National Geospatial-Intelligence Agency (except as
> otherwise directed by the President or the National Security Council),
> with appropriate representation from the intelligence community, the
> continued operation of an effective unified organization within the
> Department of Defense—
>
>> (A) for carrying out tasking of imagery collection;
>> (B) for the coordination of imagery processing and exploitation
>> activities;
>> (C) for ensuring the dissemination of imagery in a timely manner
>> to authorized recipients; and
>> (D) notwithstanding any other provision of law, for—
>>
>>> (i) prescribing technical architecture and standards
>>> related to imagery intelligence and geospatial
>>> information and ensuring compliance with such
>>> architecture and standards; and
>>> (ii) developing and fielding systems of common concern
>>> related to imagery intelligence and geospatial
>>> information;
>
> (3) through the National Reconnaissance Office (except as otherwise
> directed by the President or the National Security Council), the continued
> operation of an effective unified organization for the research and
> development, acquisition, and operation of overhead reconnaissance
> systems necessary to satisfy the requirements of all elements of the
> intelligence community;
>
> (4) through the Defense Intelligence Agency (except as otherwise
> directed by the President or the National Security Council), the continued
> operation of an effective unified system within the Department of
> Defense for the production of timely, objective military and military-
> related intelligence, based upon all sources available to the intelligence
> community, and shall ensure the appropriate dissemination of such
> intelligence to authorized recipients;
>
> (5) through the Defense Intelligence Agency (except as otherwise
> directed by the President or the National Security Council), effective

management of Department of Defense human intelligence and counterintelligence activities, including defense attaches; and

(6) that the military departments maintain sufficient capabilities to collect and produce intelligence to meet—

(A) the requirements of the Director of National Intelligence;

(B) the requirements of the Secretary of Defense or the Chairman of the Joint Chiefs of Staff;

(C) the requirements of the unified and specified combatant commands and of joint operations; and

(D) the specialized requirements of the military departments for intelligence necessary to support tactical commanders, military planners, the research and development process, the acquisition of military equipment, and training and doctrine.

(c) EXPENDITURE OF FUNDS BY THE DEFENSE INTELLIGENCE AGENCY.—(1) Subject to paragraphs (2) and (3), the Director of the Defense Intelligence Agency may expend amounts made available to the Director under the National Intelligence Program for human intelligence and counterintelligence activities for objects of a confidential, extraordinary, or emergency nature, without regard to the provisions of law or regulation relating to the expenditure of Government funds.

(2) The Director of the Defense Intelligence Agency may not expend more than five percent of the amounts made available to the Director under the National Intelligence Program for human intelligence and counterintelligence activities for a fiscal year for objects of a confidential, extraordinary, or emergency nature in accordance with paragraph (1) during such fiscal year unless—

(A) the Director notifies the congressional intelligence committees of the intent to expend the amounts; and

(B) 30 days have elapsed from the date on which the Director notifies the congressional intelligence committees in accordance with subparagraph (A).

(3) For each expenditure referred to in paragraph (1), the Director shall certify that such expenditure was made for an object of a confidential, extraordinary, or emergency nature.

(4) Not later than December 31 of each year, the Director of the Defense Intelligence Agency shall submit to the congressional intelligence committees a report on any expenditures made during the preceding fiscal year in accordance with paragraph (1).

(d) USE OF ELEMENTS OF DEPARTMENT OF DEFENSE.—The Secretary of Defense, in carrying out the functions described in this section, may use such elements of the Department of Defense as may be appropriate for the execution of those functions, in addition to, or in lieu of, the elements identified in this section.

Assistance to United States Law Enforcement Agencies

Sec. 105A. [50 U.S.C. §403–5a]

(a) Authority to Provide Assistance.—Subject to subsection (b), elements of the intelligence community may, upon the request of a United States law enforcement agency, collect information outside the United States about individuals who are not United States persons. Such elements may collect such information notwithstanding that the law enforcement agency intends to use the information collected for purposes of a law enforcement investigation or counterintelligence investigation.

(b) Limitation on Assistance by Elements of Department of Defense.—

    (1) With respect to elements within the Department of Defense, the authority in subsection (a) applies only to the following:

        (A) The National Security Agency.

        (B) The National Reconnaissance Office.

        (C) The National Geospatial-Intelligence Agency.

        (D) The Defense Intelligence Agency.

    (2) Assistance provided under this section by elements of the Department of Defense may not include the direct participation of a member of the Army, Navy, Air Force, or Marine Corps in an arrest or similar activity.

    (3) Assistance may not be provided under this section by an element of the Department of Defense if the provision of such assistance will adversely affect the military preparedness of the United States.

    (4) The Secretary of Defense shall prescribe regulations governing the exercise of authority under this section by elements of the Department of Defense, including regulations relating to the protection of sources and methods in the exercise of such authority.

(c) Definitions.—For purposes of subsection (a):

    (1) The term "United States law enforcement agency" means any department or agency of the Federal Government that the Attorney General designates as law enforcement agency for purposes of this section.

    (2) The term "United States person" means the following:

        (A) A United States citizen.

        (B) An alien known by the intelligence agency concerned to be a permanent resident alien.

        (C) An unincorporated association substantially composed of United States citizens or permanent resident aliens.

(D) A corporation incorporated in the United States, except for a corporation directed and controlled by a foreign government or governments.

DISCLOSURE OF FOREIGN INTELLIGENCE ACQUIRED IN CRIMINAL INVESTIGATIONS; NOTICE OF CRIMINAL INVESTIGATIONS OF FOREIGN INTELLIGENCE SOURCES

SEC. 105B. [50 U.S.C. §403–5b]

(a) DISCLOSURE OF FOREIGN INTELLIGENCE.—

(1) Except as otherwise provided by law and subject to paragraph (2), the Attorney General, or the head of any other department or agency of the Federal Government with law enforcement responsibilities, shall expeditiously disclose to the Director of National Intelligence, pursuant to guidelines developed by the Attorney General in consultation with the Director, foreign intelligence acquired by an element of the Department of Justice or an element of such department or agency, as the case may be, in the course of a criminal investigation.

(2) The Attorney General by regulation and in consultation with the Director may provide for exceptions to the applicability of paragraph (1) for one or more classes of foreign intelligence, or foreign intelligence with respect to one or more targets or matters, if the Attorney General determines that disclosure of such foreign intelligence under that paragraph would jeopardize an ongoing law enforcement investigation or impair other significant law enforcement interests.

(b) PROCEDURES FOR NOTICE OF CRIMINAL INVESTIGATIONS.—Not later than 180 days after the date of enactment of this section, the Attorney General, in consultation with the Director of National Intelligence, shall develop guidelines to ensure that after receipt of a report from an element of the intelligence community of activity of a foreign intelligence source or potential foreign intelligence source that may warrant investigation as criminal activity, the Attorney General provides notice to the Director, within a reasonable period of time, of his intention to commence, or decline to commence, a criminal investigation of such activity.

(c) PROCEDURES.—The Attorney General shall develop procedures for the administration of this section, including the disclosure of foreign intelligence by elements of the Department of Justice, and elements of other departments and agencies of the Federal Government, under subsection (a) and the provision of notice with respect to criminal investigations under subsection (b).

APPOINTMENT OF OFFICIALS RESPONSIBLE FOR INTELLIGENCE RELATED ACTIVITIES

SEC. 106. [50 U.S.C. §403–6]
(a) RECOMMENDATION OF DNI IN CERTAIN APPOINTMENTS.—

(1) In the event of a vacancy in a position referred to in paragraph (2), the Director of National Intelligence shall recommend to the President an individual for nomination to fill the vacancy.

(2) Paragraph (1) applies to the following positions:

(A) The Principal Deputy Director of National Intelligence.

(B) The Director of the Central Intelligence Agency.

(b) CONCURRENCE OF DNI IN APPOINTMENTS TO POSITIONS IN THE INTELLIGENCE COMMUNITY.—

(1) In the event of a vacancy in a position referred to in paragraph (2), the head of the department or agency having jurisdiction over the position shall obtain the concurrence of the Director of National Intelligence before appointing an individual to fill the vacancy or recommending to the President an individual to be nominated to fill the vacancy. If the Director does not concur in the recommendation, the head of the department or agency concerned may not fill the vacancy or make the recommendation to the President (as the case may be). In the case in which the Director does not concur in such a recommendation, the Director and the head of the department or agency concerned may advise the President directly of the intention to withhold concurrence or to make a recommendation, as the case may be.

(2) Paragraph (1) applies to the following positions:

(A) The Director of the National Security Agency.

(B) The Director of the National Reconnaissance Office.

(C) The Director of the National Geospatial-Intelligence Agency.

(D) The Assistant Secretary of State for Intelligence and Research.

(E) The Director of the Office of Intelligence of the Department of Energy.

(F) The Director of the Office of Counterintelligence of the Department of Energy.

(G) The Assistant Secretary for Intelligence and Analysis of the Department of the Treasury.

(H) The Executive Assistant Director for Intelligence of the Federal Bureau of Investigation or any successor to that position.

(I) The Under Secretary of Homeland Security for Intelligence and Analysis.

(c) CONSULTATION WITH DNI IN CERTAIN POSITIONS.—

(1) In the event of a vacancy in a position referred to in paragraph (2), the head of the department or agency having jurisdiction over the

position shall consult with the Director of National Intelligence before appointing an individual to fill the vacancy or recommending to the President an individual to be nominated to fill the vacancy.

(2) Paragraph (1) applies to the following positions:

(A) The Director of the Defense Intelligence Agency.

(B) The Assistant Commandant of the Coast Guard for Intelligence.

(C) Assistant Attorney General designated as the Assistant Attorney General for National Security under section 507A of title 28, United States Code.

NATIONAL SECURITY RESOURCES BOARD

SEC. 107. [50 U.S.C. §404]

(a) The Director of the Federal Emergency Management Agency, subject to the direction of the President, is authorized, subject to the civil-service laws and the Classification Act of 1949, to appoint and fix the compensation of such personnel as may be necessary to assist the Director in carrying out his functions.

(b) It shall be the function of the Director of the Office of Defense Mobilization to advise the President concerning the coordination of military, industrial, and civilian mobilization, including—

(1) policies concerning industrial and civilian mobilization in order to assure the most effective mobilization and maximum utilization of the Nation's manpower in the event of war.

(2) programs for the effective use in time of war of the Nation's natural and industrial resources for military and civilian needs, for the maintenance and stabilization of the civilian economy in time of war, and for the adjustment of such economy to war needs and conditions;

(3) policies for unifying, in time of war, the activities of Federal agencies and departments engaged in or concerned with production, procurement, distribution, or transportation of military or civilian supplies, materials, and products;

(4) the relationship between potential supplies of, and potential requirements for, manpower, resources, and productive facilities in time of war;

(5) policies for establishing adequate reserves of strategic and critical material, and for the conservation of these reserves;

(6) the strategic relocation of industries, services, government, and economic activities, the continuous operation of which is essential to the Nation's security.

(c) In performing his functions, the Director of the Office of Defense Mobilization shall utilize to the maximum extent the facilities and resources of the departments and agencies of the Government.

ANNUAL NATIONAL SECURITY STRATEGY REPORT

SEC. 108. [50 U.S.C. §404a]

(a)(1) The President shall transmit to Congress each year a comprehensive report on the national security strategy of the United States (hereinafter in this section referred to as a national security strategy report").

> (2) The national security strategy report for any year shall be transmitted on the date on which the President submits to Congress the budget for the next fiscal year under section 1105 of title 31, United States Code.

> (3) Not later than 150 days after the date on which a new President takes office, the President shall transmit to Congress a national security strategy report under this section. That report shall be in addition to the report for that year transmitted at the time specified in paragraph (2).

(b) Each national security strategy report shall set forth the national security strategy of the United States and shall include a comprehensive description and discussion of the following:

> (1) The worldwide interests, goals, and objectives of the United States that are vital to the national security of the United States.

> (2) The foreign policy, worldwide commitments, and national defense capabilities of the United States necessary to deter aggression and to implement the national security strategy of the United States.

> (3) The proposed short-term and long-term uses of the political, economic, military, and other elements of the national power of the United States to protect or promote the interests and achieve the goals and objectives referred to in paragraph (1).

> (4) The adequacy of the capabilities of the United States to carry out the national security strategy of the United States, including an evaluation of the balance among the capabilities of all elements of the national power of the United States to support the implementation of the national security strategy.

> (5) Such other information as may be necessary to help inform Congress on matters relating to the national security strategy of the United States.

(c) Each national security strategy report shall be transmitted in both a classified and an unclassified form. [1]

ANNUAL REPORT ON INTELLIGENCE

---

[1] *See annotation at the end of this act for additional reporting requirements, which are separately enumerated in the National Defense Authorization Act for Fiscal Year 2012.

SEC. 109. [50 U.S.C. §404d]
(a) IN GENERAL.—

(1)(A) Not later each year than the date provided in section 507, the President shall submit to the congressional intelligence committees a report on the requirements of the United States for intelligence and the activities of the intelligence community.

(B) Not later than January 31 each year, and included with the budget of the President for the next fiscal year under section 1105(a) of title 31, United States Code, the President shall submit to the appropriate congressional committees the report described in subparagraph (A).

(2) The purpose of the report is to facilitate an assessment of the activities of the intelligence community during the preceding fiscal year and to assist in the development of a mission and a budget for the intelligence community for the fiscal year beginning in the year in which the report is submitted.

(3) The report shall be submitted in unclassified form, but may include a classified annex.

(b) MATTERS COVERED.—

(1) Each report under subsection (a) shall—

(A) specify the intelligence required to meet the national security interests of the United States, and set forth an order of priority for the collection and analysis of intelligence required to meet such interests, for the fiscal year beginning in the year in which the report is submitted; and

(B) evaluate the performance of the intelligence community in collecting and analyzing intelligence required to meet such interests during the fiscal year ending in the year preceding the year in which the report is submitted, including a description of the significant successes and significant failures of the intelligence community in such collection and analysis during that fiscal year.

(2) The report shall specify matters under paragraph (1)(A) in sufficient detail to assist Congress in making decisions with respect to the allocation of resources for the matters specified.

(c) DEFINITION.—In this section, the term "appropriate congressional committees" means the following:

(1) The Committee on Appropriations and the Committee on Armed Services of the Senate.

(2) The Committee on Appropriations and the Committee on Armed Services of the House of Representatives.

NATIONAL MISSION OF THE
NATIONAL GEOSPATIAL-INTELLIGENCE AGENCY

SEC. 110. [50 U.S.C. §404e]

(a) IN GENERAL.—In addition to the Department of Defense missions set forth in section 442 of title 10, United States Code, the National Geospatial-Intelligence Agency shall support the imagery requirements of the Department of State and other departments and agencies of the United States outside the Department of Defense.

(b) REQUIREMENTS AND PRIORITIES.—The Director of National Intelligence shall establish requirements and priorities governing the collection of national intelligence by the National Geospatial-Intelligence Agency under subsection (a).

(c) CORRECTION OF DEFICIENCIES.—The Director of National Intelligence shall develop and implement such programs and policies as the Director and the Secretary of Defense jointly determine necessary to review and correct deficiencies identified in the capabilities of the National Geospatial-Intelligence Agency to accomplish assigned national missions, including support to the all-source analysis and production process. The Director shall consult with the Secretary of Defense on the development and implementation of such programs and policies. The Secretary shall obtain the advice of the Chairman of the Joint Chiefs of Staff regarding the matters on which the Director and the Secretary are to consult under the preceding sentence.

RESTRICTION ON INTELLIGENCE SHARING WITH THE UNITED NATIONS

SEC. 112. [50 U.S.C. §404g]

(a) PROVISION OF INTELLIGENCE INFORMATION TO THE UNITED NATIONS.—

(1) No United States intelligence information may be provided to the United Nations or any organization affiliated with the United Nations, or to any officials or employees thereof, unless the President certifies to the appropriate committees of Congress that the Director of National Intelligence, in consultation with the Secretary of State and the Secretary of Defense, has established and implemented procedures, and has worked with the United Nations to ensure implementation of procedures, for protecting from unauthorized disclosure United States intelligence sources and methods connected to such information.

(2) Paragraph (1) may be waived upon written certification by the President to the appropriate committees of Congress that providing such information to the United Nations or an organization affiliated with the United Nations, or to any officials or employees thereof, is in the national security interests of the United States.

(b) DELEGATION OF DUTIES.—The President may not delegate or assign the duties of the President under this section.

(c) RELATIONSHIP TO EXISTING LAW.—Nothing in this section shall be construed to—

> (1) impair or otherwise affect the authority of the Director of National Intelligence to protect intelligence sources and methods from unauthorized disclosure pursuant to section 103(c)(7) of this Act; or
>
> (2) supersede or otherwise affect the provisions of title V of this Act.

(d) DEFINITION.—As used in this section, the term "appropriate committees of Congress" means the Committee on Foreign Relations and the Select Committee on Intelligence of the Senate and the Committee on Foreign Relations and the Permanent Select Committee on Intelligence of the House of Representatives.

DETAIL OF INTELLIGENCE COMMUNITY PERSONNEL; INTELLIGENCE COMMUNITY ASSIGNMENT PROGRAM

SEC. 113. [50 U.S.C. §404h]

(a) DETAIL.—

> (1) Notwithstanding any other provision of law, the head of a department with an element in the intelligence community or the head of an intelligence community agency or element may detail any employee within that department, agency, or element to serve in any position in the Intelligence Community Assignment Program on a reimbursable or a nonreimbursable basis.
>
> (2) Nonreimbursable details may be for such periods as are agreed to between the heads of the parent and host agencies, up to a maximum of three years, except that such details may be extended for a period not to exceed one year when the heads of the parent and host agencies determine that such extension is in the public interest.

(b) BENEFITS, ALLOWANCES, TRAVEL, INCENTIVES.—

> (1) An employee detailed under subsection (a) may be authorized any benefit, allowance, travel, or incentive otherwise provided to enhance staffing by the organization from which the employee is detailed.
>
> (2) The head of an agency of an employee detailed under subsection (a) may pay a lodging allowance for the employee subject to the following conditions:
>
> > (A) The allowance shall be the lesser of the cost of the lodging or a maximum amount payable for the lodging as established jointly by the Director of National Intelligence and—
> >
> > > (i) with respect to detailed employees of the Department of Defense, the Secretary of Defense; and

(ii) with respect to detailed employees of other agencies and departments, the head of such agency or department.

(B) The detailed employee maintains a primary residence for the employee's immediate family in the local commuting area of the parent agency duty station from which the employee regularly commuted to such duty station before the detail.

(C) The lodging is within a reasonable proximity of the host agency duty station.

(D) The distance between the detailed employee's parent agency duty station and the host agency duty station is greater than 20 miles.

(E) The distance between the detailed employee's primary residence and the host agency duty station is 10 miles greater than the distance between such primary residence and the employee's parent duty station.

(F) The rate of pay applicable to the detailed employee does not exceed the rate of basic pay for grade GS–15 of the General Schedule.

NON-REIMBURSABLE DETAIL OF OTHER PERSONNEL

Sec. 113A. An officer or employee of the United States or member of the Armed Forces may be detailed to the staff of an element of the intelligence community funded through the National Intelligence Program from another element of the intelligence community or from another element of the United States Government on a non-reimbursable basis, as jointly agreed to by the heads of the receiving and detailing elements, for a period not to exceed two years. This section does not limit any other source of authority for reimbursable or non-reimbursable details.

ADDITIONAL ANNUAL REPORTS FROM THE DIRECTOR OF NATIONAL INTELLIGENCE

SEC. 114. [50 U.S.C. §404i]

(a) ANNUAL REPORT ON THE SAFETY AND SECURITY OF RUSSIAN NUCLEAR FACILITIES AND NUCLEAR MILITARY FORCES.—

(1) The Director of National Intelligence shall submit to the congressional leadership on an annual basis, and to the congressional intelligence committees on the date each year provided in section 507, an intelligence report assessing the safety and security of the nuclear facilities and nuclear military forces in Russia.

(2) Each such report shall include a discussion of the following:

(A) The ability of the Government of Russia to maintain its nuclear military forces.

(B) The security arrangements at civilian and military nuclear facilities in Russia.

(C) The reliability of controls and safety systems at civilian nuclear facilities in Russia.

(D) The reliability of command and control systems and procedures of the nuclear military forces in Russia.

(3) Each such report shall be submitted in unclassified form, but may contain a classified annex.

(b) ANNUAL REPORT ON HIRING AND RETENTION OF MINORITY EMPLOYEES.—

(1) The Director of National Intelligence shall, on an annual basis, submit to Congress a report on the employment of covered persons within each element of the intelligence community for the preceding fiscal year.

(2) Each such report shall include disaggregated data by category of covered person from each element of the intelligence community on the following:

(A) Of all individuals employed in the element during the fiscal year involved, the aggregate percentage of such individuals who are covered persons.

(B) Of all individuals employed in the element during the fiscal year involved at the levels referred to in clauses (i) and (ii), the percentage of covered persons employed at such levels:

(i) Positions at levels 1 through 15 of the General Schedule.

(ii) Positions at levels above GS–15.

(C) Of all individuals hired by the element involved during the fiscal year involved, the percentage of such individuals who are covered persons.

(3) Each such report shall be submitted in unclassified form, but may contain a classified annex.

(4) Nothing in this subsection shall be construed as providing for the substitution of any similar report required under another provision of law.

(5) In this subsection, the term "covered persons" means—

(A) racial and ethnic minorities;

(B) women; and

(C) individuals with disabilities.

(c) ANNUAL REPORT ON THREAT OF ATTACK ON THE UNITED STATES USING WEAPONS OF MASS DESTRUCTION.—

(1) Not later each year than the date provided in section 507, the Director of National Intelligence shall submit to the congressional committees specified in paragraph (3) a report assessing the following:

    (A) The current threat of attack on the United States using ballistic missiles or cruise missiles.

    (B) The current threat of attack on the United States using a chemical, biological, or nuclear weapon delivered by a system other than a ballistic missile or cruise missile.

(2) Each report under paragraph (1) shall be a national intelligence estimate, or have the formality of a national intelligence estimate.

(3) The congressional committees referred to in paragraph (1) are the following:

    (A) The congressional intelligence committees.

    (B) The Committees on Foreign Relations and Armed Services of the Senate.

    (C) The Committees on International Relations and Armed Services of the House of Representatives.

(d) CONGRESSIONAL LEADERSHIP DEFINED.—In this section, the term "congressional leadership" means the Speaker and the minority leader of the House of Representatives and the majority leader and the minority leader of the Senate.

TRAVEL ON ANY COMMON CARRIER FOR CERTAIN INTELLIGENCE COLLECTION PERSONNEL

SEC. 116. [50 U.S.C. §404k]

(a) IN GENERAL.—Notwithstanding any other provision of law, the Director of National Intelligence may authorize travel on any common carrier when such travel, in the discretion of the Director—

    (1) is consistent with intelligence community mission requirements, or

    (2) is required for cover purposes, operational needs, or other exceptional circumstances necessary for the successful performance of an intelligence community mission.

(b) AUTHORIZED DELEGATION OF DUTY.—The Director of National Intelligence may only delegate the authority granted by this section to the Principal Deputy Director of National Intelligence, or with respect to employees of the Central Intelligence Agency, to the Director of the Central Intelligence Agency, who may delegate such authority to other appropriate officials of the Central Intelligence Agency.

POW/MIA ANALYTIC CAPABILITY

SEC. 117. [50 U.S.C. §404l]

(a) REQUIREMENT.—

(1) The Director of National Intelligence shall, in consultation with the Secretary of Defense, establish and maintain in the intelligence community an analytic capability with responsibility for intelligence in support of the activities of the United States relating to individuals who, after December 31, 1990, are unaccounted for United States personnel.

(2) The analytic capability maintained under paragraph (1) shall be known as the "POW/MIA analytic capability of the intelligence community".

(b) UNACCOUNTED FOR UNITED STATES PERSONNEL.—In this section, the term "unaccounted for United States personnel" means the following:

(1) Any missing person (as that term is defined in section 1513(1) of title 10, United States Code).

(2) Any United States national who was killed while engaged in activities on behalf of the United States and whose remains have not been repatriated to the United States.

ANNUAL REPORT ON FINANCIAL INTELLIGENCE ON TERRORIST ASSETS

SEC. 118. [50 U.S.C. §404m]

(a) ANNUAL REPORT.—On an annual basis, the Secretary of the Treasury (acting through the head of the Office of Intelligence Support) shall submit a report to the appropriate congressional committees that fully informs the committees concerning operations against terrorist financial networks.

Each such report shall include with respect to the preceding one-year period—

(1) the total number of asset seizures, designations, and other actions against individuals or entities found to have engaged in financial support of terrorism;

(2) the total number of physical searches of offices, residences, or financial records of individuals or entities suspected of having engaged in financial support for terrorist activity; and

(3) whether the financial intelligence information seized in these cases has been shared on a full and timely basis with the all departments, agencies, and other entities of the United States Government involved in intelligence activities participating in the Foreign Terrorist Asset Tracking Center.

(b) IMMEDIATE NOTIFICATION FOR EMERGENCY DESIGNATION.—In the case of a designation of an individual or entity, or the assets of an individual or entity, as having been found to have engaged in terrorist activities, the Secretary of the Treasury shall report such designation within 24 hours of such a designation to the appropriate congressional committees.

(c) SUBMITTAL DATE OF REPORTS TO CONGRESSIONAL INTELLIGENCE COMMITTEES.—In the case of the reports required to be submitted under subsection (a) to the congressional intelligence committees, the submittal dates for such reports shall be as provided in section 507.

(d) APPROPRIATE CONGRESSIONAL COMMITTEES DEFINED.—In this section, the term "appropriate congressional committees" means the following:

> (1) The Permanent Select Committee on Intelligence, the Committee on Appropriations, the Committee on Armed Services, and the Committee on Financial Services of the House of Representatives.
>
> (2) The Select Committee on Intelligence, the Committee on Appropriations, the Committee on Armed Services, and the Committee on Banking, Housing, and Urban Affairs of the Senate.

NATIONAL COUNTERTERRORISM CENTER

SEC. 119. [50 U.S.C. §404o]

(a) ESTABLISHMENT OF CENTER.—There is within the Office of the Director of National Intelligence a National Counterterrorism Center.

(b) DIRECTOR OF NATIONAL COUNTERTERRORISM CENTER.—

> (1) There is a Director of the National Counterterrorism Center, who shall be the head of the National Counterterrorism Center, and who shall be appointed by the President, by and with the advice and consent of the Senate.
>
> (2) The Director of the National Counterterrorism Center may not simultaneously serve in any other capacity in the executive branch.

(c) REPORTING.—

> (1) The Director of the National Counterterrorism Center shall report to the Director of National Intelligence with respect to matters described in paragraph (2) and the President with respect to matters described in paragraph (3).
>
> (2) The matters described in this paragraph are as follows:
>
>> (A) The budget and programs of the National Counterterrorism Center.
>>
>> (B) The activities of the Directorate of Intelligence of the National Counterterrorism Center under subsection (i).
>>
>> (C) The conduct of intelligence operations implemented by other elements of the intelligence community; and
>
> (3) The matters described in this paragraph are the planning and progress of joint counterterrorism operations (other than intelligence operations).

(d) PRIMARY MISSIONS.—The primary missions of the National Counterterrorism Center shall be as follows:

(1) To serve as the primary organization in the United States Government for analyzing and integrating all intelligence possessed or acquired by the United States Government pertaining to terrorism and counterterrorism, excepting intelligence pertaining exclusively to domestic terrorists and domestic counterterrorism.

(2) To conduct strategic operational planning for counterterrorism activities, integrating all instruments of national power, including diplomatic, financial, military, intelligence, homeland security, and law enforcement activities within and among agencies.

(3) To assign roles and responsibilities as part of its strategic operational planning duties to lead Departments or agencies, as appropriate, for counterterrorism activities that are consistent with applicable law and that support counterterrorism strategic operational plans, but shall not direct the execution of any resulting operations.

(4) To ensure that agencies, as appropriate, have access to and receive all-source intelligence support needed to execute their counterterrorism plans or perform independent, alternative analysis.

(5) To ensure that such agencies have access to and receive intelligence needed to accomplish their assigned activities.

(6) To serve as the central and shared knowledge bank on known and suspected terrorists and international terror groups, as well as their goals, strategies, capabilities, and networks of contacts and support.

(e) DOMESTIC COUNTERTERRORISM INTELLIGENCE.—

(1) The Center may, consistent with applicable law, the direction of the President, and the guidelines referred to in section 102A(b), receive intelligence pertaining exclusively to domestic counterterrorism from any Federal, State, or local government or other source necessary to fulfill its responsibilities and retain and disseminate such intelligence.

(2) Any agency authorized to conduct counterterrorism activities may request information from the Center to assist it in its responsibilities, consistent with applicable law and the guidelines referred to in section 102A(b).

(f) DUTIES AND RESPONSIBILITIES OF DIRECTOR.—

(1) The Director of the National Counterterrorism Center shall—

(A) serve as the principal adviser to the Director of National Intelligence on intelligence operations relating to counterterrorism;

(B) provide strategic operational plans for the civilian and military counterterrorism efforts of the United States Government and for the effective integration of counterterrorism intelligence and operations across agency boundaries, both inside and outside the United States;

(C) advise the Director of National Intelligence on the extent to which the counterterrorism program recommendations and budget proposals of the departments, agencies, and elements of the United States Government conform to the priorities established by the President;

(D) disseminate terrorism information, including current terrorism threat analysis, to the President, the Vice President, the Secretaries of State, Defense, and Homeland Security, the Attorney General, the Director of the Central Intelligence Agency, and other officials of the executive branch as appropriate, and to the appropriate committees of Congress;

(E) support the Department of Justice and the Department of Homeland Security, and other appropriate agencies, in fulfillment of their responsibilities to disseminate terrorism information, consistent with applicable law, guidelines referred to in section 102A(b), Executive orders and other Presidential guidance, to State and local government officials, and other entities, and coordinate dissemination of terrorism information to foreign governments as approved by the Director of National Intelligence;

(F) develop a strategy for combining terrorist travel intelligence operations and law enforcement planning and operations into a cohesive effort to intercept terrorists, find terrorist travel facilitators, and constrain terrorist mobility;

(G) have primary responsibility within the United States Government for conducting net assessments of terrorist threats;

(H) consistent with priorities approved by the President, assist the Director of National Intelligence in establishing requirements for the intelligence community for the collection of terrorism information; and

(I) perform such other duties as the Director of National Intelligence may prescribe or are prescribed by law.

(2) Nothing in paragraph (1)(G) shall limit the authority of the departments and agencies of the United States to conduct net assessments.

(g) LIMITATION.—The Director of the National Counterterrorism Center may not direct the execution of counterterrorism operations.

(h) RESOLUTION OF DISPUTES.—The Director of National Intelligence shall resolve disagreements between the National Counterterrorism Center and the head of a department, agency, or element of the United States Government on designations, assignments, plans, or responsibilities under this section. The head of such a department, agency, or element may appeal the resolution of the disagreement by the Director of National Intelligence to the President.

(i) DIRECTORATE OF INTELLIGENCE.—The Director of the National Counterterrorism Center shall establish and maintain within the National Counterterrorism Center a Directorate of Intelligence which shall have primary responsibility within the United States Government for analysis of terrorism and terrorist organizations (except for purely domestic terrorism and domestic terrorist organizations) from all sources of intelligence, whether collected inside or outside the United States.

(j) DIRECTORATE OF STRATEGIC OPERATIONAL PLANNING.—

> (1) The Director of the National Counterterrorism Center shall establish and maintain within the National Counterterrorism Center a Directorate of Strategic Operational Planning which shall provide strategic operational plans for counterterrorism operations conducted by the United States Government.
>
> (2) Strategic operational planning shall include the mission, objectives to be achieved, tasks to be performed, interagency coordination of operational activities, and the assignment of roles and responsibilities.
>
> (3) The Director of the National Counterterrorism Center shall monitor the implementation of strategic operational plans, and shall obtain information from each element of the intelligence community, and from each other department, agency, or element of the United States Government relevant for monitoring the progress of such entity in implementing such plans.

NATIONAL COUNTER PROLIFERATION CENTER

SEC. 119A. [50 U.S.C. §404o-1]

(a) ESTABLISHMENT.—(1) The President shall establish a National Counter Proliferation Center, taking into account all appropriate government tools to prevent and halt the proliferation of weapons of mass destruction, their delivery systems, and related materials and technologies.

> (2) The head of the National Counter Proliferation Center shall be the Director of the National Counter Proliferation Center, who shall be appointed by the Director of National Intelligence.
>
> (3) The National Counter Proliferation Center shall be located within the Office of the Director of National Intelligence.

(b) MISSIONS AND OBJECTIVES.—In establishing the National Counter Proliferation Center, the President shall address the following missions and objectives to prevent and halt the proliferation of weapons of mass destruction, their delivery systems, and related materials and technologies:

(1) Establishing a primary organization within the United States Government for analyzing and integrating all intelligence possessed or acquired by the United States pertaining to proliferation.

(2) Ensuring that appropriate agencies have full access to and receive all-source intelligence support needed to execute their counter proliferation plans or activities, and perform independent, alternative analyses.

(3) Establishing a central repository on known and suspected proliferation activities, including the goals, strategies, capabilities, networks, and any individuals, groups, or entities engaged in proliferation.

(4) Disseminating proliferation information, including proliferation threats and analyses, to the President, to the appropriate departments and agencies, and to the appropriate committees of Congress.

(5) Conducting net assessments and warnings about the proliferation of weapons of mass destruction, their delivery systems, and related materials and technologies.

(6) Coordinating counter proliferation plans and activities of the various departments and agencies of the United States Government to prevent and halt the proliferation of weapons of mass destruction, their delivery systems, and related materials and technologies.

(7) Conducting strategic operational counter proliferation planning for the United States Government to prevent and halt the proliferation of weapons of mass destruction, their delivery systems, and related materials and technologies.

(c) NATIONAL SECURITY WAIVER.—The President may waive the requirements of this section, and any parts thereof, if the President determines that such requirements do not materially improve the ability of the United States Government to prevent and halt the proliferation of weapons of mass destruction, their delivery systems, and related materials and technologies. Such waiver shall be made in writing to Congress and shall include a description of how the missions and objectives in subsection (b) are being met.

(d) REPORT TO CONGRESS.—

(1) Not later than nine months after the implementation of this Act, the President shall submit to Congress, in classified form if necessary, the findings and recommendations of the President's Commission on Weapons of Mass Destruction established by Executive Order in February 2004, together with the views of the President regarding the establishment of a National Counter Proliferation Center.

(2) If the President decides not to exercise the waiver authority granted by subsection (c), the President shall submit to Congress from time to time updates and plans regarding the establishment of a National Counter Proliferation Center.

(e) SENSE OF CONGRESS.—It is the sense of Congress that a central feature of counter proliferation activities, consistent with the President's Proliferation Security Initiative, should include the physical interdiction, by air, sea, or land, of weapons of mass destruction, their delivery systems, and related materials and technologies, and enhanced law enforcement activities to identify and disrupt proliferation networks, activities, organizations, and persons.

NATIONAL INTELLIGENCE CENTERS

SEC. 119B. [50 U.S.C. §404o-2]

(a) AUTHORITY TO ESTABLISH.—The Director of National Intelligence may establish one or more national intelligence centers to address intelligence priorities, including, but not limited to, regional issues.

(b) RESOURCES OF DIRECTORS OF CENTERS.—

> (1) The Director of National Intelligence shall ensure that the head of each national intelligence center under subsection (a) has appropriate authority, direction, and control of such center, and of the personnel assigned to such center, to carry out the assigned mission of such center.

> (2) The Director of National Intelligence shall ensure that each national intelligence center has appropriate personnel to accomplish effectively the mission of such center.

(c) INFORMATION SHARING.—The Director of National Intelligence shall, to the extent appropriate and practicable, ensure that each national intelligence center under subsection (a) and the other elements of the intelligence community share information in order to facilitate the mission of such center.

(d) MISSION OF CENTERS.—Pursuant to the direction of the Director of National Intelligence, each national intelligence center under subsection (a) may, in the area of intelligence responsibility assigned to such center—

> (1) have primary responsibility for providing all-source analysis of intelligence based upon intelligence gathered both domestically and abroad;

> (2) have primary responsibility for identifying and proposing to the Director of National Intelligence intelligence collection and analysis and production requirements; and

> (3) perform such other duties as the Director of National Intelligence shall specify.

(e) REVIEW AND MODIFICATION OF CENTERS.—The Director of National Intelligence shall determine on a regular basis whether—

> (1) the area of intelligence responsibility assigned to each national intelligence center under subsection (a) continues to meet appropriate intelligence priorities; and

(2) the staffing and management of such center remains appropriate for the accomplishment of the mission of such center.

(f) TERMINATION.—The Director of National Intelligence may terminate any national intelligence center under subsection (a).

(g) SEPARATE BUDGET ACCOUNT.—The Director of National Intelligence shall, as appropriate, include in the National Intelligence Program budget a separate line item for each national intelligence center under subsection (a).

TITLE II—THE DEPARTMENT OF DEFENSE

DEPARTMENT OF DEFENSE

SEC. 201. [50 U.S.C. §408]

(d) Except to the extent inconsistent with the provisions of this Act, the provisions of title IV of the Revised Statutes as now of hereafter amended shall be applicable to the Department of Defense.

DEFINITIONS OF MILITARY DEPARTMENTS

SEC. 205. [50 U.S.C. §409]

(a) The term "Department of the Army" as used in this Act shall be construed to mean the Department of the Army at the seat of government and all field headquarters, forces, reserve components, installations, activities, and functions under the control or supervision of the Department of the Army.

(b) The term "Department of the Navy" as used in this Act shall be construed to mean the Department of the Navy at the seat of government; the headquarters, United States Marine Corps; the entire operating forces of the United States Navy, including naval aviation, and of the United States Marine Corps, including the reserve components of such forces; all field activities, headquarters, forces, bases, installations, activities and functions under the control or supervision of the Department of the Navy; and the United States Coast Guard when operating as a part of the Navy pursuant to law.

(c) The term "Department of the Air Force" as used in this Act shall be construed to mean the Department of the Air Force at the seat of government and all field headquarters, forces, reserve components, installations, activities, and functions under the control or supervision of the Department of the Air Force.

TITLE III—MISCELLANEOUS

NATIONAL SECURITY AGENCY VOLUNTARY SEPARATION

SEC. 301. 50 U.S.C. §409a

(a) SHORT TITLE.—This section may be cited as the "National Security Agency Voluntary Separation Act".

(b) DEFINITIONS.—For purposes of this section—

    (1) the term "Director" means the Director of the National Security Agency; and

    (2) the term "employee" means an employee of the National Security Agency, serving under an appointment without time limitation, who has been currently employed by the National Security Agency for a continuous period of at least 12 months prior to the effective date of the program established under subsection (c), except that such term does not include—

        (A) a reemployed annuitant under subchapter III of chapter 83 or chapter 84 of title 5, United States Code, or another retirement system for employees of the Government; or

        (B) an employee having a disability on the basis of which such employee is or would be eligible for disability retirement under any of the retirement systems referred to in subparagraph (A).

(c) ESTABLISHMENT OF PROGRAM.—Notwithstanding any other provision of law, the Director, in his sole discretion, may establish a program under which employees may, after October 1, 2000, be eligible for early retirement, offered separation pay to separate from service voluntarily, or both.

(d) EARLY RETIREMENT.—An employee who—

    (1) is at least 50 years of age and has completed 20 years of service; or

    (2) has at least 25 years of service, may, pursuant to regulations promulgated under this section, apply and be retired from the National Security Agency and receive benefits in accordance with chapter 83 or 84 of title 5, United States Code, if the employee has not less than 10 years of service with the National Security Agency.

(e) AMOUNT OF SEPARATION PAY AND TREATMENT FOR OTHER PURPOSES.—

    (1) AMOUNT.—Separation pay shall be paid in a lump sum and shall be equal to the lesser of—

        (A) an amount equal to the amount the employee would be entitled to receive under section 5595(c) of title 5, United States Code, if the employee were entitled to payment under such section; or

        (B) $25,000.

    (2) TREATMENT.—Separation pay shall not—

        (A) be a basis for payment, and shall not be included in the computation, of any other type of Government benefit; and

        (B) be taken into account for the purpose of determining the amount of any severance pay to which an individual may be entitled under section 5595 of title 5, United States Code, based on any other separation.

(f) REEMPLOYMENT RESTRICTIONS.—An employee who receives separation pay under such program may not be reemployed by the National Security Agency for the 12-month period beginning on the effective date of the employee's separation. An employee who receives separation pay under this section on the basis of a separation occurring on or after the date of the enactment of the Federal Workforce Restructuring Act of 1994 (Public Law 103–236; 108 Stat. 111) and accepts employment with the Government of the United States within 5 years after the date of the separation on which payment of the separation pay is based shall be required to repay the entire amount of the separation pay to the National Security Agency. If the employment is with an Executive agency (as defined by section 105 of title 5, United States Code), the Director of the Office of Personnel Management may, at the request of the head of the agency, waive the repayment if the individual involved possesses unique abilities and is the only qualified applicant available for the position. If the employment is with an entity in the legislative branch, the head of the entity or the appointing official may waive the repayment if the individual involved possesses unique abilities and is the only qualified applicant available for the position. If the employment is with the judicial branch, the Director of the Administrative Office of the United States Courts may waive the repayment if the individual involved possesses unique abilities and is the only qualified applicant available for the position.

(g) BAR ON CERTAIN EMPLOYMENT.—

(1) BAR.—An employee may not be separated from service under this section unless the employee agrees that the employee will not—

(A) act as agent or attorney for, or otherwise represent, any other person (except the United States) in any formal or informal appearance before, or, with the intent to influence, make any oral or written communication on behalf of any other person (except the United States) to the National Security Agency; or

(B) participate in any manner in the award, modification, or extension of any contract for property or services with the National Security Agency, during the 12-month period beginning on the effective date of the employee's separation from service.

(2) PENALTY.—An employee who violates an agreement under this subsection shall be liable to the United States in the amount of the separation pay paid to the employee pursuant to this section multiplied by the proportion of the 12-month period during which the employee was in violation of the agreement.

(h) LIMITATIONS.—Under this program, early retirement and separation pay may be offered only—

(1) with the prior approval of the Director;

(2) for the period specified by the Director; and

(3) to employees within such occupational groups or geographic locations, or subject to such other similar limitations or conditions, as the Director may require.

(i) REGULATIONS.—Before an employee may be eligible for early retirement, separation pay, or both, under this section, the Director shall prescribe such regulations as may be necessary to carry out this section.

(j) NOTIFICATION OF EXERCISE OF AUTHORITY.—The Director may not make an offer of early retirement, separation pay, or both, pursuant to this section until 15 days after submitting to the congressional intelligence committees a report describing the occupational groups or geographic locations, or other similar limitations or conditions, required by the Director under subsection (h), and includes the proposed regulations issued pursuant to subsection (i).

(k) REMITTANCE OF FUNDS.—In addition to any other payment that is required to be made under subchapter III of chapter 83 or chapter 84 of title 5, United States Code, the National Security Agency shall remit to the Office of Personnel Management for deposit in the Treasury of the United States to the credit of the Civil Service Retirement and Disability Fund, an amount equal to 15 percent of the final basic pay of each employee to whom a voluntary separation payment has been or is to be paid under this section. The remittance required by this subsection shall be in lieu of any remittance required by section 4(a) of the Federal Workforce Restructuring Act of 1994 (5 U.S.C. §8331 note).

AUTHORITY OF FEDERAL BUREAU OF INVESTIGATION TO AWARD PERSONAL SERVICES CONTRACTS

SEC. 302. [50 U.S.C. §409b]

(a) IN GENERAL.—The Director of the Federal Bureau of Investigation may enter into personal services contracts if the personal services to be provided under such contracts directly support the intelligence or counterintelligence missions of the Federal Bureau of Investigation.

(b) INAPPLICABILITY OF CERTAIN REQUIREMENTS.—Contracts under subsection (a) shall not be subject to the annuity offset requirements of sections 8344 and 8468 of title 5, United States Code, the requirements of section 3109 of title 5, United States Code, or any law or regulation requiring competitive contracting.

(c) CONTRACT TO BE APPROPRIATE MEANS OF SECURING SERVICES.—The Chief Contracting Officer of the Federal Bureau of Investigation shall ensure that each personal services contract entered into by the Director under this section is the appropriate means of securing the services to be provided under such contract.

ADVISORY COMMITTEES AND PERSONNEL

SEC. 303. [50 U.S.C. §405]

(a) The Director of the Federal Emergency Management Agency, the Director of National Intelligence, and the National Security Council, acting through its Executive Secretary, are authorized to appoint such advisory committees and to employ, consistent with other provisions of this Act, such part-time advisory personnel as they may deem necessary in carrying out their respective functions and the functions of agencies under their control. Persons holding other offices or positions under the United States for which they receive compensation, while serving as members of such committees, shall receive no additional compensation for such service. Retired members of the uniformed services employed by the Director of National Intelligence who hold no other office or position under the United States for which they receive compensation, other members of such committees and other part-time advisory personnel so employed may serve without compensation or may receive compensation at a daily rate not to exceed the daily equivalent of the rate of pay in effect for grade GS–18 of the General Schedule established by section 5332 of title 5, United States Code, as determined by the appointing authority.

(b) Service of an individual as a member of any such advisory committee, or in any other part-time capacity for a department or agency hereunder, shall not be considered as service bringing such individual within the provisions of section 203, 205, or 207, of title 18, United States Code, unless the act of such individual, which by such section is made unlawful when performed by an individual referred to in such section, is with respect to any particular matter which directly involves a department or agency which such person is advising or in which such department or agency is directly interested.

AUTHORIZATION FOR APPROPRIATIONS

SEC. 307. [50 U.S.C. §411]

There are hereby authorized to be appropriated such sums as may be necessary and appropriate to carry out the provisions and purposes of this Act (other than the provisions and purposes of sections 102, 103, 104, 105 and titles V, VI, and VII).

DEFINITIONS

SEC. 308. [50 U.S.C. §410]

(a) As used in this Act, the term "function" includes functions, powers, and duties.

(b) As used in this Act, the term, "Department of Defense" shall be deemed to include the military departments of the Army, the Navy, and the Air Force, and all agencies created under title II of this Act.

SEVERABILITY

SEC. 309. [50 U.S.C. §401 note]
If any provision of this Act or the application thereof to any person or circumstances is held invalid, the validity of the remainder of the Act and of the application of such provision to other persons and circumstances shall not be affected thereby.

EFFECTIVE DATE

SEC. 310. [50 U.S.C. §401 note]
(a) The first sentence of section 202 (a) and sections 1, 2, 307, 308, 309, and 310 shall take effect immediately upon the enactment of this Act.
(b) Except as provided in subsection (a), the provisions of this Act shall take effect on whichever of the following days is the earlier: The day after the day upon which the Secretary of Defense first appointed takes office, or the sixtieth day after the date of the enactment of this Act.

REPEALING AND SAVING PROVISIONS

SEC. 411. [50 U.S.C. §412]
All laws, orders, and regulations inconsistent with the provisions of this title are repealed insofar as they are inconsistent with the powers, duties, and responsibilities enacted hereby: *Provided,* That the powers, duties, and responsibilities of the Secretary of Defense under this title shall be administered in conformance with the policy and requirements for administration of budgetary and fiscal matters in the Government generally, including accounting and financial reporting, and that nothing in this title shall be construed as eliminating or modifying the powers, duties, and responsibilities of any other department, agency, or officer of the Government in connection with such matters, but no such department, agency, or officer shall exercise any such powers, duties, or responsibilities in a manner that will render ineffective the provisions of this title.

TITLE V—ACCOUNTABILITY FOR INTELLIGENCE ACTIVITIES

GENERAL CONGRESSIONAL OVERSIGHT PROVISIONS

SEC. 501. [50 U.S.C. §413]
(a)(1)The President shall ensure that the congressional intelligence committees are kept fully and currently informed of the intelligence activities of the United States, including any significant anticipated intelligence activity as required by this title.

(2) Nothing in this title shall be construed as requiring the approval of the congressional intelligence committees as a condition precedent to the initiation of any significant anticipated intelligence activity.

(b) The President shall ensure that any illegal intelligence activity is reported promptly to the congressional intelligence committees, as well as any corrective action that has been taken or is planned in connection with such illegal activity.

(c) The President and the congressional intelligence committees shall each establish such written procedures as may be necessary to carry out the provisions of this title.

(d) The House of Representatives and the Senate shall each establish, by rule or resolution of such House, procedures to protect from unauthorized disclosure all classified information, and all information relating to intelligence sources and methods, that is furnished to the congressional intelligence committees or to Members of Congress under this title. Such procedures shall be established in consultation with the Director of National Intelligence. In accordance with such procedures, each of the congressional intelligence committees shall promptly call to the attention of its respective House, or to any appropriate committee or committees of its respective House, any matter relating to intelligence activities requiring the attention of such House or such committee or committees.

(e) Nothing in this Act shall be construed as authority to withhold information from the congressional intelligence committees on the grounds that providing the information to the congressional intelligence committees would constitute the unauthorized disclosure of classified information or information relating to intelligence sources and methods.

(f) As used in this section, the term "intelligence activities" includes covert actions as defined in section 503(e), and includes financial intelligence activities.

REPORTING ON INTELLIGENCE ACTIVITIES OTHER THAN COVERT ACTIONS

SEC. 502. [50 U.S.C. §413a]

(a) IN GENERAL.—To the extent consistent with due regard for the protection from unauthorized disclosure of classified information relating to sensitive intelligence sources and methods or other exceptionally sensitive matters, the Director of National Intelligence and the heads of all departments, agencies, and other entities of the United States Government involved in intelligence activities shall—

> (1) keep the congressional intelligence committees fully and currently informed of all intelligence activities, other than a covert action (as defined in section 503(e)), which are the responsibility of, are engaged in by, or are carried out for or on behalf of, any department, agency, or

entity of the United States Government, including any significant anticipated intelligence activity and any significant intelligence failure; and

(2) furnish the congressional intelligence committees any information or material concerning intelligence activities(including the legal basis under which the intelligence activity is being or was conducted), other than covert actions, which is within their custody or control, and which is requested by either of the congressional intelligence committees in order to carry out its authorized responsibilities.

(b) FORM AND CONTENTS OF CERTAIN REPORTS.—Any report relating to a significant anticipated intelligence activity or a significant intelligence failure that is submitted to the congressional intelligence committees for purposes of subsection (a)(1) shall be in writing, and shall contain the following:

(1) A concise statement of any facts pertinent to such report.

(2) An explanation of the significance of the intelligence activity or intelligence failure covered by such report.

(c) STANDARDS AND PROCEDURES FOR CERTAIN REPORTS.—The Director of National Intelligence, in consultation with the heads of the departments, agencies, and entities referred to in subsection (a), shall establish standards and procedures applicable to reports covered by subsection (b).

PRESIDENTIAL APPROVAL AND REPORTING OF COVERT ACTIONS

SEC. 503. [50 U.S.C. §413b]

(a) The President may not authorize the conduct of a covert action by departments, agencies, or entities of the United States Government unless the President determines such an action is necessary to support identifiable foreign policy objectives of the United States and is important to the national security of the United States, which determination shall be set forth in a finding that shall meet each of the following conditions:

(1) Each finding shall be in writing, unless immediate action by the United States is required and time does not permit the preparation of a written finding, in which case a written record of the President's decision shall be contemporaneously made and shall be reduced to a written finding as soon as possible but in no event more than 48 hours after the decision is made.

(2) Except as permitted by paragraph (1), a finding may not authorize or sanction a covert action, or any aspect of any such action, which already has occurred.

(3) Each finding shall specify each department, agency, or entity of the United States Government authorized to fund or otherwise participate in any significant way in such action. Any employee, contractor, or contract

agent of a department, agency, or entity of the United States Government other than the Central Intelligence Agency directed to participate in any way in a covert action shall be subject either to the policies and regulations of the Central Intelligence Agency, or to written policies or regulations adopted by such department, agency, or entity, to govern such participation.

(4) Each finding shall specify whether it is contemplated that any third party which is not an element of, or a contractor or contract agent of, the United States Government, or is not otherwise subject to United States Government policies and regulations, will be used to fund or otherwise participate in any significant way in the covert action concerned, or be used to undertake the covert action concerned on behalf of the United States.

(5) A finding may not authorize any action that would violate the Constitution or any statute of the United States.

(b) To the extent consistent with due regard for the protection from unauthorized disclosure of classified information relating to sensitive intelligence sources and methods or other exceptionally sensitive matters, the Director of National Intelligence and the heads of all departments, agencies, and entities of the United States Government involved in a covert action—

(1) shall keep the congressional intelligence committees fully and currently informed of all covert actions which are the responsibility of, are engaged in by, or are carried out for or on behalf of, any department, agency, or entity of the United States Government, including significant failures; and

(2) shall furnish to the congressional intelligence committees any information or material concerning covert actions (including the legal basis under which the covert action is being or was conducted) which is in the possession, custody, or control of any department, agency, or entity of the United States Government and which is requested by either of the congressional intelligence committees in order to carry out its authorized responsibilities.

(c)(1) The President shall ensure that any finding approved pursuant to subsection (a) shall be reported in writing to the congressional intelligence committees as soon as possible after such approval and before the initiation of the covert action authorized by the finding, except as otherwise provided in paragraph (2) and paragraph (3).

(2) If the President determines that it is essential to limit access to the finding to meet extraordinary circumstances affecting vital interests of the United States, the finding may be reported to the chairmen and ranking minority members of the congressional intelligence committees, the Speaker and minority leader of the House of Representatives, the

majority and minority leaders of the Senate, and such other member or members of the congressional leadership as may be included by the President.

(3) Whenever a finding is not reported pursuant to paragraph (1) or (2) of this section, the President shall fully inform the congressional intelligence committees in a timely fashion and shall provide a statement of the reasons for not giving prior notice.

(4) In a case under paragraph (1), (2), or (3), a copy of the finding, signed by the President, shall be provided to the chairman of each congressional intelligence committee.

(5)(A) When access to a finding, or a notification provided under subsection (d)(1),

is limited to the Members of Congress specified in paragraph (2), a written statement of the reasons for limiting such access shall also be provided.

(B) Not later than180 days after a statement of reasons is submitted in accordance with subparagraph (A) or this subparagraph, the President shall ensure that—

(i) all members of the congressional intelligence committees are provided access to the finding or notification; or

(ii) a statement of reasons that it is essential to continue to limit access to such finding or such notification to meet extraordinary circumstances affecting vital interests of the United States is submitted to the Members of Congress specified in paragraph (2).

(d)(1) The President shall ensure that the congressional intelligence committees, or, if applicable, the Members of Congress specified in subsection (c)(2), are notified in writing of any significant change in a previously approved covert action, or any significant undertaking pursuant to a previously approved finding, in the same manner as findings are reported pursuant to subsection (c).

(2)In determining whether an activity constitutes a significant undertaking for purposes of paragraph (1), the President shall consider whether the activity—

(A) involves significant risk of loss of life;

(B) requires an expansion of existing authorities, including authorities relating to research, development, or operations;

(C) results in the expenditure of significant funds or other resources;

(D) requires notification under section 504;

(E) gives rise to a significant risk of disclosing intelligence sources or methods; or

(F) presents a reasonably foreseeable risk of serious damage to the diplomatic relations of the United States if such activity were disclosed without authorization.

(e) As used in this title, the term "covert action" means an activity or activities of the United States Government to influence political, economic, or military conditions abroad, where it is intended that the role of the United States Government will not be apparent or acknowledged publicly, but does not include—

(1) activities the primary purpose of which is to acquire intelligence, traditional counterintelligence activities, traditional activities to improve or maintain the operational security of United States Government programs, or administrative activities;

(2) traditional diplomatic or military activities or routine support to such activities;

(3) traditional law enforcement activities conducted by United States Government law enforcement agencies or routine support to such activities; or

(4) activities to provide routine support to the overt activities (other than activities described in paragraph (1), (2), or (3)) of other United States Government agencies abroad.

(f) No covert action may be conducted which is intended to influence United States political processes, public opinion, policies, or media.

(g)(1) In any case where access to a finding reported under subsection (c) or notification provided under subsection (d)(1) is not made available to all members of a congressional intelligence committee in accordance with subsection (c)(2), the President shall notify all members of such committee that such finding or such notification has been provided only to the members specified in subsection (c)(2).

(2) In any case where access to a finding reported under subsection (c) or notification provided under subsection (d)(1) is not made available to all members of a congressional intelligence committee in accordance with subsection (c)(2), the President shall provide to all members of such committee a general description regarding the finding or notification, as applicable, consistent with the reasons for not yet fully informing all members of such committee.

(3) The President shall maintain—

(A) a record of the members of Congress to whom a finding is reported under subsection (c) or notification is provided under subsection (d)(1) and the date on which each member of Congress receives such finding or notification; and

(B) each written statement provided under subsection (c)(5).'

FUNDING OF INTELLIGENCE ACTIVITIES

SEC. 504. [50 U.S.C. §414]

(a) Appropriated funds available to an intelligence agency may be obligated or expended for an intelligence or intelligence-related activity only if—

(1) those funds were specifically authorized by the Congress for use for such activities; or

(2) in the case of funds from the Reserve for Contingencies of the Central Intelligence Agency and consistent with the provisions of section 503 of this Act concerning any significant anticipated intelligence activity, the Director of the Central Intelligence Agency has notified the appropriate congressional committees of the intent to make such funds available for such activity; or

(3) in the case of funds specifically authorized by the Congress for a different activity—

(A) the activity to be funded is a higher priority intelligence or intelligence-related activity;

(B) the use of such funds for such activity supports an emergent need, improves program effectiveness, or increases efficiency; and

(C) the Director of National Intelligence, the Secretary of Defense, or the Attorney General, as appropriate, has notified the appropriate congressional committees of the intent to make such funds available for such activity;

(4) nothing in this subsection prohibits obligation or expenditure of funds available to an intelligence agency in accordance with sections 1535 and 1536 of title 31, United States Code.

(b) Funds available to an intelligence agency may not be made available for any intelligence or intelligence-related activity for which funds were denied by the Congress.

(c) No funds appropriated for, or otherwise available to, any department, agency, or entity of the United States Government may be expended, or may be directed to be expended, for any covert action, as defined in section 503(e), unless and until a Presidential finding required by subsection (a) of section 503 has been signed or otherwise issued in accordance with that subsection.

(d)(1) Except as otherwise specifically provided by law, funds available to an intelligence agency that are not appropriated funds may be obligated or expended for an intelligence or intelligence-related activity only if those funds are used for activities reported to the appropriate congressional committees pursuant to procedures which identify—

(A) the types of activities for which nonappropriated funds may be expended; and

(B) the circumstances under which an activity must be reported as a significant anticipated intelligence activity before such funds can be expended.

(2) Procedures for purposes of paragraph (1) shall be jointly agreed upon by the congressional intelligence committees and, as appropriate, the Director of National Intelligence or the Secretary of Defense.

(e) As used in this section—

(1) the term "intelligence agency" means any department, agency, or other entity of the United States involved in intelligence or intelligence-related activities;

(2) the term "appropriate congressional committees" means the Permanent Select Committee on Intelligence and the Committee on Appropriations of the House of Representatives and the Select Committee on Intelligence and the Committee on Appropriations of the Senate; and

(3) the term "specifically authorized by the Congress" means that—

(A) the activity and the amount of funds proposed to be used for that activity were identified in a formal budget request to the Congress, but funds shall be deemed to be specifically authorized for that activity only to the extent that the Congress both authorized the funds to be appropriated for that activity and appropriated the funds for that activity; or

(B) although the funds were not formally requested, the Congress both specifically authorized the appropriation of the funds for the activity and appropriated the funds for the activity.

NOTICE TO CONGRESS OF CERTAIN TRANSFERS OF DEFENSE ARTICLES AND DEFENSE SERVICES

SEC. 505. [50 U.S.C. §415]

(a)(1) The transfer of a defense article or defense service, or the anticipated transfer in any fiscal year of any aggregation of defense articles or defense services, exceeding $1,000,000 in value by an intelligence agency to a recipient outside that agency shall be considered a significant anticipated intelligence activity for the purpose of this title.

(2) Paragraph (1) does not apply if—

(A) the transfer is being made to a department, agency, or other entity of the United States (so long as there will not be a subsequent retransfer of the defense articles or defense services outside the United States Government in conjunction with an intelligence or intelligence-related activity); or

(B) the transfer—

(i) is being made pursuant to authorities contained in part II of the Foreign Assistance Act of 1961, the Arms Export Control Act, title 10 of the United States Code (including a law enacted pursuant to section 7307(a) of that title), or the Federal Property and Administrative Services Act of 1949, and

(ii) is not being made in conjunction with an intelligence or intelligence-related activity.

(3) An intelligence agency may not transfer any defense articles or defense services outside the agency in conjunction with any intelligence or intelligence-related activity for which funds were denied by the Congress.

(b) As used in this section—

(1) the term "intelligence agency" means any department, agency, or other entity of the United States involved in intelligence or intelligence-related activities;

(2) the terms "defense articles" and "defense services" mean the items on the United States Munitions List pursuant to section 38 of the Arms Export Control Act (22 CFR part 121);

(3) the term "transfer" means—

(A) in the case of defense articles, the transfer of possession of those articles; and

(B) in the case of defense services, the provision of those services; and

(4) the term "value" means—

(A) in the case of defense articles, the greater of—

(i) the original acquisition cost to the United States Government, plus the cost of improvements or other modifications made by or on behalf of the Government; or

(ii) the replacement cost; and

(B) in the case of defense services, the full cost to the Government of providing the services.

SPECIFICITY OF NATIONAL INTELLIGENCE PROGRAM BUDGET AMOUNTS FOR COUNTERTERRORISM, COUNTERPROLIFERATION, COUNTERNARCOTICS, AND COUNTERINTELLIGENCE

SEC. 506. [50 U.S.C. §415a]

(a) IN GENERAL.—The budget justification materials submitted to Congress in support of the budget of the President for a fiscal year that is submitted to Congress under section 1105(a) of title 31, United States Code, shall set forth separately the aggregate amount requested for that fiscal year for the National Intelligence Program for each of the following:

    (1) Counterterrorism.

    (2) Counterproliferation.

    (3) Counternarcotics.

    (4) Counterintelligence.

(b) ELECTION OF CLASSIFIED OR UNCLASSIFIED FORM.—
Amounts set forth under subsection (a) may be set forth in unclassified form or classified form, at the election of the Director of National Intelligence.

BUDGET TREATMENT OF COSTS OF ACQUISITION OF MAJOR SYSTEMS BY THE INTELLIGENCE COMMUNITY

SEC. 506A. [50 U.S.C. §415a-1]

(a) INDEPENDENT COST ESTIMATES.—

    (1) The Director of National Intelligence shall, in consultation with the head of each element of the intelligence community concerned, prepare an independent cost estimate of the full life-cycle cost of development, procurement, and operation of each major system to be acquired by the intelligence community.

    (2)(A) Each independent cost estimate for a major system shall, to the maximum extent practicable, specify the amount required to be appropriated and obligated to develop, procure, and operate the major system in each fiscal year of the proposed period of development, procurement, and operation of the major system.

        (B) For major system acquisitions requiring a service or capability from another acquisition or program to deliver the end-to-end functionality for the intelligence community end users, independent cost estimates shall include, to the maximum extent practicable, all estimated costs across all pertinent elements of the intelligence community. For collection programs, such cost estimates shall include the cost of new analyst training, new hardware and software for data exploitation and analysis, and any unique or additional costs for data processing, storing, and power, space, and cooling across the life cycle of the program. If such costs for processing, exploitation, dissemination, and storage are scheduled to be executed in other elements of the intelligence community, the independent cost estimate shall identify and annotate such costs for such other elements accordingly.

(3)(A) In the case of a program of the intelligence community that qualifies as a major system, an independent cost estimate shall be prepared before the submission to Congress of the budget of the President for the first fiscal year in which appropriated funds are anticipated to be obligated for the development or procurement of such major system.

(B) In the case of a program of the intelligence community for which an independent cost estimate was not previously required to be prepared under this section, including a program for which development or procurement commenced before the date of the enactment of the Intelligence Authorization Act for Fiscal Year 2004, if the aggregate future costs of development or procurement (or any combination of such activities) of the program will exceed $500,000,000 (in current fiscal year dollars), the program shall qualify as a major system for purposes of this section, and an independent cost estimate for such major system shall be prepared before the submission to Congress of the budget of the President for the first fiscal year thereafter in which appropriated funds are anticipated to be obligated for such major system.

(4) The independent cost estimate for a major system shall be updated upon—

(A) the completion of any preliminary design review associated with the major system;

(B) any significant modification to the anticipated design of the major system; or

(C) any change in circumstances that renders the current independent cost estimate for the major system inaccurate.

(5) Any update of an independent cost estimate for a major system under paragraph (4) shall meet all requirements for independent cost estimates under this section, and shall be treated as the most current independent cost estimate for the major system until further updated under that paragraph.

(b) PREPARATION OF INDEPENDENT COST ESTIMATES.—

(1) The Director shall establish within the Office of the Director of National Intelligence an office which shall be responsible for preparing independent cost estimates, and any updates thereof, under subsection (a), unless a designation is made under paragraph (2).

(2) In the case of the acquisition of a major system for an element of the intelligence community within the Department of Defense, the Director

and the Secretary of Defense shall provide that the independent cost estimate, and any updates thereof, under subsection (a) be prepared by an entity jointly designated by the Director and the Secretary in accordance with section 2434(b)(1)(A) of title 10, United States Code.

(c) UTILIZATION IN BUDGETS OF PRESIDENT.—

(1) If the budget of the President requests appropriations for any fiscal year for the development or procurement of a major system by the intelligence community, the President shall, subject to paragraph (2), request in such budget an amount of appropriations for the development or procurement, as the case may be, of the major system that is equivalent to the amount of appropriations identified in the most current independent cost estimate for the major system for obligation for each fiscal year for which appropriations are requested for the major system in such budget.

(2) If the amount of appropriations requested in the budget of the President for the development or procurement of a major system is less than the amount of appropriations identified in the most current independent cost estimate for the major system for obligation for each fiscal year for which appropriations are requested for the major system in such budget, the President shall include in the budget justification materials submitted to Congress in support of such budget—

(A) an explanation for the difference between the amount of appropriations requested and the amount of appropriations identified in the most current independent cost estimate;

(B) a description of the importance of the major system to the national security;

(C) an assessment of the consequences for the funding of all programs of the National Foreign Intelligence Program in future fiscal years if the most current independent cost estimate for the major system is accurate and additional appropriations are required in future fiscal years to ensure the continued development or procurement of the major system, including the consequences of such funding shortfalls on the major system and all other programs of the National Intelligence Program; and

(D) such other information on the funding of the major system as the President considers appropriate.

(d) INCLUSION OF ESTIMATES IN BUDGET JUSTIFICATION MATERIALS.—The budget justification materials submitted to Congress in support of the budget of the President shall include the most current independent cost estimate under this section for each major system for which appropriations are requested in such budget for any fiscal year.

(e) DEFINITIONS.—In this section:

(1) The term "budget of the President" means the budget of the President for a fiscal year as submitted to Congress under section 1105(a) of title 31, United States Code.

(2)(A) The term "independent cost estimate" means a pragmatic and neutral analysis, assessment, and quantification of all costs and risks associated with the development, acquisition, procurement, operation, and sustainment of a major system across its proposed life cycle, which shall be based on programmatic and technical specifications provided by the office within the element of the intelligence community with primary responsibility for the development, procurement, or operation of the major system.

(B) In accordance with subsection (a)(2)(B), each independent cost estimate shall include all costs required across elements of the intelligence community to develop, acquire, procure, operate, and sustain the system to provide the end-to-end intelligence functionality of the system, including—

(i) for collection programs, the cost of new analyst training, new hardware and software for data exploitation and analysis, and any unique or additional costs for data processing, storing, and power, space, and cooling across the life cycle of the program; and

(ii) costs for processing, exploitation, dissemination, and storage scheduled to be executed in other elements of the intelligence community.

(3) The term "major system" means any significant program of an element of the intelligence community with projected total development and procurement costs exceeding $500,000,000 (based on fiscal year 2010 constant dollars), which costs shall include all end-to-end program costs, including costs associated with the development and procurement of the program and any other costs associated with the development and procurement of systems required to support or utilize the program.

ANNUAL PERSONNEL LEVEL ASSESSMENTS FOR THE INTELLIGENCE COMMUNITY

Sec. 506B. [50 USC 415a-4.] (a) REQUIREMENT TO PROVIDE.— The Director of National Intelligence shall, in consultation with the head of each element of the intelligence community, prepare an annual personnel level assessment for such element that assesses the personnel levels for such element for the fiscal year following the fiscal year in which the assessment is submitted.

(b) SCHEDULE.—Each assessment required by subsection (a) shall be submitted to the congressional intelligence committees each year at the time that the

President submits to Congress the budget for a fiscal year pursuant to section 1105 of title 31, United States Code.

(c) CONTENTS.—Each assessment required by subsection (a) submitted during a fiscal year shall contain the following information for the element of the intelligence community concerned:

> (1) The budget submission for personnel costs for the upcoming fiscal year.
>
> (2) The dollar and percentage increase or decrease of such costs as compared to the personnel costs of the current fiscal year.
>
> (3) The dollar and percentage increase or decrease of such costs as compared to the personnel costs during the prior 5 fiscal years.
>
> (4) The number of full-time equivalent positions that is the basis for which personnel funds are requested for the upcoming fiscal year.
>
> (5) The numerical and percentage increase or decrease of the number referred to in paragraph (4) as compared to the number of full-time equivalent positions of the current fiscal year.
>
> (6) The numerical and percentage increase or decrease of the number referred to in paragraph (4) as compared to the number of full-time equivalent positions during the prior 5 fiscal years.
>
> (7) The best estimate of the number and costs of core contract personnel to be funded by the element for the upcoming fiscal year.
>
> (8) The numerical and percentage increase or decrease of such costs of core contract personnel as compared to the best estimate of the costs of core contract personnel of the current fiscal year.
>
> (9) The numerical and percentage increase or decrease of such number and such costs of core contract personnel as compared to the number and cost of core contract personnel during the prior 5 fiscal years.
>
> (10) A justification for the requested personnel and core contract personnel levels.
>
> (11) The best estimate of the number of intelligence of the intelligence community.
>
> (12) A statement by the Director of National Intelligence that, based on current and projected funding, the element concerned will have sufficient—
>
>> (A) internal infrastructure to support the requested personnel and core contract personnel levels;
>>
>> (B) training resources to support the requested personnel levels; and
>>
>> (C) funding to support the administrative and operational activities of the requested personnel levels.

VULNERABILITY ASSESSMENTS OF MAJOR SYSTEMS

Sec. 506C. (50 USC 415a-5.)
(a) INITIAL VULNERABILITY ASSESSMENTS.—
    (1)(A) Except as provided in subparagraph (B), the
Director of National Intelligence shall conduct and submit to the
congressional intelligence committees an initial vulnerability
assessment for each major system and its significant items of supply—
        (i) except as provided in clause (ii), prior to the
completion of Milestone B or an equivalent acquisition
decision for the major system; or
        (ii) prior to the date that is 1 year after the date of
the enactment of the Intelligence Authorization Act for
Fiscal Year 2010 in the case of a major system for which
Milestone B or an equivalent acquisition decision—
            (I) was completed prior to such date of enactment;
or
            (II) is completed on a date during the 180-day
period following such date of enactment.
    (B) The Director may submit to the congressional intelligence
committees an initial vulnerability assessment required by clause
(ii) of subparagraph (A) not later than 180 days after the date
such assessment is required to be submitted under such clause if
the Director notifies the congressional intelligence committees of
the extension of the submission date under this subparagraph and
provides a justification for such extension.
    (C) The initial vulnerability assessment of a major system and its
significant items of supply shall include use of an analysis-based
approach to—
        (i) identify vulnerabilities;
        (ii) define exploitation potential;
        (iii) examine the system's potential effectiveness;
        (iv) determine overall vulnerability; and
        (v) make recommendations for risk reduction.
    (2) If an initial vulnerability assessment for a major system is
not submitted to the congressional intelligence committees as
required by paragraph (1), funds appropriated for the acquisition
of the major system may not be obligated for a major contract
related to the major system. Such prohibition on the obligation
of funds for the acquisition of the major system shall cease to
apply on the date on which the congressional intelligence
committees receive the initial vulnerability assessment.
(b) SUBSEQUENT VULNERABILITY ASSESSMENTS.—

(1) The Director of National Intelligence shall, periodically throughout the procurement of a major system or if the Director determines that a change in circumstances warrants the issuance of a subsequent vulnerability assessment, conduct a subsequent vulnerability assessment of each major system and its significant items of supply within the National Intelligence Program.

(2) Upon the request of a congressional intelligence committee, the Director of National Intelligence may, if appropriate, recertify the previous vulnerability assessment or may conduct a subsequent vulnerability assessment of a particular major system and its significant items of supply within the National Intelligence Program.

(3) Any subsequent vulnerability assessment of a major system and its significant items of supply shall include use of an analysis-based approach and, if applicable, a testing-based approach, to monitor the exploitation potential of such system and reexamine the factors described in clauses (i) through (v) of subsection (a)(1)(C).

(c) MAJOR SYSTEM MANAGEMENT.—The Director of National Intelligence shall give due consideration to the vulnerability assessments prepared for a given major system when developing and determining the National Intelligence Program budget.

(d) CONGRESSIONAL OVERSIGHT.—

(1) The Director of National Intelligence shall provide to the congressional intelligence committees a copy of each vulnerability assessment conducted under subsection (a) or (b) not later than 10 days after the date of the completion of such assessment.

(2) The Director of National Intelligence shall provide the congressional intelligence committees with a proposed schedule for subsequent periodic vulnerability assessments of a major system under subsection (b)(1) when providing such committees with the initial vulnerability assessment under subsection (a) of such system as required by paragraph (1).

(e) DEFINITIONS.—In this section:

(1) The term "item of supply" has the meaning given that term in section 4(10) of the Office of Federal Procurement Policy Act (41 U.S.C. 403(10)).

(2) The term "major contract" means each of the 6 largest prime, associate, or Government-furnished equipment contracts under a major system that is in excess of $40,000,000 and that is not a firm, fixed price contract.

(3) The term "major system" has the meaning given that term in section 506A(e).

(4) The term "Milestone B" means a decision to enter into major system development and demonstration pursuant to guidance prescribed by the Director of National Intelligence.

(5) The term "vulnerability assessment'" means the process of identifying and quantifying vulnerabilities in a major system and its significant items of supply.

INTELLIGENCE COMMUNITY BUSINESS SYSTEM TRANSFORMATION

Sec. 506D. (50 USC 415a-6)

(a) LIMITATION ON OBLIGATION OF FUNDS.—

(1) Subject to paragraph (3), no funds appropriated to any element of the intelligence community may be obligated for an intelligence community business system transformation that will have a total cost in excess of $3,000,000 unless—

(A) the Director of the Office of Business Transformation of the Office of the Director of National Intelligence makes a certification described in paragraph (2) with respect to such intelligence community business system transformation; and

(B) such certification is approved by the board established under subsection (f).

(2) The certification described in this paragraph for an intelligence community business system transformation is a certification made by the Director of the Office of Business Transformation of the Office of the Director of National Intelligence that the intelligence community business system transformation—

(A) complies with the enterprise architecture under subsection (b) and such other policies and standards that the Director of National Intelligence considers appropriate; or

(B) is necessary—

(i) to achieve a critical national security capability or address a critical requirement; or

(ii) to prevent a significant adverse effect on a project that is needed to achieve an essential capability, taking into consideration any alternative solutions for preventing such adverse effect.

(3) With respect to a fiscal year after fiscal year 2010, the amount referred to in paragraph (1) in the matter preceding subparagraph (A) shall be equal to the sum of—

(A) the amount in effect under such paragraph (1) for the preceding fiscal year (determined after application of this paragraph), plus

(B) such amount multiplied by the annual percentage increase in the consumer price index (all items; U.S. city average) as of September of the previous fiscal year.

(b) ENTERPRISE ARCHITECTURE FOR INTELLIGENCE COMMUNITY BUSINESS SYSTEMS.—

(1) The Director of National Intelligence shall, acting through the board established under subsection (f), develop and implement an enterprise architecture to cover all intelligence community business systems, and the functions and activities supported by such business systems. The enterprise architecture shall be sufficiently defined to effectively guide, constrain, and permit implementation of interoperable intelligence community business system solutions, consistent with applicable policies and procedures established by the Director of the Office of Management and Budget.

(2) The enterprise architecture under paragraph (1) shall include the following:

(A) An information infrastructure that will enable the intelligence community to—

(i) comply with all Federal accounting, financial management, and reporting requirements;

(ii) routinely produce timely, accurate, and reliable financial information for management purposes;

(iii) integrate budget, accounting, and program information and systems; and

(iv) provide for the measurement of performance, including the ability to produce timely, relevant, and reliable cost information.

(B) Policies, procedures, data standards, and system interface requirements that apply uniformly throughout the intelligence community.

(c) RESPONSIBILITIES FOR INTELLIGENCE COMMUNITY BUSINESS SYSTEM TRANSFORMATION.—The Director of National Intelligence shall be responsible for the entire life cycle of an intelligence community business system transformation, including review, approval, and oversight of the planning, design, acquisition, deployment, operation, and maintenance of the business system transformation.

(d) INTELLIGENCE COMMUNITY BUSINESS SYSTEM INVESTMENT REVIEW.—

(1) The Director of the Office of Business Transformation of the Office of the Director of National Intelligence shall establish and implement, not later than 60 days after the enactment of the Intelligence Authorization Act for Fiscal Year 2010, an investment review process for the intelligence community business

systems for which the Director of the Office of Business Transformation is responsible.

(2) The investment review process under paragraph (1) shall—

    (A) meet the requirements of section 11312 of title 40, United States Code; and

    (B) specifically set forth the responsibilities of the Director of the Office of Business Transformation under such review process.

(3) The investment review process under paragraph (1) shall include the following elements:

    (A) Review and approval by an investment review board (consisting of appropriate representatives of the intelligence community) of each intelligence community business system as an investment before the obligation of funds for such system.

    (B) Periodic review, but not less often than annually, of every intelligence community business system investment.

    (C) Thresholds for levels of review to ensure appropriate review of intelligence community business system investments depending on the scope, complexity, and cost of the system involved.

    (D) Procedures for making certifications in accordance with the requirements of subsection (a)(2).

(e) BUDGET INFORMATION.—For each fiscal year after fiscal year 2011, the Director of National Intelligence shall include in the materials the Director submits to Congress in support of the budget for such fiscal year that is submitted to Congress under section 1105 of title 31, United States Code, the following information:

(1) An identification of each intelligence community business system for which funding is proposed in such budget.

(2) An identification of all funds, by appropriation, proposed in such budget for each such system, including—

    (A) funds for current services to operate and maintain such system;

    (B) funds for business systems modernization identified for each specific appropriation; and

    (C) funds for associated business process improvement or reengineering efforts.

(3) The certification, if any, made under subsection (a)(2) with respect to each such system.

(f) INTELLIGENCE COMMUNITY BUSINESS SYSTEM TRANSFORMATION GOVERNANCE BOARD.—

(1) The Director of National Intelligence shall establish a board within the intelligence community business system transformation governance structure (in this subsection referred to as the `Board').

(2) The Board shall—

    (A) recommend to the Director policies and procedures necessary to effectively integrate all business activities and any transformation, reform, reorganization, or process improvement initiatives undertaken within the intelligence community;

    (B) review and approve any major update of—

        (i) the enterprise architecture developed under subsection (b); and

        (ii) any plans for an intelligence community business systems modernization;

    (C) manage cross-domain integration consistent with such enterprise architecture;

    (D) coordinate initiatives for intelligence community business system transformation to maximize benefits and minimize costs for the intelligence community, and periodically report to the Director on the status of efforts to carry out an intelligence community business system transformation;

    (E) ensure that funds are obligated for intelligence community business system transformation in a manner consistent with subsection (a); and

    (F) carry out such other duties as the Director shall specify.

(g) RELATION TO ANNUAL REGISTRATION REQUIREMENTS.—Nothing in this section shall be construed to alter the requirements of section 8083 of the Department of Defense Appropriations Act, 2005 (Public Law 108-287; 118 Stat. 989), with regard to information technology systems (as defined in subsection (d) of such section).

(h) Relationship to Defense Business Enterprise Architecture.— Nothing in this section shall be construed to exempt funds authorized to be appropriated to the Department of Defense from the requirements of section 2222 of title 10, United States Code, to the extent that such requirements are otherwise applicable.

(i) RELATION TO CLINGER-COHEN ACT.—

    (1) Executive agency responsibilities in chapter 113 of title 40, United States Code, for any intelligence community business system transformation shall be exercised jointly by—

        (A) the Director of National Intelligence and the Chief

Information Officer of the Intelligence Community; and

(B) the head of the executive agency that contains the element of the intelligence community involved and the chief information officer of that executive agency.

(2) The Director of National Intelligence and the head of the executive agency referred to in paragraph (1)(B) shall enter into a Memorandum of Understanding to carry out the requirements of this section in a manner that best meets the needs of the intelligence community and the executive agency.

(j) REPORTS.—Not later than March 31 of each of the years 2011 through 2015, the Director of National Intelligence shall submit to the congressional intelligence committees a report on the compliance of the intelligence community with the requirements of this section. Each such report shall—

(1) describe actions taken and proposed for meeting the requirements of subsection (a), including—

(A) specific milestones and actual performance against specified performance measures, and any revision of such milestones and performance measures; and

(B) specific actions on the intelligence community business system transformations submitted for certification under such subsection;

(2) identify the number of intelligence community business system transformations that received a certification described in subsection (a)(2); and

(3) describe specific improvements in business operations and cost savings resulting from successful intelligence community business systems transformation efforts.

(k) DEFINITIONS.—In this section:

(1) The term "enterprise architecture" has the meaning given that term in section 3601(4) of title 44, United States Code.

2) The terms "information system" and "information technology" have the meanings given those terms in section 11101 of title 40, United States Code.

(3) The term "intelligence community business system" means an information system, including a national security system, that is operated by, for, or on behalf of an element of the intelligence community, including a financial system, mixed system, financial data feeder system, and the business infrastructure capabilities shared by the systems of the business enterprise architecture, including people, process, and technology, that build upon the core infrastructure used to support business activities, such as acquisition, financial management, logistics,

strategic planning and budgeting, installations and environment, and human resource management.

(4) The term "intelligence community business system transformation" means—

> (A) the acquisition or development of a new intelligence community business system; or
>
> (B) any significant modification or enhancement of an existing intelligence community business system (other than necessary to maintain current services).

(5) The term "national security system" has the meaning given that term in section 3542 of title 44, United States Code.

(6) The term "Office of Business Transformation of the Office of the Director of National Intelligence" includes any successor office that assumes the functions of the Office of Business Transformation of the Office of the Director of National Intelligence as carried out by the Office of Business Transformation on the date of the enactment of the Intelligence Authorization Act for Fiscal Year 2010.

REPORTS ON THE ACQUISITION OF MAJOR SYSTEMS

Sec. 506E. (50 USC 415a-7.)

(a) DEFINITIONS.—In this section:

(1) The term "cost estimate"—

> (A) means an assessment and quantification of all costs and risks associated with the acquisition of a major system based upon reasonably available information at the time the Director establishes the 2010 adjusted total acquisition cost for such system pursuant to subsection (h) or restructures such system pursuant to section 506F(c); and
>
> (B) does not mean an `independent cost estimate'.

(2) The term "critical cost growth threshold" means a percentage increase in the total acquisition cost for a major system of at least 25 percent over the total acquisition cost for the major system as shown in the current Baseline Estimate for the major system.

(3)(A) The term "current Baseline Estimate" means the projected total acquisition cost of a major system that is—

> (i) approved by the Director, or a designee of the Director, at Milestone B or an equivalent acquisition decision for the development, procurement, and construction of such system;
>
> (ii) approved by the Director at the time such system is restructured pursuant to section 506F(c); or
>
> (iii) the 2010 adjusted total acquisition cost determined pursuant to subsection (h).

         (B) A current Baseline Estimate may be in the form of an independent cost estimate.

(4) Except as otherwise specifically provided, the term "Director" means the Director of National Intelligence.

(5) The term "independent cost estimate" has the meaning given that term in section 506A(e).

(6) The term "major contract" means each of the 6 largest prime, associate, or Government-furnished equipment contracts under a major system that is in excess of $40,000,000 and that is not a firm, fixed price contract.

(7) The term "major system" has the meaning given that term in section 506A(e).

(8) The term "Milestone B" means a decision to enter into major system development and demonstration pursuant to guidance prescribed by the Director.

(9) The term "program manager" means—

         (A) the head of the element of the intelligence community that is responsible for the budget, cost, schedule, and performance of a major system; or

         (B) in the case of a major system within the Office of the Director of National Intelligence, the deputy who is responsible for the budget, cost, schedule, and performance of the major system.

(10) The term "significant cost growth threshold" means the percentage increase in the total acquisition cost for a major system of at least 15 percent over the total acquisition cost for such system as shown in the current Baseline Estimate for such system.

(11) The term "total acquisition cost" means the amount equal to the total cost for development and procurement of, and system-specific construction for, a major system.

(b) MAJOR SYSTEM COST REPORTS.—

(1) The program manager for a major system shall, on a quarterly basis, submit to the Director a major system cost report as described in paragraph (2).

(2) A major system cost report shall include the following information (as of the last day of the quarter for which the report is made):

         (A) The total acquisition cost for the major system.

         (B) Any cost variance or schedule variance in a major contract for the major system since the contract was entered into.

         (C) Any changes from a major system schedule milestones or performances that are known, expected, or anticipated by the program manager.

(D) Any significant changes in the total acquisition cost for development and procurement of any software component of the major system, schedule milestones for such software component of the major system, or expected performance of such software component of the major system that are known, expected, or anticipated by the program manager.

(3) Each major system cost report required by paragraph (1) shall be submitted not more than 30 days after the end of the reporting quarter.

(c) REPORTS FOR BREACH OF SIGNIFICANT OR CRITICAL COST GROWTH THRESHOLDS.—If the program manager of a major system for which a report has previously been submitted under subsection (b) determines at any time during a quarter that there is reasonable cause to believe that the total acquisition cost for the major system has increased by a percentage equal to or greater than the significant cost growth threshold or critical cost growth threshold and if a report indicating an increase of such percentage or more has not previously been submitted to the Director, then the program manager shall immediately submit to the Director a major system cost report containing the information, determined as of the date of the report, required under subsection (b).

(d) NOTIFICATION TO CONGRESS OF COST GROWTH.—

(1) Whenever a major system cost report is submitted to the Director, the Director shall determine whether the current acquisition cost for the major system has increased by a percentage equal to or greater than the significant cost growth threshold or the critical cost growth threshold.

(2) If the Director determines that the current total acquisition cost has increased by a percentage equal to or greater than the significant cost growth threshold or critical cost growth threshold, the Director shall submit to Congress a Major System Congressional Report pursuant to subsection (e).

(e) REQUIREMENT FOR MAJOR SYSTEM CONGRESSIONAL REPORT.—

(1) Whenever the Director determines under subsection (d) that the total acquisition cost of a major system has increased by a percentage equal to or greater than the significant cost growth threshold for the major system, a Major System Congressional Report shall be submitted to Congress not later than 45 days after the date on which the Director receives the major system cost report for such major system.

(2) If the total acquisition cost of a major system (as determined by the Director under subsection (d)) increases by a percentage equal to or greater than the critical cost growth threshold for the program or subprogram, the Director shall take actions consistent with the requirements of section 506F.

(f) MAJOR SYSTEM CONGRESSIONAL REPORT ELEMENTS.—

(1) Except as provided in paragraph (2), each Major System Congressional Report shall
include the following:

    (A) The name of the major system.

    (B) The date of the preparation of the report.

    (C) The program phase of the major system as of the date of the preparation of the report.

    (D) The estimate of the total acquisition cost for the major system expressed in constant base-year dollars and in current dollars.

    (E) The current Baseline Estimate for the major system in constant base-year dollars and in current dollars.

    (F) A statement of the reasons for any increase in total acquisition cost for the major system.

    (G) The completion status of the major system—

        (i) expressed as the percentage that the number of years for which funds have been appropriated for the major system is of the number of years for which it is planned that funds will be appropriated for the major system; and

        (ii) expressed as the percentage that the amount of funds that have been appropriated for the major system is of the total amount of funds which it is planned will be appropriated for the major system.

    (H) The fiscal year in which the major system was first authorized and in which funds for such system were first appropriated by Congress.

    (I) The current change and the total change, in dollars and expressed as a percentage, in the total acquisition cost for the major system, stated both in constant base-year dollars and in current dollars.

    (J) The quantity of end items to be acquired under the major system and the current change and total change, if any, in that quantity.

    (K) The identities of the officers responsible for management and cost control of the major system.

    (L) The action taken and proposed to be taken to control future cost growth of the major system.

    (M) Any changes made in the performance or schedule milestones of the major system and the extent to which such changes have contributed to the increase in total acquisition cost for the major system.

(N) The following contract performance assessment information with respect to each major contract under the major system:

(i) The name of the contractor.

(ii) The phase that the contract is in at the time of the preparation of the report.

(iii) The percentage of work under the contract that has been completed.

(iv) Any current change and the total change, in dollars and expressed as a percentage, in the contract cost.

(v) The percentage by which the contract is currently ahead of or behind schedule.

(vi) A narrative providing a summary explanation of the most significant occurrences, including cost and schedule variances under major contracts of the major system, contributing to the changes identified and a discussion of the effect these occurrences will have on the future costs and schedule of the major system.

(O) In any case in which one or more problems with a software component of the major system significantly contributed to the increase in costs of the major system, the action taken and proposed to be taken to solve such problems.

(2) A Major System Congressional Report prepared for a major system for which the increase in the total acquisition cost is due to termination or cancellation of the entire major system shall include only—

(A) the information described in subparagraphs (A) through (F) of paragraph (1); and

(B) the total percentage change in total acquisition cost for such system.

(g) PROHIBITION ON OBLIGATION OF FUNDS.—If a determination of an increase by a percentage equal to or greater than the significant cost growth threshold is made by the Director under subsection (d) and a Major System Congressional Report containing the information described in subsection (f) is not submitted to Congress under subsection (e)(1), or if a determination of an increase by a percentage equal to or greater than the critical cost growth threshold is made by the Director under subsection (d) and the Major System Congressional Report containing the information described in subsection (f) and section 506F(b)(3) and the certification required by section 506F(b)(2) are not submitted to Congress under subsection (e)(2), funds appropriated for construction, research, development, test, evaluation, and procurement may not be obligated for a major contract under the major system. The prohibition on the obligation of funds for a major system shall cease to apply at the end of the 45-day period that begins on the date—

(1) on which Congress receives the Major System Congressional Report under subsection (e)(1) with respect to that major system, in the case of a determination of an increase by a percentage equal to or greater than the significant cost growth threshold (as determined in subsection (d)); or

(2) on which Congress receives both the Major System Congressional Report under subsection (e)(2) and the certification of the Director under section 506F(b)(2) with respect to that major system, in the case of an increase by a percentage equal to or greater than the critical cost growth threshold (as determined under subsection (d)).

(h) TREATMENT OF COST INCREASES PRIOR TO ENACTMENT OF INTELLIGENCE AUTHORIZATION ACT FOR FISCAL YEAR 2010.—

(1) Not later than 180 days after the date of the enactment of the Intelligence Authorization Act for Fiscal Year 2010, the Director—

(A) shall, for each major system, determine if the total acquisition cost of such major system increased by a percentage equal to or greater than the significant cost growth threshold or the critical cost growth threshold prior to such date of enactment;

(B) shall establish for each major system for which the total acquisition cost has increased by a percentage equal to or greater than the significant cost growth threshold or the critical cost growth threshold prior to such date of enactment a revised current Baseline Estimate based upon an updated cost estimate;

(C) may, for a major system not described in subparagraph (B), establish a revised current Baseline Estimate based upon an updated cost estimate; and

(D) shall submit to Congress a report describing—

(i) each determination made under subparagraph (A);

(ii) each revised current Baseline Estimate established for a major system under subparagraph (B); and

(iii) each revised current Baseline Estimate established for a major system under subparagraph (C), including the percentage increase of the total acquisition cost of such major system that occurred prior to the date of the enactment of such Act.

(2) The revised current Baseline Estimate established for a major system under subparagraph (B) or (C) of paragraph (1) shall be the 2010

adjusted total acquisition cost for the major system and may include the estimated cost of conducting any vulnerability assessments for such major system required under section 506C.

(i) REQUIREMENTS TO USE BASE YEAR DOLLARS.—Any determination of a percentage increase under this section shall be stated in terms of constant base year dollars.

(j) FORM OF REPORT.—Any report required to be submitted under this section may be submitted in a classified form.

CRITICAL COST GROWTH IN MAJOR SYSTEMS

Sec. 506F. (50 USC 415a-8.) (a) REASSESSMENT OF MAJOR SYSTEM.—If the Director of National Intelligence determines under section 506E(d) that the total acquisition cost of a major system has increased by a percentage equal to or greater than the critical cost growth threshold for the major system, the Director shall—

(1) determine the root cause or causes of the critical cost growth, in accordance with applicable statutory requirements, policies, procedures, and guidance; and

(2) carry out an assessment of—

(A) the projected cost of completing the major system if current requirements are not modified;

(B) the projected cost of completing the major system based on reasonable modification of such requirements;

(C) the rough order of magnitude of the costs of any reasonable alternative system or capability; and

(D) the need to reduce funding for other systems due to the growth in cost of the major system.

(b) PRESUMPTION OF TERMINATION.—(1) After conducting the reassessment required by subsection (a) with respect to a major system, the Director shall terminate the major system unless the Director submits to Congress a Major System Congressional Report containing a certification in accordance with paragraph (2) and the information described in paragraph (3) The Director shall submit such Major System Congressional Report and certification not later than 90 days after the date the Director receives the relevant major system cost report under subsection (b) or (c) of section 506E.

(2) A certification described by this paragraph with respect to a major system is a written certification that—

(A) the continuation of the major system is essential to the national security;

(B) there are no alternatives to the major system that will provide acceptable capability to meet the intelligence requirement at less cost;

(C) the new estimates of the total acquisition cost have been determined by the Director to be reasonable;

(D) the major system is a higher priority than other systems whose funding must be reduced to accommodate the growth in cost of the major system; and

(E) the management structure for the major system is adequate to manage and control the total acquisition cost.

(3) A Major System Congressional Report accompanying a written certification under paragraph (2) shall include, in addition to the requirements of section 506E(e), the root cause analysis and assessment carried out pursuant to subsection (a), the basis for each determination made in accordance with subparagraphs (A) through (E) of paragraph (2), and a description of all funding changes made as a result of the growth in the cost of the major system, including reductions made in funding for other systems to accommodate such cost growth, together with supporting documentation.

(c) ACTIONS IF MAJOR SYSTEM NOT TERMINATED.—If the Director elects not to terminate a major system pursuant to subsection (b), the Director shall—

(1) restructure the major system in a manner that addresses the root cause or causes of the critical cost growth, as identified pursuant to subsection (a), and ensures that the system has an appropriate management structure as set forth in the certification submitted pursuant to subsection (b)(2)(E);

(2) rescind the most recent Milestone approval for the major system;

(3) require a new Milestone approval for the major system before taking any action to enter a new contract, exercise an option under an existing contract, or otherwise extend the scope of an existing contract under the system, except to the extent determined necessary by the Milestone Decision Authority, on a nondelegable basis, to ensure that the system may be restructured as intended by the Director without unnecessarily wasting resources;

(4) establish a revised current Baseline Estimate for the major system based upon an updated cost estimate; and

(5) conduct regular reviews of the major system.

(d) ACTIONS IF MAJOR SYSTEM TERMINATED.—If a major system is terminated pursuant to subsection (b), the Director shall submit to Congress a written report setting forth—

(1) an explanation of the reasons for terminating the major system;

(2) the alternatives considered to address any problems in the major system; and

(3) the course the Director plans to pursue to meet any intelligence requirements otherwise intended to be met by the major system.

(e) FORM OF REPORT.—Any report or certification required to be submitted under this section may be submitted in a classified form.

(f) WAIVER.—

(1) The Director may waive the requirements of subsections (d)(2), (e), and (g) of section 506E and subsections (a)(2), (b), (c), and (d) of this section with respect to a major system if the Director determines that at least 90 percent of the amount of the current Baseline Estimate for the major system has been expended.

(2)(A) If the Director grants a waiver under paragraph (1) with respect to a major system, the Director shall submit to the congressional intelligence committees written notice of the waiver that includes—

(i) the information described in section 506E(f); and

(ii) if the current total acquisition cost of the major system has increased by a percentage equal to or greater than the critical cost growth threshold—

(I) a determination of the root cause or causes of the critical cost growth, as described in subsection (a)(1); and

(II) a certification that includes the elements described in subparagraphs (A), (B), and (E) of subsection (b)(2).

(B) The Director shall submit the written notice required by subparagraph (A) not later than 90 days after the date that the Director receives a major system cost report under subsection (b) or (c) of section 506E that indicates that the total acquisition cost for the major system has increased by a percentage equal to or greater than the significant cost growth threshold or critical cost growth threshold.

(g) DEFINITIONS.—In this section, the terms "cost estimate", "critical cost growth threshold", "current Baseline Estimate", "major system", and "total acquisition cost" have the meaning given those terms in section 506E(a).

FUTURE BUDGET PROJECTIONS

Sec. 506G. (50 USC 415a–9.) (a) FUTURE YEAR INTELLIGENCE PLANS.—

(1) The Director of National Intelligence, with the concurrence of the Director of the Office of Management and Budget, shall provide to the

congressional intelligence committees a Future Year Intelligence Plan, as described in paragraph (2), for—

    (A) each expenditure center in the National Intelligence Program; and

    (B) each major system in the National Intelligence Program.

(2)(A) A Future Year Intelligence Plan submitted under this subsection shall include the year-by-year proposed funding for each center or system referred to in subparagraph (A) or (B) of paragraph (1), for the budget year for which the Plan is submitted and not less than the 4 subsequent fiscal years.

    (B) A Future Year Intelligence Plan submitted under subparagraph

    (B) of paragraph (1) for a major system shall include—

        (i) the estimated total life-cycle cost of such major system; and

        (ii) major milestones that have significant resource implications for such major system.

(b) LONG-TERM BUDGET PROJECTIONS.—

(1) The Director of National Intelligence, with the concurrence of the Director of the Office of Management and Budget, shall provide to the congressional intelligence committees a Long-term Budget Projection for each element of the intelligence community funded under the National Intelligence Program acquiring a major system that includes the budget for such element for the 5-year period that begins on the day after the end of the last fiscal year for which year-by-year proposed funding is included in a Future Year Intelligence Plan for such major system in accordance with subsection (a)(2)(A).

(2) A Long-term Budget Projection submitted under paragraph (1) shall include—

    (A) projections for the appropriate element of the intelligence community for—

        (i) pay and benefits of officers and employees of such element;

        (ii) other operating and support costs and minor acquisitions of such element;

        (iii) research and technology required by such element;

        (iv) current and planned major system acquisitions for such element;

        (v) any future major system acquisitions for such element; and

        (vi) any additional funding projections that the Director of National Intelligence considers appropriate;

(B) a budget projection based on effective cost and schedule execution of current or planned major system acquisitions and application of Office of Management and Budget inflation estimates to future major system acquisitions;

(C) any additional assumptions and projections that the Director of National Intelligence considers appropriate; and

(D) a description of whether, and to what extent, the total projection for each year exceeds the level that would result from applying the most recent Office of Management and Budget inflation estimate to the budget of that element of the intelligence community.

(c) SUBMISSION TO CONGRESS.—The Director of National Intelligence, with the concurrence of the Director of the Office of Management and Budget, shall submit to the congressional intelligence committees each Future Year Intelligence Plan or Long-term Budget Projection required under subsection (a) or (b) for a fiscal year at the time that the President submits to Congress the budget for such fiscal year pursuant section 1105 of title 31, United States Code.

(d) MAJOR SYSTEM AFFORDABILITY REPORT.—

(1) The Director of National Intelligence, with the concurrence of the Director of the Office of Management and Budget, shall prepare a report on the acquisition of a major system funded under the National Intelligence Program before the time that the President submits to Congress the budget for the first fiscal year in which appropriated funds are anticipated to be obligated for the development or procurement of such major system.

(2) The report on such major system shall include an assessment of whether, and to what extent, such acquisition, if developed, procured, and operated, is projected to cause an increase in the most recent Future Year Intelligence Plan and Long-term Budget Projection submitted under section 506G for an element of the intelligence community.

(3) The Director of National Intelligence shall update the report whenever an independent cost estimate must be updated pursuant to section 506A(a)(4).

(4) The Director of National Intelligence shall submit each report required by this subsection at the time that the President submits to Congress the budget for a fiscal year pursuant to section 1105 of title 31, United States Code.

(e) DEFINITIONS.—In this section:

(1) Budget year.—The term "budget year" means the next fiscal year for which the President is required to submit to Congress a budget pursuant to section 1105 of title 31, United States Code.

(2) Independent cost estimate; major system.—The terms "independent cost estimate" and "major system" have the meaning given those terms in section 506A(e).

REPORTS ON SECURITY CLEARANCES

Sec. 506H. [50 USC 415a-10.]

(a) QUADRENNIAL AUDIT OF POSITION REQUIREMENTS.—(1) The President shall every four years conduct an audit of the manner in which the executive branch determines whether a security clearance is required for a particular position in the United States Government.

    (2) Not later than 30 days after the completion of an audit conducted under paragraph (1), the President shall submit to Congress the results of such audit.

(b) REPORT ON SECURITY CLEARANCE DETERMINATIONS.—(1) Not later than February 1 of each year, the President shall submit to Congress a report on the security clearance process. Such report shall include, for each security clearance level—

    (A) the number of employees of the United States Government who—

        (i) held a security clearance at such level as of October 1 of the preceding year; and

        (ii) were approved for a security clearance at such level during the preceding fiscal year;

    (B) the number of contractors to the United States Government who—

        (i) held a security clearance at such level as of October 1 of the preceding year; and

        (ii) were approved for a security clearance at such level during the preceding fiscal year; and

    (C) for each element of the intelligence community—

        (i) the total amount of time it took to process the security clearance determination for such level that—

            (I) was among the 80 percent of security clearance determinations made during the receding fiscal year that took the shortest amount of time to complete; and

            (II) took the longest amount of time to complete;

        (ii) the total amount of time it took to process the security clearance determination for such level that—

            (I) was among the 90 percent of security clearance determinations made during the preceding fiscal year that took the shortest amount of time to complete; and

(II) took the longest amount of time to complete;

(iii) the number of pending security clearance investigations for such level as of October 1 of the preceding year that have remained pending for—

(I) 4 months or less;

(II) between 4 months and 8 months;

(III) between 8 months and one year; and

(IV) more than one year;

(iv) the percentage of reviews during the preceding fiscal year that resulted in a denial or revocation of a security clearance;

(v) the percentage of investigations during the preceding fiscal year that resulted in incomplete information;

(vi) the percentage of investigations during the preceding fiscal year that did not result in enough information to make a decision on potentially adverse information; and

(vii) for security clearance determinations completed or pending during the preceding fiscal year that have taken longer than one year to complete—

(I) the number of security clearance determinations for positions as employees of the United States Government that required more than one year to complete;

(II) the number of security clearance determinations for contractors that required more than one year to complete;

(III) the agencies that investigated and adjudicated such determinations; and

(IV) the cause of significant delays in such determinations.

(2) For purposes of paragraph (1), the President may consider—

(A) security clearances at the level of confidential and secret as one security clearance level; and

(B) security clearances at the level of top secret or higher as one security clearance level.

(c) FORM.—The results required under subsection (a)(2) and the reports required under subsection (b)(1) shall be submitted in unclassified form, but may include a classified annex.

SUMMARY OF INTELLIGENCE RELATING TO TERRORIST RECIDIVISM OF DETAINEES HELD AT UNITED STATES NAVAL STATION, GUANTANAMO BAY, CUBA

SEC. 506I. (a) IN GENERAL.—The Director of National Intelligence, in consultation with the Director of the Central Intelligence Agency and the Director of the Defense Intelligence Agency, shall make publicly available an unclassified summary of—

(1) intelligence relating to recidivism of detainees currently or formerly held at the Naval Detention Facility at Guantanamo Bay, Cuba, by the Department of Defense; and

(2) an assessment of the likelihood that such detainees will engage in terrorism or communicate with persons in terrorist organizations.

(b) UPDATES.—Not less frequently than once every 6 months, the Director of National Intelligence, in consultation with the Director of the Central Intelligence Agency and the Secretary of Defense, shall update and make publicly available an unclassified summary consisting of the information required by subsection (a) and the number of individuals formerly detained at Naval Station, Guantanamo Bay, Cuba, who are confirmed or suspected of returning to terrorist activities after release or transfer from such Naval Station.''.

(2) INITIAL UPDATE.—The initial update required by section 506I(b) of such Act, as added by paragraph (1) of this subsection, shall be made publicly available not later than 10 days after the date the first report following the date of the enactment of the Intelligence Authorization Act for Fiscal Year 2012 is submitted to members and committees of Congress pursuant to section 319 of the Supplemental Appropriations Act, 2009 (Public Law 111–32; 10 U.S.C. 801 note).

DATE OF SUBMITTAL OF VARIOUS ANNUAL AND SEMIANNUAL REPORTS TO THE CONGRESSIONAL INTELLIGENCE COMMITTEES

SEC. 507. [50 U.S.C. §415b]

(a) ANNUAL REPORTS.—

(1) The date for the submittal to the congressional intelligence committees of the following annual reports shall be the date each year provided in subsection (c)(1)(A):

(A) The annual report on the protection of the identities of covert agents required by section 603.

(B) The annual report of the Inspectors Generals of the intelligence community on proposed resources and activities of their offices required by section 8H(g) of the Inspector General Act of 1978.

(C) The annual report on the acquisition of technology relating to weapons of mass destruction and advanced conventional munitions required by section 721 of the Intelligence Authorization Act for Fiscal Year 1997 (Public Law 104-293; 50 U.S.C. §2366).

(D) The annual report on commercial activities as security for intelligence collection required by section 437(c) of title 10, United States Code.

(E) The annual report on certifications for immunity in interdiction of aircraft engaged in illicit drug trafficking required by section 1012(c)(2) of the National Defense Authorization Act for Fiscal Year 1995 (22 U.S.C. §2291–4(c)(2)).

(F) The annual report on activities under the David L. Boren National Security Education Act of 1991 (title VIII of Public Law 102–183; 50 U.S.C. §1901 et seq.) required by section 806(a) of that Act (50 U.S.C. §1906(a)).

(G) The annual report on hiring and retention of minority employees in the intelligence community required by section 114(c).

(H) The annual report on outside employment of employees of elements of the intelligence community required by section 102A(u)(2).

(I) The annual report on financial intelligence on terrorist assets required by section 118.

(2) The date for the submittal to the congressional intelligence committees of the following annual reports shall be the date each year provided in subsection (c)(1)(B):

(A) The annual report on the safety and security of Russian nuclear facilities and nuclear military forces required by section 114(a).

(B) The annual report on the threat of attack on the United States from weapons of mass destruction required by section 114(c).

(b) SEMIANNUAL REPORTS.—The dates for the submittal to the congressional intelligence committees of the following semiannual reports shall be the dates each year provided in subsection (c)(2):

(1) The semiannual reports on the Office of the Inspector General of the Central Intelligence Agency required by section 17(d)(1) of the Central Intelligence Agency Act of 1949 (50 U.S.C. §403q(d)(1)).

(2) The semiannual reports on decisions not to prosecute certain violations of law under the Classified Information Procedures Act (18 U.S.C. App.) as required by section 13 of that Act.

(3) The semiannual reports on the disclosure of information and consumer reports to the Federal Bureau of Investigation for counterintelligence purposes required by section 624(h)(2) of the Fair Credit Reporting Act (15 U.S.C. §1681u(h)(2)).

(4) The semiannual provision of information on requests for financial information for foreign counterintelligence purposes required by section 1114(a)(5)(C) of the Right to Financial Privacy Act of 1978 (12 U.S.C. §3414(a)(5)(C)).

(c) SUBMITTAL DATES FOR REPORTS.—

(1)(A) Except as provided in subsection (d), each annual report listed in subsection (a)(1) shall be submitted not later than February 1.

(B) Except as provided in subsection (d), each annual report listed in subsection (a)(2) shall be submitted not later than December 1.

(2) Except as provided in subsection (d), each semiannual report listed in subsection (b) shall be submitted not later than February 1 and August 1.

(d) POSTPONEMENT OF SUBMITTAL.—

(1) Subject to paragraph (3), the date for the submittal of—

(A) an annual report listed in subsection (a)(1) may be postponed until March 1;

(B) an annual report listed in subsection (a)(2) may be postponed until January 1; and

(C) a semiannual report listed in subsection (b) may be postponed until March 1 or September 1, as the case may be, if the official required to submit such report submits to the congressional intelligence committees a written notification of such postponement.

(2)(A) Notwithstanding any other provision of law and subject to paragraph (3), the date for the submittal to the congressional intelligence committees of any report described in subparagraph (B) may be postponed by not more than 30 days from the date otherwise specified in the provision of law for the submittal of such report if the official required to submit such report submits to the congressional intelligence committees a written notification of such postponement.

(B) A report described in this subparagraph is any report on intelligence or intelligence-related activities of the United States Government that is submitted under a provision of law requiring the submittal of only a single report.

(3)(A) The date for the submittal of a report whose submittal is postponed under paragraph (1) or (2) may be postponed beyond the time provided for the submittal of such report under such paragraph if the official required to submit such report submits to the congressional intelligence committees a written certification that preparation and submittal of such report at such time will impede the work of officers or employees of the intelligence community in a manner that will be detrimental to the national security of the United States.

(B) A certification with respect to a report under subparagraph (A) shall include a proposed submittal date for such report, and such report shall be submitted not later than that date.

CERTIFICATION OF COMPLIANCE WITH OVERSIGHT REQUIREMENTS

Sec. 508. [50 USC 415d.] The head of each element of the intelligence community shall annually submit to the congressional intelligence committees—

(1) a certification that, to the best of the knowledge of the head of such element—

(A) the head of such element is in full compliance with the requirements of this title; and

(B) any information required to be submitted by the head of such element under this Act before the date of the submission of such certification has been properly submitted; or

(2) if the head of such element is unable to submit a certification under paragraph (1), a statement—

(A) of the reasons the head of such element is unable to submit such a certification;

(B) describing any information required to be submitted by the head of such element under this Act before the date of the submission of such statement that has not been properly submitted; and

(C) that the head of such element will submit such information as soon as possible after the submission of such statement.

TITLE VI—PROTECTION OF CERTAIN NATIONAL SECURITY INFORMATION

PROTECTION OF IDENTITIES OF CERTAIN UNITED STATES UNDERCOVER INTELLIGENCE OFFICERS, AGENTS, INFORMANTS, AND SOURCES

SEC. 601. [50 U.S.C. §421]

(a) Whoever, having or having had authorized access to classified information that identifies a covert agent, intentionally discloses any information identifying such covert agent to any individual not authorized to receive classified information, knowing that the information disclosed so identifies such covert agent and that the United States is taking affirmative measures to conceal such covert agent's intelligence relationship to the United States, shall be fined under title 18, United States Code, or imprisoned not more than 15 years, or both.

(b) Whoever, as a result of having authorized access to classified information, learns the identity of a covert agent and intentionally discloses any information identifying such covert agent to any individual not authorized to receive classified information, knowing that the information disclosed so identifies such covert agent and that the United States is taking affirmative measures to conceal such covert agent's intelligence relationship to the United States, shall be fined under title 18, United States Code, or imprisoned not more than 10 years, or both.

(c) Whoever, in the course of a pattern of activities intended to identify and expose covert agents and with reason to believe that such activities would impair or impede the foreign intelligence activities of the United States, discloses any information that identifies an individual as a covert agent to any individual not authorized to receive classified information, knowing that the information disclosed so identifies such individual and that the United States is taking affirmative measures to conceal such individual's classified intelligence relationship to the United States, shall be fined under title 18, United States Code, or imprisoned not more than three years, or both.

(d) A term of imprisonment imposed under this section shall be consecutive to any other sentence of imprisonment.

DEFENSES AND EXCEPTIONS

SEC. 602. [50 U.S.C. §422]

(a) It is a defense to a prosecution under section 601 that before the commission of the offense with which the defendant is charged, the United States had publicly acknowledged or revealed the intelligence relationship to the United States of the individual the disclosure of whose intelligence relationship to the United States is the basis for the prosecution.

(b)(1) Subject to paragraph (2), no person other than a person committing an offense under section 601 shall be subject to prosecution under such section by virtue of section 2 or 4 of title 18, United States Code, or shall be subject to prosecution for conspiracy to commit an offense under such section.

(2) Paragraph (1) shall not apply (A) in the case of a person who acted in the course of a pattern of activities intended to identify and expose covert agents and with reason to believe that such activities would impair or impede the foreign intelligence activities of the United States, or (B) in the case of a person who has authorized access to classified information.

(c) It shall not be an offense under section 601 to transmit information described in such section directly to either congressional intelligence committee.

(d) It shall not be an offense under section 601 for an individual to disclose information that solely identifies himself as a covert agent.

REPORT

SEC. 603. [50 U.S.C. §423]
(a) The President, after receiving information from the Director of National Intelligence, shall submit to the congressional intelligence committees an annual report on measures to protect the identities of covert agents, including an assessment of the need, if any, for modification of this title for the purpose of improving legal protections for covert agents, and on any other matter relevant to the protection of the identities of covert agents. The date for the submittal of the report shall be the date provided in section 507.
(b) The report described in subsection (a) shall be exempt from any requirement for publication or disclosure.

EXTRATERRITORIAL JURISDICTION

SEC. 604. [50 U.S.C. §424]
There is jurisdiction over an offense under section 601 committed outside the United States if the individual committing the offense is a citizen of the United States or an alien lawfully admitted to the United States for permanent residence (as defined in section 101(a)(20) of the Immigration and Nationality Act).

PROVIDING INFORMATION TO CONGRESS

SEC. 605. [50 U.S.C. §425]
Nothing in this title may be construed as authority to withhold information from the Congress or from a committee of either House of Congress.

DEFINITIONS

SEC. 606. [50 U.S.C. §426]
For the purposes of this title:
(1) The term "classified information" means information or material designated and clearly marked or clearly represented, pursuant to the provisions of a statute or Executive order (or a regulation or order issued pursuant to a statute or Executive order), as requiring a specific degree of protection against unauthorized disclosure for reasons of national security.
(2) The term "authorized", when used with respect to access to classified information, means having authority, right, or permission pursuant to the provisions of a statute, Executive order, directive of the head of any department or agency engaged in foreign intelligence or

counterintelligence activities, order of any United States court, or provisions of any Rule of the House of Representatives or resolution of the Senate which assigns responsibility within the respective House of Congress for the oversight of intelligence activities.

(3) The term "disclose" means to communicate, provide, impart, transmit, transfer, convey, publish, or otherwise make available.

(4) The term "covert agent" means—

(A) a present or retired officer or employee of an intelligence agency or a present or retired member of the Armed Forces assigned to duty with an intelligence agency—

(i) whose identity as such an officer, employee, or member is classified information, and

(ii) who is serving outside the United States or has within the last five years served outside the United States; or

(B) a United States citizen whose intelligence relationship to the United States is classified information, and—

(i) who resides and acts outside the United States as an agent of, or informant or source of operational assistance to, an intelligence agency, or

(ii) who is at the time of the disclosure acting as an agent of, or informant to, the foreign counterintelligence or foreign counterterrorism components of the Federal Bureau of Investigation; or

(C) an individual, other than a United States citizen, whose past or present intelligence relationship to the United States is classified information and who is a present or former agent of, or a present or former informant or source of operational assistance to, an intelligence agency.

(5) The term "intelligence agency" means the Central Intelligence Agency, a foreign intelligence component of the Department of Defense, or the foreign counterintelligence or foreign counterterrorism components of the Federal Bureau of Investigation.

(6) The term "informant" means any individual who furnishes information to an intelligence agency in the course of a confidential relationship protecting the identity of such individual from public disclosure.

(7) The terms "officer" and "employee" have the meanings given such terms by section 2104 and 2105, respectively, of title 5, United States Code.

(8) The term "Armed Forces" means the Army, Navy, Air Force, Marine Corps, and Coast Guard.

(9) The term "United States", when used in a geographic sense, means all areas under the territorial sovereignty of the United States and the Trust Territory of the Pacific Islands.

(10) The term "pattern of activities" requires a series of acts with a common purpose or objective.

TITLE VII—PROTECTION OF OPERATIONAL FILES

OPERATIONAL FILES OF THE CENTRAL INTELLIGENCE AGENCY

SEC. 701. [50 U.S.C. §431]

(a) The Director of the Central Intelligence Agency, with the coordination of the Director of National Intelligence, may exempt operational files of the Central Intelligence Agency from the provisions of section 552 of title 5, United States Code (Freedom of Information Act), which require publication or disclosure, or search or review in connection therewith.

(b) In this section, the term "operational files" means—

(1) files of the National Clandestine Service which document the conduct of foreign intelligence or counterintelligence operations or intelligence or security liaison arrangements or information exchanges with foreign governments or their intelligence or security services;

(2) files of the Directorate for Science and Technology which document the means by which foreign intelligence or counterintelligence is collected through scientific and technical systems; and

(3) files of the Office of Personnel Security which document investigations conducted to determine the suitability of potential foreign intelligence or counterintelligence sources; except that files which are the sole repository of disseminated intelligence are not operational files.

(c) Notwithstanding subsection (a) of this section, exempted operational files shall continue to be subject to search and review for information concerning—

(1) United States citizens or aliens lawfully admitted for permanent residence who have requested information on themselves pursuant to the provisions of section 552 of title 5, United States Code (Freedom of Information Act), or section 552a of title 5, United States Code (Privacy Act of 1974);

(2) any special activity the existence of which is not exempt from disclosure under the provisions of section 552 of title 5, United States Code (Freedom of Information Act); or

(3) the specific subject matter of an investigation by the congressional intelligence committees, the Intelligence Oversight Board, the Department of Justice, the Office of General Counsel of the Central

Intelligence Agency, the Office of Inspector General of the Central Intelligence Agency, or the Office of the Director of National Intelligence for any impropriety, or violation of law, Executive order, or Presidential directive, in the conduct of an intelligence activity.

(d)(1) Files that are not exempted under subsection (a) of this section which contain information derived or disseminated from exempted operational files shall be subject to search and review.

(2) The inclusion of information from exempted operational files in files that are not exempted under subsection (a) of this section shall not affect the exemption under subsection (a) of this section of the originating operational files from search, review, publication, or disclosure.

(3) Records from exempted operational files which have been disseminated to and referenced in files that are not exempted under subsection (a) of this section and which have been returned to exempted operational files for sole retention shall be subject to search and review.

(e) The provisions of subsection (a) of this section shall not be superseded except by a provision of law which is enacted after the date of enactment of subsection (a), and which specifically cites and repeals or modifies its provisions.

(f) Whenever any person who has requested agency records under section 552 of title 5, United States Code (Freedom of Information Act), alleges that the Central Intelligence Agency has improperly withheld records because of failure to comply with any provision of this section, judicial review shall be available under the terms set forth in section 552(a)(4)(B) of title 5, United States Code, except that—

(1) in any case in which information specifically authorized under criteria established by an Executive order to be kept secret in the interest of national defense or foreign relations which is filed with, or produced for, the court by the Central Intelligence Agency, such information shall be examined ex parte, in camera by the court;

(2) the court shall, to the fullest extent practicable, determine issues of fact based on sworn written submissions of the parties;

(3) when a complainant alleges that requested records are improperly withheld because of improper placement solely in exempted operational files, the complainant shall support such allegation with a sworn written submission, based upon personal knowledge or otherwise admissible evidence;

(4)(A) when a complainant alleges that requested records were improperly withheld because of improper exemption of operational files, the Central Intelligence Agency shall meet its burden under section 552(a)(4)(B) of title 5, United States Code, by demonstrating to the court by sworn written submission that exempted operational files likely to contain responsive records currently perform the functions set forth in subsection (b) of this section; and

>(B) the court may not order the Central Intelligence Agency to review the content of any exempted operational file or files in order to make the demonstration required under subparagraph (A) of this paragraph, unless the complainant disputes the Central Intelligence Agency's showing with a sworn written submission based on personal knowledge or otherwise admissible evidence;

(5) in proceedings under paragraphs (3) and (4) of this subsection, the parties shall not obtain discovery pursuant to rules 26 through 36 of the Federal Rules of Civil Procedure, except that requests for admission may be made pursuant to rules 26 and 36;

(6) if the court finds under this subsection that the Central Intelligence Agency has improperly withheld requested records because of failure to comply with any provision of this section, the court shall order the Central Intelligence Agency to search and review the appropriate exempted operational file or files for the requested records and make such records, or portions thereof, available in accordance with the provisions of section 552 of title 5, United States Code (Freedom of Information Act), and such order shall be the exclusive remedy for failure to comply with this section; and

(7) if at any time following the filing of a complaint pursuant to this subsection the Central Intelligence Agency agrees to search the appropriate exempted operational file or files for the requested records, the court shall dismiss the claim based upon such complaint.

(g) DECENNIAL REVIEW OF EXEMPTED OPERATIONAL FILES—

(1) Not less than once every ten years, the Director of the Central Intelligence Agency and the Director of National Intelligence shall review the exemptions in force under subsection (a) to determine whether such exemptions may be removed from any category of exempted files or any portion thereof.

(2) The review required by paragraph (1) shall include consideration of the historical value or other public interest in the subject matter of the particular category of files or portions thereof and the potential for declassifying a significant part of the information contained therein.

(3) A complainant who alleges that the Central Intelligence Agency has improperly withheld records because of failure to comply with this subsection may seek judicial review in the district court of the United States of the district in which any of the parties reside, or in the District of Columbia. In such a proceeding, the court's review shall be limited to determining the following:

(A) Whether the Central Intelligence Agency has conducted the review required by paragraph (1) before October 15, 1994, or before the expiration of the 10-year period beginning on the date of the most recent review.

(B) Whether the Central Intelligence Agency, in fact, considered the criteria set forth in paragraph (2) in conducting the required review.

OPERATIONAL FILES OF THE
NATIONAL GEOSPATIAL-INTELLIGENCE AGENCY

SEC. 702. [50 U.S.C. §432]

(a) EXEMPTION OF CERTAIN OPERATIONAL FILES FROM SEARCH, REVIEW, PUBLICATION, OR DISCLOSURE.—

(1) The Director of the National Geospatial-Intelligence Agency, with the coordination of the Director of National Intelligence, may exempt operational files of the National Geospatial-Intelligence Agency from the provisions of section 552 of title 5, United States Code, which require publication, disclosure, search, or review in connection therewith.

(2)(A) Subject to subparagraph (B), for the purposes of this section, the term "operational files" means files of the National Geospatial-Intelligence Agency (hereafter in this section referred to as "NGA") concerning the activities of NGA that before the establishment of NGA were performed by the National Photographic Interpretation Center of the Central Intelligence Agency (NPIC), that document the means by which foreign intelligence or counterintelligence is collected through scientific and technical systems.

(B) Files which are the sole repository of disseminated intelligence are not operational files.

(3) Notwithstanding paragraph (1), exempted operational files shall continue to be subject to search and review for information concerning—

(A) United States citizens or aliens lawfully admitted for permanent residence who have requested information on themselves pursuant to the provisions of section 552 or 552a of title 5, United States Code;

(B) any special activity the existence of which is not exempt from disclosure under the provisions of section 552 of title 5, United States Code; or

(C) the specific subject matter of an investigation by any of the following for any impropriety, or violation of law, Executive order, or Presidential directive, in the conduct of an intelligence activity:

(i) The congressional intelligence committees.
(ii) The Intelligence Oversight Board.
(iii) The Department of Justice.
(iv) The Office of General Counsel of NGA.
(v) The Office of the Director of NGA.
(vi) The Office of the Inspector General of the National-Geospatial Intelligence Agency.

(4)(A) Files that are not exempted under paragraph (1) which contain information derived or disseminated from exempted operational files shall be subject to search and review.

(B) The inclusion of information from exempted operational files in files that are not exempted under paragraph (1) shall not affect the exemption under paragraph (1) of the originating operational files from search, review, publication, or disclosure.

(C) Records from exempted operational files which have been disseminated to and referenced in files that are not exempted under paragraph (1) and which have been returned to exempted operational files for sole retention shall be subject to search and review.

(5) The provisions of paragraph (1) may not be superseded except by a provision of law which is enacted after the date of the enactment of this section, and which specifically cites and repeals or modifies its provisions.

(6)(A) Except as provided in subparagraph (B), whenever any person who has requested agency records under section 552 of title 5, United States Code, alleges that NGA has withheld records improperly because of failure to comply with any provision of this section, judicial review shall be available under the terms set forth in section 552(a)(4)(B) of title 5, United States Code.

(B) Judicial review shall not be available in the manner provided for under subparagraph (A) as follows:

(i) In any case in which information specifically authorized under criteria established by an Executive order to be kept secret in the interests of national defense or foreign relations is filed with, or produced for, the court by NGA, such information shall be examined ex parte, in camera by the court.

(ii) The court shall, to the fullest extent practicable, determine the issues of fact based on sworn written submissions of the parties.

(iii) When a complainant alleges that requested records are improperly withheld because of improper placement solely in exempted operational files, the complainant shall support such allegation with a sworn written submission based upon personal knowledge or otherwise admissible evidence.

(iv)(I) When a complainant alleges that requested records were improperly withheld because of improper exemption of operational files, NGA shall meet its burden under section 552(a)(4)(B) of title 5, United States Code, by demonstrating to the court by sworn written submission that exempted operational files likely to contain responsive records currently perform the functions set forth in paragraph (2).

(II) The court may not order NGA to review the content of any exempted operational file or files in order to make the demonstration required under subclause (I), unless the complainant disputes NGA's showing with a sworn written submission based on personal knowledge or otherwise admissible evidence.

(v) In proceedings under clauses (iii) and (iv), the parties may not obtain discovery pursuant to rules 26 through 36 of the Federal Rules of Civil Procedure, except that requests for admissions may be made pursuant to rules 26 and 36.

(vi) If the court finds under this paragraph that NGA has improperly withheld requested records because of failure to comply with any provision of this subsection, the court shall order NGA to search and review the appropriate exempted operational file or files for the requested records and make such records, or portions thereof, available in accordance with the provisions of section 552 of title 5, United States Code, and such order shall be the exclusive remedy for failure to comply with this subsection.

(vii) If at any time following the filing of a complaint pursuant to this paragraph NGA agrees to search the appropriate exempted operational file or files for the requested records, the court shall dismiss the claim based upon such complaint.

(viii) Any information filed with, or produced for the court pursuant to clauses (i) and (iv) shall be coordinated with the Director of National Intelligence prior to submission to the court.

(b) DECENNIAL REVIEW OF EXEMPTED OPERATIONAL FILES.—

(1) Not less than once every 10 years, the Director of the National Geospatial-Intelligence Agency and the Director of National Intelligence shall review the exemptions in force under subsection (a)(1) to determine whether such exemptions may be removed from the category of exempted files or any portion thereof. The Director of National Intelligence must approve any determination to remove such exemptions.

(2) The review required by paragraph (1) shall include consideration of the historical value or other public interest in the subject matter of the particular category of files or portions thereof and the potential for declassifying a significant part of the information contained therein.

(3) A complainant that alleges that NGA has improperly withheld records because of failure to comply with this subsection may seek judicial review in the district court of the United States of the district in which any of the parties reside, or in the District of Columbia. In such a proceeding, the court's review shall be limited to determining the following:

(A) Whether NGA has conducted the review required by paragraph (1) before the expiration of the 10-year period beginning on the date of the enactment of this section or before the expiration of the 10-year period beginning on the date of the most recent review.

(B) Whether NGA, in fact, considered the criteria set forth in paragraph (2) in conducting the required review.

OPERATIONAL FILES OF THE NATIONAL RECONNAISSANCE OFFICE

SEC. 703. [50 U.S.C. §432a]

(a) EXEMPTION OF CERTAIN OPERATIONAL FILES FROM SEARCH, REVIEW, PUBLICATION, OR DISCLOSURE.—

(1) The Director of the National Reconnaissance Office, with the coordination of the Director of National Intelligence, may exempt operational files of the National Reconnaissance Office from the provisions of section 552 of title 5, United States Code, which require publication, disclosure, search, or review in connection therewith.

(2)(A) Subject to subparagraph (B), for the purposes of this section, the term "operational files" means files of the National Reconnaissance Office (hereafter in this section referred to as "NRO") that document the means by which foreign intelligence or counterintelligence is collected through scientific and technical systems.

(B) Files which are the sole repository of disseminated intelligence are not operational files.

(3) Notwithstanding paragraph (1), exempted operational files shall continue to be subject to search and review for information concerning—

(A) United States citizens or aliens lawfully admitted for permanent residence who have requested information on themselves pursuant to the provisions of section 552 or 552a of title 5, United States Code;

(B) any special activity the existence of which is not exempt from disclosure under the provisions of section 552 of title 5, United States Code; or

(C) the specific subject matter of an investigation by any of the following for any impropriety, or violation of law, Executive order, or Presidential directive, in the conduct of an intelligence activity:

(i) The Permanent Select Committee on Intelligence of the House of Representatives.

(ii) The Select Committee on Intelligence of the Senate.

(iii) The Intelligence Oversight Board.

(iv) The Department of Justice.

(v) The Office of General Counsel of NRO.

(vi) The Office of the Director of NRO.

(vii) The Office of the Inspector General of the NRO.

(4)(A) Files that are not exempted under paragraph (1) which contain information derived or disseminated from exempted operational files shall be subject to search and review.

(B) The inclusion of information from exempted operational files in files that are not exempted under paragraph (1) shall not affect the exemption under paragraph (1) of the originating operational files from search, review, publication, or disclosure.

(C) The declassification of some of the information contained in exempted operational files shall not affect the status of the operational file as being exempt from search, review, publication, or disclosure.

(D) Records from exempted operational files which have been disseminated to and referenced in files that are not exempted under paragraph (1) and which have been returned to exempted operational files for sole retention shall be subject to search and review.

(5) The provisions of paragraph (1) may not be superseded except by a provision of law which is enacted after the date of the enactment of this

section, and which specifically cites and repeals or modifies its provisions.

(6)(A) Except as provided in subparagraph (B), whenever any person who has requested agency records under section 552 of title 5, United States Code, alleges that NRO has withheld records improperly because of failure to comply with any provision of this section, judicial review shall be available under the terms set forth in section 552(a)(4)(B) of title 5, United States Code.

    (B) Judicial review shall not be available in the manner provided for under subparagraph (A) as follows:

        (i) In any case in which information specifically authorized under criteria established by an Executive order to be kept secret in the interests of national defense or foreign relations is filed with, or produced for, the court by NRO, such information shall be examined ex parte, in camera by the court.

        (ii) The court shall, to the fullest extent practicable, determine the issues of fact based on sworn written submissions of the parties.

        (iii) When a complainant alleges that requested records are improperly withheld because of improper placement solely in exempted operational files, the complainant shall support such allegation with a sworn written submission based upon personal knowledge or otherwise admissible evidence.

        (iv)(I) When a complainant alleges that requested records were improperly withheld because of improper exemption of operational files, NRO shall meet its burden under section 552(a)(4)(B) of title 5, United States Code, by demonstrating to the court by sworn written submission that exempted operational files likely to contain responsive records currently perform the functions set forth in paragraph (2).

            (II) The court may not order NRO to review the content of any exempted operational file or files in order to make the demonstration required under subclause (I), unless the complainant disputes NRO's showing with a sworn written submission based on personal knowledge or otherwise admissible evidence.

        (v) In proceedings under clauses (iii) and (iv), the parties may not obtain discovery pursuant to rules 26 through

36 of the Federal Rules of Civil Procedure, except that requests for admissions may be made pursuant to rules 26 and 36.

(vi) If the court finds under this paragraph that NRO has improperly withheld requested records because of failure to comply with any provision of this subsection, the court shall order NRO to search and review the appropriate exempted operational file or files for the requested records and make such records, or portions thereof, available in accordance with the provisions of section 552 of title 5, United States Code, and such order shall be the exclusive remedy for failure to comply with this subsection.

(vii) If at any time following the filing of a complaint pursuant to this paragraph NRO agrees to search the appropriate exempted operational file or files for the requested records, the court shall dismiss the claim based upon such complaint.

(viii) Any information filed with, or produced for the court pursuant to clauses (i) and (iv) shall be coordinated with the Director of National Intelligence prior to submission to the court.

(b) DECENNIAL REVIEW OF EXEMPTED OPERATIONAL FILES.—

(1) Not less than once every 10 years, the Director of the National Reconnaissance Office and the Director of National Intelligence shall review the exemptions in force under subsection (a)(1) to determine whether such exemptions may be removed from the category of exempted files or any portion thereof. The Director of National Intelligence must approve any determination to remove such exemptions.

(2) The review required by paragraph (1) shall include consideration of the historical value or other public interest in the subject matter of the particular category of files or portions thereof and the potential for declassifying a significant part of the information contained therein.

(3) A complainant that alleges that NRO has improperly withheld records because of failure to comply with this subsection may seek judicial review in the district court of the United States of the district in which any of the parties reside, or in the District of Columbia. In such a proceeding, the court's review shall be limited to determining the following:

(A) Whether NRO has conducted the review required by paragraph (1) before the expiration of the 10-year period beginning on the date of the enactment of this section or before the expiration of the 10-year period beginning on the date of the most recent review.

(B) Whether NRO, in fact, considered the criteria set forth in paragraph (2) in conducting the required review.

OPERATIONAL FILES OF THE NATIONAL SECURITY AGENCY

SEC. 704. [50 U.S.C. §432b]

(a) EXEMPTION OF CERTAIN OPERATIONAL FILES FROM SEARCH, REVIEW, PUBLICATION, OR DISCLOSURE.—The Director of the National Security Agency, in coordination with the Director of National Intelligence, may exempt operational files of the National Security Agency from the provisions of section 552 of title 5, United States Code, which require publication, disclosure, search, or review in connection therewith.

(b) OPERATIONAL FILES DEFINED.—

(1) In this section, the term "operational files" means—

(A) files of the Signals Intelligence Directorate of the National Security Agency (and any successor organization of that directorate) that document the means by which foreign intelligence or counterintelligence is collected through technical systems; and

(B) files of the Research Associate Directorate of the National Security Agency (and any successor organization of that directorate) that document the means by which foreign intelligence or counterintelligence is collected through scientific and technical systems.

(2) Files that are the sole repository of disseminated intelligence, and files that have been accessioned into the National Security Agency Archives (or any successor organization) are not operational files.

(c) SEARCH AND REVIEW FOR INFORMATION.—Notwithstanding subsection (a), exempted operational files shall continue to be subject to search and review for information concerning any of the following:

(1) United States citizens or aliens lawfully admitted for permanent residence who have requested information on themselves pursuant to the provisions of section 552 or 552a of title 5, United States Code.

(2) Any special activity the existence of which is not exempt from disclosure under the provisions of section 552 of title 5, United States Code.

(3) The specific subject matter of an investigation by any of the following for any impropriety, or violation of law, Executive order, or Presidential directive, in the conduct of an intelligence activity:

(A) The Committee on Armed Services and the Permanent Select Committee on Intelligence of the House of Representatives.

(B) The Committee on Armed Services and the Select Committee on Intelligence of the Senate.

(C) The Intelligence Oversight Board.

(D) The Department of Justice.

(E) The Office of General Counsel of the National Security Agency.

(F) The Office of the Inspector General of the Department of Defense.

(G) The Office of the Director of the National Security Agency.

(H) The Office of the Inspector General of the National Security Agency.

(d) INFORMATION DERIVED OR DISSEMINATED FROM EXEMPTED OPERATIONAL FILES.—

(1) Files that are not exempted under subsection (a) that contain information derived or disseminated from exempted operational files shall be subject to search and review.

(2) The inclusion of information from exempted operational files in files that are not exempted under subsection (a) shall not affect the exemption under subsection (a) of the originating operational files from search, review, publication, or disclosure.

(3) The declassification of some of the information contained in exempted operational files shall not affect the status of the operational file as being exempt from search, review, publication, or disclosure.

(4) Records from exempted operational files that have been disseminated to and referenced in files that are not exempted under subsection (a) and that have been returned to exempted operational files for sole retention shall be subject to search and review.

(e) SUPERCEDURE OF OTHER LAWS.—The provisions of subsection (a) may not be superseded except by a provision of law that is enacted after the date of the enactment of this section and that specifically cites and repeals or modifies such provisions.

(f) ALLEGATION; IMPROPER WITHHOLDING OF RECORDS; JUDICIAL REVIEW.—

(1) Except as provided in paragraph (2), whenever any person who has requested agency records under section 552 of title 5, United States Code, alleges that the National Security Agency has withheld records improperly because of failure to comply with any provision of this section, judicial review shall be available under the terms set forth in section 552(a)(4)(B) of title 5, United States Code.

(2) Judicial review shall not be available in the manner provided for under paragraph (1) as follows:

(A) In any case in which information specifically authorized under criteria established by an Executive order to be kept secret in the interests of national defense or foreign relations is filed with, or produced for, the court by the National Security Agency, such information shall be examined ex parte, in camera by the court.

(B) The court shall determine, to the fullest extent practicable, the issues of fact based on sworn written submissions of the parties.

(C) When a complainant alleges that requested records are improperly withheld because of improper placement solely in exempted operational files, the complainant shall support such allegation with a sworn written submission based upon personal knowledge or otherwise admissible evidence.

(D)(i) When a complainant alleges that requested records were improperly withheld because of improper exemption of operational files, the National Security Agency shall meet its burden under section 552(a)(4)(B) of title 5, United States Code, by demonstrating to the court by sworn written submission that exempted operational files likely to contain responsive records currently perform the functions set forth in subsection (b).

(ii) The court may not order the National Security Agency to review the content of any exempted operational file or files in order to make the demonstration required under clause (i), unless the complainant disputes the National Security Agency's showing with a sworn written submission based on personal knowledge or otherwise admissible evidence.

(E) In proceedings under subparagraphs (C) and (D), the parties may not obtain discovery pursuant to rules 26 through 36 of the Federal Rules of Civil Procedure, except that requests for admissions may be made pursuant to rules 26 and 36.

(F) If the court finds under this subsection that the National Security Agency has improperly withheld requested records because of failure to comply with any provision of this subsection, the court shall order the Agency to search and review the appropriate exempted operational file or files for the requested records and make such records, or portions thereof, available in accordance with the provisions of section 552 of title 5, United States Code, and such order shall be the exclusive remedy for failure to comply with this section (other than subsection (g)).

(G) If at any time following the filing of a complaint pursuant to this paragraph the National Security Agency agrees to search the appropriate exempted operational file or files for the requested records, the court shall dismiss the claim based upon such complaint.

(H) Any information filed with, or produced for the court pursuant to subparagraphs (A) and (D) shall be coordinated with the Director of National Intelligence before submission to the court.

(g) DECENNIAL REVIEW OF EXEMPTED OPERATIONAL FILES.—

(1) Not less than once every 10 years, the Director of the National Security Agency and the Director of National Intelligence shall review the exemptions in force under subsection (a) to determine whether such exemptions may be removed from a category of exempted files or any portion thereof. The Director of National Intelligence must approve any determination to remove such exemptions.

(2) The review required by paragraph (1) shall include consideration of the historical value or other public interest in the subject matter of a particular category of files or portions thereof and the potential for declassifying a significant part of the information contained therein.

(3) A complainant that alleges that the National Security Agency has improperly withheld records because of failure to comply with this subsection may seek judicial review in the district court of the United States of the district in which any of the parties reside, or in the District of Columbia. In such a proceeding, the court's review shall be limited to determining the following:

(A) Whether the National Security Agency has conducted the review required by paragraph (1) before the expiration of the 10-year period beginning on the date of the enactment of this section or before the expiration of the 10-year period beginning on the date of the most recent review.

(B) Whether the National Security Agency, in fact, considered the criteria set forth in paragraph (2) in conducting the required review.

OPERATIONAL FILES OF THE DEFENSE INTELLIGENCE AGENCY

SEC. 705. [50 U.S.C. §432c]
(a) EXEMPTION OF OPERATIONAL FILES. —The Director of the Defense Intelligence Agency, in coordination with the Director of National Intelligence,

may exempt operational files of the Defense Intelligence Agency from the provisions of section 552 of title 5, United States Code, which require publication, disclosure, search, or review in connection therewith.

(b) OPERATIONAL FILES DEFINED. —

(1) In this section, the term "operational files" means—

(A) files of the Directorate of Human Intelligence of the Defense Intelligence Agency (and any successor organization of that directorate) that document the conduct of foreign intelligence or counterintelligence operations or intelligence or security liaison arrangements or information exchanges with foreign governments or their intelligence or security services; and

(B) files of the Directorate of Technology of the Defense Intelligence Agency (and any successor organization of that directorate) that document the means by which foreign intelligence or counterintelligence is collected through technical systems.

(2) Files that are the sole repository of disseminated intelligence are not operational files.

(c) SEARCH AND REVIEW FOR INFORMATION. —Notwithstanding subsection (a), exempted operational files shall continue to be subject to search and review for information concerning:

(1) United States citizens or aliens lawfully admitted for permanent residence who have requested information on themselves pursuant to the provisions of section 552 or 552a of title 5, United States Code.

(2) Any special activity the existence of which is not exempt from disclosure under the provisions of section 552 of title 5, United States Code.

(3) The specific subject matter of an investigation by any of the following for any impropriety, or violation of law, Executive order, or Presidential directive, in the conduct of an intelligence activity:

(A) The Committee on Armed Services and the Permanent Select Committee on Intelligence of the House of Representatives.

(B) The Committee on Armed Services and the Select Committee on Intelligence of the Senate.

(C) The Intelligence Oversight Board.

(D) The Department of Justice.

(E) The Office of General Counsel of the Department of Defense or of the Defense Intelligence Agency.

(F) The Office of Inspector General of the Department of Defense or of the Defense Intelligence Agency.

(G) The Office of the Director of the Defense Intelligence Agency.

(d) INFORMATION DERIVED OR DISSEMINATED FROM EXEMPTED OPERATIONAL FILES.—

(1) Files that are not exempted under subsection (a) that contain information derived or disseminated from exempted operational files shall be subject to search and review.

(2) The inclusion of information from exempted operational files in files that are not exempted under subsection (a) shall not affect the exemption under subsection (a) of the originating operational files from search, review, publication, or disclosure.

(3) The declassification of some of the information contained in an exempted operational file shall not affect the status of the operational file as being exempt from search, review, publication, or disclosure.

(4) Records from exempted operational files that have been disseminated to and referenced in files that are not exempted under subsection (a) and that have been returned to exempted operational files for sole retention shall be subject to search and review.

(e) ALLEGATION; IMPROPER WITHHOLDING OF RECORDS; JUDICIAL REVIEW. —

(1) Except as provided in paragraph (2), whenever any person who has requested agency records under section 552 of title 5, United States Code, alleges that the Defense Intelligence Agency has withheld records improperly because of failure to comply with any provision of this section, judicial review shall be available under the terms set forth in section 552(a)(4)(B) of title 5, United States Code.

(2) Judicial review shall not be available in the manner provided under paragraph (1) as follows:

(A) In any case in which information specifically authorized under criteria established by an Executive order to be kept secret in the interest of national defense or foreign relations which is filed with, or produced for, the court by the Defense Intelligence Agency, such information shall be examined ex parte, in camera by the court.

(B) The court shall determine, to the fullest extent practicable, issues of fact based on sworn written submissions of the parties.

(C) When a complainant alleges that requested records were improperly withheld because of improper placement solely in exempted operational files, the complainant shall support such allegation with a sworn written submission based upon personal knowledge or otherwise admissible evidence.

(D)(i) When a complainant alleges that requested records were improperly withheld because of improper exemption of operational files, the Defense Intelligence Agency shall meet its burden under section 552(a)(4)(B) of title 5, United States Code, by demonstrating to the court by sworn written submission that exempted operational files likely to contain responsive records currently perform the functions set forth in subsection (b).

    (ii) The court may not order the Defense Intelligence Agency to review the content of any exempted operational file or files in order to make the demonstration required under clause (i), unless the complainant disputes the Defense Intelligence Agency's showing with a sworn written submission based on personal knowledge or otherwise admissible evidence.

(E) In proceedings under subparagraphs (C) and (D), the parties shall not obtain discovery pursuant to rules 26 through 36 of the Federal Rules of Civil Procedure, except that requests for admission may be made pursuant to rules 26 and 36.

(F) If the court finds under this subsection that the Defense Intelligence Agency has improperly withheld requested records because of failure to comply with any provision of this subsection, the court shall order the Defense Intelligence Agency to search and review the appropriate exempted operational file or files for the requested records and make such records, or portions thereof, available in accordance with the provisions of section 552 of title 5, United States Code, and such order shall be the exclusive remedy for failure to comply with this section (other than subsection (f)).

(G) If at any time following the filing of a complaint pursuant to this paragraph the Defense Intelligence Agency agrees to search the appropriate exempted operational file or files for the requested records, the court shall dismiss the claim based upon such complaint.

(H) Any information filed with, or produced for the court pursuant to subparagraphs (A) and (D) shall be coordinated with the Director of National Intelligence before submission to the court.

(f) DECENNIAL REVIEW OF EXEMPTED OPERATIONAL FILES. —

    (1) Not less than once every 10 years, the Director of the Defense Intelligence Agency and the Director of National Intelligence shall review the exemptions in force under subsection (a) to determine whether such exemptions may be removed from a category of exempted files or any portion thereof. The Director of National Intelligence must approve any determinations to remove such exemptions.

(2) The review required by paragraph (1) shall include consideration of the historical value or other public interest in the subject matter of the particular category of files or portions thereof and the potential for declassifying a significant part of the information contained therein.

(3) A complainant that alleges that the Defense Intelligence Agency has improperly withheld records because of failure to comply with this subsection may seek judicial review in the district court of the United States of the district in which any of the parties reside, or in the District of Columbia. In such a proceeding, the court's review shall be limited to determining the following:

(A) Whether the Defense Intelligence Agency has conducted the review required by paragraph (1) before the expiration of the 10-year period beginning on the date of the enactment of this section or before the expiration of the 10-year period beginning on the date of the most recent review.

(B) Whether the Defense Intelligence Agency, in fact, considered the criteria set forth in paragraph (2) in conducting the required review.

(g) TERMINATION.—This section shall cease to be effective on December 31, 2007.

PROTECTION OF CERTAIN FILES OF THE OFFICE OF THE DIRECTOR OF NATIONAL INTELLIGENCE

Sec. 706. [50 USC 432d.] (a) INAPPLICABILITY OF FOIA TO EXEMPTED OPERATIONAL FILES PROVIDED TO ODNI.—(1) Subject to paragraph (2), the provisions of section 552 of title 5, United States Code, that require search, review, publication, or disclosure of a record shall not apply to a record provided to the Office of the Director of National Intelligence by an element of the intelligence community from the exempted operational files of such element.

(2) Paragraph (1) shall not apply with respect to a record of the Office that—

(A) contains information derived or disseminated from an exempted operational file, unless such record is created by the Office for the sole purpose of organizing such exempted operational file for use by the Office;

(B) is disseminated by the Office to a person other than an officer, employee, or contractor of the Office; or

(C) is no longer designated as an exempted operational file in accordance with this title.

(b) EFFECT OF PROVIDING FILES TO ODNI.—Notwithstanding any other provision of this title, an exempted operational file that is provided to the Office by an element of the intelligence community shall not be subject to the provisions of section 552 of title 5, United States Code, that require search, review, publication, or disclosure of a record solely because such element provides such exempted operational file to the Office.

(c) SEARCH AND REVIEW FOR CERTAIN PURPOSES.—Notwithstanding subsection (a) or (b), an exempted operational file shall continue to be subject to search and review for information concerning any of the following:

> (1) United States citizens or aliens lawfully admitted for permanent residence who have requested information on themselves pursuant to the provisions of section 552 or 552a of title 5, United States Code.
>
> (2) Any special activity the existence of which is not exempt from disclosure under the provisions of section 552 of title 5, United States Code.
>
> (3) The specific subject matter of an investigation for any impropriety or violation of law, Executive order, or Presidential directive, in the conduct of an intelligence activity by any of the following:
>
>> (A) The Select Committee on Intelligence of the Senate.
>>
>> (B) The Permanent Select Committee on Intelligence of the House of Representatives.
>>
>> (C) The Intelligence Oversight Board.
>>
>> (D) The Department of Justice.
>>
>> (E) The Office of the Director of National Intelligence.
>>
>> (F) The Office of the Inspector General of the Intelligence Community.

(d) DECENNIAL REVIEW OF EXEMPTED OPERATIONAL FILES.—(1) Not less than once every 10 years, the Director of National Intelligence shall review the exemptions in force under subsection (a) to determine whether such exemptions may be removed from any category of exempted files or any portion thereof.

> (2) The review required by paragraph (1) shall include consideration of the historical value or other public interest in the subject matter of the particular category of files or portions thereof and the potential for declassifying a significant part of the information contained therein.
>
> (3) A complainant that alleges that the Director of National Intelligence has improperly withheld records because of failure to comply with this subsection may seek judicial review in the district court of the United States of the district in which any of the parties reside, or in the District of Columbia. In such a proceeding, the court's review shall be limited to determining the following:
>
>> (A) Whether the Director has conducted the review required by paragraph (1) before the expiration of the 10-year period beginning on the date of the enactment of the Intelligence Authorization Act for Fiscal Year 2010 or before the expiration

of the 10-year period beginning on the date of the most recent review.

(B) Whether the Director of National Intelligence, in fact, considered the criteria set forth in paragraph (2) in conducting the required review.

(e) SUPERSEDURE OF OTHER LAWS.—The provisions of this section may not be superseded except by a provision of law that is enacted after the date of the enactment of this section and that specifically cites and repeals or modifies such provisions.

(f) ALLEGATION; IMPROPER WITHHOLDING OF RECORDS; JUDICIAL REVIEW.—
(1) Except as provided in paragraph (2), whenever any person who has requested agency records under section 552 of title 5, United States Code, alleges that the Office has withheld records improperly because of failure to comply with any provision of this section, judicial review shall be available under the terms set forth in section 552(a)(4)(B) of title 5, United States Code.

(2) Judicial review shall not be available in the manner provided for under paragraph (1) as follows:

(A) In any case in which information specifically authorized under criteria established by an Executive order to be kept secret in the interests of national defense or foreign relations is filed with, or produced for, the court by the Office, such information shall be examined ex parte, in camera by the court.

(B) The court shall determine, to the fullest extent practicable, the issues of fact based on sworn written submissions of the parties.

(C)(i) When a complainant alleges that requested records were improperly withheld because of improper exemption of operational files, the Office may meet the burden of the Office under section 552(a)(4)(B) of title 5, United States Code, by demonstrating to the court by sworn written submission that exempted files likely to contain responsive records are records provided to the Office by an element of the intelligence community from the exempted operational files of such element.

(ii) The court may not order the Office to review the content of any exempted file in order to make the demonstration required under clause (i), unless the complainant disputes the Office's showing with a sworn written submission based on personal knowledge or otherwise admissible evidence.

(D) In proceedings under subparagraph (C), a party may not obtain discovery pursuant to rules 26 through 36 of the Federal Rules of Civil Procedure, except that requests for admissions may be made pursuant to rules 26 and 36 of the Federal Rules of Civil Procedure.

(E) If the court finds under this subsection that the Office has improperly withheld requested records because of failure to comply with any provision of this section, the court shall order the Office to search and review each appropriate exempted file for the requested records and make such records, or portions thereof, available in accordance with the provisions of section 552 of title 5, United States Code (commonly referred to as the Freedom of Information Act), and such order shall be the exclusive remedy for failure to comply with this section.

(F) If at any time following the filing of a complaint pursuant to this paragraph the Office agrees to search each appropriate exempted file for the requested records, the court shall dismiss the claim based upon such complaint.

(g) DEFINITIONS.—In this section:

(1) The term "exempted operational file" means a file of an element of the intelligence community that, in accordance with this title, is exempted from the provisions of section 552 of title 5, United States Code, that require search, review, publication, or disclosure of such file.

(2) Except as otherwise specifically provided, the term "Office" means the Office of the Director of National Intelligence.

TITLE VIII—ACCESS TO CLASSIFIED INFORMATION PROCEDURES

PROCEDURES

SEC. 801. [50 U.S.C 435]

(a) Not later than 180 days after the date of enactment of this title, the President shall, by Executive order or regulation, establish procedures to govern access to classified information which shall be binding upon all departments, agencies, and offices of the executive branch of Government. Such procedures shall, at a minimum—

(1) provide that, except as may be permitted by the President, no employee in the executive branch of Government may be given access to classified information by any department, agency, or office of the executive branch of Government unless, based upon an appropriate background investigation, such access is determined to be clearly consistent with the national security interests of the United States;

(2) establish uniform minimum requirements governing the scope and frequency of background investigations and reinvestigations for all employees in the executive branch of Government who require access to classified information as part of their official responsibilities;

(3) provide that all employees in the executive branch of Government who require access to classified information shall be required as a condition of such access to provide to the employing department or agency written consent which permits access by an authorized investigative agency to relevant financial records, other financial information, consumer reports, travel records, and computers used in the performance of Government duties, as determined by the President, in accordance with section 802 of this title, during the period of access to classified information and for a period of three years thereafter;

(4) provide that all employees in the executive branch of Government who require access to particularly sensitive classified information, as determined by the President, shall be required, as a condition of maintaining access to such information, to submit to the employing department or agency, during the period of such access, relevant information concerning their financial condition and foreign travel, as determined by the President, as may be necessary to ensure appropriate security; and

(5) establish uniform minimum standards to ensure that employees in the executive branch of Government whose access to classified information is being denied or terminated under this title are appropriately advised of the reasons for such denial or termination and are provided an adequate opportunity to respond to all adverse information which forms the basis for such denial or termination before final action by the department or agency concerned.

(b)(1) Subsection (a) shall not be deemed to limit or affect the responsibility and power of an agency head pursuant to other law or Executive order to deny or terminate access to classified information if the national security so requires. Such responsibility and power may be exercised only when the agency head determines that the procedures prescribed by subsection (a) cannot be invoked in a manner that is consistent with the national security.

(2) Upon the exercise of such responsibility, the agency head shall submit a report to the congressional intelligence committees.

REQUESTS BY AUTHORIZED INVESTIGATIVE AGENCIES

SEC. 802. [50 U.S.C. §436]

(a)(1) Any authorized investigative agency may request from any financial agency, financial institution, or holding company, or from any consumer reporting agency, such financial records, other financial information, and consumer reports as may be necessary in order to conduct any authorized law enforcement investigation, counterintelligence inquiry, or security determination. Any authorized investigative agency may also request records maintained by any commercial entity within the United States pertaining to travel by an employee in the executive branch of Government outside the United States.

 (2) Requests may be made under this section where—

  (A) the records sought pertain to a person who is or was an employee in the executive branch of Government required by the President in an Executive order or regulation, as a condition of access to classified information, to provide consent, during a background investigation and for such time as access to the information is maintained, and for a period of not more than three years thereafter, permitting access to financial records, other financial information, consumer reports, and travel records; and

  (B)(i) there are reasonable grounds to believe, based on credible information, that the person is, or may be, disclosing classified information in an unauthorized manner to a foreign power or agent of a foreign power;

   (ii) information the employing agency deems credible indicates the person has incurred excessive indebtedness or has acquired a level of affluence which cannot be explained by other information known to the agency; or

   (iii) circumstances indicate the person had the capability and opportunity to disclose classified information which is known to have been lost or compromised to a foreign power or an agent of a foreign power.

 (3) Each such request—

  (A) shall be accompanied by a written certification signed by the department or agency head or deputy department or agency head concerned, or by a senior official designated for this purpose by the department or agency head concerned (whose rank shall be no lower than Assistant Secretary or Assistant Director), and shall certify that—

   (i) the person concerned is or was an employee within the meaning of paragraph (2)(A);

   (ii) the request is being made pursuant to an authorized inquiry or investigation and is authorized under this section; and

   (iii) the records or information to be reviewed are records or information which the employee has previously agreed to make available to the authorized investigative agency for review;

(B) shall contain a copy of the agreement referred to in subparagraph (A)(iii);

(C) shall identify specifically or by category the records or information to be reviewed; and

(D) shall inform the recipient of the request of the prohibition described in subsection (b).

(b) Prohibition of Certain Disclosure—

(1) If an authorized investigative agency described in subsection (a) certifies that otherwise there may result a danger to the national security of the United States, interference with a criminal, counterterrorism, or counterintelligence investigation, interference with diplomatic relations, or danger to the life or physical safety of any person, no governmental or private entity, or officer, employee, or agent of such entity, may disclose to any person (other than those to whom such disclosure is necessary to comply with the request or an attorney to obtain legal advice or legal assistance with respect to the request) that such entity has received or satisfied a request made by an authorized investigative agency under this section.

(2) The request shall notify the person or entity to whom the request is directed of the nondisclosure requirement under paragraph (1).

(3) Any recipient disclosing to those persons necessary to comply with the request or to an attorney to obtain legal advice or legal assistance with respect to the request shall inform such persons of any applicable nondisclosure requirement. Any person who receives a disclosure under this subsection shall be subject to the same prohibitions on disclosure under paragraph (1).

(4) At the request of the authorized investigative agency, any person making or intending to make a disclosure under this section shall identify to the requesting official of the authorized investigative agency the person to whom such disclosure will be made or to whom such disclosure was made prior to the request, except that nothing in this section shall require a person to inform the requesting official of the identity of an attorney to whom disclosure was made or will be made to obtain legal advice or legal assistance with respect to the request under subsection (a).

(c)(1) Notwithstanding any other provision of law (other than section 6103 of the Internal Revenue Code of 1986), an entity receiving a request for records or information under subsection (a) shall, if the request satisfies the requirements of this section, make available such records or information within 30 days for inspection or copying, as may be appropriate, by the agency requesting such records or information.

(2) Any entity (including any officer, employee, or agent thereof) that discloses records or information for inspection or copying pursuant to this section in good faith reliance upon the certifications made by an agency pursuant to this section shall not be liable for any such disclosure to any person under this title, the constitution of any State, or any law or regulation of any State or any political subdivision of any State.

(d) Any agency requesting records or information under this section may, subject to the availability of appropriations, reimburse a private entity for any cost reasonably incurred by such entity in responding to such request, including the cost of identifying, reproducing, or transporting records or other data.

(e) An agency receiving records or information pursuant to a request under this section may disseminate the records or information obtained pursuant to such request outside the agency only—

(1) to the agency employing the employee who is the subject of the records or information;

(2) to the Department of Justice for law enforcement or counterintelligence purposes; or

(3) with respect to dissemination to an agency of the United States, if such information is clearly relevant to the authorized responsibilities of such agency.

(f) Nothing in this section may be construed to affect the authority of an investigative agency to obtain information pursuant to the Right to Financial Privacy Act (12 U.S.C. §3401 et seq.) or the Fair Credit Reporting Act (15 U.S.C. §1681 et seq.).

EXCEPTIONS

SEC. 803. [50 U.S.C. §437]
Except as otherwise specifically provided, the provisions of this title shall not apply to the President and Vice President, Members of the Congress, Justices of the Supreme Court, and Federal judges appointed by the President.

DEFINITIONS

SEC. 804. [50 U.S.C. §438]
For purposes of this title—

(1) the term "authorized investigative agency" means an agency authorized by law or regulation to conduct a counterintelligence investigation or investigations of persons who are proposed for access to

classified information to ascertain whether such persons satisfy the criteria for obtaining and retaining access to such information;

(2) the term "classified information" means any information that has been determined pursuant to Executive Order No. 12356 of April 2, 1982, or successor orders, or the Atomic Energy Act of 1954, to require protection against unauthorized disclosure and that is so designated;

(3) the term "consumer reporting agency" has the meaning given such term in section 603 of the Consumer Credit Protection Act (15 U.S.C. §1681a);

(4) the term "employee" includes any person who receives a salary or compensation of any kind from the United States Government, is a contractor of the United States Government or an employee thereof, is an unpaid consultant of the United States Government, or otherwise acts for or on behalf of the United States Government, except as otherwise determined by the President;

(5) the terms "financial agency" and "financial institution" have the meanings given to such terms in section 5312(a) of title 31, United States Code, and the term "holding company" has the meaning given to such term in section 1101(6) of the Right to Financial Privacy Act of 1978 (12 U.S.C. §3401);

(6) the terms "foreign power" and "agent of a foreign power" have the same meanings as set forth in sections 101 (a) and (b), respectively, of the Foreign Intelligence Surveillance Act of 1978 (50 U.S.C. §1801);

(7) the term "State" means each of the several States of the United States, the District of Columbia, the Commonwealth of Puerto Rico, the Commonwealth of the Northern Mariana Islands, the United States Virgin Islands, Guam, American Samoa, the Republic of the Marshall Islands, the Federated States of Micronesia, and the Republic of Palau, and any other possession of the United States; and

(8) the term "computer" means any electronic, magnetic, optical, electrochemical, or other high speed data processing device performing logical, arithmetic, or storage functions, and includes any data storage facility or communications facility directly related to or operating in conjunction with such device and any data or other information stored or contained in such device.

TITLE IX—APPLICATION OF SANCTIONS LAWS TO INTELLIGENCE ACTIVITIES

STAY OF SANCTIONS

SEC. 901. [50 U.S.C. §441]

Notwithstanding any provision of law identified in section 904, the President may stay the imposition of an economic, cultural, diplomatic, or other sanction or related action by the United States Government concerning a foreign country, organization, or person when the President determines and reports to Congress in accordance with section 903 that to proceed without delay would seriously risk the compromise of an ongoing criminal investigation directly related to the activities giving rise to the sanction or an intelligence source or method directly related to the activities giving rise to the sanction. Any such stay shall be effective for a period of time specified by the President, which period may not exceed 120 days, unless such period is extended in accordance with section 902.

EXTENSION OF STAY

SEC. 902. [50 U.S.C. §441a]
Whenever the President determines and reports to Congress in accordance with section 903 that a stay of sanctions or related actions pursuant to section 901 has not afforded sufficient time to obviate the risk to an ongoing criminal investigation or to an intelligence source or method that gave rise to the stay, he may extend such stay for a period of time specified by the President, which period may not exceed 120 days. The authority of this section may be used to extend the period of a stay pursuant to section 901 for successive periods of not more than 120 days each.

REPORTS

SEC. 903. [50 U.S.C. §441b]
Reports to Congress pursuant to sections 901 and 902 shall be submitted promptly upon determinations under this title. Such reports shall be submitted to the Committee on International Relations of the House of Representatives and the Committee on Foreign Relations of the Senate. With respect to determinations relating to intelligence sources and methods, reports shall also be submitted to the congressional intelligence committees. With respect to determinations relating to ongoing criminal investigations, reports shall also be submitted to the Committees on the Judiciary of the House of Representatives and the Senate.

LAWS SUBJECT TO STAY

SEC. 904. [50 U.S.C. §441c]
The President may use the authority of sections 901 and 902 to stay the imposition of an economic, cultural, diplomatic, or other sanction or related action by the United States Government related to the proliferation of weapons of

mass destruction, their delivery systems, or advanced conventional weapons otherwise required to be imposed by the Chemical and Biological Weapons Control and Warfare Elimination Act of 1991 (title III of Public Law 102–182); the Nuclear Proliferation Prevention Act of 1994 (title VIII of Public Law 103–236); title XVII of the National Defense Authorization Act for Fiscal Year 1991 (Public Law 101–510) (relating to the nonproliferation of missile technology); the Iran-Iraq Arms Nonproliferation Act of 1992 (title XVI of Public Law 102–484); section 573 of the Foreign Operations, Export Financing Related Programs Appropriations Act, 1994 (Public Law 103–87); section 563 of the Foreign Operations, Export Financing Related Programs Appropriations Act, 1995 (Public Law 103–306); and comparable provisions.

TITLE X—EDUCATION IN SUPPORT OF NATIONAL INTELLIGENCE

SUBTITLE A – SCIENCE AND TECHNOLOGY

SCHOLARSHIPS AND WORK-STUDY FOR PURSUIT OF GRADUATE DEGREES IN SCIENCE AND TECHNOLOGY

SEC. 1001. [50 U.S.C. §441g]

(a) PROGRAM AUTHORIZED.—The Director of National Intelligence may carry out a program to provide scholarships and work-study for individuals who are pursuing graduate degrees in fields of study in science and technology that are identified by the Director as appropriate to meet the future needs of the intelligence community for qualified scientists and engineers.

(b) ADMINISTRATION.—If the Director of National Intelligence carries out the program under subsection (a), the Director shall administer the program through the Office of the Director of National Intelligence.

(c) IDENTIFICATION OF FIELDS OF STUDY.—If the Director of National Intelligence carries out the program under subsection (a), the Director shall identify fields of study under subsection (a) in consultation with the other heads of the elements of the intelligence community.

(d) ELIGIBILITY FOR PARTICIPATION.—An individual eligible to participate in the program is any individual who—

> (1) either—
>> (A) is an employee of the intelligence community; or
>> (B) meets criteria for eligibility for employment in the intelligence community that are established by the Director of National Intelligence;
> (2) is accepted in a graduate degree program in a field of study in science or technology identified under subsection (a); and
> (3) is eligible for a security clearance at the level of Secret or above.

(e) REGULATIONS.—If the Director of National Intelligence carries out the program under subsection (a), the Director shall prescribe regulations for purposes of the administration of this section.

FRAMEWORK FOR CROSS-DISCIPLINARY EDUCATION AND TRAINING

SEC. 1002. [50 U.S.C. §441g-1]
The Director of National Intelligence shall establish an integrated framework that brings together the educational components of the intelligence community in order to promote a more effective and productive intelligence community through cross-disciplinary education and joint training.

SUBTITLE B – FOREIGN LANGUAGES PROGRAM

PROGRAM ON ADVANCEMENT OF FOREIGN LANGUAGES CRITICAL TO THE INTELLIGENCE COMMUNITY

SEC. 1011. [50 U.S.C. §441j]
(a) IN GENERAL.—The Secretary of Defense and the Director of National Intelligence may jointly carry out a program to advance skills in foreign languages that are critical to the capability of the intelligence community to carry out the national security activities of the United States (hereinafter in this subtitle referred to as the Foreign Languages Program').
(b) IDENTIFICATION OF REQUISITE ACTIONS.—In order to carry out the Foreign Languages Program, the Secretary of Defense and the Director of National Intelligence shall jointly identify actions required to improve the education of personnel in the intelligence community in foreign languages that are critical to the capability of the intelligence community to carry out the national security activities of the United States and to meet the long-term intelligence needs of the United States.

EDUCATION PARTNERSHIPS

SEC. 1012. [50 U.S.C. §441j-1]
(a) IN GENERAL.—In carrying out the Foreign Languages Program, the head of a covered element of the intelligence community may enter into one or more education partnership agreements with educational institutions in the United States in order to encourage and enhance the study in such educational institutions of foreign languages that are critical to the capability of the intelligence community to carry out the national security activities of the United States.

(b) ASSISTANCE PROVIDED UNDER EDUCATIONAL PARTNERSHIP AGREEMENTS.—Under an educational partnership agreement entered into with an educational institution pursuant to this section, the head of a covered element of the intelligence community may provide the following assistance to the educational institution:

(1) The loan of equipment and instructional materials of the element of the intelligence community to the educational institution for any purpose and duration that the head of the element considers appropriate.

(2) Notwithstanding any other provision of law relating to the transfer of surplus property, the transfer to the educational institution of any computer equipment, or other equipment, that is—

(A) commonly used by educational institutions;

(B) surplus to the needs of the element of the intelligence community; and

(C) determined by the head of the element to be appropriate for support of such agreement.

(3) The provision of dedicated personnel to the educational institution—

(A) to teach courses in foreign languages that are critical to the capability of the intelligence community to carry out the national security activities of the United States; or

(B) to assist in the development for the educational institution of courses and materials on such languages.

(4) The involvement of faculty and students of the educational institution in research projects of the element of the intelligence community.

(5) Cooperation with the educational institution in developing a program under which students receive academic credit at the educational institution for work on research projects of the element of the intelligence community.

(6) The provision of academic and career advice and assistance to students of the educational institution.

(7) The provision of cash awards and other items that the head of the element of the intelligence community considers appropriate.

VOLUNTARY SERVICES

SEC. 1013. [50 U.S.C. §441j-2]

(a) AUTHORITY TO ACCEPT SERVICES.—Notwithstanding section 1342 of title 31, United States Code, and subject to subsection (b), the Foreign Languages Program under section 1011 shall include authority for the head of a covered element of the intelligence community to accept from any dedicated personnel voluntary services in support of the activities authorized by this subtitle.

(b) REQUIREMENTS AND LIMITATIONS.—

(1) In accepting voluntary services from an individual under subsection (a), the head of a covered element of the intelligence community shall—

    (A) supervise the individual to the same extent as the head of the element would supervise a compensated employee of that element providing similar services; and

    (B) ensure that the individual is licensed, privileged, has appropriate educational or experiential credentials, or is otherwise qualified under applicable law or regulations to provide such services.

(2) In accepting voluntary services from an individual under subsection (a), the head of a covered element of the intelligence community may not—

    (A) place the individual in a policymaking position, or other position performing inherently governmental functions; or

    (B) compensate the individual for the provision of such services.

(c) AUTHORITY TO RECRUIT AND TRAIN INDIVIDUALS PROVIDING SERVICES.— The head of a covered element of the intelligence community may recruit and train individuals to provide voluntary services under subsection (a).

(d) STATUS OF INDIVIDUALS PROVIDING SERVICES.—

(1) Subject to paragraph (2), while providing voluntary services under subsection (a) or receiving training under subsection (c), an individual shall be considered to be an employee of the Federal Government only for purposes of the following provisions of law:

    (A) Section 552a of title 5, United States Code (relating to maintenance of records on individuals).

    (B) Chapter 11 of title 18, United States Code (relating to conflicts of interest).

(2)(A) With respect to voluntary services under paragraph (1) provided by an individual that are within the scope of the services accepted under that paragraph, the individual shall be deemed to be a volunteer of a governmental entity or nonprofit institution for purposes of the Volunteer Protection Act of 1997 (42 U.S.C. §14501 et seq.).

    (B) In the case of any claim against such an individual with respect to the provision of such services, section 4(d) of such Act (42 U.S.C. §14503(d)) shall not apply.

(3) Acceptance of voluntary services under this section shall have no bearing on the issuance or renewal of a security clearance.

(e) REIMBURSEMENT OF INCIDENTAL EXPENSES.—

(1) The head of a covered element of the intelligence community may reimburse an individual for incidental expenses incurred by the individual in providing voluntary services under subsection (a). The head

of a covered element of the intelligence community shall determine which expenses are eligible for reimbursement under this subsection.

(2) Reimbursement under paragraph (1) may be made from appropriated or nonappropriated funds.

(f) AUTHORITY TO INSTALL EQUIPMENT.—

(1) The head of a covered element of the intelligence community may install telephone lines and any necessary telecommunication equipment in the private residences of individuals who provide voluntary services under subsection (a).

(2) The head of a covered element of the intelligence community may pay the charges incurred for the use of equipment installed under paragraph (1) for authorized purposes.

(3) Notwithstanding section 1348 of title 31, United States Code, the head of a covered element of the intelligence community may use appropriated funds or nonappropriated funds of the element in carrying out this subsection.

REGULATIONS

SEC. 1014. [50 U.S.C. §441j-3]

(a) IN GENERAL.—The Secretary of Defense and the Director of National Intelligence shall jointly prescribe regulations to carry out the Foreign Languages Program.

(b) ELEMENTS OF THE INTELLIGENCE COMMUNITY.—The head of each covered element of the intelligence community shall prescribe regulations to carry out sections 1012 and 1013 with respect to that element including the following:

(1) Procedures to be utilized for the acceptance of voluntary services under section 1013.

(2) Procedures and requirements relating to the installation of equipment under section 1013(f).

DEFINITIONS

SEC. 1015. [50 U.S.C. §441j-4]

In this subtitle:

(1) The term "covered element of the intelligence community" means an agency, office, bureau, or element referred to in subparagraphs (B) through (L) of section 3(4).

(2) The term "educational institution" means—

(A) a local educational agency (as that term is defined in section 9101(26) of the Elementary and Secondary Education Act of 1965 (20 U.S.C. §7801(26)));

(B) an institution of higher education (as defined in section 102 of the Higher Education Act of 1965 (20 U.S.C. §1002) other than institutions referred to in subsection (a)(1)(C) of such section); or

(C) any other nonprofit institution that provides instruction of foreign languages in languages that are critical to the capability of the intelligence community to carry out national security activities of the United States.

(3) The term "dedicated personnel" means employees of the intelligence community and private citizens (including former civilian employees of the Federal Government who have been voluntarily separated, and members of the United States Armed Forces who have been honorably discharged, honorably separated, or generally discharged under honorable circumstances and rehired on a voluntary basis specifically to perform the activities authorized under this subtitle).

SUBTITLE C – ADDITIONAL EDUCATION PROGRAMS

ASSIGNMENT OF INTELLIGENCE COMMUNITY PERSONNEL AS LANGUAGE STUDENTS

SEC. 1021. [50 U.S.C. §441m]

(a) IN GENERAL.—The Director of National Intelligence, acting through the heads of the elements of the intelligence community, may assign employees of such elements in analyst positions requiring foreign language expertise as students at accredited professional, technical, or other institutions of higher education for training at the graduate or undergraduate level in foreign languages required for the conduct of duties and responsibilities of such positions.

(b) AUTHORITY FOR REIMBURSEMENT OF COSTS OF TUITION AND TRAINING.—

(1) The Director of National Intelligence may reimburse an employee assigned under subsection (a) for the total cost of the training described in that subsection, including costs of educational and supplementary reading materials.

(2) The authority under paragraph (1) shall apply to employees who are assigned on a full-time or part-time basis.

(3) Reimbursement under paragraph (1) may be made from appropriated or nonappropriated funds.

(c) RELATIONSHIP TO COMPENSATION AS AN ANALYST.—Reimbursement under this section to an employee who is an analyst is in addition to any benefits, allowances, travel expenses, or other compensation the employee is entitled to by reason of serving in such an analyst position.

PROGRAM ON RECRUITMENT AND TRAINING

Sec. 1022. (a) PROGRAM.—(1) The Director of National Intelligence shall carry out a program to ensure that selected students or former students are provided funds to continue academic training, or are reimbursed for academic training previously obtained, in areas of specialization that the Director, in consultation with the other heads of the elements of the intelligence community, identifies as areas in which the current capabilities of the intelligence community are deficient or in which future capabilities of the intelligence community are likely to be deficient.

(2) A student or former student selected for participation in the program shall commit to employment with an element of the intelligence community, following completion of appropriate academic training, under such terms and conditions as the Director considers appropriate.

(3) The program shall be known as the Pat Roberts Intelligence Scholars Program.

(b) ELEMENTS.—In carrying out the program under subsection (a), the Director shall—(1) establish such requirements relating to the academic training of participants as the Director considers appropriate to ensure that participants are prepared for employment as intelligence professionals; and

(2) periodically review the areas of specialization of the elements of the intelligence community to determine the areas in which such elements are, or are likely to be, deficient in capabilities.

(c) USE OF FUNDS.—Funds made available for the program under subsection (a) shall be used—

(1) to provide a monthly stipend for each month that a student is pursuing a course of study;

(2) to pay the full tuition of a student or former student for the completion of such course of study;

(3) to pay for books and materials that the student or former student requires or required to complete such course of study;

(4) to pay the expenses of the student or former student for travel requested by an element of the intelligence community in relation to such program; or

(5) for such other purposes the Director considers reasonably appropriate to carry out such program.

EDUCATIONAL SCHOLARSHIP PROGRAM

Sec. 1023. [50 U.S.C. 441o] The head of a department or agency containing an element of the intelligence community may establish an undergraduate or graduate training program with respect to civilian employees and prospective civilian employees of such element similar in purpose, conditions, content, and administration to the program that the Secretary of Defense is authorized to establish under section 16 of the National Security Agency Act of 1959 (50 U.S.C. 402 note).

INTELLIGENCE OFFICER TRAINING PROGRAM

Sec. 1024. [50 USC 441p] (a) PROGRAMS.—

(1) The Director of National Intelligence may carry out grant programs in accordance with subsections (b) and (c) to enhance the recruitment and retention of an ethnically and culturally diverse intelligence community workforce with capabilities critical to the national security interests of the United States.

(2) In carrying out paragraph (1), the Director shall identify the skills necessary to meet current or emergent needs of the intelligence community and the educational disciplines that will provide individuals with such skills.

(b) INSTITUTIONAL GRANT PROGRAM.—

(1) The Director may provide grants to institutions of higher education to support the establishment or continued development of programs of study in educational disciplines identified under subsection (a)(2).

(2) A grant provided under paragraph (1) may, with respect to the educational disciplines identified under subsection (a)(2), be used for the following purposes:

(A) Curriculum or program development.

(B) Faculty development.

(C) Laboratory equipment or improvements.

(D) Faculty research.

(c) GRANT PROGRAM FOR HISTORICALLY BLACK COLLEGES AND UNIVERSITIES.—(1) The Director may provide grants to historically black colleges and universities to provide programs of study in educational disciplines identified under subsection (a)(2) or described in paragraph (2).

(2) A grant provided under paragraph (1) may be used to provide programs of study in the following educational disciplines:

(A) Intermediate and advanced foreign languages deemed in the immediate interest of the intelligence community, including Farsi, Pashto, Middle Eastern, African, and South Asian dialects.

181

(B) Study abroad programs and cultural immersion programs.

(d) APPLICATION.—An institution of higher education seeking a grant under this section shall submit an application describing the proposed use of the grant at such time and in such manner as the Director may require.

(e) REPORTS.—An institution of higher education that receives a grant under this section shall submit to the Director regular reports regarding the use of such grant, including—

(1) a description of the benefits to students who participate in the course of study funded by such grant;

(2) a description of the results and accomplishments related to such course of study; and

(3) any other information that the Director may require.

(f) REGULATIONS.—The Director shall prescribe such regulations as may be necessary to carry out this section.

(g) DEFINITIONS.—In this section:

(1) The term "Director" means the Director of National Intelligence.

(2) HISTORICALLY BLACK COLLEGE AND UNIVERSITY.—The term "historically black college and university" has the meaning given the term `part B institution' in section 322 of the Higher Education Act of 1965 (20 U.S.C. 1061).

(3) The term "institution of higher education" has the meaning given the term in section 101 of the Higher Education Act of 1965 (20 U.S.C. 1001).

(4) Study abroad program.—The term "study abroad program" means a program of study that—

(A) takes places outside the geographical boundaries of the United States;

(B) focuses on areas of the world that are critical to the national security interests of the United States and are generally underrepresented in study abroad programs at institutions of higher education, including Africa, Asia, Central and Eastern Europe, Eurasia, Latin America, and the Middle East; and

(C) is a credit or noncredit program.

TITLE XI—ADDITIONAL MISCELLANEOUS PROVISIONS

APPLICABILITY TO UNITED STATES INTELLIGENCE ACTIVITIES OF FEDERAL LAWS IMPLEMENTING INTERNATIONAL TREATIES AND AGREEMENTS

SEC. 1101. [50 U.S.C. §442]

(a) IN GENERAL.—No Federal law enacted on or after the date of the enactment of the Intelligence Authorization Act for Fiscal Year 2001 that implements a treaty or other international agreement shall be construed as making unlawful an otherwise lawful and authorized intelligence activity of the United States Government or its employees, or any other person to the extent such other person is carrying out such activity on behalf of, and at the direction of, the United States, unless such Federal law specifically addresses such intelligence activity.

(b) AUTHORIZED INTELLIGENCE ACTIVITIES.—An intelligence activity shall be treated as authorized for purposes of subsection (a) if the intelligence activity is authorized by an appropriate official of the United States Government, acting within the scope of the official duties of that official and in compliance with Federal law and any applicable Presidential directive.

COUNTERINTELLIGENCE INITIATIVES

SEC. 1102. [50 U.S.C. §442a]

(a) INSPECTION PROCESS.—

In order to protect intelligence sources and methods from unauthorized disclosure, the Director of National Intelligence shall establish and implement an inspection process for all agencies and departments of the United States that handle classified information relating to the national security of the United States intended to assure that those agencies and departments maintain effective operational security practices and programs directed against counterintelligence activities.

(b) ANNUAL REVIEW OF DISSEMINATION LISTS.—

(1) The Director of National Intelligence shall establish and implement a process for all elements of the intelligence community to review, on an annual basis, individuals included on distribution lists for access to classified information. Such process shall ensure that only individuals who have a particularized need to know' (as determined by the Director) are continued on such distribution lists.

(2) Not later than October 15 of each year, the Director shall certify to the congressional intelligence committees that the review required under paragraph (1) has been conducted in all elements of the intelligence community during the preceding fiscal year.

(c) COMPLETION OF FINANCIAL DISCLOSURE STATEMENTS REQUIRED FOR ACCESS TO CERTAIN CLASSIFIED INFORMATION.—

The Director of National Intelligence shall establish and implement a process by which each head of an element of the intelligence community directs that all employees of that element, in order to be granted access to classified information referred to in subsection (a) of section 1.3 of Executive Order No. 12968 (August 2, 1995; 60 Fed. Reg. 40245; 50 U.S.C. §435 note), submit financial disclosure forms as required under subsection (b) of such section.

(d) ARRANGEMENTS TO HANDLE SENSITIVE INFORMATION.—The Director of National Intelligence shall establish, for all elements of the intelligence community, programs and procedures by which sensitive classified information relating to human intelligence is safeguarded against unauthorized disclosure by employees of those elements.

MISUSE OF THE OFFICE OF THE DIRECTOR OF NATIONAL INTELLIGENCE NAME, INITIALS, OR SEAL

Sec. 1103. [50 USC 442b.] (a) PROHIBITED ACTS.—No person may, except with the written permission of the Director of National Intelligence, or a designee of the Director, knowingly use the words "Office of the Director of National Intelligence", the initials "ODNI", the seal of the Office of the Director of National Intelligence, or any colorable imitation of such words, initials, or seal in connection with any merchandise, impersonation, solicitation, or commercial activity in a manner reasonably calculated to convey the impression that such use is approved, endorsed, or authorized by the Director of National Intelligence. (b) INJUNCTION.—Whenever it appears to the Attorney General that any person is engaged or is about to engage in an act or practice which constitutes or will constitute conduct prohibited by subsection (a), the Attorney General may initiate a civil proceeding in a district court of the United States to enjoin such act or practice. Such court shall proceed as soon as practicable to the hearing and determination of such action and may, at any time before final determination, enter such restraining orders or prohibitions, or take such other action as is warranted, to prevent injury to the United States or to any person or class of persons for whose protection the action is brought.

*Annotation:

Reporting Requirements for Section 1032 of the National Defense Authorization Act for Fiscal Year 2012 that imposes additional requirements on the annual National Security Strategy report:

SEC. 1032. NATIONAL SECURITY PLANNING GUIDANCE TO DENY SAFE HAVENS TO AL-QAEDA AND ITS VIOLENT EXTREMIST AFFILIATES.

(a) PURPOSE.—The purpose of this section is to improve interagency strategic planning and execution to more effectively integrate efforts to deny safe havens and strengthen at-risk states to further the goals of the National Security Strategy related to the disruption, dismantlement, and defeat of al-Qaeda and its violent extremist affiliates.

(b) NATIONAL SECURITY PLANNING GUIDANCE.—

(1) GUIDANCE REQUIRED.—The President shall issue classified or unclassified national security planning guidance in support of objectives stated in the national security strategy report submitted to Congress by the President pursuant to section 108 of the National Security Act of 1947 (50 U.S.C. 404a) to deny safe havens to al-Qaeda and its violent extremist affiliates and to strengthen at-risk states. Such guidance shall serve as the strategic plan that governs United States and coordinated international efforts to enhance the capacity of governmental and nongovernmental entities to work toward the goal of eliminating the ability of al-Qaeda and its violent extremist affiliates to establish or maintain safe havens.

(2) CONTENTS OF GUIDANCE.—The guidance required under paragraph (1) shall include each of the following:

(A) A prioritized list of specified geographic areas that the President determines are necessary to address and an explicit discussion and list of the criteria or rationale used to prioritize the areas on the list, including a discussion of the conditions that would hamper the ability of the United States to strengthen at-risk states or other entities in such areas.

(B) For each specified geographic area, a description, analysis, and discussion of the core problems and contributing issues that allow or could allow al-Qaeda and its violent extremist affiliates to use the area as a safe haven from which to plan and launch attacks, engage in propaganda, or raise funds and other support, including any ongoing or potential radicalization of the population, or to use the area as a key transit route for personnel, weapons, funding, or other support.

(C) A list of short-term, mid-term, and long-term goals for each specified geographic area, prioritized by importance.

(D) A description of the role and mission of each Federal department and agency involved in executing the guidance, including the Departments of Defense, Justice, Treasury, and State and the Agency for International Development.

(E) A description of gaps in United States capabilities to meet the goals listed pursuant to subparagraph (C), and the extent to which those gaps can be met through coordination with nongovernmental, international, or private sector organizations, entities, or companies.

(3) REVIEW AND UPDATE OF GUIDANCE.—The President shall review and update the guidance required under paragraph (1) as necessary. Any such review shall address each of the following:

(A) The overall progress made toward achieving the goals listed pursuant to paragraph (2)(C), including an overall assessment of the progress in denying a safe haven to al-Qaeda and its violent extremist affiliates.

(B) The performance of each Federal department and agency involved in executing the guidance.

(C) The performance of the unified country team and appropriate combatant command, or in the case of a crossborder effort, country teams in the area and the appropriate combatant command.

(D) Any addition to, deletion from, or change in the order of the prioritized list maintained pursuant to paragraph (2)(A).

(4) SPECIFIED GEOGRAPHIC AREA DEFINED.—In this subsection, the term ''specified geographic area'' means any country, subnational territory, or region—

(A) that serves or may potentially serve as a safe haven for al-Qaeda or a violent extremist affiliate of al-Qaeda—

(i) from which to plan and launch attacks, engage in propaganda, or raise funds and other support; or

(ii) for use as a key transit route for personnel, weapons, funding, or other support; and

(B) over which one or more governments or entities exert insufficient governmental or security control to deny al-Qaeda and its violent extremist affiliates the ability to establish a large scale presence.

INTELLIGENCE REFORM AND TERRORISM PREVENTION ACT OF 2004

(Public Law 108-458 of December 17, 2004; 118 STAT. 3638)

AN ACT To reform the intelligence community and the intelligence and intelligence-related activities of the United States Government, and for other purposes.

Be it enacted by the Senate and House of Representatives of the United States of America in Congress assembled,

SECTION 1. SHORT TITLE; TABLE OF CONTENTS.

(a) SHORT TITLE—This Act may be cited as the `Intelligence Reform and Terrorism Prevention Act of 2004'.
(b) TABLE OF CONTENTS—The table of contents for this Act is as follows:

TITLE I—REFORM OF THE INTELLIGENCE COMMUNITY

TITLE IV—TRANSPORTATION SECURITY

Subtitle A—National Strategy for Transportation Security

Subtitle B—Aviation Security

Subtitle C—Air Cargo Security

Subtitle D—Maritime Security

Subtitle K—Pretrial Detention of Terrorists

TITLE VII—IMPLEMENTATION OF 9/11 COMMISSION RECOMMENDATIONS

Subtitle A—Diplomacy, Foreign Aid, and the Military in the War on Terrorism

Subtitle B—Terrorist Travel and Effective Screening

Subtitle C—National Preparedness

TITLE VIII—OTHER MATTERS

Subtitle A—Intelligence Matters

Subtitle B—Department of Homeland Security Matters

Subtitle C—Homeland Security Civil Rights and Civil Liberties Protection

Subtitle D—Other Matters

TITLE I—REFORM OF THE INTELLIGENCE COMMUNITY

SEC. 1001. SHORT TITLE.

This title may be cited as the `National Security Intelligence Reform Act of 2004'.

Subtitle A—Establishment of Director of National Intelligence

REORGANIZATION AND IMPROVEMENT OF MANAGEMENT OF INTELLIGENCE COMMUNITY.

SEC. 1011.

(a) IN GENERAL—Title I of the National Security Act of 1947 (50 U.S.C. 402 et seq.) is amended by striking sections 102 through 104 and inserting the following new sections:

[Amendments omitted here—*see* the National Security Act of 1947 in this book]

(b) SENSE OF CONGRESS—It is the sense of Congress that—
(1) the human intelligence officers of the intelligence community have performed admirably and honorably in the face of great personal dangers;
(2) during an extended period of unprecedented investment and improvements in technical collection means, the human intelligence capabilities of the United States have not received the necessary and commensurate priorities;
(3) human intelligence is becoming an increasingly important capability to provide information on the asymmetric threats to the national security of the United States;
(4) the continued development and improvement of a robust and empowered and flexible human intelligence work force is critical to identifying, understanding, and countering the plans and intentions of the adversaries of the United States; and
(5) an increased emphasis on, and resources applied to, enhancing the depth and breadth of human intelligence capabilities of the United States intelligence community must be among the top priorities of the Director of National Intelligence.
(c) TRANSFORMATION OF CENTRAL INTELLIGENCE AGENCY—The Director of the Central Intelligence Agency shall, in accordance with standards developed by the Director in consultation with the Director of National Intelligence—

(1) enhance the analytic, human intelligence, and other capabilities of the Central Intelligence Agency;

(2) develop and maintain an effective language program within the Agency;

(3) emphasize the hiring of personnel of diverse backgrounds for purposes of improving the capabilities of the Agency;

(4) establish and maintain effective relationships between human intelligence and signals intelligence within the Agency at the operational level; and

(5) achieve a more effective balance within the Agency with respect to unilateral operations and liaison operations.

(d) REPORT—(1) Not later than 180 days after the date of the enactment of this Act, the Director of the Central Intelligence Agency shall submit to the Director of National Intelligence and the congressional intelligence committees a report setting forth the following:

(A) A strategy for improving the conduct of analysis (including strategic analysis) by the Central Intelligence Agency, and the progress of the Agency in implementing that strategy.

(B) A strategy for improving the human intelligence and other capabilities of the Agency, and the progress of the Agency in implementing that strategy.

(2)(A) The information in the report under paragraph (1) on the strategy referred to in paragraph (1)(B) shall—

(i) identify the number and types of personnel required to implement that strategy;

(ii) include a plan for the recruitment, training, equipping, and deployment of such personnel; and

(iii) set forth an estimate of the costs of such activities.

(B) If as of the date of the report under paragraph (1), a proper balance does not exist between unilateral operations and liaison operations, such report shall set forth the steps to be taken to achieve such balance.

REVISED DEFINITION OF NATIONAL INTELLIGENCE.

SEC. 1012.

Paragraph (5) of section 3 of the National Security Act of 1947 (50 U.S.C. 401a) is amended to read as follows:

`(5) The terms `national intelligence' and `intelligence related to national security' refer to all intelligence, regardless of the source from which derived and including information gathered within or outside the United States, that—

`(A) pertains, as determined consistent with any guidance issued by the President, to more than one United States Government agency; and
`(B) that involves—
`(i) threats to the United States, its people, property, or interests;
`(ii) the development, proliferation, or use of weapons of mass destruction; or
`(iii) any other matter bearing on United States national or homeland security.'.

JOINT PROCEDURES FOR OPERATIONAL COORDINATION BETWEEN DEPARTMENT OF DEFENSE AND CENTRAL INTELLIGENCE AGENCY.

SEC. 1013.

(a) Development of Procedures—The Director of National Intelligence, in consultation with the Secretary of Defense and the Director of the Central Intelligence Agency, shall develop joint procedures to be used by the Department of Defense and the Central Intelligence Agency to improve the coordination and deconfliction of operations that involve elements of both the Armed Forces and the Central Intelligence Agency consistent with national security and the protection of human intelligence sources and methods. Those procedures shall, at a minimum, provide the following:

(1) Methods by which the Director of the Central Intelligence Agency and the Secretary of Defense can improve communication and coordination in the planning, execution, and sustainment of operations, including, as a minimum—

(A) information exchange between senior officials of the Central Intelligence Agency and senior officers and officials of the Department of Defense when planning for such an operation commences by either organization; and

(B) exchange of information between the Secretary and the Director of the Central Intelligence Agency to ensure that senior operational officials in both the Department of Defense and the Central Intelligence Agency have knowledge of the existence of the ongoing operations of the other.

(2) When appropriate, in cases where the Department of Defense and the Central Intelligence Agency are conducting separate missions in the same geographical area, a mutual agreement on the tactical and strategic objectives for the region and a clear delineation of operational responsibilities to prevent conflict and duplication of effort.

(b) Implementation Report—Not later than 180 days after the date of the enactment of the Act, the Director of National Intelligence shall submit to the congressional defense committees (as defined in section 101 of title 10, United States Code) and the congressional intelligence committees (as defined in section 3(7) of the National Security Act of 1947 (50 U.S.C. 401a(7))) a report describing the procedures established pursuant to subsection (a) and the status of the implementation of those procedures.

ROLE OF DIRECTOR OF NATIONAL INTELLIGENCE IN APPOINTMENT OF CERTAIN OFFICIALS RESPONSIBLE FOR INTELLIGENCE-RELATED ACTIVITIES.

SEC. 1014.

Section 106 of the National Security Act of 1947 (50 U.S.C. 403-6) is amended by striking all after the heading and inserting the following:

[Amendments omitted here—*see* the National Security Act of 1947 in this book]

EXECUTIVE SCHEDULE MATTERS.

SEC. 1015.

(a) EXECUTIVE SCHEDULE LEVEL I—Section 5312 of title 5, United States Code, is amended by adding at the end the following new item:
`Director of National Intelligence.'.
(b) EXECUTIVE SCHEDULE LEVEL II—Section 5313 of title 5, United States Code, is amended by adding at the end the following new items:
`Principal Deputy Director of National Intelligence.
`Director of the National Counterterrorism Center.
`Director of the National Counter Proliferation Center.'.

(c) EXECUTIVE SCHEDULE LEVEL IV—Section 5315 of title 5, United States Code, is amended—

(1) by striking the item relating to the Assistant Directors of Central Intelligence; and

(2) by adding at the end the following new item:

`General Counsel of the Office of the National Intelligence Director.'.

INFORMATION SHARING.

SEC. 1016.

(a) DEFINITIONS—In this section:

(1) HOMELAND SECURITY INFORMATION—The term `homeland security information' has the meaning given that term in section 892(f) of the Homeland Security Act of 2002 (6 U.S.C. 482(f)).

(2) INFORMATION SHARING COUNCIL—The term `Information Sharing Council' means the Information Systems Council established by Executive Order 13356, or any successor body designated by the President, and referred to under subsection (g).

(3) INFORMATION SHARING ENVIRONMENT—The terms `information sharing environment' and `ISE' mean an approach that facilitates the sharing of terrorism and homeland security information, which may include any method determined necessary and appropriate for carrying out this section.

(4) PROGRAM MANAGER—The term `program manager' means the program manager designated under subsection (f).

(5) TERRORISM INFORMATION—The term `terrorism information'—

(A) means all information, whether collected, produced, or distributed by intelligence, law enforcement, military, homeland security, or other activities relating to—

(i) the existence, organization, capabilities, plans, intentions, vulnerabilities, means of finance or material support, or activities of foreign or international terrorist groups or individuals, or of domestic groups or individuals involved in transnational terrorism;

(ii) threats posed by such groups or individuals to the United States, United States persons, or

202

United States interests, or to those of other nations;

(iii) communications of or by such groups or individuals; or

(iv) groups or individuals reasonably believed to be assisting or associated with such groups or individuals; and

(B) includes weapons of mass destruction information.

(6) WEAPONS OF MASS DESTRUCTION INFORMATION—The term `weapons of mass destruction information' means information that could reasonably be expected to assist in the development, proliferation, or use of a weapon of mass destruction (including a chemical, biological, radiological, or nuclear weapon) that could be used by a terrorist or a terrorist organization against the United States, including information about the location of any stockpile of nuclear materials that could be exploited for use in such a weapon that could be used by a terrorist or a terrorist organization against the United States.

(b) INFORMATION SHARING ENVIRONMENT—

(1) ESTABLISHMENT—The President shall—

(A) create an information sharing environment for the sharing of terrorism information in a manner consistent with national security and with applicable legal standards relating to privacy and civil liberties;

(B) designate the organizational and management structures that will be used to operate and manage the ISE; and

(C) determine and enforce the policies, directives, and rules that will govern the content and usage of the ISE.

(2) ATTRIBUTES—The President shall, through the structures described in subparagraphs (B) and (C) of paragraph (1), ensure that the ISE provides and facilitates the means for sharing terrorism information among all appropriate Federal, State, local, and tribal entities, and the private sector through the use of policy guidelines and technologies. The President shall, to the greatest extent practicable, ensure that the ISE provides the functional equivalent of, or otherwise supports, a decentralized, distributed, and coordinated environment that—

(A) connects existing systems, where appropriate, provides no single points of failure, and allows users to

share information among agencies, between levels of government, and, as appropriate, with the private sector;
(B) ensures direct and continuous online electronic access to information;
(C) facilitates the availability of information in a form and manner that facilitates its use in analysis, investigations and operations;
(D) builds upon existing systems capabilities currently in use across the Government;
(E) employs an information access management approach that controls access to data rather than just systems and networks, without sacrificing security;
(F) facilitates the sharing of information at and across all levels of security;
(G) provides directory services, or the functional equivalent, for locating people and information;
(H) incorporates protections for individuals' privacy and civil liberties;
(I) incorporates strong mechanisms to enhance accountability and facilitate oversight, including audits, authentication, and access controls;
(J) integrates the information within the scope of the information sharing environment, including any such information in legacy technologies;
(K) integrates technologies, including all legacy technologies, through Internet-based services, consistent with appropriate security protocols and safeguards, to enable connectivity among required users at the Federal, State, and local levels;
(L) allows the full range of analytic and operational activities without the need to centralize information within the scope of the information sharing environment;
(M) permits analysts to collaborate both independently and in a group (commonly known as `collective and noncollective collaboration'), and across multiple levels of national security information and controlled unclassified information;
(N) provides a resolution process that enables changes by authorized officials regarding rules and policies for the access, use, and retention of information within the scope of the information sharing environment; and

(O) incorporates continuous, real-time, and immutable audit capabilities, to the maximum extent practicable.

(c) PRELIMINARY REPORT—Not later than 180 days after the date of the enactment of this Act, the program manager shall, in consultation with the Information Sharing Council—

(1) submit to the President and Congress a description of the technological, legal, and policy issues presented by the creation of the ISE, and the way in which these issues will be addressed;

(2) establish an initial capability to provide electronic directory services, or the functional equivalent, to assist in locating in the Federal Government intelligence and terrorism information and people with relevant knowledge about intelligence and terrorism information; and

(3) conduct a review of relevant current Federal agency capabilities, databases, and systems for sharing information.

(d) GUIDELINES AND REQUIREMENTS—As soon as possible, but in no event later than 270 days after the date of the enactment of this Act, the President shall—

(1) leverage all ongoing efforts consistent with establishing the ISE and issue guidelines for acquiring, accessing, sharing, and using information, including guidelines to ensure that information is provided in its most shareable form, such as by using tearlines to separate out data from the sources and methods by which the data are obtained;

(2) in consultation with the Privacy and Civil Liberties Oversight Board established under section 1061, issue guidelines that—

(A) protect privacy and civil liberties in the development and use of the ISE; and

(B) shall be made public, unless nondisclosure is clearly necessary to protect national security; and

(3) require the heads of Federal departments and agencies to promote a culture of information sharing by—

(A) reducing disincentives to information sharing, including over-classification of information and unnecessary requirements for originator approval, consistent with applicable laws and regulations; and

(B) providing affirmative incentives for information sharing.

(e) IMPLEMENTATION PLAN REPORT—Not later than one year after the date of the enactment of this Act, the President shall, with the assistance of the program manager, submit to Congress a report containing an implementation plan for the ISE. The report shall include the following:

(1) A description of the functions, capabilities, resources, and conceptual design of the ISE, including standards.

(2) A description of the impact on enterprise architectures of participating agencies.

(3) A budget estimate that identifies the incremental costs associated with designing, testing, integrating, deploying, and operating the ISE.

(4) A project plan for designing, testing, integrating, deploying, and operating the ISE.

(5) The policies and directives referred to in subsection (b)(1)(C), as well as the metrics and enforcement mechanisms that will be utilized.

(6) Objective, systemwide performance measures to enable the assessment of progress toward achieving the full implementation of the ISE.

(7) A description of the training requirements needed to ensure that the ISE will be adequately implemented and properly utilized.

(8) A description of the means by which privacy and civil liberties will be protected in the design and operation of the ISE.

(9) The recommendations of the program manager, in consultation with the Information Sharing Council, regarding whether, and under what conditions, the ISE should be expanded to include other intelligence information.

(10) A delineation of the roles of the Federal departments and agencies that will participate in the ISE, including an identification of the agencies that will deliver the infrastructure needed to operate and manage the ISE (as distinct from individual department or agency components that are part of the ISE), with such delineation of roles to be consistent with—

(A) the authority of the Director of National Intelligence under this title, and the amendments made by this title, to set standards for information sharing throughout the intelligence community; and

(B) the authority of the Secretary of Homeland Security and the Attorney General, and the role of the Department of Homeland Security and the Department of Justice, in coordinating with State, local, and tribal officials and the private sector.

(11) The recommendations of the program manager, in consultation with the Information Sharing Council, for a future management structure for the ISE, including whether the position of program manager should continue to remain in existence.

(f) PROGRAM MANAGER—

(1) DESIGNATION—Not later than 120 days after the date of the enactment of this Act, with notification to Congress, the President shall designate an individual as the program manager responsible for information sharing across the Federal Government. The individual designated as the program manager shall serve as program manager until removed from service or replaced by the President (at the President's sole discretion). The program manager, in consultation with the head of any affected department or agency, shall have and exercise governmentwide authority over the sharing of information within the scope of the information sharing environment, including homeland security information, terrorism information, and weapons of mass destruction information, by all Federal departments, agencies, and components, irrespective of the Federal department, agency, or component in which the program manager may be administratively located, except as otherwise expressly provided by law.

(2) DUTIES AND RESPONSIBILITIES—

(A) IN GENERAL—The program manager shall, in consultation with the Information Sharing Council—

(i) plan for and oversee the implementation of, and manage, the ISE;

(ii) assist in the development of policies, as appropriate, to foster the development and proper operation of the ISE;

(iii) consistent with the direction and policies issued by the President, the Director of National Intelligence, and the Director of the Office of Management and Budget, issue governmentwide procedures, guidelines, instructions, and functional standards, as appropriate, for the management, development, and proper operation of the ISE;

(iv) identify and resolve information sharing disputes between Federal departments, agencies, and components; and

(v) assist, monitor, and assess the implementation of the ISE by Federal departments and agencies to ensure adequate progress, technological consistency and policy compliance; and regularly report the findings to Congress.

(B) CONTENT OF POLICIES, PROCEDURES, GUIDELINES, RULES, AND STANDARDS—The policies, procedures, guidelines, rules, and standards under subparagraph (A)(ii) shall—

(i) take into account the varying missions and security requirements of agencies participating in the ISE;

(ii) address development, implementation, and oversight of technical standards and requirements;

(iii) take into account ongoing and planned efforts that support development, implementation and management of the ISE;

(iv) address and facilitate information sharing between and among departments and agencies of the intelligence community, the Department of Defense, the homeland security community and the law enforcement community;

(v) address and facilitate information sharing between Federal departments and agencies and State, tribal, and local governments;

(vi) address and facilitate, as appropriate, information sharing between Federal departments and agencies and the private sector;

(vii) address and facilitate, as appropriate, information sharing between Federal departments and agencies with foreign partners and allies; and

(viii) ensure the protection of privacy and civil liberties.

(g) INFORMATION SHARING COUNCIL—

(1) ESTABLISHMENT—There is established an Information Sharing Council that shall assist the President and the program manager in their duties under this section. The Information Sharing Council shall serve until removed from service or

208

replaced by the President (at the sole discretion of the President) with a successor body.

(2) SPECIFIC DUTIES—In assisting the President and the program manager in their duties under this section, the Information Sharing Council shall—

(A) advise the President and the program manager in developing policies, procedures, guidelines, roles, and standards necessary to establish, implement, and maintain the ISE;

(B) work to ensure coordination among the Federal departments and agencies participating in the ISE in the establishment, implementation, and maintenance of the ISE;

(C) identify and, as appropriate, recommend the consolidation and elimination of current programs, systems, and processes used by Federal departments and agencies to share information, and recommend, as appropriate, the redirection of existing resources to support the ISE;

(D) identify gaps, if any, between existing technologies, programs and systems used by Federal departments and agencies to share information and the parameters of the proposed information sharing environment;

(E) recommend solutions to address any gaps identified under subparagraph (D);

(F) recommend means by which the ISE can be extended to allow interchange of information between Federal departments and agencies and appropriate authorities of State and local governments;

(G) assist the program manager in identifying and resolving information sharing disputes between Federal departments, agencies, and components;

(H) identify appropriate personnel for assignment to the program manager to support staffing needs identified by the program manager; and

(I) recommend whether or not, and by which means, the ISE should be expanded so as to allow future expansion encompassing other relevant categories of information.

(3) CONSULTATION—In performing its duties, the Information Sharing Council shall consider input from persons and entities outside the Federal Government having significant

experience and expertise in policy, technical matters, and operational matters relating to the ISE.

(4) INAPPLICABILITY OF FEDERAL ADVISORY COMMITTEE ACT—The Information Sharing Council (including any subsidiary group of the Information Sharing Council) not be subject to the requirements of the Federal Advisory Committee Act (5 U.S.C. App.).

(5) DETAILEES—Upon a request by the Director of National Intelligence, the departments and agencies represented on the Information Sharing Council shall detail to the program manager, on a reimbursable basis, appropriate personnel identified under paragraph (2)(H).

(h) PERFORMANCE MANAGEMENT REPORTS-

(1) IN GENERAL—Not later than two years after the date of the enactment of this Act, and not later than June 30 of each year thereafter, the President shall submit to Congress a report on the state of the ISE and of information sharing across the Federal Government.

(2) CONTENT—Each report under this subsection shall include—

(A) a progress report on the extent to which the ISE has been implemented, including how the ISE has fared on the performance measures and whether the performance goals set in the preceding year have been met;

(B) objective system-wide performance goals for the following year;

(C) an accounting of how much was spent on the ISE in the preceding year;

(D) actions taken to ensure that procurement of and investments in systems and technology are consistent with the implementation plan for the ISE;

(E) the extent to which all terrorism watch lists are available for combined searching in real time through the ISE and whether there are consistent standards for placing individuals on, and removing individuals from, the watch lists, including the availability of processes for correcting errors;

(F) the extent to which State, tribal, and local officials are participating in the ISE;

(G) the extent to which private sector data, including information from owners and operators of critical infrastructure, is incorporated in the ISE, and the extent to which individuals and entities outside the government are receiving information through the ISE;

(H) the measures taken by the Federal government to ensure the accuracy of information in the ISE, in particular the accuracy of information about individuals;

(I) an assessment of the privacy and civil liberties protections of the ISE, including actions taken in the preceding year to implement or enforce privacy and civil liberties protections; and

(J) an assessment of the security protections used in the ISE.

(i) AGENCY RESPONSIBILITIES—The head of each department or agency that possesses or uses intelligence or terrorism information, operates a system in the ISE, or otherwise participates (or expects to participate) in the ISE shall—

(1) ensure full department or agency compliance with information sharing policies, procedures, guidelines, rules, and standards established under subsections (b) and (f);

(2) ensure the provision of adequate resources for systems and activities supporting operation of and participation in the ISE;

(3) ensure full department or agency cooperation in the development of the ISE to implement governmentwide information sharing; and

(4) submit, at the request of the President or the program manager, any reports on the implementation of the requirements of the ISE within such department or agency.

(j) Report on the Information Sharing Environment-

(1) IN GENERAL—Not later than 180 days after the date of enactment of the Implementing Recommendations of the 9/11 Commission Act of 2007, the President shall report to the Committee on Homeland Security and Governmental Affairs of the Senate, the Select Committee on Intelligence of the Senate, the Committee on Homeland Security of the House of Representatives, and the Permanent Select Committee on Intelligence of the House of Representatives on the feasibility of—

(A) eliminating the use of any marking or process (including `Originator Control') intended to, or having the effect of, restricting the sharing of information within the scope of the information sharing environment, including homeland security information, terrorism information, and weapons of mass destruction information, between and among participants in the information sharing environment, unless the President has—

    (i) specifically exempted categories of information from such elimination; and

    (ii) reported that exemption to the committees of Congress described in the matter preceding this subparagraph; and

(B) continuing to use Federal agency standards in effect on such date of enactment for the collection, sharing, and access to information within the scope of the information sharing environment, including homeland security information, terrorism information, and weapons of mass destruction information, relating to citizens and lawful permanent residents;

(C) replacing the standards described in subparagraph (B) with a standard that would allow mission-based or threat-based permission to access or share information within the scope of the information sharing environment, including homeland security information, terrorism information, and weapons of mass destruction information, for a particular purpose that the Federal Government, through an appropriate process established in consultation with the Privacy and Civil Liberties Oversight Board established under section 1061, has determined to be lawfully permissible for a particular agency, component, or employee (commonly known as an `authorized use' standard); and

(D) the use of anonymized data by Federal departments, agencies, or components collecting, possessing, disseminating, or handling information within the scope of the information sharing environment, including homeland security information, terrorism information, and weapons of mass destruction information, in any cases in which—

    (i) the use of such information is reasonably expected to produce results materially equivalent to the use of information that is transferred or stored in a non-anonymized form; and

    ii) such use is consistent with any mission of that department, agency, or component (including any mission under a Federal statute or directive of the President) that involves the storage, retention, sharing, or exchange of personally identifiable information.

(2) DEFINITION—In this subsection, the term `anonymized data' means data in which the individual to whom the data pertains is not identifiable with reasonable efforts, including information that has been encrypted or hidden through the use of other technology.

(k) Additional Positions—The program manager is authorized to hire not more than 40 full-time employees to assist the program manager in—

(1) activities associated with the implementation of the information sharing environment, including—

(A) implementing the requirements under subsection (b)(2); and

(B) any additional implementation initiatives to enhance and expedite the creation of the information sharing environment; and

(2) identifying and resolving information sharing disputes between Federal departments, agencies, and components under subsection (f)(2)(A)(iv).

(l) Authorization of Appropriations—There is authorized to be appropriated to carry out this section $30,000,000 for each of fiscal years 2008 and 2009.

ALTERNATIVE ANALYSIS OF INTELLIGENCE BY THE INTELLIGENCE COMMUNITY.

SEC. 1017.

(a) IN GENERAL—Not later than 180 days after the effective date of this Act, the Director of National Intelligence shall establish a process and assign an individual or entity the responsibility for ensuring that, as appropriate, elements of the intelligence community conduct alternative analysis (commonly referred to as `red-team analysis') of the information and conclusions in intelligence products.

(b) REPORT—Not later than 270 days after the effective date of this Act, the Director of National Intelligence shall provide a report to the Select Committee on Intelligence of the Senate and the Permanent Select Committee of the House of Representatives on the implementation of subsection (a).

213

PRESIDENTIAL GUIDELINES ON IMPLEMENTATION AND PRESERVATION OF AUTHORITIES.

SEC. 1018.

The President shall issue guidelines to ensure the effective implementation and execution within the executive branch of the authorities granted to the Director of National Intelligence by this title and the amendments made by this title, in a manner that respects and does not abrogate the statutory responsibilities of the heads of the departments of the United States Government concerning such departments, including, but not limited to:

(1) the authority of the Director of the Office of Management and Budget; and

(2) the authority of the principal officers of the executive departments as heads of their respective departments, including, but not limited to, under—

(A) section 199 of the Revised Statutes (22 U.S.C. 2651);

(B) title II of the Department of Energy Organization Act (42 U.S.C. 7131 et seq.);

(C) the State Department Basic Authorities Act of 1956;

(D) section 102(a) of the Homeland Security Act of 2002 (6 U.S.C. 112(a)); and

(E) sections 301 of title 5, 113(b) and 162(b) of title 10, 503 of title 28, and 301(b) of title 31, United States Code.

ASSIGNMENT OF RESPONSIBILITIES RELATING TO ANALYTIC INTEGRITY.

SEC. 1019.

(a) ASSIGNMENT OF RESPONSIBILITIES—For purposes of carrying out section 102A(h) of the National Security Act of 1947 (as added by section 1011(a)), the Director of National Intelligence shall, not later than 180 days after the date of the enactment of this Act, assign an individual or entity to be responsible for ensuring that finished intelligence products produced by any element or elements of the intelligence community are timely, objective, independent of political considerations, based upon all sources of available intelligence, and employ the standards of proper analytic tradecraft.

(b) RESPONSIBILITIES—(1) The individual or entity assigned responsibility under subsection (a)—

(A) may be responsible for general oversight and management of analysis and production, but may not be directly responsible for, or involved in, the specific production of any finished intelligence product;

(B) shall perform, on a regular basis, detailed reviews of finished intelligence product or other analytic products by an element or elements of the intelligence community covering a particular topic or subject matter;

(C) shall be responsible for identifying on an annual basis functional or topical areas of analysis for specific review under subparagraph (B); and

(D) upon completion of any review under subparagraph (B), may draft lessons learned, identify best practices, or make recommendations for improvement to the analytic tradecraft employed in the production of the reviewed product or products.

(2) Each review under paragraph (1)(B) should—

(A) include whether the product or products concerned were based on all sources of available intelligence, properly describe the quality and reliability of underlying sources, properly caveat and express uncertainties or confidence in analytic judgments, properly distinguish between underlying intelligence and the assumptions and judgments of analysts, and incorporate, where appropriate, alternative analyses; and

(B) ensure that the analytic methodologies, tradecraft, and practices used by the element or elements concerned in the production of the product or products concerned meet the standards set forth in subsection (a).

(3) Information drafted under paragraph (1)(D) should, as appropriate, be included in analysis teaching modules and case studies for use throughout the intelligence community.

(c) ANNUAL REPORTS—Not later than December 1 each year, the Director of National Intelligence shall submit to the congressional intelligence committees, the heads of the relevant elements of the intelligence community, and the heads of analytic training departments a report containing a description, and the associated findings, of each review under subsection (b)(1)(B) during such year.

(d) CONGRESSIONAL INTELLIGENCE COMMITTEES DEFINED— In this section, the term `congressional intelligence committees' means—

(1) the Select Committee on Intelligence of the Senate; and
(2) the Permanent Select Committee on Intelligence of the House of Representatives.

SAFEGUARD OF OBJECTIVITY IN INTELLIGENCE ANALYSIS.

SEC. 1020.

(a) IN GENERAL—Not later than 180 days after the effective date of this Act, the Director of National Intelligence shall identify an individual within the Office of the Director of National Intelligence who shall be available to analysts within the Office of the Director of National Intelligence to counsel, conduct arbitration, offer recommendations, and, as appropriate, initiate inquiries into real or perceived problems of analytic tradecraft or politicization, biased reporting, or lack of objectivity in intelligence analysis.

(b) REPORT—Not later than 270 days after the effective date of this Act, the Director of National Intelligence shall provide a report to the Select Committee on Intelligence of the Senate and the Permanent Select Committee on Intelligence of the House of Representatives on the implementation of subsection (a).

Subtitle B—National Counterterrorism Center, National Counter Proliferation Center, and National Intelligence Centers

NATIONAL COUNTERTERRORISM CENTER.

SEC. 1021.

Title I of the National Security Act of 1947 (50 U.S.C. 402 et seq.) is amended by adding at the end the following new section:

[Amendments omitted here—*see* the National Security Act of 1947 in this book]

NATIONAL COUNTER PROLIFERATION CENTER.

SEC. 1022.

Title I of the National Security Act of 1947, as amended by section 1021 of this Act, is further amended by adding at the end the following new section:

[Amendments omitted here—*see* the National Security Act of 1947 in this book]

NATIONAL INTELLIGENCE CENTERS.

SEC. 1023.

Title I of the National Security Act of 1947, as amended by section 1022 of this Act, is further amended by adding at the end the following new section:

[Amendments omitted here—*see* the National Security Act of 1947 in this book]

Subtitle C—Joint Intelligence Community Council

JOINT INTELLIGENCE COMMUNITY COUNCIL.

SEC. 1031.

Title I of the National Security Act of 1947 (50 U.S.C. 402 et seq.) is amended by inserting after section 101 the following new section:

[Amendments omitted here—*see* the National Security Act of 1947 in this book]

Subtitle D—Improvement of Education for the Intelligence Community

ADDITIONAL EDUCATION AND TRAINING REQUIREMENTS.

SEC. 1041.

(a) FINDINGS—Congress makes the following findings:

(1) Foreign language education is essential for the development of a highly-skilled workforce for the intelligence community.

(2) Since September 11, 2001, the need for language proficiency levels to meet required national security functions has been raised, and the ability to comprehend and articulate technical and scientific information in foreign languages has become critical.

(b) LINGUISTIC REQUIREMENTS—(1) The Director of National Intelligence shall—

(A) identify the linguistic requirements for the Office of the Director of National Intelligence;

(B) identify specific requirements for the range of linguistic skills necessary for the intelligence community, including proficiency in scientific and technical vocabularies of critical foreign languages; and

(C) develop a comprehensive plan for the Office to meet such requirements through the education, recruitment, and training of linguists.

(2) In carrying out activities under paragraph (1), the Director shall take into account education grant programs of the Department of Defense and the Department of Education that are in existence as of the date of the enactment of this Act.

(c) PROFESSIONAL INTELLIGENCE TRAINING—The Director of National Intelligence shall require the head of each element and component within the Office of the Director of National Intelligence who has responsibility for professional intelligence training to periodically review and revise the curriculum for the professional intelligence training of the senior and intermediate level personnel of such element or component in order to—

(1) strengthen the focus of such curriculum on the integration of intelligence collection and analysis throughout the Office; and

(2) prepare such personnel for duty with other departments, agencies, and elements of the intelligence community.

CROSS-DISCIPLINARY EDUCATION AND TRAINING.

SEC. 1042.

Title X of the National Security Act of 1947 (50 U.S.C. 441g) is amended by adding at the end the following new section:

[Amendments omitted here—*see* the National Security Act of 1947 in this book]

INTELLIGENCE COMMUNITY SCHOLARSHIP PROGRAM.

SEC. 1043.

Title X of the National Security Act of 1947, as amended by section 1042 of this Act, is further amended by adding at the end the following new section:

[Amendments omitted here—*see* the National Security Act of 1947 in this book]

Subtitle E—Additional Improvements of Intelligence Activities

SERVICE AND NATIONAL LABORATORIES AND THE INTELLIGENCE COMMUNITY.

SEC. 1051.

The Director of National Intelligence, in cooperation with the Secretary of Defense and the Secretary of Energy, should seek to ensure that each service laboratory of the Department of Defense and each national laboratory of the Department of Energy may, acting through the relevant Secretary and in a manner consistent with the missions and commitments of the laboratory—
(1) assist the Director of National Intelligence in all aspects of technical intelligence, including research, applied sciences, analysis, technology evaluation and assessment, and any other aspect that the relevant Secretary considers appropriate; and
(2) make available to the intelligence community, on a community-wide basis—
(A) the analysis and production services of the service and national laboratories, in a manner that maximizes the capacity and services of such laboratories; and
(B) the facilities and human resources of the service and national laboratories, in a manner that improves the technological capabilities of the intelligence community.

OPEN-SOURCE INTELLIGENCE.

SEC. 1052.

(a) Sense of Congress—It is the sense of Congress that—
(1) the Director of National Intelligence should establish an intelligence center for the purpose of coordinating the collection, analysis, production, and dissemination of open-source intelligence to elements of the intelligence community;
(2) open-source intelligence is a valuable source that must be integrated into the intelligence cycle to ensure that United States policymakers are fully and completely informed; and
(3) the intelligence center should ensure that each element of the intelligence community uses open-source intelligence consistent with the mission of such element.

(b) REQUIREMENT FOR EFFICIENT USE BY INTELLIGENCE COMMUNITY OF OPEN-SOURCE INTELLIGENCE—The Director of National Intelligence shall ensure that the intelligence community makes efficient and effective use of open-source information and analysis.

(c) Report—Not later than June 30, 2005, the Director of National Intelligence shall submit to the congressional intelligence committees a report containing the decision of the Director as to whether an open-source intelligence center will be established. If the Director decides not to establish an open-source intelligence center, such report shall also contain a description of how the intelligence community will use open-source intelligence and effectively integrate open-source intelligence into the national intelligence cycle.

(d) CONGRESSIONAL INTELLIGENCE COMMITTEES DEFINED— In this section, the term `congressional intelligence committees' means—
(1) the Select Committee on Intelligence of the Senate; and
(2) the Permanent Select Committee on Intelligence of the House of Representatives.

NATIONAL INTELLIGENCE RESERVE CORPS.

SEC. 1053.

(a) ESTABLISHMENT—The Director of National Intelligence may provide for the establishment and training of a National Intelligence Reserve Corps (in this section referred to as `National Intelligence Reserve Corps') for the temporary reemployment on a voluntary basis of former employees of elements of the intelligence community during periods of emergency, as determined by the Director.

(b) ELIGIBLE INDIVIDUALS—An individual may participate in the National Intelligence Reserve Corps only if the individual previously served as a full time employee of an element of the intelligence community.

(c) TERMS OF PARTICIPATION—The Director of National Intelligence shall prescribe the terms and conditions under which eligible individuals may participate in the National Intelligence Reserve Corps.

(d) EXPENSES—The Director of National Intelligence may provide members of the National Intelligence Reserve Corps transportation and per diem in lieu of subsistence for purposes of participating in any training that relates to service as a member of the Reserve Corps.

(e) TREATMENT OF ANNUITANTS—(1) If an annuitant receiving an annuity from the Civil Service Retirement and Disability Fund becomes temporarily reemployed pursuant to this section, such annuity shall not be discontinued thereby.

(2) An annuitant so reemployed shall not be considered an employee for the purposes of chapter 83 or 84 of title 5, United States Code.

(f) TREATMENT UNDER OFFICE OF DIRECTOR OF NATIONAL INTELLIGENCE PERSONNEL CEILING—A member of the National Intelligence Reserve Corps who is reemployed on a temporary basis pursuant to this section shall not count against any personnel ceiling applicable to the Office of the Director of National Intelligence.

Subtitle F—Privacy and Civil Liberties

PRIVACY AND CIVIL LIBERTIES OVERSIGHT BOARD.

SEC. 1061.

(a) In General—There is established as an independent agency within the executive branch a Privacy and Civil Liberties Oversight Board (referred to in this section as the `Board').

(b) Findings—Consistent with the report of the National Commission on Terrorist Attacks Upon the United States, Congress makes the following findings:

221

(1) In conducting the war on terrorism, the Government may need additional powers and may need to enhance the use of its existing powers.

(2) This shift of power and authority to the Government calls for an enhanced system of checks and balances to protect the precious liberties that are vital to our way of life and to ensure that the Government uses its powers for the purposes for which the powers were given.

(3) The National Commission on Terrorist Attacks Upon the United States correctly concluded that `The choice between security and liberty is a false choice, as nothing is more likely to endanger America's liberties than the success of a terrorist attack at home. Our history has shown us that insecurity threatens liberty. Yet, if our liberties are curtailed, we lose the values that we are struggling to defend.

(c) Purpose—The Board shall—

(1) analyze and review actions the executive branch takes to protect the Nation from terrorism, ensuring that the need for such actions is balanced with the need to protect privacy and civil liberties; and

(2) ensure that liberty concerns are appropriately considered in the development and implementation of laws, regulations, and policies related to efforts to protect the Nation against terrorism.

(d) Functions—

(1) ADVICE AND COUNSEL ON POLICY DEVELOPMENT AND IMPLEMENTATION—The Board shall—

(A) review proposed legislation, regulations, and policies related to efforts to protect the Nation from terrorism, including the development and adoption of information sharing guidelines under subsections (d) and (f) of section 1016;

(B) review the implementation of new and existing legislation, regulations, and policies related to efforts to protect the Nation from terrorism, including the implementation of information sharing guidelines under subsections (d) and (f) of section 1016;

(C) advise the President and the departments, agencies, and elements of the executive branch to ensure that privacy and civil liberties are appropriately considered in the development and implementation of such legislation, regulations, policies, and guidelines; and

222

(D) in providing advice on proposals to retain or enhance a particular governmental power, consider whether the department, agency, or element of the executive branch has established—

(i) that the need for the power is balanced with the need to protect privacy and civil liberties;

(ii) that there is adequate supervision of the use by the executive branch of the power to ensure protection of privacy and civil liberties; and

(iii) that there are adequate guidelines and oversight to properly confine its use.

(2) OVERSIGHT—The Board shall continually review—

(A) the regulations, policies, and procedures, and the implementation of the regulations, policies, and procedures, of the departments, agencies, and elements of the executive branch relating to efforts to protect the Nation from terrorism to ensure that privacy and civil liberties are protected;

(B) the information sharing practices of the departments, agencies, and elements of the executive branch relating to efforts to protect the Nation from terrorism to determine whether they appropriately protect privacy and civil liberties and adhere to the information sharing guidelines issued or developed under subsections (d) and (f) of section 1016 and to other governing laws, regulations, and policies regarding privacy and civil liberties; and

(C) other actions by the executive branch relating to efforts to protect the Nation from terrorism to determine whether such actions—

(i) appropriately protect privacy and civil liberties; and

(ii) are consistent with governing laws, regulations, and policies regarding privacy and civil liberties.

(3) RELATIONSHIP WITH PRIVACY AND CIVIL LIBERTIES OFFICERS—The Board shall—

(A) receive and review reports and other information from privacy officers and civil liberties officers under section 1062;

(B) when appropriate, make recommendations to such privacy officers and civil liberties officers regarding their activities; and

(C) when appropriate, coordinate the activities of such privacy officers and civil liberties officers on relevant interagency matters.

(4) TESTIMONY—The members of the Board shall appear and testify before Congress upon request.

(e) Reports—

(1) IN GENERAL—The Board shall—

(A) receive and review reports from privacy officers and civil liberties officers under section 1062; and

(B) periodically submit, not less than semiannually, reports—

(i)(I) to the appropriate committees of Congress, including the Committee on the Judiciary of the Senate, the Committee on the Judiciary of the House of Representatives, the Committee on Homeland Security and Governmental Affairs of the Senate, the Committee on Homeland Security of the House of Representatives, the Committee on Oversight and Government Reform of the House of Representatives, the Select Committee on Intelligence of the Senate, and the Permanent Select Committee on Intelligence of the House of Representatives; and

(II) to the President; and

(ii) which shall be in unclassified form to the greatest extent possible, with a classified annex where necessary.

(2) CONTENTS—Not less than 2 reports submitted each year under paragraph (1)(B) shall include—

(A) a description of the major activities of the Board during the preceding period;

(B) information on the findings, conclusions, and recommendations of the Board resulting from its advice and oversight functions under subsection (d);

(C) the minority views on any findings, conclusions, and recommendations of the Board resulting from its advice and oversight functions under subsection (d);

(D) each proposal reviewed by the Board under subsection (d)(1) that—

(i) the Board advised against implementation; and

(ii) notwithstanding such advice, actions were taken to implement; and

(E) for the preceding period, any requests submitted under subsection (g)(1)(D) for the issuance of subpoenas that were modified or denied by the Attorney General.

(f) Informing the Public—The Board shall—

(1) make its reports, including its reports to Congress, available to the public to the greatest extent that is consistent with the protection of classified information and applicable law; and

(2) hold public hearings and otherwise inform the public of its activities, as appropriate and in a manner consistent with the protection of classified information and applicable law.

(g) Access to Information—

(1) AUTHORIZATION—If determined by the Board to be necessary to carry out its responsibilities under this section, the Board is authorized to—

(A) have access from any department, agency, or element of the executive branch, or any Federal officer or employee of any such department, agency, or element, to all relevant records, reports, audits, reviews, documents, papers, recommendations, or other relevant material, including classified information consistent with applicable law;

(B) interview, take statements from, or take public testimony from personnel of any department, agency, or element of the executive branch, or any Federal officer or employee of any such department, agency, or element;

(C) request information or assistance from any State, tribal, or local government; and

(D) at the direction of a majority of the members of the Board, submit a written request to the Attorney General of the United States that the Attorney General require, by subpoena, persons (other than departments, agencies, and elements of the executive branch) to produce any relevant information, documents, reports, answers, records, accounts, papers, and other documentary or testimonial evidence.

(2) REVIEW OF SUBPOENA REQUEST—

(A) IN GENERAL—Not later than 30 days after the date of receipt of a request by the Board under paragraph (1)(D), the Attorney General shall—

(i) issue the subpoena as requested; or

(ii) provide the Board, in writing, with an explanation of the grounds on which the subpoena request has been modified or denied.

(B) NOTIFICATION—If a subpoena request is modified or denied under subparagraph (A)(ii), the Attorney General shall, not later than 30 days after the date of that modification or denial, notify the Committee on the Judiciary of the Senate and the Committee on the Judiciary of the House of Representatives.

(3) ENFORCEMENT OF SUBPOENA—In the case of contumacy or failure to obey a subpoena issued pursuant to paragraph (1)(D), the United States district court for the judicial district in which the subpoenaed person resides, is served, or may be found may issue an order requiring such person to produce the evidence required by such subpoena.

(4) AGENCY COOPERATION—Whenever information or assistance requested under subparagraph (A) or (B) of paragraph (1) is, in the judgment of the Board, unreasonably refused or not provided, the Board shall report the circumstances to the head of the department, agency, or element concerned without delay. The head of the department, agency, or element concerned shall ensure that the Board is given access to the information, assistance, material, or personnel the Board determines to be necessary to carry out its functions.

(h) Membership—

(1) MEMBERS—The Board shall be composed of a full-time chairman and 4 additional members, who shall be appointed by the President, by and with the advice and consent of the Senate.

(2) QUALIFICATIONS—Members of the Board shall be selected solely on the basis of their professional qualifications, achievements, public stature, expertise in civil liberties and privacy, and relevant experience, and without regard to political affiliation, but in no event shall more than 3 members of the Board be members of the same political party. The President shall, before appointing an individual who is not a member of the same political party as the President, consult with the leadership of that party, if any, in the Senate and House of Representatives.

(3) INCOMPATIBLE OFFICE—An individual appointed to the Board may not, while serving on the Board, be an elected official, officer, or employee of the Federal Government, other than in the capacity as a member of the Board.

(4) TERM—Each member of the Board shall serve a term of 6 years, except that—

> (A) a member appointed to a term of office after the commencement of such term may serve under such appointment only for the remainder of such term; and
>
> (B) upon the expiration of the term of office of a member, the member shall continue to serve until the member's successor has been appointed and qualified, except that no member may serve under this subparagraph—
>
> > (i) for more than 60 days when Congress is in session unless a nomination to fill the vacancy shall have been submitted to the Senate; or
> >
> > (ii) after the adjournment sine die of the session of the Senate in which such nomination is submitted.

(5) QUORUM AND MEETINGS—The Board shall meet upon the call of the chairman or a majority of its members. Three members of the Board shall constitute a quorum.

(i) Compensation and Travel Expenses—

> (1) COMPENSATION—
>
> > (A) CHAIRMAN—The chairman of the Board shall be compensated at the rate of pay payable for a position at level III of the Executive Schedule under section 5314 of title 5, United States Code.
> >
> > (B) MEMBERS—Each member of the Board shall be compensated at a rate of pay payable for a position at level IV of the Executive Schedule under section 5315 of title 5, United States Code, for each day during which that member is engaged in the actual performance of the duties of the Board.
>
> (2) TRAVEL EXPENSES—Members of the Board shall be allowed travel expenses, including per diem in lieu of subsistence, at rates authorized for persons employed intermittently by the Government under section 5703(b) of title 5, United States Code, while away from their homes or regular places of business in the performance of services for the Board.

(j) Staff—

(1) APPOINTMENT AND COMPENSATION—The chairman of the Board, in accordance with rules agreed upon by the Board, shall appoint and fix the compensation of a full-time executive director and such other personnel as may be necessary to enable the Board to carry out its functions, without regard to the provisions of title 5, United States Code, governing appointments in the competitive service, and without regard to the provisions of chapter 51 and subchapter III of chapter 53 of such title relating to classification and General Schedule pay rates, except that no rate of pay fixed under this subsection may exceed the equivalent of that payable for a position at level V of the Executive Schedule under section 5316 of title 5, United States Code.

(2) DETAILEES—Any Federal employee may be detailed to the Board without reimbursement from the Board, and such detailee shall retain the rights, status, and privileges of the detailee's regular employment without interruption.

(3) CONSULTANT SERVICES—The Board may procure the temporary or intermittent services of experts and consultants in accordance with section 3109 of title 5, United States Code, at rates that do not exceed the daily rate paid a person occupying a position at level IV of the Executive Schedule under section 5315 of such title.

(k) Security Clearances—

(1) IN GENERAL—The appropriate departments, agencies, and elements of the executive branch shall cooperate with the Board to expeditiously provide the Board members and staff with appropriate security clearances to the extent possible under existing procedures and requirements.

(2) RULES AND PROCEDURES—After consultation with the Secretary of Defense, the Attorney General, and the Director of National Intelligence, the Board shall adopt rules and procedures of the Board for physical, communications, computer, document, personnel, and other security relating to carrying out the functions of the Board.

(l) Treatment as Agency, Not as Advisory Committee—The Board—

(1) is an agency (as defined in section 551(1) of title 5, United States Code); and

(2) is not an advisory committee (as defined in section 3(2) of the Federal Advisory Committee Act (5 U.S.C. App.)).

(m) Authorization of Appropriations—There are authorized to be appropriated to carry out this section amounts as follows:

(1) For fiscal year 2008, $5,000,000.
(2) For fiscal year 2009, $6,650,000.
(3) For fiscal year 2010, $8,300,000.
(4) For fiscal year 2011, $10,000,000.
(5) For fiscal year 2012 and each subsequent fiscal year, such sums as may be necessary.

PRIVACY AND CIVIL LIBERTIES OFFICERS.

SEC. 1062.

(a) Designation and Functions—The Attorney General, the Secretary of Defense, the Secretary of State, the Secretary of the Treasury, the Secretary of Health and Human Services, the Secretary of Homeland Security, the Director of National Intelligence, the Director of the Central Intelligence Agency, and the head of any other department, agency, or element of the executive branch designated by the Privacy and Civil Liberties Oversight Board under section 1061 to be appropriate for coverage under this section shall designate not less than 1 senior officer to serve as the principal advisor to—

(1) assist the head of such department, agency, or element and other officials of such department, agency, or element in appropriately considering privacy and civil liberties concerns when such officials are proposing, developing, or implementing laws, regulations, policies, procedures, or guidelines related to efforts to protect the Nation against terrorism;

(2) periodically investigate and review department, agency, or element actions, policies, procedures, guidelines, and related laws and their implementation to ensure that such department, agency, or element is adequately considering privacy and civil liberties in its actions;

(3) ensure that such department, agency, or element has adequate procedures to receive, investigate, respond to, and redress complaints from individuals who allege such department, agency, or element has violated their privacy or civil liberties; and

(4) in providing advice on proposals to retain or enhance a particular governmental power the officer shall consider whether such department, agency, or element has established—

(A) that the need for the power is balanced with the need to protect privacy and civil liberties;

229

(B) that there is adequate supervision of the use by such department, agency, or element of the power to ensure protection of privacy and civil liberties; and

(C) that there are adequate guidelines and oversight to properly confine its use.

(b) Exception to Designation Authority—

(1) PRIVACY OFFICERS—In any department, agency, or element referred to in subsection (a) or designated by the Privacy and Civil Liberties Oversight Board, which has a statutorily created privacy officer, such officer shall perform the functions specified in subsection (a) with respect to privacy.

(2) CIVIL LIBERTIES OFFICERS—In any department, agency, or element referred to in subsection (a) or designated by the Board, which has a statutorily created civil liberties officer, such officer shall perform the functions specified in subsection (a) with respect to civil liberties.

(c) Supervision and Coordination—Each privacy officer or civil liberties officer described in subsection (a) or (b) shall—

(1) report directly to the head of the department, agency, or element concerned; and

(2) coordinate their activities with the Inspector General of such department, agency, or element to avoid duplication of effort.

(d) Agency Cooperation—The head of each department, agency, or element shall ensure that each privacy officer and civil liberties officer—

(1) has the information, material, and resources necessary to fulfill the functions of such officer;

(2) is advised of proposed policy changes;

(3) is consulted by decision makers; and

(4) is given access to material and personnel the officer determines to be necessary to carry out the functions of such officer.

(e) Reprisal for Making Complaint—No action constituting a reprisal, or threat of reprisal, for making a complaint or for disclosing information to a privacy officer or civil liberties officer described in subsection (a) or (b), or to the Privacy and Civil Liberties Oversight Board, that indicates a possible violation of privacy protections or civil liberties in the administration of the programs and operations of the Federal Government relating to efforts to protect the Nation from terrorism shall be taken by any Federal employee in a position to take such action, unless the complaint was made or the information was disclosed with the knowledge that it was false or with willful disregard for its truth or falsity.

(f) Periodic Reports—

    (1) IN GENERAL—The privacy officers and civil liberties officers of each department, agency, or element referred to or described in subsection (a) or (b) shall periodically, but not less than quarterly, submit a report on the activities of such officers—

        (A)(i) to the appropriate committees of Congress, including the Committee on the Judiciary of the Senate, the Committee on the Judiciary of the House of Representatives, the Committee on Homeland Security and Governmental Affairs of the Senate, the Committee on Oversight and Government Reform of the House of Representatives, the Select Committee on Intelligence of the Senate, and the Permanent Select Committee on Intelligence of the House of Representatives;

        (ii) to the head of such department, agency, or element; and

        (iii) to the Privacy and Civil Liberties Oversight Board; and

        (B) which shall be in unclassified form to the greatest extent possible, with a classified annex where necessary.

    (2) CONTENTS—Each report submitted under paragraph (1) shall include information on the discharge of each of the functions of the officer concerned, including—

        (A) information on the number and types of reviews undertaken;

        (B) the type of advice provided and the response given to such advice;

        (C) the number and nature of the complaints received by the department, agency, or element concerned for alleged violations; and

        (D) a summary of the disposition of such complaints, the reviews and inquiries conducted, and the impact of the activities of such officer.

(g) Informing the Public—Each privacy officer and civil liberties officer shall—

    (1) make the reports of such officer, including reports to Congress, available to the public to the greatest extent that is consistent with the protection of classified information and applicable law; and

231

(2) otherwise inform the public of the activities of such officer, as appropriate and in a manner consistent with the protection of classified information and applicable law.

(h) Savings Clause—Nothing in this section shall be construed to limit or otherwise supplant any other authorities or responsibilities provided by law to privacy officers or civil liberties officers.

Subtitle G—Conforming and Other Amendments

SEC. 1071. CONFORMING AMENDMENTS RELATING TO ROLES OF DIRECTOR OF NATIONAL INTELLIGENCE AND DIRECTOR OF THE CENTRAL INTELLIGENCE AGENCY.

(a) NATIONAL SECURITY ACT OF 1947—(1) The National Security Act of 1947 (50 U.S.C. 401 et seq.) is amended by striking `Director of Central Intelligence' each place it appears in the following provisions and inserting `Director of National Intelligence':

(A) Section 101(h)(2)(A) (50 U.S.C. 402(h)(2)(A)).

(B) Section 101(h)(5) (50 U.S.C. 402(h)(5)).

(C) Section 101(i)(2)(A) (50 U.S.C. 402(i)(2)(A)).

(D) Section 101(j) (50 U.S.C. 402(j)).

(E) Section 105(a) (50 U.S.C. 403-5(a)).

(F) Section 105(b)(6)(A) (50 U.S.C. 403-5(b)(6)(A)).

(G) Section 105B(a)(1) (50 U.S.C. 403-5b(a)(1)).

(H) Section 105B(b) (50 U.S.C. 403-5b(b)), the first place it appears.

(I) Section 110(b) (50 U.S.C. 404e(b)).

(J) Section 110(c) (50 U.S.C. 404e(c)).

(K) Section 112(a)(1) (50 U.S.C. 404g(a)(1)).

(L) Section 112(d)(1) (50 U.S.C. 404g(d)(1)).

(M) Section 113(b)(2)(A) (50 U.S.C. 404h(b)(2)(A)).

(N) Section 114(a)(1) (50 U.S.C. 404i(a)(1)).

(O) Section 114(b)(1) (50 U.S.C. 404i(b)(1)).

(P) Section 115(a)(1) (50 U.S.C. 404j(a)(1)).

(Q) Section 115(b) (50 U.S.C. 404j(b)).

(R) Section 115(c)(1)(B) (50 U.S.C. 404j(c)(1)(B)).

(S) Section 116(a) (50 U.S.C. 404k(a)).

(T) Section 117(a)(1) (50 U.S.C. 404l(a)(1)).

(U) Section 303(a) (50 U.S.C. 405(a)), both places it appears.

(V) Section 501(d) (50 U.S.C. 413(d)).

(W) Section 502(a) (50 U.S.C. 413a(a)).

(X) Section 502(c) (50 U.S.C. 413a(c)).
(Y) Section 503(b) (50 U.S.C. 413b(b)).
(Z) Section 504(a)(3)(C) (50 U.S.C. 414(a)(3)(C)).
(AA) Section 504(d)(2) (50 U.S.C. 414(d)(2)).
(BB) Section 506A(a)(1) (50 U.S.C. 415a-1(a)(1)).
(CC) Section 603(a) (50 U.S.C. 423(a)).
(DD) Section 702(a)(1) (50 U.S.C. 432(a)(1)).
(EE) Section 702(a)(6)(B)(viii) (50 U.S.C. 432(a)(6)(B)(viii)).
(FF) Section 702(b)(1) (50 U.S.C. 432(b)(1)), both places it appears.
(GG) Section 703(a)(1) (50 U.S.C. 432a(a)(1)).
(HH) Section 703(a)(6)(B)(viii) (50 U.S.C. 432a(a)(6)(B)(viii)).
(II) Section 703(b)(1) (50 U.S.C. 432a(b)(1)), both places it appears.
(JJ) Section 704(a)(1) (50 U.S.C. 432b(a)(1)).
(KK) Section 704(f)(2)(H) (50 U.S.C. 432b(f)(2)(H)).
(LL) Section 704(g)(1)) (50 U.S.C. 432b(g)(1)), both places it appears.
(MM) Section 1001(a) (50 U.S.C. 441g(a)).
(NN) Section 1102(a)(1) (50 U.S.C. 442a(a)(1)).
(OO) Section 1102(b)(1) (50 U.S.C. 442a(b)(1)).
(PP) Section 1102(c)(1) (50 U.S.C. 442a(c)(1)).
(QQ) Section 1102(d) (50 U.S.C. 442a(d)).
(2) That Act is further amended by striking `of Central Intelligence' each place it appears in the following provisions:
(A) Section 105(a)(2) (50 U.S.C. 403-5(a)(2)).
(B) Section 105B(a)(2) (50 U.S.C. 403-5b(a)(2)).
(C) Section 105B(b) (50 U.S.C. 403-5b(b)), the second place it appears.
(3) That Act is further amended by striking `Director' each place it appears in the following provisions and inserting `Director of National Intelligence':
(A) Section 114(c) (50 U.S.C. 404i(c)).
(B) Section 116(b) (50 U.S.C. 404k(b)).
(C) Section 1001(b) (50 U.S.C. 441g(b)).
(D) Section 1001(c) (50 U.S.C. 441g(c)), the first place it appears.
(E) Section 1001(d)(1)(B) (50 U.S.C. 441g(d)(1)(B)).
(F) Section 1001(e) (50 U.S.C. 441g(e)), the first place it appears.

(4) Section 114A of that Act (50 U.S.C. 404i-1) is amended by striking `Director of Central Intelligence' and inserting `Director of National Intelligence, the Director of the Central Intelligence Agency'

(5) Section 504(a)(2) of that Act (50 U.S.C. 414(a)(2)) is amended by striking `Director of Central Intelligence' and inserting `Director of the Central Intelligence Agency'.

(6) Section 701 of that Act (50 U.S.C. 431) is amended—

(A) in subsection (a), by striking `Operational files of the Central Intelligence Agency may be exempted by the Director of Central Intelligence' and inserting `The Director of the Central Intelligence Agency, with the coordination of the Director of National Intelligence, may exempt operational files of the Central Intelligence Agency'; and

(B) in subsection (g)(1), by striking `Director of Central Intelligence' and inserting `Director of the Central Intelligence Agency and the Director of National Intelligence'.

(7) The heading for section 114 of that Act (50 U.S.C. 404i) is amended to read as follows:

`ADDITIONAL ANNUAL REPORTS FROM THE DIRECTOR OF NATIONAL INTELLIGENCE'.

(b) CENTRAL INTELLIGENCE AGENCY ACT OF 1949—(1) The Central Intelligence Agency Act of 1949 (50 U.S.C. 403a et seq.) is amended by striking `Director of Central Intelligence' each place it appears in the following provisions and inserting `Director of National Intelligence':

(A) Section 6 (50 U.S.C. 403g).

(B) Section 17(f) (50 U.S.C. 403q(f)), both places it appears.

(2) That Act is further amended by striking `of Central Intelligence' in each of the following provisions:

(A) Section 2 (50 U.S.C. 403b).

(B) Section 16(c)(1)(B) (50 U.S.C. 403p(c)(1)(B)).

(C) Section 17(d)(1) (50 U.S.C. 403q(d)(1)).

(D) Section 20(c) (50 U.S.C. 403t(c)).

(3) That Act is further amended by striking `Director of Central Intelligence' each place it appears in the following provisions and inserting `Director of the Central Intelligence Agency':

(A) Section 14(b) (50 U.S.C. 403n(b)).

(B) Section 16(b)(2) (50 U.S.C. 403p(b)(2)).

(C) Section 16(b)(3) (50 U.S.C. 403p(b)(3)), both places it appears.

(D) Section 21(g)(1) (50 U.S.C. 403u(g)(1)).

(E) Section 21(g)(2) (50 U.S.C. 403u(g)(2)).

(c) CENTRAL INTELLIGENCE AGENCY RETIREMENT ACT—Section 101 of the Central Intelligence Agency Retirement Act (50 U.S.C. 2001) is amended by striking paragraph (2) and inserting the following new paragraph (2):

`(2) DIRECTOR—The term `Director' means the Director of the Central Intelligence Agency.'.

(d) CIA VOLUNTARY SEPARATION PAY ACT—Subsection (a)(1) of section 2 of the Central Intelligence Agency Voluntary Separation Pay Act (50 U.S.C. 2001 note) is amended to read as follows:

`(1) the term `Director' means the Director of the Central Intelligence Agency;'.

(e) FOREIGN INTELLIGENCE SURVEILLANCE ACT OF 1978—The Foreign Intelligence Surveillance Act of 1978 (50 U.S.C. 1801 et seq.) is amended by striking `Director of Central Intelligence' each place it appears and inserting `Director of National Intelligence'.

(f) CLASSIFIED INFORMATION PROCEDURES ACT—Section 9(a) of the Classified Information Procedures Act (5 U.S.C. App.) is amended by striking `Director of Central Intelligence' and inserting `Director of National Intelligence'.

(g) INTELLIGENCE AUTHORIZATION ACTS—

(1) PUBLIC LAW 103-359—Section 811(c)(6)(C) of the Counterintelligence and Security Enhancements Act of 1994 (title VIII of Public Law 103-359) is amended by striking `Director of Central Intelligence' and inserting `Director of National Intelligence'.

(2) PUBLIC LAW 107-306- (A) The Intelligence Authorization Act for Fiscal Year 2003 (Public Law 107-306) is amended by striking `Director of Central Intelligence, acting as the head of the intelligence community,' each place it appears in the following provisions and inserting `Director of National Intelligence':

(i) Section 313(a) (50 U.S.C. 404n(a)).

(ii) Section 343(a)(1) (50 U.S.C. 404n-2(a)(1))

(B) That Act is further amended by striking `Director of Central Intelligence' each place it appears in the following provisions and inserting `Director of National Intelligence':

(i) Section 904(e)(4) (50 U.S.C. 402c(e)(4)).

(ii) Section 904(e)(5) (50 U.S.C. 402c(e)(5)).

(iii) Section 904(h) (50 U.S.C. 402c(h)), each place it appears.

(iv) Section 904(m) (50 U.S.C. 402c(m)).

(C) Section 341 of that Act (50 U.S.C. 404n-1) is amended by striking `Director of Central Intelligence, acting as the head of the intelligence community, shall establish in the Central Intelligence Agency' and inserting `Director of National Intelligence shall establish within the Central Intelligence Agency'.

(D) Section 352(b) of that Act (50 U.S.C. 404-3 note) is amended by striking `Director' and inserting `Director of National Intelligence'.

(3) PUBLIC LAW 108-177- (A) The Intelligence Authorization Act for Fiscal Year 2004 (Public Law 108-177) is amended by striking `Director of Central Intelligence' each place it appears in the following provisions and inserting `Director of National Intelligence':

(i) Section 317(a) (50 U.S.C. 403-3 note).
(ii) Section 317(h)(1).
(iii) Section 318(a) (50 U.S.C. 441g note).
(iv) Section 319(b) (50 U.S.C. 403 note).
(v) Section 341(b) (28 U.S.C. 519 note).
(vi) Section 357(a) (50 U.S.C. 403 note).
(vii) Section 504(a) (117 Stat. 2634), both places it appears.

(B) Section 319(f)(2) of that Act (50 U.S.C. 403 note) is amended by striking `Director' the first place it appears and inserting `Director of National Intelligence'.

(C) Section 404 of that Act (18 U.S.C. 4124 note) is amended by striking `Director of Central Intelligence' and inserting `Director of the Central Intelligence Agency'.

OTHER CONFORMING AMENDMENTS

SEC. 1072.

(a) NATIONAL SECURITY ACT OF 1947- (1) Section 101(j) of the National Security Act of 1947 (50 U.S.C. 402(j)) is amended by striking `Deputy Director of Central Intelligence' and inserting `Principal Deputy Director of National Intelligence'.

(2) Section 105(a) of that Act (50 U.S.C. 403-5(a)) is amended by striking `The Secretary' in the matter preceding paragraph (1) and inserting `Consistent with sections 102 and 102A, the Secretary'.

(3) Section 105(b) of that Act (50 U.S.C. 403-5(b)) is amended by striking `103 and 104' in the matter preceding paragraph (1) and inserting `102 and 102A'.

(4) Section 112(d)(1) of that Act (50 U.S.C. 404g(d)(1)) is amended by striking `section 103(c)(6) of this Act' and inserting `section 102A(i) of this Act'.

(5) Section 116(b) of that Act (50 U.S.C. 404k(b)) is amended by striking `to the Deputy Director of Central Intelligence, or with respect to employees of the Central Intelligence Agency, the Director may delegate such authority to the Deputy Director for Operations' and inserting `to the Principal Deputy Director of National Intelligence, or with respect to employees of the Central Intelligence Agency, to the Director of the Central Intelligence Agency'.

(6) Section 506A(b)(1) of that Act (50 U.S.C. 415a-1(b)(1)) is amended by striking `Office of the Deputy Director of Central Intelligence' and inserting `Office of the Director of National Intelligence'.

(7) Section 701(c)(3) of that Act (50 U.S.C. 431(c)(3)) is amended by striking `Office of the Director of Central Intelligence' and inserting `Office of the Director of National Intelligence'.

(8) Section 1001(b) of that Act (50 U.S.C. 441g(b)) is amended by striking `Assistant Director of Central Intelligence for Administration' and inserting `Office of the Director of National Intelligence'.

(b) CENTRAL INTELLIGENCE AGENCY ACT OF 1949—Section 6 of the Central Intelligence Agency Act of 1949 (50 U.S.C. 403g) is amended by striking `section 103(c)(7) of the National Security Act of 1947 (50 U.S.C. 403-3(c)(7))' and inserting `section 102A(i) of the National Security Act of 1947'.

(c) CENTRAL INTELLIGENCE AGENCY RETIREMENT ACT— Section 201(c) of the Central Intelligence Agency Retirement Act (50 U.S.C. 2011(c)) is amended by striking `paragraph (6) of section 103(c) of the National Security Act of 1947 (50 U.S.C. 403-3(c)) that the Director of Central Intelligence' and inserting `section 102A(i) of the National Security Act of 1947 (50 U.S.C. 403-3(c)(1)) that the Director of National Intelligence'.

(d) INTELLIGENCE AUTHORIZATION ACTS—

(1) PUBLIC LAW 107-306—(A) Section 343(c) of the Intelligence Authorization Act for Fiscal Year 2003 (Public Law 107-306; 50 U.S.C. 404n-2(c)) is amended by striking `section 103(c)(6) of the National Security Act of 1947 (50 U.S.C. 403-3((c)(6))' and inserting `section 102A(i) of the National Security Act of 1947 (50 U.S.C. 403-3(c)(1))'.

(B)(i) Section 902 of that Act (also known as the Counterintelligence Enhancements Act of 2002) (50 U.S.C. 402b) is amended by striking `President' each place it appears and inserting `Director of National Intelligence'.

(ii) Section 902(a)(2) of that Act is amended by striking `Director of Central Intelligence' and inserting `Director of the Central Intelligence Agency'.

(C) Section 904 of that Act (50 U.S.C. 402c) is amended—

 (i) in subsection (c), by striking `Office of the Director of Central Intelligence' and inserting `Office of the Director of National Intelligence'; and

 (ii) in subsection (l), by striking `Office of the Director of Central Intelligence' and inserting `Office of the Director of National Intelligence'.

(2) PUBLIC LAW 108-177—(A) Section 317 of the Intelligence Authorization Act for Fiscal Year 2004 (Public Law 108-177; 50 U.S.C. 403-3 note) is amended—

 (i) in subsection (g), by striking `Assistant Director of Central Intelligence for Analysis and Production' and inserting `Deputy Director of National Intelligence'; and

 (ii) in subsection (h)(2)(C), by striking `Assistant Director' and inserting `Deputy Director of National Intelligence'.

(B) Section 318(e) of that Act (50 U.S.C. 441g note) is amended by striking `Assistant Director of Central Intelligence for Analysis and Production' and inserting `Deputy Director of National Intelligence'.

ELEMENTS OF INTELLIGENCE COMMUNITY UNDER NATIONAL SECURITY ACT OF 1947.

SEC. 1073.

Paragraph (4) of section 3 of the National Security Act of 1947 (50 U.S.C. 401a) is amended to read as follows:

 `(4) The term `intelligence community' includes the following:

  `(A) The Office of the Director of National Intelligence.

  `(B) The Central Intelligence Agency.

  `(C) The National Security Agency.

  `(D) The Defense Intelligence Agency.

  `(E) The National Geospatial-Intelligence Agency.

`(F) The National Reconnaissance Office.

`(G) Other offices within the Department of Defense for the collection of specialized national intelligence through reconnaissance programs.

`(H) The intelligence elements of the Army, the Navy, the Air Force, the Marine Corps, the Federal Bureau of Investigation, and the Department of Energy.

`(I) The Bureau of Intelligence and Research of the Department of State.

`(J) The Office of Intelligence and Analysis of the Department of the Treasury.

`(K) The elements of the Department of Homeland Security concerned with the analysis of intelligence information, including the Office of Intelligence of the Coast Guard.

`(L) Such other elements of any other department or agency as may be designated by the President, or designated jointly by the Director of National Intelligence and the head of the department or agency concerned, as an element of the intelligence community.'.

REDESIGNATION OF NATIONAL FOREIGN INTELLIGENCE PROGRAM AS NATIONAL INTELLIGENCE PROGRAM.

SEC. 1074.

(a) REDESIGNATION—Paragraph (6) of section 3 of the National Security Act of 1947 (50 U.S.C. 401a) is amended by striking `Foreign'.

(b) CONFORMING AMENDMENTS—(1)(A) Section 506 of the National Security Act of 1947 (50 U.S.C. 415a) is amended—

(i) in subsection (a), by striking `National Foreign Intelligence Program' and inserting `National Intelligence Program'; and

(ii) in the section heading, by striking `FOREIGN'.

(B) Section 105 of that Act (50 U.S.C. 403-5) is amended—

(i) in paragraphs (2) and (3) of subsection (a), by striking `National Foreign Intelligence Program' and inserting `National Intelligence Program'; and

(ii) in the section heading, by striking `FOREIGN'.

(2) Section 17(f) of the Central Intelligence Agency Act of 1949 (50 U.S.C. 403q(f)) is amended by striking `National Foreign Intelligence Program' and inserting `National Intelligence Program'.

REPEAL OF SUPERSEDED AUTHORITY.

SEC. 1075.

Section 111 of the National Security Act of 1947 (50 U.S.C. 404f) is repealed.

CLERICAL AMENDMENTS TO NATIONAL SECURITY ACT OF 1947.

SEC. 1076.

The table of contents in the first section of the National Security Act of 1947 is amended—
(1) by striking the items relating to sections 102 through 105 and inserting the following new items:
`Sec. 101A. Joint Intelligence Community Council.
`Sec. 102. Director of National Intelligence.
`Sec. 102A. Responsibilities and authorities of the Director of National Intelligence.
`Sec. 103. Office of the Director of National Intelligence.
`Sec. 103A. Deputy Directors of National Intelligence.
`Sec. 103B. National Intelligence Council.
`Sec. 103C. General Counsel.
`Sec. 103D. Civil Liberties Protection Officer.
`Sec. 103E. Director of Science and Technology.
`Sec. 103F. National Counterintelligence Executive.
`Sec. 104. Central Intelligence Agency.
`Sec. 104A. Director of the Central Intelligence Agency.
`Sec. 105. Responsibilities of the Secretary of Defense pertaining to the National Intelligence Program.';
(2) by striking the item relating to section 111;
(3) by striking the item relating to section 114 and inserting the following new item:
`Sec. 114. Additional annual reports from the Director of National Intelligence.';
(4) by inserting after the item relating to section 118 the following new items:
`Sec. 119. National Counterterrorism Center.
`Sec. 119A. National Counter Proliferation Center.
`Sec. 119B. National intelligence centers.

(5) by striking the item relating to section 506 and inserting the following new item:

`Sec. 506. Specificity of National Intelligence Program budget amounts for counterterrorism, counterproliferation, counternarcotics, and counterintelligence.';

and

(6) by inserting after the item relating to section 1001 the following new items:

`Sec. 1002. Framework for cross-disciplinary education and training.

`Sec. 1003. Intelligence Community Scholarship Program.'.

CONFORMING AMENDMENTS RELATING TO PROHIBITING DUAL SERVICE OF THE DIRECTOR OF THE CENTRAL INTELLIGENCE AGENCY.

SEC. 1077.

Section 1 of the Central Intelligence Agency Act of 1949 (50 U.S.C. 403a) is amended—

(1) by redesignating paragraphs (a), (b), and (c) as paragraphs (1), (2), and (3), respectively; and

(2) by striking paragraph (2), as so redesignated, and inserting the following new paragraph (2):

`(2) `Director' means the Director of the Central Intelligence Agency; and'.

AUTHORITY TO ESTABLISH INSPECTOR GENERAL FOR THE OFFICE OF THE DIRECTOR OF NATIONAL INTELLIGENCE.

SEC. 1078.

The Inspector General Act of 1978 (5 U.S.C. App.) is amended by inserting after section 8J the following new section:

`AUTHORITY TO ESTABLISH INSPECTOR GENERAL OF THE OFFICE OF THE DIRECTOR OF NATIONAL INTELLIGENCE

SEC. 8K. If the Director of National Intelligence determines that an Office of Inspector General would be beneficial to improving the operations and effectiveness of the Office of the Director of National

Intelligence, the Director of National Intelligence is authorized to establish, with any of the duties, responsibilities, and authorities set forth in this Act, an Office of Inspector General.'.

ETHICS MATTERS.

SEC. 1079.

(a) POLITICAL SERVICE OF PERSONNEL—Section 7323(b)(2)(B)(i) of title 5, United States Code, is amended—
>(1) in subclause (XII), by striking `or' at the end; and
>(2) by inserting after subclause (XIII) the following new subclause:
>>`(XIV) the Office of the Director of National Intelligence; or'.

(b) DELETION OF INFORMATION ABOUT FOREIGN GIFTS— Section 7342(f)(4) of title 5, United States Code, is amended—
>(1) by inserting `(A)' after `(4)';
>(2) in subparagraph (A), as so designated, by striking `the Director of Central Intelligence' and inserting `the Director of the Central Intelligence Agency'; and
>(3) by adding at the end the following new subparagraph:

`(B) In transmitting such listings for the Office of the Director of National Intelligence, the Director of National Intelligence may delete the information described in subparagraphs (A) and (C) of paragraphs (2) and (3) if the Director certifies in writing to the Secretary of State that the publication of such information could adversely affect United States intelligence sources.'.

(c) EXEMPTION FROM FINANCIAL DISCLOSURES—Section 105(a)(1) of the Ethics in Government Act (5 U.S.C. App.) is amended by inserting `the Office of the Director of National Intelligence,' before `the Central Intelligence Agency'.

CONSTRUCTION OF AUTHORITY OF DIRECTOR OF NATIONAL INTELLIGENCE TO ACQUIRE AND MANAGE PROPERTY AND SERVICES.

SEC. 1080.

Section 113(e) of title 40, United States Code, is amended—
>(1) in paragraph (18), by striking `or' at the end;

(2) in paragraph (19), by striking the period at the end and inserting `; or'; and
(3) by adding at the end the following new paragraph:
`(20) the Office of the Director of National Intelligence.'.

GENERAL REFERENCES.

SEC. 1081.

(a) DIRECTOR OF CENTRAL INTELLIGENCE AS HEAD OF INTELLIGENCE COMMUNITY—Any reference to the Director of Central Intelligence or the Director of the Central Intelligence Agency in the Director's capacity as the head of the intelligence community in any law, regulation, document, paper, or other record of the United States shall be deemed to be a reference to the Director of National Intelligence.
(b) DIRECTOR OF CENTRAL INTELLIGENCE AS HEAD OF CIA—Any reference to the Director of Central Intelligence or the Director of the Central Intelligence Agency in the Director's capacity as the head of the Central Intelligence Agency in any law, regulation, document, paper, or other record of the United States shall be deemed to be a reference to the Director of the Central Intelligence Agency.
(c) COMMUNITY MANAGEMENT STAFF—Any reference to the Community Management Staff in any law, regulation, document, paper, or other record of the United States shall be deemed to be a reference to the staff of the Office of the Director of National Intelligence.

Subtitle H—Transfer, Termination, Transition, and Other Provisions

TRANSFER OF COMMUNITY MANAGEMENT STAFF.

SEC. 1091.

(a) TRANSFER—There shall be transferred to the Office of the Director of National Intelligence such staff of the Community Management Staff as of the date of the enactment of this Act as the Director of National Intelligence determines to be appropriate, including all functions and activities discharged by the Community Management Staff as of that date.
(b) ADMINISTRATION—The Director of National Intelligence shall administer the Community Management Staff after the date of the enactment of this Act as a component of the Office of the Director of

National Intelligence under section 103 of the National Security Act of 1947, as amended by section 1011(a) of this Act.

TRANSFER OF TERRORIST THREAT INTEGRATION CENTER.

SEC. 1092.

(a) TRANSFER—There shall be transferred to the National Counterterrorism Center the Terrorist Threat Integration Center (TTIC) or its successor entity, including all functions and activities discharged by the Terrorist Threat Integration Center or its successor entity as of the date of the enactment of this Act.

(b) ADMINISTRATION—The Director of the National Counterterrorism Center shall administer the Terrorist Threat Integration Center after the date of the enactment of this Act as a component of the Directorate of Intelligence of the National Counterterrorism Center under section 119(i) of the National Security Act of 1947, as added by section 1021(a) of this Act.

TERMINATION OF POSITIONS OF ASSISTANT DIRECTORS OF CENTRAL INTELLIGENCE.

SEC. 1093.

(a) TERMINATION—The positions referred to in subsection (b) are hereby abolished.

(b) COVERED POSITIONS—The positions referred to in this subsection are as follows:

(1) The Assistant Director of Central Intelligence for Collection.

(2) The Assistant Director of Central Intelligence for Analysis and Production.

(3) The Assistant Director of Central Intelligence for Administration.

IMPLEMENTATION PLAN.

SEC. 1094.

The President shall transmit to Congress a plan for the implementation of this title and the amendments made by this title. The plan shall address, at a minimum, the following:

(1) The transfer of personnel, assets, and obligations to the Director of National Intelligence pursuant to this title.

(2) Any consolidation, reorganization, or streamlining of activities transferred to the Director of National Intelligence pursuant to this title.

(3) The establishment of offices within the Office of the Director of National Intelligence to implement the duties and responsibilities of the Director of National Intelligence as described in this title.

(4) Specification of any proposed disposition of property, facilities, contracts, records, and other assets and obligations to be transferred to the Director of National Intelligence.

(5) Recommendations for additional legislative or administrative action as the President considers appropriate.

DIRECTOR OF NATIONAL INTELLIGENCE REPORT ON IMPLEMENTATION OF INTELLIGENCE COMMUNITY REFORM.

SEC. 1095.

(a) REPORT—Not later than one year after the effective date of this Act, the Director of National Intelligence shall submit to the congressional intelligence committees a report on the progress made in the implementation of this title, including the amendments made by this title. The report shall include a comprehensive description of the progress made, and may include such recommendations for additional legislative or administrative action as the Director considers appropriate.

(b) CONGRESSIONAL INTELLIGENCE COMMITTEES DEFINED— In this section, the term 'congressional intelligence committees' means—

(1) the Select Committee on Intelligence of the Senate; and

(2) the Permanent Select Committee on Intelligence of the House of Representatives.

TRANSITIONAL AUTHORITIES.

SEC. 1096.

(a) IN GENERAL—Upon the request of the Director of National Intelligence, the head of any executive agency may, on a reimbursable basis, provide services or detail personnel to the Director of National Intelligence.

(b) TRANSFER OF PERSONNEL—In addition to any other authorities available under law for such purposes, in the fiscal years 2005 and 2006, the Director of National Intelligence—

(1) is authorized within the Office of the Director of National Intelligence the total of 500 new positions; and

(2) with the approval of the Director of the Office of Management and Budget, may detail not more than 150 personnel funded within the National Intelligence Program to the Office of the Director of National Intelligence for a period of not more than 2 years.

EFFECTIVE DATES.

SEC. 1097.

(a) IN GENERAL—Except as otherwise expressly provided in this Act, this title and the amendments made by this title shall take effect not later than six months after the date of the enactment of this Act.

(b) SPECIFIC EFFECTIVE DATES—(1)(A) Not later than 60 days after the date of the appointment of the first Director of National Intelligence, the Director of National Intelligence shall first appoint individuals to positions within the Office of the Director of National Intelligence.

(B) Subparagraph (A) shall not apply with respect to the Principal Deputy Director of National Intelligence.

(2) Not later than 180 days after the effective date of this Act, the President shall transmit to Congress the implementation plan required by section 1094.

(3) Not later than one year after the date of the enactment of this Act, the Director of National Intelligence shall prescribe regulations, policies, procedures, standards, and guidelines required under section 102A of the National Security Act of 1947, as amended by section 1011(a) of this Act.

Subtitle I—Other Matters

STUDY OF PROMOTION AND PROFESSIONAL MILITARY EDUCATION SCHOOL SELECTION RATES FOR MILITARY INTELLIGENCE OFFICERS.

SEC. 1101.

(a) STUDY—The Secretary of Defense shall conduct a study of the promotion selection rates, and the selection rates for attendance at professional military education schools, of intelligence officers of the Armed Forces, particularly in comparison to the rates for other officers of the same Armed Force who are in the same grade and competitive category.

(b) REPORT—The Secretary shall submit to the Committees on Armed Services of the Senate and House of Representatives a report providing the Secretary's findings resulting from the study under subsection (a) and the Secretary's recommendations (if any) for such changes in law as the Secretary considers needed to ensure that intelligence officers, as a group, are selected for promotion, and for attendance at professional military education schools, at rates not less than the rates for all line (or the equivalent) officers of the same Armed Force (both in the zone and below the zone) in the same grade. The report shall be submitted not later than April 1, 2005.

EXTENSION AND IMPROVEMENT OF AUTHORITIES OF PUBLIC INTEREST DECLASSIFICATION BOARD.

SEC. 1102.

(a) DIRECTION—Section 703(a) of the Public Interest Declassification Act of 2000 (title VII of Public Law 106-567; 114 Stat. 2856; 50 U.S.C. 435 note) is amended—
    (1) by inserting `(1)' after `ESTABLISHMENT- '; and
    (2) by adding at the end the following new paragraph:
`(2) The Board shall report directly to the President or, upon designation by the President, the Vice President, the Attorney General, or other designee of the President. The other designee of the President under this paragraph may not be an agency head or official authorized to classify information under Executive Order 12958, or any successor order.'.
(b) PURPOSES—Section 703(b) of that Act (114 Stat. 2856) is amended by adding at the end the following new paragraph:
    `(5) To review and make recommendations to the President in a timely manner with respect to any congressional request, made by the committee of jurisdiction, to declassify certain records or to reconsider a declination to declassify specific records.'.
(c) RECOMMENDATIONS ON SPECIAL SEARCHES—Section 704(c)(2)(A) of that Act (114 Stat. 2860) is amended by inserting before the period the following: `, and also including specific requests for the

declassification of certain records or for the reconsideration of declinations to declassify specific records'.

(d) DECLASSIFICATION REVIEWS—Section 704 of that Act (114 Stat. 2859) is further amended by adding at the end the following new subsection:

`(e) DECLASSIFICATION REVIEWS—If requested by the President, the Board shall review in a timely manner certain records or declinations to declassify specific records, the declassification of which has been the subject of specific congressional request described in section 703(b)(5).'.

(e) NOTIFICATION OF REVIEW—Section 706 of that Act (114 Stat. 2861) is amended by adding at the end the following new subsection:

`(f) NOTIFICATION OF REVIEW—In response to a specific congressional request for declassification review described in section 703(b)(5), the Board shall advise the originators of the request in a timely manner whether the Board intends to conduct such review.'.

(f) EXTENSION—Section 710(b) of that Act (114 Stat. 2864) is amended by striking `4 years' and inserting `8 years'.

SEVERABILITY.

SEC. 1103.

If any provision of this Act, or an amendment made by this Act, or the application of such provision to any person or circumstance is held invalid, the remainder of this Act, or the application of such provision to persons or circumstances other those to which such provision is held invalid shall not be affected thereby.

TITLE III—SECURITY CLEARANCES

SECURITY CLEARANCES.

SEC. 3001.

(a) DEFINITIONS—In this section:
    (1) The term `agency' means—
        (A) an executive agency (as that term is defined in section 105 of title 5, United States Code);
        (B) a military department (as that term is defined in section 102 of title 5, United States Code); and

(C) an element of the intelligence community.

(2) The term `authorized investigative agency' means an agency designated by the head of the agency selected pursuant to subsection (b) to conduct a counterintelligence investigation or investigation of persons who are proposed for access to classified information to ascertain whether such persons satisfy the criteria for obtaining and retaining access to such information.

(3) The term `authorized adjudicative agency' means an agency authorized by law, regulation, or direction of the Director of National Intelligence to determine eligibility for access to classified information in accordance with Executive Order 12968.

(4) The term `highly sensitive program' means—

    (A) a government program designated as a Special Access Program (as that term is defined in section 4.1(h) of Executive Order 12958 or any successor Executive order); or

    (B) a government program that applies restrictions required for—

        (i) restricted data (as that term is defined in section 11 y. of the Atomic Energy Act of 1954 (42 U.S.C. 2014(y)); or

        (ii) other information commonly referred to as `sensitive compartmented information'.

(5) The term `current investigation file' means, with respect to a security clearance, a file on an investigation or adjudication that has been conducted during—

    (A) the 5-year period beginning on the date the security clearance was granted, in the case of a Top Secret Clearance, or the date access was granted to a highly sensitive program;

    (B) the 10-year period beginning on the date the security clearance was granted in the case of a Secret Clearance; and

    (C) the 15-year period beginning on the date the security clearance was granted in the case of a Confidential Clearance.

(6) The term `personnel security investigation' means any investigation required for the purpose of determining the eligibility of any military, civilian, or government contractor personnel to access classified information.

(7) The term `periodic reinvestigations' means investigations conducted for the purpose of updating a previously completed background investigation—

> (A) every 5 years in the case of a top secret clearance or access to a highly sensitive program;
> (B) every 10 years in the case of a secret clearance; or
> (C) every 15 years in the case of a Confidential Clearance.

(8) The term `appropriate committees of Congress' means—

> (A) the Permanent Select Committee on Intelligence and the Committees on Armed Services, Homeland Security, Government Reform, and the Judiciary of the House of Representatives; and
> (B) the Select Committee on Intelligence and the Committees on Armed Services, Homeland Security and Governmental Affairs, and the Judiciary of the Senate.

(b) SELECTION OF ENTITY—Not later than 90 days after the date of the enactment of this Act, the President shall select a single department, agency, or element of the executive branch to be responsible for—

(1) directing day-to-day oversight of investigations and adjudications for personnel security clearances, including for highly sensitive programs, throughout the United States Government;

(2) developing and implementing uniform and consistent policies and procedures to ensure the effective, efficient, and timely completion of security clearances and determinations for access to highly sensitive programs, including the standardization of security questionnaires, financial disclosure requirements for security clearance applicants, and polygraph policies and procedures;

(3) serving as the final authority to designate an authorized investigative agency or authorized adjudicative agency;

(4) ensuring reciprocal recognition of access to classified information among the agencies of the United States Government, including acting as the final authority to arbitrate and resolve disputes involving the reciprocity of security clearances and access to highly sensitive programs pursuant to subsection (d);

(5) ensuring, to the maximum extent practicable, that sufficient resources are available in each agency to achieve clearance and investigative program goals; and

(6) reviewing and coordinating the development of tools and techniques for enhancing the conduct of investigations and granting of clearances.

(c) PERFORMANCE OF SECURITY CLEARANCE INVESTIGATIONS—(1) Notwithstanding any other provision of law, not later than 180 days after the date of the enactment of this Act, the President shall, in consultation with the head of the entity selected pursuant to subsection (b), select a single agency of the executive branch to conduct, to the maximum extent practicable, security clearance investigations of employees and contractor personnel of the United States Government who require access to classified information and to provide and maintain all security clearances of such employees and contractor personnel. The head of the entity selected pursuant to subsection (b) may designate other agencies to conduct such investigations if the head of the entity selected pursuant to subsection (b) considers it appropriate for national security and efficiency purposes.

(2) The agency selected under paragraph (1) shall—

(A) take all necessary actions to carry out the requirements of this section, including entering into a memorandum of understanding with any agency carrying out responsibilities relating to security clearances or security clearance investigations before the date of the enactment of this Act;

(B) as soon as practicable, integrate reporting of security clearance applications, security clearance investigations, and determinations of eligibility for security clearances, with the database required by subsection (e); and

(C) ensure that security clearance investigations are conducted in accordance with uniform standards and requirements established under subsection (b), including uniform security questionnaires and financial disclosure requirements.

(d) RECIPROCITY OF SECURITY CLEARANCE AND ACCESS DETERMINATIONS—(1) All security clearance background investigations and determinations completed by an authorized investigative agency or authorized adjudicative agency shall be accepted by all agencies.

(2) All security clearance background investigations initiated by an authorized investigative agency shall be transferable to any other authorized investigative agency.

(3)(A) An authorized investigative agency or authorized adjudicative agency may not establish additional investigative or adjudicative requirements (other than requirements for the conduct of a polygraph examination) that exceed requirements specified in Executive Orders

251

establishing security requirements for access to classified information without the approval of the head of the entity selected pursuant to subsection (b).

(B) Notwithstanding subparagraph (A), the head of the entity selected pursuant to subsection (b) may establish such additional requirements as the head of such entity considers necessary for national security purposes.

(4) An authorized investigative agency or authorized adjudicative agency may not conduct an investigation for purposes of determining whether to grant a security clearance to an individual where a current investigation or clearance of equal level already exists or has been granted by another authorized adjudicative agency.

(5) The head of the entity selected pursuant to subsection (b) may disallow the reciprocal recognition of an individual security clearance by an agency under this section on a case-by-case basis if the head of the entity selected pursuant to subsection (b) determines that such action is necessary for national security purposes.

(6) The head of the entity selected pursuant to subsection (b) shall establish a review procedure by which agencies can seek review of actions required under this section.

(e) DATABASE ON SECURITY CLEARANCES—(1) Not later than 12 months after the date of the enactment of this Act, the Director of the Office of Personnel Management shall, in cooperation with the heads of the entities selected pursuant to subsections (b) and (c), establish and commence operating and maintaining an integrated, secure, database into which appropriate data relevant to the granting, denial, or revocation of a security clearance or access pertaining to military, civilian, or government contractor personnel shall be entered from all authorized investigative and adjudicative agencies.

(2) The database under this subsection shall function to integrate information from existing Federal clearance tracking systems from other authorized investigative and adjudicative agencies into a single consolidated database.

(3) Each authorized investigative or adjudicative agency shall check the database under this subsection to determine whether an individual the agency has identified as requiring a security clearance has already been granted or denied a security clearance, or has had a security clearance revoked, by any other authorized investigative or adjudicative agency.

(4) The head of the entity selected pursuant to subsection (b) shall evaluate the extent to which an agency is submitting information to, and requesting information from, the database under this subsection as part of

a determination of whether to certify the agency as an authorized investigative agency or authorized adjudicative agency.

(5) The head of the entity selected pursuant to subsection (b) may authorize an agency to withhold information about certain individuals from the database under this subsection if the head of the entity considers it necessary for national security purposes.

(f) EVALUATION OF USE OF AVAILABLE TECHNOLOGY IN CLEARANCE INVESTIGATIONS AND ADJUDICATIONS—(1) The head of the entity selected pursuant to subsection (b) shall evaluate the use of available information technology and databases to expedite investigative and adjudicative processes for all and to verify standard information submitted as part of an application for a security clearance.

(2) The evaluation shall assess the application of the technologies described in paragraph (1) for—

>(A) granting interim clearances to applicants at the secret, top secret, and special access program levels before the completion of the appropriate full investigation;

>(B) expediting investigations and adjudications of security clearances, including verification of information submitted by the applicant;

>(C) ongoing verification of suitability of personnel with security clearances in effect for continued access to classified information;

>(D) use of such technologies to augment periodic reinvestigations;

>(E) assessing the impact of the use of such technologies on the rights of applicants to verify, correct, or challenge information obtained through such technologies; and

>(F) such other purposes as the head of the entity selected pursuant to subsection (b) considers appropriate.

(3) An individual subject to verification utilizing the technology described in paragraph (1) shall be notified of such verification, shall provide consent to such use, and shall have access to data being verified in order to correct errors or challenge information the individual believes is incorrect.

(4) Not later than one year after the date of the enactment of this Act, the head of the entity selected pursuant to subsection (b) shall submit to the President and the appropriate committees of Congress a report on the results of the evaluation, including recommendations on the use of technologies described in paragraph (1).

(g) REDUCTION IN LENGTH OF PERSONNEL SECURITY CLEARANCE PROCESS—(1) The head of the entity selected pursuant to subsection (b) shall, within 90 days of selection under that subsection, develop, in consultation with the appropriate committees of Congress and each authorized adjudicative agency, a plan to reduce the length of the personnel security clearance process.

(2)(A) To the extent practical the plan under paragraph (1) shall require that each authorized adjudicative agency make a determination on at least 90 percent of all applications for a personnel security clearance within an average of 60 days after the date of receipt of the completed application for a security clearance by an authorized investigative agency. Such 60-day average period shall include—

    (i) a period of not longer than 40 days to complete the investigative phase of the clearance review; and

    (ii) a period of not longer than 20 days to complete the adjudicative phase of the clearance review.

(B) Determinations on clearances not made within 60 days shall be made without delay.

(3)(A) The plan under paragraph (1) shall take effect 5 years after the date of the enactment of this Act.

(B) During the period beginning on a date not later than 2 years after the date after the enactment of this Act and ending on the date on which the plan under paragraph (1) takes effect, each authorized adjudicative agency shall make a determination on at least 80 percent of all applications for a personnel security clearance pursuant to this section within an average of 120 days after the date of receipt of the application for a security clearance by an authorized investigative agency. Such 120-day average period shall include—

    (i) a period of not longer than 90 days to complete the investigative phase of the clearance review; and

    (ii) a period of not longer than 30 days to complete the adjudicative phase of the clearance review.

(h) REPORTS—(1) Not later than February 15, 2006, and annually thereafter through 2011, the head of the entity selected pursuant to subsection (b) shall submit to the appropriate committees of Congress a report on the progress made during the preceding year toward meeting the requirements of this section.

(2) Each report shall include, for the period covered by such report—

    (A) the periods of time required by the authorized investigative agencies and authorized adjudicative agencies for conducting investigations, adjudicating cases, and granting clearances, from date of submission to ultimate disposition and notification to the subject and the subject's employer;

(B) a discussion of any impediments to the smooth and timely functioning of the requirements of this section; and

(C) such other information or recommendations as the head of the entity selected pursuant to subsection (b) considers appropriate.

(i) AUTHORIZATION OF APPROPRIATIONS—There is authorized to be appropriated such sums as may be necessary for fiscal year 2005 and each fiscal year thereafter for the implementation, maintenance, and operation of the database required by subsection (e).

CENTRAL INTELLIGENCE AGENCY ACT OF 1949

(Public Law 110 of June 20, 1949; 63 STAT. 208)

AN ACT To provide for the administration of the Central Intelligence Agency, established pursuant to section 102, National Security Act of 1947, and for other purposes.

Be it enacted by the Senate and House of Representatives of the United States of America in Congress assembled,

DEFINITIONS

SECTION 1. [50 U.S.C. §403a]
That when used in this Act, the term—
> (1) "Agency" means the Central Intelligence Agency;
> (2) "Director" means the Director of the Central Intelligence Agency; and
> (3) "Government agency" means any executive department, commission, council, independent establishment, corporation wholly or partly owned by the United States which is an instrumentality of the United States, board, bureau, division, service, office, officer, authority, administration, or other establishment, in the executive branch of the Government.

SEAL OF OFFICE

SEC. 2. [50 U.S.C. §403b]
The Director shall cause a seal of office to be made for the Central Intelligence Agency, of such design as the President shall approve, and judicial notice shall be taken thereof.

PROCUREMENT AUTHORITIES

SEC. 3. [50 U.S.C. §403c]
(a) PURCHASES AND CONTRACTS FOR SUPPLIES AND SERVICES.—In the performance of its functions the Central Intelligence Agency is authorized to exercise the authorities contained in sections 2304(a)(1) to (6), (10), (12), (15), (17), and sections 2305(a) to (c), 2306, 2307, 2308, 2309, 2312, and 2313 of title 10.
(b) "AGENCY HEAD" DEFINED.—In the exercise of the authorities granted in subsection (a) of this section, the term "Agency head" shall mean the Director, the Deputy Director, or the Executive of the Agency.

(c) CLASSES OF PURCHASES AND CONTRACTS; FINALITY OF DECISION; POWERS DELEGABLE.—The determinations and decisions provided in subsection (a) of this section to be made by the Agency head may be made with respect to individual purchases and contracts or with respect to classes of purchases or contracts, and shall be final. Except as provided in subsection (d) of this section, the Agency head is authorized to delegate his powers provided in this section, including the making of such determinations and decisions, in his discretion and subject to his direction, to any other officer or officers or officials of the Agency.

(d) POWERS NOT DELEGABLE; WRITTEN FINDINGS.—The power of the Agency head to make the determinations or decisions specified in paragraphs (12) and (15) of section 2304(a) and section 2307(a) of title 10 shall not be delegable. Each determination or decision required by paragraphs (12) and (15) of section 2304(a), by sections 2306 and 2313, or by section 2307(a) of title 10, shall be based upon written findings made by the official making such determinations, which findings shall be final and shall be available within the Agency for a period of at least six years following the date of the determination.

TRAVEL, ALLOWANCES, AND RELATED EXPENSES

SEC. 4. [50 U.S.C. §403e]
CENTRAL INTELLIGENCE AGENCY PERSONNEL; ALLOWANCES AND BENEFITS.—
(a) TRAVEL, ALLOWANCES, AND RELATED EXPENSES FOR OFFICERS AND EMPLOYEES ASSIGNED TO DUTY STATIONS OUTSIDE UNITED STATES.—Under such regulations as the Director may prescribe, the Agency, with respect to its officers and employees assigned to duty stations outside the several States of the United States of America, excluding Alaska and Hawaii, but including the District of Columbia, shall—

(1)(A) pay the travel expenses of officers and employees of the Agency, including expenses incurred while traveling pursuant to authorized home leave;

(B) pay the travel expenses of members of the family of an officer or employee of the Agency when proceeding to or returning from his post of duty; accompanying him on authorized home leave; or otherwise traveling in accordance with authority granted pursuant to the terms of sections 403a to 403s of this title or any other Act;

(C) pay the cost of transporting the furniture and household and personal effects of an officer or employee of the Agency to his successive posts of duty and, on the termination of his services, to his residence at time of appointment or to a point not more distant, or, upon retirement, to the place where he will reside;

(D) pay the cost of packing and unpacking, transporting to and from a place of storage, and storing the furniture and household and personal effects of an officer or employee of the Agency, when he is absent from his post of assignment under orders, or when he is assigned to a post to which he cannot take or at which he is unable to use such furniture and household and personal effects, or when it is in the public interest or more economical to authorize storage; but in no instance shall the weight or volume of the effects stored together with the weight or volume of the effects transported exceed the maximum limitations fixed by regulations, when not otherwise fixed by law;

(E) pay the cost of packing and unpacking, transporting to and from a place of storage, and storing the furniture and household and personal effects of an officer or employee of the Agency in connection with assignment or transfer to a new post, from the date of his departure from his last post or from the date of his departure, from his place of residence in the case of a new officer or employee and for not to exceed three months after arrival at the new post, or until the establishment of residence quarters, whichever shall be shorter; and in connection with separation of an officer or employee of the Agency, the cost of packing and unpacking, transporting to and from a place of storage, and storing for a period not to exceed three months, his furniture and household and personal effects; but in no instance shall the weight or volume of the effects stored together with the weight or volume of the effects transported exceed the maximum limitations fixed by regulations, when not otherwise fixed by law;

(F) pay the travel expenses and transportation costs incident to the removal of the members of the family of an officer or employee of the Agency and his furniture and household and personal effects, including automobiles, from a post at which, because of the prevalence of disturbed conditions, there is imminent danger to life and property, and the return of such persons, furniture, and effects to such post upon the cessation of such conditions; or to such other post as may in the meantime have become the post to which such officer or employee has been assigned.

(2) Charge expenses in connection with travel of personnel, their dependents, and transportation of their household goods and personal effects, involving a change of permanent station, to the appropriation for the fiscal year current when any part of either the travel or transportation

pertaining to the transfer begins pursuant to previously issued travel and transfer orders, notwithstanding the fact that such travel or transportation may not all be effected during such fiscal year, or the travel and transfer orders may have been issued during the prior fiscal year.

(3)(A) Order to any of the several States of the United States of America (including the District of Columbia, the Commonwealth of Puerto Rico, and any territory or possession of the United States) on leave of absence each officer or employee of the Agency who was a resident of the United States (as described above) at time of employment, upon completion of two years' continuous service abroad, or as soon as possible thereafter.

(B) While in the United States (as described in paragraph (3)(A) of this subsection) on leave, the service of any officer or employee shall be available for work or duties in the Agency or elsewhere as the Director may prescribe; and the time of such work or duty shall not be counted as leave.

(C) Where an officer or employee on leave returns to the United States (as described in paragraph (3)(A) of this subsection), leave of absence granted shall be exclusive of the time actually and necessarily occupied in going to and from the United States (as so described) and such time as may be necessarily occupied in awaiting transportation.

(4) Notwithstanding the provisions of any other law, transport for or on behalf of an officer or employee of the Agency, a privately owned motor vehicle in any case in which it shall be determined that water, rail, or air transportation of the motor vehicle is necessary or expedient for all or any part of the distance between points of origin and destination, and pay the costs of such transportation. Not more than one motor vehicle of any officer or employee of the Agency may be transported under authority of this paragraph during any four-year period, except that, as a replacement for such motor vehicle, one additional motor vehicle of any such officer or employee may be so transported during such period upon approval, in advance, by the Director and upon a determination, in advance, by the Director that such replacement is necessary for reasons beyond the control of the officer or employee and is in the interest of the Government. After the expiration of a period of four years following the date of transportation under authority of this paragraph of a privately owned motor vehicle of any officer or employee who has remained in continuous service outside the several States of the United States of America, excluding Alaska and Hawaii, but including the District of Columbia, during such period, the transportation of a replacement for such motor vehicle for such officer or employee may be authorized by the Director in accordance with this paragraph.

(5)(A) In the event of illness or injury requiring the hospitalization of an officer or full time employee of the Agency incurred while on assignment abroad, in a locality where there does not exist a suitable hospital or clinic, pay the travel expenses of such officer or employee by whatever means the Director deems appropriate and without regard to the Standardized Government Travel Regulations and section 5731 of title 5, to the nearest locality where a suitable hospital or clinic exists and on the recovery of such officer or employee pay for the travel expenses of the return to the post of duty of such officer or employee. If the officer or employee is too ill to travel unattended, the Director may also pay the travel expenses of an attendant;

> (B) Establish a first-aid station and provide for the services of a nurse at a post at which, in the opinion of the Director, sufficient personnel is employed to warrant such a station: Provided, That, in the opinion of the Director, it is not feasible to utilize an existing facility;
>
> (C) In the event of illness or injury requiring hospitalization of an officer or full time employee of the Agency incurred in the line of duty while such person is assigned abroad, pay for the cost of the treatment of such illness or injury at a suitable hospital or clinic;
>
> (D) Provide for the periodic physical examination of officers and employees of the Agency and for the cost of administering inoculation or vaccinations to such officers or employees.

(6) Pay the costs of preparing and transporting the remains of an officer or employee of the Agency or a member of his family who may die while in travel status or abroad, to his home or official station, or to such other place as the Director may determine to be the appropriate place of interment, provided that in no case shall the expense payable be greater than the amount which would have been payable had the destination been the home or official station.

(7) Pay the costs of travel of new appointees and their dependents, and the transportation of their household goods and personal effects, from places of actual residence in foreign countries at time of appointment to places of employment and return to their actual residences at the time of appointment or a point not more distant: Provided, That such appointees agree in writing to remain with the United States Government for a period of not less than twelve months from the time of appointment. Violation of such agreement for personal convenience of an employee or because of separation for misconduct will bar such return payments and, if determined by the Director or his designee to be in the best interests of the United States, any money expended by the United States on account

261

of such travel and transportation shall be considered as a debt due by the individual concerned to the United States.

(b) ALLOWANCES AND BENEFITS COMPARABLE TO THOSE PAID MEMBERS OF FOREIGN SERVICE; SPECIAL REQUIREMENTS; PERSONS DETAILED OR ASSIGNED FROM OTHER AGENCIES; REGULATIONS.—

(1) The Director may pay to officers and employees of the Agency, and to persons detailed or assigned to the Agency from other agencies of the Government or from the Armed Forces, allowances and benefits comparable to the allowances and benefits authorized to be paid to members of the Foreign Service under chapter 9 of title I of the Foreign Service Act of 1980 (22 U.S.C. §4081 et seq.) or any other provision of law.

(2) The Director may pay allowances and benefits related to officially authorized travel, personnel and physical security activities, operational activities, and cover-related activities (whether or not such allowances and benefits are otherwise authorized under this section or any other provision of law) when payment of such allowances and benefits is necessary to meet the special requirements of work related to such activities. Payment of allowances and benefits under this paragraph shall be in accordance with regulations prescribed by the Director. Rates for allowances and benefits under this paragraph may not be set at rates in excess of those authorized by section 5724 and 5724a of title 5 when reimbursement is provided for relocation attributable, in whole or in part, to relocation within the United States.

(3) Notwithstanding any other provision of this section or any other provision of law relating to the officially authorized travel of Government employees, the Director, in order to reflect Agency requirements not taken into account in the formulation of Government-wide travel procedures, may by regulation—

(A) authorize the travel of officers and employees of the Agency, and of persons detailed or assigned to the Agency from other agencies of the Government or from the Armed Forces who are engaged in the performance of intelligence functions, and
(B) provide for payment for such travel, in classes of cases, as determined by the Director, in which such travel is important to the performance of intelligence functions.

(4) Members of the Armed Forces may not receive benefits under both this section and title 37 for the same purpose. The Director and Secretary of Defense shall prescribe joint regulations to carry out the preceding sentence.

(5) Regulations, other than regulations under paragraph (1), issued pursuant to this subsection shall be submitted to the Permanent Select

Committee on Intelligence of the House of Representatives and the Select Committee on Intelligence of the Senate before such regulations take effect.

GENERAL AUTHORITIES OF AGENCY

SEC. 5. [50 U.S.C. §403f]

(a) IN GENERAL.—In the performance of its functions, the Central Intelligence Agency is authorized to—

(1) Transfer to and receive from other Government agencies such sums as may be approved by the Office of Management and Budget, for the performance of any of the functions or activities authorized under section 104A of the National Security Act of 1947 (50 U.S.C. 403-4a)., and any other Government agency is authorized to transfer to or receive from the Agency such sums without regard to any provisions of law limiting or prohibiting transfers between appropriations. Sums transferred to the Agency in accordance with this paragraph may be expended for the purposes and under the authority of sections 403a to 403s of this title without regard to limitations of appropriations from which transferred;

(2) Exchange funds without regard to section 3651 of the Revised Statutes;

(3) Reimburse other Government agencies for services of personnel assigned to the Agency, and such other Government agencies are authorized, without regard to provisions of law to the contrary, so to assign or detail any officer or employee for duty with the Agency;

(4) Authorize personnel designated by the Director to carry firearms to the extent necessary for the performance of the Agency's authorized functions, except that, within the United States, such authority shall be limited to the purposes of protection of classified materials and information, the training of Agency personnel and other authorized persons in the use of firearms, the protection of Agency installations and property, the protection of current and former Agency personnel and their immediate families, defectors and their immediate families, and other persons in the United States under Agency auspices, and the protection of the Director of National Intelligence and such personnel of the Office of the Director of National Intelligence as the Director of National Intelligence may designate;

(5) Make alterations, improvements, and repairs on premises rented by the Agency, and pay rent therefor;

(6) Determine and fix the minimum and maximum limits of age within which an original appointment may be made to an operational position within the Agency, notwithstanding the provision of any other law, in

accordance with such criteria as the Director, in his discretion, may prescribe; and

(7) Notwithstanding section 1341(a)(1) of title 31, enter into multiyear leases for up to 15 years.

(b) SCOPE OF AUTHORITY FOR EXPENDITURE. —

(1) The authority to enter into a multiyear lease under subsection (a)(7) of this section shall be subject to appropriations provided in advance for—

(A) the entire lease; or

(B) the first 12 months of the lease and the Government's estimated termination liability.

(2) In the case of any such lease entered into under subparagraph (B) of paragraph (1)—

(A) such lease shall include a clause that provides that the contract shall be terminated if budget authority (as defined by section 622(2) of title 2) is not provided specifically for that project in an appropriations Act in advance of an obligation of funds in respect thereto;

(B) notwithstanding section 1552 of title 31, amounts obligated for paying termination costs with respect to such lease shall remain available until the costs associated with termination of such lease are paid;

(C) funds available for termination liability shall remain available to satisfy rental obligations with respect to such lease in subsequent fiscal years in the event such lease is not terminated early, but only to the extent those funds are in excess of the amount of termination liability at the time of their use to satisfy such rental obligations; and

(D) funds appropriated for a fiscal year may be used to make payments on such lease, for a maximum of 12 months, beginning any time during such fiscal year.

(c) TRANSFERS FOR ACQUISITION OF LAND.—

(1) Sums appropriated or otherwise made available to the Agency for the acquisition of land that are transferred to another department or agency for that purpose shall remain available for 3 years.

(2) The Director shall submit to the Select Committee on Intelligence of the Senate and the Permanent Select Committee on Intelligence of the House of Representatives a report on the transfer of sums described in paragraph (1) each time that authority is exercised.

PROTECTION OF NATURE OF AGENCY'S FUNCTIONS

SEC. 6. [50 U.S.C. Sec. §403g]

In the interests of the security of the foreign intelligence activities of the United States and in order further to implement section 403-1(i) of this title that the Director of National Intelligence shall be responsible for protecting intelligence sources and methods from unauthorized disclosure, the Agency shall be exempted from the provisions of sections 1 and 2 of the Act of August 28, 1935 (49 Stat. 956, 957; 5 U.S.C. §654), and the provisions of any other law which require the publication or disclosure of the organization, functions, names, official titles, salaries, or numbers of personnel employed by the Agency: *Provided,* That in furtherance of this section, the Director of the Office of Management and Budget shall make no reports to the Congress in connection with the Agency under section 607 of the Act of June 30, 1945, as amended (5 U.S.C. §947(b)).

ADMISSION OF ESSENTIAL ALIENS; LIMITATION ON NUMBER

SEC. 7. [50 U.S.C. Sec. §403h]

Whenever the Director, the Attorney General, and the Commissioner of Immigration and Naturalization shall determine that the admission of a particular alien into the United States for permanent residence is in the interest of national security or essential to the furtherance of the national intelligence mission, such alien and his immediate family shall be admitted to the United States for permanent residence without regard to their inadmissibility under the immigration or any other laws and regulations, or to the failure to comply with such laws and regulations pertaining to admissibility: *Provided,* That the number of aliens and members of their immediate families admitted to the United States under the authority of this section shall in no case exceed one hundred persons in any one fiscal year.

APPROPRIATIONS

SEC. 8. [50 U.S.C. Sec. §403j]

CENTRAL INTELLIGENCE AGENCY; APPROPRIATIONS, EXPENDITURES.—

(a) Notwithstanding any other provisions of law, sums made available to the Agency by appropriation or otherwise may be expended for purposes necessary to carry out its functions, including—

> (1) personal services, including personal services without regard to limitations on types of persons to be employed, and rent at the seat of government and elsewhere; health-service program as authorized by law (5 U.S.C. §7901); rental of news-reporting services; purchase or rental and operation of photographic, reproduction, cryptographic, duplication, and printing machines, equipment, and devices, and radio-receiving and

radio-sending equipment and devices, including telegraph and teletype equipment; purchase, maintenance, operation, repair, and hire of passenger motor vehicles, and aircraft, and vessels of all kinds; subject to policies established by the Director, transportation of officers and employees of the Agency in Government-owned automotive equipment between their domiciles and places of employment, where such personnel are engaged in work which makes such transportation necessary, and transportation in such equipment, to and from school, of children of Agency personnel who have quarters for themselves and their families at isolated stations outside the continental United States where adequate public or private transportation is not available; printing and binding; purchase, maintenance, and cleaning of firearms, including purchase, storage, and maintenance of ammunition; subject to policies established by the Director, expenses of travel in connection with, and expenses incident to attendance at meetings of professional, technical, scientific, and other similar organizations when such attendance would be a benefit in the conduct of the work of the Agency; association and library dues; payment of premiums or costs of surety bonds for officers or employees without regard to the provisions of section 14 of title 6; payment of claims pursuant to title 28; acquisition of necessary land and the clearing of such land; construction of buildings and facilities without regard to 36 Stat. 699; 40 U.S.C. §259, 267; repair, rental, operation, and maintenance of buildings, utilities, facilities, and appurtenances; and (2) supplies, equipment, and personnel and contractual services otherwise authorized by law and regulations, when approved by the Director.

(b) The sums made available to the Agency may be expended without regard to the provisions of law and regulations relating to the expenditure of Government funds; and for objects of a confidential, extraordinary, or emergency nature, such expenditures to be accounted for solely on the certificate of the Director and every such certificate shall be deemed a sufficient voucher for the amount therein certified.

SEPARABILITY OF PROVISIONS

SEC. 9. [50 U.S.C. §403a note]
If any provision of this Act or the application of such provision to any person or circumstances, is held invalid, the remainder of this Act or the application of such provision to persons or circumstances other than those as to which it is held invalid, shall not be affected thereby.

SHORT TITLE

SEC. 10. [50 U.S.C. §401 note]
This Act may be cited as the "Central Intelligence Agency Act of 1949".

AUTHORITY TO PAY DEATH GRATUITIES

SEC. 11. [50 U.S.C. §403k]
(a)(1) The Director may pay a gratuity to the surviving dependents of any officer or employee of the Agency who dies as a result of injuries (other than from disease) sustained outside the United States and whose death—
(A) resulted from hostile or terrorist activities; or
(B) occurred in connection with an intelligence activity having a substantial element of risk.
(2) The provisions of this subsection shall apply with respect to deaths occurring after June 30, 1974.
(b) Any payment under subsection (a) of this section—
(1) shall be in an amount equal to the amount of the annual salary of the officer or employee concerned at the time of death;
(2) shall be considered a gift and shall be in lieu of payment of any lesser death gratuity authorized by any other Federal law; and
(3) shall be made under the same conditions as apply to payments authorized by section 3973 of title 22.

AUTHORITY TO ACCEPT GIFTS, DEVISES, AND BEQUESTS

SEC. 12. [50 U.S.C. §403l]
(a)(1) USE FOR OPERATIONAL PURPOSES PROHIBITED.—Subject to the provisions of this section, the Director may accept, hold, administer, and use gifts of money, securities, or other property whenever the Director determines it would be in the interest of the United States to do so.
(2) Any gift accepted under this section (and any income produced by any such gift)—
(A) may be used only for—
(i) artistic display;
(ii) purposes relating to the general welfare, education, or recreation of employees or dependents of employees of the Agency or for similar purposes; or
(iii) purposes relating to the welfare, education, or recreation of an individual described in paragraph (3); and
(B) under no circumstances may such a gift (or any income produced by any such gift) be used for operational purposes.
(3) An individual described in this paragraph is an individual who—

(A) is an employee or a former employee of the Agency who suffered injury or illness while employed by the Agency that—
    (i) resulted from hostile or terrorist activities;
    (ii) occurred in connected with an intelligence activity having a significant element of risk; or
    (iii) occurred under other circumstances determined by the Director to be analogous to the circumstances described in clause (i) or (ii);
(B) is a family member of such an employee or former employee; or
(C) is a surviving family member of an employee of the Agency who died in circumstances described in clause (i), (ii), or (iii) of subparagraph (A).

(4) The Director may not accept any gift under this section that is expressly conditioned upon any expenditure not to be met from the gift itself or from income produced by the gift unless such expenditure has been authorized by law.

(5) The Director may, in the Director's discretion, determine that an individual described in subparagraph (A) or (B) of paragraph (3) may accept a gift for the purposes described in paragraph (2)(A)(iii).

(b) SALE, EXCHANGE AND INVESTMENT OF GIFTS.—Unless otherwise restricted by the terms of the gift, the Director may sell or exchange, or invest or reinvest, any property which is accepted under this section, but any such investment may only be in interest-bearing obligations of the United States or in obligations guaranteed as to both principal and interest by the United States.

(c) DEPOSIT OF GIFTS INTO SPECIAL FUND.—There is hereby created on the books of the Treasury of the United States a fund into which gifts of money, securities, and other intangible property accepted under the authority of this section, and the earnings and proceeds thereof, shall be deposited. The assets of such fund shall be disbursed upon the order of the Director for the purposes specified in subsection (a) or (b) of this section.

(d) TAXATION OF GIFTS.—For purposes of Federal income, estate, and gift taxes, gifts accepted by the Director under this section shall be considered to be to or for the use of the United States.

(e) "GIFT" DEFINED.—For the purposes of this section, the term "gift" includes a bequest or devise.

(f) The Director, in consultation with the Director of the Office of Government Ethics, shall issue regulations to carry out the authority provided in this section. Such regulations shall ensure that such authority is exercised consistent with all relevant ethical constraints and principles, including—
    (1) the avoidance of any prohibited conflict of interest or appearance of impropriety; and

(2) a prohibition against the acceptance of a gift from a foreign government or an agent of a foreign government.

MISUSE OF AGENCY NAME, INITIALS, OR SEAL

SEC. 13. [50 U.S.C. §403m]

(a) PROHIBITED ACTS.—No person may, except with the written permission of the Director, knowingly use the words "Central Intelligence Agency", the initials "CIA", the seal of the Central Intelligence Agency, or any colorable imitation of such words, initials, or seal in connection with any merchandise, impersonation, solicitation, or commercial activity in a manner reasonably calculated to convey the impression that such use is approved, endorsed, or authorized by the Central Intelligence Agency.

(b) INJUNCTION.—Whenever it appears to the Attorney General that any person is engaged or is about to engage in an act or practice which constitutes or will constitute conduct prohibited by subsection (a) of this section, the Attorney General may initiate a civil proceeding in a district court of the United States to enjoin such act or practice. Such court shall proceed as soon as practicable to the hearing and determination of such action and may, at any time before final determination, enter such restraining orders or prohibitions, or take such other action as is warranted, to prevent injury to the United States or to any person or class of persons for whose protection the action is brought.

RETIREMENT EQUITY FOR SPOUSES OF CERTAIN EMPLOYEES

SEC. 14. [50 U.S.C. §403n]

SPECIAL PROVISIONS FOR SPOUSES OF CENTRAL INTELLIGENCE AGENCY EMPLOYEES APPLICABLE TO AGENCY PARTICIPANTS IN CIVIL SERVICE RETIREMENT AND DISABILITY SYSTEM.—

(a) MANNER AND EXTENT OF APPLICABILITY.—The provisions of sections 2002, 2031(b)(1)-(3), 2031(f), 2031(g), 2031(h)(2), 2031(i), 2031(l), 2032, 2033, 2034, 2035, 2052(b), 2071(b), 2071(d), and 2094(b) of this title establishing certain requirements, limitations, rights, entitlements, and benefits relating to retirement annuities, survivor benefits, and lump-sum payments for a spouse or former spouse of an Agency employee who is a participant in the Central Intelligence Agency Retirement and Disability System shall apply in the same manner and to the same extent in the case of an Agency employee who is a participant in the Civil Service Retirement and Disability System.

(b) REGULATIONS.—The Director of the Office of Personnel Management, in consultation with the Director of the Central Intelligence Agency, shall prescribe such regulations as may be necessary to implement the provisions of this section.

SECURITY PERSONNEL AT AGENCY INSTALLATIONS

SEC. 15. [50 U.S.C. §403o]
(a) SPECIAL POLICEMEN: FUNCTIONS AND POWERS; REGULATIONS:
PROMULGATION AND ENFORCEMENT.—

(1) The Director may authorize Agency personnel within the United States to perform the same functions as officers and agents of the Department of Homeland Security, as provided in section 1315(b)(2) of title 40, with the powers set forth in that section, except that such personnel shall perform such functions and exercise such powers—

(A) within the Agency Headquarters Compound and the property controlled and occupied by the Federal Highway Administration located immediately adjacent to such Compound;

(B) in the streets, sidewalks, and the open areas within the zone beginning at the outside boundary of such Compound and property and extending outward 500 feet;

(C) within any other Agency installation and protected property; and

(D) in the streets, sidewalks, and open areas within the zone beginning at the outside boundary of any installation or property referred to in subparagraph (C) and extending outward 500 feet.

(2) The performance of functions and exercise of powers under subparagraph (B) or (D) of paragraph (1) shall be limited to those circumstances where such personnel can identify specific and articulable facts giving such personnel reason to believe that the performance of such functions and exercise of such powers is reasonable to protect against physical damage or injury, or threats of physical damage or injury, to Agency installations, property, or employees.

(3) Nothing in this subsection shall be construed to preclude, or limit in any way, the authority of any Federal, State, or local law enforcement agency, or any other Federal police or Federal protective service.

(4) The rules and regulations enforced by such personnel shall be the rules and regulations prescribed by the Director and shall only be applicable to the areas referred to in subparagraph (A) or (C) of paragraph (1).

(b) PENALTIES FOR VIOLATIONS OF REGULATIONS.—The Director is authorized to establish penalties for violations of the rules or regulations promulgated by the Director under subsection (a) of this section. Such penalties shall not exceed those specified in section 1315(c)(2) of title 40.

(c) IDENTIFICATION.—Agency personnel designated by the Director under subsection (a) of this section shall be clearly identifiable as United States

Government security personnel while engaged in the performance of the functions to which subsection (a) of this section refers.

(d) PROTECTION OF CERTAIN CIA PERSONNEL FROM TORT LIABILITY.—

(1) Notwithstanding any other provision of law, any Agency personnel designated by the Director under subsection (a) of this section, or designated by the Director under section 403f(a)(4) of this title to carry firearms for the protection of current or former Agency personnel and their immediate families, defectors and their immediate families, and other persons in the United States under Agency auspices, shall be considered for purposes of chapter 171 of title 28, or any other provision of law relating to tort liability, to be acting within the scope of their office or employment when such Agency personnel take reasonable action, which may include the use of force, to—

(A) protect an individual in the presence of such Agency personnel from a crime of violence;

(B) provide immediate assistance to an individual who has suffered or who is threatened with bodily harm; or

(C) prevent the escape of any individual whom such Agency personnel reasonably believe to have committed a crime of violence in the presence of such Agency personnel.

(2) Paragraph (1) shall not affect the authorities of the Attorney General under section 2679 of title 28.

(3) In this subsection, the term "crime of violence" has the meaning given that term in section 16 of title 18.

HEALTH BENEFITS FOR CERTAIN FORMER SPOUSES OF CENTRAL INTELLIGENCE AGENCY EMPLOYEES

SEC. 16. [50 U.S.C. §403p]

(a) PERSONS ELIGIBLE.—Except as provided in subsection (e) of this section, any individual—

(1) formerly married to an employee or former employee of the Agency, whose marriage was dissolved by divorce or annulment before May 7, 1985;

(2) who, at any time during the eighteen-month period before the divorce or annulment became final, was covered under a health benefits plan as a member of the family of such employee or former employee; and

(3) who was married to such employee for not less than ten years during periods of service by such employee with the Agency, at least five years of which were spent outside the United States by both the employee and the former spouse,

is eligible for coverage under a health benefits plan in accordance with the provisions of this section.

(b) ENROLLMENT FOR HEALTH BENEFITS.—

(1) Any individual eligible for coverage under subsection (a) of this section may enroll in a health benefits plan for self alone or for self and family if, before the expiration of the six-month period beginning on October 1, 1986, and in accordance with such procedures as the Director of the Office of Personnel Management shall by regulation prescribe, such individual—

(A) files an election for such enrollment; and

(B) arranges to pay currently into the Employees Health Benefits Fund under section 8909 of title 5 an amount equal to the sum of the employee and agency contributions payable in the case of an employee enrolled under chapter 89 of such title in the same health benefits plan and with the same level of benefits.

(2) The Director of the Central Intelligence Agency shall, as soon as possible, take all steps practicable—

(A) to determine the identity and current address of each former spouse eligible for coverage under subsection (a) of this section; and

(B) to notify each such former spouse of that individual's rights under this section.

(3) The Director of the Office of Personnel Management, upon notification by the Director of the Central Intelligence Agency, shall waive the six-month limitation set forth in paragraph (1) in any case in which the Director of the Central Intelligence Agency determines that the circumstances so warrant.

(c) ELIGIBILITY OF FORMER WIVES OR HUSBANDS.—

(1) Notwithstanding subsections (a) and (b) of this section and except as provided in subsections (d), (e), and (f) of this section, an individual—

(A) who was divorced on or before December 4, 1991, from a participant or retired participant in the Central Intelligence Agency Retirement and Disability System or the Federal Employees Retirement System Special Category;

(B) who was married to such participant for not less than ten years during the participant's creditable service, at least five years of which were spent by the participant during the participant's service as an employee of the Agency outside the United States, or otherwise in a position the duties of which qualified the participant for designation by the Director as a participant under section 2013 of this title; and

      (C) who was enrolled in a health benefits plan as a family member at any time during the 18-month period before the date of dissolution of the marriage to such participant;

is eligible for coverage under a health benefits plan.

(2) A former spouse eligible for coverage under paragraph (1) may enroll in a health benefits plan in accordance with subsection (b)(1) of this section, except that the election for such enrollment must be submitted within 60 days after the date on which the Director notifies the former spouse of such individual's eligibility for health insurance coverage under this subsection.

(d) CONTINUATION OF ELIGIBILITY.—Notwithstanding subsections (a), (b), and (c) of this section and except as provided in subsections (e) and (f) of this section, an individual divorced on or before December 4, 1991, from a participant or retired participant in the Central Intelligence Agency Retirement and Disability System or Federal Employees' Retirement System Special Category who enrolled in a health benefits plan following the dissolution of the marriage to such participant may continue enrollment following the death of such participant notwithstanding the termination of the retirement annuity of such individual.

(e) REMARRIAGE BEFORE AGE FIFTY-FIVE; CONTINUED ENROLLMENT; RESTORED ELIGIBILITY.—

      (1) Any former spouse who remarries before age fifty-five is not eligible to make an election under subsection (b)(1) of this section.

      (2) Any former spouse enrolled in a health benefits plan pursuant to an election under subsection (b)(1) of this section or to subsection (d) of this section may continue the enrollment under the conditions of eligibility which the Director of the Office of Personnel Management shall by regulation prescribe, except that any former spouse who remarries before age fifty-five shall not be eligible for continued enrollment under this section after the end of the thirty-one-day period beginning on the date of remarriage.

      (3)(A) A former spouse who is not eligible to enroll or to continue enrollment in a health benefits plan under this section solely because of remarriage before age fifty-five shall be restored to such eligibility on the date such remarriage is dissolved by death, annulment, or divorce.

           (B) A former spouse whose eligibility is restored under subparagraph (A) may, under regulations which the Director of the Office of Personnel Management shall prescribe, enroll in a health benefits plan if such former spouse—

                (i) was an individual referred to in paragraph (1) and was an individual covered under a benefits plan as a family member at any time during the 18-month period before

273

the date of dissolution of the marriage to the Agency
employee or annuitant; or

(ii) was an individual referred to in paragraph (2) and
was an individual covered under a benefits plan
immediately before the remarriage ended the enrollment.

(f) ENROLLMENT IN HEALTH BENEFITS PLAN UNDER OTHER AUTHORITY.—No
individual may be covered by a health benefits plan under this section during any
period in which such individual is enrolled in a health benefits plan under any
other authority, nor may any individual be covered under more than one
enrollment under this section.

(g) "HEALTH BENEFITS PLAN" DEFINED.—For purposes of this section the term
"health benefits plan" means an approved health benefits plan under chapter 89
of title 5.

REPORTS OF INSPECTOR GENERAL ACTIVITIES

SEC. 17. [50 U.S.C. §403q]
INSPECTOR GENERAL FOR AGENCY.—
(a) PURPOSE; ESTABLISHMENT.—In order to—

(1) create an objective and effective office, appropriately accountable to
Congress, to initiate and conduct independently inspections,
investigations, and audits relating to programs and operations of the
Agency;

(2) provide leadership and recommend policies designed to promote
economy, efficiency, and effectiveness in the administration of such
programs and operations, and detect fraud and abuse in such programs
and operations;

(3) provide a means for keeping the Director fully and currently
informed about problems and deficiencies relating to the administration
of such programs and operations, and the necessity for and the progress
of corrective actions; and

(4) in the manner prescribed by this section, ensure that the Senate Select
Committee on Intelligence and the House Permanent Select Committee
on Intelligence (hereafter in this section referred to collectively as the
"intelligence committees") are kept similarly informed of significant
problems and deficiencies as well as the necessity for and the progress of
corrective actions,

there is hereby established in the Agency an Office of Inspector General
(hereafter in this section referred to as the "Office").

(b) APPOINTMENT; SUPERVISION; REMOVAL.—

(1) There shall be at the head of the Office an Inspector General who
shall be appointed by the President, by and with the advice and consent

274

of the Senate. This appointment shall be made without regard to political affiliation and shall be on the basis of integrity and demonstrated ability in accounting, auditing, financial analysis, law, management analysis, public administration, or investigation. Such appointment shall also be made on the basis of compliance with the security standards of the Agency and prior experience in the field of foreign intelligence.

(2) The Inspector General shall report directly to and be under the general supervision of the Director.

(3) The Director may prohibit the Inspector General from initiating, carrying out, or completing any audit, inspection, or investigation, or from issuing any subpoena, after the Inspector General has decided to initiate, carry out, or complete such audit, inspection, or investigation or to issue such subpoena, if the Director determines that such prohibition is necessary to protect vital national security interests of the United States.

(4) If the Director exercises any power under paragraph (3), he shall submit an appropriately classified statement of the reasons for the exercise of such power within seven days to the intelligence committees. The Director shall advise the Inspector General at the time such report is submitted, and, to the extent consistent with the protection of intelligence sources and methods, provide the Inspector General with a copy of any such report. In such cases, the Inspector General may submit such comments to the intelligence committees that he considers appropriate.

(5) In accordance with section 535 of title 28, the Inspector General shall report to the Attorney General any information, allegation, or complaint received by the Inspector General relating to violations of Federal criminal law that involve a program or operation of the Agency, consistent with such guidelines as may be issued by the Attorney General pursuant to subsection (b)(2) of such section. A copy of all such reports shall be furnished to the Director.

(6) The Inspector General may be removed from office only by the President. The President shall communicate in writing to the intelligence committees the reasons for any such removal not later than 30 days prior to the effect date of such removal. Nothing in this paragraph shall be construed to prohibit a personnel action otherwise authorized by law, other than transfer or removal.

(c) DUTIES AND RESPONSIBILITIES.—It shall be the duty and responsibility of the Inspector General appointed under this section—

(1) to provide policy direction for, and to plan, conduct, supervise, and coordinate independently, the inspections, investigations, and audits relating to the programs and operations of the Agency to ensure they are conducted efficiently and in accordance with applicable law and regulations;

(2) to keep the Director fully and currently informed concerning violations of law and regulations, fraud and other serious problems, abuses and deficiencies that may occur in such programs and operations, and to report the progress made in implementing corrective action;

(3) to take due regard for the protection of intelligence sources and methods in the preparation of all reports issued by the Office, and, to the extent consistent with the purpose and objective of such reports, take such measures as may be appropriate to minimize the disclosure of intelligence sources and methods described in such reports; and

(4) in the execution of his responsibilities, to comply with generally accepted government auditing standards.

(d) SEMIANNUAL REPORTS; IMMEDIATE REPORTS OF SERIOUS OR FLAGRANT PROBLEMS; REPORTS OF FUNCTIONAL PROBLEMS; REPORTS TO CONGRESS ON URGENT CONCERNS.—

(1) The Inspector General shall, not later than January 31 and July 31 of each year, prepare and submit to the Director a classified semiannual report summarizing the activities of the Office during the immediately preceding six-month periods ending December 31 (of the preceding year) and June 30, respectively. Not later than the dates each year provided for the transmittal of such reports in section 507 of the National Security Act of 1947 [50 U.S.C. §415b], the Director shall transmit such reports to the intelligence committees with any comments he may deem appropriate. Such reports shall, at a minimum, include a list of the title or subject of each inspection, investigation, review, or audit conducted during the reporting period and—

(A) a description of significant problems, abuses, and deficiencies relating to the administration of programs and operations of the Agency identified by the Office during the reporting period;

(B) a description of the recommendations for corrective action made by the Office during the reporting period with respect to significant problems, abuses, or deficiencies identified in subparagraph (A);

(C) a statement of whether corrective action has been completed on each significant recommendation described in previous semiannual reports, and, in a case where corrective action has been completed, a description of such corrective action;

(D) a certification that the Inspector General has had full and direct access to all information relevant to the performance of his functions;

(E) a description of the exercise of the subpoena authority under subsection (e)(5) of this section by the Inspector General during the reporting period; and

(F) such recommendations as the Inspector General may wish to make concerning legislation to promote economy and efficiency in the administration of programs and operations undertaken by the Agency, and to detect and eliminate fraud and abuse in such programs and operations.

(2) The Inspector General shall report immediately to the Director whenever he becomes aware of particularly serious or flagrant problems, abuses, or deficiencies relating to the administration of programs or operations. The Director shall transmit such report to the intelligence committees within seven calendar days, together with any comments he considers appropriate.

(3) In the event that—

(A) the Inspector General is unable to resolve any differences with the Director affecting the execution of the Inspector General's duties or responsibilities;

(B) an investigation, inspection, or audit carried out by the Inspector General should focus on any current or former Agency official who—

(i) holds or held a position in the Agency that is subject to appointment by the President, by and with the advice and consent of the Senate, including such a position held on an acting basis; or

(ii) holds or held the position in the Agency, including such a position held on an acting basis, of—

(I) Deputy Director;

(II) Assistant Deputy Director;

(III) Director of the National Clandestine Service;

(IV) Director of Intelligence;

(V) Director of Support; or

(VI) Director of Science and Technology;

(C) a matter requires a report by the Inspector General to the Department of Justice on possible criminal conduct by a current or former Agency official described or referred to in subparagraph (B);

(D) the Inspector General receives notice from the Department of Justice declining or approving prosecution of possible criminal conduct of any of the officials described in subparagraph (B); or

(E) the Inspector General, after exhausting all possible alternatives, is unable to obtain significant documentary information in the course of an investigation, inspection, or audit,

the Inspector General shall immediately notify and submit a report on such matter to the intelligence committees.

(4) Pursuant to Title V of the National Security Act of 1947 [50 U.S.C. §413 et seq.], the Director shall submit to the intelligence committees any report or findings and recommendations of an inspection, investigation, or audit conducted by the office which has been requested by the Chairman or Ranking Minority Member of either committee.

(5)(A) An employee of the Agency, or of a contractor to the Agency, who intends to report to Congress a complaint or information with respect to an urgent concern may report such complaint or information to the Inspector General.

(B) Not later than the end of the 14-calendar day period beginning on the date of receipt from an employee of a complaint or information under subparagraph (A), the Inspector General shall determine whether the complaint or information appears credible. Upon making such a determination, the Inspector General shall transmit to the Director notice of that determination, together with the complaint or information.

(C) Upon receipt of a transmittal from the Inspector General under subparagraph (B), the Director shall, within 7 calendar days of such receipt, forward such transmittal to the intelligence committees, together with any comments the Director considers appropriate.

(D)(i) If the Inspector General does not find credible under subparagraph (B) a complaint or information submitted under subparagraph (A), or does not transmit the complaint or information to the Director in accurate form under subparagraph (B), the employee (subject to clause (ii)) may submit the complaint or information to Congress by contacting either or both of the intelligence committees directly.

(ii) The employee may contact the intelligence committees directly as described in clause (i) only if the employee—

(I) before making such a contact, furnishes to the Director, through the Inspector General, a statement of the employee's complaint or information and notice of the employee's intent

278

to contact the intelligence committees directly; and

(II) obtains and follows from the Director, through the Inspector General, direction on how to contact the intelligence committees in accordance with appropriate security practices.

(iii) A member or employee of one of the intelligence committees who receives a complaint or information under clause (i) does so in that member or employee's official capacity as a member or employee of that committee.

(E) The Inspector General shall notify an employee who reports a complaint or information to the Inspector General under this paragraph of each action taken under this paragraph with respect to the complaint or information. Such notice shall be provided not later than 3 days after any such action is taken.

(F) An action taken by the Director or the Inspector General under this paragraph shall not be subject to judicial review.

(G) In this paragraph:

(i) The term "urgent concern" means any of the following:

(I) A serious or flagrant problem, abuse, violation of law or Executive order, or deficiency relating to the funding, administration, or operations of an intelligence activity involving classified information, but does not include differences of opinions concerning public policy matters.

(II) A false statement to Congress, or a willful withholding from Congress, on an issue of material fact relating to the funding, administration, or operation of an intelligence activity.

(III) An action, including a personnel action described in section 2302(a)(2)(A) of title 5, constituting reprisal or threat of reprisal prohibited under subsection (e)(3)(B) of this section in response to an employee's reporting an urgent concern in accordance with this paragraph.

(ii) The term "intelligence committees" means the Permanent Select Committee on Intelligence of the

House of Representatives and the Select Committee on Intelligence of the Senate.

(e) AUTHORITIES OF INSPECTOR GENERAL.—

(1) The Inspector General shall have direct and prompt access to the Director when necessary for any purpose pertaining to the performance of his duties.

(2) The Inspector General shall have access to any employee or any employee of a contractor of the Agency whose testimony is needed for the performance of his duties. In addition, he shall have direct access to all records, reports, audits, reviews, documents, papers, recommendations, or other material which relate to the programs and operations with respect to which the Inspector General has responsibilities under this section. Failure on the part of any employee or contractor to cooperate with the Inspector General shall be grounds for appropriate administrative actions by the Director, to include loss of employment or the termination of an existing contractual relationship.

(3) The Inspector General is authorized to receive and investigate complaints or information from any person concerning the existence of an activity constituting a violation of laws, rules, or regulations, or mismanagement, gross waste of funds, abuse of authority, or a substantial and specific danger to the public health and safety. Once such complaint or information has been received from an employee of the Agency—

(A) the Inspector General shall not disclose the identity of the employee without the consent of the employee, unless the Inspector General determines that such disclosure is unavoidable during the course of the investigation or the disclosure is made to an official of the Department of Justice responsible for determining whether a prosecution should be undertaken; and

(B) no action constituting a reprisal, or threat of reprisal, for making such complaint or providing such information may be taken by any employee of the Agency in a position to take such actions, unless the complaint was made or the information was disclosed with the knowledge that it was false or with willful disregard for its truth or falsity.

(4) The Inspector General shall have authority to administer to or take from any person an oath, affirmation, or affidavit, whenever necessary in the performance of his duties, which oath, affirmation, or affidavit when administered or taken by or before an employee of the Office designated by the Inspector General shall have the same force and effect as if administered or taken by or before an officer having a seal.

(5)(A) Except as provided in subparagraph (B), the Inspector General is authorized to require by subpoena the production of all information, documents, reports, answers, records, accounts, papers, and other data in any medium (including electronically stored information or any tangible thing) and documentary evidence necessary in the performance of the duties and responsibilities of the Inspector General.

(B) In the case of Government agencies, the Inspector General shall obtain information, documents, reports, answers, records, accounts, papers, and other data and evidence for the purpose specified in subparagraph (A) using procedures other than by subpoenas.

(C) The Inspector General may not issue a subpoena for or on behalf of any other element or component of the Agency.

(D) In the case of contumacy or refusal to obey a subpoena issued under this paragraph, the subpoena shall be enforceable by order of any appropriate district court of the United States.

(6) The Inspector General shall be provided with appropriate and adequate office space at central and field office locations, together with such equipment, office supplies, maintenance services, and communications facilities and services as may be necessary for the operation of such offices.

(7) Subject to applicable law and the policies of the Director, the Inspector General shall select, appoint and employ such officers and employees as may be necessary to carry out his functions. In making such selections, the Inspector General shall ensure that such officers and employees have the requisite training and experience to enable him to carry out his duties effectively. In this regard, the Inspector General shall create within his organization a career cadre of sufficient size to provide appropriate continuity and objectivity needed for the effective performance of his duties.

(8)(A) The Inspector General shall—

(i) appoint a Counsel to the Inspector General who shall report to the Inspector General; or

(ii) obtain the services of a counsel appointed by and directly reporting to another Inspector General or the Council of the Inspectors General on Integrity and Efficiency on a reimbursable basis.

(B) The counsel appointed or obtained under subparagraph (A) shall perform such functions as the Inspector General may prescribe.

(9) The Inspector General may request such information or assistance as may be necessary for carrying out his duties and responsibilities from

any Government agency. Upon request of the Inspector General for such information or assistance, the head of the Government agency involved shall, insofar as is practicable and not in contravention of any existing statutory restriction or regulation of the Government agency concerned, furnish to the Inspector General, or to an authorized designee, such information or assistance. Consistent with budgetary and personnel resources allocated by the Director, the Inspector General has final approval of—

(A) the selection of internal and external candidates for employment with the Office of Inspector General; and
(B) all other personnel decisions concerning personnel permanently assigned to the Office of Inspector General, including selection and appointment to the Senior Intelligence Service, but excluding all security-based determinations that are not within the authority of a head of other Central Intelligence Agency offices.

(f) SEPARATE BUDGET ACCOUNT.—(1) Beginning with fiscal year 1991, and in accordance with procedures to be issued by the Director of National Intelligence in consultation with the intelligence committees, the Director of National Intelligence shall include in the National Intelligence Program budget a separate account for the Office of Inspector General established pursuant to this section.

(2) For each fiscal year, the Inspector General shall transmit a budget estimate and request through the Director to the Director of National Intelligence that specifies for such fiscal year—

(A) the aggregate amount requested for the operations of the Inspector General;
(B) the amount requested for all training requirements of the Inspector General, including a certification from the Inspector General that the amount requested is sufficient to fund all training requirements for the Office; and
(C) the amount requested to support the Council of the Inspectors General on Integrity and Efficiency, including a justification for such amount.

(3) In transmitting a proposed budget to the President for a fiscal year, the Director of National Intelligence shall include for such fiscal year—

(A) the aggregate amount requested for the Inspector General of the Central Intelligence Agency;
(B) the amount requested for Inspector General training;
(C) the amount requested to support the Council of the Inspectors General on Integrity and Efficiency; and
(D) the comments of the Inspector General, if any, with respect to such proposed budget.

(4) The Director of National Intelligence shall submit to the Committee on Appropriations and the Select Committee on Intelligence of the Senate and the Committee on Appropriations and the Permanent Select Committee on Intelligence of the House of Representatives for each fiscal year—

>>(A) a separate statement of the budget estimate transmitted pursuant to paragraph (2);

>>(B) the amount requested by the Director of National Intelligence for the Inspector General pursuant to paragraph (3)(A);

>>(C) the amount requested by the Director of National Intelligence for training of personnel of the Office of the Inspector General pursuant to paragraph (3)(B);

>>(D) the amount requested by the Director of National Intelligence for support for the Council of the Inspectors General on Integrity and Efficiency pursuant to paragraph (3)(C);

>>(E) the comments of the Inspector General under paragraph (3)(D), if any, on the amounts requested pursuant to paragraph (3), including whether such amounts would substantially inhibit the Inspector General from performing the duties of the Office.

(g) TRANSFER.—There shall be transferred to the Office the office of the Agency referred to as the "Office of Inspector General." The personnel, assets, liabilities, contracts, property, records, and unexpended balances of appropriations, authorizations, allocations, and other funds employed, held, used, arising from, or available to such "Office of Inspector General" are hereby transferred to the Office established pursuant to this section.

(h) INFORMATION ON WEBSITE.—(1) The Director of the Central Intelligence Agency shall establish and maintain on the homepage of the Agency's publicly accessible website information relating to the Office of the Inspector General including methods to contact the Inspector General.

(2) The information referred to in paragraph (1) shall be obvious and facilitate accessibility to the information related to the Office of the Inspector General.

SPECIAL ANNUITY COMPUTATION RULES FOR CERTAIN EMPLOYEES' SERVICE ABROAD

SEC. 18. [50 U.S.C. §403r]

(a) OFFICERS AND EMPLOYEES TO WHOM RULES APPLY.—Notwithstanding any provision of chapter 83 of title 5, the annuity under subchapter III of such chapter of an officer or employee of the Central Intelligence Agency who retires on or after October 1, 1989, is not designated under section 2013 of this title, and has served abroad as an officer or employee of the Agency on or after January 1, 1987, shall be computed as provided in subsection (b) of this section.

(b) COMPUTATION RULES.—

(1) The portion of the annuity relating to such service abroad that is actually performed at any time during the officer's or employee's first ten years of total service shall be computed at the rate and using the percent of average pay specified in section 8339(a)(3) of title 5 that is normally applicable only to so much of an employee's total service as exceeds ten years.

(2) The portion of the annuity relating to service abroad as described in subsection (a) of this section but that is actually performed at any time after the officer's or employee's first ten years of total service shall be computed as provided in section 8339(a)(3) of title 5; but, in addition, the officer or employee shall be deemed for annuity computation purposes to have actually performed an equivalent period of service abroad during his or her first ten years of total service, and in calculating the portion of the officer's or employee's annuity for his or her first ten years of total service, the computation rate and percent of average pay specified in paragraph (1) shall also be applied to the period of such deemed or equivalent service abroad.

(3) The portion of the annuity relating to other service by an officer or employee as described in subsection (a) of this section shall be computed as provided in the provisions of section 8339(a) of title 5 that would otherwise be applicable to such service.

(4) For purposes of this subsection, the term "total service" has the meaning given such term under chapter 83 of title 5.

(c) ANNUITIES DEEMED ANNUITIES UNDER SECTION 8339 OF TITLE 5.—For purposes of subsections (f) through (m) of section 8339 of title 5, an annuity computed under this section shall be deemed to be an annuity computed under subsections (a) and (o) of section 8339 of title 5.

(d) OFFICERS AND EMPLOYEES ENTITLED TO GREATER ANNUITIES UNDER SECTION 8339 OF TITLE 5.—The provisions of subsection (a) of this section shall not apply to an officer or employee of the Central Intelligence Agency who would otherwise be entitled to a greater annuity computed under an otherwise applicable subsection of section 8339 of title 5.

SPECIAL RULES FOR DISABILITY RETIREMENT AND DEATH-IN-SERVICE BENEFITS WITH RESPECT TO CERTAIN EMPLOYEES

SEC. 19. [50 U.S.C. §403s]
(a) OFFICERS AND EMPLOYEES TO WHOM SECTION 2051 RULES APPLY.—
Notwithstanding any other provision of law, an officer or employee of the Central Intelligence Agency subject to retirement system coverage under subchapter III of chapter 83 of title 5 who—

(1) has five years of civilian service credit toward retirement under such subchapter III of chapter 83, title 5;

(2) has not been designated under section 2013 of this title as a participant in the Central Intelligence Agency Retirement and Disability System;

(3) has become disabled during a period of assignment to the performance of duties that are qualifying toward such designation under such section 2013 of this title; and

(4) satisfies the requirements for disability retirement under section 8337 of title 5—

shall, upon his own application or upon order of the Director, be retired on an annuity computed in accordance with the rules prescribed in section 2051 of this title, in lieu of an annuity computed as provided by section 8337 of title 5.

(b) Survivors of officers and employees to whom section 2052 rules apply.— Notwithstanding any other provision of law, in the case of an officer or employee of the Central Intelligence Agency subject to retirement system coverage under subchapter III of chapter 83, title 5, who—

(1) has at least eighteen months of civilian service credit toward retirement under such subchapter III of chapter 83, title 5;

(2) has not been designated under section 2013 of this title as a participant in the Central Intelligence Agency Retirement and Disability System;

(3) prior to separation or retirement from the Agency, dies during a period of assignment to the performance of duties that are qualifying toward such designation under such section 2013 of this title; and

(4) is survived by a surviving spouse, former spouse, or child as defined in section 2002 of this title, who would otherwise be entitled to an annuity under section 8341 of title 5—

such surviving spouse, former spouse, or child of such officer or employee shall be entitled to an annuity computed in accordance with section 2052 of this title, in lieu of an annuity computed in accordance with section 8341 of title 5.

(c) Annuities under this section deemed annuities under chapter 83 of title 5.— The annuities provided under subsections (a) and (b) of this section shall be deemed to be annuities under chapter 83 of title 5 for purposes of the other provisions of such chapter and other laws (including title 26) relating to such annuities, and shall be payable from the Central Intelligence Agency Retirement and Disability Fund maintained pursuant to section 2012 of this title.

GENERAL COUNSEL OF THE CENTRAL INTELLIGENCE AGENCY

SEC. 20. [50 U.S.C. §403t]

(a) APPOINTMENT.—There is a General Counsel of the Central Intelligence Agency, appointed from civilian life by the President, by and with the advice and consent of the Senate.

(b) CHIEF LEGAL OFFICER.—The General Counsel is the chief legal officer of the Central Intelligence Agency.

(c) FUNCTIONS.—The General Counsel of the Central Intelligence Agency shall perform such functions as the Director may prescribe.

CENTRAL SERVICES PROGRAM

SEC. 21. [50 U.S.C. §403u]

(a) IN GENERAL.—The Director may carry out a program under which elements of the Agency provide items and services on a reimbursable basis to other elements of the Agency, nonappropriated fund entities or instrumentalities associated or affiliated with the Agency, and other Government agencies. The Director shall carry out the program in accordance with the provisions of this section.

(b) PARTICIPATION OF AGENCY ELEMENTS.—

(1) In order to carry out the program, the Director shall—

(A) designate the elements of the Agency that are to provide items or services under the program (in this section referred to as "central service providers");

(B) specify the items or services to be provided under the program by such providers; and

(C) assign to such providers for purposes of the program such inventories, equipment, and other assets (including equipment on order) as the Director determines necessary to permit such providers to provide items or services under the program.

(2) The designation of elements and the specification of items and services under paragraph (1) shall be subject to the approval of the Director of the Office of Management and Budget.

(c) CENTRAL SERVICES WORKING CAPITAL FUND.—

(1) There is established a fund to be known as the Central Services Working Capital Fund (in this section referred to as the "Fund"). The purpose of the Fund is to provide sums for activities under the program.

(2) There shall be deposited in the Fund the following:

(A) Amounts appropriated to the Fund.

(B) Amounts credited to the Fund from payments received by central service providers under subsection (e) of this section.

(C) Fees imposed and collected under subsection (f)(1) of this section.

(D) Amounts received in payment for loss or damage to equipment or property of a central service provider as a result of activities under the program.

(E) Other receipts from the sale or exchange of equipment or property of a central service provider as a result of activities under the program.

(F) Receipts from individuals in reimbursement for utility services and meals provided under the program.

(G) Receipts from individuals for the rental of property and equipment under the program.

(H) Such other amounts as the Director is authorized to deposit in or transfer to the Fund.

(3) Amounts in the Fund shall be available, without fiscal year limitation, for the following purposes:

(A) To pay the costs of providing items or services under the program.

(B) To pay the costs of carrying out activities under subsection (f)(2) of this section.

(d) LIMITATION ON AMOUNT OF ORDERS.—The total value of all orders for items or services to be provided under the program in any fiscal year may not exceed an amount specified in advance by the Director of the Office of Management and Budget.

(e) PAYMENT FOR ITEMS AND SERVICES.—

(1) A Government agency provided items or services under the program shall pay the central service provider concerned for such items or services an amount equal to the costs incurred by the provider in providing such items or services plus any fee imposed under subsection (f) of this section. In calculating such costs, the Director shall take into account personnel costs (including costs associated with salaries, annual leave, and workers' compensation), plant and equipment costs (including depreciation of plant and equipment other than structures owned by the Agency), operation and maintenance expenses, amortized costs, and other expenses.

(2) Payment for items or services under paragraph (1) may take the form of an advanced payment by an agency from appropriations available to such agency for the procurement of such items or services.

(f) FEES.—

(1) The Director may permit a central service provider to impose and collect a fee with respect to the provision of an item or service under the program. The amount of the fee may not exceed an amount equal to four percent of the payment received by the provider for the item or service.

(2) The Director may obligate and expend amounts in the Fund that are attributable to the fees imposed and collected under paragraph (1) to acquire equipment or systems for, or to improve the equipment or systems of, central service providers and any elements of the Agency that are not designated for participation in the program in order to facilitate the designation of such elements for future participation in the program.

(g) TERMINATION.—

(1) Subject to paragraph (2), the Director of the Central Intelligence Agency and the Director of the Office of Management and Budget, acting jointly—

(A) may terminate the program under this section and the Fund at any time; and

(B) upon such termination, shall provide for the disposition of the personnel, assets, liabilities, grants, contracts, property, records, and unexpended balances of appropriations, authorizations, allocations, and other funds held, used, arising from, available to, or to be made available in connection with the program or the Fund.

(2) The Director of the Central Intelligence Agency and the Director of the Office of Management and Budget may not undertake any action under paragraph (1) until 60 days after the date on which the Directors jointly submit notice of such action to the Permanent Select Committee on Intelligence of the House of Representatives and the Select Committee on Intelligence of the Senate.

DETAIL OF EMPLOYEES

SEC. 22. [50 U.S.C. §403v]

The Director may—

(1) detail any personnel of the Agency on a reimbursable basis indefinitely to the National Reconnaissance Office without regard to any limitation under law on the duration of details of Federal Government personnel; and

(2) hire personnel for the purpose of any detail under paragraph (1).

INTELLIGENCE OPERATIONS AND COVER ENHANCEMENT AUTHORITY

Sec. 23. [50 U.S.C. §403w]

(a) DEFINITIONS.—In this section—

(1) the term "designated employee" means an employee designated by the Director of the Central Intelligence Agency under subsection (b) of this section; and

(2) the term "Federal retirement system" includes the Central Intelligence Agency Retirement and Disability System, and the Federal Employees' Retirement System (including the Thrift Savings Plan).

(b) IN GENERAL.—

(1) AUTHORITY.—Notwithstanding any other provision of law, the Director of the Central Intelligence Agency may exercise the authorities under this section in order to—

(A) protect from unauthorized disclosure—

(i) intelligence operations;

(ii) the identities of undercover intelligence officers;

(iii) intelligence sources and methods; or

(iv) intelligence cover mechanisms; or

(B) meet the special requirements of work related to collection of foreign intelligence or other authorized activities of the Agency.

(2) DESIGNATION OF EMPLOYEES.—The Director of the Central Intelligence Agency may designate any employee of the Agency who is under nonofficial cover to be an employee to whom this section applies. Such designation may be made with respect to any or all authorities exercised under this section.

(c) COMPENSATION.—The Director of the Central Intelligence Agency may pay a designated employee salary, allowances, and other benefits in an amount and in a manner consistent with the nonofficial cover of that employee, without regard to any limitation that is otherwise applicable to a Federal employee. A designated employee may accept, utilize, and, to the extent authorized by regulations prescribed under subsection (i) of this section, retain any salary, allowances, and other benefits provided under this section.

(d) RETIREMENT BENEFITS.—

(1) IN GENERAL.—The Director of the Central Intelligence Agency may establish and administer a nonofficial cover employee retirement system for designated employees (and the spouse, former spouses, and survivors of such designated employees). A designated employee may not participate in the retirement system established under this paragraph and another Federal retirement system at the same time.

(2) CONVERSION TO OTHER FEDERAL RETIREMENT SYSTEM.—

(A) IN GENERAL.—A designated employee participating in the retirement system established under paragraph (1) may convert to coverage under the Federal retirement system which would otherwise apply to that employee at any appropriate time determined by the Director of the Central Intelligence Agency (including at the time of separation of service by reason of retirement), if the Director of the Central Intelligence Agency determines that the employee's participation in the retirement system established under this subsection is no longer necessary to protect from unauthorized disclosure—

    (i) intelligence operations;

    (ii) the identities of undercover intelligence officers;

    (iii) intelligence sources and methods; or

    (iv) intelligence cover mechanisms.

(B) CONVERSION TREATMENT.—Upon a conversion under this paragraph—

    (i) all periods of service under the retirement system established under this subsection shall be deemed periods of creditable service under the applicable Federal retirement system;

    (ii) the Director of the Central Intelligence Agency shall transmit an amount for deposit in any applicable fund of that Federal retirement system that—

        (I) is necessary to cover all employee and agency contributions including—

            (aa) interest as determined by the head of the agency administering the Federal retirement system into which the employee is converting; or

            (bb) in the case of an employee converting into the Federal Employees' Retirement System, interest as determined under section 8334(e) of title 5; and

        (II) ensures that such conversion does not result in any unfunded liability to that fund; and

    (iii) in the case of a designated employee who participated in an employee investment retirement system established under paragraph (1) and is converted to coverage under subchapter III of chapter 84 of title 5, the Director of the Central Intelligence Agency may transmit any or all amounts of that designated employee in that employee investment retirement system (or similar part of that retirement system) to the Thrift Savings Fund.

(C) TRANSMITTED AMOUNTS.—

    (i) IN GENERAL.—Amounts described under subparagraph (B)(ii) shall be paid from the fund or appropriation used to pay the designated employee.

(ii) OFFSET.—The Director of the Central Intelligence Agency may use amounts contributed by the designated employee to a retirement system established under paragraph (1) to offset amounts paid under clause (i).

(D) RECORDS.—The Director of the Central Intelligence Agency shall transmit all necessary records relating to a designated employee who converts to a Federal retirement system under this paragraph (including records relating to periods of service which are deemed to be periods of creditable service under subparagraph (B)) to the head of the agency administering that Federal retirement system.

(e) HEALTH INSURANCE BENEFITS.—

(1) IN GENERAL.—The Director of the Central Intelligence Agency may establish and administer a nonofficial cover employee health insurance program for designated employees (and the family of such designated employees). A designated employee may not participate in the health insurance program established under this paragraph and the program under chapter 89 of title 5 at the same time.

(2) CONVERSION TO FEDERAL EMPLOYEES' HEALTH BENEFITS PROGRAM.—

(A) IN GENERAL.—A designated employee participating in the health insurance program established under paragraph (1) may convert to coverage under the program under chapter 89 of title 5 at any appropriate time determined by the Director of the Central Intelligence Agency (including at the time of separation of service by reason of retirement), if the Director of the Central Intelligence Agency determines that the employee's participation in the health insurance program established under this subsection is no longer necessary to protect from unauthorized disclosure—

(i) intelligence operations;

(ii) the identities of undercover intelligence officers;

(iii) intelligence sources and methods; or

(iv) intelligence cover mechanisms.

(B) CONVERSION TREATMENT.—Upon a conversion under this paragraph—

(i) the employee (and family, if applicable) shall be entitled to immediate enrollment and coverage under chapter 89 of title 5;

(ii) any requirement of prior enrollment in a health benefits plan under chapter 89 of that title for continuation of coverage purposes shall not apply;

   (iii) the employee shall be deemed to have had coverage under chapter 89 of that title from the first opportunity to enroll for purposes of continuing coverage as an annuitant; and

   (iv) the Director of the Central Intelligence Agency shall transmit an amount for deposit in the Employees' Health Benefits Fund that is necessary to cover any costs of such conversion.

  (C) TRANSMITTED AMOUNTS.—Any amount described under subparagraph (B)(iv) shall be paid from the fund or appropriation used to pay the designated employee.

(f) LIFE INSURANCE BENEFITS.—

 (1) IN GENERAL.—The Director of the Central Intelligence Agency may establish and administer a nonofficial cover employee life insurance program for designated employees (and the family of such designated employees). A designated employee may not participate in the life insurance program established under this paragraph and the program under chapter 87 of title 5 at the same time.

 (2) CONVERSION TO FEDERAL EMPLOYEES GROUP LIFE INSURANCE PROGRAM.—

  (A) IN GENERAL.—A designated employee participating in the life insurance program established under paragraph (1) may convert to coverage under the program under chapter 87 of title 5 at any appropriate time determined by the Director of the Central Intelligence Agency (including at the time of separation of service by reason of retirement), if the Director of the Central Intelligence Agency determines that the employee's participation in the life insurance program established under this subsection is no longer necessary to protect from unauthorized disclosure—

   (i) intelligence operations;

   (ii) the identities of undercover intelligence officers;

   (iii) intelligence sources and methods; or

   (iv) intelligence cover mechanisms.

  (B) CONVERSION TREATMENT.—Upon a conversion under this paragraph—

   (i) the employee (and family, if applicable) shall be entitled to immediate coverage under chapter 87 of title 5;

   (ii) any requirement of prior enrollment in a life insurance program under chapter 87 of that title for continuation of coverage purposes shall not apply;

(iii) the employee shall be deemed to have had coverage under chapter 87 of that title for the full period of service during which the employee would have been entitled to be insured for purposes of continuing coverage as an annuitant; and

(iv) the Director of the Central Intelligence Agency shall transmit an amount for deposit in the Employees' Life Insurance Fund that is necessary to cover any costs of such conversion.

(C) TRANSMITTED AMOUNTS.—Any amount described under subparagraph (B)(iv) shall be paid from the fund or appropriation used to pay the designated employee.

(g) EXEMPTION FROM CERTAIN REQUIREMENTS.—The Director of the Central Intelligence Agency may exempt a designated employee from mandatory compliance with any Federal regulation, rule, standardized administrative policy, process, or procedure that the Director of the Central Intelligence Agency determines—

(1) would be inconsistent with the nonofficial cover of that employee; and

(2) could expose that employee to detection as a Federal employee.

(h) TAXATION AND SOCIAL SECURITY.—

(1) In general.—Notwithstanding any other provision of law, a designated employee—

(A) shall file a Federal or State tax return as if that employee is not a Federal employee and may claim and receive the benefit of any exclusion, deduction, tax credit, or other tax treatment that would otherwise apply if that employee was not a Federal employee, if the Director of the Central Intelligence Agency determines that taking any action under this paragraph is necessary to—

(i) protect from unauthorized disclosure—

(I) intelligence operations;

(II) the identities of undercover intelligence officers;

(III) intelligence sources and methods; or

(IV) intelligence cover mechanisms; and

(ii) meet the special requirements of work related to collection of foreign intelligence or other authorized activities of the Agency; and

(B) shall receive social security benefits based on the social security contributions made.

293

(2) INTERNAL REVENUE SERVICE REVIEW.—The Director of the Central Intelligence Agency shall establish procedures to carry out this subsection. The procedures shall be subject to periodic review by the Internal Revenue Service.

(i) Regulations.—The Director of the Central Intelligence Agency shall prescribe regulations to carry out this section. The regulations shall ensure that the combination of salary, allowances, and benefits that an employee designated under this section may retain does not significantly exceed, except to the extent determined by the Director of the Central Intelligence Agency to be necessary to exercise the authority in subsection (b) of this section, the combination of salary, allowances, and benefits otherwise received by Federal employees not designated under this section.

(j) Finality of decisions.—Any determinations authorized by this section to be made by the Director of the Central Intelligence Agency or the Director's designee shall be final and conclusive and shall not be subject to review by any court.

(k) Subsequently enacted laws.—No law enacted after the effective date of this section shall affect the authorities and provisions of this section unless such law specifically refers to this section.

SEPARATION PAY PROGRAM FOR VOLUNTARY SEPARATION FROM SERVICE

[50 U.S.C. §403x]

(a) DEFINITIONS.—For purposes of this section—

(1) the term "Director" means the Director of the Central Intelligence Agency; and

(2) the term "employee" means an employee of the Central Intelligence Agency, serving under an appointment without time limitation, who has been currently employed for a continuous period of at least 12 months, except that such term does not include—

(A) a reemployed annuitant under subchapter III of chapter 83 or chapter 84 of title 5 or another retirement system for employees of the Government; or

(B) an employee having a disability on the basis of which such employee is or would be eligible for disability retirement under any of the retirement systems referred to in subparagraph (A).

(b) ESTABLISHMENT OF PROGRAM.—In order to avoid or minimize the need for involuntary separations due to downsizing, reorganization, transfer of function, or other similar action, the Director may establish a program under which employees may be offered separation pay to separate from service voluntarily (whether by retirement or resignation). An employee who receives separation pay under such program may not be reemployed by the Central Intelligence Agency for the 12-month period beginning on the effective date of the employee's separation. An employee who receives separation pay under this section on the basis of a separation occurring on or after March 30, 1994, and accepts employment with the Government of the United States within 5 years after the date of the separation on which payment of the separation pay is based shall be required to repay the entire amount of the separation pay to the Central Intelligence Agency. If the employment is with an Executive agency (as defined by section 105 of title 5), the Director of the Office of Personnel Management may, at the request of the head of the agency, waive the repayment if the individual involved possesses unique abilities and is the only qualified applicant available for the position. If the employment is with an entity in the legislative branch, the head of the entity or the appointing official may waive the repayment if the individual involved possesses unique abilities and is the only qualified applicant available for the position. If the employment is with the judicial branch, the Director of the Administrative Office of the United States Courts may waive the repayment if the individual involved possesses unique abilities and is the only qualified applicant available for the position.

(c) BAR ON CERTAIN EMPLOYMENT.—

    (1) BAR.—An employee may not be separated from service under this section unless the employee agrees that the employee will not –

        (A) act as agent or attorney for, or otherwise represent, any other person (except the United States) in any formal or informal appearance before, or, with the intent to influence, make any oral or written communication on behalf of any other person (except the United States) to the Central Intelligence Agency; or

        (B) participate in any manner in the award, modification, extension, or performance of any contract for property or services with the Central Intelligence Agency, during the 12-month period beginning on the effective date of the employee's separation from service.

    (2) PENALTY.—An employee who violates an agreement under this subsection shall be liable to the United States in the amount of the separation pay paid to the employee pursuant to this section times the proportion of the 12-month period during which the employee was in violation of the agreement.

(d) LIMITATIONS.—Under this program, separation pay may be offered only—

    (1) with the prior approval of the Director; and

    (2) to employees within such occupational groups or geographic locations, or subject to such other similar limitations or conditions, as the Director may require.

(e) AMOUNT AND TREATMENT FOR OTHER PURPOSES.—Such separation pay—

    (1) shall be paid in a lump sum;

(2) shall be equal to the lesser of—

    (A) an amount equal to the amount the employee would be entitled to receive under section 5595(c) of title 5, if the employee were entitled to payment under such section; or

    (B) $25,000;

(3) shall not be a basis for payment, and shall not be included in the computation, of any other type of Government benefit; and

(4) shall not be taken into account for the purpose of determining the amount of any severance pay to which an individual may be entitled under section 5595 of title 5 based on any other separation.

(f) REGULATIONS.—The Director shall prescribe such regulations as may be necessary to carry out this section.

(g) REPORTING REQUIREMENTS.—

    (1) OFFERING NOTIFICATION.—The Director may not make an offering of voluntary separation pay pursuant to this section until 30 days after submitting to the Permanent Select Committee on Intelligence of the House of Representatives and the Select Committee on Intelligence of the Senate a report describing the occupational groups or geographic locations, or other similar limitations or conditions, required by the Director under subsection (d) of this section.

    (2) Annual report.—At the end of each of the fiscal years 1993 through 1997, the Director shall submit to the President and the Permanent Select Committee on Intelligence of the House of Representatives and the Select Committee on Intelligence of the Senate a report on the effectiveness and costs of carrying out this section.

NATIONAL SECURITY AGENCY ACT OF 1959

(Pub. L. 86-36, May 29, 1959)

SECTION. 1. This Act (this note) may be cited as the 'National Security Agency Act of 1959'.

[SEC. 2. Repealed. Pub .L. 104-201, SEC. 1633, Sept. 9, 1996, 110 Stat. 2751.]

SEC. 3. (Amended section 1581(a) of Title 10, Armed Forces.)

[SEC. 4. Repealed. Pub .L. 104-201, SEC. 1633, Sept. 9, 1996, 110 Stat. 2751.]

SEC. 5. Officers and employees of the National Security Agency who are citizens or nationals of the United States may be granted additional compensation, in accordance with regulations which shall be prescribed by the Secretary of Defense, not in excess of additional compensation authorized by section 207 of the Independent Offices Appropriation Act, 1949, as amended (5 U.S.C. 118h) (see 5 U.S.C. 5941), for employees whose rates of basic compensation are fixed by statute.

SEC. 6.
(a) Except as provided in subsection (b) of this section, nothing in this Act or any other law (including, but not limited to, the first section and section 2 of the Act of August 28, 1935 (5 U.S.C. 654) (repealed by Pub. L. 86-626, title I, SEC. 101, July 12, 1960, 74 Stat. 427)) shall be construed to require the disclosure of the organization or any function of the National Security Agency, or any information with respect to the activities thereof, or of the names, titles, salaries, or number of the persons employed by such agency.
(b) The reporting requirements of section 1582 of title 10, United States Code, shall apply to positions established in the National Security Agency in the manner provided by section 4 of this Act.

[SEC. 7. Repealed. Pub. L. 89-554, SEC. 8(a), Sept. 6, 1966, 80 Stat. 660.]

SEC. 8. The foregoing provisions of this Act shall take effect on the first day of the first pay period which begins later than the thirtieth day following the date of enactment of this Act.

SEC. 9.
(a) Notwithstanding section 322 of the Act of June 30, 1932 (40 U.S.C. 278a), section 5536 of title 5, United States Code, and section 2675 of title 10, United

States Code, the Director of the National Security Agency, on behalf of the Secretary of Defense, may lease real property outside the United States, for periods not exceeding ten years, for the use of the National Security Agency for special cryptologic activities and for housing for personnel assigned to such activities.

(b) The Director of the National Security Agency, on behalf of the Secretary of Defense, may provide to certain civilian and military personnel of the Department of Defense who are assigned to special cryptologic activities outside the United States and who are designated by the Secretary of Defense for the purposes of this subsection -

    (1) allowances and benefits –

        (A) comparable to those provided by the Secretary of State to members of the Foreign Service under chapter 9 of title I of the Foreign Service Act of 1980 (22 U.S.C. 4081 et seq.) or any other provision of law; and

        (B) in the case of selected personnel serving in circumstances similar to those in which personnel of the Central Intelligence Agency serve, comparable to those provided by the Director of Central Intelligence to personnel of the Central Intelligence Agency;

    (2) housing (including heat, light, and household equipment) without cost to such personnel, if the Director of the National Security Agency, on behalf of the Secretary of Defense determines that it would be in the public interest to provide such housing; and

    (3) special retirement accrual in the same manner provided in section 303 of the Central Intelligence Agency Retirement Act (50 U.S.C. 403 note) (50 U.S.C. 2001 et seq.) and in section 18 of the Central Intelligence Agency Act of 1949 (50 U.S.C. 403r).

(c) The authority of the Director of the National Security Agency, on behalf of the Secretary of Defense, to make payments under subsections (a) and (b), and under contracts for leases entered into under subsection (a), is effective for any fiscal year only to the extent that appropriated funds are available for such purpose.

(d) Members of the Armed Forces may not receive benefits under both subsection (b)(1) and title 37, United States Code, for the same purpose. The Secretary of Defense shall prescribe such regulations as may be necessary to carry out this subsection.

(e) Regulations issued pursuant to subsection (b)(1) shall be submitted to the Permanent Select Committee on Intelligence of the House of Representatives and the Select Committee on Intelligence of the Senate before such regulations take effect.

SEC. 10.

(a) The Director of the National Security Agency shall arrange for, and shall prescribe regulations concerning, language and language-related training programs for military and civilian cryptologic personnel. In establishing programs under this section for language and language-related training, the Director –

(1) may provide for the training and instruction to be furnished, including functional and geographic area specializations;

(2) may arrange for training and instruction through other Government agencies and, in any case in which appropriate training or instruction is unavailable through Government facilities, through nongovernmental facilities that furnish training and instruction useful in the fields of language and foreign affairs;

(3) may support programs that furnish necessary language and language-related skills, including, in any case in which appropriate programs are unavailable at Government facilities, support through contracts, grants, or cooperation with nongovernmental educational institutions; and

(4) may obtain by appointment or contract the services of individuals to serve as language instructors, linguists, or special language project personnel.

(b)(1) In order to maintain necessary capability in foreign language skills and related abilities needed by the National Security Agency, the Director, without regard to subchapter IV of chapter 55 of title 5, United States Code, may provide special monetary or other incentives to encourage civilian cryptologic personnel of the Agency to acquire or retain proficiency in foreign languages or special related abilities needed by the Agency.

(2) In order to provide linguistic training and support for cryptologic personnel, the Director –

(A) may pay all or part of the tuition and other expenses related to the training of personnel who are assigned or detailed for language and language-related training, orientation, or instruction; and

(B) may pay benefits and allowances to civilian personnel in accordance with chapters 57 and 59 of title 5, United States Code, and to military personnel in accordance with chapter 7 of title 37, United States Code, and applicable provisions of title 10, United States Code, when such personnel are assigned to training at sites away from their designated duty station.

(c)(1) To the extent not inconsistent, in the opinion of the Secretary of Defense, with the operation of military cryptologic reserve units and in order to maintain necessary capability in foreign language skills and related abilities needed by the National Security Agency, the Director may establish a cryptologic linguist reserve. The cryptologic linguist reserve may consist of former or retired civilian or military cryptologic personnel of the National Security Agency and of other qualified individuals, as determined by the Director of the Agency. Each member of the cryptologic linguist reserve shall agree that, during any period of emergency (as determined by the Director), the member shall return to active civilian status with the National Security Agency and shall perform such linguistic or linguistic-related duties as the Director may assign.

(2) In order to attract individuals to become members of the cryptologic linguist reserve, the Director, without regard to subchapter IV of chapter 55 of title 5, United States Code, may provide special monetary incentives to individuals eligible to become members of the reserve who agree to become members of the cryptologic linguist reserve and to acquire or retain proficiency in foreign languages or special related abilities.

(3) In order to provide training and support for members of the cryptologic linguist reserve, the Director –

(A) may pay all or part of the tuition and other expenses related to the training of individuals in the cryptologic linguist reserve who are assigned or detailed for language and language-related training, orientation, or instruction; and

(B) may pay benefits and allowances in accordance with chapters 57 and 59 of title 5, United States Code, to individuals in the cryptologic linguist reserve who are assigned to training at sites away from their homes or regular places of business.

(d)(1) The Director, before providing training under this section to any individual, may obtain an agreement with that individual that -

(A) in the case of current employees, pertains to continuation of service of the employee, and repayment of the expenses of such training for failure to fulfill the agreement, consistent with the provisions of section 4108 of title 5, United States Code; and

(B) in the case of individuals accepted for membership in the cryptologic linguist reserve, pertains to return to service when requested, and repayment of the expenses of such training for failure to fulfill the agreement, consistent with the provisions of section 4108 of title 5, United States Code.

(2) The Director, under regulations prescribed under this section, may waive, in whole or in part, a right of recovery under an agreement made under this subsection if it is shown that the recovery would be against equity and good conscience or against the public interest.

(e)(1) Subject to paragraph (2), the Director may provide to family members of military and civilian cryptologic personnel assigned to representational duties outside the United States, in anticipation of the assignment of such personnel outside the United States or while outside the United States, appropriate orientation and language training that is directly related to the assignment abroad.

(2) Language training under paragraph (1) may not be provided to any individual through payment of the expenses of tuition or other cost of instruction at a non-Government educational institution unless appropriate instruction is not available at a Government facility.

(f) The Director may waive the applicability of any provision of chapter 41 of title 5, United States Code, to any provision of this section if he finds that such waiver is important to the performance of cryptologic functions.

(g) The authority of the Director to enter into contracts or to make grants under this section is effective for any fiscal year only to the extent that appropriated funds are available for such purpose.

(h) Regulations issued pursuant to this section shall be submitted to the Permanent Select Committee on Intelligence of the House of Representatives and the Select Committee on Intelligence of the Senate before such regulations take effect.

(i) The Director of the National Security Agency, on behalf of the Secretary of Defense, may, without regard to section 4109(a)(2)(B) of title 5, United States Code, pay travel, transportation, storage, and subsistence expenses under chapter 57 of such title to civilian and military personnel of the Department of Defense who are assigned to duty outside the United States for a period of one year or longer which involves cryptologic training, language training, or related disciplines.

SEC. 11.

(a)(1) The Director of the National Security Agency may authorize agency personnel within the United States to perform the same functions as special policemen of the General Services Administration perform under the first section of the Act entitled `An Act to authorize the Federal Works Administrator or officials of the Federal Works Agency duly authorized by him to appoint special policemen for duty upon Federal property under the jurisdiction of the Federal Works Agency, and for other purposes' (40 U.S.C. 318) with the powers set forth in that section, except that such personnel shall perform such functions and exercise such powers—

    (A) at the National Security Agency Headquarters complex and at any facilities and protected property which are solely under the administration and control of, or are used exclusively by, the National Security Agency; and

    (B) in the streets, sidewalks, and the open areas within the zone beginning at the outside boundary of such facilities or protected property and extending outward 500 feet.

(2) The performance of functions and exercise of powers under subparagraph (B) of paragraph (1) shall be limited to those circumstances where such personnel can identify specific and articulable facts giving such personnel

reason to believe that the performance of such functions and exercise of such powers is reasonable to protect against physical damage or injury, or threats of physical damage or injury, to agency installations, property, or employees. (3) Nothing in this subsection shall be construed to preclude, or limit in any way, the authority of any Federal, State, or local law enforcement agency, or any other Federal police or Federal protective service. (4) The rules and regulations enforced by such personnel shall be the rules and regulations prescribed by the Director and shall only be applicable to the areas referred to in subparagraph (A) of paragraph (1). (5) Agency personnel authorized by the Director under paragraph (1) may transport an individual apprehended under the authority of this section from the premises at which the individual was apprehended, as described in subparagraph (A) or (B) of paragraph (1), for the purpose of transferring such individual to the custody of law enforcement officials. Such transportation may be provided only to make a transfer of custody at a location within 30 miles of the premises described in subparagraphs (A) and (B) of paragraph (1).

(b) The Director of the National Security Agency is authorized to establish penalties for violations of the rules or regulations prescribed by the Director under subsection (a). Such penalties shall not exceed those specified in the fourth section of the Act referred to in subsection (a) (40 U.S.C. 318c).

(c) Agency personnel designated by the Director of the National Security Agency under subsection (a) shall be clearly identifiable as United States Government security personnel while engaged in the performance of the functions to which subsection (a) refers.

(d)(1) Notwithstanding any other provision of law, agency personnel designated by the Director of the National Security Agency under subsection (a) shall be considered for purposes of chapter 171 of title 28, United States Code, or any other provision of law relating to tort liability, to be acting within the scope of their office or employment when such agency personnel take reasonable action, which may include the use of force, to—

    (A) protect and individual in the presence of such agency personnel from a crime of violence;

    (B) provide immediate assistance to an individual who has suffered or who is threatened with bodily harm;

    (C) prevent the escape of any individual whom such agency personnel reasonably believe to have committed a crime of violence in the presence of such agency personnel; or

    (D) transport an individual pursuant to subsection (a)(2).

(2) Paragraph (1) shall not affect the authorities of the Attorney General under section 2679 of title 28, United States Code.

(3) In this subsection, the term "crime of violence" as the meaning given that term in section 16 of title 18, United States Code.

SEC. 12.

(a)(1) The Secretary of Defense (or his designee) may by regulation establish a personnel system for senior civilian cryptologic personnel in the National Security Agency to be known as the Senior Cryptologic Executive Service. The regulations establishing the Senior Cryptologic Executive Service shall –

(A) meet the requirements set forth in section 3131 of title 5, United States Code, for the Senior Executive Service;

(B) provide that positions in the Senior Cryptologic Executive Service meet requirements that are consistent with the provisions of section 3132(a)(2) of such title;

(C) provide, without regard to section 2, rates of pay for the Senior Cryptologic Executive Service that are not in excess of the maximum rate or less than the minimum rate of basic pay established for the Senior Executive Service under section 5382 of such title, and that are adjusted at the same time and to the same extent as rates of basic pay for the Senior Executive Service are adjusted;

(D) provide a performance appraisal system for the Senior Cryptologic Executive Service that conforms to the provisions of subchapter II of chapter 43 of such title;

(E) provide for removal consistent with section 3592 of such title, and removal or suspension consistent with subsections (a), (b), and (c) of section 7543 of such title (except that any hearing or appeal to which a member of the Senior Cryptologic Executive Service is entitled shall be held or decided pursuant to procedures established by regulations of the Secretary of Defense or his designee);

(F) permit the payment of performance awards to members of the Senior Cryptologic Executive Service consistent with the provisions applicable to performance awards under section 5384 of such title;

(G) provide that members of the Senior Cryptologic Executive Service may be granted sabbatical leaves consistent with the provisions of section 3396(c) of such title.(;) and

(H) provide for the recertification of members of the Senior Cryptologic Executive Service consistent with the provisions of section 3393a of such title.

(2) Except as otherwise provided in subsection (a), the Secretary of Defense (or his designee) may –

(A) make applicable to the Senior Cryptologic Executive Service any of the provisions of title 5, United States Code, applicable to applicants for or members of the Senior Executive Service; and

(B) appoint, promote, and assign individuals to positions established within the Senior Cryptologic Executive Service without regard to the provisions of title 5, United States Code, governing appointments and other personnel actions in the competitive service.

(3) The President, based on the recommendations of the Secretary of Defense, may award ranks to members of the Senior Cryptologic Executive Service in a manner consistent with the provisions of section 4507 of title 5, United States Code.

(4) Notwithstanding any other provision of this section, the Director of the National Security Agency may detail or assign any member of the Senior Cryptologic Executive Service to serve in a position outside the National Security Agency in which the member's expertise and experience may be of benefit to the National Security Agency or another Government agency. Any such member shall not by reason of such detail or assignment lose any entitlement or status associated with membership in the Senior Cryptologic Executive Service.

(b) The Secretary of Defense (or his designee) may by regulation establish a merit pay system for such employees of the National Security Agency as the Secretary of Defense (or his designee) considers appropriate. The merit pay system shall be designed to carry out purposes consistent with those set forth in section 5401(a) of title 5, United States Code.

(c) Nothing in this section shall be construed to allow the aggregate amount payable to a member of the Senior Cryptologic Executive Service under this section during any fiscal year to exceed the annual rate payable for positions at level I of the Executive Schedule (5 U.S.C. 5312) in effect at the end of such year.

SEC. 13.

(a) The Director of the National Security Agency may make grants to private individuals and institutions for the conduct of cryptologic research. An application for a grant under this section may not be approved unless the Director determines that the award of the grant would be clearly consistent with the national security.

(b) The grant program established by subsection (a) shall be conducted in accordance with the Federal Grant and Cooperative Agreement Act of 1977 (41 U.S.C. 501 et seq.) (31 U.S.C. 6301 et seq.) to the extent that such Act is consistent with and in accordance with section 6 of this Act.

(c) The authority of the Director to make grants under this section is effective for any fiscal year only to the extent that appropriated funds are available for such purpose.

SEC. 14. Funds appropriated to an entity of the Federal Government other than an element of the Department of Defense that have been specifically appropriated for the purchase of cryptologic equipment, materials, or services with respect to which the National Security Agency has been designated as the central source of procurement for the Government shall remain available for a period of three fiscal years.

SEC. 15.
(a) No person may, except with the written permission of the Director of the National Security Agency, knowingly use the words 'National Security Agency', the initials 'NSA', the seal of the National Security Agency, or any colorable imitation of such words, initials, or seal in connection with any merchandise, impersonation, solicitation, or commercial activity in a manner reasonably calculated to convey the impression that such use is approved, endorsed, or authorized by the National Security Agency.
(b) Whenever it appears to the Attorney General that any person is engaged or is about to engage in an act or practice which constitutes or will constitute conduct prohibited by subsection (a), the Attorney General may initiate a civil proceeding in a district court of the United States to enjoin such act or practice. Such court shall proceed as soon as practicable to the hearing and determination of such action and may, at any time before final determination, enter such restraining orders or prohibitions, or take such other action as is warranted, to prevent injury to the United States or to any person or class of persons for whose protection the action is brought.

SEC. 16.
(a) The purpose of this section is to establish an undergraduate training program, which may lead to the baccalaureate degree, to facilitate the recruitment of individuals, particularly minority high school students, with a demonstrated capability to develop skills critical to the mission of the National Security Agency, including mathematics, computer science, engineering, and foreign languages.
(b) The Secretary of Defense is authorized, in his discretion, to assign civilian employees of the National Security Agency as students at accredited professional, technical, and other institutions of higher learning for training at the undergraduate level in skills critical to effective performance of the mission of the Agency.
(c) The National Security Agency may pay, directly or by reimbursement to employees, expenses incident to assignments under subsection (b), in any fiscal year only to the extent that appropriated funds are available for such purpose.
(d)(1) To be eligible for assignment under subsection (b), an employee of the Agency must agree in writing –

(A) to continue in the service of the Agency for the period of the assignment and to complete the educational course of training for which the employee is assigned;

(B) to continue in the service of the Agency following completion of the assignment for a period of one-and-a-half years for each year of the assignment or part thereof;

(C) to reimburse the United States for the total cost of education (excluding the employee's pay and allowances) provided under this section to the employee if, prior to the employee's completing the educational course of training for which the employee is assigned, the assignment or the employee's employment with the Agency is terminated either by the Agency due to misconduct by the employee or by the employee voluntarily; and

(D) to reimburse the United States if, after completing the educational course of training for which the employee is assigned, the employee's employment with the Agency is terminated either by the Agency due to misconduct by the employee or by the employee voluntarily, prior to the employee's completion of the service obligation period described in subparagraph (B), in an amount that bears the same ratio to the total cost of the education (excluding the employee's pay and allowances) provided to the employee as the unserved portion of the service obligation period described in subparagraph (B) bears to the total period of the service obligation described in subparagraph (B).

(2) Subject to paragraph (3), the obligation to reimburse the United States under an agreement described in paragraph (1), including interest due on such obligation, is for all purposes a debt owing the United States.

(3)(A) A discharge in bankruptcy under title 11, United States Code, shall not release a person from an obligation to reimburse the United States required under an agreement described in paragraph (1) if the final decree of the discharge in bankruptcy is issued within five years after the last day of the combined period of service obligation described in   subparagraphs (A) and (B) of paragraph (1).

(B) The Secretary of Defense may release a person, in whole or in part, from the obligation to reimburse the United States under an agreement described in paragraph (1) when, in his discretion, the Secretary determines that equity or the interests of the United States so require.

(C) The Secretary of Defense shall permit an employee assigned under this section who, prior to commencing a second academic year of such assignment, voluntarily terminates the assignment or the employee's employment with the Agency, to satisfy his obligation under an agreement described in paragraph (1) to reimburse the United States by reimbursement according to a schedule of monthly payments which results in completion of reimbursement by a date five years after the date of termination of the assignment or employment or earlier at the option of the employee.

(e)(1) When an employee is assigned under this section to an institution, the Agency shall disclose to the institution to which the employee is assigned that the Agency employs the employee and that the Agency funds the employee's education.

(2) Agency efforts to recruit individuals at educational institutions for participation in the undergraduate training program established by this section shall be made openly and according to the common practices of universities and employers recruiting at such institutions.

(f) Chapter 41 of title 5 and subsections (a) and (b) of section 3324 of title 31, United States Code, shall not apply with respect to this section.

(g) The Secretary of Defense may issue such regulations as may be necessary to implement this section.

[SEC. 17. Repealed. Pub. L. 103-359, SEC. 806, Oct. 14, 1994, 108 Stat. 3442]

SEC. 18.

(a) The Secretary of Defense may pay the expenses referred to in section 5742(b) of title 5, United States Code, in the case of any employee of the National Security Agency who dies while on a rotational tour of duty within the United States or while in transit to or from such tour of duty.

(b) For the purposes of this section, the term 'rotational tour of duty', with respect to an employee, means a permanent change of station involving the transfer of the employee from the National Security Agency headquarters to another post of duty for a fixed period established by regulation to be followed at the end of such period by a permanent change of station involving a transfer of the employee back to such headquarters.

SEC. 19.

(a) There is established the National Security Agency Emerging Technologies Panel. The Panel is a standing panel of the National Security Agency. The Panel shall be appointed by, and shall report directly to, the Director of the National Security Agency.

(b) The Panel shall study and assess, and periodically advise the Director on, the research, development, and application of existing and emerging science and technology advances, advances in encryption, and other topics.

(c) The Federal Advisory Committee Act (5 U.S.C. App.) shall not apply with respect to the Panel.

SEC. 20.

(a) The Director may collect charges for evaluating, certifying, or validating information assurance products under the National Information Assurance Program or successor program.

(b) The charges collected under subsection (a) shall be established through a public rulemaking process in accordance with Office of Management and Budget Circular No. A-25.

(c) Charges collected under subsection (a) shall not exceed the direct costs of the program referred to in that subsection.

(d) The appropriation or fund bearing the cost of the service for which charges are collected under the program referred to in subsection (a) may be reimbursed, or the Director may require advance payment subject to such adjustment on completion of the work as may be agreed
upon.

(e) Amounts collected under this section shall be credited to the account or accounts from which costs associated with such amounts have been or will be incurred, to reimburse or offset the direct costs of the program referred to in subsection (a).

DEPARTMENT OF DEFENSE TITLE 10 AUTHORITIES

CHAPTER 4 OF TITLE 10, UNITED STATES CODE

UNDER SECRETARY OF DEFENSE FOR INTELLIGENCE

SEC. 137.

(a) There is an Under Secretary of Defense for Intelligence, appointed from civilian life by the President, by and with the advice and consent of the Senate.

(b) Subject to the authority, direction, and control of the Secretary of Defense, the Under Secretary of Defense for Intelligence shall perform such duties and exercise such powers as the Secretary of Defense may prescribe in the area of intelligence.

(c) The Under Secretary of Defense for Intelligence takes precedence in the Department of Defense after the Under Secretary of Defense for Personnel and Readiness.

CHAPTER 21 OF TITLE 10, UNITED STATES CODE

FUNDS FOR FOREIGN CRYPTOLOGIC SUPPORT

SEC. 421.

(a) The Secretary of Defense may use appropriated funds available to the Department of Defense for intelligence and communications purposes to pay for the expenses of arrangements with foreign countries for cryptologic support.

(b) The Secretary of Defense may use funds other than appropriated funds to pay for the expenses of arrangements with foreign countries for cryptologic support without regard for the provisions of law relating to the expenditure of United States Government funds, except that—

(1) no such funds may be expended, in whole or in part, by or for the benefit of the Department of Defense for a purpose for which Congress had previously denied funds; and

(2) proceeds from the sale of cryptologic items may be used only to purchase replacement items similar to the items that are sold; and

(3) the authority provided by this subsection may not be used to acquire items or services for the principal benefit of the United States.

(c) Any funds expended under the authority of subsection (a) shall be reported to the Select Committee on Intelligence of the Senate and the Permanent Select Committee on Intelligence of the House of Representatives pursuant to the provisions of title V of the National Security Act of 1947 (50 U.S.C. §413 et seq.). Funds expended under the authority of subsection (b) shall be reported pursuant to procedures jointly agreed upon by such committees and the Secretary of Defense.

USE OF FUNDS FOR CERTAIN INCIDENTAL PURPOSES

SEC. 422.

(a) COUNTERINTELLIGENCE OFFICIAL RECEPTION AND REPRESENTATION EXPENSES.—The Secretary of Defense may use funds available to the Department of Defense for counterintelligence programs to pay the expenses of hosting foreign officials in the United States under the auspices of the Department of Defense for consultation on counterintelligence matters.

(b) PROMOTIONAL ITEMS FOR RECRUITMENT PURPOSES.—The Secretary of Defense may use funds available for an intelligence element of the Department of Defense to purchase promotional items of nominal value for use in the recruitment of individuals for employment by that element.

AUTHORITY TO USE PROCEEDS FROM COUNTERINTELLIGENCE OPERATIONS OF THE MILITARY DEPARTMENTS

SEC. 423.

(a) The Secretary of Defense may authorize, without regard to the provisions of section 3302 of title 31, use of proceeds from counterintelligence operations conducted by components of the military departments to offset necessary and reasonable expenses, not otherwise prohibited by law, incurred in such operations, and to make exceptional performance awards to personnel involved in such operations, if use of appropriated funds to meet such expenses or to make such awards would not be practicable.

(b) As soon as the net proceeds from such counterintelligence operations are no longer necessary for the conduct of those operations, such proceeds shall be deposited into the Treasury as miscellaneous receipts.

(c) The Secretary of Defense shall establish policies and procedures to govern acquisition, use, management, and disposition of proceeds from counterintelligence operations conducted by components of the military departments or the Defense Intelligence Agency, including effective internal systems of accounting and administrative controls.

DISCLOSURE OF ORGANIZATIONAL AND PERSONNEL INFORMATION: EXEMPTION FOR SPECIFIED INTELLIGENCE AGENCIES

SEC. 424.

(a) EXEMPTION FROM DISCLOSURE.—Except as required by the President or as provided in subsection (c), no provision of law shall be construed to require the disclosure of—

(1) the organization or any function of an organization of the Department of Defense named in subsection (b); or

(2) the number of persons employed by or assigned or detailed to any such organization or the name, official title, occupational series, grade, or salary of any such person.

(b) COVERED ORGANIZATIONS.—This section applies to the following organizations of the Department of Defense:

(1) The Defense Intelligence Agency.

(2) The National Reconnaissance Office.

(3) The National Geospatial-Intelligence Agency.

(c) PROVISION OF INFORMATION TO CONGRESS.—Subsection (a) does not apply with respect to the provision of information to Congress.

PROHIBITION OF UNAUTHORIZED USE OF NAME, INITIALS, OR SEAL: SPECIFIED INTELLIGENCE AGENCIES

SEC. 425.

(a) PROHIBITION.—Except with the written permission of both the Secretary of Defense and the Director of National Intelligence, no person may knowingly use, in connection with any merchandise, retail product, impersonation, solicitation, or commercial activity in a manner reasonably calculated to convey the impression that such use is approved, endorsed, or authorized by the Secretary and the Director, any of the following (or any colorable imitation thereof):

(1) The words "Defense Intelligence Agency", the initials "DIA", or the seal of the Defense Intelligence Agency.

(2) The words "National Reconnaissance Office", the initials "NRO", or the seal of the National Reconnaissance Office.

(3) The words "National Imagery and Mapping Agency", the initials "NIMA", or the seal of the National Imagery and Mapping Agency.

(4) The words "Defense Mapping Agency", the initials "DMA", or the seal of the Defense Mapping Agency.

(5) The words "National Geospatial-Intelligence Agency", the initials "NGA," or the seal of the National Geospatial-Intelligence Agency.

(b) AUTHORITY TO ENJOIN VIOLATIONS.—Whenever it appears to the Attorney General that any person is engaged or is about to engage in an act or practice which constitutes or will constitute conduct prohibited by subsection (a), the Attorney General may initiate a civil proceeding in a district court of the United States to enjoin such act or practice. Such court shall proceed as soon as practicable to the hearing and determination of such action and may, at any time before final determination, enter such restraining orders or prohibitions, or take such other actions as is warranted, to prevent injury to the United States or to any person or class of persons for whose protection the action is brought.

INTEGRATION OF DEPARTMENT OF DEFENSE INTELLIGENCE, SURVEILLANCE, AND RECONNAISSANCE CAPABILITIES

SEC. 426.

(a) ISR INTEGRATION COUNCIL.—

(1) The Under Secretary of Defense for Intelligence shall establish an Intelligence, Surveillance, and Reconnaissance Integration Council—

    (A) to assist the Under Secretary with respect to matters relating to the integration of intelligence, surveillance, and reconnaissance capabilities, and coordination of related developmental activities, of the military departments, intelligence agencies of the Department of Defense, and relevant combatant commands; and

    (B) otherwise to provide a means to facilitate the integration of such capabilities and the coordination of such developmental activities.

(2) The Council shall be composed of—

    (A) the senior intelligence officers of the armed forces and the United States Special Operations Command;

    (B) the Director of Operations of the Joint Staff; and

    (C) the directors of the intelligence agencies of the Department of Defense.

(3) The Under Secretary of Defense for Intelligence shall invite the participation of the Director of National Intelligence (or that Director's representative) in the proceedings of the Council.

(4) Each Secretary of a military department may designate an officer or employee of such military department to attend the proceedings of the Council as a representative of such military department.

(b) ISR INTEGRATION ROADMAP.—

(1) The Under Secretary of Defense for Intelligence shall develop a comprehensive plan, to be known as the "Defense Intelligence, Surveillance, and Reconnaissance Integration Roadmap", to guide the development and integration of the Department of Defense intelligence, surveillance, and reconnaissance capabilities for the 15-year period of fiscal years 2004 through 2018.

(2) The Under Secretary shall develop the Defense Intelligence, Surveillance, and Reconnaissance Integration Roadmap in consultation with the Intelligence, Surveillance, and Reconnaissance Integration Council and the Director of National Intelligence.

DEFENSE INDUSTRIAL SECURITY

SEC. 428.

(a) RESPONSIBILITY FOR DEFENSE INDUSTRIAL SECURITY.—The Secretary of Defense shall be responsible for the protection of classified information disclosed to contractors of the Department of Defense.

(b) CONSISTENCY WITH EXECUTIVE ORDERS AND DIRECTIVES.—The Secretary shall carry out the responsibility assigned under subsection (a) in a manner consistent with Executive Order 12829 (or any successor order to such executive order) and consistent with policies relating to the National Industrial Security Program (or any successor to such program).

(c) PERFORMANCE OF INDUSTRIAL SECURITY FUNCTIONS FOR OTHER AGENCIES.—The Secretary may perform industrial security functions for other agencies of the Federal government upon request or upon designation of the Department of Defense as executive agent for the National Industrial Security Program (or any successor to such program).

(d) REGULATIONS AND POLICY GUIDANCE.—The Secretary shall prescribe, and from time to time revise, such regulations and policy guidance as are necessary to ensure the protection of classified information disclosed to contractors of the Department of Defense.

(e) DEDICATION OF RESOURCES.—The Secretary shall ensure that sufficient resources are provided to staff, train, and support such personnel as are necessary to fully protect classified information disclosed to contractors of the Department of Defense.

(f) BIENNIAL REPORT.—The Secretary shall report biennially to the congressional defense committees on expenditures and activities of the Department of Defense in carrying out the requirements of this section. The Secretary shall submit the report at or about the same time that the President's budget is submitted pursuant to section 1105 (a) of title 31 in odd numbered years. The report shall be in an unclassified form (with a classified annex if necessary) and shall cover the activities of the Department of Defense in the preceding two fiscal years, including the following:

(1) The workforce responsible for carrying out the requirements of this section, including the number and experience of such workforce; training in the performance of industrial security functions; performance metrics; and resulting assessment of overall quality.

(2) A description of funds authorized, appropriated, or reprogrammed to carry out the requirements of this section, the budget execution of such funds, and the adequacy of budgets provided for performing such purpose.

(3) Statistics on the number of contractors handling classified information of the Department of Defense, and the percentage of such contractors who are subject to foreign ownership, control, or influence.

(4) Statistics on the number of violations identified, enforcement actions taken, and the percentage of such violations occurring at facilities of contractors subject to foreign ownership, control, or influence.

(5) An assessment of whether major contractors implementing the program have adequate enforcement programs and have trained their employees adequately in the requirements of the program.

(6) Trend data on attempts to compromise classified information disclosed to contractors of the Department of Defense to the extent that such data are available.

APPROPRIATIONS FOR DEFENSE INTELLIGENCE ELEMENTS: ACCOUNTS FOR TRANSFERS; TRANSFER AUTHORITY

SEC. 429.

(a) ACCOUNTS FOR APPROPRIATIONS FOR DEFENSE INTELLIGENCE ELEMENTS.— The Secretary of Defense may transfer appropriations of the Department of Defense which are available for the activities of Defense intelligence elements to an account or accounts established for receipt of such transfers. Each such account may also receive transfers from the Director of National Intelligence if made pursuant to Section 102A of the National Security Act of 1947 (50 U.S.C. 403–1), and transfers and reimbursements arising from transactions, as authorized by law, between a Defense intelligence element and another entity. Appropriation balances in each such account may be transferred back to the account or accounts from which such appropriations originated as appropriation refunds.

(b) RECORDATION OF TRANSFERS.—Transfers made pursuant to subsection (a) shall be recorded as expenditure transfers.

(c) AVAILABILITY OF FUNDS.—Funds transferred pursuant to subsection (a) shall remain available for the same time period and for the same purpose as the appropriation from which transferred, and shall remain subject to the same limitations provided in the act making the appropriation.

(d) OBLIGATION AND EXPENDITURE OF FUNDS.—Unless otherwise specifically authorized by law, funds transferred pursuant to subsection (a) shall only be obligated and expended in accordance H. R. 1892—20 with chapter 15 of title 31 and all other applicable provisions of law.

(e) DEFENSE INTELLIGENCE ELEMENT DEFINED.—In this section, the term 'Defense intelligence element' means any of the Department of Defense agencies, offices, and elements included within the definition of 'intelligence community' under section 3(4) of the National Security Act of 1947 (50 U.S.C. 401a(4)).''.

AUTHORITY TO ENGAGE IN COMMERCIAL ACTIVITIES AS SECURITY FOR INTELLIGENCE COLLECTION ACTIVITIES

SEC. 431.

(a) AUTHORITY.—The Secretary of Defense, subject to the provisions of this subchapter, may authorize the conduct of those commercial activities necessary to provide security for authorized intelligence collection activities abroad undertaken by the Department of Defense. No commercial activity may be initiated pursuant to this subchapter after December 31, 2006.

(b) INTERAGENCY COORDINATION AND SUPPORT.—Any such activity shall—

(1) be coordinated with, and (where appropriate) be supported by, the Director of Central Intelligence; and

(2) to the extent the activity takes place within the United States, be coordinated with, and (where appropriate) be supported by, the Director of the Federal Bureau of Investigation.

(c) DEFINITIONS.—In this subchapter:

(1) The term "commercial activities" means activities that are conducted in a manner consistent with prevailing commercial practices and includes—

(A) the acquisition, use, sale, storage and disposal of goods and services;

(B) entering into employment contracts and leases and other agreements for real and personal property;

(C) depositing funds into and withdrawing funds from domestic and foreign commercial business or financial institutions;

(D) acquiring licenses, registrations, permits, and insurance; and

(E) establishing corporations, partnerships, and other legal entities.

(2) The term "intelligence collection activities" means the collection of foreign intelligence and counterintelligence information.

USE, DISPOSITION, AND AUDITING OF FUNDS

SEC. 432.

(a) USE OF FUNDS.—Funds generated by a commercial activity authorized pursuant to this subchapter may be used to offset necessary and reasonable expenses arising from that activity. Use of such funds for that purpose shall be kept to the minimum necessary to conduct the activity concerned in a secure manner. Any funds generated by the activity in excess of those required for that purpose shall be deposited, as often as may be practicable, into the Treasury as miscellaneous receipts.

(b) AUDITS.—

(1) The Secretary of Defense shall assign an organization within the Department of Defense to have auditing responsibility with respect to activities authorized under this subchapter.

(2) That organization shall audit the use and disposition of funds generated by any commercial activity authorized under this subchapter not less often than annually. The results of all such audits shall be

promptly reported to the intelligence committees (as defined in section 437 (d) of this title).

RELATIONSHIP WITH OTHER FEDERAL LAWS

SEC. 433.

(a) IN GENERAL.—Except as provided by subsection (b), a commercial activity conducted pursuant to this subchapter shall be carried out in accordance with applicable Federal law.

(b) AUTHORIZATION OF WAIVERS WHEN NECESSARY TO MAINTAIN SECURITY.—

(1) If the Secretary of Defense determines, in connection with a commercial activity authorized pursuant to section 431 of this title, that compliance with certain Federal laws or regulations pertaining to the management and administration of Federal agencies would create an unacceptable risk of compromise of an authorized intelligence activity, the Secretary may, to the extent necessary to prevent such compromise, waive compliance with such laws or regulations.

(2) Any determination and waiver by the Secretary under paragraph (1) shall be made in writing and shall include a specification of the laws and regulations for which compliance by the commercial activity concerned is not required consistent with this section.

(3) The authority of the Secretary under paragraph (1) may be delegated only to the Deputy Secretary of Defense, an Under Secretary of Defense, an Assistant Secretary of Defense, or a Secretary of a military department.

(c) FEDERAL LAWS AND REGULATIONS.—For purposes of this section, Federal laws and regulations pertaining to the management and administration of Federal agencies are only those Federal laws and regulations pertaining to the following:

(1) The receipt and use of appropriated and nonappropriated funds.

(2) The acquisition or management of property or services.

(3) Information disclosure, retention, and management.

(4) The employment of personnel.

(5) Payments for travel and housing.

(6) The establishment of legal entities or government instrumentalities.

(7) Foreign trade or financial transaction restrictions that would reveal the commercial activity as an activity of the United States Government.

RESERVATION OF DEFENSES AND IMMUNITIES

SEC. 434.

The submission to judicial proceedings in a State or other legal jurisdiction, in connection with a commercial activity undertaken pursuant to this subchapter, shall not constitute a waiver of the defenses and immunities of the United States.

LIMITATIONS

SEC. 435.

(a) LAWFUL ACTIVITIES.—Nothing in this subchapter authorizes the conduct of any intelligence activity that is not otherwise authorized by law or Executive order.

(b) DOMESTIC ACTIVITIES.—Personnel conducting commercial activity authorized by this subchapter may only engage in those activities in the United States to the extent necessary to support intelligence activities abroad.

(c) PROVIDING GOODS AND SERVICES TO THE DEPARTMENT OF DEFENSE.— Commercial activity may not be undertaken within the United States for the purpose of providing goods and services to the Department of Defense, other than as may be necessary to provide security for the activities subject to this subchapter.

(d) NOTICE TO UNITED STATES PERSONS.—

(1) In carrying out a commercial activity authorized under this subchapter, the Secretary of Defense may not permit an entity engaged in such activity to employ a United States person in an operational, managerial, or supervisory position, and may not assign or detail a United States person to perform operational, managerial, or supervisory duties for such an entity, unless that person is informed in advance of the intelligence security purpose of that activity.

(2) In this subsection, the term "United States person" means an individual who is a citizen of the United States or an alien lawfully admitted to the United States for permanent residence.

REGULATIONS

SEC. 436.

The Secretary of Defense shall prescribe regulations to implement the authority provided in this subchapter. Such regulations shall be consistent with this subchapter and shall at a minimum—

(1) specify all elements of the Department of Defense who are authorized to engage in commercial activities pursuant to this subchapter;

(2) require the personal approval of the Secretary or Deputy Secretary of Defense for all sensitive activities to be authorized pursuant to this subchapter;

(3) specify all officials who are authorized to grant waivers of laws or regulations pursuant to section 433 (b) of this title, or to approve the establishment or conduct of commercial activities pursuant to this subchapter;

(4) designate a single office within the Defense Intelligence Agency to be responsible for the management and supervision of all activities authorized under this subchapter;

(5) require that each commercial activity proposed to be authorized under this subchapter be subject to appropriate legal review before the activity is authorized; and

(6) provide for appropriate internal audit controls and oversight for such activities.

CONGRESSIONAL OVERSIGHT

SEC. 437.

(a) PROPOSED REGULATIONS.—Copies of regulations proposed to be prescribed under section 436 of this title (including any proposed revision to such regulations) shall be submitted to the intelligence committees not less than 30 days before they take effect.

(b) CURRENT INFORMATION.—Consistent with title V of the National Security Act of 1947 (50 U.S.C. §413 et seq.), the Secretary of Defense shall ensure that the intelligence committees are kept fully and currently informed of actions taken pursuant to this subchapter, including any significant anticipated activity to be authorized pursuant to this subchapter.

NATIONAL IMAGERY AND MAPPING AGENCY ACT OF 1996

Chapter 22 Of Title 10, United States Code

SUBCHAPTER I—MISSIONS AND AUTHORITY

ESTABLISHMENT

SECTION. 441.

(a) ESTABLISHMENT.—The National Geospatial-Intelligence Agency is a combat support agency of the Department of Defense and has significant national missions.

(b) DIRECTOR.—

(1) The Director of the National Geospatial-Intelligence Agency is the head of the agency.

(2) Upon a vacancy in the position of Director, the Secretary of Defense shall recommend to the President an individual for appointment to the position.

(3) If an officer of the armed forces on active duty is appointed to the position of Director, the position shall be treated as having been designated by the President as a position of importance and responsibility for purposes of section 601 of this title and shall carry the grade of lieutenant general, or, in the case of an officer of the Navy, vice admiral.

(c) DIRECTOR OF NATIONAL INTELLIGENCE COLLECTION TASKING AUTHORITY.—Unless otherwise directed by the President, the Director of National Intelligence shall have authority (except as otherwise agreed by the Director and the Secretary of Defense) to—

(1) approve collection requirements levied on national imagery collection assets;

(2) determine priorities for such requirements; and

(3) resolve conflicts in such priorities.

(d) AUTHORITY AND CONTINUED IMPROVEMENT OF IMAGERY INTELLIGENCE SUPPORT TO ALL-SOURCE ANALYSIS AND PRODUCTION FUNCTION.—The Secretary of Defense, in consultation with the Director of National Intelligence, shall take all necessary steps to ensure the full availability and continued improvement of imagery intelligence support for all-source analysis and production.

MISSIONS

SEC. 442.

(a) NATIONAL SECURITY MISSIONS.—

319

(1) The National Geospatial-Intelligence Agency shall, in support of the national security objectives of the United States, provide geospatial intelligence consisting of the following:

(A) Imagery.

(B) Imagery intelligence.

(C) Geospatial information.

(2)

(A) As directed by the Director of National Intelligence, the National Geospatial-Intelligence Agency shall develop a system to facilitate the analysis, dissemination, and incorporation of likenesses, videos, and presentations produced by ground-based platforms, including handheld or clandestine photography taken by or on behalf of human intelligence collection organizations or available as open-source information, into the National System for Geospatial Intelligence.

(B) The authority provided by this paragraph does not include authority for the National Geospatial-Intelligence Agency to manage tasking of handheld or clandestine photography taken by or on behalf of human intelligence collection organizations.

(3) Geospatial intelligence provided in carrying out paragraphs (1) and (2) shall be timely, relevant, and accurate.

(b) NAVIGATION INFORMATION.—The National Geospatial-Intelligence Agency shall improve means of navigating vessels of the Navy and the merchant marine by providing, under the authority of the Secretary of Defense, accurate and inexpensive nautical charts, sailing directions, books on navigation, and manuals of instructions for the use of all vessels of the United States and of navigators generally.

(c) MAPS, CHARTS, ETC.—The National Geospatial-Intelligence Agency shall prepare and distribute maps, charts, books, and geodetic products as authorized under subchapter II of this chapter.

(d) NATIONAL MISSIONS.—The National Geospatial-Intelligence Agency also has national missions as specified in section 110(a) of the National Security Act of 1947 (50 U.S.C. 404e(a)).

(e) SYSTEMS.—The National Geospatial-Intelligence Agency may, in furtherance of a mission of the Agency, design, develop, deploy, operate, and maintain systems related to the processing and dissemination of imagery intelligence and geospatial information that may be transferred to, accepted or used by, or used on behalf of—

(1) the armed forces, including any combatant command, component of a combatant command, joint task force, or tactical unit; or

(2) any other department or agency of the United States.

IMAGERY INTELLIGENCE AND GEOSPATIAL INFORMATION:

SUPPORT FOR FOREIGN COUNTRIES

SEC. 443.

(a) USE OF APPROPRIATED FUNDS.—The Director of the National Geospatial-Intelligence Agency may use appropriated funds available to the National Geospatial-Intelligence Agency to provide foreign countries with imagery intelligence and geospatial information support.

(b) USE OF FUNDS OTHER THAN APPROPRIATED FUNDS.—The Director may use funds other than appropriated funds to provide foreign countries with imagery intelligence and geospatial information support, notwithstanding provisions of law relating to the expenditure of funds of the United States, except that—

(1) no such funds may be expended, in whole or in part, by or for the benefit of the National Geospatial-Intelligence Agency for a purpose for which Congress had previously denied funds;

(2) proceeds from the sale of imagery intelligence or geospatial information items may be used only to purchase replacement items similar to the items that are sold; and

(3) the authority provided by this subsection may not be used to acquire items or services for the principal benefit of the United States.

(c) ACCOMMODATION PROCUREMENTS.—The authority under this section may be exercised to conduct accommodation procurements on behalf of foreign countries.

(d) COORDINATION WITH DIRECTOR OF NATIONAL INTELLIGENCE.—The Director of the Agency shall coordinate with the Director of National Intelligence any action under this section that involves imagery intelligence or intelligence products or involves providing support to an intelligence or security service of a foreign country.

SUPPORT FROM CENTRAL INTELLIGENCE AGENCY

SEC. 444.

(a) SUPPORT AUTHORIZED.—The Director of the Central Intelligence Agency may provide support in accordance with this section to the Director of the National Geospatial-Intelligence Agency. The Director of the National Geospatial-Intelligence Agency may accept support provided under this section.

(b) ADMINISTRATIVE AND CONTRACT SERVICES.—

(1) In furtherance of the national intelligence effort, the Director of the Central Intelligence Agency may provide administrative and contract services to the National Geospatial-Intelligence Agency as if that agency were an organizational element of the Central Intelligence Agency.

(2) Services provided under paragraph (1) may include the services of security police. For purposes of section 15 of the Central Intelligence Agency

Act of 1949 (50 U.S.C. 403o), an installation of the National Geospatial-Intelligence Agency that is provided security police services under this section shall be considered an installation of the Central Intelligence Agency. (3) Support provided under this subsection shall be provided under terms and conditions agreed upon by the Secretary of Defense and the Director of the Central Intelligence Agency.

(c) DETAIL OF PERSONNEL.—The Director of the Central Intelligence Agency may detail personnel of the Central Intelligence Agency indefinitely to the National Geospatial-Intelligence Agency without regard to any limitation on the duration of interagency details of Federal Government personnel.

(d) REIMBURSABLE OR NONREIMBURSABLE SUPPORT.—Support under this section may be provided and accepted on either a reimbursable basis or a nonreimbursable basis.

(e) AUTHORITY TO TRANSFER FUNDS.—

(1) The Director of the National Geospatial-Intelligence Agency may transfer funds available for that agency to the Director of the Central Intelligence Agency for the Central Intelligence Agency.

(2) The Director of the Central Intelligence Agency —

(A) may accept funds transferred under paragraph (1); and

(B) shall expend such funds, in accordance with the Central Intelligence Agency Act of 1949 (50 U.S.C. 403a et seq.), to provide administrative and contract services or detail personnel to the National Geospatial-Intelligence Agency under this section.

PROTECTION OF AGENCY IDENTIFICATIONS AND ORGANIZATIONAL INFORMATION

SEC. 445.
[Repealed. Pub. L. 105–107, title V, SEC. 503(c), Nov. 20, 1997, 111 Stat. 2262]

SUBCHAPTER II—MAPS, CHARTS, AND GEODETIC PRODUCTS

MAPS, CHARTS, AND BOOKS

SEC. 451.
The Secretary of Defense may—

(1) have the National Geospatial-Intelligence Agency prepare maps, charts, and nautical books required in navigation and have those materials published and furnished to navigators; and

(2) buy the plates and copyrights of existing maps, charts, books on navigation, and sailing directions and instructions.

PILOT CHARTS

SEC. 452.

(a) There shall be conspicuously printed on pilot charts prepared in the National Geospatial-Intelligence Agency the following: "Prepared from data furnished by the National Geospatial-Intelligence Agency of the Department of Defense and by the Department of Commerce, and published at the National Geospatial-Intelligence Agency under the authority of the Secretary of Defense".

(b) The Secretary of Commerce shall furnish to the National Geospatial-Intelligence Agency, as quickly as possible, all meteorological information received by the Secretary that is necessary for, and of the character used in, preparing pilot charts.

SALE OF MAPS, CHARTS, AND NAVIGATIONAL PUBLICATIONS: PRICES; USE OF PROCEEDS

SEC. 453.

(a) PRICES.—All maps, charts, and other publications offered for sale by the National Geospatial-Intelligence Agency shall be sold at prices and under regulations that may be prescribed by the Secretary of Defense.

(b) USE OF PROCEEDS TO PAY FOREIGN LICENSING FEES.—

(1) The Secretary of Defense may pay any NGA foreign data acquisition fee out of the proceeds of the sale of maps, charts, and other publications of the Agency, and those proceeds are hereby made available for that purpose.

(2) In this subsection, the term "NGA foreign data acquisition fee" means any licensing or other fee imposed by a foreign country or international organization for the acquisition or use of data or products by the National Geospatial-Intelligence Agency.

EXCHANGE OF MAPPING, CHARTING, AND GEODETIC DATA WITH FOREIGN COUNTRIES, INTERNATIONAL ORGANIZATIONS, NONGOVERNMENTAL ORGANIZATIONS, AND ACADEMIC INSTITUTIONS

SEC. 454.

(a) FOREIGN COUNTRIES AND INTERNATIONAL ORGANIZATIONS.—The Secretary of Defense may authorize the National Geospatial-Intelligence Agency to exchange or furnish mapping, charting, and geodetic data, supplies and services to a foreign country or international organization pursuant to an agreement for the production or exchange of such data.

(b) NONGOVERNMENTAL ORGANIZATIONS AND ACADEMIC INSTITUTIONS.—The Secretary may authorize the National Geospatial-Intelligence Agency to exchange or furnish mapping, charting, and geodetic data, supplies, and services relating to areas outside of the United States to a nongovernmental organization or an academic institution engaged in geospatial information research or production of such areas pursuant to an agreement for the production or exchange of such data.

MAPS, CHARTS, AND GEODETIC DATA: PUBLIC AVAILABILITY; EXCEPTIONS

SEC. 455.

(a) The National Geospatial-Intelligence Agency shall offer for sale maps and charts at scales of 1:500,000 and smaller, except those withheld in accordance with subsection (b) or those specifically authorized under criteria established by Executive order to be kept secret in the interest of national defense or foreign policy and in fact properly classified pursuant to such Executive order.

(b)(1) Notwithstanding any other provision of law, the Secretary of Defense may withhold from public disclosure any geodetic product in the possession of, or under the control of, the Department of Defense—

(A) that was obtained or produced, or that contains information that was provided, pursuant to an international agreement that restricts disclosure of such product or information to government officials of the agreeing parties or that restricts use of such product or information to government purposes only;

(B) that contains information that the Secretary of Defense has determined in writing would, if disclosed, reveal sources and methods, or capabilities, used to obtain source material for production of the geodetic product; or

(C) that contains information that the Director of the National Geospatial-Intelligence Agency has determined in writing would, if disclosed, jeopardize or interfere with ongoing military or intelligence operations, reveal military operational or contingency plans, or reveal, jeopardize, or compromise military or intelligence capabilities.

(2) In this subsection, the term "geodetic product" means imagery, imagery intelligence, or geospatial information.

(c) (1) Regulations to implement this section (including any amendments to such regulations) shall be published in the Federal Register for public comment for a period of not less than 30 days before they take effect.

(2) Regulations under this section shall address the conditions under which release of geodetic products authorized under subsection (b) to be withheld from public disclosure would be appropriate—

(A) in the case of allies of the United States; and

(B) in the case of qualified United States contractors (including contractors that are small business concerns) who need such products for use in the performance of contracts with the United States.

CIVIL ACTIONS BARRED

SEC. 456.

(a) CLAIMS BARRED.—No civil action may be brought against the United States on the basis of the content of a navigational aid prepared or disseminated by the National Geospatial-Intelligence Agency.

(b) NAVIGATIONAL AIDS COVERED.—Subsection (a) applies with respect to a navigational aid in the form of a map, a chart, or a publication and any other form or medium of product or information in which the National Geospatial-Intelligence Agency prepares or disseminates navigational aids.

OPERATIONAL FILES PREVIOUSLY MAINTAINED BY OR CONCERNING ACTIVITIES OF NATIONAL PHOTOGRAPHIC INTERPRETATION CENTER: AUTHORITY TO WITHHOLD FROM PUBLIC DISCLOSURE

SEC. 457.

(a) AUTHORITY.—The Secretary of Defense may withhold from public disclosure operational files described in subsection (b) to the same extent that operational files may be withheld under section 701 of the National Security Act of 1947 (50 U.S.C. 431).

(b) COVERED OPERATIONAL FILES.—The authority under subsection (a) applies to operational files in the possession of the National Geospatial-Intelligence Agency that—

(1) as of September 22, 1996, were maintained by the National Photographic Interpretation Center; or

(2) concern the activities of the Agency that, as of such date, were performed by the National Photographic Interpretation Center.

(c) OPERATIONAL FILES DEFINED.—In this section, the term "operational files" has the meaning given that term in section 701(b) of the National Security Act of 1947 (50 U.S.C. 431 (b)).

SUBCHAPTER III—PERSONNEL MANAGEMENT

MANAGEMENT RIGHTS

SEC. 461.

(a) SCOPE.—If there is no obligation under the provisions of chapter 71 of title 5 for the head of an agency of the United States to consult or negotiate with a labor organization on a particular matter by reason of that matter being covered by a provision of law or a Governmentwide regulation, the Director of the National Geospatial-Intelligence Agency is not obligated to consult or negotiate with a labor organization on that matter even if that provision of law or regulation is inapplicable to the National Geospatial-Intelligence Agency.

(b) BARGAINING UNITS.—The Director of the National Geospatial-Intelligence Agency shall accord exclusive recognition to a labor organization under section 7111 of title 5 only for a bargaining unit that was recognized as appropriate for the Defense Mapping Agency on September 30, 1996.

(c) TERMINATION OF BARGAINING UNIT COVERAGE OF POSITION MODIFIED TO AFFECT NATIONAL SECURITY DIRECTLY.—

(1) If the Director of the National Geospatial-Intelligence Agency determines that the responsibilities of a position within a collective bargaining unit should be modified to include intelligence, counterintelligence, investigative, or security duties not previously assigned to that position and that the performance of the newly assigned duties directly affects the national security of the United States, then, upon such a modification of the responsibilities of that position, the position shall cease to be covered by the collective bargaining unit and the employee in that position shall cease to be entitled to representation by a labor organization accorded exclusive recognition for that collective bargaining unit.

(2) A determination described in paragraph (1) that is made by the Director of the National Geospatial-Intelligence Agency may not be reviewed by the Federal Labor Relations Authority or any court of the United States.

FINANCIAL ASSISTANCE TO CERTAIN EMPLOYEES IN ACQUISITION OF CRITICAL SKILLS

SEC. 462.

The Secretary of Defense may establish an undergraduate training program with respect to civilian employees of the National Geospatial-Intelligence Agency that is similar in purpose, conditions, content, and administration to the program established by the Secretary of Defense under section 16 of the National Security Agency Act of 1959 (50 U.S.C. 402 note) for civilian employees of the National Security Agency.

SUBCHAPTER IV—DEFINITIONS

DEFINITIONS

SEC. 467.

In this chapter:

(1) The term "function" means any duty, obligation, responsibility, privilege, activity, or program.

(2)(A) The term "imagery" means, except as provided in subparagraph (B), a likeness or presentation of any natural or manmade feature or related object or activity and the positional data acquired at the same time the likeness or representation was acquired, including—

(i) products produced by space-based national intelligence reconnaissance systems; and

(ii) likenesses or presentations produced by satellites, airborne platforms, unmanned aerial vehicles, or other similar means.

(B) Such term does not include handheld or clandestine photography taken by or on behalf of human intelligence collection organizations.

(3) The term "imagery intelligence" means the technical, geographic, and intelligence information derived through the interpretation or analysis of imagery and collateral materials.

(4) The term "geospatial information" means information that identifies the geographic location and characteristics of natural or constructed features and boundaries on the earth and includes—

(A) statistical data and information derived from, among other things, remote sensing, mapping, and surveying technologies; and

(B) mapping, charting, geodetic data, and related products.

(5) The term "geospatial intelligence" means the exploitation and analysis of imagery and geospatial information to describe, assess, and visually depict physical features and geographically referenced activities on the earth. Geospatial intelligence consists of imagery, imagery intelligence, and geospatial information.

HOMELAND SECURITY ACT OF 2002

(Public Law 107-296 of November 25, 2002; 116 STAT. 2135)

Be it enacted by the Senate and House of Representatives of the United States of America in Congress assembled,

SHORT TITLE; TABLE OF CONTENTS.

SECTION 1. [6 U.S.C. §101 note]
(a) SHORT TITLE.—This Act may be cited as the "Homeland Security Act of 2002".

(b) TABLE OF CONTENTS.—The table of contents for this Act is as follows:

DEFINITIONS

SEC. 2. [6 U.S.C. §101]
In this Act, the following definitions apply:

(1) Each of the terms "American homeland" and "homeland" means the United States.

(2) The term "appropriate congressional committee" means any committee of the House of Representatives or the Senate having legislative or oversight jurisdiction under the Rules of the House of Representatives or the Senate, respectively, over the matter concerned.

(3) The term "assets" includes contracts, facilities, property, records, unobligated or unexpended balances of appropriations, and other funds or resources(other than personnel).

(4) The term "critical infrastructure" has the meaning given that term in section 1016(e) of Public Law 107-56(42 U.S.C. §5195c(e)).

(5) The term "Department" means the Department of Homeland Security.

(6) The term "emergency response providers" includes Federal, State, and local governmental and nongovernmental emergency public safety, fire, law enforcement, emergency response, emergency medical(including hospital emergency facilities), and related personnel, agencies, and authorities.

(7) The term "executive agency" means an executive agency and a military department, as defined, respectively, in sections 105 and 102 of title 5, United States Code.

(8) The term "functions" includes authorities, powers, rights, privileges, immunities, programs, projects, activities, duties, and responsibilities.

(9) The term "intelligence component of the Department: means any element or entity of the Department that collects, gathers, processes, analyzes, produces, or disseminates intelligence information within the scope of the information sharing environment, including homeland security information, terrorism information, and weapons of mass destruction information, or national intelligence, as defined under section 3(5) of the National Security Act of 1947 (50 U.S.C. §401a(5)), except—

> (A) the United States Secret Service; and
>
> (B) the Coast Guard, when operating under the direct authority of the Secretary of Defense or Secretary of the Navy pursuant to section 3 of title 14, United States Code, except that nothing in this paragraph shall affect or diminish the authority and responsibilities of the Commandant of the Coast Guard to command or control the Coast Guard as an armed force or the authority of the Director of National Intelligence with respect to the Coast Guard as an element of the intelligence community (as defined under section 3(4) of the National Security Act of 1947 (50 U.S.C. §401a(4)).

(10) The term "key resources" means publicly or privately controlled resources essential to the minimal operations of the economy and government.

(11) The term "local government" means—

> (A) a county, municipality, city, town, township, local public authority, school district, special district, intrastate district, council of governments(regardless of whether the council of governments is incorporated as a nonprofit corporation under State law), regional or interstate government entity, or agency or instrumentality of a local government;
>
> (B) an Indian tribe or authorized tribal organization, or in Alaska a Native village or Alaska Regional Native Corporation; and

   (C) a rural community, unincorporated town or village, or other
    public entity.

(12) The term "major disaster" has the meaning given in section 102(2)
of the Robert T. Stafford Disaster Relief and Emergency Assistance
Act(42 U.S.C. §5122).

(13) The term "personnel" means officers and employees.

(14) The term "Secretary" means the Secretary of Homeland Security.

(15) The term "State" means any State of the United States, the District
of Columbia, the Commonwealth of Puerto Rico, the Virgin Islands,
Guam, American Samoa, the Commonwealth of the Northern Mariana
Islands, and any possession of the United States.

(16) The term "terrorism" means any activity that—

   (A) involves an act that—

     (i) is dangerous to human life or potentially destructive
     of critical infrastructure or key resources; and

     (ii) is a violation of the criminal laws of the United
     States or of any State or other subdivision of the United
     States; and

   (B) appears to be intended—

     (i) to intimidate or coerce a civilian population;

     (ii) to influence the policy of a government by
     intimidation or coercion; or

     (iii) to affect the conduct of a government by mass
     destruction, assassination, or kidnapping.

(17)(A) The term "United States", when used in a geographic sense,
means any State of the United States, the District of Columbia, the
Commonwealth of Puerto Rico, the Virgin Islands, Guam, American
Samoa, the Commonwealth of the Northern Mariana Islands, any
possession of the United States, and any waters within the jurisdiction of
the United States.

   (B) Nothing in this paragraph or any other provision of this Act
   shall be construed to modify the definition of "United States" for
   the purposes of the Immigration and Nationality Act or any other
   immigration or nationality law.

(18) The term "voluntary preparedness standards" means a common set
of criteria for preparedness, disaster management, emergency
management, and business continuity programs, such as the American
National Standards Institute's National Fire Protection Association
Standard on Disaster/Emergency Management and Business Continuity
Programs (ANSI/NFPA 1600).

TITLE I—DEPARTMENT OF HOMELAND SECURITY

EXECUTIVE DEPARTMENT; MISSION

SEC. 101. [6 U.S.C. §111]

(a) ESTABLISHMENT.—There is established a Department of Homeland Security, as an executive department of the United States within the meaning of title 5, United States Code.

(b) MISSION.—

(1) IN GENERAL.—The primary mission of the Department is to—

(A) prevent terrorist attacks within the United States;

(B) reduce the vulnerability of the United States to terrorism;

(C) minimize the damage, and assist in the recovery, from terrorist attacks that do occur within the United States;

(D) carry out all functions of entities transferred to the Department, including by acting as a focal point regarding natural and manmade crises and emergency planning;

(E) ensure that the functions of the agencies and subdivisions within the Department that are not related directly to securing the homeland are not diminished or neglected except by a specific explicit Act of Congress;

(F) ensure that the overall economic security of the United States is not diminished by efforts, activities, and programs aimed at securing the homeland;

(G) monitor connections between illegal drug trafficking and terrorism, coordinate efforts to sever such connections, and otherwise contribute to efforts to interdict illegal drug trafficking; and

(H) monitor connections between illegal drug trafficking and terrorism, coordinate efforts to sever such connections, and otherwise contribute to efforts to interdict illegal drug trafficking.

(2) RESPONSIBILITY FOR INVESTIGATING AND PROSECUTING TERRORISM.—Except as specifically provided by law with respect to entities transferred to the Department under this Act, primary responsibility for investigating and prosecuting acts of terrorism shall be vested not in the Department, but rather in Federal, State, and local law enforcement agencies with jurisdiction over the acts in question.

SECRETARY; FUNCTIONS

SEC. 102. [6 U.S.C. §112]

(a) SECRETARY.—

(1) IN GENERAL.—There is a Secretary of Homeland Security, appointed by the President, by and with the advice and consent of the Senate.

(2) HEAD OF DEPARTMENT.—The Secretary is the head of the Department and shall have direction, authority, and control over it.

(3) Functions vested in secretary.—All functions of all officers, employees, and organizational units of the Department are vested in the Secretary.

(b) FUNCTIONS.—The Secretary—

(1) except as otherwise provided by this Act, may delegate any of the Secretary's functions to any officer, employee, or organizational unit of the Department;

(2) shall have the authority to make contracts, grants, and cooperative agreements, and to enter into agreements with other executive agencies, as may be necessary and proper to carry out the Secretary's responsibilities under this Act or otherwise provided by law; and

(3) shall take reasonable steps to ensure that information systems and databases of the Department are compatible with each other and with appropriate databases of other Departments.

(c) COORDINATION WITH NON-FEDERAL ENTITIES.—With respect to homeland security, the Secretary shall coordinate through the Office of State and Local Coordination(established under section 801)(including the provision of training and equipment) with State and local government personnel, agencies, and authorities, with the private sector, and with other entities, including by:

(1) coordinating with State and local government personnel, agencies, and authorities, and with the private sector, to ensure adequate planning, equipment, training, and exercise activities;

(2) coordinating and, as appropriate, consolidating, the Federal Government's communications and systems of communications relating to homeland security with State and local government personnel, agencies, and authorities, the private sector, other entities, and the public; and

(3) distributing or, as appropriate, coordinating the distribution of, warnings and information to State and local government personnel, agencies, and authorities and to the public.

(d) MEETINGS OF NATIONAL SECURITY COUNCIL.—The Secretary may, subject to the direction of the President, attend and participate in meetings of the National Security Council.

(e) ISSUANCE OF REGULATIONS.—The issuance of regulations by the Secretary shall be governed by the provisions of chapter 5 of title 5, United States Code, except as specifically provided in this Act, in laws granting regulatory authorities that are transferred by this Act, and in laws enacted after the date of enactment of this Act.

(f) SPECIAL ASSISTANT TO THE SECRETARY.—The Secretary shall appoint a Special Assistant to the Secretary who shall be responsible for—

(1) creating and fostering strategic communications with the private sector to enhance the primary mission of the Department to protect the American homeland;

(2) advising the Secretary on the impact of the Department's policies, regulations, processes, and actions on the private sector;

(3) interfacing with other relevant Federal agencies with homeland security missions to assess the impact of these agencies' actions on the private sector;

(4) creating and managing private sector advisory councils composed of representatives of industries and associations designated by the Secretary to—

(A) advise the Secretary on private sector products, applications, and solutions as they relate to homeland security challenges;

(B) advise the Secretary on homeland security policies, regulations, processes, and actions that affect the participating industries and associations; and

(C) advise the Secretary on private sector preparedness issues, including effective methods for—

(i) promoting voluntary preparedness standards to the private sector; and

(ii) assisting the private sector in adopting voluntary preparedness standards;

(5) working with Federal laboratories, federally funded research and development centers, other federally funded organizations, academia, and the private sector to develop innovative approaches to address homeland security challenges to produce and deploy the best available technologies for homeland security missions;

(6) promoting existing public-private partnerships and developing new public-private partnerships to provide for collaboration and mutual support to address homeland security challenges;

(7) assisting in the development and promotion of private sector best practices to secure critical infrastructure;

(8) providing information to the private sector regarding voluntary preparedness standards and the business justification for preparedness

and promoting to the private sector the adoption of voluntary preparedness standards;

(9) coordinating industry efforts, with respect to functions of the Department of Homeland Security, to identify private sector resources and capabilities that could be effective in supplementing Federal, State, and local government agency efforts to prevent or respond to a terrorist attack;

(10) coordinating with the Directorate of Border and Transportation Security and the Assistant Secretary for Trade Development of the Department of Commerce on issues related to the travel and tourism industries; and

(11) consulting with the Office of State and Local Government Coordination and Preparedness on all matters of concern to the private sector, including the tourism industry.

(g) STANDARDS POLICY.—All standards activities of the Department shall be conducted in accordance with section 12(d) of the National Technology Transfer Advancement Act of 1995(15 U.S.C. §272 note) and Office of Management and Budget Circular A-119.

OTHER OFFICERS

SEC. 103. [6 U.S.C. §113]

(a) DEPUTY SECRETARY; UNDER SECRETARIES.—There are the following officers, appointed by the President, by and with the advice and consent of the Senate:

(1) A Deputy Secretary of Homeland Security, who shall be the Secretary's first assistant for purposes of subchapter III of chapter 33 of title 5, United States Code.

(2) An Under Secretary for Science and Technology.

(3) An Under Secretary for Border and Transportation Security.

(4) An Administrator of the Federal Emergency Management Agency

(5) A Director of the Bureau of Citizenship and Immigration Services.

(6) An Under Secretary for Management.

(7) A Director of the Office of Counternarcotics Enforcement .

(8) An Under Secretary responsible for overseeing critical infrastructure protection, cybersecurity, and other related programs of the Department.

(9) Not more than 12 Assistant Secretaries.

(10) A General Counsel, who shall be the chief legal officer of the Department.

(b) INSPECTOR GENERAL.—There shall be in the Department an Office of Inspector General and an Inspector General at the head of such office, as provided in the Inspector General Act of 1978(5 U.S.C. App.).

(c) COMMANDANT OF THE COAST GUARD.—To assist the Secretary in the performance of the Secretary's functions, there is a Commandant of the Coast Guard, who shall be appointed as provided in section 44 of title 14, United States Code, and who shall report directly to the Secretary. In addition to such duties as may be provided in this Act and as assigned to the Commandant by the Secretary, the duties of the Commandant shall include those required by section 2 of title 14, United States Code.

(d) OTHER OFFICERS.—To assist the Secretary in the performance of the Secretary's functions, there are the following officers, appointed by the President:

(1) A Director of the Secret Service.

(2) A Chief Information Officer.

(3) An Officer for Civil Rights and Civil Liberties.

(4) A Director for Domestic Nuclear Detection

(e) CHIEF FINANCIAL OFFICER. There shall be in the Department a Chief Financial Officer, as provided in chapter 9 of title 31, United States Code [31 U.S.C. §§901 et seq,].

(f) PERFORMANCE OF SPECIFIC FUNCTIONS.—Subject to the provisions of this Act, every officer of the Department shall perform the functions specified by law for the official's office or prescribed by the Secretary.

TITLE II—INFORMATION ANALYSIS AND INFRASTRUCTURE PROTECTION

SUBTITLE A—INFORMATION AND ANALYSIS AND INFRASTRUCTURE PROTECTION; ACCESS TO INFORMATION

INFORMATION AND ANALYSIS AND INFRASTRUCTURE PROTECTION; ACCESS TO INFORMATION

SEC. 201. [6 U.S.C. §121]

(a) INTELLIGENCE AND ANALYSIS AND INFRASTRUCTURE PROTECTION.—There shall be in the Department an Office of Intelligence and Analysis and an Office of Infrastructure Protection.

(b) Under Secretary for Intelligence and Analysis and Assistant Secretary for Infrastructure Protection—

(1) OFFICE OF INTELLIGENCE AND ANALYSIS.—The Office of Intelligence and Analysis shall be headed by an Under Secretary for Intelligence and Analysis, who shall be appointed by the President, by and with the advice and consent of the Senate.

(2) CHIEF INTELLIGENCE OFFICER.—The Under Secretary for Intelligence and Analysis shall serve as the Chief Intelligence Officer of the Department.

(3) OFFICE OF INFRASTRUCTURE PROTECTION.—The Office of Infrastructure Protection shall be headed by an Assistant Secretary for Infrastructure Protection, who shall be appointed by the President.

(c) DISCHARGE OF RESPONSIBILITIES.—The Secretary shall ensure that the responsibilities of the Department relating to information analysis and infrastructure protection, including those described in subsection (d), are carried out through the Under Secretary for Intelligence and Analysis or the Assistant Secretary for Infrastructure Protection, as appropriate.

(d) RESPONSIBILITIES OF SECRETARY RELATING TO INTELLIGENCE AND ANALYSIS AND INFRASTRUCTURE PROTECTION.—The responsibilities of the Secretary relating to intelligence analysis and infrastructure protection shall be as follows:

(1) To access, receive, and analyze law enforcement information, intelligence information, and other information from agencies of the Federal Government, State and local government agencies(including law enforcement agencies), and private sector entities, and to integrate such information, in support of the mission responsibilities of the Department and the functions of the National Counterterrorism Center established under section 119 of the National Security Act of 1947 (50 U.S.C. §404o), in order to—

(A) identify and assess the nature and scope of terrorist threats to the homeland;

(B) detect and identify threats of terrorism against the United States; and

(C) understand such threats in light of actual and potential vulnerabilities of the homeland.

(2) To carry out comprehensive assessments of the vulnerabilities of the key resources and critical infrastructure of the United States, including the performance of risk assessments to determine the risks posed by particular types of terrorist attacks within the United States(including an assessment of the probability of success of such attacks and the feasibility and potential efficacy of various countermeasures to such attacks).

(3) To integrate relevant information, analyses, and vulnerability assessments(whether such information, analyses, or assessments are provided or produced by the Department or others) in order to identify priorities for protective and support measures by the Department, other agencies of the Federal Government, State and local government agencies and authorities, the private sector, and other entities.

(4) To ensure, pursuant to section 202, the timely and efficient access by the Department to all information necessary to discharge the responsibilities under this section, including obtaining such information from other agencies of the Federal Government.

(5) To develop a comprehensive national plan for securing the key resources and critical infrastructure of the United States, including power production, generation, and distribution systems, information technology and telecommunications systems(including satellites), electronic financial and property record storage and transmission systems, emergency preparedness communications systems, and the physical and technological assets that support such systems.

(6) To recommend measures necessary to protect the key resources and critical infrastructure of the United States in coordination with other agencies of the Federal Government and in cooperation with State and local government agencies and authorities, the private sector, and other entities.

(7) To review, analyze, and make recommendations for improvements to the policies and procedures governing the sharing of information within the scope of the information sharing environment established under section 1016 of the Intelligence Reform and Terrorism Prevention Act of 2004 (6 U.S.C. §485), including homeland security information, terrorism information, and weapons of mass destruction information, and any policies, guidelines, procedures, instructions, or standards established under that section.

(8) To disseminate, as appropriate, information analyzed by the Department within the Department, to other agencies of the Federal Government with responsibilities relating to homeland security, and to agencies of State and local governments and private sector entities with such responsibilities in order to assist in the deterrence, prevention, preemption of, or response to, terrorist attacks against the United States.

(9) To consult with the Director of National Intelligence and other appropriate intelligence, law enforcement, or other elements of the Federal Government to establish collection priorities and strategies for information, including law enforcement-related information, relating to threats of terrorism against the United States through such means as the representation of the Department in discussions regarding requirements and priorities in the collection of such information.

(10) To consult with State and local governments and private sector entities to ensure appropriate exchanges of information, including law enforcement-related information, relating to threats of terrorism against the United States.

(11) To ensure that—

(A) any material received pursuant to this Act is protected from unauthorized disclosure and handled and used only for the performance of official duties; and

(B) any intelligence information under this Act is shared, retained, and disseminated consistent with the authority of the Director of National Intelligence to protect intelligence sources and methods under the National Security Act of 1947(50 U.S.C. §401 et seq.) and related procedures and, as appropriate, similar authorities of the Attorney General concerning sensitive law enforcement information.

(12) To request additional information from other agencies of the Federal Government, State and local government agencies, and the private sector relating to threats of terrorism in the United States, or relating to other areas of responsibility assigned by the Secretary, including the entry into cooperative agreements through the Secretary to obtain such information.

(13) To establish and utilize, in conjunction with the chief information officer of the Department, a secure communications and information technology infrastructure, including data-mining and other advanced analytical tools, in order to access, receive, and analyze data and information in furtherance of the responsibilities under this section, and to disseminate information acquired and analyzed by the Department, as appropriate.

(14) To ensure, in conjunction with the chief information officer of the Department, that any information databases and analytical tools developed or utilized by the Department—

(A) are compatible with one another and with relevant information databases of other agencies of the Federal Government; and

(B) treat information in such databases in a manner that complies with applicable Federal law on privacy.

(15) To coordinate training and other support to the elements and personnel of the Department, other agencies of the Federal Government, and State and local governments that provide information to the Department, or are consumers of information provided by the Department, in order to facilitate the identification and sharing of information revealed in their ordinary duties and the optimal utilization of information received from the Department.

(16) To coordinate with elements of the intelligence community and with Federal, State, and local law enforcement agencies, and the private sector, as appropriate.

(17) To provide intelligence and information analysis and support to other elements of the Department.

(18) To coordinate and enhance integration among the intelligence components of the Department, including through strategic oversight of the intelligence activities of such components.

(19) To establish the intelligence collection, processing, analysis, and dissemination priorities, policies, processes, standards, guidelines, and procedures for the intelligence components of the Department, consistent with any directions from the President and, as applicable, the Director of National Intelligence.

(20) To establish a structure and process to support the missions and goals of the intelligence components of the Department.

(21) To ensure that, whenever possible, the Department—

>(A) produces and disseminates unclassified reports and analytic products based on open-source information; and

>(B) produces and disseminates such reports and analytic products contemporaneously with reports or analytic products concerning the same or similar information that the Department produced and disseminated in a classified format.

(22) To establish within the Office of Intelligence and Analysis an internal continuity of operations plan.

(23) Based on intelligence priorities set by the President, and guidance from the Secretary and, as appropriate, the Director of National Intelligence—

>(A) to provide to the heads of each intelligence component of the Department guidance for developing the budget pertaining to the activities of such component; and

>(B) to present to the Secretary a recommendation for a consolidated budget for the intelligence components of the Department, together with any comments from the heads of such components.

(24) To perform such other duties relating to such responsibilities as the Secretary may provide.

(25) To prepare and submit to the Committee on Homeland Security and Governmental Affairs of the Senate and the Committee on Homeland Security in the House of Representatives, and to other appropriate congressional committees having jurisdiction over the critical infrastructure or key resources, for each sector identified in the National Infrastructure Protection Plan, a report on the comprehensive assessments carried out by the Secretary of the critical infrastructure and key resources of the United States, evaluating threat, vulnerability, and consequence, as required under this subsection. Each such report—

(A) shall contain, if applicable, actions or countermeasures recommended or taken by the Secretary or the head of another Federal agency to address issues identified in the assessments;
(B) shall be required for fiscal year 2007 and each subsequent fiscal year and shall be submitted not later than 35 days after the last day of the fiscal year covered by the report; and
(C) may be classified.

(e) STAFF.—

(1) IN GENERAL.—The Secretary shall provide the Office of Intelligence and Analysis and Office of Infrastructure Protection with a staff of analysts having appropriate expertise and experience to assist the such offices in discharging responsibilities under this section.
(2) PRIVATE SECTOR ANALYSTS.—Analysts under this subsection may include analysts from the private sector.
(3) SECURITY CLEARANCES.—Analysts under this subsection shall possess security clearances appropriate for their work under this section.

(f) DETAIL OF PERSONNEL.—

(1) IN GENERAL.—In order to assist the Office of Intelligence and Analysis and Office of Infrastructure Protection in discharging responsibilities under this section, personnel of the agencies referred to in paragraph(2) may be detailed to the Department for the performance of analytic functions and related duties.
(2) COVERED AGENCIES.—The agencies referred to in this paragraph are as follows:

(A) The Department of State.
(B) The Central Intelligence Agency.
(C) The Federal Bureau of Investigation.
(D) The National Security Agency.
(E) The National Geospatial-Intelligence Agency.
(F) The Defense Intelligence Agency.
(G) Any other agency of the Federal Government that the President considers appropriate.

(3) COOPERATIVE AGREEMENTS.—The Secretary and the head of the agency concerned may enter into cooperative agreements for the purpose of detailing personnel under this subsection.
(4) BASIS.—The detail of personnel under this subsection may be on a reimbursable or non-reimbursable basis.

(g) FUNCTIONS TRANSFERRED.—In accordance with title XV, there shall be transferred to the Secretary, for assignment to the U Office of Intelligence and Analysis and Office of Infrastructure Protection under this section, the functions, personnel, assets, and liabilities of the following:

(1) The National Infrastructure Protection Center of the Federal Bureau of Investigation(other than the Computer Investigations and Operations Section), including the functions of the Attorney General relating thereto.

(2) The National Communications System of the Department of Defense, including the functions of the Secretary of Defense relating thereto.

(3) The Critical Infrastructure Assurance Office of the Department of Commerce, including the functions of the Secretary of Commerce relating thereto.

(4) The National Infrastructure Simulation and Analysis Center of the Department of Energy and the energy security and assurance program and activities of the Department, including the functions of the Secretary of Energy relating thereto.

(5) The Federal Computer Incident Response Center of the General Services Administration, including the functions of the Administrator of General Services relating thereto.

(h) INCLUSION OF CERTAIN ELEMENTS OF THE DEPARTMENT AS ELEMENTS OF THE INTELLIGENCE COMMUNITY.—Section 3(4) of the National Security Act of 1947(50 U.S.C. §401(a)) is amended—

(1) by striking "and" at the end of subparagraph(I);

(2) by redesignating subparagraph(J) as subparagraph(K); and

(3) by inserting after subparagraph(I) the following new subparagraph:

"(J) the elements of the Department of Homeland Security concerned with the analyses of foreign intelligence information; and".

ACCESS TO INFORMATION

SEC. 202. [6 U.S.C. §122]

(a) IN GENERAL.—

(1) THREAT AND VULNERABILITY INFORMATION.—Except as otherwise directed by the President, the Secretary shall have such access as the Secretary considers necessary to all information, including reports, assessments, analyses, and unevaluated intelligence relating to threats of terrorism against the United States and to other areas of responsibility assigned by the Secretary, and to all information concerning infrastructure or other vulnerabilities of the United States to terrorism, whether or not such information has been analyzed, that may be collected, possessed, or prepared by any agency of the Federal Government.

(2) OTHER INFORMATION.—The Secretary shall also have access to other information relating to matters under the responsibility of the Secretary that may be collected, possessed, or prepared by an agency of the Federal Government as the President may further provide.

(b) MANNER OF ACCESS.—Except as otherwise directed by the President, with respect to information to which the Secretary has access pursuant to this section—

(1) the Secretary may obtain such material upon request, and may enter into cooperative arrangements with other executive agencies to provide such material or provide Department officials with access to it on a regular or routine basis, including requests or arrangements involving broad categories of material, access to electronic databases, or both; and

(2) regardless of whether the Secretary has made any request or entered into any cooperative arrangement pursuant to paragraph(1), all agencies of the Federal Government shall promptly provide to the Secretary—

(A) all reports(including information reports containing intelligence which has not been fully evaluated), assessments, and analytical information relating to threats of terrorism against the United States and to other areas of responsibility assigned by the Secretary;

(B) all information concerning the vulnerability of the infrastructure of the United States, or other vulnerabilities of the United States, to terrorism, whether or not such information has been analyzed;

(C) all other information relating to significant and credible threats of terrorism against the United States, whether or not such information has been analyzed; and

(D) such other information or material as the President may direct.

(c) TREATMENT UNDER CERTAIN LAWS.—The Secretary shall be deemed to be a Federal law enforcement, intelligence, protective, national defense, immigration, or national security official, and shall be provided with all information from law enforcement agencies that is required to be given to the Director of Central Intelligence, under any provision of the following:

(1) The USA PATRIOT Act of 2001(Public Law 107-56).

(2) Section 2517(6) of title 18, United States Code.

(3) Rule 6(e)(3)(C) of the Federal Rules of Criminal Procedure.

(d) ACCESS TO INTELLIGENCE AND OTHER INFORMATION.—

(1) ACCESS BY ELEMENTS OF FEDERAL GOVERNMENT.—Nothing in this title shall preclude any element of the intelligence community(as that term is defined in section 3(4) of the National Security Act of 1947(50 U.S.C. §401a(4)), or any other element of the Federal Government with responsibility for analyzing terrorist threat information, from receiving any intelligence or other information relating to terrorism.

(2) SHARING OF INFORMATION.—The Secretary, in consultation with the Director of Central Intelligence, shall work to ensure that intelligence or

other information relating to terrorism to which the Department has access is appropriately shared with the elements of the Federal Government referred to in paragraph(1), as well as with State and local governments, as appropriate.

(3) To integrate relevant information, analysis, and vulnerability assessments (regardless of whether such information, analysis or assessments are provided by or produced by the Department) in order to—

(A) identify priorities for protective and support measures regarding terrorist and other threats to homeland security by the Department, other agencies of the Federal Government, State, and local government agencies and authorities, the private sector, and other entities; and

(B) prepare finished intelligence and information products in both classified and unclassified formats, as appropriate, whenever reasonably expected to be of benefit to a State, local, or tribal government (including a State, local, or tribal law enforcement agency) or a private sector entity.

HOMELAND SECURITY ADVISORY SYSTEM

SEC. 203. [6 U.S.C. §124]

(a) REQUIREMENT.—The Secretary shall administer the Homeland Security Advisory System in accordance with this section to provide advisories or warnings regarding the threat or risk that acts of terrorism will be committed on the homeland to Federal, State, local, and tribal government authorities and to the people of the United States, as appropriate. The Secretary shall exercise primary responsibility for providing such advisories or warnings.

(b) REQUIRED ELEMENTS.—In administering the Homeland Security Advisory System, the Secretary shall—

(1) establish criteria for the issuance and revocation of such advisories or warnings;

(2) develop a methodology, relying on the criteria established under paragraph (1), for the issuance and revocation of such advisories or warnings;

(3) provide, in each such advisory or warning, specific information and advice regarding appropriate protective measures and countermeasures that may be taken in response to the threat or risk, at the maximum level of detail practicable to enable individuals, government entities, emergency response providers, and the private sector to act appropriately;

(4) whenever possible, limit the scope of each such advisory or warning to a specific region, locality, or economic sector believed to be under threat or at risk; and

(5) not, in issuing any advisory or warning, use color designations as the exclusive means of specifying homeland security threat conditions that are the subject of the advisory or warning.

HOMELAND SECURITY INFORMATION SHARING

SEC. 204. [6 U.S.C. §124A]

(a) INFORMATION SHARING.—Consistent with section 1016 of the Intelligence Reform and Terrorism Prevention Act of 2004 (6 U.S.C. §485), the Secretary, acting through the Under Secretary for Intelligence and Analysis, shall integrate the information and standardize the format of the products of the intelligence components of the Department containing homeland security information, terrorism information, weapons of mass destruction information, or national intelligence (as defined in section 3(5) of the National Security Act of 1947 (50 U.S.C. §401a(5))) except for any internal security protocols or personnel information of such intelligence components, or other administrative processes that are administered by any chief security officer of the Department.

(b) INFORMATION SHARING AND KNOWLEDGE MANAGEMENT OFFICERS.—For each intelligence component of the Department, the Secretary shall designate an information sharing and knowledge management officer who shall report to the Under Secretary for Intelligence and Analysis regarding coordinating the different systems used in the Department to gather and disseminate homeland security information or national intelligence (as defined in section 3(5) of the National Security Act of 1947 (50 U.S.C. §401a(5))).

(c) STATE, LOCAL, AND PRIVATE-SECTOR SOURCES OF INFORMATION—

(1) ESTABLISHMENT OF BUSINESS PROCESSES.—The Secretary, acting through the Under Secretary for Intelligence and Analysis or the Assistant Secretary for Infrastructure Protection, as appropriate, shall—

(A) establish Department-wide procedures for the review and analysis of information provided by State, local, and tribal governments and the private sector;

(B) as appropriate, integrate such information into the information gathered by the Department and other departments and agencies of the Federal Government; and

(C) make available such information, as appropriate, within the Department and to other departments and agencies of the Federal Government.

(2) FEEDBACK.—The Secretary shall develop mechanisms to provide feedback regarding the analysis and utility of information provided by

any entity of State, local, or tribal government or the private sector that provides such information to the Department.

(d) TRAINING AND EVALUATION OF EMPLOYEES—

(1) TRAINING.—The Secretary, acting through the Under Secretary for Intelligence and Analysis or the Assistant Secretary for Infrastructure Protection, as appropriate, shall provide to employees of the Department opportunities for training and education to develop an understanding of—

(A) the definitions of homeland security information and national intelligence (as defined in section 3(5) of the National Security Act of 1947 (50 U.S.C. §401a(5))); and

(B) how information available to such employees as part of their duties—

(i) might qualify as homeland security information or national intelligence; and

(ii) might be relevant to the Office of Intelligence and Analysis and the intelligence components of the Department.

(2) EVALUATIONS.—The Under Secretary for Intelligence and Analysis shall—

(A) on an ongoing basis, evaluate how employees of the Office of Intelligence and Analysis and the intelligence components of the Department are utilizing homeland security information or national intelligence, sharing information within the Department, as described in this title, and participating in the information sharing environment established under section 1016 of the Intelligence Reform and Terrorism Prevention Act of 2004 (6 U.S.C. §485); and

(B) provide to the appropriate component heads regular reports regarding the evaluations under subparagraph (A).

COMPREHENSIVE INFORMATION TECHNOLOGY NETWORK ARCHITECTURE

SEC. 205. [6 U.S.C. §124B]

(a) ESTABLISHMENT.—The Secretary, acting through the Under Secretary for Intelligence and Analysis, shall establish, consistent with the policies and procedures developed under section 1016 of the Intelligence Reform and Terrorism Prevention Act of 2004 (6 U.S.C. §485), and consistent with the enterprise architecture of the Department, a comprehensive information technology network architecture for the Office of Intelligence and Analysis that connects the various databases and related information technology assets of the Office of Intelligence and Analysis and the intelligence components of the

Department in order to promote internal information sharing among the intelligence and other personnel of the Department.

(b) COMPREHENSIVE INFORMATION TECHNOLOGY NETWORK ARCHITECTURE DEFINED.—The term "comprehensive information technology network architecture" means an integrated framework for evolving or maintaining existing information technology and acquiring new information technology to achieve the strategic management and information resources management goals of the Office of Intelligence and Analysis.

COORDINATION WITH INFORMATION SHARING ENVIRONMENT

SEC. 206. [6 U.S.C. §124C]

(a) GUIDANCE.—All activities to comply with sections 203, 204, and 205 shall be—

> (1) consistent with any policies, guidelines, procedures, instructions, or standards established under section 1016 of the Intelligence Reform and Terrorism Prevention Act of 2004 (6 U.S.C. §485);
>
> (2) implemented in coordination with, as appropriate, the program manager for the information sharing environment established under that section;
>
> (3) consistent with any applicable guidance issued by the Director of National Intelligence; and
>
> (4) consistent with any applicable guidance issued by the Secretary relating to the protection of law enforcement information or proprietary information.

(b) CONSULTATION.—In carrying out the duties and responsibilities under this subtitle, the Under Secretary for Intelligence and Analysis shall take into account the views of the heads of the intelligence components of the Department.

INTELLIGENCE COMPONENTS

SEC. 207. [6 U.S.C. §124D]

Subject to the direction and control of the Secretary, and consistent with any applicable guidance issued by the Director of National Intelligence, the responsibilities of the head of each intelligence component of the Department are as follows:

> (1) To ensure that the collection, processing, analysis, and dissemination of information within the scope of the information sharing environment, including homeland security information, terrorism information, weapons of mass destruction information, and national intelligence (as defined in section 3(5) of the National Security Act of 1947 (50 U.S.C. §401a(5))), are carried out effectively and efficiently in support of the

intelligence mission of the Department, as led by the Under Secretary for Intelligence and Analysis.

(2) To otherwise support and implement the intelligence mission of the Department, as led by the Under Secretary for Intelligence and Analysis.

(3) To incorporate the input of the Under Secretary for Intelligence and Analysis with respect to performance appraisals, bonus or award recommendations, pay adjustments, and other forms of commendation.

(4) To coordinate with the Under Secretary for Intelligence and Analysis in developing policies and requirements for the recruitment and selection of intelligence officials of the intelligence component.

(5) To advise and coordinate with the Under Secretary for Intelligence and Analysis on any plan to reorganize or restructure the intelligence component that would, if implemented, result in realignments of intelligence functions.

(6) To ensure that employees of the intelligence component have knowledge of, and comply with, the programs and policies established by the Under Secretary for Intelligence and Analysis and other appropriate officials of the Department and that such employees comply with all applicable laws and regulations.

(7) To perform such other activities relating to such responsibilities as the Secretary may provide.

TRAINING FOR EMPLOYEES OF INTELLIGENCE COMPONENTS

SEC. 208. [6 U.S.C. §124E]
The Secretary shall provide training and guidance for employees, officials, and senior executives of the intelligence components of the Department to develop knowledge of laws, regulations, operations, policies, procedures, and programs that are related to the functions of the Department relating to the collection, processing, analysis, and dissemination of information within the scope of the information sharing environment, including homeland security information, terrorism information, and weapons of mass destruction information, or national intelligence (as defined in section 3(5) of the National Security Act of 1947 (50 U.S.C. §401a(5))).

INTELLIGENCE TRAINING DEVELOPMENT FOR STATE AND LOCAL GOVERNMENT OFFICIALS

SEC. 209. [6 U.S.C. §124F]
(a) CURRICULUM.—The Secretary, acting through the Under Secretary for Intelligence and Analysis, shall—

(1) develop a curriculum for training State, local, and tribal government officials, including law enforcement officers, intelligence analysts, and other emergency response providers, in the intelligence cycle and Federal laws, practices, and regulations regarding the development, handling, and review of intelligence and other information; and

(2) ensure that the curriculum includes executive level training for senior level State, local, and tribal law enforcement officers, intelligence analysts, and other emergency response providers.

(b) TRAINING.—To the extent possible, the Federal Law Enforcement Training Center and other existing Federal entities with the capacity and expertise to train State, local, and tribal government officials based on the curriculum developed under subsection (a) shall be used to carry out the training programs created under this section. If such entities do not have the capacity, resources, or capabilities to conduct such training, the Secretary may approve another entity to conduct such training.

(c) CONSULTATION.—In carrying out the duties described in subsection (a), the Under Secretary for Intelligence and Analysis shall consult with the Director of the Federal Law Enforcement Training Center, the Attorney General, the Director of National Intelligence, the Administrator of the Federal Emergency Management Agency, and other appropriate parties, such as private industry, institutions of higher education, nonprofit institutions, and other intelligence agencies of the Federal Government.

INFORMATION SHARING INCENTIVES

SEC. 210. [6 U.S.C. §124G]

(a) AWARDS.—In making cash awards under chapter 45 of title 5, United States Code, the President or the head of an agency, in consultation with the program manager designated under section 1016 of the Intelligence Reform and Terrorism Prevention Act of 2004 (6 U.S.C. §485), may consider the success of an employee in appropriately sharing information within the scope of the information sharing environment established under that section, including homeland security information, terrorism information, and weapons of mass destruction information, or national intelligence (as defined in section 3(5) of the National Security Act of 1947 (50 U.S.C. §401a(5)), in a manner consistent with any policies, guidelines, procedures, instructions, or standards established by the President or, as appropriate, the program manager of that environment for the implementation and management of that environment.

(b) OTHER INCENTIVES.—The head of each department or agency described in section 1016(i) of the Intelligence Reform and Terrorism Prevention Act of 2004 (6 U.S.C. §485(i)), in consultation with the program manager designated under section 1016 of the Intelligence Reform and Terrorism Prevention Act of 2004 (6

U.S.C. §485), shall adopt best practices regarding effective ways to educate and motivate officers and employees of the Federal Government to participate fully in the information sharing environment, including—

(1) promotions and other nonmonetary awards; and

(2) publicizing information sharing accomplishments by individual employees and, where appropriate, the tangible end benefits that resulted.

DEPARTMENT OF HOMELAND SECURITY STATE, LOCAL, AND REGIONAL FUSION CENTER INITIATIVE

SEC. 210A. [6 U.S.C. §124H]

(a) ESTABLISHMENT.—The Secretary, in consultation with the program manager of the information sharing environment established under section 1016 of the Intelligence Reform and Terrorism Prevention Act of 2004 (6 U.S.C. §485), the Attorney General, the Privacy Officer of the Department, the Officer for Civil Rights and Civil Liberties of the Department, and the Privacy and Civil Liberties Oversight Board established under section 1061 of the Intelligence Reform and Terrorism Prevention Act of 2004 (5 U.S.C. §601 note), shall establish a Department of Homeland Security State, Local, and Regional Fusion Center Initiative to establish partnerships with State, local, and regional fusion centers.

(b) DEPARTMENT SUPPORT AND COORDINATION.—Through the Department of Homeland Security State, Local, and Regional Fusion Center Initiative, and in coordination with the principal officials of participating State, local, or regional fusion centers and the officers designated as the Homeland Security Advisors of the States, the Secretary shall—

(1) provide operational and intelligence advice and assistance to State, local, and regional fusion centers;

(2) support efforts to include State, local, and regional fusion centers into efforts to establish an information sharing environment;

(3) conduct tabletop and live training exercises to regularly assess the capability of individual and regional networks of State, local, and regional fusion centers to integrate the efforts of such networks with the efforts of the Department;

(4) coordinate with other relevant Federal entities engaged in homeland security-related activities;

(5) provide analytic and reporting advice and assistance to State, local, and regional fusion centers;

(6) review information within the scope of the information sharing environment, including homeland security information, terrorism information, and weapons of mass destruction information, that is gathered by State, local, and regional fusion centers, and to incorporate

such information, as appropriate, into the Department's own such information;

(7) provide management assistance to State, local, and regional fusion centers;

(8) serve as a point of contact to ensure the dissemination of information within the scope of the information sharing environment, including homeland security information, terrorism information, and weapons of mass destruction information;

(9) facilitate close communication and coordination between State, local, and regional fusion centers and the Department;

(10) provide State, local, and regional fusion centers with expertise on Department resources and operations;

(11) provide training to State, local, and regional fusion centers and encourage such fusion centers to participate in terrorism threat-related exercises conducted by the Department; and

(12) carry out such other duties as the Secretary determines are appropriate.

(c) PERSONNEL ASSIGNMENT.—

(1) IN GENERAL.—The Under Secretary for Intelligence and Analysis shall, to the maximum extent practicable, assign officers and intelligence analysts from components of the Department to participating State, local, and regional fusion centers.

(2) PERSONNEL SOURCES.—Officers and intelligence analysts assigned to participating fusion centers under this subsection may be assigned from the following Department components, in coordination with the respective component head and in consultation with the principal officials of participating fusion centers:

(A) Office of Intelligence and Analysis.

(B) Office of Infrastructure Protection.

(C) Transportation Security Administration.

(D) United States Customs and Border Protection.

(E) United States Immigration and Customs Enforcement.

(F) United States Coast Guard.

(G) Other components of the Department, as determined by the Secretary.

(3) QUALIFYING CRITERIA—

(A) IN GENERAL.—The Secretary shall develop qualifying criteria for a fusion center to participate in the assigning of Department officers or intelligence analysts under this section.

(B) CRITERIA.—Any criteria developed under subparagraph (A) may include—

(i) whether the fusion center, through its mission and governance structure, focuses on a broad counterterrorism approach, and whether that broad approach is pervasive through all levels of the organization;

(ii) whether the fusion center has sufficient numbers of adequately trained personnel to support a broad counterterrorism mission;

(iii) whether the fusion center has—

(I) access to relevant law enforcement, emergency response, private sector, open source, and national security data; and

(II) the ability to share and analytically utilize that data for lawful purposes;

(iv) whether the fusion center is adequately funded by the State, local, or regional government to support its counterterrorism mission; and

(v) the relevancy of the mission of the fusion center to the particular source component of Department officers or intelligence analysts.

(4) PREREQUISITE.—

(A) INTELLIGENCE ANALYSIS, PRIVACY, AND CIVIL LIBERTIES TRAINING.—Before being assigned to a fusion center under this section, an officer or intelligence analyst shall undergo—

(i) appropriate intelligence analysis or information sharing training using an intelligence-led policing curriculum that is consistent with—

(I) standard training and education programs offered to Department law enforcement and intelligence personnel; and

(II) the Criminal Intelligence Systems Operating Policies under part 23 of title 28, Code of Federal Regulations (or any corresponding similar rule or regulation);

(ii) appropriate privacy and civil liberties training that is developed, supported, or sponsored by the Privacy Officer appointed under section 222 and the Officer for Civil Rights and Civil Liberties of the Department, in consultation with the Privacy and Civil Liberties Oversight Board established under section 1061 of the Intelligence Reform and Terrorism Prevention Act of 2004 (5 U.S.C. §601 note); and

(iii) such other training prescribed by the Under Secretary for Intelligence and Analysis.

(B) PRIOR WORK EXPERIENCE IN AREA.—In determining the eligibility of an officer or intelligence analyst to be assigned to a fusion center under this section, the Under Secretary for Intelligence and Analysis shall consider the familiarity of the officer or intelligence analyst with the State, locality, or region, as determined by such factors as whether the officer or intelligence analyst—

(i) has been previously assigned in the geographic area; or

(ii) has previously worked with intelligence officials or law enforcement or other emergency response providers from that State, locality, or region.

(5) EXPEDITED SECURITY CLEARANCE PROCESSING.—The Under Secretary for Intelligence and Analysis—

(A) shall ensure that each officer or intelligence analyst assigned to a fusion center under this section has the appropriate security clearance to contribute effectively to the mission of the fusion center; and

(B) may request that security clearance processing be expedited for each such officer or intelligence analyst and may use available funds for such purpose.

(6) FURTHER QUALIFICATIONS.—Each officer or intelligence analyst assigned to a fusion center under this section shall satisfy any other qualifications the Under Secretary for Intelligence and Analysis may prescribe.

(d) RESPONSIBILITIES.—An officer or intelligence analyst assigned to a fusion center under this section shall—

(1) assist law enforcement agencies and other emergency response providers of State, local, and tribal governments and fusion center personnel in using information within the scope of the information sharing environment, including homeland security information, terrorism information, and weapons of mass destruction information, to develop a comprehensive and accurate threat picture;

(2) review homeland security-relevant information from law enforcement agencies and other emergency response providers of State, local, and tribal government;

(3) create intelligence and other information products derived from such information and other homeland security-relevant information provided by the Department; and

(4) assist in the dissemination of such products, as coordinated by the Under Secretary for Intelligence and Analysis, to law enforcement agencies and other emergency response providers of State, local, and tribal government, other fusion centers, and appropriate Federal agencies.

(e) BORDER INTELLIGENCE PRIORITY.—

(1) IN GENERAL.—The Secretary shall make it a priority to assign officers and intelligence analysts under this section from United States Customs and Border Protection, United States Immigration and Customs Enforcement, and the Coast Guard to participating State, local, and regional fusion centers located in jurisdictions along land or maritime borders of the United States in order to enhance the integrity of and security at such borders by helping Federal, State, local, and tribal law enforcement authorities to identify, investigate, and otherwise interdict persons, weapons, and related contraband that pose a threat to homeland security.

(2) BORDER INTELLIGENCE PRODUCTS.—When performing the responsibilities described in subsection (d), officers and intelligence analysts assigned to participating State, local, and regional fusion centers under this section shall have, as a primary responsibility, the creation of border intelligence products that—

(A) assist State, local, and tribal law enforcement agencies in deploying their resources most efficiently to help detect and interdict terrorists, weapons of mass destruction, and related contraband at land or maritime borders of the United States;

(B) promote more consistent and timely sharing of border security-relevant information among jurisdictions along land or maritime borders of the United States; and

(C) enhance the Department's situational awareness of the threat of acts of terrorism at or involving the land or maritime borders of the United States.

(f) DATABASE ACCESS.—In order to fulfill the objectives described under subsection (d), each officer or intelligence analyst assigned to a fusion center under this section shall have appropriate access to all relevant Federal databases and information systems, consistent with any policies, guidelines, procedures, instructions, or standards established by the President or, as appropriate, the program manager of the information sharing environment for the implementation and management of that environment.

(g) CONSUMER FEEDBACK.—

(1) IN GENERAL.—The Secretary shall create a voluntary mechanism for any State, local, or tribal law enforcement officer or other emergency response provider who is a consumer of the intelligence or other

information products referred to in subsection (d) to provide feedback to the Department on the quality and utility of such intelligence products.

(2) REPORT.—Not later than one year after the date of the enactment of the Implementing Recommendations of the 9/11 Commission Act of 2007, and annually thereafter, the Secretary shall submit to the Committee on Homeland Security and Governmental Affairs of the Senate and the Committee on Homeland Security of the House of Representatives a report that includes a description of the consumer feedback obtained under paragraph (1) and, if applicable, how the Department has adjusted its production of intelligence products in response to that consumer feedback.

(h) RULE OF CONSTRUCTION.—

(1) IN GENERAL.—The authorities granted under this section shall supplement the authorities granted under section 201(d) and nothing in this section shall be construed to abrogate the authorities granted under section 201(d).

(2) PARTICIPATION.—Nothing in this section shall be construed to require a State, local, or regional government or entity to accept the assignment of officers or intelligence analysts of the Department into the fusion center of that State, locality, or region.

(i) GUIDELINES.—The Secretary, in consultation with the Attorney General, shall establish guidelines for fusion centers created and operated by State and local governments, to include standards that any such fusion center shall—

(1) collaboratively develop a mission statement, identify expectations and goals, measure performance, and determine effectiveness for that fusion center;

(2) create a representative governance structure that includes law enforcement officers and other emergency response providers and, as appropriate, the private sector;

(3) create a collaborative environment for the sharing of intelligence and information among Federal, State, local, and tribal government agencies (including law enforcement officers and other emergency response providers), the private sector, and the public, consistent with any policies, guidelines, procedures, instructions, or standards established by the President or, as appropriate, the program manager of the information sharing environment;

(4) leverage the databases, systems, and networks available from public and private sector entities, in accordance with all applicable laws, to maximize information sharing;

(5) develop, publish, and adhere to a privacy and civil liberties policy consistent with Federal, State, and local law;

(6) provide, in coordination with the Privacy Officer of the Department and the Officer for Civil Rights and Civil Liberties of the Department, appropriate privacy and civil liberties training for all State, local, tribal, and private sector representatives at the fusion center;

(7) ensure appropriate security measures are in place for the facility, data, and personnel;

(8) select and train personnel based on the needs, mission, goals, and functions of that fusion center;

(9) offer a variety of intelligence and information services and products to recipients of fusion center intelligence and information; and

(10) incorporate law enforcement officers, other emergency response providers, and, as appropriate, the private sector, into all relevant phases of the intelligence and fusion process, consistent with the mission statement developed under paragraph (1), either through full time representatives or liaison relationships with the fusion center to enable the receipt and sharing of information and intelligence.

(j) DEFINITIONS.—In this section—

(1) the term "fusion center" means a collaborative effort of 2 or more Federal, State, local, or tribal government agencies that combines resources, expertise, or information with the goal of maximizing the ability of such agencies to detect, prevent, investigate, apprehend, and respond to criminal or terrorist activity;

(2) the term "information sharing environment" means the information sharing environment established under section 1016 of the Intelligence Reform and Terrorism Prevention Act of 2004 (6 U.S.C. §485);

(3) the term "intelligence analyst" means an individual who regularly advises, administers, supervises, or performs work in the collection, gathering, analysis, evaluation, reporting, production, or dissemination of information on political, economic, social, cultural, physical, geographical, scientific, or military conditions, trends, or forces in foreign or domestic areas that directly or indirectly affect national security;

(4) the term "intelligence-led policing" means the collection and analysis of information to produce an intelligence end product designed to inform law enforcement decision making at the tactical and strategic levels; and

(5) the term "terrorism information" has the meaning given that term in section 1016 of the Intelligence Reform and Terrorism Prevention Act of 2004 (6 U.S.C. §485).

(k) Authorization of Appropriations.—There is authorized to be appropriated $10,000,000 for each of fiscal years 2008 through 2012, to carry out this section, except for subsection (i), including for hiring officers and intelligence analysts to replace officers and intelligence analysts who are assigned to fusion centers under this section.

HOMELAND SECURITY INFORMATION SHARING FELLOWS PROGRAM

SEC. 210B. [6 U.S.C. §124I]

(a) ESTABLISHMENT.—

(1) IN GENERAL.—The Secretary, acting through the Under Secretary for Intelligence and Analysis, and in consultation with the Chief Human Capital Officer, shall establish a fellowship program in accordance with this section for the purpose of—

(A) detailing State, local, and tribal law enforcement officers and intelligence analysts to the Department in accordance with subchapter VI of chapter 33 of title 5, United States Code, to participate in the work of the Office of Intelligence and Analysis in order to become familiar with—

(i) the relevant missions and capabilities of the Department and other Federal agencies; and

(ii) the role, programs, products, and personnel of the Office of Intelligence and Analysis; and

(B) promoting information sharing between the Department and State, local, and tribal law enforcement officers and intelligence analysts by assigning such officers and analysts to—

(i) serve as a point of contact in the Department to assist in the representation of State, local, and tribal information requirements;

(ii) identify information within the scope of the information sharing environment, including homeland security information, terrorism information, and weapons of mass destruction information, that is of interest to State, local, and tribal law enforcement officers, intelligence analysts, and other emergency response providers;

(iii) assist Department analysts in preparing and disseminating products derived from information within the scope of the information sharing environment, including homeland security information, terrorism information, and weapons of mass destruction information, that are tailored to State, local, and tribal law enforcement officers and intelligence analysts and designed to prepare for and thwart acts of terrorism; and

368

(iv) assist Department analysts in preparing products derived from information within the scope of the information sharing environment, including homeland security information, terrorism information, and weapons of mass destruction information, that are tailored to State, local, and tribal emergency response providers and assist in the dissemination of such products through appropriate Department channels.

(2) PROGRAM NAME.—The program under this section shall be known as the "Homeland Security Information Sharing Fellows Program."

(b) ELIGIBILITY.—

(1) IN GENERAL.—In order to be eligible for selection as an Information Sharing Fellow under the program under this section, an individual shall—

(A) have homeland security-related responsibilities;

(B) be eligible for an appropriate security clearance;

(C) possess a valid need for access to classified information, as determined by the Under Secretary for Intelligence and Analysis;

(D) be an employee of an eligible entity; and

(E) have undergone appropriate privacy and civil liberties training that is developed, supported, or sponsored by the Privacy Officer and the Officer for Civil Rights and Civil Liberties, in consultation with the Privacy and Civil Liberties Oversight Board established under section 1061 of the Intelligence Reform and Terrorism Prevention Act of 2004 (5 U.S.C. §601 note).

(2) ELIGIBLE ENTITIES.—In this subsection, the term "eligible entity" means—

(A) a State, local, or regional fusion center;

(B) a State or local law enforcement or other government entity that serves a major metropolitan area, suburban area, or rural area, as determined by the Secretary;

(C) a State or local law enforcement or other government entity with port, border, or agricultural responsibilities, as determined by the Secretary;

(D) a tribal law enforcement or other authority; or

(E) such other entity as the Secretary determines is appropriate.

(c) OPTIONAL PARTICIPATION.—No State, local, or tribal law enforcement or other government entity shall be required to participate in the Homeland Security Information Sharing Fellows Program.

(d) PROCEDURES FOR NOMINATION AND SELECTION.—

(1) IN GENERAL.—The Under Secretary for Intelligence and Analysis shall establish procedures to provide for the nomination and selection of individuals to participate in the Homeland Security Information Sharing Fellows Program.

(2) LIMITATIONS.—The Under Secretary for Intelligence and Analysis shall—

 (A) select law enforcement officers and intelligence analysts representing a broad cross-section of State, local, and tribal agencies; and

 (B) ensure that the number of Information Sharing Fellows selected does not impede the activities of the Office of Intelligence and Analysis.

RURAL POLICING INSTITUTE

SEC. 210C. [6 U.S.C. §124J]

(a) IN GENERAL.—The Secretary shall establish a Rural Policing Institute, which shall be administered by the Federal Law Enforcement Training Center, to target training to law enforcement agencies and other emergency response providers located in rural areas. The Secretary, through the Rural Policing Institute, shall—

 (1) evaluate the needs of law enforcement agencies and other emergency response providers in rural areas;

 (2) develop expert training programs designed to address the needs of law enforcement agencies and other emergency response providers in rural areas as identified in the evaluation conducted under paragraph (1), including training programs about intelligence-led policing and protections for privacy, civil rights, and civil liberties;

 (3) provide the training programs developed under paragraph (2) to law enforcement agencies and other emergency response providers in rural areas; and

 (4) conduct outreach efforts to ensure that local and tribal governments in rural areas are aware of the training programs developed under paragraph (2) so they can avail themselves of such programs.

(b) CURRICULA.—The training at the Rural Policing Institute established under subsection (a) shall—

 (1) be configured in a manner so as not to duplicate or displace any law enforcement or emergency response program of the Federal Law Enforcement Training Center or a local or tribal government entity in existence on the date of enactment of the Implementing Recommendations of the 9/11 Commission Act of 2007; and

 (2) to the maximum extent practicable, be delivered in a cost-effective manner at facilities of the Department, on closed military installations

with adequate training facilities, or at facilities operated by the
participants.

(c) DEFINITION.—In this section, the term "rural" means an area that is not
located in a metropolitan statistical area, as defined by the Office of Management
and Budget.

(d) AUTHORIZATION OF APPROPRIATIONS.—There are authorized to be
appropriated to carry out this section (including for contracts, staff, and
equipment)—

> (1) $10,000,000 for fiscal year 2008; and
>
> (2) $5,000,000 for each of fiscal years 2009 through 2013.

INTERAGENCY THREAT ASSESSMENT AND COORDINATION GROUP

SEC. 210D. [6 U.S.C. §124K]

(a) IN GENERAL.—To improve the sharing of information within the scope of the
information sharing environment established under section 1016 of the
Intelligence Reform and Terrorism Prevention Act of 2004 (6 U.S.C. §485) with
State, local, tribal, and private sector officials, the Director of National
Intelligence, through the program manager for the information sharing
environment, in coordination with the Secretary, shall coordinate and oversee the
creation of an Interagency Threat Assessment and Coordination Group (referred
to in this section as the "ITACG").

(b) COMPOSITION OF ITACG.—The ITACG shall consist of—

> (1) an ITACG Advisory Council to set policy and develop processes for
> the integration, analysis, and dissemination of federally-coordinated
> information within the scope of the information sharing environment,
> including homeland security information, terrorism information, and
> weapons of mass destruction information; and
>
> (2) an ITACG Detail comprised of State, local, and tribal homeland
> security and law enforcement officers and intelligence analysts detailed
> to work in the National Counterterrorism Center with Federal
> intelligence analysts for the purpose of integrating, analyzing, and
> assisting in the dissemination of federally-coordinated information
> within the scope of the information sharing environment, including
> homeland security information, terrorism information, and weapons of
> mass destruction information, through appropriate channels identified by
> the ITACG Advisory Council.

(c) RESPONSIBILITIES OF PROGRAM MANAGER.—The program manager shall—

> (1) monitor and assess the efficacy of the ITACG;
>
> (2) not later than 180 days after the date of the enactment of the
> Implementing Recommendations of the 9/11 Commission Act of 2007,
> and at least annually thereafter, submit to the Secretary, the Attorney

General, the Director of National Intelligence, the Committee on Homeland Security and Governmental Affairs of the Senate and the Committee on Homeland Security of the House of Representatives a report on the progress of the ITACG; and

(3) in each report required by paragraph (2) submitted after the date of the enactment of the Reducing Over–Classification Act, include an assessment of whether the detailees under subsection (d)(5) have appropriate access to all relevant information, as required by subsection (g)(2)(C).

(d) RESPONSIBILITIES OF SECRETARY.—The Secretary, or the Secretary's designee, in coordination with the Director of the National Counterterrorism Center and the ITACG Advisory Council, shall—

(1) create policies and standards for the creation of information products derived from information within the scope of the information sharing environment, including homeland security information, terrorism information, and weapons of mass destruction information, that are suitable for dissemination to State, local, and tribal governments and the private sector;

(2) evaluate and develop processes for the timely dissemination of federally-coordinated information within the scope of the information sharing environment, including homeland security information, terrorism information, and weapons of mass destruction information, to State, local, and tribal governments and the private sector;

(3) establish criteria and a methodology for indicating to State, local, and tribal governments and the private sector the reliability of information within the scope of the information sharing environment, including homeland security information, terrorism information, and weapons of mass destruction information, disseminated to them;

(4) educate the intelligence community about the requirements of the State, local, and tribal homeland security, law enforcement, and other emergency response providers regarding information within the scope of the information sharing environment, including homeland security information, terrorism information, and weapons of mass destruction information;

(5) establish and maintain the ITACG Detail, which shall assign an appropriate number of State, local, and tribal homeland security and law enforcement officers and intelligence analysts to work in the National Counterterrorism Center who shall—

(A) educate and advise National Counterterrorism Center intelligence analysts about the requirements of the State, local, and tribal homeland security and law enforcement officers, and other emergency response providers regarding information within the scope of the information sharing environment, including homeland security information, terrorism information, and weapons of mass destruction information;

(B) assist National Counterterrorism Center intelligence analysts in integrating, analyzing, and otherwise preparing versions of products derived from information within the scope of the information sharing environment, including homeland security information, terrorism information, and weapons of mass destruction information that are unclassified or classified at the lowest possible level and suitable for dissemination to State, local, and tribal homeland security and law enforcement agencies in order to help deter and prevent terrorist attacks;

(C) implement, in coordination with National Counterterrorism Center intelligence analysts, the policies, processes, procedures, standards, and guidelines developed by the ITACG Advisory Council;

(D) assist in the dissemination of products derived from information within the scope of the information sharing environment, including homeland security information, terrorism information, and weapons of mass destruction information, to State, local, and tribal jurisdictions only through appropriate channels identified by the ITACG Advisory Council;

(E) make recommendations, as appropriate, to the Secretary or the Secretary's designee, for the further dissemination of intelligence products that could likely inform or improve the security of a State, local, or tribal government, (including a State, local, or tribal law enforcement agency) or a private sector entity; and

(F) report directly to the senior intelligence official from the Department under paragraph (6);

(6) detail a senior intelligence official from the Department of Homeland Security to the National Counterterrorism Center, who shall—

(A) manage the day-to-day operations of the ITACG Detail;

(B) report directly to the Director of the National Counterterrorism Center or the Director's designee; and

(C) in coordination with the Director of the Federal Bureau of Investigation, and subject to the approval of the Director of the National Counterterrorism Center, select a deputy from the pool of available detailees from the Federal Bureau of Investigation in the National Counterterrorism Center;

(7) establish, within the ITACG Advisory Council, a mechanism to select law enforcement officers and intelligence analysts for placement in the

National Counterterrorism Center consistent with paragraph (5), using criteria developed by the ITACG Advisory Council that shall encourage participation from a broadly representative group of State, local, and tribal homeland security and law enforcement agencies; and

(8) compile an annual assessment of the ITACG Detail's performance, including summaries of customer feedback, in preparing, disseminating, and requesting the dissemination of intelligence products intended for State, local and tribal government (including State, local, and tribal law enforcement agencies) and private sector entities; and

(9) provide the assessment developed pursuant to paragraph (8) to the program manager for use in the annual reports required by subsection (c)(2).

(e) MEMBERSHIP.—The Secretary, or the Secretary's designee, shall serve as the chair of the ITACG Advisory Council, which shall include—

(1) representatives of—

(A) the Department;

(B) the Federal Bureau of Investigation;

(C) the National Counterterrorism Center;

(D) the Department of Defense;

(E) the Department of Energy;

(F) the Department of State; and

(G) other Federal entities as appropriate;

(2) the program manager of the information sharing environment, designated under section 1016(f) of the Intelligence Reform and Terrorism Prevention Act of 2004 (6 U.S.C. §485(f)), or the program manager's designee; and

(3) executive level law enforcement and intelligence officials from State, local, and tribal governments.

(f) CRITERIA.—The Secretary, in consultation with the Director of National Intelligence, the Attorney General, and the program manager of the information sharing environment established under section 1016 of the Intelligence Reform and Terrorism Prevention Act of 2004 (6 U.S.C. §485), shall—

(1) establish procedures for selecting members of the ITACG Advisory Council and for the proper handling and safeguarding of products derived from information within the scope of the information sharing environment, including homeland security information, terrorism information, and weapons of mass destruction information, by those members; and

(2) ensure that at least 50 percent of the members of the ITACG Advisory Council are from State, local, and tribal governments.

(g) OPERATIONS.—

(1) IN GENERAL.—Beginning not later than 90 days after the date of enactment of the Implementing Recommendations of the 9/11

Commission Act of 2007, the ITACG Advisory Council shall meet regularly, but not less than quarterly, at the facilities of the National Counterterrorism Center of the Office of the Director of National Intelligence.

(2) MANAGEMENT.—Pursuant to section 119(f)(E) of the National Security Act of 1947 (50 U.S.C. §404o(f)(E)), the Director of the National Counterterrorism Center, acting through the senior intelligence official from the Department of Homeland Security detailed pursuant to subsection (d)(6), shall ensure that—

> (A) the products derived from information within the scope of the information sharing environment, including homeland security information, terrorism information, and weapons of mass destruction information, prepared by the National Counterterrorism Center and the ITACG Detail for distribution to State, local, and tribal homeland security and law enforcement agencies reflect the requirements of such agencies and are produced consistently with the policies, processes, procedures, standards, and guidelines established by the ITACG Advisory Council;

> (B) in consultation with the ITACG Advisory Council and consistent with sections 102A(f)(1)(B)(iii) and 119(f)(E) of the National Security Act of 1947 (50 U.S.C. §402 et seq.), all products described in subparagraph (A) are disseminated through existing channels of the Department and the Department of Justice and other appropriate channels to State, local, and tribal government officials and other entities;

> (C) all detailees under subsection (d)(5) have appropriate access to all relevant information within the scope of the information sharing environment, including homeland security information, terrorism information, and weapons of mass destruction information, available at the National Counterterrorism Center in order to accomplish the objectives under that paragraph;

> (D) all detailees under subsection (d)(5) have the appropriate security clearances and are trained in the procedures for handling, processing, storing, and disseminating classified products derived from information within the scope of the information sharing environment, including homeland security information, terrorism information, and weapons of mass destruction information; and

> (E) all detailees under subsection (d)(5) complete appropriate privacy and civil liberties training.

(h) INAPPLICABILITY OF THE FEDERAL ADVISORY COMMITTEE ACT.—The Federal Advisory Committee Act (5 U.S.C. App.) shall not apply to the ITACG or any subsidiary groups thereof.

(i) Authorization of Appropriations.—There are authorized to be appropriated such sums as may be necessary for each of fiscal years 2008 through 2012 to carry out this section, including to obtain security clearances for the State, local, and tribal participants in the ITACG.

NATIONAL ASSET DATABASE

SEC. 210E. [6 U.S.C. §124L]

(a) ESTABLISHMENT.—

    (1) NATIONAL ASSET DATABASE.—The Secretary shall establish and maintain a national database of each system or asset that—

        (A) the Secretary, in consultation with appropriate homeland security officials of the States, determines to be vital and the loss, interruption, incapacity, or destruction of which would have a negative or debilitating effect on the economic security, public health, or safety of the United States, any State, or any local government; or

        (B) the Secretary determines is appropriate for inclusion in the database.

    (2) PRIORITIZED CRITICAL INFRASTRUCTURE LIST.—In accordance with Homeland Security Presidential Directive-7, as in effect on January 1, 2007, the Secretary shall establish and maintain a single classified prioritized list of systems and assets included in the database under paragraph (1) that the Secretary determines would, if destroyed or disrupted, cause national or regional catastrophic effects.

(b) USE OF DATABASE.—The Secretary shall use the database established under subsection (a)(1) in the development and implementation of Department plans and programs as appropriate.

(c) MAINTENANCE OF DATABASE—

    (1) IN GENERAL.—The Secretary shall maintain and annually update the database established under subsection (a)(1) and the list established under subsection (a)(2), including—

        (A) establishing data collection guidelines and providing such guidelines to the appropriate homeland security official of each State;

        (B) regularly reviewing the guidelines established under subparagraph (A), including by consulting with the appropriate homeland security officials of States, to solicit feedback about the guidelines, as appropriate;

(C) after providing the homeland security official of a State with the guidelines under subparagraph (A), allowing the official a reasonable amount of time to submit to the Secretary any data submissions recommended by the official for inclusion in the database established under subsection (a)(1);

(D) examining the contents and identifying any submissions made by such an official that are described incorrectly or that do not meet the guidelines established under subparagraph (A); and

(E) providing to the appropriate homeland security official of each relevant State a list of submissions identified under subparagraph (D) for review and possible correction before the Secretary finalizes the decision of which submissions will be included in the database established under subsection (a)(1).

(2) ORGANIZATION OF INFORMATION IN DATABASE.—The Secretary shall organize the contents of the database established under subsection (a)(1) and the list established under subsection (a)(2) as the Secretary determines is appropriate. Any organizational structure of such contents shall include the categorization of the contents—

(A) according to the sectors listed in National Infrastructure Protection Plan developed pursuant to Homeland Security Presidential Directive-7; and

(B) by the State and county of their location.

(3) PRIVATE SECTOR INTEGRATION.—The Secretary shall identify and evaluate methods, including the Department's Protected Critical Infrastructure Information Program, to acquire relevant private sector information for the purpose of using that information to generate any database or list, including the database established under subsection (a)(1) and the list established under subsection (a)(2).

(4) RETENTION OF CLASSIFICATION.—The classification of information required to be provided to Congress, the Department, or any other department or agency under this section by a sector-specific agency, including the assignment of a level of classification of such information, shall be binding on Congress, the Department, and that other Federal agency.

(d) REPORTS.—

(1) REPORT REQUIRED.—Not later than 180 days after the date of the enactment of the Implementing Recommendations of the 9/11 Commission Act of 2007, and annually thereafter, the Secretary shall submit to the Committee on Homeland Security and Governmental Affairs of the Senate and the Committee on Homeland Security of the House of Representatives a report on the database established under subsection (a)(1) and the list established under subsection (a)(2).

(2) CONTENTS OF REPORT.—Each such report shall include the following:

(A) The name, location, and sector classification of each of the systems and assets on the list established under subsection (a)(2).

(B) The name, location, and sector classification of each of the systems and assets on such list that are determined by the Secretary to be most at risk to terrorism.

(C) Any significant challenges in compiling the list of the systems and assets included on such list or in the database established under subsection (a)(1).

(D) Any significant changes from the preceding report in the systems and assets included on such list or in such database.

(E) If appropriate, the extent to which such database and such list have been used, individually or jointly, for allocating funds by the Federal Government to prevent, reduce, mitigate, or respond to acts of terrorism.

(F) The amount of coordination between the Department and the private sector, through any entity of the Department that meets with representatives of private sector industries for purposes of such coordination, for the purpose of ensuring the accuracy of such database and such list.

(G) Any other information the Secretary deems relevant.

(3) CLASSIFIED INFORMATION.—The report shall be submitted in unclassified form but may contain a classified annex.

(e) INSPECTOR GENERAL STUDY.—By not later than two years after the date of enactment of the Implementing Recommendations of the 9/11 Commission Act of 2007, the Inspector General of the Department shall conduct a study of the implementation of this section.

(f) NATIONAL INFRASTRUCTURE PROTECTION CONSORTIUM.—The Secretary may establish a consortium to be known as the "National Infrastructure Protection Consortium". The Consortium may advise the Secretary on the best way to identify, generate, organize, and maintain any database or list of systems and assets established by the Secretary, including the database established under subsection (a)(1) and the list established under subsection (a)(2). If the Secretary establishes the National Infrastructure Protection Consortium, the Consortium may—

(1) be composed of national laboratories, Federal agencies, State and local homeland security organizations, academic institutions, or national Centers of Excellence that have demonstrated experience working with and identifying critical infrastructure and key resources; and

(2) provide input to the Secretary on any request pertaining to the contents of such database or such list.

378

CLASSIFIED INFORMATION ADVISORY OFFICER

SEC. 210F. [6 U.S.C. §124M]

(a) REQUIREMENT TO ESTABLISH.—The Secretary shall identify and designate within the Department a Classified Information Advisory Officer, as described in this section.

(b) RESPONSIBILITIES.—The responsibilities of the Classified Information Advisory Officer shall be as follows:

(1) To develop and disseminate educational materials and to develop and administer training programs to assist state, local, and tribal governments (including state, local, and tribal law enforcement agencies) and private sector entities—

(A) in developing plans and policies to respond to requests related to classified information without communicating such information to individuals who lack appropriate security clearances;

(B) regarding the appropriate procedures for challenging classification designations of information received by personnel of such entities; and

(C) on the means by which such personnel may apply for security clearances.

(2) To inform the Under Secretary for Intelligence and Analysis on policies and procedures that could facilitate the sharing of classified information with such personnel, as appropriate.

(c) INITIAL DESIGNATION.—Not later than 90 days after the date of the enactment of the Reducing Over–Classification Act, the Secretary shall—

(1) designate the initial Classified Information Advisory Officer; and

(2) submit to the Committee on Homeland Security and Governmental Affairs of the Senate and the Committee on Homeland Security of the House of Representatives a written notification of the designation.

TITLE V—EMERGENCY PREPAREDNESS AND RESPONSE

Sec. 515. National Operations Center. [6 U.S.C. §321D]

(a) Definition

In this section, the term "situational awareness" means information gathered from a variety of sources that, when communicated to emergency managers and decision makers, can form the basis for incident management decisionmaking.

(b) Establishment

The National Operations Center is the principal operations center for the Department and shall—

(1) provide situational awareness and a common operating picture for the entire Federal Government, and for State, local, and tribal governments as appropriate, in the event of a natural disaster, act of terrorism, or other man-made disaster; and

(2) ensure that critical terrorism and disaster-related information reaches government decision-makers.

(c) State and local fire service representation

(1) Establishment of position

The Secretary shall, in consultation with the Administrator of the United States Fire Administration, establish a fire service position at the National Operations Center established under subsection (b) to ensure the effective sharing of information between the Federal Government and State and local fire services.

(2) Designation of position

The Secretary shall designate, on a rotating basis, a State or local fire service official for the position described in paragraph (1).

(3) Management

The Secretary shall manage the position established pursuant to paragraph (1) in accordance with such rules, regulations, and practices as govern other similar rotating positions at the National Operations Center.

TITLE VIII–COORDINATION WITH NON-FEDERAL ENTITIES; INSPECTOR GENERAL; UNITED STATES SECRET SERVICE; COAST GUARD; GENERAL PROVISIONS

Subtitle A—Coordination with Non-Federal Entities

Sec. 801. Office for State and Local Government Coordination

[6 U.S.C. §361]

(a) Establishment

There is established within the Office of the Secretary the Office for State and Local Government Coordination, to oversee and coordinate departmental programs for and relationships with State and local governments.

(b) Responsibilities

The Office established under subsection (a) of this section shall—

(1) coordinate the activities of the Department relating to State and local government;

(2) assess, and advocate for, the resources needed by State and local government to implement the national strategy for combating terrorism;

(**3**) provide State and local government with regular information, research, and technical support to assist local efforts at securing the homeland; and

(**4**) develop a process for receiving meaningful input from State and local government to assist the development of the national strategy for combating terrorism and other homeland security activities.

SUBTITLE I—INFORMATION SHARING

SHORT TITLE; FINDINGS; AND SENSE OF CONGRESS.

SEC. 891. [6 U.S.C. §481]

(a) SHORT TITLE.—This subtitle may be cited as the "Homeland Security Information Sharing Act".

(b) FINDINGS.—Congress finds the following:

(1) The Federal Government is required by the Constitution to provide for the common defense, which includes terrorist attack.

(2) The Federal Government relies on State and local personnel to protect against terrorist attack.

(3) The Federal Government collects, creates, manages, and protects classified and sensitive but unclassified information to enhance homeland security.

(4) Some homeland security information is needed by the State and local personnel to prevent and prepare for terrorist attack.

(5) The needs of State and local personnel to have access to relevant homeland security information to combat terrorism must be reconciled with the need to preserve the protected status of such information and to protect the sources and methods used to acquire such information.

(6) Granting security clearances to certain State and local personnel is one way to facilitate the sharing of information regarding specific terrorist threats among Federal, State, and local levels of government.

(7) Methods exist to declassify, redact, or otherwise adapt classified information so it may be shared with State and local personnel without the need for granting additional security clearances.

(8) State and local personnel have capabilities and opportunities to gather information on suspicious activities and terrorist threats not possessed by Federal agencies.

(9) The Federal Government and State and local governments and agencies in other jurisdictions may benefit from such information.

(10) Federal, State, and local governments and intelligence, law enforcement, and other emergency preparation and response agencies

must act in partnership to maximize the benefits of information gathering and analysis to prevent and respond to terrorist attacks.

(11) Information systems, including the National Law Enforcement Telecommunications System and the Terrorist Threat Warning System, have been established for rapid sharing of classified and sensitive but unclassified information among Federal, State, and local entities.

(12) Increased efforts to share homeland security information should avoid duplicating existing information systems.

(c) SENSE OF CONGRESS.—It is the sense of Congress that Federal, State, and local entities should share homeland security information to the maximum extent practicable, with special emphasis on hard-to-reach urban and rural communities.

FACILITATING HOMELAND SECURITY INFORMATION SHARING PROCEDURES

SEC. 892. [6 U.S.C. §482]

(a) PROCEDURES FOR DETERMINING EXTENT OF SHARING OF HOMELAND SECURITY INFORMATION.—

(1) The President shall prescribe and implement procedures under which relevant Federal agencies—

(A) share relevant and appropriate homeland security information with other Federal agencies, including the Department, and appropriate State and local personnel;

(B) identify and safeguard homeland security information that is sensitive but unclassified; and

(C) to the extent such information is in classified form, determine whether, how, and to what extent to remove classified information, as appropriate, and with which such personnel it may be shared after such information is removed.

(2) The President shall ensure that such procedures apply to all agencies of the Federal Government.

(3) Such procedures shall not change the substantive requirements for the classification and safeguarding of classified information.

(4) Such procedures shall not change the requirements and authorities to protect sources and methods.

(b) PROCEDURES FOR SHARING OF HOMELAND SECURITY INFORMATION.—

(1) Under procedures prescribed by the President, all appropriate agencies, including the intelligence community, shall, through information sharing systems, share homeland security information with Federal agencies and appropriate State and local personnel to the extent such information may be shared, as determined in accordance with subsection(a), together with assessments of the credibility of such information.

(2) Each information sharing system through which information is shared under paragraph(1) shall—

(A) have the capability to transmit unclassified or classified information, though the procedures and recipients for each capability may differ;

(B) have the capability to restrict delivery of information to specified subgroups by geographic location, type of organization, position of a recipient within an organization, or a recipient's need to know such information;

(C) be configured to allow the efficient and effective sharing of information; and

(D) be accessible to appropriate State and local personnel.

(3) The procedures prescribed under paragraph(1) shall establish conditions on the use of information shared under paragraph(1)—

(A) to limit the redissemination of such information to ensure that such information is not used for an unauthorized purpose;

(B) to ensure the security and confidentiality of such information;

(C) to protect the constitutional and statutory rights of any individuals who are subjects of such information; and

(D) to provide data integrity through the timely removal and destruction of obsolete or erroneous names and information.

(4) The procedures prescribed under paragraph(1) shall ensure, to the greatest extent practicable, that the information sharing system through which information is shared under such paragraph include existing information sharing systems, including, but not limited to, the National Law Enforcement Telecommunications System, the Regional Information Sharing System, and the Terrorist Threat Warning System of the Federal Bureau of Investigation.

(5) Each appropriate Federal agency, as determined by the President, shall have access to each information sharing system through which information is shared under paragraph(1), and shall therefore have access to all information, as appropriate, shared under such paragraph.

(6) The procedures prescribed under paragraph(1) shall ensure that appropriate State and local personnel are authorized to use such information sharing systems—

(A) to access information shared with such personnel; and

(B) to share, with others who have access to such information sharing systems, the homeland security information of their own jurisdictions, which shall be marked appropriately as pertaining to potential terrorist activity.

(7) Under procedures prescribed jointly by the Director of Central Intelligence and the Attorney General, each appropriate Federal agency, as determined by the President, shall review and assess the information shared under paragraph(6) and integrate such information with existing intelligence.

(c) SHARING OF CLASSIFIED INFORMATION AND SENSITIVE BUT UNCLASSIFIED INFORMATION WITH STATE AND LOCAL PERSONNEL.—

(1) The President shall prescribe procedures under which Federal agencies may, to the extent the President considers necessary, share with appropriate State and local personnel homeland security information that remains classified or otherwise protected after the determinations prescribed under the procedures set forth in subsection(a).

(2) It is the sense of Congress that such procedures may include 1 or more of the following means:

(A) Carrying out security clearance investigations with respect to appropriate State and local personnel.

(B) With respect to information that is sensitive but unclassified, entering into nondisclosure agreements with appropriate State and local personnel.

(C) Increased use of information-sharing partnerships that include appropriate State and local personnel, such as the Joint Terrorism Task Forces of the Federal Bureau of Investigation, the Anti-Terrorism Task Forces of the Department of Justice, and regional Terrorism Early Warning Groups.

(3)(A) The Secretary shall establish a program to provide appropriate training to officials described in subparagraph(B) in order to assist such officials in—

(i) identifying sources of potential terrorist threats through such methods as the Secretary determines appropriate;

(ii) reporting information relating to such potential terrorist threats to the appropriate Federal agencies in the appropriate form and manner;

(iii) assuring that all reported information is systematically submitted to and passed on by the Department for use by appropriate Federal agencies; and

(iv) understanding the mission and roles of the intelligence community to promote more effective information sharing among Federal, State, and local officials and representatives of the private sector to prevent terrorist attacks against the United States.

(B) The officials referred to in subparagraph (A) are officials of State and local government agencies and representatives of private sector entities with responsibilities relating to the oversight and management of first responders, counterterrorism activities, or critical infrastructure.

(C) The Secretary shall consult with the Attorney General to ensure that the training program established in subparagraph(A) does not duplicate the training program established in section 908 of the USA PATRIOT Act (Public Law 107-56; 28 U.S.C. §509 note).

(D) The Secretary shall carry out this paragraph in consultation with the Director of Central Intelligence and the Attorney General.

(d) RESPONSIBLE OFFICIALS.—For each affected Federal agency, the head of such agency shall designate an official to administer this Act with respect to such agency.

(e) FEDERAL CONTROL OF INFORMATION.—Under procedures prescribed under this section, information obtained by a State or local government from a Federal agency under this section shall remain under the control of the Federal agency, and a State or local law authorizing or requiring such a government to disclose information shall not apply to such information.

(f) DEFINITIONS.—As used in this section:

(1) The term "homeland security information" means any information possessed by a Federal, State, or local agency that—

(A) relates to the threat of terrorist activity;

(B) relates to the ability to prevent, interdict, or disrupt terrorist activity;

(C) would improve the identification or investigation of a suspected terrorist or terrorist organization; or

(D) would improve the response to a terrorist act.

(2) The term "intelligence community" has the meaning given such term in section 3(4) of the National Security Act of 1947(50 U.S.C. §401a(4)).

(3) The term "State and local personnel" means any of the following persons involved in prevention, preparation, or response for terrorist attack:

(A) State Governors, mayors, and other locally elected officials.

(B) State and local law enforcement personnel and firefighters.

(C) Public health and medical professionals.

(D) Regional, State, and local emergency management agency personnel, including State adjutant generals.

(E) Other appropriate emergency response agency personnel.

385

(F) Employees of private-sector entities that affect critical infrastructure, cyber, economic, or public health security, as designated by the Federal Government in procedures developed pursuant to this section.

(4) The term "State" includes the District of Columbia and any commonwealth, territory, or possession of the United States.

(g) CONSTRUCTION.—Nothing in this Act shall be construed as authorizing any department, bureau, agency, officer, or employee of the Federal Government to request, receive, or transmit to any other Government entity or personnel, or transmit to any State or local entity or personnel otherwise authorized by this Act to receive homeland security information, any information collected by the Federal Government solely for statistical purposes in violation of any other provision of law relating to the confidentiality of such information.

REPORT

SEC. 893. [6 U.S.C. §483]

(a) REPORT REQUIRED.—Not later than 12 months after the date of the enactment of this Act, the President shall submit to the congressional committees specified in subsection(b) a report on the implementation of section 892. The report shall include any recommendations for additional measures or appropriation requests, beyond the requirements of section 892, to increase the effectiveness of sharing of information between and among Federal, State, and local entities.

(b) SPECIFIED CONGRESSIONAL COMMITTEES.—The congressional committees referred to in subsection(a) are the following committees:

(1) The Permanent Select Committee on Intelligence and the Committee on the Judiciary of the House of Representatives.

(2) The Select Committee on Intelligence and the Committee on the Judiciary of the Senate.

AUTHORIZATION OF APPROPRIATIONS

SEC. 894. [6 U.S.C. §484]

There are authorized to be appropriated such sums as may be necessary to carry out section 892.

AUTHORITY TO SHARE GRAND JURY INFORMATION

SEC. 895.

Rule 6(e) of the Federal Rules of Criminal Procedure [18 U.S.C. App.] is amended—

(1) in paragraph(2), by inserting ", or of guidelines jointly issued by the Attorney General and Director of Central Intelligence pursuant to Rule 6," after "Rule 6"; and

(2) in paragraph(3)—

    (A) in subparagraph(A)(ii), by inserting "or of a foreign government" after "(including personnel of a state or subdivision of a state";

    (B) in subparagraph(C)(i)—

        (i) in subclause(I), by inserting before the semicolon the following: "or, upon a request by an attorney for the government, when sought by a foreign court or prosecutor for use in an official criminal investigation";

        (ii) in subclause(IV)—

            (I) by inserting "or foreign" after "may disclose a violation of State";

            (II) by inserting "or of a foreign government" after "to an appropriate official of a State or subdivision of a State"; and

            (III) by striking "or" at the end;

        (iii) by striking the period at the end of subclause(V) and inserting "; or"; and

        (iv) by adding at the end the following:

            "(VI) when matters involve a threat of actual or potential attack or other grave hostile acts of a foreign power or an agent of a foreign power, domestic or international sabotage, domestic or international terrorism, or clandestine intelligence gathering activities by an intelligence service or network of a foreign power or by an agent of a foreign power, within the United States or elsewhere, to any appropriate federal, state, local, or foreign government official for the purpose of preventing or responding to such a threat."; and

    (C) in subparagraph(C)(iii)—

        (i) by striking "Federal";

        (ii) by inserting "or clause (i)(VI)" after "clause (i)(V)"; and

        (iii) by adding at the end the following: "Any state, local, or foreign official who receives information pursuant to clause (i)(VI) shall use that information only consistent with such guidelines as the Attorney General and Director of Central Intelligence shall jointly issue.".

AUTHORITY TO SHARE ELECTRONIC, WIRE, AND ORAL INTERCEPTION INFORMATION

SEC. 896.
Section 2517 of title 18, United States Code, is amended by adding at the end the following:

"(7) Any investigative or law enforcement officer, or other Federal official in carrying out official duties as such Federal official, who by any means authorized by this chapter, has obtained knowledge of the contents of any wire, oral, or electronic communication, or evidence derived there from, may disclose such contents or derivative evidence to a foreign investigative or law enforcement officer to the extent that such disclosure is appropriate to the proper performance of the official duties of the officer making or receiving the disclosure, and foreign investigative or law enforcement officers may use or disclose such contents or derivative evidence to the extent such use or disclosure is appropriate to the proper performance of their official duties.

"(8) Any investigative or law enforcement officer, or other Federal official in carrying out official duties as such Federal official, who by any means authorized by this chapter, has obtained knowledge of the contents of any wire, oral, or electronic communication, or evidence derived there from, may disclose such contents or derivative evidence to any appropriate Federal, State, local, or foreign government official to the extent that such contents or derivative evidence reveals a threat of actual or potential attack or other grave hostile acts of a foreign power or an agent of a foreign power, domestic or international sabotage, domestic or international terrorism, or clandestine intelligence gathering activities by an intelligence service or network of a foreign power or by an agent of a foreign power, within the United States or elsewhere, for the purpose of preventing or responding to such a threat. Any official who receives information pursuant to this provision may use that information only as necessary in the conduct of that person's official duties subject to any limitations on the unauthorized disclosure of such information, and any State, local, or foreign official who receives information pursuant to this provision may use that information only consistent with such guidelines as the Attorney General and Director of Central Intelligence shall jointly issue.".

FOREIGN INTELLIGENCE INFORMATION

SEC. 897.

(a) DISSEMINATION AUTHORIZED.—Section 203(d)(1) of the Uniting and Strengthening America by Providing Appropriate Tools Required to Intercept and Obstruct Terrorism (USA PATRIOT ACT) Act of 2001(Public Law 107-56; 50 U.S.C. §403-5d) is amended by adding at the end the following: "Consistent with the responsibility of the Director of Central Intelligence to protect intelligence sources and methods, and the responsibility of the Attorney General to protect sensitive law enforcement information, it shall be lawful for information revealing a threat of actual or potential attack or other grave hostile acts of a foreign power or an agent of a foreign power, domestic or international sabotage, domestic or international terrorism, or clandestine intelligence gathering activities by an intelligence service or network of a foreign power or by an agent of a foreign power, within the United States or elsewhere, obtained as part of a criminal investigation to be disclosed to any appropriate Federal, State, local, or foreign government official for the purpose of preventing or responding to such a threat. Any official who receives information pursuant to this provision may use that information only as necessary in the conduct of that person's official duties subject to any limitations on the unauthorized disclosure of such information, and any State, local, or foreign official who receives information pursuant to this provision may use that information only consistent with such guidelines as the Attorney General and Director of Central Intelligence shall jointly issue.".

(b) CONFORMING AMENDMENTS.—Section 203(c) of that Act is amended—

  (1) by striking "section 2517(6)" and inserting "paragraphs (6) and (8) of section 2517 of title 18, United States Code,"; and

  (2) by inserting "and (VI)" after "Rule 6(e)(3)(C)(i)(V)".

INFORMATION ACQUIRED FROM ELECTRONIC SURVEILLANCE

SEC. 898.

Section 106(k)(1) of the Foreign Intelligence Surveillance Act of 1978 (50 U.S.C. §1806) is amended by inserting after "law enforcement officers" the following: "or law enforcement personnel of a State or political subdivision of a State(including the chief executive officer of that State or political subdivision who has the authority to appoint or direct the chief law enforcement officer of that State or political subdivision)".

INFORMATION ACQUIRED FROM A PHYSICAL SEARCH

SEC. 899.

Section 305(k)(1) of the Foreign Intelligence Surveillance Act of 1978 (50 U.S.C. §1825) is amended by inserting after "law enforcement officers" the following: "or law enforcement personnel of a State or political subdivision of a State(including the chief executive officer of that State or political subdivision who has the authority to appoint or direct the chief law enforcement officer of that State or political subdivision)".

TITLE XV—TRANSITION

Subtitle B—Transitional Provisions

SEC. 1512. SAVINGS PROVISIONS. [6 U.S.C. §552]
(a) COMPLETED ADMINISTRATIVE ACTIONS.—(1) Completed administrative actions of an agency shall not be affected by the enactment of this Act or the transfer of such agency to the Department, but shall continue in effect according to their terms until amended, modified, superseded, terminated, set aside, or revoked in accordance with law by an officer of the United States or a court of competent jurisdiction, or by operation of law.
(2) For purposes of paragraph (1), the term "completed administrative action" includes orders, determinations, rules, regulations, personnel actions, permits, agreements, grants, contracts, certificates, licenses, registrations, and privileges.
(b) PENDING PROCEEDINGS.—Subject to the authority of the Secretary under this Act—
(1) pending proceedings in an agency, including notices of proposed rulemaking, and applications for licenses, permits, certificates, grants, and financial assistance, shall continue notwithstanding the enactment of this Act or the transfer of the agency to the Department, unless discontinued or modified under the same terms and conditions and to the same extent that such discontinuance could have occurred if such enactment or transfer had not occurred; and
(2) orders issued in such proceedings, and appeals therefrom, and payments made pursuant to such orders, shall issue in the same manner and on the same terms as if this Act had not been enacted or the agency had not been transferred, and any such orders shall continue in effect until amended, modified, superseded, terminated, set aside, or revoked by an officer of the United States or a court of competent jurisdiction, or by operation of law.
(c) PENDING CIVIL ACTIONS.—Subject to the authority of the Secretary under this Act, pending civil actions shall continue notwithstanding the enactment of this Act or the transfer of an agency to the Department, and in such civil actions, proceedings shall be had, appeals taken, and judgments rendered and enforced in the same manner and with the same effect as if such enactment or transfer had not occurred.
(d) REFERENCES.—References relating to an agency that is transferred to the

Department in statutes, Executive orders, rules, regulations, directives, or delegations of authority that precede such transfer or the effective date of this Act shall be deemed to refer, as appropriate, to the Department, to its officers, employees, or agents, or to its corresponding organizational units or functions. Statutory reporting requirements that applied in relation to such an agency immediately before the effective date of this Act shall continue to apply following such transfer if they refer to the agency by name.

(e) EMPLOYMENT PROVISIONS.—(1) Notwithstanding the generality of the foregoing (including subsections (a) and (d)), in and for the Department the Secretary may, in regulations prescribed jointly with the Director of the Office of Personnel Management, adopt the rules, procedures, terms, and conditions, established by statute, rule, or regulation before the effective date of this Act, relating to employment in any agency transferred to the Department pursuant to this Act; and

(2) except as otherwise provided in this Act, or under authority granted by this Act, the transfer pursuant to this Act of personnel shall not alter the terms and conditions of employment, including compensation, of any employee so transferred.

(f) STATUTORY REPORTING REQUIREMENTS.—Any statutory reporting requirement that applied to an agency, transferred to the Department under this Act, immediately before the effective date of this Act shall continue to apply following that transfer if the statutory requirement refers to the agency by name.

COUNTERINTELLIGENCE AND SECURITY ENHANCEMENTS ACT OF 1994

Title VIII of the Intelligence Authorization Act for Fiscal Year 1995

(Public Law 103-359 of October 14, 1994)

COORDINATION OF COUNTERINTELLIGENCE ACTIVITIES

SEC. 811(50 U.S.C. §402a)

(a) ESTABLISHMENT OF COUNTERINTELLIGENCE POLICY BOARD. There is established within the executive branch of Government a National Counterintelligence Policy Board (in this section referred to as the "Board"). The Board shall report to the President through the National Security Council.

(b) CHAIRPERSON. The National Counterintelligence Executive under section 902 of the Counterintelligence Enhancement Act of 2002 shall serve as the chairperson of the Board.

(c) MEMBERSHIP. The membership of the National Counterintelligence Policy Board shall consist of the following:

> (1) The National Counterintelligence Executive.
>
> (2) Senior personnel of departments and elements of the United States Government, appointed by the head of the department or element concerned, as follows:
>
>> (A) The Department of Justice, including the Federal Bureau of Investigation.
>>
>> (B) The Department of Defense, including the Joint Chiefs of Staff.
>>
>> (C) The Department of State.
>>
>> (D) The Department of Energy.
>>
>> (E) The Central Intelligence Agency.
>>
>> (F) Any other department, agency, or element of the United States Government specified by the President.

(d) FUNCTIONS AND DISCHARGE OF FUNCTIONS.

> (1) The Board shall—
>
>> (A) serve as the principal mechanism for—
>>
>>> (i) developing policies and procedures for the approval of the President to govern the conduct of counterintelligence activities; and
>>>
>>> (ii) upon the direction of the President, resolving conflicts that arise between elements of the Government conducting such activities; and
>>
>> (B) act as an interagency working group to—

(i) ensure the discussion and review of matters relating to the implementation of the Counterintelligence Enhancement Act of 2002; and

(ii) provide advice to the National Counterintelligence Executive on priorities in the implementation of the National Counterintelligence Strategy produced by the Office of the National Counterintelligence Executive under section 904(e)(2) of that Act.

(2) The Board may, for purposes of carrying out its functions under this section, establish such interagency boards and working groups as the Board considers appropriate.

(e) COORDINATION OF COUNTERINTELLIGENCE MATTERS WITH THE FEDERAL BUREAU OF INVESTIGATION.

(1) Except as provided in paragraph (5), the head of each department or agency within the executive branch shall ensure that—

(A) the Federal Bureau of Investigation is advised immediately of any information, regardless of its origin, which indicates that classified information is being, or may have been, disclosed in an unauthorized manner to a foreign power or an agent of a foreign power;

(B) following a report made pursuant to subparagraph (A), the Federal Bureau of Investigation is consulted with respect to all subsequent actions which may be undertaken by the department or agency concerned to determine the source of such loss or compromise; and

(C) where, after appropriate consultation with the department or agency concerned, the Federal Bureau of Investigation undertakes investigative activities to determine the source of the loss or compromise, the Federal Bureau of Investigation is given complete and timely access to the employees and records of the department or agency concerned for purposes of such investigative activities.

(2) Except as provided in paragraph (5), the Director of the Federal Bureau of Investigation shall ensure that espionage information obtained by the Federal Bureau of Investigation pertaining to the personnel, operations, or information of departments or agencies of the executive branch, is provided through appropriate channels in a timely manner to the department or agency concerned, and that such departments or agencies are consulted in a timely manner with respect to espionage investigations undertaken by the Federal Bureau of Investigation which involve the personnel, operations, or information of such department or agency.

(3) (A) The Director of the Federal Bureau of Investigation shall submit to the head of the department or agency concerned a written assessment of the potential impact of the actions of the department or agency on a counterintelligence investigation.

(B) The head of the department or agency concerned shall—

(i) use an assessment under subparagraph (A) as an aid in determining whether, and under what circumstances, the subject of an investigation under paragraph (1) should be left in place for investigative purposes; and

(ii) notify in writing the Director of the Federal Bureau of Investigation of such determination.

(C) The Director of the Federal Bureau of Investigation and the head of the department or agency concerned shall continue to consult, as appropriate, to review the status of an investigation covered by this paragraph, and to reassess, as appropriate, a determination of the head of the department or agency concerned to leave a subject in place for investigative purposes.

(4) (A) The Federal Bureau of Investigation shall notify appropriate officials within the executive branch, including the head of the department or agency concerned, of the commencement of a full field espionage investigation with respect to an employee within the executive branch.

(B) A department or agency may not conduct a polygraph examination, interrogate, or otherwise take any action that is likely to alert an employee covered by a notice under subparagraph (A) of an investigation described in that subparagraph without prior coordination and consultation with the Federal Bureau of Investigation.

(5) Where essential to meet extraordinary circumstances affecting vital national security interests of the United States, the President may on a case-by-case basis waive the requirements of paragraph (1), (2) or (3), as they apply to the head of a particular department or agency, or the Director of the Federal Bureau of Investigation. Such waiver shall be in writing and shall fully state the justification for such waiver. Within thirty days, the President shall notify the Select Committee on Intelligence of the Senate and the Permanent Select Committee on Intelligence of the House of Representatives that such waiver has been issued, and at that time or as soon as national security considerations permit, provide these committees with a complete explanation of the circumstances which necessitated such waiver.

(6) Nothing in this section may be construed to alter the existing jurisdictional arrangements between the Federal Bureau of Investigation

and the Department of Defense with respect to investigations of persons subject to the Uniform Code of Military Justice, nor to impose additional reporting requirements upon the Department of Defense with respect to such investigations beyond those required by existing law and executive branch policy.

(7) As used in this section, the terms "foreign power" and "agent of a foreign power" have the same meanings as set forth in sections 101 (a) and (b), respectively, of the Foreign Intelligence Surveillance Act of 1978.

COUNTERINTELLIGENCE ENHANCEMENT ACT OF 2002

Title IX of the Intelligence Authorization Act for Fiscal Year 2003

(Public Law 107-306 of November 27, 2002' 116 STAT. 2383)

SHORT TITLE; PURPOSE

SECTION. 901. [50 U.S.C. §401 note.]
(a) SHORT TITLE.—This title may be cited as the "Counterintelligence Enhancement Act of 2002".
(b) PURPOSE.—The purpose of this title is to facilitate the enhancement of the counterintelligence activities of the United States Government by—
> (1) enabling the counterintelligence community of the United States Government to fulfill better its mission of identifying, assessing, prioritizing, and countering the intelligence threats to the United States;
> (2) ensuring that the counterintelligence community of the United States Government acts in an efficient and effective manner; and
> (3) providing for the integration of all the counterintelligence activities of the United States Government.

NATIONAL COUNTERINTELLIGENCE EXECUTIVE

SEC. 902. [50 U.S.C. §402b]
(a) ESTABLISHMENT.—
> (1) There shall be a National Counterintelligence Executive, who shall be appointed by the Director of National Intelligence.
> (2) It is the sense of Congress that the Director of National Intelligence should seek the views of the Attorney General, Secretary of Defense, and Director of the Central Intelligence Agency in selecting an individual for appointment as the Executive.

(b) MISSION.—The mission of the National Counterintelligence Executive shall be to serve as the head of national counterintelligence for the United States Government.
(c) DUTIES.—Subject to the direction and control of the Director of National Intelligence, the duties of the National Counterintelligence Executive are as follows:
> (1) To carry out the mission referred to in subsection (b).
> (2) To act as chairperson of the National Counterintelligence Policy Board under section 811 of the Counterintelligence and Security Enhancements Act of 1994 (title VIII of Public Law 103-359; 50 U.S.C. §402a), as amended by section 903 of this Act.

(3) To act as head of the Office of the National Counterintelligence Executive under section 904.

(4) To participate as an observer on such boards, committees, and entities of the executive branch as the Director of National Intelligence considers appropriate for the discharge of the mission and functions of the Executive and the Office of the National Counterintelligence Executive under section 904.

OFFICE OF THE COUNTERINTELLIGENCE EXECUTIVE

SEC. 904. [50 U.S.C. §402c]

(a) ESTABLISHMENT.—There shall be an Office of the National Counterintelligence Executive.

(b) HEAD OF OFFICE.—The National Counterintelligence Executive shall be the head of the Office of the National Counterintelligence Executive.

(c) LOCATION OF OFFICE.—The Office of the National Counterintelligence Executive shall be located in the Office of the Director of National Intelligence.

(d) FUNCTIONS.—Subject to the direction and control of the National Counterintelligence Executive, the functions of the Office of the National Counterintelligence Executive shall be as follows:

(1) NATIONAL THREAT IDENTIFICATION AND PRIORITIZATION ASSESSMENT.—Subject to subsection (e), in consultation with appropriate department and agencies of the United States Government, and private sector entities, to produce a strategic planning assessment of the counterintelligence requirements of the United States to be known as the National Threat Identification and Prioritization Assessment.

(2) NATIONAL COUNTERINTELLIGENCE STRATEGY.

(A) REQUIREMENT TO PRODUCE—Subject to subsection (e), in consultation with appropriate department and agencies of the United States Government, and private sector entities, and based on the most current National Threat Identification and Prioritization Assessment under paragraph (1), to produce a strategy for the counterintelligence programs and activities of the United States Government to be known as the National Counterintelligence Strategy.

(B) REVISION AND REQUIREMENT—The National Counterintelligence Strategy shall be revised or updated at least once every three years and shall be aligned with the strategy and policies of the Director of National Intelligence.

(3) IMPLEMENTATION OF NATIONAL COUNTERINTELLIGENCE STRATEGY.—To evaluate on an ongoing basis the implementation of the National Counterintelligence Strategy and to submit to the President periodic reports on such evaluation, including a discussion of any

shortfalls in the implementation of the Strategy and recommendations for remedies for such shortfalls.

(4) NATIONAL COUNTERINTELLIGENCE STRATEGIC ANALYSES.—As directed by the Director of National Intelligence and in consultation with appropriate elements of the departments and agencies of the United States Government, to oversee and coordinate the production of strategic analyses of counterintelligence matters, including the production of counterintelligence damage assessments and assessments of lessons learned from counterintelligence activities.

(5) NATIONAL COUNTERINTELLIGENCE PROGRAM BUDGET.—In consultation with the Director of National Intelligence—

>   (A) to coordinate the development of budgets and resource allocation plans for the counterintelligence programs and activities of the Department of Defense, the Federal Bureau of Investigation, the Central Intelligence Agency, and other appropriate elements of the United States Government;

>   (B) to ensure that the budgets and resource allocation plans developed under subparagraph (A) address the objectives and priorities for counterintelligence under the National Counterintelligence Strategy; and

>   (C) to submit to the National Security Council periodic reports on the activities undertaken by the Office under subparagraphs (A) and (B).

(6) NATIONAL COUNTERINTELLIGENCE COLLECTION AND TARGETING COORDINATION.—To develop priorities for counterintelligence investigations and operations, and for collection of counterintelligence, for purposes of the National Counterintelligence Strategy, except that the Office may not—

>   (A) carry out any counterintelligence investigations or operations; or

>   (B) establish its own contacts, or carry out its own activities, with foreign intelligence services.

(7) NATIONAL COUNTERINTELLIGENCE OUTREACH, WATCH, AND WARNING.—

>   (A) COUNTERINTELLIGENCE VULNERABILITY SURVEYS.—To carry out and coordinate surveys of the vulnerability of the United States Government, and the private sector, to intelligence threats in order to identify the areas, programs, and activities that require protection from such threats.

>   (B) OUTREACH.—To carry out and coordinate outreach programs and activities on counterintelligence to other elements of the United States Government, and the private sector, and to

coordinate the dissemination to the public of warnings on intelligence threats to the United States.

(C) RESEARCH AND DEVELOPMENT.—To ensure that research and development programs and activities of the United States Government, and the private sector, direct attention to the needs of the counterintelligence community for technologies, products, and services.

(D) TRAINING AND PROFESSIONAL DEVELOPMENT.—To develop policies and standards for training and professional development of individuals engaged in counterintelligence activities and to manage the conduct of joint training exercises for such personnel.

(e) ADDITIONAL REQUIREMENTS REGARDING NATIONAL THREAT IDENTIFICATION AND PRIORITIZATION ASSESSMENT AND NATIONAL COUNTERINTELLIGENCE STRATEGY.—

(1) A National Threat Identification and Prioritization Assessment under subsection (d)(1), and any modification of such assessment, shall not go into effect until approved by the President.

(2) A National Counterintelligence Strategy under subsection (d)(2), and any modification of such strategy, shall not go into effect until approved by the President.

(3) The National Counterintelligence Executive shall submit to the congressional intelligence committees each National Threat Identification and Prioritization Assessment, or modification thereof, and each National Counterintelligence Strategy, or modification thereof, approved under this section.

(4) In this subsection, the term "congressional intelligence committees" means—

(A) the Select Committee on Intelligence of the Senate; and

(B) the Permanent Select Committee on Intelligence of the House of Representatives.

(f) PERSONNEL.—

(1) Personnel of the Office of the National Counterintelligence Executive may consist of personnel employed by the Office or personnel on detail from any other department, agency, or element of the Federal Government. Any such detail may be on a reimbursable or nonreimbursable basis, at the election of the head of the agency detailing such personnel.

(2) Notwithstanding section 104(d) or any other provision of law limiting the period of the detail of personnel on a nonreimbursable basis, the detail of an officer or employee of United States or a member of the Armed Forces under paragraph (1) on a nonreimbursable basis may be

for any period in excess of one year that the National Counterintelligence Executive and the head of the department, agency, or element concerned consider appropriate.

(g) TREATMENT OF ACTIVITIES UNDER CERTAIN ADMINISTRATIVE LAWS.—The files of the Office shall be treated as operational files of the Central Intelligence Agency for purposes of section 701 of the National Security Act of 1947 (50 U.S.C. §431) to the extent such files meet criteria under subsection (b) of that section for treatment of files as operational files of an element of the Agency.

(h) OVERSIGHT BY CONGRESS.—The location of the Office of the National Counterintelligence Executive within the Office of the Director of National Intelligence shall not be construed as affecting access by Congress, or any committee of Congress, to—

(1) any information, document, record, or paper in the possession of the Office; or

(2) any personnel of the Office.

(i) CONSTRUCTION.—Nothing in this section shall be construed as affecting the authority of the Director of National Intelligence, the Secretary of Defense, the Secretary of State, the Attorney General, or the Director of the Federal Bureau of Investigation as provided or specified under the National Security Act of 1947 or under other provisions of law.

NATIONAL SECURITY ACT
COUNTERINTELLIGENCE INITIATIVES

SEC. 1102. [50 U.S.C. §442a]

(a) INSPECTION PROCESS.—

In order to protect intelligence sources and methods from unauthorized disclosure, the Director of National Intelligence shall establish and implement an inspection process for all agencies and departments of the United States that handle classified information relating to the national security of the United States intended to assure that those agencies and departments maintain effective operational security practices and programs directed against counterintelligence activities.

(b) ANNUAL REVIEW OF DISSEMINATION LISTS.—

The Director of National Intelligence shall establish and implement a process for all elements of the intelligence community to review, on an annual basis, individuals included on distribution lists for access to classified information. Such process shall ensure that only individuals who have a particularized need to know' (as determined by the Director) are continued on such distribution lists.

(c) COMPLETION OF FINANCIAL DISCLOSURE STATEMENTS REQUIRED FOR ACCESS TO CERTAIN CLASSIFIED INFORMATION.—

The Director of National Intelligence shall establish and implement a process by which each head of an element of the intelligence community directs that all employees of that element, in order to be granted access to classified information referred to in subsection (a) of section 1.3 of Executive Order No. 12968 (August 2, 1995; 60 Fed. Reg. 40245; 50 U.S.C. §435 note), submit financial disclosure forms as required under subsection (b) of such section.

(d) ARRANGEMENTS TO HANDLE SENSITIVE INFORMATION.—

The Director of National Intelligence shall establish, for all elements of the intelligence community, programs and procedures by which sensitive classified information relating to human intelligence is safeguarded against unauthorized disclosure by employees of those elements.

CLASSIFIED INFORMATION PROCEDURES ACT

(Public Law 96–456 of October 15, 1980; 94 STAT. 2025)

AN ACT To provide certain pretrial, trial, and appellate procedures for criminal cases involving classified information.

Be it enacted by the Senate and House of Representatives of the United States of America in Congress assembled,

DEFINITIONS

SECTION 1. [18 U.S.C. App. §1]
(a) "Classified information", as used in this Act, means any information or material that has been determined by the United States Government pursuant to an Executive order, statute, or regulation, to require protection against unauthorized disclosure for reasons of national security and any restricted data, as defined in paragraph r. of section 11 of the Atomic Energy Act of 1954 (42 U.S.C. §2014(y)).
(b) "National security", as used in this Act, means the national defense and foreign relations of the United States.

PRETRIAL CONFERENCE

SEC. 2. [18 U.S.C. App. §2]
At any time after the filing of the indictment or information, any party may move for a pretrial conference to consider matters relating to classified information that may arise in connection with the prosecution. Following such motion, or on its own motion, the court shall promptly hold a pretrial conference to establish the timing of requests for discovery, the provision of notice required by section 5 of this Act, and the initiation of the procedure established by section 6 of this Act. In addition, at the pretrial conference the court may consider any matters which relate to classified information or which may promote a fair and expeditious trial. No admission made by the defendant or by any attorney for the defendant at such a conference may be used against the defendant unless the admission is in writing and is signed by the defendant and by the attorney for the defendant.

PROTECTIVE ORDERS

SEC. 3. [18 U.S.C. App. §3]

Upon motion of the United States, the court shall issue an order to protect against the disclosure of any classified information disclosed by the United States to any defendant in any criminal case in a district court of the United States.

DISCOVERY OF CLASSIFIED INFORMATION BY DEFENDANTS

SEC. 4. [18 U.S.C. App. §4]
The court, upon a sufficient showing, may authorize the United States to delete specified items of classified information from documents to be made available to the defendant through discovery under the Federal Rules of Criminal Procedure, to substitute a summary of the information for such classified documents, or to substitute a statement admitting relevant facts that the classified information would tend to prove. The court may permit the United States to make a request for such authorization in the form of a written statement to be inspected by the court alone. If the court enters an order granting relief following such an ex parte showing, the entire text of the statement of the United States shall be sealed and preserved in the records of the court to be made available to the appellate court in the event of an appeal.

NOTICE OF DEFENDANT'S INTENTION TO DISCLOSE CLASSIFIED INFORMATION

SEC. 5. [18 U.S.C. App. §5]
(a) NOTICE BY DEFENDANT.—If a defendant reasonably expects to disclose or to cause the disclosure of classified information in any manner in connection with any trial or pretrial proceeding involving the criminal prosecution of such defendant, the defendant shall, within the time specified by the court or, where no time is specified, within thirty days prior to trial, notify the attorney for the United States and the court in writing. Such notice shall include a brief description of the classified information. Whenever a defendant learns of additional classified information he reasonably expects to disclose at any such proceeding, he shall notify the attorney for the United States and the court in writing as soon as possible thereafter and shall include a brief description of the classified information. No defendant shall disclose any information known or believed to be classified in connection with a trial or pretrial proceeding until notice has been given under this subsection and until the United States has been afforded a reasonable opportunity to seek a determination pursuant to the procedure set forth in section 6 of this Act, and until the time for the United States to appeal such determination under section 7 has expired or any appeal under section 7 by the United States is decided.
(b) FAILURE TO COMPLY.—If the defendant fails to comply with the requirements of subsection (a) the court may preclude disclosure of any classified

information not made the subject of notification and may prohibit the examination by the defendant of any witness with respect to any such information.

PROCEDURES FOR CASES INVOLVING CLASSIFIED INFORMATION

SEC. 6. [18 U.S.C. App. §6]

(a) MOTION FOR HEARING.—Within the time specified by the court for the filing of a motion under this section, the United States may request the court to conduct a hearing to make all determinations concerning the use, relevance, or admissibility of classified information that would otherwise be made during the trial or pretrial proceeding. Upon such a request, the court shall conduct such a hearing. Any hearing held pursuant to this subsection (or any portion of such hearing specified in the request of the Attorney General) shall be held in camera if the Attorney General certifies to the court in such petition that a public proceeding may result in the disclosure of classified information. As to each item of classified information, the court shall set forth in writing the basis for its determination. Where the United States' motion under this subsection is filed prior to the trial or pretrial proceeding, the court shall rule prior to the commencement of the relevant proceeding.

(b) NOTICE.—

(1) Before any hearing is conducted pursuant to a request by the United States under subsection (a), the United States shall provide the defendant with notice of the classified information that is at issue. Such notice shall identify the specific classified information at issue whenever that information previously has been made available to the defendant by the United States. When, the United States has not previously made the information available to the defendant in connection with the case, the information may be described by generic category, in such form as the court may approve, rather than by identification of the specific information of concern to the United States.

(2) Whenever the United States requests a hearing under subsection (a), the court, upon request of the defendant, may order the United States to provide the defendant, prior to trial, such details as to the portion of the indictment or information at issue in the hearing as are needed to give the defendant fair notice to prepare for the hearing.

(c) ALTERNATIVE PROCEDURE FOR DISCLOSURE OF CLASSIFIED INFORMATION.—

(1) Upon any determination by the court authorizing the disclosure of specific classified information under the procedures established by this

section, the United States may move that, in lieu of the disclosure of such specific classified information, the court order—

(A) the substitution for such classified information of a statement admitting relevant facts that the specific classified information would tend to prove; or

(B) the substitution for such classified information of a summary of the specific classified information. The court shall grant such a motion of the United States if it finds that the statement or summary will provide the defendant with substantially the same ability to make his defense as would disclosure of the specific classified information. The court shall hold a hearing on any motion under this section. Any such hearing shall be held in camera at the request of the Attorney General.

(2) The United States may, in connection with a motion under paragraph (1), submit to the court an affidavit of the Attorney General certifying that disclosure of classified information would cause identifiable damage to the national security of the United States and explaining the basis for the classification of such information. If so requested by the United States, the court shall examine such affidavit in camera and ex parte.

(d) SEALING OF RECORDS OF IN CAMERA HEARINGS.—If at the close of an in camera hearing under this Act (or any portion of a hearing under this Act that is held in camera) the court determines that the classified information at issue may not be disclosed or elicited at the trial or pretrial proceeding, the record of such in camera hearing shall be sealed and preserved by the court for use in the event of an appeal. The defendant may seek reconsideration of the court's determination prior to or during trial.

(e) PROHIBITION ON DISCLOSURE OF CLASSIFIED INFORMATION BY DEFENDANT, RELIEF FOR DEFENDANT WHEN UNITED STATES OPPOSES DISCLOSURE.—

(1) Whenever the court denies a motion by the United States that it issue an order under subsection (c) and the United States files with the court an affidavit of the Attorney General objecting to disclosure of the classified information at issue, the court shall order that the defendant not disclose or cause the disclosure of such information.

(2) Whenever a defendant is prevented by an order under paragraph (1) from disclosing or causing the disclosure of classified information, the court shall dismiss the indictment or information; except that, when the court determines that the interests of justice would not be served by dismissal of the indictment or information, the court shall order such other action, in lieu of dismissing the indictment or information, as the court determines is appropriate. Such action may include, but need not be limited to—

(A) dismissing specified counts of the indictment or information;

(B) finding against the United States on any issue as to which the excluded classified information relates; or

(C) striking or precluding all or part of the testimony of a witness.

An order under this paragraph shall not take effect until the court has afforded the United States an opportunity to appeal such order under section 7, and thereafter to withdraw its objection to the disclosure of the classified information at issue.

(f) RECIPROCITY.—Whenever the court determines pursuant to subsection (a) that classified information may be disclosed in connection with a trial or pretrial proceeding, the court shall, unless the interests of fairness do not so require, order the United States to provide the defendant with the information it expects to use to rebut the classified information. The court may place the United States under a continuing duty to disclose such rebuttal information. If the United States fails to comply with its obligation under this subsection, the court may exclude any evidence not made the subject of a required disclosure and may prohibit the examination by the United States of any witness with respect to such information.

INTERLOCUTORY APPEAL

SEC. 7. [18 U.S.C. App. §7]

(a) An interlocutory appeal by the United States taken before or after the defendant has been placed in jeopardy shall lie to a court of appeals from a decision or order of a district court in a criminal case authorizing the disclosure of classified information, imposing sanctions for nondisclosure of classified information, or refusing a protective order sought by the United States to prevent the disclosure of classified information.

(b) An appeal taken pursuant to this section either before or during trial shall be expedited by the court of appeals. Prior to trial, an appeal shall be taken within fourteen days after the decision or order appealed from and the trial shall not commence until the appeal is resolved. If an appeal is taken during trial, the trial court shall adjourn the trial until the appeal is resolved and the court of appeals (1) shall hear argument on such appeal within four days of the adjournment of the trial, excluding intermediate weekends and holidays, (2) may dispense with written briefs other than the supporting materials previously submitted to the trial court, (3) shall render its decision within four days of argument on appeal, excluding intermediate weekends and holidays and (4) may dispense with the issuance of a written opinion in rendering its decision. Such appeal and decision shall not affect the right of the defendant, in a subsequent appeal from a judgment of conviction to claim as error reversal by the trial court on remand of a ruling appealed from during trial.

INTRODUCTION OF CLASSIFIED INFORMATION

SEC. 8. [18 U.S.C. App. §8]

(a) CLASSIFIED STATUS.—Writings, recordings, and photographs containing classified information may be admitted into evidence without change in their classification status.

(b) PRECAUTIONS BY COURT.—The court, in order to prevent unnecessary disclosure of classified information involved in any criminal proceeding, may order admission into evidence of only part of a writing, recording, or photograph, or may order admission into evidence of the whole writing, recording, or photograph with excision of some or all of the classified information contained therein, unless the whole ought in fairness be considered.

(c) TAKING OF TESTIMONY.—During the examination of a witness in any criminal proceeding, the United States may object to any question or line of inquiry that may require the witness to disclose classified information not previously found to be admissible. Following such an objection, the court shall take such suitable action to determine whether the response is admissible as will safeguard against the compromise of any classified information. Such action may include requiring the United States to provide the court with a proffer of the witness' response to the question or line of inquiry and requiring the defendant to provide the court with a proffer of the nature of the information he seeks to elicit.

SECURITY PROCEDURES

SEC. 9. [18 U.S.C. App. §9]

(a) Within one hundred and twenty days of the date of the enactment of this Act, the Chief Justice of the United States, in consultation with the Attorney General, the Director of National Intelligence, and the Secretary of Defense, shall prescribe rules establishing procedures for the protection against unauthorized disclosure of any classified information in the custody of the United States district courts, courts of appeal, or Supreme Court. Such rules, and any changes in such rules, shall be submitted to the appropriate committees of Congress and shall become effective forty-five days after such submission.

(b) Until such time as rules under subsection (a) first become effective, the Federal courts shall in each case involving classified information adopt procedures to protect against the unauthorized disclosure of such information.

COORDINATION REQUIREMENTS RELATING TO THE PROSECUTION OF CASES INVOLVING CLASSIFIED INFORMATION

SEC. 9A. [18 U.S.C. App. §9A]

(a) BRIEFINGS REQUIRED.—The Assistant Attorney General for the Criminal Division or the Assistant Attorney General for National Security, as appropriate, and the appropriate United States attorney, or the designees of such officials, shall provide briefings to the senior agency official, or the designee of such official, with respect to any case involving classified information that originated in the agency of such senior agency official.

(b) TIMING OF BRIEFINGS.—Briefings under subsection (a) with respect to a case shall occur—

> (1) as soon as practicable after the Department of Justice and the United States attorney concerned determine that a prosecution or potential prosecution could result; and
>
> (2) at such other times thereafter as are necessary to keep the senior agency official concerned fully and currently informed of the status of the prosecution.

(c) SENIOR AGENCY OFFICIAL DEFINED.—In this section, the term "senior agency official" has the meaning given that term in section 1.1 of Executive Order No. 12958.

IDENTIFICATION OF INFORMATION RELATED TO THE NATIONAL DEFENSE

SEC. 10. [18 U.S.C. App. §10]
In any prosecution in which the United States must establish that material relates to the national defense or constitutes classified information, the United States shall notify the defendant, within the time before trial specified by the court, of the portions of the material that it reasonably expects to rely upon to establish the national defense or classified information element of the offense.

AMENDMENT TO THE ACT

SEC. 11. [18 U.S.C. App. §11]
Sections 1 through 10 of this Act may be amended as provided in section 2076, title 28, United States Code.

ATTORNEY GENERAL GUIDELINES

SEC. 12. [18 U.S.C. App. §12]
(a) Within one hundred and eighty days of enactment of this Act, the Attorney General shall issue guidelines specifying the factors to be used by the Department of Justice in rendering a decision whether to prosecute a violation of Federal law in which, in the judgment of the Attorney General, there is a possibility that classified information will be revealed. Such guidelines shall be transmitted to the appropriate committees of Congress.

(b) When the Department of Justice decides not to prosecute a violation of Federal law pursuant to subsection (a), an appropriate official of the Department of Justice shall prepare written findings detailing the reasons for the decision not to prosecute. The findings shall include—

> (1) the intelligence information which the Department of Justice officials believe might be disclosed,
> (2) the purpose for which the information might be disclosed,
> (3) the probability that the information would be disclosed, and
> (4) the possible consequences such disclosure would have on the national security.

REPORTS TO CONGRESS

SEC. 13. [18 U.S.C. App. §13]

(a) Consistent with applicable authorities and duties, including those conferred by the Constitution upon the executive and legislative branches, the Attorney General shall report orally or in writing semiannually to the Permanent Select Committee on Intelligence of the United States House of Representatives, the Select Committee on Intelligence of the United States Senate, and the chairmen and ranking minority members of the Committees on the Judiciary of the Senate and House of Representatives on all cases where a decision not to prosecute a violation of Federal law pursuant to section 12(a) has been made.

(b) In the case of the semiannual reports (whether oral or written) required to be submitted under subsection (a) to the Permanent Select Committee on Intelligence of the House of Representatives and the Select Committee on Intelligence of the Senate, the submittal dates for such reports shall be as provided in section 507 of the National Security Act of 1947.

(c) The Attorney General shall deliver to the appropriate committees of Congress a report concerning the operation and effectiveness of this Act and including suggested amendments to this Act. For the first three years this Act is in effect, there shall be a report each year. After three years, such reports shall be delivered as necessary.

FUNCTIONS OF ATTORNEY GENERAL MAY BE EXERCISED BY DEPUTY ATTORNEY GENERAL OR A DESIGNATED ASSISTANT ATTORNEY GENERAL

SEC. 14. [18 U.S.C. App. §14]

The functions and duties of the Attorney General under this Act may be exercised by the Deputy Attorney General , the Associate Attorney General, or by an Assistant Attorney General designated by the Attorney General for such purpose and may not be delegated to any other official.

EFFECTIVE DATE

SEC. 15. [18 U.S.C. App. §15]
The provisions of this Act shall become effective upon the date of the enactment of this Act, but shall not apply to any prosecution in which an indictment or information was filed before such date.

SHORT TITLE

SEC. 16. [18 U.S.C. App. §16]
That this Act may be cited as the "Classified Information Procedures Act".

FOREIGN INTELLIGENCE SURVEILLANCE ACT OF 1978

(Public Law 95–511 of October 25, 1978; 92 STAT. 1783)

AN ACT To authorize electronic surveillance to obtain foreign intelligence information.

Be it enacted by the Senate and House of Representatives of the United States of America in Congress assembled,

SHORT TITLE

That this Act may be cited as the "Foreign Intelligence Surveillance Act of 1978".

TABLE OF CONTENTS

413

TITLE I—ELECTRONIC SURVEILLANCE WITHIN THE UNITED STATES FOR FOREIGN INTELLIGENCE PURPOSES

DEFINITIONS

SECTION 101. [50 U.S.C. §1801]
As used in this title:
(a) "Foreign power" means—
>(1) a foreign government or any component, thereof, whether or not recognized by the United States;
>(2) a faction of a foreign nation or nations, not substantially composed of United States persons;
>(3) an entity that is openly acknowledged by a foreign government or governments to be directed and controlled by such foreign government or governments;
>(4) a group engaged in international terrorism or activities in preparation therefor;
>(5) a foreign-based political organization, not substantially composed of United States persons;
>(6) an entity that is directed and controlled by a foreign government or governments; or
>(7) an entity not substantially composed of United States persons that is engaged in the international proliferation of weapons of mass destruction.

(b) "Agent of a foreign power" means—
>(1) any person other than a United States person, who—
>>(A) acts in the United States as an officer or employee of a foreign power, or as a member of a foreign power as defined in subsection (a)(4);
>>(B) acts for or on behalf of a foreign power which engages in clandestine intelligence activities in the United States contrary to the interests of the United States, when the circumstances of such person's presence in the United States indicate that such person may engage in such activities in the United States, or when such person knowingly aids or abets any person in the conduct of such

activities or knowingly conspires with any person to engage in such activities;

(C) engages in international terrorism or activities in preparation therefore [sic];

(D) engages in the international proliferation of weapons of mass destruction, or activities in preparation therefor; or

(E) engages in the international proliferation of weapons of mass destruction, or activities in preparation therefor for or on behalf of a foreign power; or

(2) any person who—

(A) knowingly engages in clandestine intelligence gathering activities for or on behalf of a foreign power, which activities involve or may involve a violation of the criminal statutes of the United States;

(B) pursuant to the direction of an intelligence service or network of a foreign power, knowingly engages in any other clandestine intelligence activities for or on behalf of such foreign power, which activities involve or are about to involve a violation of the criminal statutes of the United States;

(C) knowingly engages in sabotage or international terrorism, or activities that are in preparation therefor, for or on behalf of a foreign power;

(D) knowingly enters the United States under a false or fraudulent identity for or on behalf of a foreign power or, while in the United States, knowingly assumes a false or fraudulent identity for or on behalf of a foreign power; or

(E) knowingly aids or abets any person in the conduct of activities described in subparagraph (A), (B), or (C) or knowingly conspires with any person to engage in activities described in subparagraph (A), (B), or (C).

(c) "International terrorism" means activities that—

(1) involve violent acts or acts dangerous to human life that are a violation of the criminal laws of the United States or of any State, or that would be a criminal violation if committed within the jurisdiction of the United States or any State;

(2) appear to be intended—

(A) to intimidate or coerce a civilian population;

(B) to influence the policy of a government by intimidation or coercion; or

(C) to affect the conduct of a government by assassination or kidnapping; and

(3) occur totally outside the United States, or transcend national boundaries in terms of the means by which they are accomplished, the persons they appear intended to coerce or intimidate, or the locale in which their perpetrators operate or seek asylum.

(d) "Sabotage" means activities that involve a violation of chapter 105 of title 18, United States Code, or that would involve such a violation if committed against the United States.

(e) "Foreign intelligence information" means—

(1) information that relates to, and if concerning a United States person is necessary to, the ability of the United States to protect against—

(A) actual or potential attack or other grave hostile acts of a foreign power or an agent of a foreign power;

(B) sabotage, international terrorism, or the international proliferation of weapons of mass destruction by a foreign power or an agent of a foreign power; or

(C) clandestine intelligence activities by an intelligence service or network of a foreign power or by an agent of a foreign power; or

(2) information with respect to a foreign power or foreign territory that relates to, and if concerning a United States person is necessary to—

(A) the national defense or the security of the United States; or

(B) the conduct of the foreign affairs of the United States.

(f) "Electronic surveillance" means—

(1) the acquisition by an electronic, mechanical, or other surveillance device of the contents of any wire or radio communications sent by or intended to be received by a particular, known United States person who is in the United States, if the contents are acquired by intentionally targeting that United States person, under circumstances in which a person has a reasonable expectation of privacy and a warrant would be required for law enforcement purposes;

(2) the acquisition by an electronic, mechanical, or other surveillance device of the contents of any wire communication to or from a person in the United States, without the consent of any party thereto, if such acquisition occurs in the United States, but does not include the acquisition of those communications of computer trespassers that would be permissible under section 2511(2)(i) of title 18, United States Code;

(3) the intentional acquisition by an electronic, mechanical, or other surveillance device of the contents of any radio communication, under circumstances in which a person has a reasonable expectation of privacy and a warrant would be required for law enforcement purposes, and if both the sender and all intended recipients are located within the United States; or

(4) the installation or use of an electronic, mechanical, or other surveillance device in the United States for monitoring to acquire information, other than from a wire or radio communication, under circumstances in which a person has a reasonable expectation of privacy and a warrant would be required for law enforcement purposes.

(g) "Attorney General" means the Attorney General of the United States (or Acting Attorney General), the Deputy Attorney General, or, upon, the designation of the Attorney General, the Assistant Attorney General designated as the Assistant Attorney General for National Security under section 507A of title 28, United States Code.

(h) "Minimization procedures", with respect to electronic surveillance, means—

(1) specific procedures, which shall be adopted by the Attorney General, that are reasonably designed in light of the purpose and technique of the particular surveillance, to minimize the acquisition and retention, and prohibit the dissemination, of nonpublicly available information concerning unconsenting United States persons consistent with the need of the United States to obtain, produce, and disseminate foreign intelligence information;

(2) procedures that require that nonpublicly available information, which is not foreign intelligence information, as defined in subsection (c)(1), shall not be disseminated in a manner that identifies any United States person, without such person's consent, unless such person's identity is necessary to understand foreign intelligence information or assess its importance;

(3) notwithstanding paragraphs (1) and (2), procedures that allow for the retention and dissemination of information that is evidence of a crime which has been, is being, or is about to be committed and that is to be retained or disseminated for law enforcement purposes; and

(4) notwithstanding paragraphs (1), (2), and (3), with respect to any electronic surveillance approved pursuant to section 102(a), procedures that require that no contents of any communication to which a United States person is a party shall be disclosed, disseminated, or used for any purpose or retained for longer than 72 hours unless a court order under section 105 is obtained or unless the Attorney General determines that the information indicates a threat of death or serious bodily harm to any person.

(i) "United States person" means a citizen of the United States, an alien lawfully admitted for permanent residence (as defined in section 101(a)(20) of the Immigration and Nationality Act), an unincorporated association a substantial number of members of which are citizens of the United States or aliens lawfully admitted for permanent residence, or a corporation which is incorporated in the

United States, but does not include a corporation or an association which is a foreign power, as defined in subsection (a) (1), (2), or (3).

(j) "United States", when used in a geographic sense, means all areas under the territorial sovereignty of the United States and the Trust Territory of the Pacific Islands.

(k) "Aggrieved person" means a person who is the target of an electronic surveillance or any other person whose communications or activities were subject to electronic surveillance.

(l) "Wire communication" means any communications while it is being carried by a wire, cable, or other like connection furnished or operated by any person engaged as a common carrier in providing or operating such facilities for the transmission of interstate or foreign communications.

(m) "Person" means any individual, including any officer or employee of the Federal Government, or any group, entity, association, corporation, or foreign power.

(n) "Contents", when used with respect to a communication, includes any information concerning the identity of the parties to such communications or the existence, substance, purport, or meaning of that communication.

(o) "State" means any State of the United States, the District of Columbia, the Commonwealth of Puerto Rico, the Trust Territory of the Pacific Islands, an any territory or possession of the
United States.

(p) `Weapon of mass destruction' means—

> (1) any explosive, incendiary, or poison gas device that is designed, intended, or has the capability to cause a mass casualty incident;
>
> (2) any weapon that is designed, intended, or has the capability to cause death or serious bodily injury to a significant number of persons through the release, dissemination, or impact of toxic or poisonous chemicals or their precursors;
>
> (3) any weapon involving a biological agent, toxin, or vector (as such terms are defined in section 178 of title 18, United States Code) that is designed, intended, or has the capability to cause death, illness, or serious bodily injury to a significant number of persons; or
>
> (4) any weapon that is designed, intended, or has the capability to release radiation or radioactivity causing death, illness, or serious bodily injury to a significant number of persons.'.

AUTHORIZATION FOR ELECTRONIC SURVEILLANCE
FOR FOREIGN INTELLIGENCE PURPOSES

SEC. 102. [50 U.S.C. §1802]

(a)(1) Notwithstanding any other law, the President, through the Attorney General, may authorize electronic surveillance without a court order under this title to acquire foreign intelligence information for periods of up to one year if the Attorney General certifies in writing under oath that—

(A) the electronic surveillance is solely directed at—

(i) the acquisition of the contents of communications transmitted by means of communications used exclusively between or among foreign powers, as defined in section 101(a) (1), (2), or (3); or

(ii) the acquisition of technical intelligence, other than the spoken communications of individuals, from property or premises under the open and exclusive control of a foreign power, as defined in section 101(a) (1), (2), or (3);

(B) there is no substantial likelihood that the surveillance will acquire the contents of any communications to which a United States person is a party; and

(C) the proposed minimization procedures with respect to such surveillance meet the definition of minimization procedures under section 101(h); and if the Attorney General reports such minimization procedures and any changes thereto to the House Permanent Select Committee on Intelligence and the Senate Select Committee on Intelligence at least thirty days prior to their effective date, unless the Attorney General determines immediate action is required and notifies the committees immediately of such minimization procedures and the reason for their becoming effective immediately.

(2) An electronic surveillance authorized by this subsection may be conducted only in accordance with the Attorney General's certification and the minimization procedures adopted by him. The Attorney General shall assess compliance with such procedures and shall report such assessments to the House Permanent Select Committee on Intelligence and the Senate Select Committee on Intelligence under the provisions of section 108(a).

(3) The Attorney General shall immediately transmit under seal to the court established under section 103(a) a copy of his certification. Such certification shall be maintained under security measures established by the Chief Justice with the concurrence of the Attorney General, in consultation with the Director of National Intelligence, and shall remain sealed unless—

(A) an application for a court order with respect to the surveillance is made under sections 101(h)(4) and 104; or

(B) the certification is necessary to determine the legality of the surveillance under section 106(f).

(4) With respect to electronic surveillance authorized by this subsection, the Attorney General may direct a specified communication common carrier to—

(A) furnish all information, facilities, or technical assistance necessary to accomplish the electronic surveillance in such a manner as will protect its secrecy and produce a minimum of interference with the services that such carrier is providing its customers; and

(B) maintain under security procedures approved by the Attorney General and the Director of National Intelligence any records concerning the surveillance or the aid furnished which such carrier wishes to retain.

The Government shall compensate, at the prevailing rate, such carrier for furnishing such aid.

(b) Applications for a court order under this title are authorized if the President has, by written authorization, empowered the Attorney General [sic] to approve applications to the court having jurisdiction under section 103, and a judge to whom an application is made may, notwithstanding any other law, grant an order, in conformity with section 105, approving electronic surveillance of a foreign power or an agent of a foreign power for the purpose of obtaining foreign intelligence information, except that the court shall not have jurisdiction to grant any order approving electronic surveillance directed solely as described in paragraph (1)(A) of subsection (a) unless such surveillance may involve the acquisition of communications of any United States person.

DESIGNATION OF JUDGES

SEC. 103. [50 U.S.C. §1803]

(a)(1) The Chief Justice of the United States shall publicly designate 11 district court judges from at least seven of the United States judicial circuits of whom no fewer than 3 shall reside within 20 miles of the District of Columbia who shall constitute a court which shall have jurisdiction to hear applications for and grant orders approving electronic surveillance anywhere within the United States under the procedures set forth in this Act, except that no judge designated under this subsection (except when sitting en banc under paragraph (2)) shall hear the same application for electronic surveillance under this Act which has been denied previously by another judge designated under this subsection. If any judge so designated denies an application for an order authorizing electronic surveillance under this Act, such judge shall provide immediately for the record a written statement of each reason for his decision and, on motion of the United States, the record shall be transmitted, under seal, to the court of review established in subsection (b).

> (2)(A) The court established under this subsection may, on its own initiative, or upon the request of the Government in any proceeding or a party under section 501(f) or paragraph (4) or (5) of section 702(h), hold a hearing or rehearing, en banc, when ordered by a majority of the judges that constitute such court upon a determination that—
>
>> (i) en banc consideration is necessary to secure or maintain uniformity of the court's decisions; or
>> (ii) the proceeding involves a question of exceptional importance.
>
> (B) Any authority granted by this Act to a judge of the court established under this subsection may be exercised by the court en banc. When exercising such authority, the court en banc shall comply with any requirements of this Act on the exercise of such authority.
>
> (C) For purposes of this paragraph, the court en banc shall consist of all judges who constitute the court established under this subsection.

(b) The Chief Justice shall publicly designate three judges, one of whom shall be publicly designate as the presiding judge, from the United States district courts or courts of appeals who together shall comprise a court of review which shall have jurisdiction to review the denial of any application made under this Act. If such court determines that the application was properly denied, the court shall immediately provide for the record a written statement of each reason for its decision and, on petition of the United States for a writ of certiorari, the record shall be transmitted under seal to the Supreme Court, which shall have jurisdiction to review such decision.

(c) Proceedings under this Act shall be conducted as expeditiously as possible. The record of proceedings under this Act, including applications made and orders granted, shall be maintained under security measures established by the Chief Justice in consultation with the Attorney General and the Director of National Intelligence.

(d) Each judge designated under this section shall so serve for a maximum of seven years and shall not be eligible for redesignation, except that the judges first designated under subsection (a) shall be designated for terms of from one to seven years so that one term expires each year, and that judges first designated under subsection (b) shall be designated for terms of three, five, and seven years.

> (e)(1) Three judges designated under subsection (a) who reside within 20 miles of the District of Columbia, or, if all of such judges are unavailable, other judges of the court established under subsection (a) as may be designated by the presiding judge of such court, shall comprise a

petition review pool which shall have jurisdiction to review petitions filed pursuant to section 1861(f)(1) or 1881a(h)(4).

(2) Not later than 60 days after the date of the enactment of the USA PATRIOT Improvement and Reauthorization Act of 2005, the court established under subsection (a) shall adopt and, consistent with the protection of national security, publish procedures for the review of petitions filed pursuant to section 1861(f)(1) or 1881a(h)(4) by the panel established under paragraph (1). Such procedures shall provide that review of a petition shall be conducted in camera and shall also provide for the designation of an acting presiding judge.

(f)(1) A judge of the court established under subsection (a), the court established under subsection (b) or a judge of that court, or the Supreme Court of the United States or a justice of that court, may, in accordance with the rules of their respective courts, enter a stay of an order or an order modifying an order of the court established under subsection (a) or the court established under subsection (b) entered under any title of this Act, while the court established under subsection (a) conducts a rehearing, while an appeal is pending to the court established under subsection (b), or while a petition of certiorari is pending in the Supreme Court of the United States, or during the pendency of any review by that court.

(2) The authority described in paragraph (1) shall apply to an order entered under any provision of this Act.

(g)(1) The courts established pursuant to subsections (a) and (b) may establish such rules and procedures, and take such actions, as are reasonably necessary to administer their responsibilities under this Act.

(2) The rules and procedures established under paragraph (1), and any modifications of such rules and procedures, shall be recorded, and shall be transmitted to the following:

(A) All of the judges on the court established pursuant to subsection (a).

(B) All of the judges on the court of review established pursuant to subsection (b).

(C) The Chief Justice of the United States.

(D) The Committee on the Judiciary of the Senate.

(E) The Select Committee on Intelligence of the Senate.

(F) The Committee on the Judiciary of the House of Representatives.

(G) The Permanent Select Committee on Intelligence of the House of Representatives.

(3) The transmissions required by paragraph (2) shall be submitted in unclassified form, but may include a classified annex.

(h) Nothing in this Act shall be construed to reduce or contravene the inherent authority of the court established under subsection (a) to determine or enforce compliance with an order or a rule of such court or with a procedure approved by such court.

APPLICATION FOR AN ORDER

SEC. 104. [50 U.S.C. §1804]
(a) Each application for an order approving electronic surveillance under this title shall be made by a Federal officer in writing upon oath or affirmation to a judge having jurisdiction under section 103. Each application shall require the approval of the Attorney General based upon his finding that it satisfies the criteria and requirements of such application as set forth in this title. It shall include—

(1) the identity of the Federal officer making the application;

(2) the identity, if known, or a description of the specific target of the electronic surveillance;

(3) a statement of the facts and circumstances relied upon by the applicant to justify his belief that—

(A) the target of the electronic surveillance is a foreign power or an agent of a foreign power; and

(B) each of the facilities or places at which the electronic surveillance is directed is being used, or is about to be used, by a foreign power or an agent of a foreign power;

(4) a statement of the proposed minimization procedures;

(5) a description of the nature of the information sought and the type of communications or activities to be subjected to the surveillance;

(6) a certification or certifications by the Assistant to the President for National Security Affairs, an executive branch official or officials designated by the President from among those executive officers employed in the area of national security or defense and appointed by the President with the advice and consent of the Senate, or the Deputy Director of the Federal Bureau of Investigation, if designated by the President as a certifying official —

(A) that the certifying official deems the information sought to be foreign intelligence information;

(B) that a significant purpose of the surveillance is to obtain foreign intelligence information;

(C) that such information cannot reasonably be obtained by normal investigative techniques;

(D) that designates the type of foreign intelligence information being sought according to the categories described in section 101(e); and

(E) including a statement of the basis for the certification that—
(i) the information sought is the type of foreign intelligence information designated; and
(ii) such information cannot reasonably be obtained by normal investigative techniques;

(7) a summary statement of the means by which the surveillance will be effected and a statement whether physical entry is required to effect the surveillance;

(8) a statement of the facts concerning all previous applications that have been made to any judge under this title involving any of the persons, facilities, or places specified in the application, and the action taken on each previous application; and

(9) a statement of the period of time for which the electronic surveillance is required to be maintained, and if the nature of the intelligence gathering is such that the approval of the use of electronic surveillance under this title should not automatically terminate when the described type of information has first been obtained, a description of facts supporting the belief that additional information of the same type will be obtained thereafter.

(b) The Attorney General may require any other affidavit or certification from any other officer in connection with the application.

(c) The judge may require the applicant to furnish such other information as may be necessary to make the determinations required by section 105.

(d) (1)(A) Upon written request of the Director of the Federal Bureau of Investigation, the Secretary of Defense, the Secretary of State, or the Director of National Intelligence, or the Director of the Central Intelligence Agency, the Attorney General shall personally review under subsection (a) an application under that subsection for a target described in section 101(b)(2).

(B) Except when disabled or otherwise unavailable to make a request referred to in subparagraph (A), an official referred to in that subparagraph may not delegate the authority to make a request referred to in that subparagraph.

(C) Each official referred to in subparagraph (A) with authority to make a request under that subparagraph shall take appropriate actions in advance to ensure that delegation of such authority is clearly established in the event such official is disabled or otherwise unavailable to make such request.

(2)(A) If as a result of a request under paragraph (1) the Attorney General determines not to approve an application under the second sentence of subsection (a) for purposes of making the application under this section, the Attorney General shall provide written notice of the determination to the official making the request for the review of the application under that paragraph. Except when disabled or otherwise unavailable to make a determination under the preceding sentence, the Attorney General may not delegate the responsibility to make a determination under that sentence. The Attorney General shall take appropriate actions in advance to ensure that delegation of such responsibility is clearly established in the event the Attorney General is disabled or otherwise unavailable to make such determination.

(B) Notice with respect to an application under subparagraph (A) shall set forth the modifications, if any, of the application that are necessary in order for the Attorney General to approve the application under the second sentence of subsection (a) for purposes of making the application under this section.

(C) Upon review of any modifications of an application set forth under subparagraph (B), the official notified of the modifications under this paragraph shall modify the application if such official determines that such modification is warranted. Such official shall supervise the making of any modification under this subparagraph. Except when disabled or otherwise unavailable to supervise the making of any modification under the preceding sentence, such official may not delegate the responsibility to supervise the making of any modification under that preceding sentence. Each such official shall take appropriate actions in advance to ensure that delegation of such responsibility is clearly established in the event such official is disabled or otherwise unavailable to supervise the making of such modification.

ISSUANCE OF AN ORDER

SEC. 105. [50 U.S.C. §1805]

(a) Upon an application made pursuant to section 104, the judge shall enter an ex parte order as requested or as modified approving the electronic surveillance if he finds that—

(1) the application has been made by a Federal officer and approved by the Attorney General;

(2) on the basis of the facts submitted by the applicant there is probable cause to believe that—

(A) the target of the electronic surveillance is a foreign power or an agent of a foreign power: Provided, That no United States person may be considered a foreign power or an agent of a foreign power solely upon the basis of activities protected by the first amendment to the Constitution of the United States; and

(B) each of the facilities or places at which the electronic surveillance is directed is being used, or is about to be used, by a foreign power or an agent of a foreign power;

(3) the proposed minimization procedures meet the definition of minimization procedures under section 101(h); and

(4) the application which has been filed contains all statements and certifications required by section 104 and, if the target is a United States person, the certification or certifications are not clearly erroneous on the basis of the statement made under section 104(a)(7)(E) and any other information furnished under section 104(d).

(b) In determining whether or not probable cause exists for purposes of an order under subsection (a)(2), a judge may consider past activities of the target, as well as facts and circumstances relating to current or future activities of the target.

(c) (1) SPECIFICATIONS.—An order approving an electronic surveillance under this section shall specify—

(A) the identity, if known, or a description of the specific target of the electronic surveillance identified or described in the application pursuant to section 104(a)(3) of this Act;

(B) the nature and location of each of the facilities or places at which the electronic surveillance will be directed, if known;

(C) the type of information sought to be acquired and the type of communications or activities to be subjected to the surveillance;

(D) the means by which the electronic surveillance will be effected and whether physical entry will be used to effect the surveillance; and

(E) the period of time during which the electronic surveillance is approved.

(2) DIRECTIONS.—An order approving an electronic surveillance under this section shall direct—

(A) that the minimization procedures be followed;

(B) that, upon the request of the applicant, a specified communication or other common carrier, landlord, custodian, or other specified person, or in circumstances where the Court finds, based upon specific facts provided in the application, that the actions of the target of the application may have the effect of thwarting the identification of a specified person, such other persons, furnish the applicant forthwith all information, facilities, or technical assistance necessary to accomplish the electronic surveillance in such a manner as will protect its secrecy and produce a minimum of interference with the services that such carrier, landlord, custodian, or other person is providing that target of electronic surveillance;

(C) that such carrier, landlord, custodian, or other person maintain under security procedures approved by the Attorney General and the Director of National Intelligence any records concerning the surveillance or the aid furnished that such person wishes to retain; and

(D) that the applicant compensate, at the prevailing rate, such carrier, landlord, custodian, or other person for furnishing such aid.

(3) SPECIAL DIRECTIONS FOR CERTAIN ORDERS.—An order approving an electronic surveillance under this section in circumstances where the nature and location of each of the facilities or places at which the surveillance will be directed is unknown shall direct the applicant to provide notice to the court within ten days after the date on which surveillance begins to be directed at any new facility or place, unless the court finds good cause to justify a longer period of up to 60 days, of—

(A) the nature and location of each new facility or place at which the electronic surveillance is directed;

(B) the facts and circumstances relied upon by the applicant to justify the applicant's belief that each new facility or place at which the electronic surveillance is directed is or was being used, or is about to be used, by the target of the surveillance;

(C) a statement of any proposed minimization procedures that differ from those contained in the original application or order, that may be necessitated by a change in the facility or place at which the electronic surveillance is directed; and

(D) the total number of electronic surveillances that have been or are being conducted under the authority of the order.

(d)(1) An order issued under this section may approve an electronic surveillance for the period necessary to achieve its purpose, or for ninety days, whichever is less, except that

(A) 1 an order under this section shall approve an electronic surveillance targeted against a foreign power, as defined in section 101(a), (1), (2), or (3), for the period specified in the application or for one year, whichever is less, and

(B) an order under this Act for a surveillance targeted against an agent of a foreign power, who is not a United States person may be for the period specified in the application or for 120 days, whichever is less.

(2) Extensions of an order issued under this title may be granted on the same basis as an original order upon an application for an extension and new findings made in the same manner as required for an original order, except that

(A) an extension of an order under this Act for a surveillance targeted against a foreign power, a defined in paragraph (5), (6), or (7) of section 101(a), or against a foreign power as defined in section 101(a)(4) that is not a United States person, may be for a period not to exceed one year if the judge finds probable cause to believe that no communication of any individual United States person will be acquired during the period, and

(B) an extension of an order under this Act for a surveillance targeted against an agent of a foreign power who is not a United States person may be for a period not to exceed 1 year.

(3) At or before the end of the period of time for which electronic surveillance is approved by an order or an extension, the judge may assess compliance with the minimization procedures by reviewing the circumstances under which information concerning United States persons was acquired, retained, or disseminated.

(e)(1) Notwithstanding any other provision of this title, the Attorney General may authorize the emergency employment of electronic surveillance if the Attorney General—

(A) reasonably determines that an emergency situation exists with respect to the employment of electronic surveillance to obtain foreign intelligence information before an order authorizing such surveillance can with due diligence be obtained;

(B) reasonably determines that the factual basis for the issuance of an order under this title to approve such electronic surveillance exists;

(C) informs, either personally or through a designee, a judge having jurisdiction under section 103 at the time of such authorization that the decision has been made to employ emergency electronic surveillance; and

(D) makes an application in accordance with this title to a judge having jurisdiction under section 103 as soon as practicable, but not later than 7 days after the Attorney General authorizes such surveillance.

(2) If the Attorney General authorizes the emergency employment of electronic surveillance under paragraph (1), the Attorney General shall require that the minimization procedures required by this title for the issuance of a judicial order be followed.

(3) In the absence of a judicial order approving such electronic surveillance, the surveillance shall terminate when the information sought is obtained, when the application for the order is denied, or after the expiration of 7 days from the time of authorization by the Attorney General, whichever is earliest.

(4) A denial of the application made under this subsection may be reviewed as provided in section 103.

(5) In the event that such application for approval is denied, or in any other case where the electronic surveillance is terminated and no order is issued approving the surveillance, no information obtained or evidence derived from such surveillance shall be received in evidence or otherwise disclosed in any trial, hearing, or other proceeding in or before any court, grand jury, department, office, agency, regulatory body, legislative committee, or other authority of the United States, a State, or political subdivision thereof, and no information concerning any United States person acquired from such surveillance shall subsequently be used or disclosed in any other manner by Federal officers or employees without the consent of such person, except with the approval of the Attorney General if the information indicates a threat of death or serious bodily harm to any person.

(6) The Attorney General shall assess compliance with the requirements of paragraph (5).

(f) Notwithstanding any other provision of this Act, officers, employees, or agents of the United States are authorized in the normal course of their official duties to conduct electronic surveillance not targeted against the communications of any particular person or persons, under procedures approved by the Attorney General, solely to—

(1) test the capability of electronic equipment, if—

(A) it is not reasonable to obtain the consent of the persons incidentally subjected to the surveillance;

(B) the test is limited in extent and duration to that necessary to determine to capability of the equipment;

(C) the contents of any communication acquired are retained and used only for the purpose of determining the capability of the equipment, are disclosed only to test personnel, and are destroyed before or immediately upon completion of the test; and

(D) Provided, That the test may exceed ninety days only with the prior approval of the Attorney General;

(2) determine the existence and capability of electronic surveillance equipment being used by persons not authorized to conduct electronic surveillance, if—

(A) it is not reasonable to obtain the consent of persons incidentally subjected to the surveillance;

(B) such electronic surveillance is limited in extent and duration to that necessary to determine the existence and capability of such equipment; and

(C) any information acquired by such surveillance is used only to enforce chapter 119 of title 18, United States Code, or section 705 of the Communications Act of 1934, or to protect information from unauthorized surveillance; or

(3) train intelligence personnel in the use of electronic surveillance equipment, if—

(A) it is not reasonable to—

(i) obtain the consent of the persons incidentally subjected to the surveillance;

(ii) train persons in the course of surveillances otherwise authorized by this title; or

(iii) train persons in the use of such equipment without engaging in electronic surveillance;

(B) such electronic surveillance is limited in extent and duration to that necessary to train the personnel in the use of the equipment; and

(C) no contents of any communication acquired are retained or disseminated for any purpose, but are destroyed as soon as reasonably possible.

(g) Certifications made by the Attorney General pursuant to section 102(a) and applications made and orders granted under this title shall be retained for a period of at least ten years from the date of the certification or application.

(h) No cause of action shall lie in any court against any provider of a wire or electronic communication service, landlord, custodian, or other person (including any officer, employee, agent, or other specified person thereof) that furnishes any information, facilities, or technical assistance in accordance with a court order or request for emergency assistance under this Act for electronic surveillance or physical search.

(i) In any case in which the Government makes an application to a judge under this title to conduct electronic surveillance involving communications and the judge grants such application, upon the request of the applicant, the judge shall also authorize the installation and use of pen registers and trap and trace devices, and direct the disclosure of the information set forth in section 402(d)(2).

USE OF INFORMATION

SEC. 106. [50 U.S.C. §1806]

(a) Information acquired from an electronic surveillance conducted pursuant to this title concerning any United States person may be used and disclosed by Federal officers and employees without the consent of the United States person only in accordance with the minimization procedures required by this title. No otherwise privileged communication obtained in accordance with, or in violation of, the provisions of this Act shall lose its privileged character. No information acquired from an electronic surveillance pursuant to this title may be used or disclosed by Federal officers or employees except for lawful purposes.

(b) No information acquired pursuant to this title shall be disclosed for law enforcement purposes unless such disclosure is accompanied by a statement that such information, or any information derived therefrom, may only be used in a criminal proceeding with the advance authorization of the Attorney General.

(c) Whenever the Government intends to enter into evidence or otherwise use or disclose in any trial, hearing, or other proceeding in or before any court, department, officer, agency, regulatory body, or other authority of the United States, against an aggrieved person, any information obtained or derived from an electronic surveillance of that aggrieved person pursuant to the authority of this Act, the Government shall, prior to the trial, hearing, or other proceeding or at a reasonable time prior to an effort to so disclose or so use that information or submit it in evidence, notify the aggrieved person and the court or other authority in which the information is to be disclosed or used that the Government intends to so disclose or so use such information.

(d) Whenever any State or political subdivision thereof intends to enter into evidence or otherwise use or disclose in any trial, hearing, or other proceeding in or before any court, department, officer, agency, regulatory body, or other authority of a State or a political subdivision thereof, against an aggrieved person any information obtained or derived from an electronic surveillance of that aggrieved person pursuant to the authority of this Act, the State or political subdivision thereof shall notify the aggrieved person, the court or other authority in which the information is to be disclosed or used, and the Attorney General that the State or political subdivision thereof intends to so disclose or so use such information.

(e) Any person against whom evidence obtained or derived from an electronic surveillance to which he is an aggrieved person is to be, or has been, introduced or otherwise used or disclosed in any trial, hearing, or other proceeding in or before any court, department, officer, agency, regulatory body, or other authority of the United States, a State, or a political subdivision thereof, may move to suppress the evidence obtained or derived from such electronic surveillance on the grounds that—

> (1) the information was unlawfully acquired; or
>
> (2) the surveillance was not made in conformity with an order of authorization or approval. Such a motion shall be made before the trial, hearing, or other proceeding unless there was no opportunity to make such a motion or the person was not aware of the grounds of the motion.

(f) [IN CAMERA AND EX PARTE REVIEW BY DISTRICT COURT.—] Whenever a court or other authority is notified pursuant to subsection (c) or (d), or whenever a motion is made pursuant to subsection (e), or whenever any motion or request is made by an aggrieved person pursuant to any other statute or rule of the United States or any State before any court or other authority of the United States or any State to discover or obtain applications or orders or other materials relating to electronic surveillance or to discover, obtain, or suppress evidence or information obtained or derived from electronic surveillance under this Act, the United States district court or, where the motion is made before another authority, the United States district court in the same district as the authority, shall, notwithstanding any other law, if the Attorney General files an affidavit under oath that disclosure or an adversary hearing would harm the national security of the United States, review in camera and ex parte the application, order, and such other materials relating to the surveillance as may be necessary to determine whether the surveillance of the aggrieved person was lawfully authorized and conducted. In making this determination, the court may disclose to the aggrieved person, under appropriate security procedures and protective orders, portions of the application, order, or other materials relating to the surveillance only where such disclosure is necessary to make an accurate determination of the legality of the surveillance.

(g) If the United States district court pursuant to subsection (f) determine that the surveillance was not lawfully authorized or conducted, it shall, in accordance with the requirements of law, suppress the evidence which was unlawfully obtained or derived from electronic surveillance of the aggrieved person or otherwise grant the motion of the aggrieved person. If the court determines that the surveillance was lawfully authorized and conducted, it shall deny the motion of the aggrieved person except to the extent that due process requires discovery or disclosure.

(h) Orders granting motions or requests under subsection (g), decisions under this section that electronic surveillance was not lawfully authorized or conducted, and orders of the United States district court requiring review or granting disclosure of applications, orders, or other materials relating to a surveillance shall be final orders and binding upon all courts of the United States and the several States except a United States court of appeals and the Supreme Court.

(i) In circumstances involving the unintentional acquisition by an electronic, mechanical, or other surveillance device of the contents of any communication, under circumstances in which a person has a reasonable expectation of privacy and a warrant would be required for law enforcement purposes, and if both the sender and all intended recipients are located within the United States, such contents shall be destroyed upon recognition, unless the Attorney General determines that the contents indicates a threat of death or serious bodily harm to any person.

(j) If an emergency employment of electronic surveillance is authorized under section 105(e) and a subsequent order approving the surveillance is not obtained, the judge shall cause to be served on any United States person named in the application and on such other United States persons subject to electronic surveillance as the judge may determine in his discretion it is in the interest of justice to serve, notice of—

    (1) the fact of the application;

    (2) the period of the surveillance; and

    (3) the fact that during the period information was or was not obtained.

On an ex parte showing of good cause to the judge the serving of the notice required by this subsection may be postponed or suspended for a period not to exceed ninety days. Thereafter, on a further ex parte showing of good cause, the court shall forego ordering the serving of the notice required under this subsection.

(k)(1) Federal officers who conduct electronic surveillance to acquire foreign intelligence information under this title may consult with Federal law enforcement officers or law enforcement personnel of a State or political subdivision of a State (including the chief executive officer of that State or political subdivision who has the authority to appoint or direct the chief law enforcement officer of that State or political subdivision) to coordinate efforts to investigate or protect against—

    (A) actual or potential attack or other grave hostile acts of a foreign power or an agent of a foreign power;

    (B) sabotage, international terrorism, or the international proliferation of weapons of mass destruction by a foreign power or an agent of a foreign power; or

    (C) clandestine intelligence activities by an intelligence service or network of a foreign power or by an agent of a foreign power.

(2) Coordination authorized under paragraph (1) shall not preclude the certification required by section 104(a)(7)(B) or the entry of an order under section 105.

REPORT OF ELECTRONIC SURVEILLANCE

SEC. 107. [50 U.S.C. §1807]

In April of each year, the Attorney General shall transmit to the Administrative Office of the United States Court and to Congress a report setting forth with respect to the preceding calendar year—

(a) the total number of applications made for orders and extensions of orders approving electronic surveillance under this title; and

(b) the total number of such orders and extensions either granted, modified, or denied.

CONGRESSIONAL OVERSIGHT

SEC. 108. [50 U.S.C. §1808]

(a)(1) On a semiannual basis the Attorney General shall fully inform the House Permanent Select Committee on Intelligence and the Senate Select Committees on Intelligence and the Committee on the Judiciary of the Senate concerning all electronic surveillance under this title. Nothing in this title shall be deemed to limit the authority and responsibility of the appropriate committees of each House of Congress to obtain such information as they may need to carry out their respective functions and duties.

    (2) Each report under the first sentence of paragraph (1) shall include a description of—

        (A) the total number of applications made for orders and extensions of orders approving electronic surveillance under this title where the nature and location of each facility or place at which the electronic surveillance will be directed is unknown;

        (B) each criminal case in which information acquired under this Act has been authorized for use at trial during the period covered by such report; and

        (C) the total number of emergency employments of electronic surveillance under section 105(e) and the total number of subsequent orders approving or denying such electronic surveillance.

(b) On or before one year after the effective date of this Act and on the same day each year for four years thereafter, the Permanent Select Committee on Intelligence and the Senate Select Committee on Intelligence shall report respectively to the House of Representatives and the Senate, concerning the implementation of this Act. Said reports shall include but not be limited to an analysis and recommendations concerning whether this Act should be (1) amended, (2) repealed, or (3) permitted to continue in effect without amendment.

PENALTIES

SEC. 109. [50 U.S.C. §1809]

(a) OFFENSE.—A person is guilty of an offense if he intentionally—

    (1) engages in electronic surveillance under color of law except as authorized by this Act, chapter 119, 121, or 206 of title 18, United States Code, or any express statutory authorization that is an additional exclusive means for conducting electronic surveillance under section 112; or

    (2) disclose or uses information obtained under color of law by electronic surveillance, knowing or having reason to known that the information was obtained through electronic surveillance not authorized by this Act, chapter 119, 121, or 206 of title 18, United States Code, or

any express statutory authorization that is an additional exclusive means for conducting electronic surveillance under section 112.

(b) DEFENSE.—It is a defense to a prosecution under subsection (a) that the defendant was a law enforcement or investigative officer engaged in the course of his official duties and the electronic surveillance was authorized by and conducted pursuant to a search warrant or court order of a court of competent jurisdiction.

(c) PENALTY.—An offense in this section is punishable by a fine of not more than $10,000 or imprisonment for not more than five years, or both.

(d) JURISDICTION.—There is Federal jurisdiction over an offense under this section if the person committing the offense was an officer or employee of the United States at the time the offense was committed.

CIVIL LIABILITY

SEC. 110. [50 U.S.C. §1810]
CIVIL ACTION.—An aggrieved person, other than a foreign power or an agent of a foreign power, as defined in section 101 (a) or (b)(1)(A), respectively, who has been subjected to an electronic surveillance or about whom information obtained by electronic surveillance of such person has been disclosed or used in violation of section 109 shall have a cause of action against any person who committed such violation and shall be entitled to recover—

(a) actual damages, but not less than liquidated damages of $1,000 or $100 per day for each day of violation, whichever is greater;

(b) punitive damages; and

(c) reasonable attorney's fees and other investigation and litigation costs reasonably incurred.

AUTHORIZATION DURING TIME OF WAR

SEC. 111. [50 U.S.C. §1811]
Notwithstanding any other law, the President, through the Attorney General, may authorize electronic surveillance without a court order under this title to acquire foreign intelligence information for a period not to exceed fifteen calendar days following a declaration of war by the Congress.

STATEMENT OF EXCLUSIVE MEANS BY WHICH ELECTRONIC SURVEILLANCE AND INTERCEPTION OF CERTAIN COMMUNICATIONS MAY BE CONDUCTED

SEC. 112. [50 U.S.C. § 1812]
(a) Except as provided in subsection (b), the procedures of chapters 119, 121, and 206 of title 18, United States Code, and this Act shall be the exclusive means by

which electronic surveillance and the interception of domestic wire, oral, or electronic communications may be conducted.

(b) Only an express statutory authorization for electronic surveillance or the interception of domestic wire, oral, or electronic communications, other than as an amendment to this Act or chapters 119, 121, or 206 of title 18, United States Code, shall constitute an additional exclusive means for the purpose of subsection (a).

TITLE II—CONFORMING AMENDMENTS

AMENDMENTS TO CHAPTER 119 OF TITLE 18, UNITED STATES CODE

SEC. 201.

Chapter 119 of title 18, United States Code, is amended as follows:

(a) Section 2511(2)(a)(ii) is amended to read as follows:

> "(ii) Notwithstanding any other law, communication common carriers, their officers, employees, and agents, landlords, custodians, or other persons, are authorized to provide information, facilities, or technical assistance to persons authorized by law to intercept wire or oral communications or to conduct electronic surveillance, as defined in section 101 of the Foreign Intelligence Surveillance Act of 1978, if the common carrier, its officers, employees, or agent, landlord, custodian, or other specified person, has been provided with—

"(A) a court order directing such assistance signed by the authorizing judge, or

"(B) a certification in writing by a person specified in section 2518(7) of title or the Attorney General of the United States that no warrant or court order is required by law, that all statutory requirements have been met, and that the specified assistance is required, setting forth the period of time during which the provision of the information, facilities, or technical assistance is authorized and specifying the information, facilities, or technical assistance required. No communications common carrier, officer, employee, or agent thereof, or landlord, custodian, or other specified person shall disclose the existence of any interception or surveillance or the device used to accomplish the interception or surveillance with respect to which the person has been furnished an order or certification under this subparagraph, except as may otherwise be required by legal process and then only after prior notification of the Attorney General or to the principal prosecuting attorney of a State or any political subdivision of a State, as may be appropriate. Any violation of this subparagraph by a communication common carrier or an officer, employee, or agent thereof, shall render the carrier liable for the civil damages provided for in section 2520. No cause of action shall lie in any court against any communication common carrier, its officers, employees, or agents, landlord, custodian, or other specified person for providing information, facilities, or assistance in accordance with the terms of an order or certification under this subparagraph.".

(b) Section 2511(2) is amended by adding at the end thereof the following new provisions:

"(e) Notwithstanding any other provision of this Act or section 605 or 606 of the Communications Act of 1934, it shall not be unlawful for an officer, employee, or agent of the United States in the normal course of his official duty to conduct electronic surveillance, as defined in section 101 of the Foreign Intelligence Surveillance Act of 1978, as authorized by that Act.
"(f) Nothing contained in this chapter, or section 605 of the Communications Act of 1934, shall be deemed to affect the acquisition by the United States Government of foreign intelligence information from international or foreign communications by a means other than electronic surveillance as defined in section 101 of the Foreign Intelligence Surveillance Act of 1978, and procedures in this chapter and the Foreign Intelligence Surveillance Act of 1978 shall be the exclusive means by which electronic surveillance, as defined in section 101 of such Act, and the interception of domestic wire and oral communications may be conducted.".

(c) Section 2511(3) is repealed.
(d) Section 2518(1) is amended by inserting "under this chapter" after "communication".
(e) Section 2518(4) is amended by inserting "under this chapter" after both appearances of "wire or oral communication".
(f) Section 2518(9) is amended by striking out "intercepted" and inserting "intercepted pursuant to this chapter" after "communication".
(g) Section 2518(10) is amended by striking out "intercepted" and inserting "intercepted pursuant to this chapter" after the first appearance of "communication".
(h) Section 2519(3) is amended by inserting "pursuant to this chapter" after "wire or oral communications" and after "granted or denied".

TITLE III—PHYSICAL SEARCHES WITHIN
THE UNITED STATES FOR FOREIGN INTELLIGENCE PURPOSES

DEFINITIONS

SEC. 301. [50 U.S.C. §1821]

As used in this title:

(1) The terms "foreign power", "agent of a foreign power", "international terrorism", "sabotage", "foreign intelligence information", "Attorney General", "United States person", " 'United States', 'person', 'weapon of mass destruction', and 'State' " shall have the same meanings as in section 101 of this Act, except as specifically provided by this title.

(2) "Aggrieved person" means a person whose premises, property, information, or material is the target of physical search or any other person whose premises, property, information, or material was subject to physical search.

(3) "Foreign Intelligence Surveillance Court" means the court established by section 103(a) of this Act.

(4) "Minimization procedures" with respect to physical search, means—

(A) specific procedures, which shall be adopted by the Attorney General, that are reasonably designed in light of the purposes and technique of the particular physical search, to minimize the acquisition and retention, and prohibit the dissemination, of nonpublicly available information concerning unconsenting United States persons consistent with the need of the United States to obtain, produce, and disseminate foreign intelligence information;

(B) procedures that require that nonpublicly available information, which is not foreign intelligence information, as defined in section 101(e)(1) of this Act, shall not be disseminated in a manner that identifies any United States person, without such person's consent, unless such person's identity is necessary to understand such foreign intelligence information or assess its importance;

(C) notwithstanding subparagraphs (A) and (B), procedures that allow for the retention and dissemination of information that is evidence of a crime which has been, is being, or is about to be committed and that is to be retained or disseminated for law enforcement purposes; and

(D) notwithstanding subparagraphs (A), (B), and (C), with respect to any physical search approved pursuant to section 302(a), procedures that require that no information, material, or property of a United States person shall be disclosed, disseminated, or used for any purpose or retained for longer than 72 hours unless a court order under section 304 is obtained or unless the Attorney General determines that the information indicates a threat of death or serious bodily harm to any person. (5) "Physical search" means any physical intrusion within the United States into premises or property (including examination of the interior of property by technical means) that is intended to result in a seizure, reproduction, inspection, or alteration of information, material, or property, under circumstances in which a person has a reasonable expectation of privacy and a warrant would be required for law enforcement purposes, but does not include (A) "electronic surveillance", as defined in section 101(f) of this Act, or (B) the acquisition by the United States Government of foreign intelligence information from international or foreign communications, or foreign intelligence activities conducted in accordance with otherwise applicable Federal law involving a foreign electronic communications system, utilizing a means other than electronic surveillance as defined in section 101(f) of this Act.

AUTHORIZATION OF PHYSICAL SEARCHES FOR FOREIGN INTELLIGENCE PURPOSES

SEC. 302. [50 U.S.C. §1822]
(a)(1) Notwithstanding any other provision of law, the President, acting through the Attorney General, may authorize physical searches without a court order under this title to acquire foreign intelligence information for periods of up to one year if—

    (A) the Attorney General certifies in writing under oath that—
        (i) the physical search is solely directed at premises, information, material, or property used exclusively by, or under the open and exclusive control of, a foreign power or powers (as defined in section 101(a) (1), (2), or (3));
        (ii) there is no substantial likelihood that the physical search will involve the premises, information, material, or property of a United States person; and

(iii) the proposed minimization procedures with respect to such physical search meet the definition of minimization procedures under paragraphs (1) through (4) of section 301(4); and

(B) the Attorney General reports such minimization procedures and any changes thereto to the Permanent Select Committee on Intelligence of the House of Representatives and the Select Committee on Intelligence of the Senate at least 30 days before their effective date, unless the Attorney General determines that immediate action is required and notifies the committees immediately of such minimization procedures and the reason for their becoming effective immediately.

(2) A physical search authorized by this subsection may be conducted only in accordance with the certification and minimization procedures adopted by the Attorney General. The Attorney General shall assess compliance with such procedures and shall report such assessments to the Permanent Select Committee on Intelligence of the House of Representatives and the Select Committee on Intelligence of the Senate under the provisions of section 306.

(3) The Attorney General shall immediately transmit under seal to the Foreign Intelligence Surveillance Court a copy of the certification. Such certification shall be maintained under security measures established by the Chief Justice of the United States with the concurrence of the Attorney General, in consultation with the Director of National Intelligence, and shall remain sealed unless—

(A) an application for a court order with respect to the physical search is made under section 301(4) and section 303; or

(B) the certification is necessary to determine the legality of the physical search under section 305(g).

(4)(A) With respect to physical searches authorized by this subsection, the Attorney General may direct a specified landlord, custodian, or other specified person to—

(i) furnish all information, facilities, or assistance necessary to accomplish the physical search in such a manner as will protect its secrecy and produce a minimum of interference with the services that such landlord, custodian, or other person is providing the target of the physical search; and

(ii) maintain under security procedures approved by the Attorney General and the Director of National Intelligence any records concerning the search or the aid furnished that such person wishes to retain.

(B) The Government shall compensate, at the prevailing rate, such landlord, custodian, or other person for furnishing such aid.

(b) Applications for a court order under this title are authorized if the President has, by written authorization, empowered the Attorney General to approve applications to the Foreign Intelligence Surveillance Court. Notwithstanding any other provision of law, a judge of the court to whom application is made may grant an order in accordance with section 304 approving a physical search in the United States of the premises, property, information, or material of a foreign power or an agent of a foreign power for the purpose of collecting foreign intelligence information.

(c) The Foreign Intelligence Surveillance Court shall have jurisdiction to hear applications for and grant orders approving a physical search for the purpose of obtaining foreign intelligence information anywhere within the United States under the procedures set forth in this title, except that no judge (except when sitting en banc) shall hear the same application which has been denied previously by another judge designated under section 103(a) of this Act. If any judge so designated denies an application for an order authorizing a physical search under this title, such judge shall provide immediately for the record a written statement of each reason for such decision and, on motion of the United States, the record shall be transmitted, under seal, to the court of review established under section 103(b).

(d) The court of review established under section 103(b) shall have jurisdiction to review the denial of any application made under this title. If such court determines that the application was properly denied, the court shall immediately provide for the record a written statement of each reason for its decision and, on petition of the United States for a writ of certiorari, the record shall be transmitted under seal to the Supreme Court, which shall have jurisdiction to review such decision.

(e) Judicial proceedings under this title shall be concluded as expeditiously as possible. The record of proceedings under this title, including applications made and orders granted, shall be maintained under security measures established by the Chief Justice of the United States in consultation with the Attorney General and the Director of National Intelligence.

APPLICATION FOR AN ORDER

SEC. 303. [50 U.S.C. §1823]

(a) Each application for an order approving a physical search under this title shall be made by a Federal officer in writing upon oath or affirmation to a judge of the Foreign Intelligence Surveillance Court. Each application shall require the approval of the Attorney General based upon the Attorney General's finding that it satisfies the criteria and requirements for such application as set forth in this title. Each application shall include—

(1) the identity of the Federal officer making the application;

(2) the identity, if known, or a description of the target of the search, and a description of the premises or property to be searched and of the information, material, or property to be seized, reproduced, or altered;

(3) a statement of the facts and circumstances relied upon by the applicant to justify the applicant's belief that—

> (A) the target of the physical search is a foreign power or an agent of a foreign power;
>
> (B) the premises or property to be searched contains foreign intelligence information; and
>
> (C) the premises or property to be searched is or is about to be owned, used, possessed by, or is in transit to or from a foreign power or an agent of a foreign power;

(4) a statement of the proposed minimization procedures;

(5) a statement of the nature of the foreign intelligence sought and the manner in which the physical search is to be conducted;

(6) a certification or certifications by the Assistant to the President for National Security Affairs, an executive branch official or officials designated by the President from among those executive branch officers employed in the area of national security or defense and appointed by the President, by and with the advice and consent of the Senate, or the Deputy Director of the Federal Bureau of Investigation, if designated by the President as a certifying official—

> (A) that the certifying official deems the information sought to be foreign intelligence information;
>
> (B) that a significant purpose of the search is to obtain foreign intelligence information;
>
> (C) that such information cannot reasonably be obtained by normal investigative techniques;
>
> (D) that designates the type of foreign intelligence information being sought according to the categories described in section 101(e); and
>
> (E) includes a statement explaining the basis for the certifications required by subparagraphs (C) and (D);

(7) where the physical search involves a search of the residence of a United States person, the Attorney General shall state what investigative techniques have previously been utilized to obtain the foreign intelligence information concerned and the degree to which these techniques resulted in acquiring such information; and

(8) a statement of the facts concerning all previous applications that have been made to any judge under this title involving any of the persons, premises, or property specified in the application, and the action taken on each previous application.

(b) The Attorney General may require any other affidavit or certification from any other officer in connection with the application.

(c) The judge may require the applicant to furnish such other information as may be necessary to make the determinations required by section 304.

(d)(1)(A) Upon written request of the Director of the Federal Bureau of Investigation, the Secretary of Defense, the Secretary of State, or the Director of National Intelligence, the Attorney General shall personally review under subsection (a) an application under that subsection for a target described in section 101(b)(2).

(B) Except when disabled or otherwise unavailable to make a request referred to in subparagraph (A), an official referred to in that subparagraph may not delegate the authority to make a request referred to in that subparagraph.

(C) Each official referred to in subparagraph (A) with authority to make a request under that subparagraph shall take appropriate actions in advance to ensure that delegation of such authority is clearly established in the event such official is disabled or otherwise unavailable to make such request.

(2)(A) If as a result of a request under paragraph (1) the Attorney General determines not to approve an application under the second sentence of subsection (a) for purposes of making the application under this section, the Attorney General shall provide written notice of the determination to the official making the request for the review of the application under that paragraph. Except when disabled or otherwise unavailable to make a determination under the preceding sentence, the Attorney General may not delegate the responsibility to make a determination under that sentence. The Attorney General shall take appropriate actions in advance to ensure that delegation of such responsibility is clearly established in the event the Attorney General is disabled or otherwise unavailable to make such determination.

(B) Notice with respect to an application under subparagraph (A) shall set forth the modifications, if any, of the application that are necessary in order for the Attorney General to approve the application under the second sentence of subsection (a) for purposes of making the application under this section.

(C) Upon review of any modifications of an application set forth under subparagraph (B), the official notified of the modifications under this paragraph shall modify the application if such official determines that such modification is warranted. Such official shall supervise the making of any modification under this subparagraph. Except when disabled or otherwise unavailable to supervise the making of any modification under the preceding sentence, such official may not delegate the responsibility to supervise the making of any modification under that preceding sentence. Each such official shall take appropriate actions in advance to ensure that delegation of such responsibility is clearly established in the event such official is disabled or otherwise unavailable to supervise the making of such modification.

ISSUANCE OF AN ORDER

SEC. 304. [50 U.S.C. §§1824]
(a) Upon an application made pursuant to section 303, the judge shall enter an ex parte order as requested or as modified approving the physical search if the judge finds that—

(1) the application has been made by a Federal officer and approved by the Attorney General;

(2) on the basis of the facts submitted by the applicant there is probable cause to believe that—

(A) the target of the physical search is a foreign power or an agent of a foreign power, except that no United States person may be considered an agent of a foreign power solely upon the basis of activities protected by the first amendment to the Constitution of the United States; and

(B) the premises or property to be searched is or is about to be owned, used, possessed by, or is in transit to or from an agent of a foreign power or a foreign power;

(3) the proposed minimization procedures meet the definition of minimization contained in this title; and

(4) the application which has been filed contains all statements and certifications required by section 303, and, if the target is a United States person, the certification or certifications are not clearly erroneous on the basis of the statement made under section 303(a)(6)(E) and any other information furnished under section 303(c).

(b) In determining whether or not probable cause exists for purposes of an order under subsection (a)(2), a judge may consider past activities of the target, as well as facts and circumstances relating to current or future activities of the target.
(c) An order approving a physical search under this section shall—

(1) specify—

(A) the identity, if known, or a description of the target of the physical search;

(B) the nature and location of each of the premises or property to be searched;

(C) the type of information, material, or property to be seized, altered, or reproduced;

(D) a statement of the manner in which the physical search is to be conducted and, whenever more than one physical search is authorized under the order, the authorized scope of each search and what minimization procedures shall apply to the information acquired by each search; and

(E) the period of time during which physical searches are approved; and

(2) direct—

(A) that the minimization procedures be followed;

(B) that, upon the request of the applicant, a specified landlord, custodian, or other specified person furnish the applicant forthwith all information, facilities, or assistance necessary to accomplish the physical search in such a manner as will protect its secrecy and produce a minimum of interference with the services that such landlord, custodian, or other person is providing the target of the physical search;

(C) that such landlord, custodian, or other person maintain under security procedures approved by the Attorney General and the Director of National Intelligence any records concerning the search or the aid furnished that such person wishes to retain;

(D) that the applicant compensate, at the prevailing rate, such landlord, custodian, or other person for furnishing such aid; and

(E) that the Federal officer conducting the physical search promptly report to the court the circumstances and results of the physical search.

(d)(1) An order issued under this section may approve a physical search for the period necessary to achieve its purpose, or for 90 days, whichever is less, except that

(A) an order under this section shall approve a physical search targeted against a foreign power, as defined in paragraph (1), (2), or (3) of section 101(a), for the period specified in the application or for one year, whichever is less, and

(B) an order under this section for a physical search targeted against an agent of a foreign power who is not a United States person may be for the period specified in the application or for 120 days, whichever is less.

(2) Extensions of an order issued under this title may be granted on the same basis as the original order upon an application for an extension and new findings made in the same manner as required for the original order, except that an extension of an order under this Act for a physical search targeted against a foreign power, as defined in paragraph (5), (6), or (7) of section 101(a), or against a foreign power, as defined in section 101(a)(4), that is not a United States person, or against an agent of a foreign power who is not a United States person, may be for a period not to exceed one year if the judge finds probable cause to believe that no property of any individual United States person will be acquired during the period.

(3) At or before the end of the period of time for which a physical search is approved by an order or an extension, or at any time after a physical search is carried out, the judge may assess compliance with the minimization procedures by reviewing the circumstances under which information concerning United States persons was acquired, retained, or disseminated.

(e)(1) Notwithstanding any other provision of this title, the Attorney General may authorize the emergency employment of a physical search if the Attorney General—

(A) reasonably determines that an emergency situation exists with respect to the employment of a physical search to obtain foreign intelligence information before an order authorizing such physical search can with due diligence be obtained;

(B) reasonably determines that the factual basis for issuance of an order under this title to approve such physical search exists;

(C) informs, either personally or through a designee, a judge of the Foreign Intelligence Surveillance Court at the time of such authorization that the decision has been made to employ an emergency physical search; and

(D) makes an application in accordance with this title to a judge of the Foreign Intelligence Surveillance Court as soon as practicable, but not more than 7 days after the Attorney General authorizes such physical search.

(2) If the Attorney General authorizes the emergency employment of a physical search under paragraph (1), the Attorney General shall require that the minimization procedures required by this title for the issuance of a judicial order be followed.

(3) In the absence of a judicial order approving such physical search, the physical search shall terminate when the information sought is obtained, when the application for the order is denied, or after the expiration of 7

days from the time of authorization by the Attorney General, whichever is earliest.

(4) A denial of the application made under this subsection may be reviewed as provided in section 103.

(5) In the event that such application for approval is denied, or in any other case where the physical search is terminated and no order is issued approving the physical search, no information obtained or evidence derived from such physical search shall be received in evidence or otherwise disclosed in any trial, hearing, or other proceeding in or before any court, grand jury, department, office, agency, regulatory body, legislative committee, or other authority of the United States, a State, or political subdivision thereof, and no information concerning any United States person acquired from such physical search shall subsequently be used or disclosed in any other manner by Federal officers or employees without the consent of such person, except with the approval of the Attorney General if the information indicates a threat of death or serious bodily harm to any person.

(6) The Attorney General shall assess compliance with the requirements of paragraph (5).

(f) Applications made and orders granted under this title shall be retained for a period of at least 10 years from the date of the application.

USE OF INFORMATION

SEC. 305. [50 U.S.C. §1825]

(a) Information acquired from a physical search conducted pursuant to this title concerning any United States person may be used and disclosed by Federal officers and employees without the consent of the United States person only in accordance with the minimization procedures required by this title. No information acquired from a physical search pursuant to this title may be used or disclosed by Federal officers or employees except for lawful purposes.

(b) Where a physical search authorized and conducted pursuant to section 304 involves the residence of a United States person, and, at any time after the search the Attorney General determines there is no national security interest in continuing to maintain the secrecy of the search, the Attorney General shall provide notice to the United States person whose residence was searched of the fact of the search conducted pursuant to this Act and shall identify any property of such person seized, altered, or reproduced during such search.

(c) No information acquired pursuant to this title shall be disclosed for law enforcement purposes unless such disclosure is accompanied by a statement that such information, or any information derived therefrom, may only be used in a criminal proceeding with the advance authorization of the Attorney General.

(d) Whenever the United States intends to enter into evidence or otherwise use or disclose in any trial, hearing, or other proceeding in or before any court, department, officer, agency, regulatory body, or other authority of the United States, against an aggrieved person, any information obtained or derived from a physical search pursuant to the authority of this Act, the United States shall, prior to the trial, hearing, or the other proceeding or at a reasonable time prior to an effort to so disclose or so use that information or submit it in evidence, notify the aggrieved person and the court or other authority in which the information is to be disclosed or used that the United States intends to so disclose or so use such information.

(e) Whenever any State or political subdivision thereof intends to enter into evidence or otherwise use or disclose in any trial, hearing, or other proceeding in or before any court, department, officer, agency, regulatory body, or other authority of a State or a political subdivision thereof against an aggrieved person any information obtained or derived from a physical search pursuant to the authority of this Act, the State or political subdivision thereof shall notify the aggrieved person, the court or other authority in which the information is to be disclosed or used, and the Attorney General that the State or political subdivision thereof intends to so disclose or so use such information.

(f)(1) Any person against whom evidence obtained or derived from a physical search to which he is an aggrieved person is to be, or has been, introduced or otherwise used or disclosed in any trial, hearing, or other proceeding in or before any court, department, officer, agency, regulatory body, or other authority of the United States, a State, or a political subdivision thereof, may move to suppress the evidence obtained or derived from such search on the grounds that—

(A) the information was unlawfully acquired; or

(B) the physical search was not made in conformity with an order of authorization or approval.

(2) Such a motion shall be made before the trial, hearing, or other proceeding unless there was no opportunity to make such a motion or the person was not aware of the grounds of the motion.

(g) Whenever a court or other authority is notified pursuant to subsection (d) or (e), or whenever a motion is made pursuant to subsection (f), or whenever any motion or request is made by an aggrieved person pursuant to any other statute or rule of the United States or any State before any court or other authority of the United States or any State to discover or obtain applications or orders or other materials relating to a physical search authorized by this title or to discover, obtain, or suppress evidence or information obtained or derived from a physical search authorized by this title, the United States district court or, where the motion is made before another authority, the United States district court in the same district as the authority shall, notwithstanding any other provision of law, if the Attorney General files an affidavit under oath that disclosure or any adversary hearing would harm the national security of the United States, review in camera and ex parte the application, order, and such other materials relating to the physical search as may be necessary to determine whether the physical search of the aggrieved person was lawfully authorized and conducted. In making this determination, the court may disclose to the aggrieved person, under appropriate security procedures and protective orders, portions of the application, order, or other materials relating to the physical search, or may require the Attorney General to provide to the aggrieved person a summary of such materials, only where such disclosure is necessary to make an accurate determination of the legality of the physical search.

(h) If the United States district court pursuant to subsection (g) determines that the physical search was not lawfully authorized or conducted, it shall, in accordance with the requirements of law, suppress the evidence which was unlawfully obtained or derived from the physical search of the aggrieved person or otherwise grant the motion of the aggrieved person. If the court determines that the physical search was lawfully authorized or conducted, it shall deny the motion of the aggrieved person except to the extent that due process requires discovery or disclosure.

(i) Orders granting motions or requests under subsection (h), decisions under this section that a physical search was not lawfully authorized or conducted, and orders of the United States district court requiring review or granting disclosure of applications, orders, or other materials relating to the physical search shall be final orders and binding upon all courts of the United States and the several States except a United States Court of Appeals or the Supreme Court.

(j)(1) If an emergency execution of a physical search is authorized under section 304(d) and a subsequent order approving the search is not obtained, the judge shall cause to be served on any United States person named in the application and on such other United States persons subject to the search as the judge may determine in his discretion it is in the interests of justice to serve, notice of—

(A) the fact of the application;

(B) the period of the search; and

(C) the fact that during the period information was or was not obtained.

(2) On an ex parte showing of good cause to the judge, the serving of the notice required by this subsection may be postponed or suspended for a period not to exceed 90 days. Thereafter, on a further ex parte showing of good cause, the court shall forego ordering the serving of the notice required under this subsection.

(k)(1) Federal officers who conduct physical searches to acquire foreign intelligence information under this title may consult with Federal law enforcement officers or law enforcement personnel of a State or political subdivision of a State (including the chief executive officer of that State or political subdivision who has the authority to appoint or direct the chief law enforcement officer of that State or political subdivision) to coordinate efforts to investigate or protect against—

(A) actual or potential attack or other grave hostile acts of a foreign power or an agent of a foreign power;

(B) sabotage, international terrorism, or the international proliferation of weapons of mass destruction by a foreign power or an agent of a foreign power; or

(C) clandestine intelligence activities by an intelligence service or network of a foreign power or by an agent of a foreign power.

(2) Coordination authorized under paragraph (1) shall not preclude the certification required by section 303(a)(6) or the entry of an order under section 304.

CONGRESSIONAL OVERSIGHT

SEC. 306. [50 U.S.C. §1826]

On a semiannual basis the Attorney General shall fully inform the Permanent Select Committee on Intelligence of the House of Representatives and the Select Committee on Intelligence of the Senate and the Committee on the Judiciary of the Senate concerning all physical searches conducted pursuant to this title. On a semiannual basis the Attorney General shall also provide to those committees and the Committee on the Judiciary of the House of Representatives a report setting forth with respect to the preceding six-month period—

(1) the total number of applications made for orders approving physical searches under this title;

(2) the total number of such orders either granted, modified, or denied;

(3) the number of physical searches which involved searches of the residences, offices, or personal property of United States persons, and the number of occasions, if any, where the Attorney General provided notice pursuant to section 305(b); and

(4) the total number of emergency physical searches authorized by the Attorney General under section 304(e) and the total number of subsequent orders approving or denying such physical searches.

PENALTIES

SEC. 307. [50 U.S.C. §1827]

(a) A person is guilty of an offense if he intentionally—

(1) under color of law for the purpose of obtaining foreign intelligence information, executes a physical search within the United States except as authorized by statute; or

(2) discloses or uses information obtained under color of law by physical search within the United States, knowing or having reason to know that the information was obtained through physical search not authorized by statute, for the purpose of obtaining intelligence information.

(b) It is a defense to a prosecution under subsection (a) that the defendant was a law enforcement or investigative officer engaged in the course of his official duties and the physical search was authorized by and conducted pursuant to a search warrant or court order of a court of competent jurisdiction.

(c) An offense described in this section is punishable by a fine of not more than $10,000 or imprisonment for not more than five years, or both.

(d) There is Federal jurisdiction over an offense under this section if the person committing the offense was an officer or employee of the United States at the time the offense was committed.

CIVIL LIABILITY

SEC. 308. [50 U.S.C. §1828]

An aggrieved person, other than a foreign power or an agent of a foreign power, as defined in section 101 (a) or (b)(1)(A), respectively, of this Act, whose premises, property, information, or material has been subjected to a physical search within the United States or about whom information obtained by such a physical search has been disclosed or used in violation of section 307 shall have a cause of action against any person who committed such violation and shall be entitled to recover—

(1) actual damages, but not less than liquidated damages of $1,000 or $100 per day for each day of violation, whichever is greater;

(2) punitive damages; and

(3) reasonable attorney's fees and other investigative and litigation costs reasonably incurred.

AUTHORIZATION DURING TIME OF WAR

SEC. 309. [50 U.S.C. §1829]

Notwithstanding any other provision of law, the President, through the Attorney General, may authorize physical searches without a court order under this title to acquire foreign intelligence information for a period not to exceed 15 calendar days following a declaration of war by the Congress.

452

TITLE IV—PEN REGISTERS AND TRAP AND TRACE DEVICES FOR FOREIGN INTELLIGENCE PURPOSES

DEFINITIONS

SEC. 401. [50 U.S.C. §1841]
As used in this title:

 (1) The terms "foreign power", "agent of a foreign power", "international terrorism", "foreign intelligence information", "Attorney General", "United States person", "United States", "person", and "State" shall have the same meanings as in section 101 of this Act.

 (2) The terms "pen register" and "trap and trace device" have the meanings given such terms in section 3127 of title 18, United States Code.

 (3) The term "aggrieved person" means any person—

  (A) whose telephone line was subject to the installation or use of a pen register or trap and trace device authorized by this title; or

  (B) whose communication instrument or device was subject to the use of a pen register or trap and trace device authorized by this title to capture incoming electronic or other communications impulses.

PEN REGISTERS AND TRAP AND TRACE DEVICES FOR FOREIGN INTELLIGENCE AND INTERNATIONAL TERRORISM INVESTIGATIONS

SEC. 402. [50 U.S.C. §1842]
(a)(1) Notwithstanding any other provision of law, the Attorney General or a designated attorney for the Government may make an application for an order or an extension of an order authorizing or approving the installation and use of a pen register or trap and trace device for any investigation to obtain foreign intelligence information not concerning a United States person or to protect against international terrorism or clandestine intelligence activities, provided that such investigation of a United States person is not conducted solely upon the basis of activities protected by the first amendment to the Constitution which is being conducted by the Federal Bureau of Investigation under such guidelines as the Attorney General approves pursuant to Executive Order No. 12333, or a successor order.

 (2) The authority under paragraph (1) is in addition to the authority under title I of this Act to conduct the electronic surveillance referred to in that paragraph.

(b) Each application under this section shall be in writing under oath or affirmation to—

(1) a judge of the court established by section 103(a) of this Act; or

(2) a United States Magistrate Judge under chapter 43 of title 28, United States Code, who is publicly designated by the Chief Justice of the United States to have the power to hear applications for and grant orders approving the installation and use of a pen register or trap and trace device on behalf of a judge of that court.

(c) Each application under this section shall require the approval of the Attorney General, or a designated attorney for the Government, and shall include—

(1) the identity of the Federal officer seeking to use the pen register or trap and trace device covered by the application; and

(2) a certification by the applicant that the information likely to be obtained is foreign intelligence information not concerning a United States person or is relevant to an ongoing investigation to protect against international terrorism or clandestine intelligence activities, provided that such investigation of a United States person is not conducted solely upon the basis of activities protected by the first amendment to the Constitution.

(d)(1) Upon an application made pursuant to this section, the judge shall enter an ex parte order as requested, or as modified, approving the installation and use of a pen register or trap and trace device if the judge finds that the application satisfies the requirements of this section.

(2) An order issued under this section—

(A) shall specify—

(i) the identity, if known, of the person who is the subject of the investigation;

(ii) the identity, if known, of the person to whom is leased or in whose name is listed the telephone line or other facility to which the pen register or trap and trace device is to be attached or applied;

(iii) the attributes of the communications to which the order applies, such as the number or other identifier, and, if known, the location of the telephone line or other facility to which the pen register or trap and trace device is to be attached or applied and, in the case of a trap and trace device, the geographic limits of the trap and trace order;

(B) shall direct that—

(i) upon request of the applicant, the provider of a wire or electronic communication service, landlord, custodian, or other person shall furnish any information, facilities, or technical assistance necessary to accomplish the installation and operation of the pen register or trap

454

and trace device in such a manner as will protect its secrecy and produce a minimum amount of interference with the services that such provider, landlord, custodian, or other person is providing the person concerned;

(ii) such provider, landlord, custodian, or other person—

(I) shall not disclose the existence of the investigation or of the pen register or trap and trace device to any person unless or until ordered by the court; and

(II) shall maintain, under security procedures approved by the Attorney General and the Director of National Intelligence pursuant to section 105(b)(2)(C) of this Act, any records concerning the pen register or trap and trace device or the aid furnished; and

(iii) the applicant shall compensate such provider, landlord, custodian, or other person for reasonable expenses incurred by such provider, landlord, custodian, or other person in providing such information, facilities, or technical assistance; and

(C) shall direct that, upon the request of the applicant, the provider of a wire or electronic communication service shall disclose to the Federal officer using the pen register or trap and trace device covered by the order—

(i) in the case of the customer or subscriber using the service covered by the order (for the period specified by the order)—

(I) the name of the customer or subscriber;

(II) the address of the customer or subscriber;

(III) the telephone or instrument number, or other subscriber number or identifier, of the customer or subscriber, including any temporarily assigned network address or associated routing or transmission information;

(IV) the length of the provision of service by such provider to the customer or subscriber and the types of services utilized by the customer or subscriber;

(V) in the case of a provider of local or long distance telephone service, any local or long distance telephone records of the customer or subscriber;

(VI) if applicable, any records reflecting period of usage (or sessions) by the customer or subscriber; and

(VII) any mechanisms and sources of payment for such service, including the number of any credit card or bank account utilized for payment for such service; and

(ii) if available, with respect to any customer or subscriber of incoming or outgoing communications to or from the service covered by the order—

(I) the name of such customer or subscriber;

(II) the address of such customer or subscriber;

(III) the telephone or instrument number, or other subscriber number or identifier, of such customer or subscriber, including any temporarily assigned network address or associated routing or transmission information; and

(IV) the length of the provision of service by such provider to such customer or subscriber and the types of services utilized by such customer or subscriber.

(e)(1) Except as provided in paragraph (2), an order issued under this section shall authorize the installation and use of a pen register or trap and trace device for a period not to exceed 90 days. Extensions of such an order may be granted, but only upon an application for an order under this section and upon the judicial finding required by subsection (d). The period of extension shall be for a period not to exceed 90 days.

(2) In the case of an application under subsection (c) where the applicant has certified that the information likely to be obtained is foreign intelligence information not concerning a United States person, an order, or an extension of an order, under the section may be for a period not to exceed one year.

(f) No cause of action shall lie in any court against any provider of a wire or electronic communication service, landlord, custodian, or other person (including any officer, employee, agent, or other specified person thereof) that furnishes any information, facilities, or technical assistance under subsection (d) in accordance with the terms of an order issued under this section.

(g) Unless otherwise ordered by the judge, the results of a pen register or trap and trace device shall be furnished at reasonable intervals during regular business hours for the duration of the order to the authorized Government official or officials.

AUTHORIZATION DURING EMERGENCIES

SEC. 403. [50 U.S.C. §1843]

(a) Notwithstanding any other provision of this Act, when the Attorney General makes a determination described in subsection (b), the Attorney General may authorize the installation and use of a pen register or trap and trace device on an emergency basis to gather foreign intelligence information not concerning a United States person or information to protect against international terrorism or clandestine intelligence activities, provided that such investigation of a United States person is not conducted solely upon the basis of activities protected by the first amendment to the Constitution if—

(1) a judge referred to in section 402(b) of this Act is informed by the Attorney General or his designee at the time of such authorization that the decision has been made to install and use the pen register or trap and trace device, as the case may be, on an emergency basis; and

(2) an application in accordance with section 402 of this Act is made to such judge as soon as practicable, but not more than 7 days, after the Attorney General authorizes the installation and use of the pen register or trap and trace device, as the case may be, under this section.

(b) A determination under this subsection is a reasonable determination by the Attorney General that—

(1) an emergency requires the installation and use of a pen register or trap and trace device to obtain foreign intelligence information not concerning a United States person or information to protect against international terrorism or clandestine intelligence activities, provided that such investigation of a United States person is not conducted solely upon the basis of activities protected by the first amendment to the Constitution before an order authorizing the installation and use of the pen register or trap and trace device, as the case may be, can with due diligence be obtained under section 402 of this Act; and

(2) the factual basis for issuance of an order under such section 402 to approve the installation and use of the pen register or trap and trace device, as the case may be, exists.

(c)(1) In the absence of an order applied for under subsection (a)(2) approving the installation and use of a pen register or trap and trace device authorized under this section, the installation and use of the pen register or trap and trace device, as the case may be, shall terminate at the earlier of—

(A) when the information sought is obtained;

(B) when the application for the order is denied under section 402 of this Act; or

(C) 7 days after the time of the authorization by the Attorney General.

(2) In the event that an application for an order applied for under subsection (a)(2) is denied, or in any other case where the installation and use of a pen register or trap and trace device under this section is terminated and no order under section 402 of this Act is issued approving the installation and use of the pen register or trap and trace device, as the case may be, no information obtained or evidence derived from the use of the pen register or trap and trace device, as the case may be, shall be received in evidence or otherwise disclosed in any trial, hearing, or other proceeding in or before any court, grand jury, department, office, agency, regulatory body, legislative committee, or other authority of the United States, a State, or political subdivision thereof, and no information concerning any United States person acquired from the use of the pen register or trap and trace device, as the case may be, shall subsequently be used or disclosed in any other manner by Federal officers or employees without the consent of such person, except with the approval of the Attorney General if the information indicates a threat of death or serious bodily harm to any person.

AUTHORIZATION DURING TIME OF WAR

SEC. 404. [50 U.S.C. §1844]
Notwithstanding any other provision of law, the President, through the Attorney General, may authorize the use of a pen register or trap and trace device without a court order under this title to acquire foreign intelligence information for a period not to exceed 15 calendar days following a declaration of war by Congress.

USE OF INFORMATION

SEC. 405. [50 U.S.C. §1845]
(a)(1) Information acquired from the use of a pen register or trap and trace device installed pursuant to this title concerning any United States person may be used and disclosed by Federal officers and employees without the consent of the United States person only in accordance with the provisions of this section.

(2) No information acquired from a pen register or trap and trace device installed and used pursuant to this title may be used or disclosed by Federal officers or employees except for lawful purposes.

(b) No information acquired pursuant to this title shall be disclosed for law enforcement purposes unless such disclosure is accompanied by a statement that such information, or any information derived therefrom, may only be used in a criminal proceeding with the advance authorization of the Attorney General.

(c) Whenever the United States intends to enter into evidence or otherwise use or disclose in any trial, hearing, or other proceeding in or before any court, department, officer, agency, regulatory body, or other authority of the United States against an aggrieved person any information obtained or derived from the use of a pen register or trap and trace device pursuant to this title, the United States shall, before the trial, hearing, or the other proceeding or at a reasonable time before an effort to so disclose or so use that information or submit it in evidence, notify the aggrieved person and the court or other authority in which the information is to be disclosed or used that the United States intends to so disclose or so use such information.

(d) Whenever any State or political subdivision thereof intends to enter into evidence or otherwise use or disclose in any trial, hearing, or other proceeding in or before any court, department, officer, agency, regulatory body, or other authority of the State or political subdivision thereof against an aggrieved person any information obtained or derived from the use of a pen register or trap and trace device pursuant to this title, the State or political subdivision thereof shall notify the aggrieved person, the court or other authority in which the information is to be disclosed or used, and the Attorney General that the State or political subdivision thereof intends to so disclose or so use such information.

(e)(1) Any aggrieved person against whom evidence obtained or derived from the use of a pen register or trap and trace device is to be, or has been, introduced or otherwise used or disclosed in any trial, hearing, or other proceeding in or before any court, department, officer, agency, regulatory body, or other authority of the United States, or a State or political subdivision thereof, may move to suppress the evidence obtained or derived from the use of the pen register or trap and trace device, as the case may be, on the grounds that—

    (A) the information was unlawfully acquired; or

    (B) the use of the pen register or trap and trace device, as the case may be, was not made in conformity with an order of authorization or approval under this title.

(2) A motion under paragraph (1) shall be made before the trial, hearing, or other proceeding unless there was no opportunity to make such a motion or the aggrieved person concerned was not aware of the grounds of the motion.

(f)(1) Whenever a court or other authority is notified pursuant to subsection (c) or (d), whenever a motion is made pursuant to subsection (e), or whenever any motion or request is made by an aggrieved person pursuant to any other statute or rule of the United States or any State before any court or other authority of the United States or any State to discover or obtain applications or orders or other materials relating to the use of a pen register or trap and trace device authorized by this title or to discover, obtain, or suppress evidence or information obtained or derived from the use of a pen register or trap and trace device authorized by this title, the United States district court or, where the motion is made before another authority, the United States district court in the same district as the authority shall, notwithstanding any other provision of law and if the Attorney General files an affidavit under oath that disclosure or any adversary hearing would harm the national security of the United States, review in camera and ex parte the application, order, and such other materials relating to the use of the pen register or trap and trace device, as the case may be, as may be necessary to determine whether the use of the pen register or trap and trace device, as the case may be, was lawfully authorized and conducted.

> (2) In making a determination under paragraph (1), the court may disclose to the aggrieved person, under appropriate security procedures and protective orders, portions of the application, order, or other materials relating to the use of the pen register or trap and trace device, as the case may be, or may require the Attorney General to provide to the aggrieved person a summary of such materials, only where such disclosure is necessary to make an accurate determination of the legality of the use of the pen register or trap and trace device, as the case may be.

(g)(1) If the United States district court determines pursuant to subsection (f) that the use of a pen register or trap and trace device was not lawfully authorized or conducted, the court may, in accordance with the requirements of law, suppress the evidence which was unlawfully obtained or derived from the use of the pen register or trap and trace device, as the case may be, or otherwise grant the motion of the aggrieved person.

> (2) If the court determines that the use of the pen register or trap and trace device, as the case may be, was lawfully authorized or conducted, it may deny the motion of the aggrieved person except to the extent that due process requires discovery or disclosure.

(h) Orders granting motions or requests under subsection (g), decisions under this section that the use of a pen register or trap and trace device was not lawfully authorized or conducted, and orders of the United States district court requiring review or granting disclosure of applications, orders, or other materials relating to the installation and use of a pen register or trap and trace device shall be final orders and binding upon all courts of the United States and the several States except a United States Court of Appeals or the Supreme Court.

CONGRESSIONAL OVERSIGHT

SEC. 406. [50 U.S.C. §1846]
(a) On a semiannual basis, the Attorney General shall fully inform the Permanent Select Committee on Intelligence of the House of Representatives and the Select

Committee on Intelligence of the Senate and the Committee on the Judiciary of the House of Representatives and the Committee on the Judiciary of the Senate concerning all uses of pen registers and trap and trace devices pursuant to this title.

(b) On a semiannual basis, the Attorney General shall also provide to the committees referred to in subsection (a) and to the Committees on the Judiciary of the House of Representatives and the Senate a report setting forth with respect to the preceding 6-month period—

> (1) the total number of applications made for orders approving the use of pen registers or trap and trace devices under this title;
>
> (2) the total number of such orders either granted, modified, or denied; and
>
> (3) the total number of pen registers and trap and trace devices whose installation and use was authorized by the Attorney General on an emergency basis under section 403, and the total number of subsequent orders approving or denying the installation and use of such pen registers and trap and trace devices.

TITLE V—ACCESS TO CERTAIN BUSINESS RECORDS FOR FOREIGN INTELLIGENCE PURPOSES

ACCESS TO CERTAIN BUSINESS RECORDS FOR FOREIGN INTELLIGENCE AND INTERNATIONAL TERRORISM INVESTIGATIONS

SEC. 501. [50 U.S.C. §1861]

> (a)(1) Subject to paragraph (3), the Director of the Federal Bureau of Investigation or a designee of the Director (whose rank shall be no lower than Assistant Special Agent in Charge) may make an application for an order requiring the production of any tangible things (including books, records, papers, documents, and other items) for an investigation to obtain foreign intelligence information not concerning a United States person or to protect against international terrorism or clandestine intelligence activities, provided that such investigation of a United States person is not conducted solely upon the basis of activities protected by the first amendment to the Constitution.
>
> (2) An investigation conducted under this section shall
>
> > (A) be conducted under guidelines approved by the Attorney General under Executive Order 12333 (or a successor order); and
> >
> > (B) not be conducted of a United States person solely upon the basis of activities protected by the first amendment to the Constitution of the United States.

(3) In the case of an application for an order requiring the production of library circulation records, library patron lists, book sales records, book customer lists, firearms sales records, tax return records, educational records, or medical records containing information that would identify a person, the Director of the Federal Bureau of Investigation may delegate the authority to make such application to either the Deputy Director of the Federal Bureau of Investigation or the Executive Assistant Director for National Security (or any successor position). The Deputy Director or the Executive Assistant Director may not further delegate such authority.

(b) Each application under this section

    (1) shall be made to—

        (A) a judge of the court established by section 103(a) of this Act; or

        (B) a United States Magistrate Judge under chapter 43 of Title 28, who is publicly designated by the Chief Justice of the United States to have the power to hear applications and grant orders for the production of tangible things under this section on behalf of a judge of that court; and

    (2) shall include—

        (A) a statement of facts showing that there are reasonable grounds to believe that the tangible things sought are relevant to an authorized investigation (other than a threat assessment) conducted in accordance with subsection (a)(2) of this section to obtain foreign intelligence information not concerning a United States person or to protect against international terrorism or clandestine intelligence activities, such things being presumptively relevant to an authorized investigation if the applicant shows in the statement of the facts that they pertain to—

            (i) a foreign power or an agent of a foreign power;

            (ii) the activities of a suspected agent of a foreign power who is the subject of such authorized investigation; or

            (iii) an individual in contact with, or known to, a suspected agent of a foreign power who is the subject of such authorized investigation; and

        (B) an enumeration of the minimization procedures adopted by the Attorney General under subsection (g) of this section that are applicable to the retention and dissemination by the Federal Bureau of Investigation of any tangible things to be made available to the Federal Bureau of Investigation based on the order requested in such application.

(c)(1) Upon an application made pursuant to this section, if the judge finds that the application meets the requirements of subsections (a) and (b) of this section, the judge shall enter an ex parte order as requested, or as modified, approving the release of tangible things. Such order shall direct that minimization procedures adopted pursuant to subsection (g) of this section be followed.

(2) An order under this subsection—

(A) shall describe the tangible things that are ordered to be produced with sufficient particularity to permit them to be fairly identified;

(B) shall include the date on which the tangible things must be provided, which shall allow a reasonable period of time within which the tangible things can be assembled and made available;

(C) shall provide clear and conspicuous notice of the principles and procedures described in subsection (d) of this section;

(D) may only require the production of a tangible thing if such thing can be obtained with a subpoena duces tecum issued by a court of the United States in aid of a grand jury investigation or with any other order issued by a court of the United States directing the production of records or tangible things; and

(E) shall not disclose that such order is issued for purposes of an investigation described in subsection (a) of this section.

(d)(1) No person shall disclose to any other person that the Federal bureau of investigation has sought or obtained tangible things pursuant to an order under this section, other than to

(A) those persons to whom disclosure is necessary to comply with such order;

(B) an attorney to obtain legal advice or assistance with respect to the production of things in response to the order; or

(C) other persons as permitted by the Director of the Federal Bureau of Investigation or the designee of the Director.

(2)(A) A person to whom disclosure is made pursuant to paragraph (1) shall be subject to the nondisclosure requirements applicable to a person to whom an order is directed under this section in the same manner as such person.

(B) Any person who discloses to a person described in subparagraph (A), (B), or (C) of paragraph (1) that the Federal Bureau of Investigation has sought or obtained tangible things pursuant to an order under this section shall notify such person of the nondisclosure requirements of this subsection.

(C) At the request of the Director of the Federal Bureau of Investigation or the designee of the Director, any person making or intending to make a disclosure under subparagraph (A) or (C) of paragraph (1) shall identify to the Director or such designee the person to whom such disclosure will be made or to whom such disclosure was made prior to the request.

(e) A person who, in good faith, produces tangible things under an order pursuant to this section shall not be liable to any other person for such production. Such production shall not be deemed to constitute a waiver of any privilege in any other proceeding or context.

(f) [JUDICIAL REVIEW OF FISA ORDERS .—]

(1) In this subsection—

(A) the term "production order" means an order to produce any tangible thing under this section; and

(B) the term "nondisclosure order" means an order imposed under subsection (d) of this section.

(2)(A)(i) A person receiving a production order may challenge the legality of that order by filing a petition with the pool established by section 103(e)(1) of this Act. Not less than 1 year after the date of the issuance of the production order, the recipient of a production order may challenge the nondisclosure order imposed in connection with such production order by filing a petition to modify or set aside such nondisclosure order, consistent with the requirements of subparagraph (C), with the pool established by 103(e)(1) of this Act.

(ii) The presiding judge shall immediately assign a petition under clause (i) to 1 of the judges serving in the pool established by 103(e)(1) of this Act. Not later than 72 hours after the assignment of such petition, the assigned judge shall conduct an initial review of the petition. If the assigned judge determines that the petition is frivolous, the assigned judge shall immediately deny the petition and affirm the production order or nondisclosure order. If the assigned judge determines the petition is not frivolous, the assigned judge shall promptly consider the petition in accordance with the procedures established under 103(e)(2) of this Act.

(iii) The assigned judge shall promptly provide a written statement for the record of the reasons for any determination under this subsection. Upon the request of the Government, any order setting aside a nondisclosure order shall be stayed pending review pursuant to paragraph (3).

(B) A judge considering a petition to modify or set aside a production order may grant such petition only if the judge finds

464

that such order does not meet the requirements of this section or is otherwise unlawful. If the judge does not modify or set aside the production order, the judge shall immediately affirm such order, and order the recipient to comply therewith.

(C)(i) A judge considering a petition to modify or set aside a nondisclosure order may grant such petition only if the judge finds that there is no reason to believe that disclosure may endanger the national security of the United States, interfere with a criminal, counterterrorism, or counterintelligence investigation, interfere with diplomatic relations, or endanger the life or physical safety of any person.

    (ii) If, upon filing of such a petition, the Attorney General, Deputy Attorney General, an Assistant Attorney General, or the Director of the Federal Bureau of Investigation certifies that disclosure may endanger the national security of the United States or interfere with diplomatic relations, such certification shall be treated as conclusive, unless the judge finds that the certification was made in bad faith.

    (iii) If the judge denies a petition to modify or set aside a nondisclosure order, the recipient of such order shall be precluded for a period of 1 year from filing another such petition with respect to such nondisclosure order.

(D) Any production or nondisclosure order not explicitly modified or set aside consistent with this subsection shall remain in full effect.

(3) A petition for review of a decision under paragraph (2) to affirm, modify, or set aside an order by the Government or any person receiving such order shall be made to the court of review established under 103(b) of this Act, which shall have jurisdiction to consider such petitions. The court of review shall provide for the record a written statement of the reasons for its decision and, on petition by the Government or any person receiving such order for writ of certiorari, the record shall be transmitted under seal to the Supreme Court of the United States, which shall have jurisdiction to review such decision.

(4) Judicial proceedings under this subsection shall be concluded as expeditiously as possible. The record of proceedings, including petitions filed, orders granted, and statements of reasons for decision, shall be maintained under security measures established by the Chief Justice of the United States, in consultation with the Attorney General and the Director of National Intelligence.

(5) All petitions under this subsection shall be filed under seal. In any proceedings under this subsection, the court shall, upon request of the Government, review ex parte and in camera any Government submission, or portions thereof, which may include classified information.

(g) MINIMIZATION PROCEDURES.—

(1) IN GENERAL.—Not later than 180 days after March 9, 2006, the Attorney General shall adopt specific minimization procedures governing the retention and dissemination by the Federal Bureau of Investigation of any tangible things, or information therein, received by the Federal Bureau of Investigation in response to an order under this subchapter.

(2) DEFINED.—In this section, the term "minimization procedures" means—

(A) specific procedures that are reasonably designed in light of the purpose and technique of an order for the production of tangible things, to minimize the retention, and prohibit the dissemination, of nonpublicly available information concerning unconsenting United States persons consistent with the need of the United States to obtain, produce, and disseminate foreign intelligence information;

(B) procedures that require that nonpublicly available information, which is not foreign intelligence information, as defined in 103(e)(1) of this Act, shall not be disseminated in a manner that identifies any United States person, without such person's consent, unless such person's identity is necessary to understand foreign intelligence information or assess its importance; and

(C) notwithstanding subparagraphs (A) and (B), procedures that allow for the retention and dissemination of information that is evidence of a crime which has been, is being, or is about to be committed and that is to be retained or disseminated for law enforcement purposes.

(h) USE OF INFORMATION.—Information acquired from tangible things received by the Federal Bureau of Investigation in response to an order under this subchapter concerning any United States person may be used and disclosed by Federal officers and employees without the consent of the United States person only in accordance with the minimization procedures adopted pursuant to subsection (g) of this section. No otherwise privileged information acquired from tangible things received by the Federal Bureau of Investigation in accordance with the provisions of this subchapter shall lose its privileged character. No information acquired from tangible things received by the Federal Bureau of

Investigation in response to an order under this subchapter may be used or disclosed by Federal officers or employees except for lawful purposes.

CONGRESSIONAL OVERSIGHT

SEC. 502. [50 U.S.C. §1862]

(a) On an annual basis, the Attorney General shall fully inform the Permanent Select Committee on Intelligence of the House of Representatives and the Select Committee on Intelligence and the Committee on the Judiciary of the Senate concerning all requests for the production of tangible things under section 501 of this Act.

(b) In April of each year, the Attorney General shall submit to the House and Senate Committees on the Judiciary and the House Permanent Select Committee on Intelligence and the Senate Select Committee on Intelligence a report setting forth with respect to the preceding calendar year—

> (1) the total number of applications made for orders approving requests for the production of tangible things under section 501 of this Act;
>
> (2) the total number of such orders either granted, modified, or denied; and
>
> (3) the number of such orders either granted, modified, or denied for the production of each of the following:
>
>> (A) Library circulation records, library patron lists, book sales records, or book customer lists.
>>
>> (B) Firearms sales records.
>>
>> (C) Tax return records.
>>
>> (D) Educational records.
>>
>> (E) Medical records containing information that would identify a person.

(c)(1) In April of each year, the Attorney General shall submit to Congress a report setting forth with respect to the preceding year—

>> (A) the total number of applications made for orders approving requests for the production of tangible things under section 501 of this Act; and
>>
>> (B) the total number of such orders either granted, modified, or denied.

> (2) Each report under this subsection shall be submitted in unclassified form.

TITLE VI—REPORTING REQUIREMENT

SEMIANNUAL REPORT OF THE ATTORNEY GENERAL

SEC. 601. [50 U.S.C. §1871]

(a) REPORT.—On a semiannual basis, the Attorney General shall submit to the Permanent Select Committee on Intelligence of the House of Representatives, the Select Committee on Intelligence of the Senate, and the Committees on the Judiciary of the House of Representatives and the Senate, in a manner consistent with the protection of the national security, a report setting forth with respect to the preceding 6-month period—

> (1) the aggregate number of persons targeted for orders issued under this Act, including a breakdown of those targeted for—
>> (A) electronic surveillance under section 105;
>> (B) physical searches under section 304;
>> (C) pen registers under section 402;
>> (D) access to records under section 501;
>> (E) acquisitions under section 703; and
>> (F) acquisitions under section 704;
>
> (2) the number of individuals covered by an order issued pursuant to section 101(b)(1)(C);
>
> (3) the number of times that the Attorney General has authorized that information obtained under this Act may be used in a criminal proceeding or any information derived therefrom may be used in a criminal proceeding;
>
> (4) a summary of significant legal interpretations of this Act involving matters before the Foreign Intelligence Surveillance Court or the Foreign Intelligence Surveillance Court of Review, including interpretations presented in applications or pleadings filed with the Foreign Intelligence Surveillance Court or the Foreign Intelligence Surveillance Court of Review by the Department of Justice; and
>
> (5) copies of all decisions, orders, or opinions of the Foreign Intelligence Surveillance Court or Foreign Intelligence Surveillance Court of Review that include significant construction or interpretation of the provisions of this Act.

(b) FREQUENCY.—The first report under this section shall be submitted not later than 6 months after the date of enactment of this section. Subsequent reports under this section shall be submitted semi-annually thereafter.

(c) SUBMISSIONS TO CONGRESS.—The Attorney General shall submit to the committees of Congress referred to in subsection (a)—

> (1) a copy of any decision, order, or opinion issued by the Foreign Intelligence Surveillance Court or the Foreign Intelligence Surveillance Court of Review that includes significant construction or interpretation of any provision of this Act, and any pleadings, applications, or memoranda of law associated with such decision, order, or opinion, not later than 45 days after such decision, order, or opinion is issued; and

(2) a copy of each such decision, order, or opinion, and any pleadings, applications, or memoranda of law associated with such decision, order, or opinion, that was issued during the 5-year period ending on the date of the enactment of the FISA Amendments Act of 2008 and not previously submitted in a report under subsection (a).

(d) PROTECTION OF NATIONAL SECURITY.—The Attorney General, in consultation with the Director of National Intelligence, may authorize redactions of materials described in subsection (c) that are provided to the committees of Congress referred to in subsection (a), if such redactions are necessary to protect the national security of the United States and are limited to sensitive sources and methods information or the identities of targets.

(e) DEFINITIONS.—In this section:

(1) FOREIGN INTELLIGENCE SURVEILLANCE COURT.—The term `Foreign Intelligence Surveillance Court' means the court established under section 103(a).

(2) FOREIGN INTELLIGENCE SURVEILLANCE COURT OF REVIEW.—The term `Foreign Intelligence Surveillance Court of Review' means the court established under section 103(b).

TITLE VII—ADDITIONAL PROCEDURES REGARDING CERTAIN PERSONS OUTSIDE THE UNITED STATES

DEFINITIONS

SEC. 701. [50 U.S.C. §1881]

(a) IN GENERAL.—The terms `agent of a foreign power', `Attorney General', `contents', `electronic surveillance', `foreign intelligence information', `foreign power', `person', `United States', and `United States person' have the meanings given such terms in section 101, except as specifically provided in this title.

(b) ADDITIONAL DEFINITIONS.—

(1) CONGRESSIONAL INTELLIGENCE COMMITTEES.—The term `congressional intelligence committees' means—

(A) the Select Committee on Intelligence of the Senate; and

(B) the Permanent Select Committee on Intelligence of the House of Representatives.

(2) FOREIGN INTELLIGENCE SURVEILLANCE COURT.—The terms `Foreign Intelligence Surveillance Court' and `Court' mean the court established under section 103(a).

(3) FOREIGN INTELLIGENCE SURVEILLANCE COURT OF REVIEW; COURT OF REVIEW.—The terms `Foreign Intelligence Surveillance Court of Review' and `Court of Review' mean the court established under section 103(b).

(4) ELECTRONIC COMMUNICATION SERVICE PROVIDER.—The term `electronic communication service provider' means—

(A) a telecommunications carrier, as that term is defined in section 3 of the Communications Act of 1934 (47 U.S.C. 153);

(B) a provider of electronic communication service, as that term is defined in section 2510 of title 18, United States Code;

(C) a provider of a remote computing service, as that term is defined in section 2711 of title 18, United States Code;

(D) any other communication service provider who has access to wire or electronic communications either as such communications are transmitted or as such communications are stored; or

(E) an officer, employee, or agent of an entity described in subparagraph (A), (B), (C), or (D).

(5) INTELLIGENCE COMMUNITY.—The term `intelligence community' has the meaning given the term in section 3(4) of the National Security Act of 1947 (50 U.S.C. 401a(4)).

PROCEDURES FOR TARGETING CERTAIN PERSONS OUTSIDE THE UNITED STATES OTHER THAN UNITED STATES PERSONS

SEC. 702. [50 U.S.C. §1881a]

(a) AUTHORIZATION.—Notwithstanding any other provision of law, upon the issuance of an order in accordance with subsection (i)(3) or a determination under subsection (c)(2), the Attorney General and the Director of National Intelligence may authorize jointly, for a period of up to 1 year from the effective date of the authorization, the targeting of persons reasonably believed to be located outside the United States to acquire foreign intelligence information.

(b) LIMITATIONS.—An acquisition authorized under subsection (a)—

(1) may not intentionally target any person known at the time of acquisition to be located in the United States;

(2) may not intentionally target a person reasonably believed to be located outside the United States if the purpose of such acquisition is to target a particular, known person reasonably believed to be in the United States;

(3) may not intentionally target a United States person reasonably believed to be located outside the United States;

(4) may not intentionally acquire any communication as to which the sender and all intended recipients are known at the time of the acquisition to be located in the United States; and

(5) shall be conducted in a manner consistent with the fourth amendment to the Constitution of the United States.

(c) CONDUCT OF ACQUISITION.—

    (1) IN GENERAL.—An acquisition authorized under subsection (a) shall be conducted only in accordance with—

        (A) the targeting and minimization procedures adopted in accordance with subsections (d) and (e); and

        (B) upon submission of a certification in accordance with subsection (g), such certification.

    (2) DETERMINATION.—A determination under this paragraph and for purposes of subsection (a) is a determination by the Attorney General and the Director of National Intelligence that exigent circumstances exist because, without immediate implementation of an authorization under subsection (a), intelligence important to the national security of the United States may be lost or not timely acquired and time does not permit the issuance of an order pursuant to subsection (i)(3) prior to the implementation of such authorization.

    (3) TIMING OF DETERMINATION.—The Attorney General and the Director of National Intelligence may make the determination under paragraph (2)—

        (A) before the submission of a certification in accordance with subsection (g); or

        (B) by amending a certification pursuant to subsection (i)(1)(C) at any time during which judicial review under subsection (i) of such certification is pending.

    (4) CONSTRUCTION.—Nothing in title I shall be construed to require an application for a court order under such title for an acquisition that is targeted in accordance with this section at a person reasonably believed to be located outside the United States.

(d) TARGETING PROCEDURES.—

    (1) REQUIREMENT TO ADOPT.—The Attorney General, in consultation with the Director of National Intelligence, shall adopt targeting procedures that are reasonably designed to—

        (A) ensure that any acquisition authorized under subsection (a) is limited to targeting persons reasonably believed to be located outside the United States; and

        (B) prevent the intentional acquisition of any communication as to which the sender and all intended recipients are known at the time of the acquisition to be located in the United States.

    (2) JUDICIAL REVIEW.—The procedures adopted in accordance with paragraph (1) shall be subject to judicial review pursuant to subsection (i).

(e) MINIMIZATION PROCEDURES.—

471

(1) REQUIREMENT TO ADOPT.—The Attorney General, in consultation with the Director of National Intelligence, shall adopt minimization procedures that meet the definition of minimization procedures under section 101(h) or 301(4), as appropriate, for acquisitions authorized under subsection (a).

(2) JUDICIAL REVIEW.—The minimization procedures adopted in accordance with paragraph (1) shall be subject to judicial review pursuant to subsection (i).

(f) GUIDELINES FOR COMPLIANCE WITH LIMITATIONS.—

(1) REQUIREMENT TO ADOPT.—The Attorney General, in consultation with the Director of National Intelligence, shall adopt guidelines to ensure—

(A) compliance with the limitations in subsection (b); and

(B) that an application for a court order is filed as required by this Act.

(2) SUBMISSION OF GUIDELINES.—The Attorney General shall provide the guidelines adopted in accordance with paragraph (1) to—

(A) the congressional intelligence committees;

(B) the Committees on the Judiciary of the Senate and the House of Representatives; and

(C) the Foreign Intelligence Surveillance Court.

(g) CERTIFICATION.—

(1) IN GENERAL.—

(A) REQUIREMENT.—Subject to subparagraph (B), prior to the implementation of an authorization under subsection (a), the Attorney General and the Director of National Intelligence shall provide to the Foreign Intelligence Surveillance Court a written certification and any supporting affidavit, under oath and under seal, in accordance with this subsection.

(B) EXCEPTION.—If the Attorney General and the Director of National Intelligence make a determination under subsection (c)(2) and time does not permit the submission of a certification under this subsection prior to the implementation of an authorization under subsection (a), the Attorney General and the Director of National Intelligence shall submit to the Court a certification for such authorization as soon as practicable but in no event later than 7 days after such determination is made.

(2) REQUIREMENTS.—A certification made under this subsection shall—

(A) attest that—

(i) there are procedures in place that have been approved, have been submitted for approval, or will be submitted with the certification for approval by the

472

Foreign Intelligence Surveillance Court that are reasonably designed to—

(I) ensure that an acquisition authorized under subsection (a) is limited to targeting persons reasonably believed to be located outside the United States; and

(II) prevent the intentional acquisition of any communication as to which the sender and all intended recipients are known at the time of the acquisition to be located in the United States;

(ii) the minimization procedures to be used with respect to such acquisition—

(I) meet the definition of minimization procedures under section 101(h) or 301(4), as appropriate; and

(II) have been approved, have been submitted for approval, or will be submitted with the certification for approval by the Foreign Intelligence Surveillance Court;

(iii) guidelines have been adopted in accordance with subsection (f) to ensure compliance with the limitations in subsection (b) and to ensure that an application for a court order is filed as required by this Act;

(iv) the procedures and guidelines referred to in clauses (i), (ii), and (iii) are consistent with the requirements of the fourth amendment to the Constitution of the United States;

(v) a significant purpose of the acquisition is to obtain foreign intelligence information;

(vi) the acquisition involves obtaining foreign intelligence information from or with the assistance of an electronic communication service provider; and

(vii) the acquisition complies with the limitations in subsection (b);

(B) include the procedures adopted in accordance with subsections (d) and (e);

(C) be supported, as appropriate, by the affidavit of any appropriate official in the area of national security who is—

(i) appointed by the President, by and with the advice and consent of the Senate; or

(ii) the head of an element of the intelligence community;

    (D) include—
        (i) an effective date for the authorization that is at least
      30 days after the submission of the written certification
      to the court; or
        (ii) if the acquisition has begun or the effective date is
      less than 30 days after the submission of the written
      certification to the court, the date the acquisition began
      or the effective date for the acquisition; and
   (E) if the Attorney General and the Director of National
   Intelligence make a determination under subsection (c)(2),
   include a statement that such determination has been made.
  (3) CHANGE IN EFFECTIVE DATE.—The Attorney General and the
Director of National Intelligence may advance or delay the effective date
referred to in paragraph (2)(D) by submitting an amended certification in
accordance with subsection (i)(1)(C) to the Foreign Intelligence
Surveillance Court for review pursuant to subsection (i).
  (4) LIMITATION.—A certification made under this subsection is not
required to identify the specific facilities, places, premises, or property at
which an acquisition authorized under subsection (a) will be directed or
conducted.
  (5) MAINTENANCE OF CERTIFICATION.—The Attorney General or a
designee of the Attorney General shall maintain a copy of a certification
made under this subsection.
  (6) REVIEW.—A certification submitted in accordance with this
subsection shall be subject to judicial review pursuant to subsection (i).

(h) DIRECTIVES AND JUDICIAL REVIEW OF DIRECTIVES—
  (1) AUTHORITY.—With respect to an acquisition authorized under
subsection (a), the Attorney General and the Director of National
Intelligence may direct, in writing, an electronic communication service
provider to—
   (A) immediately provide the Government with all information,
   facilities, or assistance necessary to accomplish the acquisition in
   a manner that will protect the secrecy of the acquisition and
   produce a minimum of interference with the services that such
   electronic communication service provider is providing to the
   target of the acquisition; and
   (B) maintain under security procedures approved by the Attorney
   General and the Director of National Intelligence any records
   concerning the acquisition or the aid furnished that such
   electronic communication service provider wishes to maintain.

(2) COMPENSATION.—The Government shall compensate, at the prevailing rate, an electronic communication service provider for providing information, facilities, or assistance in accordance with a directive issued pursuant to paragraph (1).

(3) RELEASE FROM LIABILITY.—No cause of action shall lie in any court against any electronic communication service provider for providing any information, facilities, or assistance in accordance with a directive issued pursuant to paragraph (1).

(4) CHALLENGING OF DIRECTIVES.—

(A) AUTHORITY TO CHALLENGE.—An electronic communication service provider receiving a directive issued pursuant to paragraph (1) may file a petition to modify or set aside such directive with the Foreign Intelligence Surveillance Court, which shall have jurisdiction to review such petition.

(B) ASSIGNMENT.—The presiding judge of the Court shall assign a petition filed under subparagraph (A) to 1 of the judges serving in the pool established under section 103(e)(1) not later than 24 hours after the filing of such petition.

(C) STANDARDS FOR REVIEW.—A judge considering a petition filed under subparagraph (A) may grant such petition only if the judge finds that the directive does not meet the requirements of this section, or is otherwise unlawful.

(D) PROCEDURES FOR INITIAL REVIEW.—A judge shall conduct an initial review of a petition filed under subparagraph (A) not later than 5 days after being assigned such petition. If the judge determines that such petition does not consist of claims, defenses, or other legal contentions that are warranted by existing law or by a nonfrivolous argument for extending, modifying, or reversing existing law or for establishing new law, the judge shall immediately deny such petition and affirm the directive or any part of the directive that is the subject of such petition and order the recipient to comply with the directive or any part of it. Upon making a determination under this subparagraph or promptly thereafter, the judge shall provide a written statement for the record of the reasons for such determination.

(E) PROCEDURES FOR PLENARY REVIEW.—If a judge determines that a petition filed under subparagraph (A) requires plenary review, the judge shall affirm, modify, or set aside the directive that is the subject of such petition not later than 30 days after being assigned such petition. If the judge does not set aside the directive, the judge shall immediately affirm or affirm with modifications the directive, and order the recipient to comply with the directive in its entirety or as modified. The judge shall provide a written statement for the record of the reasons for a determination under this subparagraph.

(F) CONTINUED EFFECT.—Any directive not explicitly modified or set aside under this paragraph shall remain in full effect.

(G) CONTEMPT OF COURT.—Failure to obey an order issued under this paragraph may be punished by the Court as contempt of court.

(5) ENFORCEMENT OF DIRECTIVES.—

(A) ORDER TO COMPEL.—If an electronic communication service provider fails to comply with a directive issued pursuant to paragraph (1), the Attorney General may file a petition for an order to compel the electronic communication service provider to comply with the directive with the Foreign Intelligence Surveillance Court, which shall have jurisdiction to review such petition.

(B) ASSIGNMENT.—The presiding judge of the Court shall assign a petition filed under subparagraph (A) to 1 of the judges serving in the pool established under section 103(e)(1) not later than 24 hours after the filing of such petition.

(C) PROCEDURES FOR REVIEW.—A judge considering a petition filed under subparagraph (A) shall, not later than 30 days after being assigned such petition, issue an order requiring the electronic communication service provider to comply with the directive or any part of it, as issued or as modified, if the judge finds that the directive meets the requirements of this section and is otherwise lawful. The judge shall provide a written statement for the record of the reasons for a determination under this paragraph.

(D) CONTEMPT OF COURT.—Failure to obey an order issued under this paragraph may be punished by the Court as contempt of court.

(E) PROCESS.—Any process under this paragraph may be served in any judicial district in which the electronic communication service provider may be found.

(6) APPEAL.—

(A) APPEAL TO THE COURT OF REVIEW.—The Government or an electronic communication service provider receiving a directive issued pursuant to paragraph (1) may file a petition with the Foreign Intelligence Surveillance Court of Review for review of a decision issued pursuant to paragraph (4) or (5). The Court of

Review shall have jurisdiction to consider such petition and shall provide a written statement for the record of the reasons for a decision under this subparagraph.

(B) CERTIORARI TO THE SUPREME COURT.—The Government or an electronic communication service provider receiving a directive issued pursuant to paragraph (1) may file a petition for a writ of certiorari for review of a decision of the Court of Review issued under subparagraph (A). The record for such review shall be transmitted under seal to the Supreme Court of the United States, which shall have jurisdiction to review such decision.

(i) JUDICIAL REVIEW OF CERTIFICATIONS AND PROCEDURES.—

(1) IN GENERAL.—

(A) REVIEW BY THE FOREIGN INTELLIGENCE SURVEILLANCE COURT.—The Foreign Intelligence Surveillance Court shall have jurisdiction to review a certification submitted in accordance with subsection (g) and the targeting and minimization procedures adopted in accordance with subsections (d) and (e), and amendments to such certification or such procedures.

(B) TIME PERIOD FOR REVIEW.—The Court shall review a certification submitted in accordance with subsection (g) and the targeting and minimization procedures adopted in accordance with subsections (d) and (e) and shall complete such review and issue an order under paragraph (3) not later than 30 days after the date on which such certification and such procedures are submitted.

(C) AMENDMENTS.—The Attorney General and the Director of National Intelligence may amend a certification submitted in accordance with subsection (g) or the targeting and minimization procedures adopted in accordance with subsections (d) and (e) as necessary at any time, including if the Court is conducting or has completed review of such certification or such procedures, and shall submit the amended certification or amended procedures to the Court not later than 7 days after amending such certification or such procedures. The Court shall review any amendment under this subparagraph under the procedures set forth in this subsection. The Attorney General and the Director of National Intelligence may authorize the use of an amended certification or amended procedures pending the Court's review of such amended certification or amended procedures.

(2) REVIEW.—The Court shall review the following:

(A) CERTIFICATION.—A certification submitted in accordance with subsection (g) to determine whether the certification contains all the required elements.

(B) TARGETING PROCEDURES.—The targeting procedures adopted in accordance with subsection (d) to assess whether the procedures are reasonably designed to—

(i) ensure that an acquisition authorized under subsection (a) is limited to targeting persons reasonably believed to be located outside the United States; and

(ii) prevent the intentional acquisition of any communication as to which the sender and all intended recipients are known at the time of the acquisition to be located in the United States.

(C) MINIMIZATION PROCEDURES.—The minimization procedures adopted in accordance with subsection (e) to assess whether such procedures meet the definition of minimization procedures under section 101(h) or section 301(4), as appropriate.

(3) ORDERS.—

(A) APPROVAL.—If the Court finds that a certification submitted in accordance with subsection (g) contains all the required elements and that the targeting and minimization procedures adopted in accordance with subsections (d) and (e) are consistent with the requirements of those subsections and with the fourth amendment to the Constitution of the United States, the Court shall enter an order approving the certification and the use, or continued use in the case of an acquisition authorized pursuant to a determination under subsection (c)(2), of the procedures for the acquisition.

(B) CORRECTION OF DEFICIENCIES.—If the Court finds that a certification submitted in accordance with subsection (g) does not contain all the required elements, or that the procedures adopted in accordance with subsections (d) and (e) are not consistent with the requirements of those subsections or the fourth amendment to the Constitution of the United States, the Court shall issue an order directing the Government to, at the Government's election and to the extent required by the Court's order—

(i) correct any deficiency identified by the Court's order not later than 30 days after the date on which the Court issues the order; or

(ii) cease, or not begin, the implementation of the authorization for which such certification was submitted.

(C) REQUIREMENT FOR WRITTEN STATEMENT.—In support of an order under this subsection, the Court shall provide, simultaneously with the order, for the record a written statement of the reasons for the order.

(4) APPEAL.—

(A) APPEAL TO THE COURT OF REVIEW.—The Government may file a petition with the Foreign Intelligence Surveillance Court of Review for review of an order under this subsection. The Court of Review shall have jurisdiction to consider such petition. For any decision under this subparagraph affirming, reversing, or modifying an order of the Foreign Intelligence Surveillance Court, the Court of Review shall provide for the record a written statement of the reasons for the decision.

(B) CONTINUATION OF ACQUISITION PENDING REHEARING OR APPEAL.—Any acquisition affected by an order under paragraph (3)(B) may continue—

(i) during the pendency of any rehearing of the order by the Court en banc; and

(ii) if the Government files a petition for review of an order under this section, until the Court of Review enters an order under subparagraph (C).

(C) IMPLEMENTATION PENDING APPEAL.—Not later than 60 days after the filing of a petition for review of an order under paragraph (3)(B) directing the correction of a deficiency, the Court of Review shall determine, and enter a corresponding order regarding, whether all or any part of the correction order, as issued or modified, shall be implemented during the pendency of the review.

(D) CERTIORARI TO THE SUPREME COURT.—The Government may file a petition for a writ of certiorari for review of a decision of the Court of Review issued under subparagraph (A). The record for such review shall be transmitted under seal to the Supreme Court of the United States, which shall have jurisdiction to review such decision.

(5) SCHEDULE.—

(A) REAUTHORIZATION OF AUTHORIZATIONS IN EFFECT.—If the Attorney General and the Director of National Intelligence seek to reauthorize or replace an authorization issued under subsection (a), the Attorney General and the Director of National Intelligence shall, to the extent practicable, submit to the Court the certification prepared in accordance with subsection (g) and the procedures adopted in accordance with subsections (d) and (e) at least 30 days prior to the expiration of such authorization. (B) REAUTHORIZATION OF ORDERS, AUTHORIZATIONS, AND DIRECTIVES.—If the Attorney General and the Director of National Intelligence seek to reauthorize or replace an authorization issued under subsection (a) by filing a certification pursuant to subparagraph (A), that authorization, and any directives issued thereunder and any order related thereto, shall remain in effect, notwithstanding the expiration provided for in subsection (a), until the Court issues an order with respect to such certification under paragraph (3) at which time the provisions of that paragraph and paragraph (4) shall apply with respect to such certification.

(j) JUDICIAL PROCEEDINGS.—

(1) EXPEDITED JUDICIAL PROCEEDINGS.—Judicial proceedings under this section shall be conducted as expeditiously as possible.

(2) TIME LIMITS.—A time limit for a judicial decision in this section shall apply unless the Court, the Court of Review, or any judge of either the Court or the Court of Review, by order for reasons stated, extends that time as necessary for good cause in a manner consistent with national security.

(k) MAINTENANCE AND SECURITY OF RECORDS AND PROCEEDINGS.—

(1) STANDARDS.—The Foreign Intelligence Surveillance Court shall maintain a record of a proceeding under this section, including petitions, appeals, orders, and statements of reasons for a decision, under security measures adopted by the Chief Justice of the United States, in consultation with the Attorney General and the Director of National Intelligence.

(2) FILING AND REVIEW.—All petitions under this section shall be filed under seal. In any proceedings under this section, the Court shall, upon request of the Government, review ex parte and in camera any Government submission, or portions of a submission, which may include classified information.

(3) RETENTION OF RECORDS.—The Attorney General and the Director of National Intelligence shall retain a directive or an order issued under this section for a period of not less than 10 years from the date on which such directive or such order is issued.

(l) ASSESSMENTS AND REVIEWS.—

(1) SEMIANNUAL ASSESSMENT.—Not less frequently than once every 6 months, the Attorney General and Director of National Intelligence shall assess compliance with the targeting and minimization procedures

adopted in accordance with subsections (d) and (e) and the guidelines adopted in accordance with subsection (f) and shall submit each assessment to—

    (A) the Foreign Intelligence Surveillance Court; and

    (B) consistent with the Rules of the House of Representatives, the Standing Rules of the Senate, and Senate Resolution 400 of the 94th Congress or any successor Senate resolution—

        (i) the congressional intelligence committees; and

        (ii) the Committees on the Judiciary of the House of Representatives and the Senate.

(2) AGENCY ASSESSMENT.—The Inspector General of the Department of Justice and the Inspector General of each element of the intelligence community authorized to acquire foreign intelligence information under subsection (a), with respect to the department or element of such Inspector General—

    (A) are authorized to review compliance with the targeting and minimization procedures adopted in accordance with subsections (d) and (e) and the guidelines adopted in accordance with subsection (f);

    (B) with respect to acquisitions authorized under subsection (a), shall review the number of disseminated intelligence reports containing a reference to a United States-person identity and the number of United States-person identities subsequently disseminated by the element concerned in response to requests for identities that were not referred to by name or title in the original reporting;

    (C) with respect to acquisitions authorized under subsection (a), shall review the number of targets that were later determined to be located in the United States and, to the extent possible, whether communications of such targets were reviewed; and

    (D) shall provide each such review to—

        (i) the Attorney General;

        (ii) the Director of National Intelligence; and

        (iii) consistent with the Rules of the House of Representatives, the Standing Rules of the Senate, and Senate Resolution 400 of the 94th Congress or any successor Senate resolution—

            (I) the congressional intelligence committees; and

            (II) the Committees on the Judiciary of the House of Representatives and the Senate.

(3) ANNUAL REVIEW.—

(A) REQUIREMENT TO CONDUCT.—The head of each element of the intelligence community conducting an acquisition authorized under subsection (a) shall conduct an annual review to determine whether there is reason to believe that foreign intelligence information has been or will be obtained from the acquisition. The annual review shall provide, with respect to acquisitions authorized under subsection (a)—

(i) an accounting of the number of disseminated intelligence reports containing a reference to a United States-person identity;

(ii) an accounting of the number of United States-person identities subsequently disseminated by that element in response to requests for identities that were not referred to by name or title in the original reporting;

(iii) the number of targets that were later determined to be located in the United States and, to the extent possible, whether communications of such targets were reviewed; and

(iv) a description of any procedures developed by the head of such element of the intelligence community and approved by the Director of National Intelligence to assess, in a manner consistent with national security, operational requirements and the privacy interests of United States persons, the extent to which the acquisitions authorized under subsection (a) acquire the communications of United States persons, and the results of any such assessment.

(B) USE OF REVIEW.—The head of each element of the intelligence community that conducts an annual review under subparagraph (A) shall use each such review to evaluate the adequacy of the minimization procedures utilized by such element and, as appropriate, the application of the minimization procedures to a particular acquisition authorized under subsection (a).

(C) PROVISION OF REVIEW.—The head of each element of the intelligence community that conducts an annual review under subparagraph (A) shall provide such review to—

(i) the Foreign Intelligence Surveillance Court;

(ii) the Attorney General;

(iii) the Director of National Intelligence; and

(iv) consistent with the Rules of the House of Representatives, the Standing Rules of the Senate, and

Senate Resolution 400 of the 94th Congress or any successor Senate resolution—
>> (I) the congressional intelligence committees; and
>> (II) the Committees on the Judiciary of the House of Representatives and the Senate.

CERTAIN ACQUISITIONS INSIDE THE UNITED STATES TARGETING UNITED STATES PERSONS OUTSIDE THE UNITED STATES

SEC. 703. [50 U.S.C. §1881b]

(a) JURISDICTION OF THE FOREIGN INTELLIGENCE SURVEILLANCE COURT.—

(1) IN GENERAL.—The Foreign Intelligence Surveillance Court shall have jurisdiction to review an application and to enter an order approving the targeting of a United States person reasonably believed to be located outside the United States to acquire foreign intelligence information, if the acquisition constitutes electronic surveillance or the acquisition of stored electronic communications or stored electronic data that requires an order under this Act, and such acquisition is conducted within the United States.

(2) LIMITATION.—If a United States person targeted under this subsection is reasonably believed to be located in the United States during the effective period of an order issued pursuant to subsection (c), an acquisition targeting such United States person under this section shall cease unless the targeted United States person is again reasonably believed to be located outside the United States while an order issued pursuant to subsection (c) is in effect. Nothing in this section shall be construed to limit the authority of the Government to seek an order or authorization under, or otherwise engage in any activity that is authorized under, any other title of this Act.

(b) APPLICATION.—

(1) IN GENERAL.—Each application for an order under this section shall be made by a Federal officer in writing upon oath or affirmation to a judge having jurisdiction under subsection (a)(1). Each application shall require the approval of the Attorney General based upon the Attorney General's finding that it satisfies the criteria and requirements of such application, as set forth in this section, and shall include—

>> (A) the identity of the Federal officer making the application;
>> (B) the identity, if known, or a description of the United States person who is the target of the acquisition;

(C) a statement of the facts and circumstances relied upon to justify the applicant's belief that the United States person who is the target of the acquisition is—

    (i) a person reasonably believed to be located outside the United States; and

    (ii) a foreign power, an agent of a foreign power, or an officer or employee of a foreign power;

(D) a statement of proposed minimization procedures that meet the definition of minimization procedures under section 101(h) or 301(4), as appropriate;

(E) a description of the nature of the information sought and the type of communications or activities to be subjected to acquisition;

(F) a certification made by the Attorney General or an official specified in section 104(a)(6) that—

    (i) the certifying official deems the information sought to be foreign intelligence information;

    (ii) a significant purpose of the acquisition is to obtain foreign intelligence information;

    (iii) such information cannot reasonably be obtained by normal investigative techniques;

    (iv) designates the type of foreign intelligence information being sought according to the categories described in section 101(e); and

    (v) includes a statement of the basis for the certification that—

        (I) the information sought is the type of foreign intelligence information designated; and

        (II) such information cannot reasonably be obtained by normal investigative techniques;

(G) a summary statement of the means by which the acquisition will be conducted and whether physical entry is required to effect the acquisition;

(H) the identity of any electronic communication service provider necessary to effect the acquisition, provided that the application is not required to identify the specific facilities, places, premises, or property at which the acquisition authorized under this section will be directed or conducted;

(I) a statement of the facts concerning any previous applications that have been made to any judge of the Foreign Intelligence Surveillance Court involving the United States person specified in the application and the action taken on each previous application; and

(J) a statement of the period of time for which the acquisition is required to be maintained, provided that such period of time shall not exceed 90 days per application.

(2) OTHER REQUIREMENTS OF THE ATTORNEY GENERAL.—The Attorney General may require any other affidavit or certification from any other officer in connection with the application.

(3) OTHER REQUIREMENTS OF THE JUDGE.—The judge may require the applicant to furnish such other information as may be necessary to make the findings required by subsection (c)(1).

(c) ORDER.—

(1) FINDINGS.—Upon an application made pursuant to subsection (b), the Foreign Intelligence Surveillance Court shall enter an ex parte order as requested or as modified by the Court approving the acquisition if the Court finds that—

(A) the application has been made by a Federal officer and approved by the Attorney General;

(B) on the basis of the facts submitted by the applicant, for the United States person who is the target of the acquisition, there is probable cause to believe that the target is—

(i) a person reasonably believed to be located outside the United States; and

(ii) a foreign power, an agent of a foreign power, or an officer or employee of a foreign power;

(C) the proposed minimization procedures meet the definition of minimization procedures under section 101(h) or 301(4), as appropriate; and

(D) the application that has been filed contains all statements and certifications required by subsection (b) and the certification or certifications are not clearly erroneous on the basis of the statement made under subsection (b)(1)(F)(v) and any other information furnished under subsection (b)(3).

(2) PROBABLE CAUSE.—In determining whether or not probable cause exists for purposes of paragraph (1)(B), a judge having jurisdiction under subsection (a)(1) may consider past activities of the target and facts and circumstances relating to current or future activities of the target. No United States person may be considered a foreign power, agent of a foreign power, or officer or employee of a foreign power solely upon the basis of activities protected by the first amendment to the Constitution of the United States.

(3) REVIEW.—

(A) LIMITATION ON REVIEW.—Review by a judge having jurisdiction under subsection (a)(1) shall be limited to that required to make the findings described in paragraph (1).

(B) REVIEW OF PROBABLE CAUSE.—If the judge determines that the facts submitted under subsection (b) are insufficient to establish probable cause under paragraph (1)(B), the judge shall enter an order so stating and provide a written statement for the record of the reasons for the determination. The Government may appeal an order under this subparagraph pursuant to subsection (f).

(C) REVIEW OF MINIMIZATION PROCEDURES.—If the judge determines that the proposed minimization procedures referred to in paragraph (1)(C) do not meet the definition of minimization procedures under section 101(h) or 301(4), as appropriate, the judge shall enter an order so stating and provide a written statement for the record of the reasons for the determination. The Government may appeal an order under this subparagraph pursuant to subsection (f).

(D) REVIEW OF CERTIFICATION.—If the judge determines that an application pursuant to subsection (b) does not contain all of the required elements, or that the certification or certifications are clearly erroneous on the basis of the statement made under subsection (b)(1)(F)(v) and any other information furnished under subsection (b)(3), the judge shall enter an order so stating and provide a written statement for the record of the reasons for the determination. The Government may appeal an order under this subparagraph pursuant to subsection (f).

(4) SPECIFICATIONS.—An order approving an acquisition under this subsection shall specify—

(A) the identity, if known, or a description of the United States person who is the target of the acquisition identified or described in the application pursuant to subsection (b)(1)(B);

(B) if provided in the application pursuant to subsection (b)(1)(H), the nature and location of each of the facilities or places at which the acquisition will be directed;

(C) the nature of the information sought to be acquired and the type of communications or activities to be subjected to acquisition;

(D) a summary of the means by which the acquisition will be conducted and whether physical entry is required to effect the acquisition; and

(E) the period of time during which the acquisition is approved.

(5) DIRECTIVES.—An order approving an acquisition under this subsection shall direct—

(A) that the minimization procedures referred to in paragraph (1)(C), as approved or modified by the Court, be followed;

(B) if applicable, an electronic communication service provider to provide to the Government forthwith all information, facilities, or assistance necessary to accomplish the acquisition authorized under such order in a manner that will protect the secrecy of the acquisition and produce a minimum of interference with the services that such electronic communication service provider is providing to the target of the acquisition;

(C) if applicable, an electronic communication service provider to maintain under security procedures approved by the Attorney General any records concerning the acquisition or the aid furnished that such electronic communication service provider wishes to maintain; and

(D) if applicable, that the Government compensate, at the prevailing rate, such electronic communication service provider for providing such information, facilities, or assistance.

(6) DURATION.—An order approved under this subsection shall be effective for a period not to exceed 90 days and such order may be renewed for additional 90-day periods upon submission of renewal applications meeting the requirements of subsection (b).

(7) COMPLIANCE.—At or prior to the end of the period of time for which an acquisition is approved by an order or extension under this section, the judge may assess compliance with the minimization procedures referred to in paragraph (1)(C) by reviewing the circumstances under which information concerning United States persons was acquired, retained, or disseminated.

(d) EMERGENCY AUTHORIZATION.—

(1) AUTHORITY FOR EMERGENCY AUTHORIZATION.—Notwithstanding any other provision of this Act, if the Attorney General reasonably determines that—

(A) an emergency situation exists with respect to the acquisition of foreign intelligence information for which an order may be obtained under subsection (c) before an order authorizing such acquisition can with due diligence be obtained, and

(B) the factual basis for issuance of an order under this subsection to approve such acquisition exists,

the Attorney General may authorize such acquisition if a judge having jurisdiction under subsection (a)(1) is informed by the Attorney General, or a designee of the Attorney General, at the time of such authorization that the decision has been made to conduct such acquisition and if an application in accordance with this section is made to a judge of the Foreign Intelligence Surveillance Court as soon as practicable, but not more than 7 days after the Attorney General authorizes such acquisition.

(2) MINIMIZATION PROCEDURES.—If the Attorney General authorizes an acquisition under paragraph (1), the Attorney General shall require that the minimization procedures referred to in subsection (c)(1)(C) for the issuance of a judicial order be followed.

(3) TERMINATION OF EMERGENCY AUTHORIZATION.—In the absence of a judicial order approving an acquisition under paragraph (1), such acquisition shall terminate when the information sought is obtained, when the application for the order is denied, or after the expiration of 7 days from the time of authorization by the Attorney General, whichever is earliest.

(4) USE OF INFORMATION.—If an application for approval submitted pursuant to paragraph (1) is denied, or in any other case where the acquisition is terminated and no order is issued approving the acquisition, no information obtained or evidence derived from such acquisition, except under circumstances in which the target of the acquisition is determined not to be a United States person, shall be received in evidence or otherwise disclosed in any trial, hearing, or other proceeding in or before any court, grand jury, department, office, agency, regulatory body, legislative committee, or other authority of the United States, a State, or political subdivision thereof, and no information concerning any United States person acquired from such acquisition shall subsequently be used or disclosed in any other manner by Federal officers or employees without the consent of such person, except with the approval of the Attorney General if the information indicates a threat of death or serious bodily harm to any person.

(e) RELEASE FROM LIABILITY.—No cause of action shall lie in any court against any electronic communication service provider for providing any information, facilities, or assistance in accordance with an order or request for emergency assistance issued pursuant to subsection (c) or (d), respectively.

(f) APPEAL.—

(1) APPEAL TO THE FOREIGN INTELLIGENCE SURVEILLANCE COURT OF REVIEW.—The Government may file a petition with the Foreign Intelligence Surveillance Court of Review for review of an order issued pursuant to subsection (c). The Court of Review shall have jurisdiction to consider such petition and shall provide a written statement for the record of the reasons for a decision under this paragraph.

(2) CERIORARI TO THE SUPREME COURT.—The Government may file a petition for a writ of certiorari for review of a decision of the Court of

Review issued under paragraph (1). The record for such review shall be transmitted under seal to the Supreme Court of the United States, which shall have jurisdiction to review such decision.

(g) CONSTRUCTION.—Except as provided in this section, nothing in this Act shall be construed to require an application for a court order for an acquisition that is targeted in accordance with this section at a United States person reasonably believed to be located outside the United States.

OTHER ACQUISITIONS TARGETING UNITED STATES PERSONS OUTSIDE THE UNITED STATES

SEC. 704. [50 U.S.C. §1881c]

(a) JURISDICTION AND SCOPE.—

(1) JURISDICTION.—The Foreign Intelligence Surveillance Court shall have jurisdiction to enter an order pursuant to subsection (c).

(2) SCOPE.—No element of the intelligence community may intentionally target, for the purpose of acquiring foreign intelligence information, a United States person reasonably believed to be located outside the United States under circumstances in which the targeted United States person has a reasonable expectation of privacy and a warrant would be required if the acquisition were conducted inside the United States for law enforcement purposes, unless a judge of the Foreign Intelligence Surveillance Court has entered an order with respect to such targeted United States person or the Attorney General has authorized an emergency acquisition pursuant to subsection (c) or (d), respectively, or any other provision of this Act.

(3) LIMITATIONS.—

(A) MOVING OR MISIDENTIFIED TARGETS.—If a United States person targeted under this subsection is reasonably believed to be located in the United States during the effective period of an order issued pursuant to subsection (c), an acquisition targeting such United States person under this section shall cease unless the targeted United States person is again reasonably believed to be located outside the United States during the effective period of such order.

(B) APPLICABILITY.—If an acquisition for foreign intelligence purposes is to be conducted inside the United States and could be authorized under section 703, the acquisition may only be conducted if authorized under section 703 or in accordance with another provision of this Act other than this section.

(C) CONSTRUCTION.—Nothing in this paragraph shall be construed to limit the authority of the Government to seek an

order or authorization under, or otherwise engage in any activity
that is authorized under, any other title of this Act.

(b) APPLICATION.—Each application for an order under this section shall be
made by a Federal officer in writing upon oath or affirmation to a judge having
jurisdiction under subsection (a)(1). Each application shall require the approval
of the Attorney General based upon the Attorney General's finding that it satisfies
the criteria and requirements of such application as set forth in this section and
shall include—

(1) the identity of the Federal officer making the application;

(2) the identity, if known, or a description of the specific United States
person who is the target of the acquisition;

(3) a statement of the facts and circumstances relied upon to justify the
applicant's belief that the United States person who is the target of the
acquisition is—

(A) a person reasonably believed to be located outside the United
States; and

(B) a foreign power, an agent of a foreign power, or an officer or
employee of a foreign power;

(4) a statement of proposed minimization procedures that meet the
definition of minimization procedures under section 101(h) or 301(4), as
appropriate;

(5) a certification made by the Attorney General, an official specified in
section 104(a)(6), or the head of an element of the intelligence
community that—

(A) the certifying official deems the information sought to be
foreign intelligence information; and

(B) a significant purpose of the acquisition is to obtain foreign
intelligence information;

(6) a statement of the facts concerning any previous applications that
have been made to any judge of the Foreign Intelligence Surveillance
Court involving the United States person specified in the application and
the action taken on each previous application; and

(7) a statement of the period of time for which the acquisition is required
to be maintained, provided that such period of time shall not exceed 90
days per application.

(c) ORDER.—

(1) FINDINGS.—Upon an application made pursuant to subsection (b),
the Foreign Intelligence Surveillance Court shall enter an ex parte order
as requested or as modified by the Court if the Court finds that—

(A) the application has been made by a Federal officer and
approved by the Attorney General;

(B) on the basis of the facts submitted by the applicant, for the United States person who is the target of the acquisition, there is probable cause to believe that the target is—

(i) a person reasonably believed to be located outside the United States; and

(ii) a foreign power, an agent of a foreign power, or an officer or employee of a foreign power;

(C) the proposed minimization procedures, with respect to their dissemination provisions, meet the definition of minimization procedures under section 101(h) or 301(4), as appropriate; and

(D) the application that has been filed contains all statements and certifications required by subsection (b) and the certification provided under subsection (b)(5) is not clearly erroneous on the basis of the information furnished under subsection (b).

(2) PROBABLE CAUSE.—In determining whether or not probable cause exists for purposes of paragraph (1)(B), a judge having jurisdiction under subsection (a)(1) may consider past activities of the target and facts and circumstances relating to current or future activities of the target. No United States person may be considered a foreign power, agent of a foreign power, or officer or employee of a foreign power solely upon the basis of activities protected by the first amendment to the Constitution of the United States.

(3) REVIEW.—

(A) LIMITATIONS ON REVIEW.—Review by a judge having jurisdiction under subsection (a)(1) shall be limited to that required to make the findings described in paragraph (1). The judge shall not have jurisdiction to review the means by which an acquisition under this section may be conducted.

(B) REVIEW OF PROBABLE CAUSE.—If the judge determines that the facts submitted under subsection (b) are insufficient to establish probable cause to issue an order under this subsection, the judge shall enter an order so stating and provide a written statement for the record of the reasons for such determination. The Government may appeal an order under this subparagraph pursuant to subsection (e).

(C) REVIEW OF MINIMIZATION PROCEDURES.—If the judge determines that the minimization procedures applicable to dissemination of information obtained through an acquisition under this subsection do not meet the definition of minimization procedures under section 101(h) or 301(4), as appropriate, the judge shall enter an order so stating and provide a written statement for the record of the reasons for such determination.

The Government may appeal an order under this subparagraph pursuant to subsection (e).

(D) SCOPE OF REVIEW OF CERTIFICATION.—If the judge determines that an application under subsection (b) does not contain all the required elements, or that the certification provided under subsection (b)(5) is clearly erroneous on the basis of the information furnished under subsection (b), the judge shall enter an order so stating and provide a written statement for the record of the reasons for such determination. The Government may appeal an order under this subparagraph pursuant to subsection (e).

(4) DURATION.—An order under this paragraph shall be effective for a period not to exceed 90 days and such order may be renewed for additional 90-day periods upon submission of renewal applications meeting the requirements of subsection (b).

(5) COMPLIANCE.—At or prior to the end of the period of time for which an order or extension is granted under this section, the judge may assess compliance with the minimization procedures referred to in paragraph (1)(C) by reviewing the circumstances under which information concerning United States persons was disseminated, provided that the judge may not inquire into the circumstances relating to the conduct of the acquisition.

(d) EMERGENCY AUTHORIZATION.—

(1) AUTHORITY FOR EMERGENCY AUTHORIZATION.—Notwithstanding any other provision of this section, if the Attorney General reasonably determines that—

(A) an emergency situation exists with respect to the acquisition of foreign intelligence information for which an order may be obtained under subsection (c) before an order under that subsection can, with due diligence, be obtained, and

(B) the factual basis for the issuance of an order under this section exists,

the Attorney General may authorize the emergency acquisition if a judge having jurisdiction under subsection (a)(1) is informed by the Attorney General or a designee of the Attorney General at the time of such authorization that the decision has been made to conduct such acquisition and if an application in accordance with this section is made to a judge of the Foreign Intelligence Surveillance Court as soon as practicable, but not more than 7 days after the Attorney General authorizes such acquisition.

(2) MINIMIZATION PROCEDURES.—If the Attorney General authorizes an emergency acquisition under paragraph (1), the Attorney General shall require that the minimization procedures referred to in subsection (c)(1)(C) be followed.

(3) TERMINATION OF EMERGENCY AUTHORIZATION.—In the absence of an order under subsection (c), an emergency acquisition under paragraph (1) shall terminate when the information sought is obtained, if the application for the order is denied, or after the expiration of 7 days from the time of authorization by the Attorney General, whichever is earliest.

(4) USE OF INFORMATION.—If an application submitted to the Court pursuant to paragraph (1) is denied, or in any other case where the acquisition is terminated and no order with respect to the target of the acquisition is issued under subsection (c), no information obtained or evidence derived from such acquisition, except under circumstances in which the target of the acquisition is determined not to be a United States person, shall be received in evidence or otherwise disclosed in any trial, hearing, or other proceeding in or before any court, grand jury, department, office, agency, regulatory body, legislative committee, or other authority of the United States, a State, or political subdivision thereof, and no information concerning any United States person acquired from such acquisition shall subsequently be used or disclosed in any other manner by Federal officers or employees without the consent of such person, except with the approval of the Attorney General if the information indicates a threat of death or serious bodily harm to any person.

(e) APPEAL.—

(1) APPEAL TO THE COURT OF REVIEW.—The Government may file a petition with the Foreign Intelligence Surveillance Court of Review for review of an order issued pursuant to subsection (c). The Court of Review shall have jurisdiction to consider such petition and shall provide a written statement for the record of the reasons for a decision under this paragraph.

(2) CERTIORARI TO THE SUPREME COURT.—The Government may file a petition for a writ of certiorari for review of a decision of the Court of Review issued under paragraph (1). The record for such review shall be transmitted under seal to the Supreme Court of the United States, which shall have jurisdiction to review such decision.

JOINT APPLICATIONS AND CONCURRENT AUTHORIZATIONS

SEC. 705. [50 U.S.C. §1881d]

(a) JOINT APPLICATIONS AND ORDERS.—If an acquisition targeting a United States person under section 703 or 704 is proposed to be conducted both inside and outside the United States, a judge having jurisdiction under section 703(a)(1) or 704(a)(1) may issue simultaneously, upon the request of the Government in a joint application complying with the requirements of sections 703(b) and 704(b), orders under sections 703(c) and 704(c), as appropriate.

(b) CONCURRENT AUTHORIZATION.—If an order authorizing electronic surveillance or physical search has been obtained under section 105 or 304, the Attorney General may authorize, for the effective period of that order, without an order under section 703 or 704, the targeting of that United States person for the purpose of acquiring foreign intelligence information while such person is reasonably believed to be located outside the United States.

USE OF INFORMATION ACQUIRED UNDER TITLE VII

SEC. 706. [50 U.S.C. §1881e]

(a) INFORMATION ACQUIRED UNDER SECTION 702.—Information acquired from an acquisition conducted under section 702 shall be deemed to be information acquired from an electronic surveillance pursuant to title I for purposes of section 106, except for the purposes of subsection (j) of such section.

(b) INFORMATION ACQUIRED UNDER SECTION 703.—Information acquired from an acquisition conducted under section 703 shall be deemed to be information acquired from an electronic surveillance pursuant to title I for purposes of section 106.

CONGRESSIONAL OVERSIGHT

SEC. 707. [50 U.S.C. §1881f]

(a) SEMIANNUAL REPORT.—Not less frequently than once every 6 months, the Attorney General shall fully inform, in a manner consistent with national security, the congressional intelligence committees and the Committees on the Judiciary of the Senate and the House of Representatives, consistent with the Rules of the House of Representatives, the Standing Rules of the Senate, and Senate Resolution 400 of the 94th Congress or any successor Senate resolution, concerning the implementation of this title.

(b) CONTENT.—Each report under subsection (a) shall include—

    (1) with respect to section 702—

        (A) any certifications submitted in accordance with section 702(g) during the reporting period;

        (B) with respect to each determination under section 702(c)(2), the reasons for exercising the authority under such section;

        (C) any directives issued under section 702(h) during the reporting period;

(D) a description of the judicial review during the reporting period of such certifications and targeting and minimization procedures adopted in accordance with subsections (d) and (e) of section 702 and utilized with respect to an acquisition under such section, including a copy of an order or pleading in connection with such review that contains a significant legal interpretation of the provisions of section 702;

(E) any actions taken to challenge or enforce a directive under paragraph (4) or (5) of section 702(h);

(F) any compliance reviews conducted by the Attorney General or the Director of National Intelligence of acquisitions authorized under section 702(a);

(G) a description of any incidents of noncompliance—

    (i) with a directive issued by the Attorney General and the Director of National Intelligence under section 702(h), including incidents of noncompliance by a specified person to whom the Attorney General and Director of National Intelligence issued a directive under section 702(h); and

    (ii) by an element of the intelligence community with procedures and guidelines adopted in accordance with subsections (d), (e), and (f) of section 702; and

(H) any procedures implementing section 702;

(2) with respect to section 703—

(A) the total number of applications made for orders under section 703(b);

(B) the total number of such orders—

    (i) granted;

    (ii) modified; and

    (iii) denied; and

(C) the total number of emergency acquisitions authorized by the Attorney General under section 703(d) and the total number of subsequent orders approving or denying such acquisitions; and

(3) with respect to section 704—

(A) the total number of applications made for orders under section 704(b);

(B) the total number of such orders—

    (i) granted;

    (ii) modified; and

    (iii) denied; and

(C) the total number of emergency acquisitions authorized by the Attorney General under section 704(d) and the total number of subsequent orders approving or denying such applications.

SAVINGS PROVISION

SEC. 708. [50 U.S.C. §1881g]
Nothing in this title shall be construed to limit the authority of the Government to seek an order or authorization under, or otherwise engage in any activity that is authorized under, any other title of this Act.

TITLE VIII—PROTECTION OF PERSONS ASSISTING THE GOVERNMENT

DEFINITIONS

SEC. 801. [50 U.S.C. §1885]
In this title:
  (1) ASSISTANCE.—The term `assistance' means the provision of, or the provision of access to, information (including communication contents, communications records, or other information relating to a customer or communication), facilities, or another form of assistance.
  (2) CIVIL ACTION.—The term `civil action' includes a covered civil action.
  (3) CONGRESSIONAL INTELLIGENCE COMMITTEES.—The term `congressional intelligence committees' means—
      (A) the Select Committee on Intelligence of the Senate; and
      (B) the Permanent Select Committee on Intelligence of the House of Representatives.
  (4) CONTENTS.—The term `contents' has the meaning given that term in section 101(n).
  (5) COVERED CIVIL ACTION.—The term `covered civil action' means a civil action filed in a Federal or State court that—
      (A) alleges that an electronic communication service provider furnished assistance to an element of the intelligence community; and
      (B) seeks monetary or other relief from the electronic communication service provider related to the provision of such assistance.
  (6) ELECTRONIC COMMUNICATION SERVICE PROVIDER.—The term `electronic communication service provider' means—

(A) a telecommunications carrier, as that term is defined in section 3 of the Communications Act of 1934 (47 U.S.C. 153);

(B) a provider of electronic communication service, as that term is defined in section 2510 of title 18, United States Code;

(C) a provider of a remote computing service, as that term is defined in section 2711 of title 18, United States Code;

(D) any other communication service provider who has access to wire or electronic communications either as such communications are transmitted or as such communications are stored;

(E) a parent, subsidiary, affiliate, successor, or assignee of an entity described in subparagraph (A), (B), (C), or (D); or

(F) an officer, employee, or agent of an entity described in subparagraph (A), (B), (C), (D), or (E).

(7) INTELLIGENCE COMMUNITY.—The term `intelligence community' has the meaning given the term in section 3(4) of the National Security Act of 1947 (50 U.S.C. 401a(4)).

(8) PERSON.—The term `person' means—

(A) an electronic communication service provider; or

(B) a landlord, custodian, or other person who may be authorized or required to furnish assistance pursuant to—

(i) an order of the court established under section 103(a) directing such assistance;

(ii) a certification in writing under section 2511(2)(a)(ii)(B) or 2709(b) of title 18, United States Code; or

(iii) a directive under section 102(a)(4), 105B(e), as added by section 2 of the Protect America Act of 2007 (Public Law 110-55), or 702(h).

(9) STATE.—The term `State' means any State, political subdivision of a State, the Commonwealth of Puerto Rico, the District of Columbia, and any territory or possession of the United States, and includes any officer, public utility commission, or other body authorized to regulate an electronic communication service provider.

PROCEDURES FOR IMPLEMENTING STATUTORY DEFENSES

SEC. 802. [50 U.S.C. §1885a]

(a) REQUIREMENT FOR CERTIFICATION.—Notwithstanding any other provision of law, a civil action may not lie or be maintained in a Federal or State court against any person for providing assistance to an element of the intelligence community, and shall be promptly dismissed, if the Attorney General certifies to the district court of the United States in which such action is pending that—

    (1) any assistance by that person was provided pursuant to an order of the court established under section 103(a) directing such assistance;

    (2) any assistance by that person was provided pursuant to a certification in writing under section 2511(2)(a)(ii)(B) or 2709(b) of title 18, United States Code;

    (3) any assistance by that person was provided pursuant to a directive under section 102(a)(4), 105B(e), as added by section 2 of the Protect America Act of 2007 (Public Law 110-55), or 702(h) directing such assistance;

    (4) in the case of a covered civil action, the assistance alleged to have been provided by the electronic communication service provider was—

        (A) in connection with an intelligence activity involving communications that was—

            (i) authorized by the President during the period beginning on September 11, 2001, and ending on January 17, 2007; and

            (ii) designed to detect or prevent a terrorist attack, or activities in preparation for a terrorist attack, against the United States; and

        (B) the subject of a written request or directive, or a series of written requests or directives, from the Attorney General or the head of an element of the intelligence community (or the deputy of such person) to the electronic communication service provider indicating that the activity was—

            (i) authorized by the President; and

            (ii) determined to be lawful; or

    (5) the person did not provide the alleged assistance.

(b) JUDICIAL REVIEW.—

    (1) REVIEW OF CERTIFICATIONS.—A certification under subsection (a) shall be given effect unless the court finds that such certification is not supported by substantial evidence provided to the court pursuant to this section.

    (2) SUPPLEMENTAL MATERIALS.—In its review of a certification under subsection (a), the court may examine the court order, certification, written request, or directive described in subsection (a) and any relevant court order, certification, written request, or directive submitted pursuant to subsection (d).

(c) LIMITATIONS ON DISCLOSURE.—If the Attorney General files a declaration under section 1746 of title 28, United States Code, that disclosure of a certification made pursuant to subsection (a) or the supplemental materials provided pursuant to subsection (b) or (d) would harm the national security of the United States, the court shall—

> (1) review such certification and the supplemental materials in camera and ex parte; and
>
> (2) limit any public disclosure concerning such certification and the supplemental materials, including any public order following such in camera and ex parte review, to a statement as to whether the case is dismissed and a description of the legal standards that govern the order, without disclosing the paragraph of subsection (a) that is the basis for the certification.

(d) ROLE OF THE PARTIES.—Any plaintiff or defendant in a civil action may submit any relevant court order, certification, written request, or directive to the district court referred to in subsection (a) for review and shall be permitted to participate in the briefing or argument of any legal issue in a judicial proceeding conducted pursuant to this section, but only to the extent that such participation does not require the disclosure of classified information to such party. To the extent that classified information is relevant to the proceeding or would be revealed in the determination of an issue, the court shall review such information in camera and ex parte, and shall issue any part of the court's written order that would reveal classified information in camera and ex parte and maintain such part under seal.

(e) NONDELEGATION.—The authority and duties of the Attorney General under this section shall be performed by the Attorney General (or Acting Attorney General) or the Deputy Attorney General.

(f) APPEAL.—The courts of appeals shall have jurisdiction of appeals from interlocutory orders of the district courts of the United States granting or denying a motion to dismiss or for summary judgment under this section.

(g) REMOVAL.—A civil action against a person for providing assistance to an element of the intelligence community that is brought in a State court shall be deemed to arise under the Constitution and laws of the United States and shall be removable under section 1441 of title 28, United States Code.

(h) RELATIONSHIP TO OTHER LAWS.—Nothing in this section shall be construed to limit any otherwise available immunity, privilege, or defense under any other provision of law.

(i) APPLICABILITY.—This section shall apply to a civil action pending on or filed after the date of the enactment of the FISA Amendments Act of 2008.

PREEMPTION

SEC. 803. [50 U.S.C. §1885b]
(a) IN GENERAL.—No State shall have authority to—

(1) conduct an investigation into an electronic communication service provider's alleged assistance to an element of the intelligence community;

(2) require through regulation or any other means the disclosure of information about an electronic communication service provider's alleged assistance to an element of the intelligence community;

(3) impose any administrative sanction on an electronic communication service provider for assistance to an element of the intelligence community; or

(4) commence or maintain a civil action or other proceeding to enforce a requirement that an electronic communication service provider disclose information concerning alleged assistance to an element of the intelligence community.

(b) SUITS BY THE UNITED STATES.—The United States may bring suit to enforce the provisions of this section.

(c) JURISDICTION.—The district courts of the United States shall have jurisdiction over any civil action brought by the United States to enforce the provisions of this section.

(d) APPLICATION.—This section shall apply to any investigation, action, or proceeding that is pending on or commenced after the date of the enactment of the FISA Amendments Act of 2008.

REPORTING

SEC. 804. [50 U.S.C. §1885c]

(a) SEMIANNUAL REPORT.—Not less frequently than once every 6 months, the Attorney General shall, in a manner consistent with national security, the Rules of the House of Representatives, the Standing Rules of the Senate, and Senate Resolution 400 of the 94th Congress or any successor Senate resolution, fully inform the congressional intelligence committees, the Committee on the Judiciary of the Senate, and the Committee on the Judiciary of the House of Representatives concerning the implementation of this title.

(b) CONTENT.—Each report made under subsection (a) shall include—

(1) any certifications made under section 802;

(2) a description of the judicial review of the certifications made under section 802; and

(3) any actions taken to enforce the provisions of section 803.

SELECTED ADDITIONAL PROVISIONS OF
THE FISA AMENDMENTS ACT OF 2008

REVIEW OF PREVIOUS ACTIONS

Sec. 301.

(a) DEFINITIONS.—In this section:

(1) APPROPRIATE COMMITTEES OF CONGRESS.—The term ``appropriate committees of Congress'' means—

(A) the Select Committee on Intelligence and the Committee on the Judiciary of the Senate; and

(B) the Permanent Select Committee on Intelligence and the Committee on the Judiciary of the House of Representatives.

(2) FOREIGN INTELLIGENCE SURVEILLANCE COURT.—The term ``Foreign Intelligence Surveillance Court'' means the court established under section 103(a) of the Foreign Intelligence Surveillance Act of 1978 (50 U.S.C. 1803(a)).

(3) PRESIDENT'S SURVEILLANCE PROGRAM AND PROGRAM.—The terms ``President's Surveillance Program'' and ``Program'' mean the intelligence activity involving communications that was authorized by the President during the period beginning on September 11, 2001, and ending on January 17, 2007, including the program referred to by the President in a radio address on December 17, 2005 (commonly known as the Terrorist Surveillance Program).

(b) Reviews.—

(1) REQUIREMENT TO CONDUCT.—The Inspectors General of the Department of Justice, the Office of the Director of National Intelligence, the National Security Agency, the Department of Defense, and any other element of the intelligence community that participated in the President's Surveillance Program, shall complete a comprehensive review of, with respect to the oversight authority and responsibility of each such Inspector General—

(A) all of the facts necessary to describe the establishment, implementation, product, and use of the product of the Program;

(B) access to legal reviews of the Program and access to information about the Program;

(C) communications with, and participation of, individuals and entities in the private sector related to the Program;

(D) interaction with the Foreign Intelligence Surveillance Court and transition to court orders related to the Program; and

(E) any other matters identified by any such Inspector General that would enable that Inspector General to complete a review of the Program, with respect to such Department or element.

(2) COOPERATION AND COORDINATION.—

(A) COOPERATION.—Each Inspector General required to conduct a review under paragraph (1) shall—

(i) work in conjunction, to the extent practicable, with any other Inspector General required to conduct such a review; and

(ii) utilize, to the extent practicable, and not unnecessarily duplicate or delay, such reviews or audits that have been completed or are being undertaken by any such Inspector General or by any other office of the Executive Branch related to the Program.

(B) INTEGRATION OF OTHER REVIEWS.—The Counsel of the Office of Professional Responsibility of the Department of Justice shall provide the report of any investigation conducted by such Office on matters relating to the Program, including any investigation of the process through which legal reviews of the Program were conducted and the substance of such reviews, to the Inspector General of the Department of Justice, who shall integrate the factual findings and conclusions of such investigation into its review.

(C) COORDINATION.—The Inspectors General shall designate one of the Inspectors General required to conduct a review under paragraph (1) that is appointed by the President, by and with the advice and consent of the Senate, to coordinate the conduct of the reviews and the preparation of the reports.

(c) REPORTS.—

(1) PRELIMINARY REPORTS.—Not later than 60 days after the date of the enactment of this Act, the Inspectors General of the Department of Justice, the Office of the Director of National Intelligence, the National Security Agency, the Department of Defense, and any other Inspector General required to conduct a review under subsection (b)(1), shall submit to the appropriate committees of Congress an interim report that describes the planned scope of such review.

(2) FINAL REPORT.—Not later than 1 year after the date of the enactment of this Act, the Inspectors General of the Department of Justice, the Office of the Director of National Intelligence, the National Security Agency, the Department of Defense, and any other Inspector General required to conduct a review under subsection (b)(1), shall submit to the appropriate committees of Congress, in a manner consistent with

national security, a comprehensive report on such reviews that includes any recommendations of any such Inspectors General within the oversight authority and responsibility of any such Inspector General with respect to the reviews.

(3) FORM.—A report under this subsection shall be submitted in unclassified form, but may include a classified annex. The unclassified report shall not disclose the name or identity of any individual or entity of the private sector that participated in the Program or with whom there was communication about the Program, to the extent that information is classified.

(d) RESOURCES.—

(1) EXPEDITED SECURITY CLEARANCE.—The Director of National Intelligence shall ensure that the process for the investigation and adjudication of an application by an Inspector General or any appropriate staff of an Inspector General for a security clearance necessary for the conduct of the review under subsection (b)(1) is carried out as expeditiously as possible.

(2) ADDITIONAL PERSONNEL FOR THE INSPECTORS GENERAL.—An Inspector General required to conduct a review under subsection (b)(1) and submit a report under subsection (c) is authorized to hire such additional personnel as may be necessary to carry out such review and prepare such report in a prompt and timely manner. Personnel authorized to be hired under this paragraph—

(A) shall perform such duties relating to such a review as the relevant Inspector General shall direct; and

(B) are in addition to any other personnel authorized by law.

(3) TRANSFER OF PERSONNEL.—The Attorney General, the Secretary of Defense, the Director of National Intelligence, the Director of the National Security Agency, or the head of any other element of the intelligence community may transfer personnel to the relevant Office of the Inspector General required to conduct a review under subsection (b)(1) and submit a report under subsection (c) and, in addition to any other personnel authorized by law, are authorized to fill any vacancy caused by such a transfer. Personnel transferred under this paragraph shall perform such duties relating to such review as the relevant Inspector General shall direct.

SEVERABILITY

SEC. 401 [50 U.S.C. 1801 note]
If any provision of this Act, any amendment made by this Act, or the application thereof to any person or circumstances is held invalid, the validity of the

remainder of the Act, of any such amendments, and of the application of such provisions to other persons and circumstances shall not be affected thereby.

REPEALS

SEC. 403.

(a) REPEAL OF PROTECT AMERICA ACT OF 2007 PROVISIONS.—

    (1) AMENDMENTS TO FISA.—

        (A) IN GENERAL.—Except as provided in section 404, sections 105A, 105B, and 105C of the Foreign Intelligence Surveillance Act of 1978 (50 U.S.C. 1805a, 1805b, and 1805c) are repealed.

        (B) TECHNICAL AND CONFORMING AMENDMENTS.—

            (i) TABLE OF CONTENTS.—The table of contents in the first section of the Foreign Intelligence Surveillance Act of 1978 (50 U.S.C. 1801 et seq.) is amended by striking the items relating to sections 105A, 105B, and 105C.

            (ii) CONFORMING AMENDMENTS.—Except as provided in section 404, section 103(e) of the Foreign Intelligence Surveillance Act of 1978 (50 U.S.C. 1803(e)) is amended—

                (I) in paragraph (1), by striking ``105B(h) or 501(f)(1)" and inserting ``501(f)(1) or 702(h)(4)"; and

                (II) in paragraph (2), by striking ``105B(h) or 501(f)(1)" and inserting ``501(f)(1) or 702(h)(4)".

    (2) REPORTING REQUIREMENTS.—Except as provided in section 404, section 4 of the Protect America Act of 2007 (Public Law 110-55; 121 Stat. 555) is repealed.

    (3) [50 USC 1803 note.] TRANSITION PROCEDURES.—Except as provided in section 404, subsection (b) of section 6 of the Protect America Act of 2007 (Public Law 110-55; 121 Stat. 556) is repealed.

(b) FISA AMENDMENTS ACT OF 2008.—

    (1) [50 USC 1881 note.] IN GENERAL.—Except as provided in section 404, effective December 31, 2012, title VII of the Foreign Intelligence Surveillance Act of 1978, [50 USC 1881-1881g.] as amended by section 101(a), is repealed.

    (2) [18 USC 2511 note.] TECHNICAL AND CONFORMING AMENDMENTS.—Effective December 31, 2012—

        (A) the table of contents in the first section of such Act (50 U.S.C. 1801 et seq.) is amended by striking the items related to title VII;

(B) except as provided in section 404, section 601(a)(1) of such Act (50 U.S.C. 1871(a)(1)) is amended to read as such section read on the day before the date of the enactment of this Act; and
(C) except as provided in section 404, section 2511(2)(a)(ii)(A) of title 18, United States Code, is amended by striking ``or a court order pursuant to section 704 of the Foreign Intelligence Surveillance Act of 1978".

TRANSITION PROCEDURES

SEC. 404.
(a) TRANSITION PROCEDURES FOR PROTECT AMERICA ACT OF 2007 PROVISIONS.—

(1) CONTINUED EFFECT OF ORDERS, AUTHORIZATIONS, DIRECTIVES.— Except as provided in paragraph (7), notwithstanding any other provision of law, any order, authorization, or directive issued or made pursuant to section 105B of the Foreign Intelligence Surveillance Act of 1978, as added by section 2 of the Protect America Act of 2007 (Public Law 110-55; 121 Stat. 552), shall continue in effect until the expiration of such order, authorization, or directive.

(2) APPLICABILITY OF PROTECT AMERICA ACT OF 2007 TO CONTINUED ORDERS, AUTHORIZATIONS, DIRECTIVES.—Notwithstanding any other provision of this Act, any amendment made by this Act, or the Foreign Intelligence Surveillance Act of 1978 (50 U.S.C. 1801 et seq.)—

(A) subject to paragraph (3), section 105A of such Act, as added by section 2 of the Protect America Act of 2007 (Public Law 110-55; 121 Stat. 552), shall continue to apply to any acquisition conducted pursuant to an order, authorization, or directive referred to in paragraph (1); and

(B) sections 105B and 105C of the Foreign Intelligence Surveillance Act of 1978, as added by sections 2 and 3, respectively, of the Protect America Act of 2007, shall continue to apply with respect to an order, authorization, or directive referred to in paragraph (1) until the later of—

(i) the expiration of such order, authorization, or directive; or
(ii) the date on which final judgment is entered for any petition or other litigation relating to such order, authorization, or directive.

(3) USE OF INFORMATION.—Information acquired from an acquisition conducted pursuant to an order, authorization, or directive referred to in paragraph (1) shall be deemed to be information acquired from an

electronic surveillance pursuant to title I of the Foreign Intelligence Surveillance Act of 1978 (50 U.S.C. 1801 et seq.) for purposes of section 106 of such Act (50 U.S.C. 1806), except for purposes of subsection (j) of such section.

(4) PROTECTION FROM LIABILITY.—Subsection (l) of section 105B of the Foreign Intelligence Surveillance Act of 1978, as added by section 2 of the Protect America Act of 2007, shall continue to apply with respect to any directives issued pursuant to such section 105B.

(5) JURISDICTION OF FOREIGN INTELLIGENCE SURVEILLANCE COURT.— Notwithstanding any other provision of this Act or of the Foreign Intelligence Surveillance Act of 1978 (50 U.S.C. 1801 et seq.), section 103(e) of the Foreign Intelligence Surveillance Act (50 U.S.C. 1803(e)), as amended by section 5(a) of the Protect America Act of 2007 (Public Law 110-55; 121 Stat. 556), shall continue to apply with respect to a directive issued pursuant to section 105B of the Foreign Intelligence Surveillance Act of 1978, as added by section 2 of the Protect America Act of 2007, until the later of—

(A) the expiration of all orders, authorizations, or directives referred to in paragraph (1); or

(B) the date on which final judgment is entered for any petition or other litigation relating to such order, authorization, or directive.

(6) REPORTING REQUIREMENTS.—

(A) CONTINUED APPLICABILITY.—Notwithstanding any other provision of this Act, any amendment made by this Act, the Protect America Act of 2007 (Public Law 110-55), or the Foreign Intelligence Surveillance Act of 1978 (50 U.S.C. 1801 et seq.), section 4 of the Protect America Act of 2007 shall continue to apply until the date that the certification described in subparagraph (B) is submitted.

(B) CERTIFICATION.—The certification described in this subparagraph is a certification—

(i) made by the Attorney General;

(ii) submitted as part of a semi-annual report required by section 4 of the Protect America Act of 2007;

(iii) that states that there will be no further acquisitions carried out under section 105B of the Foreign Intelligence Surveillance Act of 1978, as added by section 2 of the Protect America Act of 2007, after the date of such certification; and

(iv) that states that the information required to be included under such section 4 relating to any acquisition conducted under such section 105B has been included in a semi-annual report required by such section 4.

(7) REPLACEMENT OF ORDERS, AUTHORIZATIONS, AND DIRECTIVES.—

(A) IN GENERAL.—If the Attorney General and the Director of National Intelligence seek to replace an authorization issued pursuant to section 105B of the Foreign Intelligence Surveillance Act of 1978, as added by section 2 of the Protect America Act of 2007 (Public Law 110-55), with an authorization under section 702 of the Foreign Intelligence Surveillance Act of 1978 (as added by section 101(a) of this Act), the Attorney General and the Director of National Intelligence shall, to the extent practicable, submit to the Foreign Intelligence Surveillance Court (as such term is defined in section 701(b)(2) of such Act (as so added)) a certification prepared in accordance with subsection (g) of such section 702 and the procedures adopted in accordance with subsections (d) and (e) of such section 702 at least 30 days before the expiration of such authorization.

(B) CONTINUATION OF EXISTING ORDERS.—If the Attorney General and the Director of National Intelligence seek to replace an authorization made pursuant to section 105B of the Foreign Intelligence Surveillance Act of 1978, as added by section 2 of the Protect America Act of 2007 (Public Law 110-55; 121 Stat. 522), by filing a certification in accordance with subparagraph (A), that authorization, and any directives issued thereunder and any order related thereto, shall remain in effect, notwithstanding the expiration provided for in subsection (a) of such section 105B, until the Foreign Intelligence Surveillance Court (as such term is defined in section 701(b)(2) of the Foreign Intelligence Surveillance Act of 1978 (as so added)) issues an order with respect to that certification under section 702(i)(3) of such Act (as so added) at which time the provisions of that section and of section 702(i)(4) of such Act (as so added) shall apply.

(8) EFFECTIVE DATE.—Paragraphs (1) through (7) shall take effect as if enacted on August 5, 2007.

(b) TRANSITION PROCEDURES FOR FISA AMENDMENTS ACT OF 2008 PROVISIONS.—

(1) ORDERS IN EFFECT ON DECEMBER 31, 2012.—Notwithstanding any other provision of this Act, any amendment made by this Act, or the Foreign Intelligence Surveillance Act of 1978 (50 U.S.C. 1801 et seq.), any order, authorization, or directive issued or made under title VII of the Foreign Intelligence Surveillance Act of 1978, as amended by section

101(a), shall continue in effect until the date of the expiration of such order, authorization, or directive.

(2) APPLICABILITY OF TITLE VII OF FISA TO CONTINUED ORDERS, AUTHORIZATIONS, DIRECTIVES.—Notwithstanding any other provision of this Act, any amendment made by this Act, or the Foreign Intelligence Surveillance Act of 1978 (50 U.S.C. 1801 et seq.), with respect to any order, authorization, or directive referred to in paragraph (1), title VII of such Act, as amended by section 101(a), shall continue to apply until the later of—

(A) the expiration of such order, authorization, or directive; or

(B) the date on which final judgment is entered for any petition or other litigation relating to such order, authorization, or directive.

(3) CHALLENGE OF DIRECTIVES; PROTECTION FROM LIABILITY; USE OF INFORMATION.—Notwithstanding any other provision of this Act or of the Foreign Intelligence Surveillance Act of 1978 (50 U.S.C. 1801 et seq.)—

(A) section 103(e) of such Act, as amended by section 403(a)(1)(B)(ii), shall continue to apply with respect to any directive issued pursuant to section 702(h) of such Act, as added by section 101(a);

(B) section 702(h)(3) of such Act (as so added) shall continue to apply with respect to any directive issued pursuant to section 702(h) of such Act (as so added);

(C) section 703(e) of such Act (as so added) shall continue to apply with respect to an order or request for emergency assistance under that section;

(D) section 706 of such Act (as so added) shall continue to apply to an acquisition conducted under section 702 or 703 of such Act (as so added); and

(E) section 2511(2)(a)(ii)(A) of title 18, United States Code, as amended by section 101(c)(1), shall continue to apply to an order issued pursuant to section 704 of the Foreign Intelligence Surveillance Act of 1978, as added by section 101(a).

(4) REPORTING REQUIREMENTS.—

(A) CONTINUED APPLICABILITY.—Notwithstanding any other provision of this Act or of the Foreign Intelligence Surveillance Act of 1978 (50 U.S.C. 1801 et seq.), section 601(a) of such Act (50 U.S.C. 1871(a)), as amended by section 101(c)(2), and sections 702(l) and 707 of such Act, as added by section 101(a), shall continue to apply until the date that the certification described in subparagraph (B) is submitted.

(B) CERTIFICATION.—The certification described in this subparagraph is a certification—

>> (i) made by the Attorney General;

>> (ii) submitted to the Select Committee on Intelligence of the Senate, the Permanent Select Committee on Intelligence of the House of Representatives, and the Committees on the Judiciary of the Senate and the House of Representatives;

>> (iii) that states that there will be no further acquisitions carried out under title VII of the Foreign Intelligence Surveillance Act of 1978, as amended by section 101(a), after the date of such certification; and

>> (iv) that states that the information required to be included in a review, assessment, or report under section 601 of such Act, as amended by section 101(c), or section 702(l) or 707 of such Act, as added by section 101(a), relating to any acquisition conducted under title VII of such Act, as amended by section 101(a), has been included in a review, assessment, or report under such section 601, 702(l), or 707.

(5) TRANSITION PROCEDURES CONCERNING THE TARGETING OF UNITED STATES PERSONS OVERSEAS.—Any authorization in effect on the date of enactment of this Act under section 2.5 of Executive Order 12333 to intentionally target a United States person reasonably believed to be located outside the United States shall continue in effect, and shall constitute a sufficient basis for conducting such an acquisition targeting a United States person located outside the United States until the earlier of—

> (A) the date that authorization expires; or

> (B) the date that is 90 days after the date of the enactment of this Act.

UNITING AND STRENGTHENING AMERICA BY PROVIDING APPOPRIATE TOOLS REQUIRED TO INTERCEPT AND OBSTRUCT TERRORISM (USA PATRIOT) ACT OF 2001

(Public Law 107-56 of October 26, 2001; 115 STAT. 252)

An Act To deter and punish terrorist acts in the United States and around the world, to enhance law enforcement investigatory tools, and for other purposes.

Be it enacted by the Senate and House of Representatives of the United States of America in Congress assembled,

SHORT TITLE AND TABLE OF CONTENTS

SECTION 1.
(a) SHORT TITLE.—This Act may be cited as the "Uniting and Strengthening America by Providing Appropriate Tools Required to Intercept and Obstruct Terrorism (USA Patriot Act) Act of 2001".
(b) TABLE OF CONTENTS.—The table of contents for this Act is as follows:

TITLE II – ENHANCED SURVEILLANCE PROCEDURES

AUTHORITY TO INTERCEPT WIRE, ORAL, AND ELECTRONIC COMMUNICATIONS RELATING TO TERRORISM

SEC. 201.
Section 2516(1) of title 18, United States Code, is amended—
(1) by redesignating paragraph (p), as so redesignated by section 434(2) of the Antiterrorism and Effective Death Penalty Act of 1996 (Public Law 104-132; 110 Stat. 1274), as paragraph (r); and
(2) by inserting after paragraph (p), as so redesignated by section 201(3) of the Illegal Immigration Reform and Immigrant Responsibility Act of

1996 (division C of Public Law 104-208; 110 Stat. 3009-565), the following new paragraph:

"(q) any criminal violation of section 229 (relating to chemical weapons); or sections 2332, 2332a, 2332b, 2332d, 2339A, or 2339B of this title (relating to terrorism); or".

AUTHORITY TO INTERCEPT WIRE, ORAL, AND ELECTRONIC COMMUNICATIONS RELATING TO COMPUTER FRAUD AND ABUSE OFFENSES

SEC. 202.
Section 2516(1)(c) of title 18, United States Code, is amended by striking "and section 1341 (relating to mail fraud)," and inserting "section 1341 (relating to mail fraud), a felony violation of section 1030 (relating to computer fraud and abuse),".

AUTHORITY TO SHARE CRIMINAL INVESTIGATIVE INFORMATION

SEC. 203.
(a) AUTHORITY TO SHARE GRAND JURY INFORMATION.—
    (1) IN GENERAL.—Rule 6(e)(3)(C) of the Federal Rules of Criminal Procedure is amended to read as follows:

"(C)(i) Disclosure otherwise prohibited by this rule of matters occurring before the grand jury may also be made—
    "(I) when so directed by a court preliminarily to or in connection with a judicial proceeding;
    "(II) when permitted by a court at the request of the defendant, upon a showing that grounds may exist for a motion to dismiss the indictment because of matters occurring before the grand jury;
    "(III) when the disclosure is made by an attorney for the government to another Federal grand jury;
    "(IV) when permitted by a court at the request of an attorney for the government, upon a showing that such matters may disclose a violation of State criminal law, to an appropriate official of a State or subdivision of a State for the purpose of enforcing such law; or

"(V) when the matters involve foreign intelligence or counterintelligence (as defined in section 3 of the National Security Act of 1947 (50 U.S.C. §401a)), or foreign intelligence information (as defined in clause (iv) of this subparagraph), to any Federal law enforcement, intelligence, protective, immigration, national defense, or national security official in order to assist the official receiving that information in the performance of his official duties.

"(ii) If the court orders disclosure of matters occurring before the grand jury, the disclosure shall be made in such manner, at such time, and under such conditions as the court may direct.

"(iii) Any Federal official to whom information is disclosed pursuant to clause (i)(V) of this subparagraph may use that information only as necessary in the conduct of that person's official duties subject to any limitations on the unauthorized disclosure of such information. Within a reasonable time after such disclosure, an attorney for the government shall file under seal a notice with the court stating the fact that such information was disclosed and the departments, agencies, or entities to which the disclosure was made.

"(iv) In clause (i)(V) of this subparagraph, the term 'foreign intelligence information' means—

"(I) information, whether or not concerning a United States person, that relates to the ability of the United States to protect against—

"(aa) actual or potential attack or other grave hostile acts of a foreign power or an agent of a foreign power;

"(bb) sabotage or international terrorism by a foreign power or an agent of a foreign power; or

"(cc) clandestine intelligence activities by an intelligence service or network of a foreign power or by an agent of foreign power; or

"(II) information, whether or not concerning a United States person, with respect to a foreign power or foreign territory that relates to—

> "(aa) the national defense or the security of the United States; or
>
> "(bb) the conduct of the foreign affairs of the United States.".

(2) CONFORMING AMENDMENT.—Rule 6(e)(3)(D) of the Federal Rules of Criminal Procedure is amended by striking "(e)(3)(C)(i)" and inserting "(e) (3)(C)(i)(I)".

(b) AUTHORITY TO SHARE ELECTRONIC, WIRE, AND ORAL INTERCEPTION INFORMATION.—

(1) LAW ENFORCEMENT.—Section 2517 of title 18, United States Code, is amended by inserting at the end the following:

"(6) Any investigative or law enforcement officer, or attorney for the Government, who by any means authorized by this chapter, has obtained knowledge of the contents of any wire, oral, or electronic communication, or evidence derived therefrom, may disclose such contents to any other Federal law enforcement, intelligence, protective, immigration, national defense, or national security official to the extent that such contents include foreign intelligence or counterintelligence (as defined in section 3 of the National Security Act of 1947 (50 U.S.C. §401a)), or foreign intelligence information (as defined in subsection (19) of section 2510 of this title), to assist the official who is to receive that information in the performance of his official duties. Any Federal official who receives information pursuant to this provision may use that information only as necessary in the conduct of that person's official duties subject to any limitations on the unauthorized disclosure of such information.".

(2) DEFINITION.—Section 2510 of title 18, United States Code, is amended by—

    (A) in paragraph (17), by striking "and" after the semicolon;

    (B) in paragraph (18), by striking the period and inserting "; and"; and

    (C) by inserting at the end the following:

"(19) 'foreign intelligence information' means—

    "(A) information, whether or not concerning a United States person, that relates to the ability of the United States to protect against—

        "(i) actual or potential attack or other grave hostile acts of a foreign power or an agent of a foreign power;

"(ii) sabotage or international terrorism by a foreign power or an agent of a foreign power; or

"(iii) clandestine intelligence activities by an intelligence service or network of a foreign power or by an agent of a foreign power; or

"(B) information, whether or not concerning a United States person, with respect to a foreign power or foreign territory that relates to—

"(i) the national defense or the security of the United States; or

"(ii) the conduct of the foreign affairs of the United States.".

(c) PROCEDURES.—The Attorney General shall establish procedures for the disclosure of information pursuant to section 2517(6) and Rule 6(e)(3)(C)(i)(V) of the Federal Rules of Criminal Procedure that identifies a United States person, as defined in section 101 of the Foreign Intelligence Surveillance Act of 1978 (50 U.S.C. §1801)).

(d) FOREIGN INTELLIGENCE INFORMATION.—

(1) IN GENERAL.—Notwithstanding any other provision of law, it shall be lawful for foreign intelligence or counterintelligence (as defined in section 3 of the National Security Act of 1947 (50 U.S.C. §401a)) or foreign intelligence information obtained as part of a criminal investigation to be disclosed to any Federal law enforcement, intelligence, protective, immigration, national defense, or national security official in order to assist the official receiving that information in the performance of his official duties. Any Federal official who receives information pursuant to this provision may use that information only as necessary in the conduct of that person's official duties subject to any limitations on the unauthorized disclosure of such information.

(2) DEFINITION.—In this subsection, the term "foreign intelligence information" means—

(A) information, whether or not concerning a United States person, that relates to the ability of the United States to protect against—

(i) actual or potential attack or other grave hostile acts of a foreign power or an agent of a foreign power;

(ii) sabotage or international terrorism by a foreign power or an agent of a foreign power; or

(iii) clandestine intelligence activities by an intelligence service or network of a foreign power or by an agent of a foreign power; or

B) information, whether or not concerning a United States person, with respect to a foreign power or foreign territory that relates to—

(i) the national defense or the security of the United States; or

(ii) the conduct of the foreign affairs of the United States.

CLARIFICATION OF INTELLIGENCE EXCEPTIONS FROM LIMITATIONS ON INTERCEPTION AND DISCLOSURE OF WIRE, ORAL, AND ELECTRONIC COMMUNICATIONS

SEC. 204.

Section 2511(2)(f) of title 18, United States Code, is amended—

(1) by striking "this chapter or chapter 121" and inserting "this chapter or chapter 121 or 206 of this title"; and

(2) by striking "wire and oral" and inserting "wire, oral, and electronic".

EMPLOYMENT OF TRANSLATORS BY THE FEDERAL BUREAU OF INVESTIGATION

SEC. 205.

(a) AUTHORITY.—The Director of the Federal Bureau of Investigation is authorized to expedite the employment of personnel as translators to support counterterrorism investigations and operations without regard to applicable Federal personnel requirements and limitations.

(b) SECURITY REQUIREMENT.—The Director of the Federal Bureau of Investigation shall establish such security requirements as are necessary for the personnel employed as translators under subsection (a).

(c) REPORT.—The Attorney General shall report to the Committees on the Judiciary of the House of Representatives and the Senate on—

(1) the number of translators employed by the FBI and other components of the Department of Justice;

(2) any legal or practical impediments to using translators employed by other Federal, State, or local agencies, on a full, part-time, or shared basis; and

(3) the needs of the FBI for specific translation services in certain languages, and recommendations for meeting those needs.

ROVING SURVEILLANCE AUTHORITY UNDER THE FOREIGN INTELLIGENCE SURVEILLANCE ACT OF 1978

SEC. 206.

Section 105(c)(2)(B) of the Foreign Intelligence Surveillance Act of 1978 (50 U.S.C. §1805(c)(2)(B)) is amended by inserting ", or in circumstances where the Court finds that the actions of the target of the application may have the effect of thwarting the identification of a specified person, such other persons," after "specified person".

DURATION OF FISA SURVEILLANCE OF NON-UNITED STATES PERSONS WHO ARE AGENTS OF A FOREIGN POWER

SEC. 207.

(a) DURATION.—

(1) SURVEILLANCE.—Section 105(e)(1) of the Foreign Intelligence Surveillance Act of 1978 (50 U.S.C. §1805(e)(1)) is amended by—

(A) inserting "(A)" after "except that"; and

(B) inserting before the period the following: ", and (B) an order under this Act for a surveillance targeted against an agent of a foreign power, as defined in section 101(b)(1)(A) may be for the period specified in the application or for 120 days, whichever is less".

(2) PHYSICAL SEARCH.—Section 304(d)(1) of the Foreign Intelligence Surveillance Act of 1978 (50 U.S.C. §1824(d)(1)) is amended by—

(A) striking "forty-five" and inserting "90";

(B) inserting "(A)" after "except that"; and

(C) inserting before the period the following: ", and (B) an order under this section for a physical search targeted against an agent of a foreign power as defined in section 101(b)(1)(A) may be for the period specified in the application or for 120 days, whichever is less".

(b) EXTENSION.—

(1) IN GENERAL.—Section 105(d)(2) of the Foreign Intelligence Surveillance Act of 1978 (50 U.S.C. §1805(d)(2)) is amended by—

(A) inserting "(A)" after "except that"; and

(B) inserting before the period the following: ", and (B) an extension of an order under this Act for a surveillance targeted against an agent of a foreign power as defined in section 101(b)(1)(A) may be for a period not to exceed 1 year".

(2) DEFINED TERM.—Section 304(d)(2) of the Foreign Intelligence Surveillance Act of 1978 (50 U.S.C. §1824(d)(2) is amended by inserting after "not a United States person," the following: "or against an agent of a foreign power as defined in section 101(b)(1)(A),".

DESIGNATION OF JUDGES

SEC. 208.

Section 103(a) of the Foreign Intelligence Surveillance Act of 1978 (50 U.S.C. §1803(a)) is amended by—

(1) striking "seven district court judges" and inserting "11 district court judges"; and

(2) inserting "of whom no fewer than 3 shall reside within 20 miles of the District of Columbia" after "circuits".

SEIZURE OF VOICE-MAIL MESSAGES PURSUANT TO WARRANTS

SEC. 209.

Title 18, United States Code, is amended—

(1) in section 2510—

(A) in paragraph (1), by striking beginning with "and such" and all that follows through "communication"; and

(B) in paragraph (14), by inserting "wire or" after "transmission of"; and

(2) in subsections (a) and (b) of section 2703—

(A) by striking "CONTENTS OF ELECTRONIC" and inserting "CONTENTS OF WIRE OR ELECTRONIC" each place it appears;

(B) by striking "contents of an electronic" and inserting "contents of a wire or electronic" each place it appears; and

(C) by striking "any electronic" and inserting "any wire or electronic" each place it appears.

SCOPE OF SUBPOENAS FOR RECORDS OF ELECTRONIC COMMUNICATIONS

SEC. 210.

Section 2703(c)(2) of title 18, United States Code, as redesignated by section 212, is amended—

(1) by striking "entity the name, address, local and long distance telephone toll billing records, telephone number or other subscriber number or identity, and length of service of a subscriber" and inserting the following: "entity the—

"(A) name;

"(B) address;

"(C) local and long distance telephone connection records, or records of session times and durations;

"(D) length of service (including start date) and types of service utilized;

"(E) telephone or instrument number or other subscriber number or identity, including any temporarily assigned network address; and

"(F) means and source of payment for such service (including any credit card or bank account number),

of a subscriber"; and

(2) by striking "and the types of services the subscriber or customer utilized,".

CLARIFICATION OF SCOPE

SEC. 211.

Section 631 of the Communications Act of 1934 (47 U.S.C. §551) is amended—
(1) in subsection (c)(2)—

(A) in subparagraph (B), by striking "or";

(B) in subparagraph (C), by striking the period at the end and inserting "; or"; and

(C) by inserting at the end the following:

"(D) to a government entity as authorized under chapters 119, 121, or 206 of title 18, United States Code, except that such disclosure shall not include records revealing cable subscriber selection of video programming from a cable operator."; and

(2) in subsection (h), by striking "A governmental entity" and inserting "Except as provided in subsection (c)(2)(D), a governmental entity".

EMERGENCY DISCLOSURE OF ELECTRONIC COMMUNICATIONS TO PROTECT LIFE AND LIMB

SEC. 212.

(a) DISCLOSURE OF CONTENTS.—

(1) IN GENERAL.—Section 2702 of title 18, United States Code, is amended—

(A) by striking the section heading and inserting the following:
"§2702. Voluntary disclosure of customer communications or records";

(B) in subsection (a)—

(i) in paragraph (2)(A), by striking "and" at the end;

525

(ii) in paragraph (2)(B), by striking the period and inserting "; and"; and

(iii) by inserting after paragraph (2) the following:

"(3) a provider of remote computing service or electronic communication service to the public shall not knowingly divulge a record or other information pertaining to a subscriber to or customer of such service (not including the contents of communications covered by paragraph (1) or (2)) to any governmental entity.";

(C) in subsection (b), by striking "EXCEPTIONS.—A person or entity" and inserting "EXCEPTIONS FOR DISCLOSURE OF COMMUNICATIONS.—A provider described in subsection (a)";

(D) in subsection (b)(6)—

(i) in subparagraph (A)(ii), by striking "or";

(ii) in subparagraph (B), by striking the period and inserting "; or"; and

(iii) by adding after subparagraph (B) the following:

"(C) if the provider reasonably believes that an emergency involving immediate danger of death or serious physical injury to any person requires disclosure of the information without delay."; and

(E) by inserting after subsection (b) the following:

"(c) EXCEPTIONS FOR DISCLOSURE OF CUSTOMER RECORDS.—A provider described in subsection (a) may divulge a record or other information pertaining to a subscriber to or customer of such service (not including the contents of communications covered by subsection (a)(1) or (a)(2))—

"(1) as otherwise authorized in section 2703;

"(2) with the lawful consent of the customer or subscriber;

"(3) as may be necessarily incident to the rendition of the service or to the protection of the rights or property of the provider of that service;

"(4) to a governmental entity, if the provider reasonably believes that an emergency involving immediate danger of death or serious physical injury to any person justifies disclosure of the information; or

"(5) to any person other than a governmental entity.".

(2) TECHNICAL AND CONFORMING AMENDMENT.—The table of sections for chapter 121 of title 18, United States Code, is amended by striking the item relating to section 2702 and inserting the following:

"2702.   Voluntary disclosure of customer communications or records.".

(b) REQUIREMENTS FOR GOVERNMENT ACCESS.—

    (1) IN GENERAL.—Section 2703 of title 18, United States Code, is amended—

        (A) by striking the section heading and inserting the following:

"2703.   Required disclosure of customer communications or records";

        (B) in subsection (c) by redesignating paragraph (2) as paragraph (3);

        (C) in subsection (c)(1)—

            (i) by striking "(A) Except as provided in subparagraph (B), a provider of electronic communication service or remote computing service may" and inserting "A governmental entity may require a provider of electronic communication service or remote computing service to";

            (ii) by striking "covered by subsection (a) or (b) of this section) to any person other than a governmental entity.

"(B) A provider of electronic communication service or remote computing service shall disclose a record or other information pertaining to a subscriber to or customer of such service (not including the contents of communications covered by subsection (a) or (b) of this section) to a governmental entity' and inserting ')";

            (iii) by redesignating subparagraph (C) as paragraph (2);

            (iv) by redesignating clauses (i), (ii), (iii), and (iv) as subparagraphs (A), (B), (C), and (D), respectively;

            (v) in subparagraph (D) (as redesignated) by striking the period and inserting "; or"; and

            (vi) by inserting after subparagraph (D) (as redesignated) the following:

"(E) seeks information under paragraph (2)."; and

        (D) in paragraph (2) (as redesignated) by striking "subparagraph (B)" and insert "paragraph (1)".

    (2) TECHNICAL AND CONFORMING AMENDMENT.—The table of sections for chapter 121 of title 18, United States Code, is amended by striking the item relating to section 2703 and inserting the following:

"2703.   Required disclosure of customer communications or records.".

AUTHORITY FOR DELAYING NOTICE OF THE EXECUTION OF A WARRANT

SEC. 213.

Section 3103a of title 18, United States Code, is amended—
>   (1) by inserting "(a) IN GENERAL.—" before "In addition"; and
>   (2) by adding at the end the following:

"(b) DELAY.—With respect to the issuance of any warrant or court order under this section, or any other rule of law, to search for and seize any property or material that constitutes evidence of a criminal offense in violation of the laws of the United States, any notice required, or that may be required, to be given may be delayed if—
>   "(1) the court finds reasonable cause to believe that providing immediate notification of the execution of the warrant may have an adverse result (as defined in section 2705);
>   "(2) the warrant prohibits the seizure of any tangible property, any wire or electronic communication (as defined in section 2510), or, except as expressly provided in chapter 121, any stored wire or electronic information, except where the court finds reasonable necessity for the seizure; and
>   "(3) the warrant provides for the giving of such notice within a reasonable period of its execution, which period may thereafter be extended by the court for good cause shown.".

PEN REGISTER AND TRAP AND TRACE AUTHORITY UNDER FISA

SEC. 214.

(a) APPLICATIONS AND ORDERS.—Section 402 of the Foreign Intelligence Surveillance Act of 1978 (50 U.S.C. §1842) is amended—
>   (1) in subsection (a)(1), by striking "for any investigation to gather foreign intelligence information or information concerning international terrorism" and inserting "for any investigation to obtain foreign intelligence information not concerning a United States person or to protect against international terrorism or clandestine intelligence activities, provided that such investigation of a United States person is not conducted solely upon the basis of activities protected by the first amendment to the Constitution";
>   (2) by amending subsection (c)(2) to read as follows:

"(2) a certification by the applicant that the information likely to be obtained is foreign intelligence information not concerning a United States person or is relevant to an ongoing investigation to protect against international terrorism or clandestine intelligence activities, provided that such investigation of a United States person is not conducted solely upon the basis of activities protected by the first amendment to the Constitution.";

(3) by striking subsection (c)(3); and
(4) by amending subsection (d)(2)(A) to read as follows:

"(A) shall specify—
"(i) the identity, if known, of the person who is the subject of the investigation;
"(ii) the identity, if known, of the person to whom is leased or in whose name is listed the telephone line or other facility to which the pen register or trap and trace device is to be attached or applied;
"(iii) the attributes of the communications to which the order applies, such as the number or other identifier, and, if known, the location of the telephone line or other facility to which the pen register or trap and trace device is to be attached or applied and, in the case of a trap and trace device, the geographic limits of the trap and trace order.".

(b) AUTHORIZATION DURING EMERGENCIES.—Section 403 of the Foreign Intelligence Surveillance Act of 1978 (50 U.S.C. §1843) is amended—
(1) in subsection (a), by striking "foreign intelligence information or information concerning international terrorism" and inserting "foreign intelligence information not concerning a United States person or information to protect against international terrorism or clandestine intelligence activities, provided that such investigation of a United States person is not conducted solely upon the basis of activities protected by the first amendment to the Constitution"; and
(2) in subsection (b)(1), by striking "foreign intelligence information or information concerning international terrorism" and inserting "foreign intelligence information not concerning a United States person or information to protect against international terrorism or clandestine intelligence activities, provided that such investigation of a United States person is not conducted solely upon the basis of activities protected by the first amendment to the Constitution".

ACCESS TO RECORDS AND OTHER ITEMS UNDER THE FOREIGN INTELLIGENCE SURVEILLANCE ACT

SEC. 215.

Title V of the Foreign Intelligence Surveillance Act of 1978 (50 U.S.C. §1861 et seq.) is amended by striking sections 501 through 503 and inserting the following:

"ACCESS TO CERTAIN BUSINESS RECORDS FOR FOREIGN INTELLIGENCE AND INTERNATIONAL TERRORISM INVESTIGATIONS

"SEC. 501.

"(a)(1) The Director of the Federal Bureau of Investigation or a designee of the Director (whose rank shall be no lower than Assistant Special Agent in Charge) may make an application for an order requiring the production of any tangible things (including books, records, papers, documents, and other items) for an investigation to protect against international terrorism or clandestine intelligence activities, provided that such investigation of a United States person is not conducted solely upon the basis of activities protected by the first amendment to the Constitution.

"(2) An investigation conducted under this section shall—

"(A) be conducted under guidelines approved by the Attorney General under Executive Order 12333 (or a successor order); and

"(B) not be conducted of a United States person solely upon the basis of activities protected by the first amendment to the Constitution of the United States.

"(b) Each application under this section—

"(1) shall be made to—

"(A) a judge of the court established by section 103(a); or

"(B) a United States Magistrate Judge under chapter 43 of title 28, United States Code, who is publicly designated by the Chief Justice of the United States to have the power to hear applications and grant orders for the production of tangible things under this section on behalf of a judge of that court; and

"(2) shall specify that the records concerned are sought for an authorized investigation conducted in accordance with subsection (a)(2) to obtain foreign intelligence information not concerning a United States person or to protect against international terrorism or clandestine intelligence activities.

"(c)(1) Upon an application made pursuant to this section, the judge shall enter an ex parte order as requested, or as modified, approving the release of records if the judge finds that the application meets the requirements of this section.

"(2) An order under this subsection shall not disclose that it is issued for purposes of an investigation described in subsection (a).

"(d) No person shall disclose to any other person (other than those persons necessary to produce the tangible things under this section) that the Federal Bureau of Investigation has sought or obtained tangible things under this section.

"(e) A person who, in good faith, produces tangible things under an order pursuant to this section shall not be liable to any other person for such production. Such production shall not be deemed to constitute a waiver of any privilege in any other proceeding or context.

"CONGRESSIONAL OVERSIGHT

"SEC. 502.

"(a) On a semiannual basis, the Attorney General shall fully inform the Permanent Select Committee on Intelligence of the House of Representatives and the Select Committee on Intelligence of the Senate concerning all requests for the production of tangible things under section 402.

"(b) On a semiannual basis, the Attorney General shall provide to the Committees on the Judiciary of the House of Representatives and the Senate a report setting forth with respect to the preceding 6-month period—

"(1) the total number of applications made for orders approving requests for the production of tangible things under section 402; and

"(2) the total number of such orders either granted, modified, or denied.".

MODIFICATION OF AUTHORITIES RELATING TO USE OF PEN REGISTERS AND TRAP AND TRACE DEVICES

SEC. 216.

(a) GENERAL LIMITATIONS.—Section 3121(c) of title 18, United States Code, is amended—

(1) by inserting "or trap and trace device" after "pen register";

(2) by inserting ", routing, addressing," after "dialing"; and

(3) by striking "call processing" and inserting "the processing and transmitting of wire or electronic communications so as not to include the contents of any wire or electronic communications".

(b) ISSUANCE OF ORDERS.—

(1) IN GENERAL.—Section 3123(a) of title 18, United States Code, is amended to read as follows:

"(a) IN GENERAL.—

"(1) ATTORNEY FOR THE GOVERNMENT.—Upon an application made under section 3122(a)(1), the court shall enter an ex parte order authorizing the installation and use of a pen register or trap and trace device anywhere within the United States, if the court finds that the attorney for the Government has certified to the court that the information likely to be obtained by such installation and use is relevant to an ongoing criminal investigation. The order, upon service of that order, shall apply to any person or entity providing wire or electronic communication service in the United States whose assistance may facilitate the execution of the order. Whenever such an order is served on any person or entity not specifically named in the order, upon request of such person or entity, the attorney for the Government or law enforcement or investigative officer that is serving the order shall provide written or electronic certification that the order applies to the person or entity being served.

"(2) STATE INVESTIGATIVE OR LAW ENFORCEMENT OFFICERS.—Upon an application made under section 3122(a)(2), the court shall enter an ex parte order authorizing the installation and use of a pen register or trap and trace device within the jurisdiction of the court, if the court finds that the State law enforcement or investigative officer has certified to the court that the information likely to be obtained by such installation and use is relevant to an ongoing criminal investigation.

"(3)(A) Where the law enforcement agency implementing an ex parte order under this subsection seeks to do so by installing and using its own pen register or trap and trace device on a packet-switched data network of a provider of electronic communication service to the public, the agency shall ensure that a record will be maintained which will identify—

"(i) any officer or officers who installed the device and any officer or officers who accessed the device to obtain information from the network;

"(ii) the date and time the device was installed, the date and time the device was uninstalled, and the date, time, and duration of each time the device is accessed to obtain information;

"(iii) the configuration of the device at the time of its installation and any subsequent modification thereof; and

"(iv) any information which has been collected by the device.

To the extent that the pen register or trap and trace device can be set automatically to record this information electronically, the record shall be maintained electronically throughout the installation and use of such device.

"(B) The record maintained under subparagraph (A) shall be provided ex parte and under seal to the court which entered the ex parte order authorizing the installation and use of the device within 30 days after termination of the order (including any extensions thereof).".

(2) CONTENTS OF ORDER.—Section 3123(b)(1) of title 18, United States Code, is amended—

(A) in subparagraph (A)—

(i) by inserting "or other facility" after "telephone line"; and

(ii) by inserting before the semicolon at the end "or applied"; and

(B) by striking subparagraph (C) and inserting the following:

"(C) the attributes of the communications to which the order applies, including the number or other identifier and, if known, the location of the telephone line or other facility to which the pen register or trap and trace device is to be attached or applied, and, in the case of an order authorizing installation and use of a trap and trace device under subsection (a)(2), the geographic limits of the order; and".

(3) NONDISCLOSURE REQUIREMENTS.—Section 3123(d)(2) of title 18, United States Code, is amended—

(A) by inserting "or other facility" after "the line"; and

(B) by striking ", or who has been ordered by the court" and inserting "or applied, or who is obligated by the order".

(c) DEFINITIONS.—

(1) COURT OF COMPETENT JURISDICTION.—Section 3127(2) of title 18, United States Code, is amended by striking subparagraph (A) and inserting the following:

"(A) any district court of the United States (including a magistrate judge of such a court) or any United States court of appeals having jurisdiction over the offense being investigated; or".

(2) PEN REGISTER.—Section 3127(3) of title 18, United States Code, is amended—

> (A) by striking "electronic or other impulses" and all that follows through "is attached" and inserting "dialing, routing, addressing, or signaling information transmitted by an instrument or facility from which a wire or electronic communication is transmitted, provided, however, that such information shall not include the contents of any communication"; and
>
> (B) by inserting "or process" after "device" each place it appears.

(3) TRAP AND TRACE DEVICE.—Section 3127(4) of title 18, United States Code, is amended—

> (A) by striking "of an instrument" and all that follows through the semicolon and inserting "or other dialing, routing, addressing, and signaling information reasonably likely to identify the source of a wire or electronic communication, provided, however, that such information shall not include the contents of any communication;"; and
>
> (B) by inserting "or process" after "a device".

(4) CONFORMING AMENDMENT.—Section 3127(1) of title 18, United States Code, is amended—

> (A) by striking "and"; and
>
> (B) by inserting ", and 'contents' " after "electronic communication service".

(5) TECHNICAL AMENDMENT.—Section 3124(d) of title 18, United States Code, is amended by striking "the terms of".

(6) CONFORMING AMENDMENT.—Section 3124(b) of title 18, United States Code, is amended by inserting "or other facility" after "the appropriate line".

INTERCEPTION OF COMPUTER TRESPASSER COMMUNICATIONS

SEC. 217.

Chapter 119 of title 18, United States Code, is amended—

> (1) in section 2510—
>
> > (A) in paragraph (18), by striking "and" at the end;
> >
> > (B) in paragraph (19), by striking the period and inserting a semicolon; and
> >
> > (C) by inserting after paragraph (19) the following:

"(20) 'protected computer' has the meaning set forth in section 1030;
"(21) 'computer trespasser'—

"(A) means a person who accesses a protected computer without authorization and thus has no reasonable expectation of privacy in any communication transmitted to, through, or from the protected computer; and

"(B) does not include a person known by the owner or operator of the protected computer to have an existing contractual relationship with the owner or operator of the protected computer for access to all or part of the protected computer."; and

(2) in section 2511(2), by inserting at the end the following:

"(i) It shall not be unlawful under this chapter for a person acting under color of law to intercept the wire or electronic communications of a computer trespasser transmitted to, through, or from the protected computer, if—

"(I) the owner or operator of the protected computer authorizes the interception of the computer trespasser's communications on the protected computer;

"(II) the person acting under color of law is lawfully engaged in an investigation;

"(III) the person acting under color of law has reasonable grounds to believe that the contents of the computer trespasser's communications will be relevant to the investigation; and

"(IV) such interception does not acquire communications other than those transmitted to or from the computer trespasser."

FOREIGN INTELLIGENCE INFORMATION

SEC. 218.
Sections 104(a)(7)(B) and section 303(a)(7)(B) (50 U.S.C. §1804(a)(7)(B) and 1823(a)(7)(B)) of the Foreign Intelligence Surveillance Act of 1978 are each amended by striking "the purpose" and inserting "a significant purpose".

SINGLE-JURISDICTION SEARCH WARRANTS FOR TERRORISM

SEC. 219.

Rule 41(a) of the Federal Rules of Criminal Procedure is amended by inserting after "executed" the following: "and (3) in an investigation of domestic terrorism or international terrorism (as defined in section 2331 of title 18, United States Code), by a Federal magistrate judge in any district in which activities related to the terrorism may have occurred, for a search of property or for a person within or outside the district".

NATIONWIDE SERVICE OF SEARCH WARRANTS FOR ELECTRONIC EVIDENCE

SEC. 220.

(a) IN GENERAL.—Chapter 121 of title 18, United States Code, is amended—
  (1) in section 2703, by striking "under the Federal Rules of Criminal Procedure" every place it appears and inserting "using the procedures described in the Federal Rules of Criminal Procedure by a court with jurisdiction over the offense under investigation"; and
  (2) in section 2711—
    (A) in paragraph (1), by striking "and";
    (B) in paragraph (2), by striking the period and inserting "; and"; and
    (C) by inserting at the end the following:
  "(3) the term 'court of competent jurisdiction' has the meaning assigned by section 3127, and includes any Federal court within that definition, without geographic limitation.".

(b) CONFORMING AMENDMENT.—Section 2703(d) of title 18, United States Code, is amended by striking "described in section 3127(2)(A)".

TRADE SANCTIONS

SEC. 221.

(a) IN GENERAL.—The Trade Sanctions Reform and Export Enhancement Act of 2000 (Public Law 106-387; 114 Stat. 1549A-67) is amended—
  (1) by amending section 904(2)(C) to read as follows:
    "(C) used to facilitate the design, development, or production of chemical or biological weapons, missiles, or weapons of mass destruction.";
  (2) in section 906(a)(1)—
    (A) by inserting ", the Taliban or the territory of Afghanistan controlled by the Taliban," after "Cuba"; and
    (B) by inserting ", or in the territory of Afghanistan controlled by the Taliban," after "within such country"; and

(3) in section 906(a)(2), by inserting ", or to any other entity in Syria or North Korea" after "Korea".

(b) APPLICATION OF THE TRADE SANCTIONS REFORM AND EXPORT ENHANCEMENT ACT.—Nothing in the Trade Sanctions Reform and Export Enhancement Act of 2000 shall limit the application or scope of any law establishing criminal or civil penalties, including any Executive order or regulation promulgated pursuant to such laws (or similar or successor laws), for the unlawful export of any agricultural commodity, medicine, or medical device to—

(1) a foreign organization, group, or person designated pursuant to Executive Order No. 12947 of January 23, 1995, as amended;

(2) a Foreign Terrorist Organization pursuant to the Antiterrorism and Effective Death Penalty Act of 1996 (Public Law 104-132);

(3) a foreign organization, group, or person designated pursuant to Executive Order No. 13224 (September 23, 2001);

(4) any narcotics trafficking entity designated pursuant to Executive Order No. 12978 (October 21, 1995) or the Foreign Narcotics Kingpin Designation Act (Public Law 106-120); or

(5) any foreign organization, group, or persons subject to any restriction for its involvement in weapons of mass destruction or missile proliferation.

ASSISTANCE TO LAW ENFORCEMENT AGENCIES

SEC. 222.

Nothing in this Act shall impose any additional technical obligation or requirement on a provider of a wire or electronic communication service or other person to furnish facilities or technical assistance. A provider of a wire or electronic communication service, landlord, custodian, or other person who furnishes facilities or technical assistance pursuant to section 216 shall be reasonably compensated for such reasonable expenditures incurred in providing such facilities or assistance.

CIVIL LIABILITY FOR CERTAIN UNAUTHORIZED DISCLOSURES

SEC. 223.

(a) Section 2520 of title 18, United States Code, is amended—

(1) in subsection (a), after "entity", by inserting ", other than the United States,";

(2) by adding at the end the following:

"(f) ADMINISTRATIVE DISCIPLINE.—If a court or appropriate department or agency determines that the United States or any of its departments or agencies has violated any provision of this chapter, and the court or appropriate department or agency finds that the circumstances surrounding the violation raise serious questions about whether or not an officer or employee of the United States acted willfully or intentionally with respect to the violation, the department or agency shall, upon receipt of a true and correct copy of the decision and findings of the court or appropriate department or agency promptly initiate a proceeding to determine whether disciplinary action against the officer or employee is warranted. If the head of the department or agency involved determines that disciplinary action is not warranted, he or she shall notify the Inspector General with jurisdiction over the department or agency concerned and shall provide the Inspector General with the reasons for such determination.''; and

        (3) by adding a new subsection (g), as follows:

"(g) IMPROPER DISCLOSURE IS VIOLATION.—Any willful disclosure or use by an investigative or law enforcement officer or governmental entity of information beyond the extent permitted by section 2517 is a violation of this chapter for purposes of section 2520(a).''.

(b) Section 2707 of title 18, United States Code, is amended—
        (1) in subsection (a), after "entity", by inserting ", other than the United States,'';
        (2) by striking subsection (d) and inserting the following:

"(d) ADMINISTRATIVE DISCIPLINE.—If a court or appropriate department or agency determines that the United States or any of its departments or agencies has violated any provision of this chapter, and the court or appropriate department or agency finds that the circumstances surrounding the violation raise serious questions about whether or not an officer or employee of the United States acted willfully or intentionally with respect to the violation, the department or agency shall, upon receipt of a true and correct copy of the decision and findings of the court or appropriate department or agency promptly initiate a proceeding to determine whether disciplinary action against the officer or employee is warranted. If the head of the department or agency involved determines that disciplinary action is not warranted, he or she shall notify the Inspector General with jurisdiction over the department or agency concerned and shall provide the Inspector General with the reasons for such determination.''; and

        (3) by adding a new subsection (g), as follows:

"(g) IMPROPER DISCLOSURE.—Any willful disclosure of a 'record', as that term is defined in section 552a(a) of title 5, United States Code, obtained by an investigative or law enforcement officer, or a governmental entity, pursuant to section 2703 of this title, or from a device installed pursuant to section 3123 or 3125 of this title, that is not a disclosure made in the proper performance of the official functions of the officer or governmental entity making the disclosure, is a violation of this chapter. This provision shall not apply to information previously lawfully disclosed (prior to the commencement of any civil or administrative proceeding under this chapter) to the public by a Federal, State, or local governmental entity or by the plaintiff in a civil action under this chapter.".

(c)(1) Chapter 121 of title 18, United States Code, is amended by adding at the end the following:

"§ 2712. Civil actions against the United States

"(a) IN GENERAL.—Any person who is aggrieved by any willful violation of this chapter or of chapter 119 of this title or of sections 106(a), 305(a), or 405(a) of the Foreign Intelligence Surveillance Act of 1978 (50 U. S.C. 1801 et seq.) may commence an action in United States District Court against the United States to recover money damages. In any such action, if a person who is aggrieved successfully establishes such a violation of this chapter or of chapter 119 of this title or of the above specific provisions of title 50, the Court may assess as damages—

"(1) actual damages, but not less than $10,000, whichever amount is greater; and

"(2) litigation costs, reasonably incurred.

"(b) PROCEDURES.—(1) Any action against the United States under this section may be commenced only after a claim is presented to the appropriate department or agency under the procedures of the Federal Tort Claims Act, as set forth in title 28, United States Code.

"(2) Any action against the United States under this section shall be forever barred unless it is presented in writing to the appropriate Federal agency within 2 years after such claim accrues or unless action is begun within 6 months after the date of mailing, by certified or registered mail, of notice of final denial of the claim by the agency to which it was presented. The claim shall accrue on the date upon which the claimant first has a reasonable opportunity to discover the violation.

"(3) Any action under this section shall be tried to the court without a jury.

"(4) Notwithstanding any other provision of law, the procedures set forth in section 106(f), 305(g), or 405(f) of the Foreign Intelligence Surveillance Act of 1978 (50 U.S.C. §1801 et seq.) shall be the exclusive means by which materials governed by those sections may be reviewed.

"(5) An amount equal to any award against the United States under this section shall be reimbursed by the department or agency concerned to the fund described in section 1304 of title 31, United States Code, out of any appropriation, fund, or other account (excluding any part of such appropriation, fund, or account that is available for the enforcement of any Federal law) that is available for the operating expenses of the department or agency concerned.

"(c) ADMINISTRATIVE DISCIPLINE.—If a court or appropriate department or agency determines that the United States or any of its departments or agencies has violated any provision of this chapter, and the court or appropriate department or agency finds that the circumstances surrounding the violation raise serious questions about whether or not an officer or employee of the United States acted willfully or intentionally with respect to the violation, the department or agency shall, upon receipt of a true and correct copy of the decision and findings of the court or appropriate department or agency promptly initiate a proceeding to determine whether disciplinary action against the officer or employee is warranted. If the head of the department or agency involved determines that disciplinary action is not warranted, he or she shall notify the Inspector General with jurisdiction over the department or agency concerned and shall provide the Inspector General with the reasons for such determination.

"(d) EXCLUSIVE REMEDY.—Any action against the United States under this subsection shall be the exclusive remedy against the United States for any claims within the purview of this section.

"(e) STAY OF PROCEEDINGS.—(1) Upon the motion of the United States, the court shall stay any action commenced under this section if the court determines that civil discovery will adversely affect the ability of the Government to conduct a related investigation or the prosecution of a related criminal case. Such a stay shall toll the limitations periods of paragraph (2) of subsection (b).

"(2) In this subsection, the terms 'related criminal case' and 'related investigation' mean an actual prosecution or investigation in progress at the time at which the request for the stay or any subsequent motion to lift the stay is made. In determining whether an investigation or a criminal case is related to an action commenced under this section, the court shall consider the degree of similarity between the parties, witnesses, facts, and circumstances involved in the 2 proceedings, without requiring that any one or more factors be identical.

"(3) In requesting a stay under paragraph (1), the Government may, in appropriate cases, submit evidence ex parte in order to avoid disclosing any matter that may adversely affect a related investigation or a related criminal case. If the Government makes such an ex parte submission, the plaintiff shall be given an opportunity to make a submission to the court, not ex parte, and the court may, in its discretion, request further information from either party.".

(2) The table of sections at the beginning of chapter 121 is amended to read as follows:

"2712.   Civil action against the United States.".

SUNSET

SEC. 224.

(a) IN GENERAL.—Except as provided in subsection (b), this title and the amendments made by this title (other than sections 203(a), 203(c), 205, 208, 210, 211, 213, 216, 219, 221, and 222, and the amendments made by those sections) shall cease to have effect on December 31, 2005.

(b) EXCEPTION.—With respect to any particular foreign intelligence investigation that began before the date on which the provisions referred to in subsection (a) cease to have effect, or with respect to any particular offense or potential offense that began or occurred before the date on which such provisions cease to have effect, such provisions shall continue in effect.

IMMUNITY FOR COMPLIANCE WITH FISA WIRETAP

SEC. 225.

Section 105 of the Foreign Intelligence Surveillance Act of 1978 (50 U.S. C. 1805) is amended by inserting after subsection (g) the following:

"(h) No cause of action shall lie in any court against any provider of a wire or electronic communication service, landlord, custodian, or other person (including any officer, employee, agent, or other specified person thereof) that furnishes any information, facilities, or technical assistance in accordance with a court order or request for emergency assistance under this Act.".

TITLE VIII—STRENGTHENING THE CRIMINAL LAWS AGAINST TERRORISM

DEFINITION OF DOMESTIC TERRORISM

SEC. 802.

(a) DOMESTIC TERRORISM DEFINED.—Section 2331 of title 18, United States Code, is amended—

(1) in paragraph (1)(B)(iii), by striking "by assassination or kidnapping" and inserting "by mass destruction, assassination, or kidnapping";

(2) in paragraph (3), by striking "and";

(3) in paragraph (4), by striking the period at the end and inserting "; and"; and

(4) by adding at the end the following:

"(5) the term 'domestic terrorism' means activities that—

    "(A) involve acts dangerous to human life that are a violation of the criminal laws of the United States or of any State;

    "(B) appear to be intended—

        "(i) to intimidate or coerce a civilian population;

        "(ii) to influence the policy of a government by intimidation or coercion; or

        "(iii) to affect the conduct of a government by mass destruction, assassination, or kidnapping; and

    "(C) occur primarily within the territorial jurisdiction of the United States.".

(b) CONFORMING AMENDMENT.—Section 3077(1) of title 18, United States Code, is amended to read as follows:

    "(1) 'act of terrorism' means an act of domestic or international terrorism as defined in section 2331;".

PROHIBITION AGAINST HARBORING TERRORISTS

SEC. 803.

(a) IN GENERAL.—Chapter 113B of title 18, United States Code, is amended by adding after section 2338 the following new section:

"§ 2339. Harboring or concealing terrorists

"(a) Whoever harbors or conceals any person who he knows, or has reasonable grounds to believe, has committed, or is about to commit, an offense under section 32 (relating to destruction of aircraft or aircraft facilities), section 175 (relating to biological weapons), section 229 (relating to chemical weapons), section 831 (relating to nuclear materials), paragraph (2) or (3) of section 844(f) (relating to arson and bombing of government property risking or causing injury or death), section 1366(a) (relating to the destruction of an energy facility), section 2280 (relating to violence against maritime navigation), section 2332a (relating to weapons of mass destruction), or section 2332b (relating to acts of terrorism transcending national boundaries) of this title, section 236(a) (relating to sabotage of nuclear facilities or fuel) of the Atomic Energy Act of 1954 (42

U.S.C. §2284(a)), or section 46502 (relating to aircraft piracy) of title 49, shall be fined under this title or imprisoned not more than ten years, or both.".

"(b) A violation of this section may be prosecuted in any Federal judicial district in which the underlying offense was committed, or in any other Federal judicial district as provided by law.".

(b) TECHNICAL AMENDMENT.—The chapter analysis for chapter 113B of title 18, United States Code, is amended by inserting after the item for section 2338 the following:

"2339.   Harboring or concealing terrorists.".

JURISDICTION OVER CRIMES COMMITTED AT U.S. FACILITIES ABROAD

SEC. 804.

Section 7 of title 18, United States Code, is amended by adding at the end the following:

"(9) With respect to offenses committed by or against a national of the United States as that term is used in section 101 of the Immigration and Nationality Act—

"(A) the premises of United States diplomatic, consular, military or other United States Government missions or entities in foreign States, including the buildings, parts of buildings, and land appurtenant or ancillary thereto or used for purposes of those missions or entities, irrespective of ownership; and

"(B) residences in foreign States and the land appurtenant or ancillary thereto, irrespective of ownership, used for purposes of those missions or entities or used by United States personnel assigned to those missions or entities.

Nothing in this paragraph shall be deemed to supersede any treaty or international agreement with which this paragraph conflicts. This paragraph does not apply with respect to an offense committed by a person described in section 3261(a) of this title.".

MATERIAL SUPPORT FOR TERRORISM

SEC. 805.

(a) IN GENERAL.—Section 2339A of title 18, United States Code, is amended—

(1) in subsection (a)—

(A) by striking ", within the United States,";

(B) by inserting "229," after "175,";

(C) by inserting "1993," after "1992,";

(D) by inserting ", section 236 of the Atomic Energy Act of 1954 (42 U.S.C. §2284)," after "of this title";

(E) by inserting "or 60123(b)" after "46502"; and

(F) by inserting at the end the following: "A violation of this section may be prosecuted in any Federal judicial district in which the underlying offense was committed, or in any other Federal judicial district as provided by law."; and

(2) in subsection (b)—

(A) by striking "or other financial securities" and inserting "or monetary instruments or financial securities"; and

(B) by inserting "expert advice or assistance," after "training,".

(b) TECHNICAL AMENDMENT.—Section 1956(c)(7)(D) of title 18, United States Code, is amended by inserting "or 2339B" after "2339A".

ASSETS OF TERRORIST ORGANIZATIONS

SEC. 806.

Section 981(a)(1) of title 18, United States Code, is amended by inserting at the end the following:

"(G) All assets, foreign or domestic—

"(i) of any individual, entity, or organization engaged in planning or perpetrating any act of domestic or international terrorism (as defined in section 2331) against the United States, citizens or residents of the United States, or their property, and all assets, foreign or domestic, affording any person a source of influence over any such entity or organization;

"(ii) acquired or maintained by any person with the intent and for the purpose of supporting, planning, conducting, or concealing an act of domestic or international terrorism (as defined in section 2331) against the United States, citizens or residents of the United States, or their property; or

"(iii) derived from, involved in, or used or intended to be used to commit any act of domestic or international terrorism (as defined in section 2331) against the United States, citizens or residents of the United States, or their property.".

TECHNICAL CLARIFICATION RELATING TO

PROVISION OF MATERIAL SUPPORT TO TERRORISM

SEC. 807.

No provision of the Trade Sanctions Reform and Export Enhancement Act of 2000 (title IX of Public Law 106-387) shall be construed to limit or otherwise affect section 2339A or 2339B of title 18, United States Code.

DEFINITION OF FEDERAL CRIME OF TERRORISM

SEC. 808.

Section 2332b of title 18, United States Code, is amended—

(1) in subsection (f), by inserting "and any violation of section 351(e), 844(e), 844(f)(1), 956(b), 1361, 1366(b), 1366(c), 1751(e), 2152, or 2156 of this title," before "and the Secretary"; and

(2) in subsection (g)(5)(B), by striking clauses (i) through (iii) and inserting the following:

"(i) section 32 (relating to destruction of aircraft or aircraft facilities), 37 (relating to violence at international airports), 81 (relating to arson within special maritime and territorial jurisdiction), 175 or 175b (relating to biological weapons), 229 (relating to chemical weapons), subsection (a), (b), (c), or (d) of section 351 (relating to congressional, cabinet, and Supreme Court assassination and kidnapping), 831 (relating to nuclear materials), 842(m) or (n) (relating to plastic explosives), 844(f)(2) or (3) (relating to arson and bombing of Government property risking or causing death), 844(i) (relating to arson and bombing of property used in interstate commerce), 930(c) (relating to killing or attempted killing during an attack on a Federal facility with a dangerous weapon), 956(a)(1) (relating to conspiracy to murder, kidnap, or maim persons abroad), 1030(a)(1) (relating to protection of computers), 1030(a)(5)(A)(i) resulting in damage as defined in 1030(a)(5)(B)(ii) through (v) (relating to protection of computers), 1114 (relating to killing or attempted killing of officers and employees of the United States), 1116 (relating to murder or manslaughter of foreign officials, official guests, or internationally protected persons), 1203 (relating to hostage taking), 1362 (relating to destruction of communication lines, stations, or systems), 1363 (relating to injury to buildings or property within special maritime and territorial jurisdiction of the United States), 1366(a) (relating to destruction of an energy facility), 1751(a), (b), (c), or (d) (relating to Presidential and Presidential staff assassination and kidnapping), 1992 (relating to wrecking trains), 1993 (relating to terrorist attacks and other acts of violence against mass transportation systems), 2155 (relating to destruction of national defense materials, premises, or utilities), 2280 (relating to violence against maritime navigation), 2281 (relating to violence against maritime fixed platforms), 2332 (relating to certain homicides and other violence against United States nationals occurring outside of the United States), 2332a (relating to use of weapons of mass destruction), 2332b (relating to acts of terrorism transcending national boundaries), 2339 (relating to harboring terrorists), 2339A (relating to providing material support to terrorists), 2339B (relating to providing material support to terrorist organizations), or 2340A (relating to torture) of this title;

"(ii) section 236 (relating to sabotage of nuclear facilities or fuel) of the Atomic Energy Act of 1954 (42 U.S.C. §2284); or

"(iii) section 46502 (relating to aircraft piracy), the second sentence of section 46504 (relating to assault on a flight crew with a dangerous weapon), section 46505(b)(3) or (c) (relating to explosive or incendiary devices, or endangerment of human life by means of weapons, on aircraft), section 46506 if homicide or attempted homicide is involved (relating to application of certain criminal laws to acts on aircraft), or section 60123(b) (relating to destruction of interstate gas or hazardous liquid pipeline facility) of title 49.".

TITLE X—MISCELLANEOUS

DEFINITION OF "ELECTRONIC SURVEILLANCE"

SEC. 1003.
 Section 101(f)(2) of the Foreign Intelligence Surveillance Act (50 U.S.C. §1801(f)(2)) is amended by adding at the end before the semicolon the following:

", but does not include the acquisition of those communications of computer trespassers that would be permissible under section 2511(2)(i) of title 18, United States Code".

USA PATRIOT IMPROVEMENT AND REAUTHORIZATION ACT OF 2005

(Public Law 109-177 of March 9, 2006, 120 STAT. 192)

AN ACT To extend and modify authorities needed to combat terrorism, and for other purposes.

Be it enacted by the Senate and House of Representatives of the United States of America in Congress assembled,

SHORT TITLE; TABLE OF CONTENTS

SECTION 1.
(a) SHORT TITLE.—This Act may be cited as the "USA PATRIOT Improvement and Reauthorization Act of 2005".
(b) TABLE OF CONTENTS.—The table of contents for this Act is as follows:

TITLE I—USA PATRIOT IMPROVEMENT AND REAUTHORIZATION ACT

REFERENCE TO, AND MODIFICATION OF SHORT TITLE FOR, USA PATRIOT ACT

SEC. 101.

(a) REFERENCES TO USA PATRIOT ACT.—A reference in this Act to the USA PATRIOT Act shall be deemed a reference to the Uniting and Strengthening America by Providing Appropriate Tools Required to Intercept and Obstruct Terrorism Act (USA PATRIOT Act) of 2001.

(b) MODIFICATION OF SHORT TITLE OF USA PATRIOT ACT.—Section 1(a) of the USA PATRIOT Act is amended to read as follows:

"(a) SHORT TITLE.—This Act may be cited as the 'Uniting and Strengthening America by Providing Appropriate Tools Required to Intercept and Obstruct Terrorism Act of 2001' or the 'USA PATRIOT Act'.".

USA PATRIOT ACT SUNSET PROVISIONS

SEC. 102.

(a) IN GENERAL.—Section 224 of the USA PATRIOT Act is repealed.

(b) SECTIONS 206 AND 215 SUNSET.—

(1) IN GENERAL.—Effective December 31, 2009, the Foreign Intelligence Surveillance Act of 1978 is amended so that sections 501, 502, and 105(c)(2) read as they read on October 25, 2001.

(2) EXCEPTION.—With respect to any particular foreign intelligence investigation that began before the date on which the provisions referred to in paragraph (1) cease to have effect, or with respect to any particular offense or potential offense that began or occurred before the date on which such provisions cease to have effect, such provisions shall continue in effect.

EXTENSION OF SUNSET RELATING TO INDIVIDUAL TERRORISTS AS AGENTS OF FOREIGN POWERS

SEC. 103.

Section 6001(b) of the Intelligence Reform and Terrorism Prevention Act of 2004 (Public Law 108-458; 118 Stat. 3742) is amended to read as follows:

"(b) SUNSET.—

"(1) IN GENERAL.—Except as provided in paragraph (2), the amendment made by subsection (a) shall cease to have effect on June 1, 2015.

"(2) EXCEPTION.—With respect to any particular foreign intelligence investigation that began before the date on which the provisions referred to in paragraph (1) cease to have effect, or with respect to any particular offense or potential offense that began or occurred before the date on which the provisions cease to have effect, such provisions shall continue in effect.".

SECTION 233B AND THE MATERIAL SUPPORT SECTIONS OF TITLE 18, UNITED STATES CODE

SEC. 104.

Section 6603 of the Intelligence Reform and Terrorism Prevention Act of 2004 (Public Law 108-458; 118 Stat. 3762) is amended by striking subsection (g).

DURATION OF FISA SURVEILLANCE OF NON-UNITED STATES PERSONS UNDER SECTION 207 OF THE USA PATRIOT ACT

SEC. 105.

(a) ELECTRONIC SURVEILLANCE.—Section 105(e) of the Foreign Intelligence Surveillance Act of 1978 (50 U.S.C. §1805(e)) is amended—

(1) in paragraph (1)(B), by striking ", as defined in section 101(b)(1)(A)" and inserting "who is not a United States person"; and

(2) in subsection (2)(B), by striking "as defined in section 101(b)(1)(A)" and inserting "who is not a United States person".

(b) PHYSICAL SEARCH.—Section 304(d) of such Act (50 U.S.C. §1824(d)) is amended—

(1) in paragraph (1)(B), by striking "as defined in section 101(b)(1)(A)" and inserting "who is not a United States person"; and

(2) in paragraph (2), by striking "as defined in section 101(b)(1)(A)" and inserting "who is not a United States person".

(c) PEN REGISTERS, TRAP AND TRACE DEVICES.—Section 402(e) of such Act (50 U.S.C. §1842(e)) is amended—

(1) by striking "(e) An" and inserting "(e)(1) Except as provided in paragraph (2), an"; and

(2) by adding at the end the following new paragraph:

"(2) In the case of an application under subsection (c) where the applicant has certified that the information likely to be obtained is foreign intelligence information not concerning a United States person, an order, or an extension of an order, under this section may be for a period not to exceed one year.".

ACCESS TO CERTAIN BUSINESS RECORDS UNDER SECTION 215 OF THE USA PATRIOT ACT

SEC. 106.

(a) DIRECTOR APPROVAL FOR CERTAIN APPLICATIONS.—Subsection (a) of section 501 of the Foreign Intelligence Surveillance Act of 1978 (50 U.S.C. §1861(a)) is amended—

(1) in paragraph (1), by striking "The Director" and inserting "Subject to paragraph (3), the Director"; and

(2) by adding at the end the following:

"(3) In the case of an application for an order requiring the production of library circulation records, library patron lists, book sales records, book customer lists, firearms sales records, tax return records, educational records, or medical records containing information that would identify a person, the Director of the Federal Bureau of Investigation may delegate the authority to make such application to either the Deputy Director of the Federal Bureau of Investigation or the Executive Assistant Director for National Security (or any successor position). The Deputy Director or the Executive Assistant Director may not further delegate such authority.".

(b) FACTUAL BASIS FOR REQUESTED ORDER.—Subsection (b)(2) of such section is amended to read as follows:

"(2) shall include—
"(A) a statement of facts showing that there are reasonable grounds to believe that the tangible things sought are relevant to an authorized investigation (other than a threat assessment) conducted in accordance with subsection (a)(2) to obtain foreign intelligence information not concerning a United States person or to protect against international terrorism or clandestine intelligence activities, such things being presumptively relevant to an authorized investigation if the applicant shows in the statement of the facts that they pertain to—
"(i) a foreign power or an agent of a foreign power;
"(ii) the activities of a suspected agent of a foreign power who is the subject of such authorized investigation; or
"(iii) an individual in contact with, or known to, a suspected agent of a foreign power who is the subject of such authorized investigation; and
"(B) an enumeration of the minimization procedures adopted by the Attorney General under subsection (g) that are applicable to the retention and dissemination by the Federal Bureau of Investigation of any tangible things to be made available to the Federal Bureau of Investigation based on the order requested in such application.".

(c) CLARIFICATION OF JUDICIAL DISCRETION.—Subsection (c)(1) of such section is amended to read as follows:

"(c)(1) Upon an application made pursuant to this section, if the judge finds that the application meets the requirements of subsections (a) and (b), the judge shall enter an ex parte order as requested, or as modified, approving the release of tangible things. Such order shall direct that minimization procedures adopted pursuant to subsection (g) be followed.".

(d) ADDITIONAL PROTECTIONS.—Subsection (c)(2) of such section is amended to read as follows:

"(2) An order under this subsection—

"(A) shall describe the tangible things that are ordered to be produced with sufficient particularity to permit them to be fairly identified;

"(B) shall include the date on which the tangible things must be provided, which shall allow a reasonable period of time within which the tangible things can be assembled and made available;

"(C) shall provide clear and conspicuous notice of the principles and procedures described in subsection (d);

"(D) may only require the production of a tangible thing if such thing can be obtained with a subpoena duces tecum issued by a court of the United States in aid of a grand jury investigation or with any other order issued by a court of the United States directing the production of records or tangible things; and

"(E) shall not disclose that such order is issued for purposes of an investigation described in subsection (a).".

(e) PROHIBITIONS ON DISCLOSURE.—Subsection (d) of such section is amended to read as follows:

"(d)(1) No person shall disclose to any other person that the Federal Bureau of Investigation has sought or obtained tangible things pursuant to an order under this section, other than to—

"(A) those persons to whom disclosure is necessary to comply with such order;

"(B) an attorney to obtain legal advice or assistance with respect to the production of things in response to the order; or

"(C) other persons as permitted by the Director of the Federal Bureau of Investigation or the designee of the Director.

"(2)(A) A person to whom disclosure is made pursuant to paragraph (1) shall be subject to the nondisclosure requirements applicable to a person to whom an order is directed under this section in the same manner as such person.

"(B) Any person who discloses to a person described in subparagraph (A), (B), or (C) of paragraph (1) that the Federal Bureau of Investigation has sought or obtained tangible things pursuant to an order under this section shall notify such person of the nondisclosure requirements of this subsection.

"(C) At the request of the Director of the Federal Bureau of Investigation or the designee of the Director, any person making or intending to make a disclosure under this section shall identify to the Director or such designee the person to whom such disclosure will be made or to whom such disclosure was made prior to the request, but in no circumstance shall a person be required to inform the Director or such designee that the person intends to consult an attorney to obtain legal advice or legal assistance.".

(f) JUDICIAL REVIEW.—

(1) PETITION REVIEW POOL.—Section 103 of the Foreign Intelligence Surveillance Act of 1978 (50 U.S.C. §1803) is amended by adding at the end the following new subsection:

"(e)(1) Three judges designated under subsection (a) who reside within 20 miles of the District of Columbia, or, if all of such judges are unavailable, other judges of the court established under subsection (a) as may be designated by the presiding judge of such court, shall comprise a petition review pool which shall have jurisdiction to review petitions filed pursuant to section 501(f)(1).

"(2) Not later than 60 days after the date of the enactment of the USA PATRIOT Improvement and Reauthorization Act of 2005, the court established under subsection (a) shall adopt and, consistent with the protection of national security, publish procedures for the review of petitions filed pursuant to section 501(f)(1) by the panel established under paragraph (1). Such procedures shall provide that review of a petition shall be conducted in camera and shall also provide for the designation of an acting presiding judge.".

(2) PROCEEDINGS.—Section 501 of the Foreign Intelligence Surveillance Act of 1978 (50 U.S.C. §1861) is further amended by adding at the end the following new subsection:

"(f)(1) A person receiving an order to produce any tangible thing under this section may challenge the legality of that order by filing a petition with the pool established by section 103(e)(1). The presiding judge shall immediately assign the petition to one of the judges serving in such pool. Not later than 72 hours after the assignment of such petition, the assigned judge shall conduct an initial review of the petition. If the assigned judge determines that the petition is frivolous, the assigned judge shall immediately deny the petition and affirm the order. If the assigned judge determines the petition is not frivolous, the assigned judge shall promptly consider the petition in accordance with the procedures established pursuant to section 103(e)(2). The judge considering the petition may modify or set aside the order only if the judge finds that the order does not meet the requirements of this section or is otherwise unlawful. If the judge does not modify or set aside the order, the judge shall immediately affirm the order and order the recipient to comply therewith. The assigned judge shall promptly provide a written statement for the record of the reasons for any determination under this paragraph.

"(2) A petition for review of a decision to affirm, modify, or set aside an order by the United States or any person receiving such order shall be to the court of review established under section 103(b), which shall have jurisdiction to consider such petitions. The court of review shall provide for the record a written statement of the reasons for its decision and, on petition of the United States or any person receiving such order for writ of certiorari, the record shall be transmitted under seal to the Supreme Court, which shall have jurisdiction to review such decision.

"(3) Judicial proceedings under this subsection shall be concluded as expeditiously as possible. The record of proceedings, including petitions filed, orders granted, and statements of reasons for decision, shall be maintained under security measures established by the Chief Justice of the United States in consultation with the Attorney General and the Director of National Intelligence.

"(4) All petitions under this subsection shall be filed under seal. In any proceedings under this subsection, the court shall, upon request of the government, review ex parte and in camera any government submission, or portions thereof, which may include classified information.".

(g) MINIMIZATION PROCEDURES AND USE OF INFORMATION.—Section 501 of the Foreign Intelligence Surveillance Act of 1978 (50 U.S.C. §1861) is further amended by adding at the end the following new subsections:

"(g) MINIMIZATION PROCEDURES.—

"(1) IN GENERAL.—Not later than 180 days after the date of the enactment of the USA PATRIOT Improvement and Reauthorization Act of 2005, the Attorney General shall adopt specific minimization procedures governing the retention and dissemination by the Federal Bureau of Investigation of any tangible things, or information therein, received by the Federal Bureau of Investigation in response to an order under this title.

"(2) DEFINED.—In this section, the term 'minimization procedures' means—

"(A) specific procedures that are reasonably designed in light of the purpose and technique of an order for the production of tangible things, to minimize the retention, and prohibit the dissemination, of nonpublicly available information concerning unconsenting United States persons consistent with the need of the United States to obtain, produce, and disseminate foreign intelligence information;

"(B) procedures that require that nonpublicly available information, which is not foreign intelligence information, as defined in section 101(e)(1), shall not be disseminated in a manner that identifies any United States person, without such person's consent, unless such person's identity is necessary to understand foreign intelligence information or assess its importance; and

"(C) notwithstanding subparagraphs (A) and (B), procedures that allow for the retention and dissemination of information that is evidence of a crime which has been, is being, or is about to be committed and that is to be retained or disseminated for law enforcement purposes.

"(h) USE OF INFORMATION.—Information acquired from tangible things received by the Federal Bureau of Investigation in response to an order under this title concerning any United States person may be used and disclosed by Federal officers and employees without the consent of the United States person only in accordance with the minimization procedures adopted pursuant to subsection (g). No otherwise privileged information acquired from tangible things received by the Federal Bureau of Investigation in accordance with the provisions of this title shall lose its privileged character. No information acquired from tangible things received by the Federal Bureau of Investigation in response to an order under this title may be used or disclosed by Federal officers or employees except for lawful purposes.".

(h) ENHANCED OVERSIGHT.—Section 502 of the Foreign Intelligence Surveillance Act of 1978 (50 U.S.C. §1862) is amended—

    (1) in subsection (a)—

        (A) by striking "semiannual basis" and inserting "annual basis"; and

        (B) by inserting "and the Committee on the Judiciary" after "and the Select Committee on Intelligence";

    (2) in subsection (b)—

        (A) by striking "On a semiannual basis" and all that follows through "the preceding 6-month period" and inserting "In April of each year, the Attorney General shall submit to the House and Senate Committees on the Judiciary and the House Permanent Select Committee on Intelligence and the Senate Select Committee on Intelligence a report setting forth with respect to the preceding calendar year";

        (B) in paragraph (1), by striking "and" at the end;

        (C) in paragraph (2), by striking the period at the end and inserting "; and"; and

(D) by adding at the end the following new paragraph:

"(3) the number of such orders either granted, modified, or denied for the production of each of the following:

"(A) Library circulation records, library patron lists, book sales records, or book customer lists.

"(B) Firearms sales records.

"(C) Tax return records.

"(D) Educational records.

"(E) Medical records containing information that would identify a person."; and

(3) by adding at the end the following new subsection:

"(c)(1) In April of each year, the Attorney General shall submit to Congress a report setting forth with respect to the preceding year—

"(A) the total number of applications made for orders approving requests for the production of tangible things under section 501; and

"(B) the total number of such orders either granted, modified, or denied.

"(2) Each report under this subsection shall be submitted in unclassified form.".

AUDIT ON ACCESS TO CERTAIN BUSINESS RECORDS FOR FOREIGN INTELLIGENCE PURPOSES

SEC. 106A.

(a) AUDIT.—The Inspector General of the Department of Justice shall perform a comprehensive audit of the effectiveness and use, including any improper or illegal use, of the investigative authority provided to the Federal Bureau of Investigation under title V of the Foreign Intelligence Surveillance Act of 1978 (50 U.S.C. §1861 et seq.).

(b) REQUIREMENTS.—The audit required under subsection (a) shall include—

(1) an examination of each instance in which the Attorney General, any other officer, employee, or agent of the Department of Justice, the Director of the Federal Bureau of Investigation, or a designee of the Director, submitted an application to the Foreign Intelligence Surveillance Court (as such term is defined in section 301(3) of the Foreign Intelligence Surveillance Act of 1978 (50 U.S.C. §1821(3))) for an order under section 501 of such Act during the calendar years of 2002 through 2006, including—

(A) whether the Federal Bureau of Investigation requested that the Department of Justice submit an application and the request was not submitted to the court (including an examination of the basis for not submitting the application);

(B) whether the court granted, modified, or denied the application (including an examination of the basis for any modification or denial);

(2) the justification for the failure of the Attorney General to issue implementing procedures governing requests for the production of tangible things under such section in a timely fashion, including whether such delay harmed national security;

(3) whether bureaucratic or procedural impediments to the use of such requests for production prevent the Federal Bureau of Investigation from taking full advantage of the authorities provided under section 501 of such Act;

(4) any noteworthy facts or circumstances relating to orders under such section, including any improper or illegal use of the authority provided under such section; and

(5) an examination of the effectiveness of such section as an investigative tool, including—

(A) the categories of records obtained and the importance of the information acquired to the intelligence activities of the Federal Bureau of Investigation or any other Department or agency of the Federal Government;

(B) the manner in which such information is collected, retained, analyzed, and disseminated by the Federal Bureau of Investigation, including any direct access to such information (such as access to "raw data") provided to any other Department, agency, or instrumentality of Federal, State, local, or tribal governments or any private sector entity;

(C) with respect to calendar year 2006, an examination of the minimization procedures adopted by the Attorney General under section 501(g) of such Act and whether such minimization procedures protect the constitutional rights of United States persons;

(D) whether, and how often, the Federal Bureau of Investigation utilized information acquired pursuant to an order under section 501 of such Act to produce an analytical intelligence product for distribution within the Federal Bureau of Investigation, to the intelligence community (as such term is defined in section 3(4) of the National Security Act of 1947 (50 U.S.C. §401a(4))), or to other Federal, State, local, or tribal government Departments, agencies, or instrumentalities; and

(E) whether, and how often, the Federal Bureau of Investigation provided such information to law enforcement authorities for use in criminal proceedings.

(c) SUBMISSION DATES.—

(1) PRIOR YEARS.—Not later than one year after the date of the enactment of this Act, or upon completion of the audit under this section for calendar years 2002, 2003, and 2004, whichever is earlier, the Inspector General of the Department of Justice shall submit to the Committee on the Judiciary and the Permanent Select Committee on Intelligence of the House of Representatives and the Committee on the Judiciary and the Select Committee on Intelligence of the Senate a report containing the results of the audit conducted under this section for calendar years 2002, 2003, and 2004.

(2) CALENDAR YEARS 2005 AND 2006.—Not later than December 31, 2007, or upon completion of the audit under this section for calendar years 2005 and 2006, whichever is earlier, the Inspector General of the Department of Justice shall submit to the Committee on the Judiciary and the Permanent Select Committee on Intelligence of the House of Representatives and the Committee on the Judiciary and the Select Committee on Intelligence of the Senate a report containing the results of the audit conducted under this section for calendar years 2005 and 2006.

(d) PRIOR NOTICE TO ATTORNEY GENERAL AND DIRECTOR OF NATIONAL INTELLIGENCE; COMMENTS.—

(1) NOTICE.—Not less than 30 days before the submission of a report under subsection (c)(1) or (c)(2), the Inspector General of the Department of Justice shall provide such report to the Attorney General and the Director of National Intelligence.

(2) COMMENTS.—The Attorney General or the Director of National Intelligence may provide comments to be included in the reports submitted under subsections (c)(1) and (c)(2) as the Attorney General or the Director of National Intelligence may consider necessary.

(e) UNCLASSIFIED FORM.—The reports submitted under subsections (c)(1) and (c)(2) and any comments included under subsection (d)(2) shall be in unclassified form, but may include a classified annex.

ENHANCED OVERSIGHT OF GOOD-FAITH EMERGENCY DISCLOSURES UNDER SECTION 212 OF THE USA PATRIOT ACT

SEC. 107.

(a) Enhanced Oversight.—Section 2702 of title 18, United States Code, is amended by adding at the end the following:

"(d) Reporting of Emergency Disclosures.—On an annual basis, the Attorney General shall submit to the Committee on the Judiciary of the House of Representatives and the Committee on the Judiciary of the Senate a report containing—

"(1) the number of accounts from which the Department of Justice has received voluntary disclosures under subsection (b)(8); and

"(2) a summary of the basis for disclosure in those instances where—

"(A) voluntary disclosures under subsection (b)(8) were made to the Department of Justice; and

"(B) the investigation pertaining to those disclosures was closed without the filing of criminal charges.".

(b) Technical Amendments to Conform Communications and Customer Records Exceptions.—

(1) Voluntary Disclosures.—Section 2702 of title 18, United States Code, is amended—

(A) in subsection (b)(8), by striking "Federal, State, or local"; and

(B) by striking paragraph (4) of subsection (c) and inserting the following:

"(4) to a governmental entity, if the provider, in good faith, believes that an emergency involving danger of death or serious physical injury to any person requires disclosure without delay of information relating to the emergency;".

(2) Definitions.—Section 2711 of title 18, United States Code, is amended—

(A) in paragraph (2), by striking "and" at the end;

(B) in paragraph (3), by striking the period at the end and inserting "; and"; and

(C) by adding at the end the following:

"(4) the term 'governmental entity' means a department or agency of the United States or any State or political subdivision thereof.".

(c) Additional Exception.—Section 2702(a) of title 18, United States Code, is amended by inserting "or (c)" after "Except as provided in subsection (b)".

Multipoint Electronic Surveillance under Section 206 of the USA Patriot Act

SEC. 108.

(a) INCLUSION OF SPECIFIC FACTS IN APPLICATION.—

(1) APPLICATION.—Section 104(a)(3) of the Foreign Intelligence Surveillance Act of 1978 (50 U.S.C. §1804(a)(3)) is amended by inserting "specific" after "description of the".

(2) ORDER.—Subsection (c) of section 105 of the Foreign Intelligence Surveillance Act of 1978 (50 U.S.C. §1805(c)) is amended—

(A) in paragraph (1)(A) by striking "target of the electronic surveillance" and inserting "specific target of the electronic surveillance identified or described in the application pursuant to section 104(a)(3)"; and

(B) in paragraph (2)(B), by striking "where the Court finds" and inserting "where the Court finds, based upon specific facts provided in the application,".

(b) ADDITIONAL DIRECTIONS.—Such subsection is further amended—

(1) by striking "An order approving" and all that follows through "specify" and inserting "(1) SPECIFICATIONS—An order approving an electronic surveillance under this section shall specify";

(2) in paragraph (1)(F), by striking "; and" and inserting a period;

(3) in paragraph (2), by striking "direct" and inserting "DIRECTIONS— An order approving an electronic surveillance under this section shall direct"; and

(4) by adding at the end the following new paragraph:

"(3) SPECIAL DIRECTIONS FOR CERTAIN ORDERS.—An order approving an electronic surveillance under this section in circumstances where the nature and location of each of the facilities or places at which the surveillance will be directed is unknown shall direct the applicant to provide notice to the court within ten days after the date on which surveillance begins to be directed at any new facility or place, unless the court finds good cause to justify a longer period of up to 60 days, of—

"(A) the nature and location of each new facility or place at which the electronic surveillance is directed;

"(B) the facts and circumstances relied upon by the applicant to justify the applicant's belief that each new facility or place at which the electronic surveillance is directed is or was being used, or is about to be used, by the target of the surveillance;

"(C) a statement of any proposed minimization procedures that differ from those contained in the original application or order, that may be necessitated by a change in the facility or place at which the electronic surveillance is directed; and

"(D) the total number of electronic surveillances that have been or are being conducted under the authority of the order.".

(c) ENHANCED OVERSIGHT.—

(1) REPORT TO CONGRESS.—Section 108(a)(1) of the Foreign Intelligence Surveillance Act of 1978 (50 U.S.C. §1808(a)(1)) is amended by inserting ", and the Committee on the Judiciary of the Senate," after "Senate Select Committee on Intelligence".

(2) MODIFICATION OF SEMIANNUAL REPORT REQUIREMENT ON ACTIVITIES UNDER FOREIGN INTELLIGENCE SURVEILLANCE ACT OF 1978.—Paragraph (2) of section 108(a) of the Foreign Intelligence Surveillance Act of 1978 (50 U.S.C. §1808(a)) is amended to read as follows:

"(2) Each report under the first sentence of paragraph (1) shall include a description of—

"(A) the total number of applications made for orders and extensions of orders approving electronic surveillance under this title where the nature and location of each facility or place at which the electronic surveillance will be directed is unknown;

"(B) each criminal case in which information acquired under this Act has been authorized for use at trial during the period covered by such report; and

"(C) the total number of emergency employments of electronic surveillance under section 105(f) and the total number of subsequent orders approving or denying such electronic surveillance.".

ENHANCED CONGRESSIONAL OVERSIGHT

SEC. 109.

(a) EMERGENCY PHYSICAL SEARCHES.—Section 306 of the Foreign Intelligence Surveillance Act of 1978 (50 U.S.C. §1826) is amended—

(1) in the first sentence, by inserting ", and the Committee on the Judiciary of the Senate," after "the Senate";

(2) in the second sentence, by striking "and the Committees on the Judiciary of the House of Representatives and the Senate" and inserting "and the Committee on the Judiciary of the House of Representatives";

(3) in paragraph (2), by striking "and" at the end;

(4) in paragraph (3), by striking the period at the end and inserting "; and"; and

(5) by adding at the end the following:

"(4) the total number of emergency physical searches authorized by the Attorney General under section 304(e) and the total number of subsequent orders approving or denying such physical searches.".

(b) EMERGENCY PEN REGISTERS AND TRAP AND TRACE DEVICES.—Section 406(b) of the Foreign Intelligence Surveillance Act of 1978 (50 U.S.C. §1846(b)) is amended—

(1) in paragraph (1), by striking "and" at the end;

(2) in paragraph (2), by striking the period at the end and inserting "; and"; and

(3) by adding at the end the following:

"(3) the total number of pen registers and trap and trace devices whose installation and use was authorized by the Attorney General on an emergency basis under section 403, and the total number of subsequent orders approving or denying the installation and use of such pen registers and trap and trace devices.".

(c) ADDITIONAL REPORT.—At the beginning and midpoint of each fiscal year, the Secretary of Homeland Security shall submit to the Committees on the Judiciary of the House of Representatives and the Senate, a written report providing a description of internal affairs operations at U.S. Citizenship and Immigration Services, including the general state of such operations and a detailed description of investigations that are being conducted (or that were conducted during the previous six months) and the resources devoted to such investigations. The first such report shall be submitted not later than April 1, 2006.

(d) RULES AND PROCEDURES FOR FISA COURTS.—Section 103 of the Foreign Intelligence Surveillance Act of 1978 (50 U.S.C. §1803) is amended by adding at the end the following:

"(f)(1) The courts established pursuant to subsections (a) and (b) may establish such rules and procedures, and take such actions, as are reasonably necessary to administer their responsibilities under this Act.

"(2) The rules and procedures established under paragraph (1), and any modifications of such rules and procedures, shall be recorded, and shall be transmitted to the following:

"(A) All of the judges on the court established pursuant to subsection (a).

"(B) All of the judges on the court of review established pursuant to subsection (b).

"(C) The Chief Justice of the United States.

"(D) The Committee on the Judiciary of the Senate.

"(E) The Select Committee on Intelligence of the Senate.

"(F) The Committee on the Judiciary of the House of Representatives.

"(G) The Permanent Select Committee on Intelligence of the House of Representatives.

"(3) The transmissions required by paragraph (2) shall be submitted in unclassified form, but may include a classified annex.".

JUDICIAL REVIEW OF NATIONAL SECURITY LETTERS

SEC. 115.

Chapter 223 of title 18, United States Code, is amended—

(1) by inserting at the end of the table of sections the following new item:

"3511. Judicial review of requests for information."; and

(2) by inserting after section 3510 the following:

"§3511. Judicial review of requests for information

"(a) The recipient of a request for records, a report, or other information under section 2709(b) of this title, section 626(a) or (b) or 627(a) of the Fair Credit Reporting Act, section 1114(a)(5)(A) of the Right to Financial Privacy Act, or section 802(a) of the National Security Act of 1947 may, in the United States district court for the district in which that person or entity does business or resides, petition for an order modifying or setting aside the request. The court may modify or set aside the request if compliance would be unreasonable, oppressive, or otherwise unlawful.

"(b)(1) The recipient of a request for records, a report, or other information under section 2709(b) of this title, section 626(a) or (b) or 627(a) of the Fair Credit Reporting Act, section 1114(a)(5)(A) of the Right to Financial Privacy Act, or section 802(a) of the National Security Act of 1947, may petition any court described in subsection (a) for an order modifying or setting aside a nondisclosure requirement imposed in connection with such a request.

"(2) If the petition is filed within one year of the request for records, a report, or other information under section 2709(b) of this title, section 626(a) or (b) or 627(a) of the Fair Credit Reporting Act, section 1114(a)(5)(A) of the Right to Financial Privacy Act, or section 802(a) of the National Security Act of 1947, the court may modify or set aside such a nondisclosure requirement if it finds that there is no reason to believe that disclosure may endanger the national security of the United States, interfere with a criminal, counterterrorism, or counterintelligence investigation, interfere with diplomatic relations, or endanger the life or physical safety of any person. If, at the time of the petition, the Attorney General, Deputy Attorney General, an Assistant Attorney General, or the Director of the Federal Bureau of Investigation, or in the case of a request by a department, agency, or instrumentality of the Federal Government other than the Department of Justice, the head or deputy head of such department, agency, or instrumentality, certifies that disclosure may endanger the national security of the United States or interfere with diplomatic relations, such certification shall be treated as conclusive unless the court finds that the certification was made in bad faith.

"(3) If the petition is filed one year or more after the request for records, a report, or other information under section 2709(b) of this title, section 626(a) or (b) or 627(a) of the Fair Credit Reporting Act, section 1114(a)(5)(A) of the Right to Financial Privacy Act, or section 802(a) of the National Security Act of 1947, the Attorney General, Deputy Attorney General, an Assistant Attorney General, or the Director of the Federal Bureau of Investigation, or his designee in a position not lower than Deputy Assistant Director at Bureau headquarters or a Special Agent in Charge in a Bureau field office designated by the Director, or in the case of a request by a department, agency, or instrumentality of the Federal Government other than the Federal Bureau of Investigation, the head or deputy head of such department, agency, or instrumentality, within ninety days of the filing of the petition, shall either terminate the nondisclosure requirement or re-certify that disclosure may result in a danger to the national security of the United States, interference with a criminal, counterterrorism, or counterintelligence investigation, interference with diplomatic relations, or danger to the life or physical safety of any person. In the event of re-certification, the court may modify or set aside such a nondisclosure requirement if it finds that there is no reason to believe that disclosure may endanger the national security of the United States, interfere with a criminal, counterterrorism, or counterintelligence investigation, interfere with diplomatic relations, or endanger the life or physical safety of any person. If the recertification that disclosure may endanger the national security of the United States or interfere with diplomatic relations is made by the Attorney General, Deputy Attorney General, an Assistant Attorney General, or the Director of the Federal Bureau of Investigation, such certification shall be treated as conclusive unless the court finds that the recertification was made in bad faith. If the court denies a petition for an order modifying or setting aside a nondisclosure requirement under this paragraph, the recipient shall be precluded for a period of one year from filing another petition to modify or set aside such nondisclosure requirement.

"(c) In the case of a failure to comply with a request for records, a report, or other information made to any person or entity under section 2709(b) of this title, section 626(a) or (b) or 627(a) of the Fair Credit Reporting Act, section 1114(a)(5)(A) of the Right to Financial Privacy Act, or section 802(a) of the National Security Act of 1947, the Attorney General may invoke the aid of any district court of the United States within the jurisdiction in which the investigation is carried on or the person or entity resides, carries on business, or may be found, to compel compliance with the request. The court may issue an order requiring the person or entity to comply with the request. Any failure to obey the order of the court may be punished by the court as contempt thereof. Any process under this section may be served in any judicial district in which the person or entity may be found.

"(d) In all proceedings under this section, subject to any right to an open hearing in a contempt proceeding, the court must close any hearing to the extent necessary to prevent an unauthorized disclosure of a request for records, a report, or other information made to any person or entity under section 2709(b) of this title, section 626(a) or (b) or 627(a) of the Fair Credit Reporting Act, section 1114(a)(5)(A) of the Right to Financial Privacy Act, or section 802(a) of the National Security Act of 1947. Petitions, filings, records, orders, and subpoenas must also be kept under seal to the extent and as long as necessary to prevent the unauthorized disclosure of a request for records, a report, or other information made to any person or entity under section 2709(b) of this title, section 626(a) or (b) or 627(a) of the Fair Credit Reporting Act, section 1114(a)(5)(A) of the Right to Financial Privacy Act, or section 802(a) of the National Security Act of 1947.

"(e) In all proceedings under this section, the court shall, upon request of the government, review ex parte and in camera any government submission or portions thereof, which may include classified information.".

CONFIDENTIALITY OF NATIONAL SECURITY LETTERS

SEC. 116.
(a) Section 2709(c) of title 18, United States Code, is amended to read:

"(c) PROHIBITION OF CERTAIN DISCLOSURE.—
    "(1) If the Director of the Federal Bureau of Investigation, or his designee in a position not lower than Deputy Assistant Director at Bureau headquarters or a Special Agent in Charge in a Bureau field office designated by the Director, certifies that otherwise there may result a danger to the national security of the United States, interference with a criminal, counterterrorism, or counterintelligence investigation,

interference with diplomatic relations, or danger to the life or physical safety of any person, no wire or electronic communications service provider, or officer, employee, or agent thereof, shall disclose to any person (other than those to whom such disclosure is necessary to comply with the request or an attorney to obtain legal advice or legal assistance with respect to the request) that the Federal Bureau of Investigation has sought or obtained access to information or records under this section.

"(2) The request shall notify the person or entity to whom the request is directed of the nondisclosure requirement under paragraph (1).

"(3) Any recipient disclosing to those persons necessary to comply with the request or to an attorney to obtain legal advice or legal assistance with respect to the request shall inform such person of any applicable nondisclosure requirement. Any person who receives a disclosure under this subsection shall be subject to the same prohibitions on disclosure under paragraph (1).

"(4) At the request of the Director of the Federal Bureau of Investigation or the designee of the Director, any person making or intending to make a disclosure under this section shall identify to the Director or such designee the person to whom such disclosure will be made or to whom such disclosure was made prior to the request, but in no circumstance shall a person be required to inform the Director or such designee that the person intends to consult an attorney to obtain legal advice or legal assistance.".

(b) Section 626(d) of the Fair Credit Reporting Act (15 U.S.C. §1681u(d)) is amended to read:

"(d) CONFIDENTIALITY.—

"(1) If the Director of the Federal Bureau of Investigation, or his designee in a position not lower than Deputy Assistant Director at Bureau headquarters or a Special Agent in Charge in a Bureau field office designated by the Director, certifies that otherwise there may result a danger to the national security of the United States, interference with a criminal, counterterrorism, or counterintelligence investigation, interference with diplomatic relations, or danger to the life or physical safety of any person, no consumer reporting agency or officer, employee, or agent of a consumer reporting agency shall disclose to any person (other than those to whom such disclosure is necessary to comply with the request or an attorney to obtain legal advice or legal assistance with respect to the request) that the Federal Bureau of Investigation has sought or obtained the identity of financial institutions or a consumer report respecting any consumer under subsection (a), (b), or (c), and no consumer reporting agency or officer, employee, or agent of a consumer reporting agency shall include in any consumer report any information that would indicate that the Federal Bureau of Investigation has sought or obtained such information on a consumer report.

"(2) The request shall notify the person or entity to whom the request is directed of the nondisclosure requirement under paragraph (1).

"(3) Any recipient disclosing to those persons necessary to comply with the request or to an attorney to obtain legal advice or legal assistance with respect to the request shall inform such persons of any applicable nondisclosure requirement. Any person who receives a disclosure under this subsection shall be subject to the same prohibitions on disclosure under paragraph (1).

"(4) At the request of the Director of the Federal Bureau of Investigation or the designee of the Director, any person making or intending to make a disclosure under this section shall identify to the Director or such designee the person to whom such disclosure will be made or to whom such disclosure was made prior to the request, but in no circumstance shall a person be required to inform the Director or such designee that the person intends to consult an attorney to obtain legal advice or legal assistance.".

(c) Section 627(c) of the Fair Credit Reporting Act (15 U.S.C. §1681v(c)) is amended to read:

"(c) CONFIDENTIALITY.—

"(1) If the head of a government agency authorized to conduct investigations of intelligence or counterintelligence activities or analysis related to international terrorism, or his designee, certifies that otherwise there may result a danger to the national security of the United States, interference with a criminal, counterterrorism, or counterintelligence investigation, interference with diplomatic relations, or danger to the life or physical safety of any person, no consumer reporting agency or officer, employee, or agent of such consumer reporting agency, shall disclose to any person (other than those to whom such disclosure is necessary to comply with the request or an attorney to obtain legal advice or legal assistance with respect to the request), or specify in any consumer report, that a government agency has sought or obtained access to information under subsection (a).

"(2) The request shall notify the person or entity to whom the request is directed of the nondisclosure requirement under paragraph (1).

"(3) Any recipient disclosing to those persons necessary to comply with the request or to any attorney to obtain legal advice or legal assistance with respect to the request shall inform such persons of any applicable nondisclosure requirement. Any person who receives a disclosure under this subsection shall be subject to the same prohibitions on disclosure under paragraph (1).

"(4) At the request of the authorized Government agency, any person making or intending to make a disclosure under this section shall identify to the requesting official of the authorized Government agency the person to whom such disclosure will be made or to whom such disclosure was made prior to the request, but in no circumstance shall a person be required to inform such requesting official that the person intends to consult an attorney to obtain legal advice or legal assistance.".

(d) Section 1114(a)(3) of the Right to Financial Privacy Act (12 U.S.C. §3414(a)(3)) is amended to read as follows:

"(3)(A) If the Government authority described in paragraph (1) or the Secret Service, as the case may be, certifies that otherwise there may result a danger to the national security of the United States, interference with a criminal, counterterrorism, or counterintelligence investigation, interference with diplomatic relations, or danger to the life or physical safety of any person, no financial institution, or officer, employee, or agent of such institution, shall disclose to any person (other than those to whom such disclosure is necessary to comply with the request or an attorney to obtain legal advice or legal assistance with respect to the request) that the Government authority or the Secret Service has sought or obtained access to a customer's financial records.

"(B) The request shall notify the person or entity to whom the request is directed of the nondisclosure requirement under subparagraph (A).

"(C) Any recipient disclosing to those persons necessary to comply with the request or to an attorney to obtain legal advice or legal assistance with respect to the request shall inform such persons of any applicable nondisclosure requirement. Any person who receives a disclosure under this subsection shall be subject to the same prohibitions on disclosure under subparagraph (A).

"(D) At the request of the authorized Government agency or the Secret Service, any person making or intending to make a disclosure under this section shall identify to the requesting official of the authorized Government agency or the Secret Service the person to whom such disclosure will be made or to whom such disclosure was made prior to the request, but in no circumstance shall a person be required to inform such requesting official that the person intends to consult an attorney to obtain legal advice or legal assistance.".

(e) Section 1114(a)(5)(D) of the Right to Financial Privacy Act (12 U.S.C. §3414(a)(5)(D)) is amended to read:

"(D) PROHIBITION OF CERTAIN DISCLOSURE.—

"(i) If the Director of the Federal Bureau of Investigation, or his designee in a position not lower than Deputy Assistant Director at Bureau headquarters or a Special Agent in Charge in a Bureau field office designated by the Director, certifies that otherwise there may result a danger to the national security of the United States, interference with a criminal, counterterrorism, or counterintelligence investigation, interference with diplomatic relations, or danger to the life or physical safety of any person, no financial institution, or officer, employee, or agent of such institution, shall disclose to any person (other than those to whom such disclosure is necessary to comply with the request or an attorney to obtain legal advice or legal assistance with respect to the request) that the Federal Bureau of Investigation has sought or obtained access to a customer's or entity's financial records under subparagraph (A).

"(ii) The request shall notify the person or entity to whom the request is directed of the nondisclosure requirement under clause (i).

"(iii) Any recipient disclosing to those persons necessary to comply with the request or to an attorney to obtain legal advice or legal assistance with respect to the request shall inform such persons of any applicable nondisclosure requirement. Any person who receives a disclosure under this subsection shall be subject to the same prohibitions on disclosure under clause (i).

"(iv) At the request of the Director of the Federal Bureau of Investigation or the designee of the Director, any person making or intending to make a disclosure under this section shall identify to the Director or such designee the person to whom such disclosure will be made or to whom such disclosure was made prior to the request, but in no circumstance shall a person be required to inform the Director or such designee that the person intends to consult an attorney to obtain legal advice or legal assistance.".

(f) Section 802(b) of the National Security Act of 1947 (50 U.S.C. §436(b)) is amended to read as follows:

"(b) PROHIBITIONS OF CERTAIN DISCLOSURE.—

"(1) If an authorized investigative agency described in subsection (a) certifies that otherwise there may result a danger to the national security of the United States, interference with a criminal, counterterrorism, or counterintelligence investigation, interference with diplomatic relations, or danger to the life or physical safety of any person, no governmental or private entity, or officer, employee, or agent of such entity, may disclose to any person (other than those to whom such disclosure is necessary to comply with the request or an attorney to obtain legal advice or legal assistance with respect to the request) that such entity has received or satisfied a request made by an authorized investigative agency under this section.

"(2) The request shall notify the person or entity to whom the request is directed of the nondisclosure requirement under paragraph (1).

"(3) Any recipient disclosing to those persons necessary to comply with the request or to an attorney to obtain legal advice or legal assistance with respect to the request shall inform such persons of any applicable nondisclosure requirement. Any person who receives a disclosure under this subsection shall be subject to the same prohibitions on disclosure under paragraph (1).

"(4) At the request of the authorized investigative agency, any person making or intending to make a disclosure under this section shall identify to the requesting official of the authorized investigative agency the person to whom such disclosure will be made or to whom such disclosure was made prior to the request, but in no circumstance shall a person be required to inform such official that the person intends to consult an attorney to obtain legal advice or legal assistance.".

VIOLATIONS OF NONDISCLOSURE PROVISIONS OF NATIONAL SECURITY LETTERS

SEC. 117.

Section 1510 of title 18, United States Code, is amended by adding at the end the following:

"(e) Whoever, having been notified of the applicable disclosure prohibitions or confidentiality requirements of section 2709(c)(1) of this title, section 626(d)(1) or 627(c)(1) of the Fair Credit Reporting Act (15 U.S.C. §1681u(d)(1) or 1681v(c)(1)), section 1114(a)(3)(A) or 1114(a)(5)(D)(i) of the Right to Financial Privacy Act (12 U.S.C. §3414(a)(3)(A) or 3414(a)(5)(D)(i)), or section 802(b)(1) of the National Security Act of 1947 (50 U.S.C. §436(b)(1)), knowingly and with the intent to obstruct an investigation or judicial proceeding violates such prohibitions or requirements applicable by law to such person shall be imprisoned for not more than five years, fined under this title, or both.".

REPORTS ON NATIONAL SECURITY LETTERS

SEC. 118.

(a) EXISTING REPORTS.—Any report made to a committee of Congress regarding national security letters under section 2709(c)(1) of title 18, United States Code, section 626(d) or 627(c) of the Fair Credit Reporting Act (15 U.S.C. §1681u(d) or 1681v(c)), section 1114(a)(3) or 1114(a)(5)(D) of the Right to Financial Privacy Act (12 U.S.C. §3414(a)(3) or 3414(a)(5)(D)), or section 802(b) of the National Security Act of 1947 (50 U.S.C. §436(b)) shall also be made to the Committees on the Judiciary of the House of Representatives and the Senate.

(b) ENHANCED OVERSIGHT OF FAIR CREDIT REPORTING ACT COUNTERTERRORISM NATIONAL SECURITY LETTER.—Section 627 of the Fair Credit Reporting Act (15 U.S.C. §1681(v)) is amended by inserting at the end the following new subsection:

"(f) REPORTS TO CONGRESS.—(1) On a semi-annual basis, the Attorney General shall fully inform the Committee on the Judiciary, the Committee on Financial Services, and the Permanent Select Committee on Intelligence of the House of Representatives and the Committee on the Judiciary, the Committee on Banking, Housing, and Urban Affairs, and the Select Committee on Intelligence of the Senate concerning all requests made pursuant to subsection (a).

> "(2) In the case of the semiannual reports required to be submitted under paragraph (1) to the Permanent Select Committee on Intelligence of the House of Representatives and the Select Committee on Intelligence of the Senate, the submittal dates for such reports shall be as provided in section 507 of the National Security Act of 1947 (50 U.S.C. §415b).".

(c) REPORT ON REQUESTS FOR NATIONAL SECURITY LETTERS.—

> (1) IN GENERAL.—In April of each year, the Attorney General shall submit to Congress an aggregate report setting forth with respect to the preceding year the total number of requests made by the Department of

Justice for information concerning different United States persons under—

> (A) section 2709 of title 18, United States Code (to access certain communication service provider records), excluding the number of requests for subscriber information;
>
> (B) section 1114 of the Right to Financial Privacy Act (12 U.S.C. §3414) (to obtain financial institution customer records);
>
> (C) section 802 of the National Security Act of 1947 (50 U.S.C. §436) (to obtain financial information, records, and consumer reports);
>
> (D) section 626 of the Fair Credit Reporting Act (15 U.S.C. §1681u) (to obtain certain financial information and consumer reports); and
>
> (E) section 627 of the Fair Credit Reporting Act (15 U.S.C. §1681v) (to obtain credit agency consumer records for counterterrorism investigations).

(2) UNCLASSIFIED FORM.—The report under this section shall be submitted in unclassified form.

(d) NATIONAL SECURITY LETTER DEFINED.—In this section, the term "national security letter" means a request for information under one of the following provisions of law:

(1) Section 2709(a) of title 18, United States Code (to access certain communication service provider records).

(2) Section 1114(a)(5)(A) of the Right to Financial Privacy Act (12 U.S.C. §3414(a)(5)(A)) (to obtain financial institution customer records).

(3) Section 802 of the National Security Act of 1947 (50 U.S.C. §436) (to obtain financial information, records, and consumer reports).

(4) Section 626 of the Fair Credit Reporting Act (15 U.S.C. §1681u) (to obtain certain financial information and consumer reports).

(5) Section 627 of the Fair Credit Reporting Act (15 U.S.C. §1681v) (to obtain credit agency consumer records for counterterrorism investigations).

AUDIT OF USE OF NATIONAL SECURITY LETTERS

SEC. 119.

(a) AUDIT.—The Inspector General of the Department of Justice shall perform an audit of the effectiveness and use, including any improper or illegal use, of national security letters issued by the Department of Justice.

(b) REQUIREMENTS.—The audit required under subsection (a) shall include—

(1) an examination of the use of national security letters by the Department of Justice during calendar years 2003 through 2006;

(2) a description of any noteworthy facts or circumstances relating to such use, including any improper or illegal use of such authority; and

(3) an examination of the effectiveness of national security letters as an investigative tool, including—

(A) the importance of the information acquired by the Department of Justice to the intelligence activities of the Department of Justice or to any other department or agency of the Federal Government;

(B) the manner in which such information is collected, retained, analyzed, and disseminated by the Department of Justice, including any direct access to such information (such as access to "raw data") provided to any other department, agency, or instrumentality of Federal, State, local, or tribal governments or any private sector entity;

(C) whether, and how often, the Department of Justice utilized such information to produce an analytical intelligence product for distribution within the Department of Justice, to the intelligence community (as such term is defined in section 3(4) of the National Security Act of 1947 (50 U.S.C. §401a(4))), or to other Federal, State, local, or tribal government departments, agencies, or instrumentalities;

(D) whether, and how often, the Department of Justice provided such information to law enforcement authorities for use in criminal proceedings;

(E) with respect to national security letters issued following the date of the enactment of this Act, an examination of the number of occasions in which the Department of Justice, or an officer or employee of the Department of Justice, issued a national security letter without the certification necessary to require the recipient of such letter to comply with the nondisclosure and confidentiality requirements potentially applicable under law; and

(F) the types of electronic communications and transactional information obtained through requests for information under section 2709 of title 18, United States Code, including the types of dialing, routing, addressing, or signaling information obtained, and the procedures the Department of Justice uses if content information is obtained through the use of such authority.

(c) SUBMISSION DATES.—

(1) PRIOR YEARS.—Not later than one year after the date of the enactment of this Act, or upon completion of the audit under this section

for calendar years 2003 and 2004, whichever is earlier, the Inspector General of the Department of Justice shall submit to the Committee on the Judiciary and the Permanent Select Committee on Intelligence of the House of Representatives and the Committee on the Judiciary and the Select Committee on Intelligence of the Senate a report containing the results of the audit conducted under this subsection for calendar years 2003 and 2004.

(2) CALENDAR YEARS 2005 AND 2006.—Not later than December 31, 2007, or upon completion of the audit under this subsection for calendar years 2005 and 2006, whichever is earlier, the Inspector General of the Department of Justice shall submit to the Committee on the Judiciary and the Permanent Select Committee on Intelligence of the House of Representatives and the Committee on the Judiciary and the Select Committee on Intelligence of the Senate a report containing the results of the audit conducted under this subsection for calendar years 2005 and 2006.

(d) PRIOR NOTICE TO ATTORNEY GENERAL AND DIRECTOR OF NATIONAL INTELLIGENCE; COMMENTS.—

(1) NOTICE.—Not less than 30 days before the submission of a report under subsection (c)(1) or (c)(2), the Inspector General of the Department of Justice shall provide such report to the Attorney General and the Director of National Intelligence.

(2) COMMENTS.—The Attorney General or the Director of National Intelligence may provide comments to be included in the reports submitted under subsection (c)(1) or (c)(2) as the Attorney General or the Director of National Intelligence may consider necessary.

(e) UNCLASSIFIED FORM.—The reports submitted under subsection (c)(1) or (c)(2) and any comments included under subsection (d)(2) shall be in unclassified form, but may include a classified annex.

(f) MINIMIZATION PROCEDURES FEASIBILITY.—Not later than February 1, 2007, or upon completion of review of the report submitted under subsection (c)(1), whichever is earlier, the Attorney General and the Director of National Intelligence shall jointly submit to the Committee on the Judiciary and the Permanent Select Committee on Intelligence of the House of Representatives and the Committee on the Judiciary and the Select Committee on Intelligence of the Senate a report on the feasibility of applying minimization procedures in the context of national security letters to ensure the protection of the constitutional rights of United States persons.

(g) NATIONAL SECURITY LETTER DEFINED.—In this section, the term "national security letter" means a request for information under one of the following provisions of law:

(1) Section 2709(a) of title 18, United States Code (to access certain communication service provider records).

(2) Section 1114(a)(5)(A) of the Right to Financial Privacy Act (12 U.S.C. §3414(a)(5)(A)) (to obtain financial institution customer records).

(3) Section 802 of the National Security Act of 1947 (50 U.S.C. §436) (to obtain financial information, records, and consumer reports).

(4) Section 626 of the Fair Credit Reporting Act (15 U.S.C. §1681u) (to obtain certain financial information and consumer reports).

(5) Section 627 of the Fair Credit Reporting Act (15 U.S.C. §1681v) (to obtain credit agency consumer records for counterterrorism investigations).

USA PATRIOT ACT SECTION 214; AUTHORITY FOR DISCLOSURE OF ADDITIONAL INFORMATION IN CONNECTION WITH ORDERS FOR PEN REGISTER AND TRAP AND TRACE AUTHORITY UNDER FISA

SEC. 128.

(a) RECORDS.—Section 402(d)(2) of the Foreign Intelligence Surveillance Act of 1978 (50 U.S.C. §1842(d)(2)) is amended—

(1) in subparagraph (A)—

(A) in clause (ii), by adding "and" at the end; and

(B) in clause (iii), by striking the period at the end and inserting a semicolon;

(2) in subparagraph (B)(iii), by striking the period at the end and inserting "; and"; and

(3) by adding at the end the following:

"(C) shall direct that, upon the request of the applicant, the provider of a wire or electronic communication service shall disclose to the Federal officer using the pen register or trap and trace device covered by the order—

"(i) in the case of the customer or subscriber using the service covered by the order (for the period specified by the order)—

"(I) the name of the customer or subscriber;

"(II) the address of the customer or subscriber;

"(III) the telephone or instrument number, or other subscriber number or identifier, of the customer or subscriber, including any temporarily assigned network address or associated routing or transmission information;

"(IV) the length of the provision of service by such provider to the customer or subscriber and the types of services utilized by the customer or subscriber;

"(V) in the case of a provider of local or long distance telephone service, any local or long distance telephone records of the customer or subscriber;

"(VI) if applicable, any records reflecting period of usage (or sessions) by the customer or subscriber; and

"(VII) any mechanisms and sources of payment for such service, including the number of any credit card or bank account utilized for payment for such service; and

"(ii) if available, with respect to any customer or subscriber of incoming or outgoing communications to or from the service covered by the order—

"(I) the name of such customer or subscriber;

"(II) the address of such customer or subscriber;

"(III) the telephone or instrument number, or other subscriber number or identifier, of such customer or subscriber, including any temporarily assigned network address or associated routing or transmission information; and

"(IV) the length of the provision of service by such provider to such customer or subscriber and the types of services utilized by such customer or subscriber.".

(b) ENHANCED OVERSIGHT.—Section 406(a) of the Foreign Intelligence Surveillance Act of 1978 (50 U.S.C. §1846(a)) is amended by inserting ", and the Committee on the Judiciary of the House of Representatives and the Committee on the Judiciary of the Senate," after "of the Senate".

DETAINEE TREATMENT ACT OF 2005

Title X of Division A of the Defense Appropriations Act of Fiscal Year 2006

(Public Law 109-148 of December 30, 2007, Title X; 119 STAT. 2739)[1]

TITLE X—MATTERS RELATING TO DETAINEES

SHORT TITLE

SECTION. 1001.
This title may be cited as the "Detainee Treatment Act of 2005".

UNIFORM STANDARDS FOR THE INTERROGATION OF PERSONS UNDER THE DETENTION OF THE DEPARTMENT OF DEFENSE

SEC. 1002.
(a) IN GENERAL.—No person in the custody or under the effective control of the Department of Defense or under detention in a Department of Defense facility shall be subject to any treatment or technique of interrogation not authorized by and listed in the United States Army Field Manual on Intelligence Interrogation.
(b) APPLICABILITY.—Subsection (a) shall not apply with respect to any person in the custody or under the effective control of the Department of Defense pursuant to a criminal law or immigration law of the United States.
(c) CONSTRUCTION.—Nothing in this section shall be construed to affect the rights under the United States Constitution of any person in the custody or under the physical jurisdiction of the United States.

PROHIBITION ON CRUEL, INHUMAN, OR DEGRADING TREATMENT OR PUNISHMENT OF PERSONS UNDER CUSTODY OR CONTROL OF THE UNITED STATES GOVERNMENT

SEC. 1003.
(a) IN GENERAL.—No individual in the custody or under the physical control of the United States Government, regardless of nationality or physical location, shall be subject to cruel, inhuman, or degrading treatment or punishment.
(b) CONSTRUCTION.—Nothing in this section shall be construed to impose any geographical limitation on the applicability of the prohibition against cruel, inhuman, or degrading treatment or punishment under this section.

---

[1] Congress passed an identical version of the Detainee Treatment Act of 2005 as title XIV of the National Defense Authorization Act of 2006, Pub. L. 109-163.

(c) LIMITATION ON SUPERSEDURE.—The provisions of this section shall not be superseded, except by a provision of law enacted after the date of the enactment of this Act which specifically repeals, modifies, or supersedes the provisions of this section.

(d) CRUEL, INHUMAN, OR DEGRADING TREATMENT OR PUNISHMENT DEFINED.—In this section, the term "cruel, inhuman, or degrading treatment or punishment" means the cruel, unusual, and inhumane treatment or punishment prohibited by the Fifth, Eighth, and Fourteenth Amendments to the Constitution of the United States, as defined in the United States Reservations, Declarations and Understandings to the United Nations Convention Against Torture and Other Forms of Cruel, Inhuman or Degrading Treatment or Punishment done at New York, December 10, 1984.

PROTECTION OF UNITED STATES GOVERNMENT PERSONNEL ENGAGED IN AUTHORIZED INTERROGATIONS[2]

SEC. 1004.

(a) PROTECTION OF UNITED STATES GOVERNMENT PERSONNEL.—In any civil action or criminal prosecution against an officer, employee, member of the Armed Forces, or other agent of the United States Government who is a United States person, arising out of the officer, employee, member of the Armed Forces, or other agent's engaging in specific operational practices, that involve detention and interrogation of aliens who the President or his designees have determined are believed to be engaged in or associated with international terrorist activity that poses a serious, continuing threat to the United States, its interests, or its allies, and that were officially authorized and determined to be lawful at the time that they were conducted, it shall be a defense that such officer, employee, member of the Armed Forces, or other agent did not know that the practices were unlawful and a person of ordinary sense and understanding would not know the practices were unlawful. Good faith reliance on advice of counsel should be an important factor, among others, to consider in assessing whether a person of ordinary sense and understanding would have known the practices to be unlawful. Nothing in this section shall be construed to limit or extinguish any

---

[2] Sec. 8(b) of the Military Commissions Act of 2006, Pub. L. 109-366, provides the following: "Protection of Personnel - Sec. 1004 of the Detainee Treatment Act of 2005 (42 U.S.C. 2000dd-1) shall apply with respect to any criminal prosecution that –
    (1) relates to the detention and interrogation of aliens described in such section;
    (2) is grounded in section 2441(c)(3) of title 18, United States Code; and
    (3) relates to actions occurring between September 11, 2001, and December 30, 2005.

defense or protection otherwise available to any person or entity from suit, civil or criminal liability, or damages, or to provide immunity from prosecution for any criminal offense by the proper authorities.

(b) COUNSEL.—The United States Government shall provide or employ counsel, and pay counsel fees, court costs, bail, and other expenses incident to the representation of an officer, employee, member of the Armed Forces, or other agent described in subsection (a), with respect to any civil action or criminal prosecution or investigation arising out of practices described in that subsection whether before United States courts or agencies, foreign courts or agencies, or international courts or agencies, under the same conditions, and to the same extent, to which such services and payments are authorized under section 1037 of title 10, United States Code.

PROCEDURES FOR STATUS REVIEW OF DETAINEES OUTSIDE OF THE UNITED STATES

SEC. 1005.

(a) SUBMITTAL OF PROCEDURES FOR STATUS REVIEW OF DETAINEES AT GUANTANAMO BAY, CUBA, AND IN AFGHANISTAN AND IRAQ.—

> (1) IN GENERAL.—Not later than 180 days after the date of the enactment of this Act, the Secretary of Defense shall submit to the Committee on Armed Services and the Committee on the Judiciary of the Senate and the Committee on Armed Services and the Committee on the Judiciary of the House of Representatives a report setting forth—
>
>> (A) the procedures of the Combatant Status Review Tribunals and the Administrative Review Boards established by direction of the Secretary of Defense that are in operation at Guantanamo Bay, Cuba, for determining the status of the detainees held at Guantanamo Bay or to provide an annual review to determine the need to continue to detain an alien who is a detainee; and
>>
>> (B) the procedures in operation in Afghanistan and Iraq for a determination of the status of aliens detained in the custody or under the physical control of the Department of Defense in those countries.
>
> (2) DESIGNATED CIVILIAN OFFICIAL.—The procedures submitted to Congress pursuant to paragraph (1)(A) shall ensure that the official of the Department of Defense who is designated by the President or Secretary of Defense to be the final review authority within the Department of Defense with respect to decisions of any such tribunal or board (referred to as the "Designated Civilian Official") shall be a civilian officer of the Department of Defense holding an office to which appointments are

required by law to be made by the President, by and with the advice and consent of the Senate.

(3) CONSIDERATION OF NEW EVIDENCE.—The procedures submitted under paragraph (1)(A) shall provide for periodic review of any new evidence that may become available relating to the enemy combatant status of a detainee.

(b) CONSIDERATION OF STATEMENTS DERIVED WITH COERCION.—

(1) ASSESSMENT.—The procedures submitted to Congress pursuant to subsection (a)(1)(A) shall ensure that a Combatant Status Review Tribunal or Administrative Review Board, or any similar or successor administrative tribunal or board, in making a determination of status or disposition of any detainee under such procedures, shall, to the extent practicable, assess—

(A) whether any statement derived from or relating to such detainee was obtained as a result of coercion; and

(B) the probative value (if any) of any such statement.

(2) APPLICABILITY.—Paragraph (1) applies with respect to any proceeding beginning on or after the date of the enactment of this Act.

(c) REPORT ON MODIFICATION OF PROCEDURES.—The Secretary of Defense shall submit to the committees specified in subsection (a)(1) a report on any modification of the procedures submitted under subsection (a). Any such report shall be submitted not later than 60 days before the date on which such modification goes into effect.

(d) ANNUAL REPORT.—

(1) REPORT REQUIRED.—The Secretary of Defense shall submit to Congress an annual report on the annual review process for aliens in the custody of the Department of Defense outside the United States. Each such report shall be submitted in unclassified form, with a classified annex, if necessary. The report shall be submitted not later than December 31 each year.

(2) ELEMENTS OF REPORT.—Each such report shall include the following with respect to the year covered by the report:

(A) The number of detainees whose status was reviewed.

(B) The procedures used at each location.

(e) JUDICIAL REVIEW OF DETENTION OF ENEMY COMBATANTS.—

(1) IN GENERAL.—Section 2241 of title 28, United States Code, is amended by adding at the end the following:

"(e) Except as provided in section 1005 of the Detainee Treatment Act of 2005, no court, justice, or judge shall have jurisdiction to hear or consider—

"(1) an application for a writ of habeas corpus filed by or on behalf of an alien detained by the Department of Defense at Guantanamo Bay, Cuba; or

"(2) any other action against the United States or its agents relating to any aspect of the detention by the Department of Defense of an alien at Guantanamo Bay, Cuba, who—

> "(A) is currently in military custody; or
>
> "(B) has been determined by the United States Court of Appeals for the District of Columbia Circuit in accordance with the procedures set forth in section 1005(e) of the Detainee Treatment Act of 2005 to have been properly detained as an enemy combatant.".

(2) REVIEW OF DECISION OF COMBATANT STATUS REVIEW TRIBUNALS OF PROPRIETY OF DETENTION.—

> (A) IN GENERAL.—Subject to subparagraphs (B), (C), and (D), the United States Court of Appeals for the District of Columbia Circuit shall have exclusive jurisdiction to determine the validity of any final decision of a Combatant Status Review Tribunal that an alien is properly detained as an enemy combatant.
>
> (B) LIMITATION ON CLAIMS.—The jurisdiction of the United States Court of Appeals for the District of Columbia Circuit under this paragraph shall be limited to claims brought by or on behalf of an alien—
>
>> (i) who is, at the time a request for review by such court is filed, detained by the United States; and
>>
>> (ii) for whom a Combatant Status Review Tribunal has been conducted, pursuant to applicable procedures specified by the Secretary of Defense.
>
> (C) SCOPE OF REVIEW.—The jurisdiction of the United States Court of Appeals for the District of Columbia Circuit on any claims with respect to an alien under this paragraph shall be limited to the consideration of—
>
>> (i) whether the status determination of the Combatant Status Review Tribunal with regard to such alien was consistent with the standards and procedures specified by the Secretary of Defense for Combatant Status Review Tribunals (including the requirement that the conclusion of the Tribunal be supported by a preponderance of the evidence and allowing a rebuttable presumption in favor of the Government's evidence); and

(ii) to the extent the Constitution and laws of the United States are applicable, whether the use of such standards and procedures to make the determination is consistent with the Constitution and laws of the United States.

(D) TERMINATION OR RELEASE FROM CUSTODY.—The jurisdiction of the United States Court of Appeals for the District of Columbia Circuit with respect to the claims of an alien under this paragraph shall cease upon the release of such alien from the custody of the Department of Defense.

(3) RESPONDENT.— The Secretary of Defense shall be the named respondent in any appeal to the United States Court of Appeals for the District of Columbia Circuit under this subsection.[3]

(f) CONSTRUCTION.—Nothing in this section shall be construed to confer any constitutional right on an alien detained as an enemy combatant outside the United States.

(g) UNITED STATES DEFINED.—For purposes of this section, the term "United States", when used in a geographic sense, is as defined in section 101(a)(38) of the Immigration and Nationality Act and, in particular, does not include the United States Naval Station, Guantanamo Bay, Cuba.

(h) EFFECTIVE DATE.—

(1) IN GENERAL.—This section shall take effect on the date of the enactment of this Act.

(2) REVIEW OF COMBATANT STATUS TRIBUNAL AND MILITARY COMMISSION DECISIONS.—Paragraphs (2) and (3) of subsection (e) shall apply with respect to any claim whose review is governed by one of such paragraphs and that is pending on or after the date of the enactment of this Act.

TRAINING OF IRAQI FORCES REGARDING TREATMENT OF DETAINEES

SEC. 1006.

(a) REQUIRED POLICIES.—

(1) IN GENERAL.—The Secretary of Defense shall ensure that policies are prescribed regarding procedures for military and civilian personnel of the Department of Defense and contractor personnel of the Department of Defense in Iraq that are intended to ensure that members of the Armed Forces, and all persons acting on behalf of the Armed Forces or within

---

[3] Paragraph (3) struck by section 1803 of the Military Commissions Act of 2009 (MCA), Pub. L. 111-84, and section 1075(d)(21) of the Ike Skelton National Defense Authorization Act for Fiscal Year 2011, Pub. L. 111-383, which amended section 1803 of the MCA.

facilities of the Armed Forces, ensure that all personnel of Iraqi military forces who are trained by Department of Defense personnel and contractor personnel of the Department of Defense receive training regarding the international obligations and laws applicable to the humane detention of detainees, including protections afforded under the Geneva Conventions and the Convention Against Torture.

(2) ACKNOWLEDGEMENT OF TRAINING.—The Secretary shall ensure that, for all personnel of the Iraqi Security Forces who are provided training referred to in paragraph (1), there is documented acknowledgment of such training having been provided.

(3) DEADLINE FOR POLICIES TO BE PRESCRIBED.—The policies required by paragraph (1) shall be prescribed not later than 180 days after the date of the enactment of this Act.

(b) ARMY FIELD MANUAL.—

(1) TRANSLATION.—The Secretary of Defense shall provide for the United States Army Field Manual on Intelligence Interrogation to be translated into Arabic and any other language the Secretary determines appropriate for use by members of the Iraqi military forces.

(2) DISTRIBUTION.—The Secretary of Defense shall provide for such manual, as translated, to be provided to each unit of the Iraqi military forces trained by Department of Defense personnel or contractor personnel of the Department of Defense.

(c) TRANSMITTAL OF REGULATIONS.—Not less than 30 days after the date on which regulations, policies, and orders are first prescribed under subsection (a), the Secretary of Defense shall submit to the Committee on Armed Services of the Senate and the Committee on Armed Services of the House of Representatives copics of such regulations, policies, or orders, together with a report on steps taken to the date of the report to implement this section.

(d) ANNUAL REPORT.—Not less than one year after the date of the enactment of this Act, and annually thereafter, the Secretary of Defense shall submit to the Committee on Armed Services of the Senate and the Committee on Armed Services of the House of Representatives a report on the implementation of this section. This division may be cited as the "Department of Defense Appropriations Act, 2006".

TITLE 10, CHAPTER 47A, UNITED STATES CODE , MILITARY COMMISSIONS

CHAPTER 47A OF TITLE 10, UNITED STATES CODE [1]

CHAPTER 47A—MILITARY COMMISSIONS

---

[1] Codifying the Military Commissions Act of 2006, the Military Commissions Act of 2009 and the 2011 and 2012 amendments thereto. Statutory provisions related to chapter 47A are included at the end of this segment.

SEC. 948a. DEFINITIONS.

In this chapter:

(1) ALIEN.—The term "alien" means an individual who is not a citizen of the United States.

(2) CLASSIFIED INFORMATION.—The term "classified information" means the following:

(A) Any information or material that has been determined

by the United States Government pursuant to statute, Executive order, or regulation to require protection against unauthorized disclosure for reasons of national security.

(B) Any restricted data, as that term is defined in section 11 y. of the Atomic Energy Act of 1954 (42 U.S.C. 2014(y)).

(3) COALITION PARTNER.—The term "coalition partner", with respect to hostilities engaged in by the United States, means any State or armed force directly engaged along with the United States in such hostilities or providing direct operational support to the United States in connection with such hostilities.

(4) GENEVA CONVENTION RELATIVE TO THE TREATMENT OF PRISONERS OF WAR.—The term "Geneva Convention Relative to the Treatment of Prisoners of War" means the Convention Relative to the Treatment of Prisoners of War, done at Geneva August 12, 1949 (6 UST 3316).

(5) GENEVA CONVENTIONS.—The term "Geneva Conventions" means the international conventions signed at Geneva on August 12, 1949.

(6) PRIVILEGED BELLIGERENT.—The term "privileged belligerent" means an individual belonging to one of the eight categories enumerated in Article 4 of the Geneva Convention Relative to the Treatment of Prisoners of War.

(7) UNPRIVILEGED ENEMY BELLIGERENT.—The term "unprivileged enemy belligerent" means an individual (other than a privileged belligerent) who—

(A) has engaged in hostilities against the United States or its coalition partners;

(B) has purposefully and materially supported hostilities against the United States or its coalition partners; or

(C) was a part of al Qaeda at the time of the alleged offense under this chapter.

(8) NATIONAL SECURITY.—The term "national security" means the national defense and foreign relations of the United States.

(9) HOSTILITIES.—The term "hostilities" means any conflict subject to the laws of war.

SEC. 948b. MILITARY COMMISSIONS GENERALLY.

(a) PURPOSE.—This chapter establishes procedures governing the use of military commissions to try alien unprivileged enemy belligerents for violations of the law of war and other offenses triable by military commission.

(b) AUTHORITY FOR MILITARY COMMISSIONS UNDER THIS

CHAPTER.—The President is authorized to establish military commissions under this chapter for offenses triable by military commission as provided in this chapter.

(c) CONSTRUCTION OF PROVISIONS.—The procedures for military commissions set forth in this chapter are based upon the procedures for trial by general courts-martial under chapter 47 of this title (the Uniform Code of Military Justice). Chapter 47 of this title does not, by its terms, apply to trial by military commission except as specifically provided therein or in this chapter, and many of the provisions of chapter 47 of this title are by their terms inapplicable to military commissions. The judicial construction and application of chapter 47 of this title, while instructive, is therefore not of its own force binding on military commissions established under this chapter.

(d) INAPPLICABILITY OF CERTAIN PROVISIONS.—

    (1) The following provisions of this title shall not apply to trial by military commission under this chapter:

        (A) Section 810 (article 10 of the Uniform Code of Military Justice), relating to speedy trial, including any rule of courtsmartial relating to speedy trial.

        (B) Sections 831(a), (b), and (d) (articles 31(a), (b), and (d) of the Uniform Code of Military Justice), relating to compulsory self-incrimination.

        (C) Section 832 (article 32 of the Uniform Code of Military Justice), relating to pretrial investigation.

    (2) Other provisions of chapter 47 of this title shall apply to trial by military commission under this chapter only to the extent provided by the terms of such provisions or by this chapter.

(e) GENEVA CONVENTIONS NOT ESTABLISHING PRIVATE RIGHT OF ACTION.—No alien unprivileged enemy belligerent subject to trial by military commission under this chapter may invoke the Geneva Conventions as a basis for a private right of action.

SEC. 948c. PERSONS SUBJECT TO MILITARY COMMISSIONS.

Any alien unprivileged enemy belligerent is subject to trial by military commission as set forth in this chapter.

SEC. 948d. JURISDICTION OF MILITARY COMMISSIONS.

A military commission under this chapter shall have jurisdiction to try persons subject to this chapter for any offense made punishable by this chapter, sections 904 and 906 of this title (articles 104 and 106 of the Uniform Code of Military Justice), or the law of war, whether such offense was committed before, on, or after September 11, 2001, and may, under such limitations as the President may prescribe, adjudge any punishment not forbidden by this chapter, including the penalty of death when specifically authorized under this chapter. A military commission is a competent tribunal to make a finding sufficient for jurisdiction.

SEC. 948h. Who May Convene Military Commissions.

Military commissions under this chapter may be convened by the Secretary of Defense or by any officer or official of the United States designated by the Secretary for that purpose.

SEC. 948i. Who May Serve on Military Commissions.

(a) IN GENERAL.—Any commissioned officer of the armed forces on active duty is eligible to serve on a military commission under this chapter, including commissioned officers of the reserve components of the armed forces on active duty, commissioned officers of the National Guard on active duty in Federal service, or retired commissioned officers recalled to active duty.

(b) DETAIL OF MEMBERS.—When convening a military commission under this chapter, the convening authority shall detail as members thereof such members of the armed forces eligible under subsection (a) who, in the opinion of the convening authority, are best qualified for the duty by reason of age, education, training, experience, length of service, and judicial temperament. No member of an armed force is eligible to serve as a member of a military commission when such member is the accuser or a witness for the prosecution or has acted as an investigator or counsel in the same case.

(c) EXCUSE OF MEMBERS.—Before a military commission under this chapter is assembled for the trial of a case, the convening authority may excuse a member from participating in the case.

SEC. 948j. Military Judge of a Military Commission.

(a) DETAIL OF MILITARY JUDGE.—A military judge shall be detailed to each military commission under this chapter. The Secretary of Defense shall prescribe regulations providing for the manner in which military judges are so detailed to military commissions. The military judge shall preside over each military commission to which such military judge has been detailed.

(b) ELIGIBILITY.—A military judge shall be a commissioned officer of the armed forces who is a member of the bar of a Federal court, or a member of the bar of the highest court of a State, and who is certified to be qualified for duty under section 826 of this title (article 26 of the Uniform Code of Military Justice) as a military judge of general courts-martial by the Judge Advocate General of the armed force of which such military judge is a member.

(c) INELIGIBILITY OF CERTAIN INDIVIDUALS.—No person is eligible to act as military judge in a case of a military commission under this chapter if such person is the accuser or a witness or has acted as investigator or a counsel in the same case.

(d) CONSULTATION WITH MEMBERS; INELIGIBILITY TO VOTE.—
A military judge detailed to a military commission under this chapter may not consult with the members except in the presence of the accused (except as otherwise provided in section 949d of this title), trial counsel, and defense counsel, nor may such military judge vote with the members.

(e) OTHER DUTIES.—A commissioned officer who is certified to be qualified for duty as a military judge of a military commission under this chapter may perform such other duties as are assigned to such officer by or with the approval of the Judge Advocate General of the armed force of which such officer is a member or the designee of such Judge Advocate General.

(f) PROHIBITION ON EVALUATION OF FITNESS BY CONVENING AUTHORITY.—The convening authority of a military commission under this chapter may not prepare or review any report concerning the effectiveness, fitness, or efficiency of a military judge detailed to the military commission which relates to such judge's performance of duty as a military judge on the military commission.

SEC. 948k. DETAIL OF TRIAL COUNSEL AND DEFENSE COUNSEL.
(a) DETAIL OF COUNSEL GENERALLY.—

> (1) Trial counsel and military defense counsel shall be detailed for each military commission under this chapter.
>
> (2) Assistant trial counsel and assistant and associate defense counsel may be detailed for a military commission under this chapter.
>
> (3) Military defense counsel for a military commission under this chapter shall be detailed as soon as practicable.
>
> (4) The Secretary of Defense shall prescribe regulations Providing for the manner in which trial counsel and military Defense counsel are detailed for military commissions under this chapter and for the persons who are authorized to detail such counsel for such military commissions.

(b) TRIAL COUNSEL.—Subject to subsection (e), a trial counsel detailed for a military commission under this chapter shall be—

> (1) a judge advocate (as that term is defined in section 801 of this title (article 1 of the Uniform Code of Military Justice)) who is—
>
>> (A) a graduate of an accredited law school or a member of the bar of a Federal court or of the highest court of a State; and
>>
>> (B) certified as competent to perform duties as trial counsel before general courts-martial by the Judge Advocate General of the armed force of which such judge advocate is a member; or
>
> (2) a civilian who is—

(A) a member of the bar of a Federal court or of the highest court of a State; and

(B) otherwise qualified to practice before the military commission pursuant to regulations prescribed by the Secretary of Defense.

(c) DEFENSE COUNSEL.—

(1) Subject to subsection (e), a military defense counsel detailed for a military commission under this chapter shall be a judge advocate (as so defined) who is—

(A) a graduate of an accredited law school or a member of the bar of a Federal court or of the highest court of a State; and

(B) certified as competent to perform duties as defense counsel before general courts-martial by the Judge Advocate General of the armed force of which such judge advocate is a member.

(2) The Secretary of Defense shall prescribe regulations for the appointment and performance of defense counsel in capital cases under this chapter.

(d) CHIEF PROSECUTOR; CHIEF DEFENSE COUNSEL.—

(1) The Chief Prosecutor in a military commission under this chapter shall meet the requirements set forth in subsection (b)(1).

(2) The Chief Defense Counsel in a military commission under this chapter shall meet the requirements set forth in subsection (c)(1).

(e) INELIGIBILITY OF CERTAIN INDIVIDUALS.—No person who has acted as an investigator, military judge, or member of a military commission under this chapter in any case may act later as trial counsel or military defense counsel in the same case. No person who has acted for the prosecution before a military commission under this chapter may act later in the same case for the defense, nor may any person who has acted for the defense before a military commission under this chapter act later in the same case for the prosecution.

SEC. 948l. DETAIL OR EMPLOYMENT OF REPORTERS AND INTERPRETERS.

(a) COURT REPORTERS.—Under such regulations as the Secretary of Defense may prescribe, the convening authority of a military commission under this chapter shall detail to or employ for the military commission qualified court reporters, who shall prepare a verbatim record of the proceedings of and testimony taken before the military commission.

(b) INTERPRETERS.—Under such regulations as the Secretary of Defense may prescribe, the convening authority of a military commission under this chapter may detail to or employ for the military commission interpreters who shall interpret for the military commission, and, as necessary, for trial counsel and defense counsel for the military commission, and for the accused.

(c) TRANSCRIPT; RECORD.—The transcript of a military commission under this chapter shall be under the control of the convening authority of the military commission, who shall also be responsible for preparing the record of the proceedings of the military commission.

SEC. 948m. NUMBER OF MEMBERS; EXCUSE OF MEMBERS; ABSENT AND ADDITIONAL MEMBERS.

(a) NUMBER OF MEMBERS.—

(1) Except as provided in paragraph (2), a military commission under this chapter shall have at least five members.

(2) In a case in which the accused before a military commission under this chapter may be sentenced to a penalty of death, the military commission shall have the number of members prescribed by section 949m(c) of this title.

(b) EXCUSE OF MEMBERS.—No member of a military commission under this chapter may be absent or excused after the military commission has been assembled for the trial of a case unless excused—

(1) as a result of challenge;

(2) by the military judge for physical disability or other good cause; or

(3) by order of the convening authority for good cause.

(c) ABSENT AND ADDITIONAL MEMBERS.—Whenever a military commission under this chapter is reduced below the number of members required by subsection (a), the trial may not proceed unless the convening authority details new members sufficient to provide not less than such number. The trial may proceed with the new members present after the recorded evidence previously introduced before the members has been read to the military commission in the presence of the military judge, the accused (except as provided in section 949d of this title), and counsel for both sides.

SEC. 948q. CHARGES AND SPECIFICATIONS.

(a) CHARGES AND SPECIFICATIONS.—Charges and specifications against an accused in a military commission under this chapter shall be signed by a person subject to chapter 47 of this title under oath before a commissioned officer of the armed forces authorized to administer oaths and shall state—

(1) that the signer has personal knowledge of, or reason to believe, the matters set forth therein; and

(2) that such matters are true in fact to the best of the signer's knowledge and belief.

(b) NOTICE TO ACCUSED.—Upon the swearing of the charges and specifications in accordance with subsection (a), the accused shall be informed of the charges and specifications against the accused as soon as practicable.

SEC. 948r. EXCLUSION OF STATEMENTS OBTAINED BY TORTURE OR CRUEL, INHUMAN, OR DEGRADING TREATMENT; PROHIBITION OF SELF-INCRIMINATION; ADMISSION OF OTHER STATEMENTS OF THE ACCUSED.

(a) EXCLUSION OF STATEMENTS OBTAIN BY TORTURE OR CRUEL, INHUMAN, OR DEGRADING TREATMENT.—No statement obtained by the use of torture or by cruel, inhuman, or degrading treatment (as defined by section 1003 of the Detainee Treatment Act of 2005 (42 U.S.C. 2000dd)), whether or not under color of law, shall be admissible in a military commission under this chapter, except against a person accused of torture or such treatment as evidence that the statement was made.

(b) SELF-INCRIMINATION PROHIBITED.—No person shall be required to testify against himself or herself at a proceeding of a military commission under this chapter.

(c) OTHER STATEMENTS OF THE ACCUSED.—A statement of the accused may be admitted in evidence in a military commission under this chapter only if the military judge finds—

    (1) that the totality of the circumstances renders the statement reliable and possessing sufficient probative value; and

    (2) that—

        (A) the statement was made incident to lawful conduct during military operations at the point of capture or during closely related active combat engagement, and the interests of justice would best be served by admission of the statement into evidence; or

        (B) the statement was voluntarily given.

(d) DETERMINATION OF VOLUNTARINESS.—In determining for purposes of subsection (c)(2)(B) whether a statement was voluntarily given, the military judge shall consider the totality of the circumstances, including, as appropriate, the following:

    (1) The details of the taking of the statement, accounting for the circumstances of the conduct of military and intelligence operations during hostilities.

    (2) The characteristics of the accused, such as military training, age, and education level.

    (3) The lapse of time, change of place, or change in identity of the questioners between the statement sought to be admitted and any prior questioning of the accused.

SEC. 948s. SERVICE OF CHARGES.

The trial counsel assigned to a case before a military commission under this chapter shall cause to be served upon the accused and military defense counsel a copy of the charges upon which trial is to be had in English and, if appropriate, in another language that the accused understands, sufficiently in advance of trial to prepare a defense.

SEC. 949a. RULES.

(a) PROCEDURES AND RULES OF EVIDENCE.—Pretrial, trial, and post-trial procedures, including elements and modes of proof, for cases triable by military commission under this chapter may be prescribed by the Secretary of Defense. Such procedures may not be contrary to or inconsistent with this chapter. Except as otherwise provided in this chapter or chapter 47 of this title, the procedures and rules of evidence applicable in trials by general courts-martial of the United States shall apply in trials by military commission under this chapter.

(b) EXCEPTIONS.—

> (1) In trials by military commission under this chapter, the Secretary of Defense, in consultation with the Attorney General, may make such exceptions in the applicability of the procedures and rules of evidence otherwise applicable in general courts-martial as may be required by the unique circumstances of the conduct of military and intelligence operations during hostilities or by other practical need consistent with this chapter.
>
> (2) Notwithstanding any exceptions authorized by paragraph (1), the procedures and rules of evidence in trials by military commission under this chapter shall include, at a minimum, the following rights of the accused:
>
>> (A) To present evidence in the accused's defense, to Crossexamine the witnesses who testify against the accused, and to examine and respond to all evidence admitted against the accused on the issue of guilt or innocence and for sentencing, as provided for by this chapter.
>>
>> (B) To be present at all sessions of the military commission (other than those for deliberations or voting), except when excluded under section 949d of this title.
>>
>> (C)(i) When none of the charges sworn against the accused are capital, to be represented before a military commission by civilian counsel if provided at no expense to the Government, and by either the defense counsel detailed or the military counsel of the accused's own selection, if reasonably available.

(ii) When any of the charges sworn against the accused are capital, to be represented before a military commission in accordance with clause (i) and, to the greatest extent practicable, by at least one additional counsel who is learned in applicable law relating to capital cases and who, if necessary, may be a civilian and compensated in accordance with regulations prescribed by the Secretary of Defense.

(D) To self-representation, if the accused knowingly and competently waives the assistance of counsel, subject to the provisions of paragraph (4).

(E) To the suppression of evidence that is not reliable or probative.

(F) To the suppression of evidence the probative value of which is substantially outweighed by—

(i) the danger of unfair prejudice, confusion of the issues, or misleading the members; or

(ii) considerations of undue delay, waste of time, or needless presentation of cumulative evidence.

(3) In making exceptions in the applicability in trials by military commission under this chapter from the procedures and rules otherwise applicable in general courts-martial, the Secretary of Defense may provide the following:

(A) Evidence seized outside the United States shall not be excluded from trial by military commission on the grounds that the evidence was not seized pursuant to a search warrant or authorization.

(B) A statement of the accused that is otherwise admissible shall not be excluded from trial by military commission on grounds of alleged coercion or compulsory self-incrimination so long as the evidence complies with the provisions of section 948r of this title.

(C) Evidence shall be admitted as authentic so long as—

(i) the military judge of the military commission Determines that there is sufficient evidence that the evidence is what it is claimed to be; and

(ii) the military judge instructs the members that they may consider any issue as to authentication or identification of evidence in determining the weight, if any, to be given to the evidence.

(D) Hearsay evidence not otherwise admissible under the rules of evidence applicable in trial by general courts-martial

may be admitted in a trial by military commission only if—
(i) the proponent of the evidence makes known to the adverse party, sufficiently in advance to provide the adverse party with a fair opportunity to meet the evidence, the proponent's intention to offer the evidence, and the particulars of the evidence (including information on the circumstances under which the evidence was obtained); and
(ii) the military judge, after taking into account all of the circumstances surrounding the taking of the statement, including the degree to which the statement is corroborated, the indicia of reliability within the statement itself, and whether the will of the declarant was overborne, determines that—
(I) the statement is offered as evidence of a material fact;
(II) the statement is probative on the point for which it is offered;
(III) direct testimony from the witness is not available as a practical matter, taking into consideration the physical location of the witness, the unique circumstances of military and intelligence operations during hostilities, and the adverse impacts on military or intelligence operations that would likely result from the production of the witness; and
(IV) the general purposes of the rules of evidence and the interests of justice will best be served by admission of the statement into evidence.

(4)(A) The accused in a military commission under this chapter who exercises the right to self-representation under paragraph (2)(D) shall conform the accused's deportment and the conduct of the defense to the rules of evidence, procedure, and decorum applicable to trials by military commission.
(B) Failure of the accused to conform to the rules described in subparagraph (A) may result in a partial or total revocation by the military judge of the right of self-representation under paragraph (2)(D). In such case, the military counsel of the accused or an appropriately authorized civilian counsel shall perform the functions necessary for the defense.

(c) DELEGATION OF AUTHORITY TO PRESCRIBE REGULATIONS.—

The Secretary of Defense may delegate the authority of the Secretary to prescribe regulations under this chapter.

(d) NOTICE TO CONGRESS OF MODIFICATION OF RULES.—Not later than 60 days before the date on which any proposed modification of the rules in effect for military commissions under this chapter goes into effect, the Secretary of Defense shall submit to the Committee on Armed Services of the Senate and the Committee on Armed Services of the House of Representatives a report describing the proposed modification.

SEC. 949b. UNLAWFULLY INFLUENCING ACTION OF MILITARY COMMISSION AND UNITED STATES COURT OF MILITARY COMMISSION REVIEW.

(a) MILITARY COMMISSIONS.—

(1) No authority convening a military commission under this chapter may censure, reprimand, or admonish the military commission, or any member, military judge, or counsel thereof, with respect to the findings or sentence adjudged by the military commission, or with respect to any other exercises of its or their functions in the conduct of the proceedings.

(2) No person may attempt to coerce or, by any unauthorized means, influence—

(A) the action of a military commission under this chapter, or any member thereof, in reaching the findings or sentence in any case;

(B) the action of any convening, approving, or reviewing authority with respect to their judicial acts; or

(C) the exercise of professional judgment by trial counsel or defense counsel.

(3) The provisions of this subsection shall not apply with respect to—

(A) general instructional or informational courses in military justice if such courses are designed solely for the purpose of instructing members of a command in the substantive and procedural aspects of military commissions; or

(B) statements and instructions given in open proceedings by a military judge or counsel.

(b) UNITED STATES COURT OF MILITARY COMMISSION REVIEW.—

(1) No person may attempt to coerce or, by any unauthorized means, influence—

(A) the action of a judge on the United States Court of Military Commissions Review in reaching a decision on the findings or sentence on appeal in any case; or

(B) the exercise of professional judgment by trial counsel or defense counsel appearing before the United States Court of Military Commission Review.

(2) No person may censure, reprimand, or admonish a judge on the United States Court of Military Commission Review, or counsel thereof, with respect to any exercise of their functions in the conduct of proceedings under this chapter.

(3) The provisions of this subsection shall not apply with respect to—

(A) general instructional or informational courses in military justice if such courses are designed solely for the purpose of instructing members of a command in the substantive and procedural aspects of military commissions; or

(B) statements and instructions given in open proceedings by a judge on the United States Court of Military Commission Review, or counsel.

(4) No appellate military judge on the United States Court of Military Commission Review may be reassigned to other duties, except under circumstances as follows:

(A) The appellate military judge voluntarily requests to be reassigned to other duties and the Secretary of Defense, or the designee of the Secretary, in consultation with the Judge Advocate General of the armed force of which the appellate military judge is a member, approves such reassignment.

(B) The appellate military judge retires or otherwise separates from the armed forces.

(C) The appellate military judge is reassigned to other duties by the Secretary of Defense, or the designee of the Secretary, in consultation with the Judge Advocate General of the armed force of which the appellate military judge is a member, based on military necessity and such reassignment is consistent with service rotation regulations (to the extent such regulations are applicable).

(D) The appellate military judge is withdrawn by the Secretary of Defense, or the designee of the Secretary, in consultation with the Judge Advocate General of the armed force of which the appellate military judge is a member, for good cause consistent with applicable procedures under chapter 47 of this title (the Uniform Code of Military Justice).

(c) PROHIBITION ON CONSIDERATION OF ACTIONS ON COMMISSION IN EVALUATION OF FITNESS.—In the preparation of an effectiveness, fitness, or efficiency report or any other report or document used in whole or in part for the purpose of determining whether a commissioned officer of the armed forces is qualified to be advanced in grade, or in determining the assignment or transfer of any such officer or whether any such officer should be retained on active duty, no person may—

(1) consider or evaluate the performance of duty of any member of a military commission under this chapter; or

(2) give a less favorable rating or evaluation to any commissioned officer because of the zeal with which such officer, in acting as counsel, represented any accused before a military commission under this chapter.

SEC. 949c. DUTIES OF TRIAL COUNSEL AND DEFENSE COUNSEL.

(a) TRIAL COUNSEL.—The trial counsel of a military commission under this chapter shall prosecute in the name of the United States.

(b) DEFENSE COUNSEL.—

(1) The accused shall be represented in the accused's defense before a military commission under this chapter as provided in this subsection.

(2) The accused may be represented by military counsel detailed under section 948k of this title or by military counsel of the accused's own selection, if reasonably available.

(3) The accused may be represented by civilian counsel if retained by the accused, provided that such civilian counsel—

(A) is a United States citizen;

(B) is admitted to the practice of law in a State, district, or possession of the United States, or before a Federal court;

(C) has not been the subject of any sanction of disciplinary action by any court, bar, or other competent governmental authority for relevant misconduct;

(D) has been determined to be eligible for access to information classified at the level Secret or higher; and

(E) has signed a written agreement to comply with all applicable regulations or instructions for counsel, including any rules of court for conduct during the proceedings.

(4) If the accused is represented by civilian counsel, military counsel shall act as associate counsel.

(5) The accused is not entitled to be represented by more than one military counsel. However, the person authorized under regulations prescribed under section 948k of this title to detail counsel, in such person's sole discretion, may detail additional military counsel to represent the accused.

(6) Defense counsel may cross-examine each witness for the prosecution who testifies before a military commission under this chapter.

(7) Civilian defense counsel shall protect any classified information received during the course of representation of the accused in accordance with all applicable law governing the protection of classified nformation, and may not divulge such information to any person not authorized to receive it.

SEC. 949d. SESSIONS.

(a) SESSIONS WITHOUT PRESENCE OF MEMBERS.—

(1) At any time after the service of charges which have been referred for trial by military commission under this chapter, the military judge may call the military commission into session without the presence of the members for the purpose of—

(A) hearing and determining motions raising defenses or objections which are capable of determination without trial of the issues raised by a plea of not guilty;

(B) hearing and ruling upon any matter which may be ruled upon by the military judge under this chapter, whether or not the matter is appropriate for later consideration or decision by the members;

(C) if permitted by regulations prescribed by the Secretary of Defense, receiving the pleas of the accused; and

(D) performing any other procedural function which may be performed by the military judge under this chapter or under rules prescribed pursuant to section 949a of this title and which does not require the presence of the members.

(2) Except as provided in subsections (b), (c), and (d), any proceedings under paragraph (1) shall be conducted in the presence of the accused, defense counsel, and trial counsel, and shall be made part of the record.

(b) DELIBERATION OR VOTE OF MEMBERS.—When the members of a military commission under this chapter deliberate or vote, only the members may be present.

(c) CLOSURE OF PROCEEDINGS.—

(1) The military judge may close to the public all or part of the proceedings of a military commission under this chapter.

(2) The military judge may close to the public all or a portion of the proceedings under paragraph (1) only upon making a specific finding that such closure is necessary to—

(A) protect information the disclosure of which could reasonably be expected to cause damage to the national security, including intelligence or law enforcement sources, methods, or activities; or

(B) ensure the physical safety of individuals.

(3) A finding under paragraph (2) may be based upon a presentation, including a presentation ex parte or in camera, by either trial counsel or defense counsel.

(d) EXCLUSION OF ACCUSED FROM CERTAIN PROCEEDINGS.—
The military judge may exclude the accused from any portion of a proceeding upon a determination that, after being warned by the military judge, the accused persists in conduct that justifies exclusion from the courtroom—

    (1) to ensure the physical safety of individuals; or

    (2) to prevent disruption of the proceedings by the accused.

SEC. 949e. CONTINUANCES.

The military judge in a military commission under this chapter may, for reasonable cause, grant a continuance to any party for such time, and as often, as may appear to be just.

SEC. 949f. CHALLENGES.

(a) CHALLENGES AUTHORIZED.—The military judge and members of a military commission under this chapter may be challenged by the accused or trial counsel for cause stated to the military commission. The military judge shall determine the relevance and validity of challenges for cause, and may not receive a challenge to more than one person at a time. Challenges by trial counsel shall ordinarily be presented and decided before those by the accused are offered.

(b) PEREMPTORY CHALLENGES.—The accused and trial counsel are each entitled to one peremptory challenge, but the military judge may not be challenged except for cause.

(c) CHALLENGES AGAINST ADDITIONAL MEMBERS.—Whenever additional members are detailed to a military commission under this chapter, and after any challenges for cause against such additional members are presented and decided, the accused and trial counsel are each entitled to one peremptory challenge against members not previously subject to peremptory challenge.

SEC. 949g. OATHS.

(a) IN GENERAL.—

    (1) Before performing their respective duties in a military commission under this chapter, military judges, members, trial counsel, defense counsel, reporters, and interpreters shall take an oath to perform their duties faithfully.

    (2) The form of the oath required by paragraph (1), the time and place of the taking thereof, the manner of recording thereof, and whether the oath shall be taken for all cases in which duties are to be performed or for a particular case, shall be as provided in regulations prescribed by the Secretary of Defense. The regulations may provide that—

> (A) an oath to perform faithfully duties as a military judge, trial counsel, or defense counsel may be taken at any time by any judge advocate or other person certified to be qualified or competent for the duty; and
>
> (B) if such an oath is taken, such oath need not again be taken at the time the judge advocate or other person is detailed to that duty.

(b) WITNESSES.—Each witness before a military commission under this chapter shall be examined on oath.

(c) OATH DEFINED.—In this section, the term "oath" includes an affirmation.

SEC. 949h. FORMER JEOPARDY.

(a) IN GENERAL.—No person may, without the person's consent, be tried by a military commission under this chapter a second time for the same offense.

(b) SCOPE OF TRIAL.—No proceeding in which the accused has been found guilty by military commission under this chapter upon any charge or specification is a trial in the sense of this section until the finding of guilty has become final after review of the case has been fully completed.

SEC. 949i. PLEAS OF THE ACCUSED.

(a) PLEA OF NOT GUILTY.—If an accused in a military commission under this chapter after a plea of guilty sets up matter inconsistent with the plea, or if it appears that the accused has entered the plea of guilty through lack of understanding of its meaning and effect, or if the accused fails or refuses to plead, a plea of not guilty shall be entered in the record, and the military commission shall proceed as though the accused had pleaded not guilty.

(b) FINDING OF GUILT AFTER GUILTY PLEA.—With respect to any charge or specification to which a plea of guilty has been made by the accused in a military commission under this chapter and accepted by the military judge, a finding of guilty of the charge or specification may be entered immediately without a vote. The finding shall constitute the finding of the military commission unless the plea of guilty is withdrawn prior to announcement of the sentence, in which event the proceedings shall continue as though the accused had pleaded not guilty.

SEC. 949j. OPPORTUNITY TO OBTAIN WITNESSES AND OTHER EVIDENCE.

(a) IN GENERAL.—

> (1) Defense counsel in a military commission under this chapter shall have a reasonable opportunity to obtain witnesses and other evidence as provided in regulations prescribed by the Secretary of Defense. The opportunity to obtain witnesses and evidence shall be comparable to the

opportunity available to a criminal defendant in a court of the United States under article III of the Constitution.

(2) Process issued in military commissions under this chapter to compel witnesses to appear and testify and to compel the production of other evidence—

> (A) shall be similar to that which courts of the United States having criminal jurisdiction may lawfully issue; and
>
> (B) shall run to any place where the United States shall have jurisdiction thereof.

(b) DISCLOSURE OF EXCULPATORY EVIDENCE.—

> (1) As soon as practicable, trial counsel in a military commission under this chapter shall disclose to the defense the existence of any evidence that reasonably tends to—
>
> > (A) negate the guilt of the accused of an offense charged; or
> >
> > (B) reduce the degree of guilt of the accused with respect to an offense charged.
>
> (2) The trial counsel shall, as soon as practicable, disclose to the defense the existence of evidence that reasonably tends to impeach the credibility of a witness whom the government intends to call at trial.
>
> (3) The trial counsel shall, as soon as practicable upon a finding of guilt, disclose to the defense the existence of evidence that is not subject to paragraph (1) or paragraph (2) but that reasonably may be viewed as mitigation evidence at sentencing.
>
> (4) The disclosure obligations under this subsection encompass evidence that is known or reasonably should be known to any government officials who participated in the investigation and prosecution of the case against the defendant.

SEC. 949k. DEFENSE OF LACK OF MENTAL RESPONSIBILITY.

(a) AFFIRMATIVE DEFENSE.—It is an affirmative defense in a trial by military commission under this chapter that, at the time of the commission of the acts constituting the offense, the accused, as a result of a severe mental disease or defect, was unable to appreciate the nature and quality or the wrongfulness of the acts. Mental disease or defect does not otherwise constitute a defense.

(b) BURDEN OF PROOF.—The accused in a military commission under this chapter has the burden of proving the defense of lack of mental responsibility by clear and convincing evidence.

(c) FINDINGS FOLLOWING ASSERTION OF DEFENSE.—Whenever lack of mental responsibility of the accused with respect to an offense is properly at issue in a military commission under this chapter, the military judge shall instruct the members as to the defense of lack of mental responsibility under this section and shall charge the members to find the accused—

    (1) guilty;

    (2) not guilty; or

    (3) subject to subsection (d), not guilty by reason of lack of mental responsibility.

(d) MAJORITY VOTE REQUIRED FOR FINDING.—The accused shall be found not guilty by reason of lack of mental responsibility under subsection (c)(3) only if a majority of the members present at the time the vote is taken determines that the defense of lack of mental responsibility has been established.

SEC. 949l. VOTING AND RULINGS.

(a) VOTE BY SECRET WRITTEN BALLOT.—Voting by members of a military commission under this chapter on the findings and on the sentence shall be by secret written ballot.

(b) RULINGS.—

    (1) The military judge in a military commission under this chapter shall rule upon all questions of law, including the admissibility of evidence and all interlocutory questions arising during the proceedings.

    (2) Any ruling made by the military judge upon a question of law or an interlocutory question (other than the factual issue of mental responsibility of the accused) is conclusive and constitutes the ruling of the military commission. However, a military judge may change such a ruling at any time during the trial.

(c) INSTRUCTIONS PRIOR TO VOTE.—Before a vote is taken of the findings of a military commission under this chapter, the military judge shall, in the presence of the accused and counsel, instruct the members as to the elements of the offense and charge the members—

    (1) that the accused must be presumed to be innocent until the accused's guilt is established by legal and competent evidence beyond a reasonable doubt;

    (2) that in the case being considered, if there is a reasonable doubt as to the guilt of the accused, the doubt must be resolved in favor of the accused and the accused must be acquitted;

    (3) that, if there is reasonable doubt as to the degree of guilt, the finding must be in a lower degree as to which there is no reasonable doubt; and

    (4) that the burden of proof to establish the guilt of the accused beyond a reasonable doubt is upon the United States.

SEC. 949m. NUMBER OF VOTES REQUIRED.

(a) CONVICTION.—No person may be convicted by a military commission under this chapter of any offense, except as provided in section 949i(b) of this title or by concurrence of two-thirds of the members present at the time the vote is taken.

(b) SENTENCES.—

(1) Except as provided in paragraphs (2) and (3), sentences shall be determined by a military commission by the concurrence of two-thirds of the members present at the time the vote is taken.

(2) No person may be sentenced to death by a military commission, except insofar as—

(A) the penalty of death has been expressly authorized under this chapter, chapter 47 of this title, or the law of war for an offense of which the accused has been found guilty;

(B) trial counsel expressly sought the penalty of death by filing an appropriate notice in advance of trial;

(C) the accused was convicted of the offense by the concurrence of all the members present at the time the vote is taken; and

(D) all members present at the time the vote was taken concurred in the sentence of death.

(3) No person may be sentenced to life imprisonment, or to confinement for more than 10 years, by a military commission under this chapter except by the concurrence of three-fourths of the members present at the time the vote is taken.

(c) NUMBER OF MEMBERS REQUIRED FOR PENALTY OF DEATH.—

(1) Except as provided in paragraph (2), in a case in which the penalty of death is sought, the number of members of the military commission under this chapter shall be not less than 12 members.

(2) In any case described in paragraph (1) in which 12 members are not reasonably available for a military commission because of physical conditions or military exigencies, the convening authority shall specify a lesser number of members for the military commission (but not fewer than 9 members), and the military commission may be assembled, and the trial held, with not less than the number of members so specified. In any such case, the convening authority shall make a detailed written statement, to be appended to the record, stating why a greater number of members were not reasonably available.

SEC. 949n. MILITARY COMMISSION TO ANNOUNCE ACTION.

A military commission under this chapter shall announce its findings and sentence to the parties as soon as determined.

SEC. 949o. RECORD OF TRIAL.

(a) RECORD; AUTHENTICATION.—Each military commission under this chapter shall keep a separate, verbatim, record of the proceedings in each case brought before it, and the record shall be authenticated by the signature of the military judge. If the record cannot be authenticated by the military judge by reason of death, disability, or absence, it shall be authenticated by the signature of the trial counsel or by a member of the commission if the trial counsel is unable to authenticate it by reason of death, disability, or absence. Where appropriate, and as provided in regulations prescribed by the Secretary of Defense, the record of a military commission under this chapter may contain a classified annex.

(b) COMPLETE RECORD REQUIRED.—A complete record of the proceedings and testimony shall be prepared in every military commission under this chapter.

(c) PROVISION OF COPY TO ACCUSED.—A copy of the record of the proceedings of the military commission under this chapter shall be given the accused as soon as it is authenticated. If the record contains classified information, or a classified annex, the accused shall receive a redacted version of the record consistent with the requirements of subchapter V of this chapter. Defense counsel shall have access to the unredacted record, as provided in regulations prescribed by the Secretary of Defense.

SEC. 949p–1. PROTECTION OF CLASSIFIED INFORMATION: APPLICABILITY OF SUBCHAPTER.

(a) PROTECTION OF CLASSIFIED INFORMATION.—Classified information shall be protected and is privileged from disclosure if disclosure would be detrimental to the national security. Under no circumstances may a military judge order the release of classified information to any person not authorized to receive such information.

(b) ACCESS TO EVIDENCE.—Any information admitted into evidence pursuant to any rule, procedure, or order by the military judge shall be provided to the accused.

(c) DECLASSIFICATION.—Trial counsel shall work with the original classification authorities for evidence that may be used at trial to ensure that such evidence is declassified to the maximum extent possible, consistent with the requirements of national security. A decision not to declassify evidence under this section shall not be subject to review by a military commission or upon appeal.

(d) CONSTRUCTION OF PROVISIONS.—The judicial construction of the Classified Information Procedures Act (18 U.S.C. App.) shall be authoritative in the interpretation of this subchapter, except to the extent that such construction is inconsistent with the specific requirements of this chapter.

SEC. 949p–2. PRETRIAL CONFERENCE.

(a) MOTION.—At any time after service of charges, any party may move for a pretrial conference to consider matters relating to classified information that may arise in connection with the prosecution.

(b) CONFERENCE.—Following a motion under subsection (a), or sua sponte, the military judge shall promptly hold a pretrial conference. Upon request by either party, the court shall hold such conference ex parte to the extent necessary to protect classified information from disclosure, in accordance with the practice of the Federal courts under the Classified Information Procedures Act (18 U.S.C. App.).

(c) MATTERS TO BE ESTABLISHED AT PRETRIAL CONFERENCE.—

(1) TIMING OF SUBSEQUENT ACTIONS.—At the pretrial conference, the military judge shall establish the timing of—

(A) requests for discovery;

(B) the provision of notice required by section 949p–5 of this title; and

(C) the initiation of the procedure established by section 949p–6 of this title.

(2) OTHER MATTERS.—At the pretrial conference, the military judge may also consider any matter—

(A) which relates to classified information; or

(B) which may promote a fair and expeditious trial.

(d) EFFECT OF ADMISSIONS BY ACCUSED AT PRETRIAL CONFERENCE.—

No admission made by the accused or by any counsel for the accused at a pretrial conference under this section may be used against the accused unless the admission is in writing and is signed by the accused and by the counsel for the accused.

SEC. 949p–3. PROTECTIVE ORDERS.

Upon motion of the trial counsel, the military judge shall issue an order to protect against the disclosure of any classified information that has been disclosed by the United States to any accused in any military commission under this chapter or that has otherwise been provided to, or obtained by, any such accused in any such military commission.

SEC. 949p–4. DISCOVERY OF, AND ACCESS TO, CLASSIFIED INFORMATION BY THE ACCUSED.

(a) LIMITATIONS ON DISCOVERY OR ACCESS BY THE ACCUSED.—

(1) DECLARATIONS BY THE UNITED STATES OF DAMAGE TO NATIONAL SECURITY.—In any case before a military commission in which the United States seeks to delete, withhold, or otherwise obtain other relief with respect to the discovery of or access to any classified information, the trial counsel shall submit a declaration invoking the United States' classified information privilege and setting forth the damage to the national security that the discovery of or access to such

information reasonably could be expected to cause. The declaration shall be signed by a knowledgeable United States official possessing authority to classify information.

(2) STANDARD FOR AUTHORIZATION OF DISCOVERY OR ACCESS.—Upon the submission of a declaration under paragraph (1), the military judge may not authorize the discovery of or access to such classified information unless the military judge determines that such classified information would be noncumulative, relevant, and helpful to a legally cognizable defense, rebuttal of the prosecution's case, or to sentencing, in accordance with standards generally applicable to discovery of or access to classified information in Federal criminal cases. If the discovery of or access to such classified information is authorized, it shall be addressed in accordance with the requirements of subsection (b).

(b) DISCOVERY OF CLASSIFIED INFORMATION.—

(1) SUBSTITUTIONS AND OTHER RELIEF.—The military judge, in assessing the accused's discovery of or access to classified information under this section, may authorize the United States—

(A) to delete or withhold specified items of classified information;

(B) to substitute a summary for classified information; or

(C) to substitute a statement admitting relevant facts that the classified information or material would tend to prove.

(2) EX PARTE PRESENTATIONS.—The military judge shall permit the trial counsel to make a request for an authorization under paragraph (1) in the form of an ex parte presentation to the extent necessary to protect classified information, in accordance with the practice of the Federal courts under the Classified Information Procedures Act (18 U.S.C. App.). If the military judge enters an order granting relief following such an ex parte showing, the entire presentation (including the text of any written submission, verbatim transcript of the ex parte oral conference or hearing, and any exhibits received by the court as part of the ex parte presentation) shall be sealed and preserved in the records of the military commission to be made available to the appellate court in the event of an appeal.

(3) ACTION BY MILITARY JUDGE.—The military judge shall grant the request of the trial counsel to substitute a summary or to substitute a statement admitting relevant facts, or to provide other relief in accordance with paragraph (1), if the military judge finds that the summary, statement, or other relief would provide the accused with substantially the same ability to make a defense as would discovery of or access to the specific classified information.

(c) RECONSIDERATION.—An order of a military judge authorizing a request of the trial counsel to substitute, summarize, withhold, or prevent access to classified information under this section is not subject to a motion for reconsideration by the accused, if such order was entered pursuant to an ex parte showing under this section.

SEC. 949p–5. NOTICE BY ACCUSED OF INTENTION TO DISCLOSE CLASSIFIED INFORMATION.

(a) NOTICE BY ACCUSED.—

(1) NOTIFICATION OF TRIAL COUNSEL AND MILITARY JUDGE.—If an accused reasonably expects to disclose, or to cause the disclosure of, classified information in any manner in connection with any trial or pretrial proceeding involving the prosecution of such accused, the accused shall, within the time specified by the military judge or, where no time is specified, within 30 days before trial, notify the trial counsel and the military judge in writing. Such notice shall include a brief description of the classified information. Whenever the accused learns of additional classified information the accused reasonably expects to disclose, or to cause the disclosure of, at any such proceeding, the accused shall notify trial counsel and the military judge in writing as soon as possible thereafter and shall include a brief description of the classified information.

(2) LIMITATION ON DISCLOSURE BY ACCUSED.—No accused shall disclose, or cause the disclosure of, any information known or believed to be classified in connection with a trial or pretrial proceeding until—

(A) notice has been given under paragraph (1); and

(B) the United States has been afforded a reasonable opportunity to seek a determination pursuant to the procedure set forth in section 949p–6 of this title and the time for the United States to appeal such determination under section 950d of this title has expired or any appeal under that section by the United States is decided.

(b) FAILURE TO COMPLY.—If the accused fails to comply with the requirements of subsection (a), the military judge—

(1) may preclude disclosure of any classified information not made the subject of notification; and

(2) may prohibit the examination by the accused of any witness with respect to any such information.

SEC. 949p–6. PROCEDURE FOR CASES INVOLVING CLASSIFIED INFORMATION.

(a) MOTION FOR HEARING.—

(1) REQUEST FOR HEARING.—Within the time specified by the military judge for the filing of a motion under this section, either party may request the military judge to conduct a hearing to make all determinations concerning the use, relevance, or admissibility of classified information that would otherwise be made during the trial or pretrial proceeding.

(2) CONDUCT OF HEARING.—Upon a request by either party under paragraph (1), the military judge shall conduct such a hearing and shall rule prior to conducting any further proceedings.

(3) IN CAMERA HEARING UPON DECLARATION TO COURT BY APPROPRIATE OFFICIAL OF RISK OF DISCLOSURE OF CLASSIFIED INFORMATION.—Any hearing held pursuant to this subsection (or any portion of such hearing specified in the request of a knowledgeable United States official) shall be held in camera if a knowledgeable United States official possessing authority to classify information submits to the military judge a declaration that a public proceeding may result in the disclosure of classified information. Classified information is not subject to disclosure under this section unless the information is relevant and necessary to an element of the offense or a legally cognizable defense and is otherwise admissible in evidence.

(4) MILITARY JUDGE TO MAKE DETERMINATIONS IN WRITING.—As to each item of classified information, the military judge shall set forth in writing the basis for the determination.

(b) NOTICE AND USE OF CLASSIFIED INFORMATION BY THE GOVERNMENT.—

(1) NOTICE TO ACCUSED.—Before any hearing is conducted pursuant to a request by the trial counsel under subsection (a), trial counsel shall provide the accused with notice of the classified information that is at issue. Such notice shall identify the specific classified information at issue whenever that information previously has been made available to the accused by the United States. When the United States has not previously made the information available to the accused in connection with the case the information may be described by generic category, in such forms as the military judge may approve, rather than by identification of the specific information of concern to the United States.

(2) ORDER BY MILITARY JUDGE UPON REQUEST OF ACCUSED.—Whenever the trial counsel requests a hearing under subsection (a), the military judge, upon request of the accused, may order the trial counsel to provide the accused, prior to trial, such details as to

the portion of the charge or specification at issue in the hearing as are needed to give the accused fair notice to prepare for the hearing.

(c) SUBSTITUTIONS.—

(1) IN CAMERA PRETRIAL HEARING.—Upon request of the trial counsel pursuant to the Military Commission Rules of Evidence, and in accordance with the security procedures established by the military judge, the military judge shall conduct a classified in camera pretrial hearing concerning the admissibility of classified information.

(2) PROTECTION OF SOURCES, METHODS, AND ACTIVITIES BY WHICH EVIDENCE ACQUIRED.—When trial counsel seeks to introduce evidence before a military commission under this chapter and the Executive branch has classified the sources, methods, or activities by which the United States acquired the evidence, the military judge shall permit trial counsel to introduce the evidence, including a substituted evidentiary foundation pursuant to the procedures described in subsection (d), while protecting from disclosure information identifying those sources, methods, or activities, if—

(A) the evidence is otherwise admissible; and

(B) the military judge finds that—

(i) the evidence is reliable; and

(ii) the redaction is consistent with affording the accused a fair trial.

(d) ALTERNATIVE PROCEDURE FOR DISCLOSURE OF CLASSIFIED INFORMATION.—

(1) MOTION BY THE UNITED STATES.—Upon any determination by the military judge authorizing the disclosure of specific classified information under the procedures established by this section, the trial counsel may move that, in lieu of the disclosure of such specific classified information, the military judge order

(A) the substitution for such classified information of a statement admitting relevant facts that the specific classified information would tend to prove;

(B) the substitution for such classified information of a summary of the specific classified information; or

(C) any other procedure or redaction limiting the disclosure of specific classified information.

(2) ACTION ON MOTION.—The military judge shall grant such a motion of the trial counsel if the military judge finds that the statement, summary, or other procedure or redaction will provide the defendant with substantially the same ability to make his defense as would disclosure of the specific classified information.

(3) HEARING ON MOTION.—The military judge shall hold a hearing on any motion under this subsection. Any such hearing shall be held in camera at the request of a knowledgeable United States official possessing authority to classify information.

(4) SUBMISSION OF STATEMENT OF DAMAGE TO NATIONAL SECURITY IF DISCLOSURE ORDERED.—The trial counsel may, in connection with a motion under paragraph (1), submit to the military judge a declaration signed by a knowledgeable United States official possessing authority to classify information certifying that disclosure of classified information would cause identifiable damage to the national security of the United States and explaining the basis for the classification of such information. If so requested by the trial counsel, the military judge shall examine such declaration during an ex parte presentation.

(e) SEALING OF RECORDS OF IN CAMERA HEARINGS.—If at the close of an in camera hearing under this section (or any portion of a hearing under this section that is held in camera), the military judge determines that the classified information at issue may not be disclosed or elicited at the trial or pretrial proceeding, the record of such in camera hearing shall be sealed and preserved for use in the event of an appeal. The accused may seek reconsideration of the military judge's determination prior to or during trial.

(f) PROHIBITION ON DISCLOSURE OF CLASSIFIED INFORMATION BY THE ACCUSED; RELIEF FOR ACCUSED WHEN THE UNITED STATES OPPOSES DISCLOSURE.—

(1) ORDER TO PREVENT DISCLOSURE BY ACCUSED.— Whenever the military judge denies a motion by the trial counsel that the judge issue an order under subsection (a), (c), or (d) and the trial counsel files with the military judge a declaration signed by a knowledgeable United States official possessing authority to classify information objecting to disclosure of the classified information at issue, the military judge shall order that the accused not disclose or cause the disclosure of such information.

(2) RESULT OF ORDER UNDER PARAGRAPH (1).—Whenever an accused is prevented by an order under paragraph (1) from disclosing or causing the disclosure of classified information, the military judge shall dismiss the case, except that, when the military judge determines that the interests of justice would not be served by dismissal of the case, the military judge shall order such other action, in lieu of dismissing the charge or specification, as the military judge determines is appropriate. Such action may include, but need not be limited to, the following:

(A) Dismissing specified charges or specifications.

(B) Finding against the United States on any issue

618

as to which the excluded classified information relates.

(C) Striking or precluding all or part of the testimony of a witness.

(3) TIME FOR THE UNITED STATES TO SEEK INTERLOCUTORY APPEAL.—An order under paragraph (2) shall not take effect until the military judge has afforded the United States—

(A) an opportunity to appeal such order under section 950d of this title; and

(B) an opportunity thereafter to withdraw its objection to the disclosure of the classified information at issue.

(g) RECIPROCITY.—

(1) DISCLOSURE OF REBUTTAL INFORMATION.—Whenever the military judge determines that classified information may be disclosed in connection with a trial or pretrial proceeding, the military judge shall, unless the interests of fairness do not so require, order the United States to provide the accused with the information it expects to use to rebut the classified information. The military judge may place the United States under a continuing duty to disclose such rebuttal information.

(2) SANCTION FOR FAILURE TO COMPLY.—If the United States fails to comply with its obligation under this subsection, the military judge—

(A) may exclude any evidence not made the subject of a required disclosure; and

(B) may prohibit the examination by the United States of any witness with respect to such information.

SEC. 949p–7. INTRODUCTION OF CLASSIFIED INFORMATION INTO EVIDENCE.

(a) PRESERVATION OF CLASSIFICATION STATUS.—Writings, recordings, and photographs containing classified information may be admitted into evidence in proceedings of military commissions under this chapter without change in their classification status.

(b) PRECAUTIONS BY MILITARY JUDGES.—

(1) PRECAUTIONS IN ADMITTING CLASSIFIED INFORMATION INTO EVIDENCE.—The military judge in a trial by military commission, in order to prevent unnecessary disclosure of classified information, may order admission into evidence of only part of a writing, recording, or photograph, or may order admission into evidence of the whole writing, recording, or photograph with excision of some or all of the classified information contained therein, unless the whole ought in fairness be considered.

(2) CLASSIFIED INFORMATION KEPT UNDER SEAL.—
The military judge shall allow classified information offered or Accepted into evidence to remain under seal during the trial, even if such evidence is disclosed in the military commission, and may, upon motion by the United States, seal exhibits containing classified information for any period after trial as necessary to prevent a disclosure of classified information when a knowledgeable United States official possessing authority to classify information submits to the military judge a declaration setting forth the damage to the national security that the disclosure of such information reasonably could be expected to cause.

(c) TAKING OF TESTIMONY.—
(1) OBJECTION BY TRIAL COUNSEL.—During the examination of a witness, trial counsel may object to any question or line of inquiry that may require the witness to disclose classified information not previously found to be admissible.

(2) ACTION BY MILITARY JUDGE.—Following an objection under paragraph (1), the military judge shall take such suitable action to determine whether the response is admissible as will safeguard against the compromise of any classified information. Such action may include requiring trial counsel to provide the military judge with a proffer of the witness' response to the question or line of inquiry and requiring the accused to provide the military judge with a proffer of the nature of the information sought to be elicited by the accused. Upon request, the military judge may accept an ex parte proffer by trial counsel to the extent necessary to protect classified information from disclosure, in accordance with the practice of the Federal courts under the Classified Information Procedures Act (18 U.S.C. App.).

(d) DISCLOSURE AT TRIAL OF CERTAIN STATEMENTS PREVIOUSLY MADE BY A WITNESS.—
(1) MOTION FOR PRODUCTION OF STATEMENTS IN POSSESSION OF THE UNITED STATES.—After a witness called by the trial counsel has testified on direct examination, the military judge, on motion of the accused, may order production of statements of the witness in the possession of the United States which relate to the subject matter as to which the witness has testified. This paragraph does not preclude discovery or assertion of a privilege otherwise authorized.

(2) INVOCATION OF PRIVILEGE BY THE UNITED STATES.—
If the United States invokes a privilege, the trial counsel may provide the prior statements of the witness to the military judge during an ex parte presentation to the extent necessary to protect classified information from disclosure, in accordance with the practice of the Federal courts under the Classified Information Procedures Act (18 U.S.C. App.).

(3) ACTION BY MILITARY JUDGE ON MOTION.—If the military judge finds that disclosure of any portion of the statement identified by the United States as classified would be detrimental to the national security in the degree to warrant classification under the applicable Executive Order, statute, or regulation, that such portion of the statement is consistent with the testimony of the witness, and that the disclosure of such portion is not necessary to afford the accused a fair trial, the military judge shall excise that portion from the statement. If the military judge finds that such portion of the statement is inconsistent with the testimony of the witness or that its disclosure is necessary to afford the accused a fair trial, the military judge, shall, upon the request of the trial counsel, review alternatives to disclosure in accordance with section 949p–6(d) of this title.

SEC. 949s. CRUEL OR UNUSUAL PUNISHMENTS PROHIBITED.

Punishment by flogging, or by branding, marking, or tattooing on the body, or any other cruel or unusual punishment, may not be adjudged by a military commission under this chapter or inflicted under this chapter upon any person subject to this chapter. The use of irons, single or double, except for the purpose of safe custody, is prohibited under this chapter.

SEC. 949t. MAXIMUM LIMITS.

The punishment which a military commission under this chapter may direct for an offense may not exceed such limits as the President or Secretary of Defense may prescribe for that offense.

SEC. 949u. EXECUTION OF CONFINEMENT.

(a) IN GENERAL.—Under such regulations as the Secretary of Defense may prescribe, a sentence of confinement adjudged by a military commission under this chapter may be carried into execution by confinement—

(1) in any place of confinement under the control of any of the armed forces; or

(2) in any penal or correctional institution under the control of the United States or its allies, or which the United States may be allowed to use.

(b) TREATMENT DURING CONFINEMENT BY OTHER THAN THE ARMED FORCES.—Persons confined under subsection (a)(2) in a penal or correctional institution not under the control of an armed force are subject to the same discipline and treatment as persons confined or committed by the courts of the United States or of the State, District of Columbia, or place in which the institution is situated.

SEC. 950a. ERROR OF LAW; LESSER INCLUDED OFFENSE.

(a) ERROR OF LAW.—A finding or sentence of a military commission under this chapter may not be held incorrect on the ground of an error of law unless the error materially prejudices the substantial rights of the accused.

(b) LESSER INCLUDED OFFENSE.—Any reviewing authority with the power to approve or affirm a finding of guilty by a military commission under this chapter may approve or affirm, instead, so much of the finding as includes a lesser included offense.

SEC. 950b. REVIEW BY THE CONVENING AUTHORITY.

(a) NOTICE TO CONVENING AUTHORITY OF FINDINGS AND SENTENCE.—The findings and sentence of a military commission under this chapter shall be reported in writing promptly to the convening authority after the announcement of the sentence.

(b) SUBMITTAL OF MATTERS BY ACCUSED TO CONVENING AUTHORITY.—

(1) The accused may submit to the convening authority matters for consideration by the convening authority with respect to the findings and the sentence of the military commission under this chapter.

(2)(A) Except as provided in subparagraph (B), a submittal under paragraph (1) shall be made in writing within 20 days after the accused has been give an authenticated record of trial under section 949o(c) of this title.

(B) If the accused shows that additional time is required for the accused to make a submittal under paragraph (1), the convening authority may, for good cause, extend the applicable period under subparagraph (A) for not more than an additional 20 days.

(3) The accused may waive the accused's right to make a submittal to the convening authority under paragraph (1). Such a waiver shall be made in writing, and may not be revoked. For the purposes of subsection (c)(2), the time within which the accused may make a submittal under this subsection shall be deemed to have expired upon the submittal of a waiver under this paragraph to the convening authority.

(c) ACTION BY CONVENING AUTHORITY.—

(1) The authority under this subsection to modify the findings and sentence of a military commission under this chapter is a matter of the sole discretion and prerogative of the convening authority.

(2) The convening authority is not required to take action on the findings of a military commission under this chapter. If the convening authority takes action on the findings, the convening authority may, in the sole discretion of the convening authority, only—

(A) dismiss any charge or specification by setting aside a finding of guilty thereto; or

(B) change a finding of guilty to a charge to a finding of guilty to an offense that is a lesser included offense of the offense stated in the charge.

(3)(A) The convening authority shall take action on the sentence of a military commission under this chapter.

(B) Subject to regulations prescribed by the Secretary of Defense, action under this paragraph may be taken only after consideration of any matters submitted by the accused under subsection (b) or after the time for submitting such matters expires, whichever is earlier.

(C) In taking action under this paragraph, the convening authority may, in the sole discretion of the convening authority, approve, disapprove, commute, or suspend the sentence in whole or in part. The convening authority may not increase a sentence beyond that which is found by the military commission.

(4) The convening authority shall serve on the accused or on defense counsel notice of any action taken by the convening authority under this subsection.

(d) ORDER OF REVISION OR REHEARING.—

(1) Subject to paragraphs (2) and (3), the convening authority of a military commission under this chapter may, in the sole discretion of the convening authority, order a proceeding in revision or a rehearing.

(2)(A) Except as provided in subparagraph (B), a proceeding in revision may be ordered by the convening authority if—

(i) there is an apparent error or omission in the record; or

(ii) the record shows improper or inconsistent action by the military commission with respect to the findings or sentence that can be rectified without material prejudice to the substantial rights of the accused.

(B) In no case may a proceeding in revision—

(i) reconsider a finding of not guilty of a specification or a ruling which amounts to a finding of not guilty;

(ii) reconsider a finding of not guilty of any charge, unless there has been a finding of guilty under a specification laid under that charge, which sufficiently alleges a violation; or

(iii) increase the severity of the sentence unless the sentence prescribed for the offense is mandatory.

(3) A rehearing may be ordered by the convening authority if the convening authority disapproves the findings and sentence and states the reasons for disapproval of the findings. If the convening authority

disapproves the finding and sentence and does not order a rehearing, the convening authority shall dismiss the charges. A rehearing as to the findings may not be ordered by the convening authority when there is a lack of sufficient evidence in the record to support the findings. A rehearing as to the sentence may be ordered by the convening authority if the convening authority disapproves the sentence.

SEC. 950c. APPELLATE REFERRAL; WAIVER OR WITHDRAWAL OF APPEAL.

(a) AUTOMATIC REFERRAL FOR APPELLATE REVIEW.—Except as provided in subsection (b), in each case in which the final decision of a military commission under this chapter (as approved by the convening authority) includes a finding of guilty, the convening authority shall refer the case to the United States Court of Military Commission Review. Any such referral shall be made in accordance with procedures prescribed under regulations of the Secretary.

(b) WAIVER OF RIGHT OF REVIEW.—

(1) Except in a case in which the sentence as approved under section 950b of this title extends to death, an accused may file with the convening authority a statement expressly waiving the right of the accused to appellate review by the United States Court of Military Commission Review under section 950f of this title of the final decision of the military commission under this chapter.

(2) A waiver under paragraph (1) shall be signed by both the accused and a defense counsel.

(3) A waiver under paragraph (1) must be filed, if at all, within 10 days after notice of the action is served on the accused or on defense counsel under section 950b(c)(4) of this title. The convening authority, for good cause, may extend the period for such filing by not more than 30 days.

(c) WITHDRAWAL OF APPEAL.—Except in a case in which the sentence as approved under section 950b of this title extends to death, the accused may withdraw an appeal at any time.

(d) EFFECT OF WAIVER OR WITHDRAWAL.—A waiver of the right to appellate review or the withdrawal of an appeal under this section bars review under section 950f of this title.

SEC. 950d. INTERLOCUTORY APPEALS BY THE UNITED STATES.

(a) INTERLOCUTORY APPEAL.—Except as provided in subsection (b), in a trial by military commission under this chapter, the United States may take an interlocutory appeal to the United States Court of Military Commission Review of any order or ruling of the military judge—

(1) that terminates proceedings of the military commission with respect to a charge or specification;

(2) that excludes evidence that is substantial proof of a fact material in the proceeding;

(3) that relates to a matter under subsection (c) or (d) of section 949d of this title; or

(4) that, with respect to classified information—

(A) authorizes the disclosure of such information;

(B) imposes sanctions for nondisclosure of such information; or

(C) refuses a protective order sought by the United States to prevent the disclosure of such information.

(b) LIMITATION.—The United States may not appeal under subsection (a) an order or ruling that is, or amounts to, a finding of not guilty by the military commission with respect to a charge or specification.

(c) SCOPE OF APPEAL RIGHT WITH RESPECT TO CLASSIFIED INFORMATION.—The United States has the right to appeal under paragraph (4) of subsection (a) whenever the military judge enters an order or ruling that would require the disclosure of classified information, without regard to whether the order or ruling appealed from was entered under this chapter, another provision of law, a rule, or otherwise. Any such appeal may embrace any preceding order, ruling, or reasoning constituting the basis of the order or ruling that would authorize such disclosure.

(d) TIMING AND ACTION ON INTERLOCUTORY APPEALS RELATING TO CLASSIFIED INFORMATION.—

(1) APPEAL TO BE EXPEDITED.—An appeal taken pursuant to paragraph (4) of subsection (a) shall be expedited by the United States Court of Military Commission Review.

(2) APPEALS BEFORE TRIAL.—If such an appeal is taken before trial, the appeal shall be taken within 10 days after the order or ruling from which the appeal is made and the trial shall not commence until the appeal is decided.

(3) APPEALS DURING TRIAL.—If such an appeal is taken during trial, the military judge shall adjourn the trial until the appeal is decided, and the court of appeals—

(A) shall hear argument on such appeal within 4 days of the adjournment of the trial (excluding weekends and holidays);

(B) may dispense with written briefs other than the supporting materials previously submitted to the military judge;

(C) shall render its decision within four days of argument on appeal (excluding weekends and holidays); and

(D) may dispense with the issuance of a written opinion in rendering its decision.

(e) NOTICE AND TIMING OF OTHER APPEALS.—The United States shall take an appeal of an order or ruling under subsection (a), other than an appeal under paragraph (4) of that subsection, by filing a notice of appeal with the military judge within 5 days after the date of the order or ruling.

(f) METHOD OF APPEAL.—An appeal under this section shall be forwarded, by means specified in regulations prescribed by the Secretary of Defense, directly to the United States Court of Military Commission Review.

(g) APPEALS COURT TO ACT ONLY WITH RESPECT TO MATTER OF LAW.—In ruling on an appeal under paragraph (1), (2), or (3) of subsection (a), the appeals court may act only with respect to matters of law.

(h) SUBSEQUENT APPEAL RIGHTS OF ACCUSED NOT AFFECTED.— An appeal under paragraph (4) of subsection (a), and a decision on such appeal, shall not affect the right of the accused, in a subsequent appeal from a judgment of conviction, to claim as error reversal by the military judge on remand of a ruling appealed from during trial.

SEC. 950e. Rehearings.

(a) COMPOSITION OF MILITARY COMMISSION FOR REHEARING.— Each rehearing under this chapter shall take place before a military commission under this chapter composed of members who were not members of the military commission which first heard the case.

(b) SCOPE OF REHEARING.—

> (1) Upon a rehearing—
>> (A) the accused may not be tried for any offense of which the accused was found not guilty by the first military commission; and
>> (B) no sentence in excess of or more than the original sentence may be imposed unless—
>>> (i) the sentence is based upon a finding of guilty of an offense not considered upon the merits in the original proceedings; or
>>> (ii) the sentence prescribed for the offense is mandatory.
>
> (2) Upon a rehearing, if the sentence approved after the first military commission was in accordance with a pretrial agreement and the accused at the rehearing changes his plea with respect to the charges or specifications upon which the pretrial agreement was based, or otherwise does not comply with pretrial agreement, the sentence as to those charges or specifications may include any punishment not in excess of that lawfully adjudged at the first military commission.

SEC. 950f. Review by United States Court of Military Commission Review.

626

(a) ESTABLISHMENT.—There is a court of record to be known as the "United States Court of Military Commission Review" (in this section referred to as the "Court"). The Court shall consist of one or more panels, each composed of not less than three judges on the Court. For the purpose of reviewing decisions of military commissions under this chapter, the Court may sit in panels or as a whole, in accordance with rules prescribed by the Secretary of Defense.

(b) JUDGES.—

(1) Judges on the Court shall be assigned or appointed in a manner consistent with the provisions of this subsection.

(2) The Secretary of Defense may assign persons who are appellate military judges to be judges on the Court. Any judge so assigned shall be a commissioned officer of the armed forces, and shall meet the qualifications for military judges prescribed by section 948j(b) of this title.

(3) The President may appoint, by and with the advice and consent of the Senate, additional judges to the United States Court of Military Commission Review.

(4) No person may serve as a judge on the Court in any case in which that person acted as a military judge, counsel, or reviewing official.

(c) CASES TO BE REVIEWED.—The Court shall, in accordance with procedures prescribed under regulations of the Secretary, review the record in each case that is referred to the Court by the convening authority under section 950c of this title with respect to any matter properly raised by the accused.

(d) STANDARD AND SCOPE OF REVIEW.—In a case reviewed by the Court under this section, the Court may act only with respect to the findings and sentence as approved by the convening authority. The Court may affirm only such findings of guilty, and the sentence or such part or amount of the sentence, as the Court finds correct in law and fact and determines, on the basis of the entire record, should be approved. In considering the record, the Court may weigh the evidence, judge the credibility of witnesses, and determine controverted questions of fact, recognizing that the military commission saw and heard the witnesses.

(e) REHEARINGS.—If the Court sets aside the findings or sentence, the Court may, except where the setting aside is based on lack of sufficient evidence in the record to support the findings, order a rehearing. If the Court sets aside the findings or sentence and does not order a rehearing, the Court shall order that the charges be dismissed.

SEC. 950g. REVIEW BY UNITED STATES COURT OF APPEALS FOR THE DISTRICT OF COLUMBIA CIRCUIT; WRIT OF CERTIORARI TO SUPREME COURT.

(a) EXCLUSIVE APPELLATE JURISDICTION.—Except as provided in subsection (b), the United States Court of Appeals for the District of Columbia Circuit shall have exclusive jurisdiction to determine the validity of a final judgment rendered by a military commission (as approved by the convening authority and, where applicable, as affirmed or set aside as incorrect in law by the United States Court of Military Commission Review) under this chapter.

(b) EXHAUSTION OF OTHER APPEALS.—The United States Court of Appeals for the District of Columbia Circuit may not review a final judgment described in subsection (a) until all other appeals under this chapter have been waived or exhausted.

(c) TIME FOR SEEKING REVIEW.—A petition for review by the United States Court of Appeals for the District of Columbia Circuit must be filed in the Court of Appeals—

> (1) not later than 20 days after the date on which written notice of the final decision of the United States Court of Military Commission Review is served on the parties; or

> (2) if the accused submits, in the form prescribed by section 950c of this title, a written notice waiving the right of the accused to review by the United States Court of Military Commission Review, not later than 20 days after the date on which such notice is submitted.

(d) SCOPE AND NATURE OF REVIEW.—The United States Court of Appeals for the District of Columbia Circuit may act under this section only with respect to the findings and sentence as approved by the convening authority and as affirmed or set aside as incorrect in law by the United States Court of Military Commission Review, and shall take action only with respect to matters of law, including the sufficiency of the evidence to support the verdict.

(e) REVIEW BY SUPREME COURT.—The Supreme Court may review by writ of certiorari pursuant to section 1254 of title 28 the final judgment of the United States Court of Appeals for the District of Columbia Circuit under this section.

SEC. 950h. APPELLATE COUNSEL.

(a) APPOINTMENT.—The Secretary of Defense shall, by regulation, establish procedures for the appointment of appellate counsel for the United States and for the accused in military commissions under this chapter. Appellate counsel shall meet the qualifications of counsel for appearing before military commissions under this chapter.

(b) REPRESENTATION OF UNITED STATES.—Appellate counsel appointed under subsection (a)—

> (1) shall represent the United States in any appeal or review proceeding under this chapter before the United States Court of Military Commission Review; and

(2) may, when requested to do so by the Attorney General in a case arising under this chapter, represent the United States before the United States Court of Appeals for the District of Columbia Circuit or the Supreme Court.

(c) REPRESENTATION OF ACCUSED.—The accused shall be represented by appellate counsel appointed under subsection (a) before the United States Court of Military Commission Review, the United States Court of Appeals for the District of Columbia Circuit, and the Supreme Court, and by civilian counsel if retained by the accused. Any such civilian counsel shall meet the qualifications under paragraph (3) of section 949c(b) of this title for civilian counsel appearing before military commissions under this chapter and shall be subject to the requirements of paragraph (7) of that section.

SEC. 950i. EXECUTION OF SENTENCE; SUSPENSION OF SENTENCE.

(a) IN GENERAL.—The Secretary of Defense is authorized to carry out a sentence imposed by a military commission under this chapter in accordance with such procedures as the Secretary may prescribe.

(b) EXECUTION OF SENTENCE OF DEATH ONLY UPON APPROVAL BY THE PRESIDENT.—If the sentence of a military commission under this chapter extends to death, that part of the sentence providing for death may not be executed until approved by the President. In such a case, the President may commute, remit, or suspend the sentence, or any part thereof, as he sees fit.

(c) EXECUTION OF SENTENCE OF DEATH ONLY UPON FINAL JUDGMENT OF LEGALITY OF PROCEEDINGS.—

(1) If the sentence of a military commission under this chapter extends to death, the sentence may not be executed until there is a final judgment as to the legality of the proceedings (and with respect to death, approval under subsection (b)).

(2) A judgment as to legality of proceedings is final for purposes of paragraph (1) when review is completed in accordance with the judgment of the United States Court of Military Commission Review and—

(A) the time for the accused to file a petition for review by the United States Court of Appeals for the District of Columbia Circuit has expired, the accused has not filed a timely petition for such review, and the case is not otherwise under review by the Court of Appeals; or

(B) review is completed in accordance with the judgment of the United States Court of Appeals for the District of Columbia Circuit and—

(i) a petition for a writ of certiorari is not timely filed;

(ii) such a petition is denied by the Supreme Court; or

(iii) review is otherwise completed in accordance with

the judgment of the Supreme Court.

(d) SUSPENSION OF SENTENCE.—The Secretary of the Defense, or the convening authority acting on the case (if other than the Secretary), may suspend the execution of any sentence or part thereof in the case, except a sentence of death.

SEC. 950j. FINALITY OF PROCEEDINGS, FINDINGS, AND SENTENCES.

The appellate review of records of trial provided by this chapter, and the proceedings, findings, and sentences of military commissions as approved, reviewed, or affirmed as required by this chapter, are final and conclusive. Orders publishing the proceedings of military commissions under this chapter are binding upon all departments, courts, agencies, and officers of the United States, subject only to action by the Secretary or the convening authority as provided in section 950i(c) of this title and the authority of the President.

SEC. 950p. DEFINITIONS; CONSTRUCTION OF CERTAIN OFFENSES; COMMON CIRCUMSTANCES.

(a) DEFINITIONS.—In this subchapter:

(1) The term "military objective" means combatants and those objects during hostilities which, by their nature, location, purpose, or use, effectively contribute to the war-fighting or war-sustaining capability of an opposing force and whose total or partial destruction, capture, or neutralization would constitute a definite military advantage to the attacker under the circumstances at the time of an attack.

(2) The term "protected person" means any person entitled to protection under one or more of the Geneva Conventions, including civilians not taking an active part in hostilities, military personnel placed out of combat by sickness, wounds, or detention, and military medical or religious personnel.

(3) The term "protected property" means any property specifically protected by the law of war, including buildings dedicated to religion, education, art, science, or charitable purposes, historic monuments, hospitals, and places where the sick and wounded are collected, but only if and to the extent such property is not being used for military purposes or is not otherwise a military objective. The term includes objects properly identified by one of the distinctive emblems of the Geneva Conventions, but does not include civilian property that is a military objective.

(b) CONSTRUCTION OF CERTAIN OFFENSES.—The intent required for offenses under paragraphs (1), (2), (3), (4), and (12) of section 950t of this title precludes the applicability of such offenses with regard to collateral damage or to death, damage, or injury incident to a lawful attack.

(c) COMMON CIRCUMSTANCES.—An offense specified in this Subchapter is triable by military commission under this chapter only if the offense is committed in the context of and associated with hostilities.

(d) EFFECT.—The provisions of this subchapter codify offenses that have traditionally been triable by military commission. This chapter does not establish new crimes that did not exist before the date of the enactment of this subchapter, as amended by the National Defense Authorization Act for Fiscal Year 2010, but rather codifies those crimes for trial by military commission. Because the provisions of this subchapter codify offenses that have traditionally been triable under the law of war or otherwise triable by military commission, this subchapter does not preclude trial for offenses that occurred before the date of the enactment of this subchapter, as so amended.

SEC. 950q. PRINCIPALS.

Any person punishable under this chapter who—

> (1) commits an offense punishable by this chapter, or aids, abets, counsels, commands, or procures its commission; (2) causes an act to be done which if directly performed by him would be punishable by this chapter; or (3) is a superior commander who, with regard to acts punishable by this chapter, knew, had reason to know, or should have known, that a subordinate was about to commit such acts or had done so and who failed to take the necessary and reasonable measures to prevent such acts or to punish the perpetrators thereof, is a principal.

SEC. 950r. ACCESSORY AFTER THE FACT.

Any person subject to this chapter who, knowing that an offense punishable by this chapter has been committed, receives, comforts, or assists the offender in order to hinder or prevent his apprehension, trial, or punishment shall be punished as a military commission under this chapter may direct.

SEC. 950s. CONVICTION OF LESSER OFFENSES.

An accused may be found guilty of an offense necessarily included in the offense charged or of an attempt to commit either the offense charged or an attempt to commit either the offense charged or an offense necessarily included therein.

SEC. 950t. CRIMES TRIABLE BY MILITARY COMMISSION.

The following offenses shall be triable by military commission under this chapter at any time without limitation:

> (1) MURDER OF PROTECTED PERSONS.—Any person subject to this chapter who intentionally kills one or more protected persons shall

be punished by death or such other punishment as a military commission under this chapter may direct.

(2) ATTACKING CIVILIANS.—Any person subject to this chapter who intentionally engages in an attack upon a civilian population as such, or individual civilians not taking active part in hostilities, shall be punished, if death results to one or more of the victims, by death or such other punishment as a military commission under this chapter may direct, and, if death does not result to any of the victims, by such punishment, other than death, as a military commission under this chapter may direct.

(3) ATTACKING CIVILIAN OBJECTS.—Any person subject to this chapter who intentionally engages in an attack upon a civilian object that is not a military objective shall be punished as a military commission under this chapter may direct.

(4) ATTACKING PROTECTED PROPERTY.—Any person subject to this chapter who intentionally engages in an attack upon protected property shall be punished as a military commission under this chapter may direct.

(5) PILLAGING.—Any person subject to this chapter who intentionally and in the absence of military necessity appropriates or seizes property for private or personal use, without the consent of a person with authority to permit such appropriation or seizure, shall be punished as a military commission under this chapter may direct.

(6) DENYING QUARTER.—Any person subject to this chapter who, with effective command or control over subordinate groups, declares, orders, or otherwise indicates to those groups that there shall be no survivors or surrender accepted, with the intent to threaten an adversary or to conduct hostilities such that there would be no survivors or surrender accepted, shall be punished as a military commission under this chapter may direct.

(7) TAKING HOSTAGES.—Any person subject to this chapter who, having knowingly seized or detained one or more persons, threatens to kill, injure, or continue to detain such person or persons with the intent of compelling any nation, person other than the hostage, or group of persons to act or refrain from acting as an explicit or implicit condition for the safety or release of such person or persons, shall be punished, if death results to one or more of the victims, by death or such other punishment as a military commission under this chapter may direct, and, if death does not result to any of the victims, by such punishment, other than death, as a military commission under this chapter may direct.

(8) EMPLOYING POISON OR SIMILAR WEAPONS.—Any person subject to this chapter who intentionally, as a method of warfare, employs a substance or weapon that releases a substance that causes

death or serious and lasting damage to health in the ordinary course of events, through its asphyxiating, bacteriological, or toxic properties, shall be punished, if death results to one or more of the victims, by death or such other punishment as a military commission under this chapter may direct, and, if death does not result to any of the victims, by such punishment, other than death, as a military commission under this chapter may direct.

(9) USING PROTECTED PERSONS AS A SHIELD.—Any person subject to this chapter who positions, or otherwise takes advantage of, a protected person with the intent to shield a military objective from attack. or to shield, favor, or impede military operations, shall be punished, if death results to one or more of the victims, by death or such other punishment as a military commission under this chapter may direct, and, if death does not result to any of the victims, by such punishment, other than death, as a military commission under this chapter may direct.

(10) USING PROTECTED PROPERTY AS A SHIELD.—Any person subject to this chapter who positions, or otherwise takes advantage of the location of, protected property with the intent to shield a military objective from attack, or to shield, favor, or impede military operations, shall be punished as a military commission under this chapter may direct.

(11) TORTURE.—

    (A) OFFENSE.—Any person subject to this chapter who commits an act specifically intended to inflict severe physical or mental pain or suffering (other than pain or suffering incidental to lawful sanctions) upon another person within his custody or physical control for the purpose of obtaining information or a confession, punishment, intimidation, coercion, or any reason based on discrimination of any kind, shall be punished, if death results to one or more of the victims, by death or such other punishment as a military commission under this chapter may direct, and, if death does not result to any of the victims, by such punishment, other than death, as a military commission under this chapter may direct.

    (B) SEVERE MENTAL PAIN OR SUFFERING DEFINED.— In this paragraph, the term "severe mental pain or suffering" has the meaning given that term in section 2340(2) of title 18.

(12) CRUEL OR INHUMAN TREATMENT.—Any person subject to this chapter who subjects another person in their custody or under their physical control, regardless of nationality or physical location, to cruel or inhuman treatment that constitutes a grave breach of common Article 3 of the Geneva Conventions shall be punished, if death results to the victim, by death or such other punishment as a military commission

under this chapter may direct, and, if death does not result to the victim, by such punishment, other than death, as a military commission under this chapter may direct.

(13) INTENTIONALLY CAUSING SERIOUS BODILY INJURY.—

    (A) OFFENSE.—Any person subject to this chapter who intentionally causes serious bodily injury to one or more persons, including privileged belligerents, in violation of the law of war shall be punished, if death results to one or more of the victims, by death or such other punishment as a military commission under this chapter may direct, and, if death does not result to any of the victims, by such punishment, other than death, as a military commission under this chapter may direct.

    (B) SERIOUS BODILY INJURY DEFINED.—In this paragraph,
the term "serious bodily injury" means bodily injury which involves—

        (i) a substantial risk of death;

        (ii) extreme physical pain;

        (iii) protracted and obvious disfigurement; or

        (iv) protracted loss or impairment of the function of a bodily member, organ, or mental faculty.

(14) MUTILATING OR MAIMING.—Any person subject to this chapter who intentionally injures one or more protected persons by disfiguring the person or persons by any mutilation of the person or persons, or by permanently disabling any member, limb, or organ of the body of the person or persons, without any legitimate medical or dental purpose, shall be punished, if death results to one or more of the victims, by death or such other punishment as a military commission under this chapter may direct, and, if death does not result to any of the victims, by such punishment, other than death, as a military commission under this chapter may direct.

(15) MURDER IN VIOLATION OF THE LAW OF WAR.—Any person subject to this chapter who intentionally kills one or more persons, including privileged belligerents, in violation of the law of war shall be punished by death or such other punishment as a military commission under this chapter may direct.

(16) DESTRUCTION OF PROPERTY IN VIOLATION OF THE LAW OF WAR.—Any person subject to this chapter who intentionally destroys property belonging to another person in violation of the law of war shall punished as a military commission under this chapter may direct.

(17) USING TREACHERY OR PERFIDY.—Any person subject

to this chapter who, after inviting the confidence or belief of one or more persons that they were entitled to, or obliged to accord, protection under the law of war, intentionally makes use of that confidence or belief in killing, injuring, or capturing such person or persons shall be punished, if death results to one or more of the victims, by death or such other punishment as a military commission under this chapter may direct, and, if death does not result to any of the victims, by such punishment, other than death, as a military commission under this chapter may direct.

(18) IMPROPERLY USING A FLAG OF TRUCE.—Any person subject to this chapter who uses a flag of truce to feign an intention to negotiate, surrender, or otherwise suspend hostilities when there is no such intention shall be punished as a military commission under this chapter may direct.

(19) IMPROPERLY USING A DISTINCTIVE EMBLEM.—Any person subject to this chapter who intentionally uses a distinctive emblem recognized by the law of war for combatant purposes in a manner prohibited by the law of war shall be punished as a military commission under this chapter may direct.

(20) INTENTIONALLY MISTREATING A DEAD BODY.—Any person subject to this chapter who intentionally mistreats the body of a dead person, without justification by legitimate military necessary, shall be punished as a military commission under this chapter may direct.

(21) RAPE.—Any person subject to this chapter who forcibly or with coercion or threat of force wrongfully invades the body of a person by penetrating, however slightly, the anal or genital opening of the victim with any part of the body of the accused, or with any foreign object, shall be punished as a military commission under this chapter may direct.

(22) SEXUAL ASSAULT OR ABUSE.—Any person subject to this chapter who forcibly or with coercion or threat of force engages in sexual contact with one or more persons, or causes one or more persons to engage in sexual contact, shall be punished as a military commission under this chapter may direct.

(23) HIJACKING OR HAZARDING A VESSEL OR AIRCRAFT.— Any person subject to this chapter who intentionally seizes, exercises unauthorized control over, or endangers the safe navigation of a vessel or aircraft that is not a legitimate military objective shall be punished, if death results to one or more of the victims, by death or such other punishment as a military commission under this chapter may direct, and, if death does not result to any of the victims, by such punishment, other than death, as a military commission under this chapter may direct.

(24) TERRORISM.—Any person subject to this chapter who intentionally kills or inflicts great bodily harm on one or more

protected persons, or intentionally engages in an act that evinces a wanton disregard for human life, in a manner calculated to influence or affect the conduct of government or civilian population by intimidation or coercion, or to retaliate against government conduct, shall be punished, if death results to one or more of the victims, by death or such other punishment as a military commission under this chapter may direct, and, if death does not result to any of the victims, by such punishment, other than death, as a military commission under this chapter may direct.

(25) PROVIDING MATERIAL SUPPORT FOR TERRORISM.—

    (A) OFFENSE.—Any person subject to this chapter who provides material support or resources, knowing or intending that they are to be used in preparation for, or in carrying out, an act of terrorism (as set forth in paragraph (24) of this section), or who intentionally provides material support or resources to an international terrorist organization engaged in hostilities against the United States, knowing that such organization has engaged or engages in terrorism (as so set forth), shall be punished as a military commission under this chapter may direct.

    (B) MATERIAL SUPPORT OR RESOURCES DEFINED.—In this paragraph, the term "material support or resources" has the meaning given that term in section 2339A(b) of title 18.

(26) WRONGFULLY AIDING THE ENEMY.—Any person subject to this chapter who, in breach of an allegiance or duty to the United States, knowingly and intentionally aids an enemy of the United States, or one of the co-belligerents of the enemy, shall be punished as a military commission under this chapter may direct.

(27) SPYING.—Any person subject to this chapter who, in violation of the law of war and with intent or reason to believe that it is to be used to the injury of the United States or to the advantage of a foreign power, collects or attempts to collect information by clandestine means or while acting under false pretenses, for the purpose of conveying such information to an enemy of the United States, or one of the co-belligerents of the enemy, shall be punished by death or such other punishment as a military commission under this chapter may direct.

(28) ATTEMPTS.—

    (A) IN GENERAL.—Any person subject to this chapter who attempts to commit any offense punishable by this chapter shall be punished as a military commission under this chapter may direct.

    (B) SCOPE OF OFFENSE.—An act, done with specific intent to commit an offense under this chapter, amounting to more than mere preparation and tending, even though failing, to effect its commission, is an attempt to commit that offense.

(C) EFFECT OF CONSUMMATION.—Any person subject to this chapter may be convicted of an attempt to commit an offense although it appears on the trial that the offense was consummated.

(29) CONSPIRACY.—Any person subject to this chapter who conspires to commit one or more substantive offenses triable by military commission under this subchapter, and who knowingly does any overt act to effect the object of the conspiracy, shall be punished, if death results to one or more of the victims, by death or such other punishment as a military commission under this chapter may direct, and, if death does not result to any of the victims, by such punishment, other than death, as a military commission under this chapter may direct.

(30) SOLICITATION.—Any person subject to this chapter who solicits or advises another or others to commit one or more substantive offenses triable by military commission under this chapter shall, if the offense solicited or advised is attempted or committed, be punished with the punishment provided for the commission of the offense, but, if the offense solicited or advised is not committed or attempted, shall be punished as a military commission under this chapter may direct.

(31) CONTEMPT.—A military commission under this chapter may punish for contempt any person who uses any menacing word, sign, or gesture in its presence, or who disturbs its proceedings by any riot or disorder.

(32) PERJURY AND OBSTRUCTION OF JUSTICE.—A military commission under this chapter may try offenses and impose such punishment as the military commission may direct for perjury, false testimony, or obstruction of justice related to the military commission.

*Statutory Provisions Related to Title 10, Chapter 47A, United States Code

(Public Law 111-84 of October 28, 2009; 123 STAT. 2574)

SEC. 1803. CONFORMING AMENDMENTS.
(a) UNIFORM CODE OF MILITARY JUSTICE.—
(1) PERSONS SUBJECT TO UCMJ.—Paragraph (13) of section 802(a) of title 10, United States Code (article 2(a) of the Uniform Code of Military Justice), is amended to read as follows:
(13) Individuals belonging to one of the eight categories enumerated in Article 4 of the Convention Relative to the Treatment of Prisoners of War, done at Geneva August 12, 1949 (6 UST 3316), who violate the law of war.
(2) CONSTRUCTION OF MILITARY COMMISSIONS WITH COURTSMARTIAL.—
Section 839 of such title (article 39 of the Uniform Code of Military Justice) is amended by adding at the end the following new subsection:
(d) The findings, holdings, interpretations, and other precedents of military commissions under chapter 47A of this title—
(1) may not be introduced or considered in any hearing, trial, or other proceeding of a court-martial under this chapter; and
(2) may not form the basis of any holding, decision, or other determination of a court-martial.
~~(b) APPELLATE REVIEW UNDER DETAINEE TREATMENT ACT OF 2005. Section 1005(e) of the Detainee Treatment Act of 2005 (title X of Public Law 109-359; 10 U.S.C. 801 note) is amended by striking paragraph (3).~~
(b) APPELLATE REVIEW UNDER DETAINEE TREATMENT ACT OF 2005.—
(1) DEPARTMENT OF DEFENSE, EMERGENCY SUPPLEMENTAL APPROPRIATIONS TO ADDRESS HURRICANES IN THE GULF OF MEXICO, AND PANDEMIC INFLUENZA ACT, 2006.—Section 1005(e) of the Detainee Treatment Act of 2005 (title X of Public Law 109–148; 10 U.S.C. 801 note) is amended by striking paragraph (3).
(2) NATIONAL DEFENSE AUTHORIZATION ACT FOR FISCAL YEAR 2006.—Section 1405(e) of the Detainee Treatment Act of 2005 (Public Law 109–163; 10 U.S.C. 801 note) is amended by striking paragraph (3).

SEC. 1804. PROCEEDINGS UNDER PRIOR STATUTE.
(a) PRIOR CONVICTIONS.—The amendment made by section 1802

shall have no effect on the validity of any conviction pursuant to chapter 47A of title 10, United States Code (as such chapter was in effect on the day before the date of the enactment of this Act).

(b) COMPOSITION OF MILITARY COMMISSIONS.—Notwithstanding the amendment made by section 1802—

(1) any commission convened pursuant to chapter 47A of title 10, United States Code (as such chapter was in effect on the day before the date of the enactment of this Act), shall be deemed to have been convened pursuant to chapter 47A of title 10, United States Code (as amended by section 1802);

(2) any member of the Armed Forces detailed to serve on a commission pursuant to chapter 47A of title 10, United States Code (as in effect on the day before the date of the enactment of this Act), shall be deemed to have been detailed pursuant to chapter 47A of title 10, United States Code (as so amended);

(3) any military judge detailed to a commission pursuant to chapter 47A of title 10, United States Code (as in effect on the day before the date of the enactment of this Act), shall be deemed to have been detailed pursuant to chapter 47A of title 10, United States Code (as so amended);

(4) any trial counsel or defense counsel detailed for a commission pursuant to chapter 47A of title 10, United States Code (as in effect on the day before the date of the enactment of this Act), shall be deemed to have been detailed pursuant to chapter 47A of title 10, United States Code (as so amended);

(5) any court reporters detailed to or employed by a commission pursuant to chapter 47A of title 10, United States Code (as in effect on the day before the date of the enactment of this Act), shall be deemed to have been detailed or employed pursuant to chapter 47A of title 10, United States Code (as so amended); and

(6) any appellate military judge or other duly appointed appellate judge on the Court of Military Commission Review pursuant to chapter 47A of title 10, United States Code (as in effect on the day before the date of the enactment of this Act), shall be deemed to have been detailed or appointed to the United States Court of Military Commission Review pursuant to chapter 47A of title 10, United States Code (as so amended).

(c) CHARGES AND SPECIFICATIONS.—Notwithstanding the amendment made by section 1802—

(1) any charges or specifications sworn or referred pursuant to chapter 47A of title 10, United States Code (as such chapter was in effect on the day before the date of the enactment of this Act), shall be deemed to have been sworn or referred pursuant to chapter 47A of title 10, United States Code (as amended by section 1802); and

639

(2) any charges or specifications described in paragraph (1) may be amended, without prejudice, as needed to properly allege jurisdiction under chapter 47A of title 10, United States Code (as so amended), and crimes triable under such chapter.

(d) PROCEDURES AND REQUIREMENTS.—

(1) IN GENERAL.—Except as provided in subsections (a) through (c) and subject to paragraph (2), any commission convened pursuant to chapter 47A of title 10, United States Code (as such chapter was in effect on the day before the date of the enactment of this Act), shall be conducted after the date of the enactment of this Act in accordance with the procedures and requirements of chapter 47A of title 10, United States Code (as amended by section 1802).

(2) TEMPORARY CONTINUATION OF PRIOR PROCEDURES AND REQUIREMENTS.—Any military commission described in paragraph (1) may be conducted in accordance with any procedures and requirements of chapter 47A of title 10, United States Code (as in effect on the day before the date of the enactment of this Act), that are not inconsistent with the provisions of chapter 47A of title 10, United States Code, (as so amended), until the earlier of—

(A) the date of the submittal to Congress under section 1805 of the revised rules for military commissions under chapter 47A of title 10, United States Code (as so amended); or

(B) the date that is 90 days after the date of the enactment of this Act.

SEC. 1805. SUBMITTAL TO CONGRESS OF REVISED RULES FOR MILITARY COMMISSIONS.

(a) DEADLINE FOR SUBMITTAL.—Not later than 90 days after the date of the enactment of this Act, the Secretary of Defense shall submit to the Committees on Armed Services of the Senate and the House of Representatives the revised rules for military commissions prescribed by the Secretary for purposes of chapter 47A of title 10, United States Code (as amended by section 1802).

(b) TREATMENT OF REVISED RULES UNDER REQUIREMENT FOR NOTICE AND WAIT REGARDING MODIFICATION OF RULES.—The revised rules submitted to Congress under subsection (a) shall not be treated as a modification of the rules in effect for military commissions for purposes of section 949a(d) of title 10, United States Code (as so amended).

SEC. 1806. ANNUAL REPORTS TO CONGRESS ON TRIALS BY MILITARY COMMISSION.

(a) ANNUAL REPORTS REQUIRED.—Not later than January 31of each year, the Secretary of Defense shall submit to the Committees on Armed Services of the Senate and the House of Representatives a report on any trials conducted by military commissions under chapter 47A of title 10, United States Code (as amended by section 1802), during the preceding year.

(b) FORM.—Each report under this section shall be submitted in unclassified form, but may include a classified annex.

SEC. 1807. SENSE OF CONGRESS ON MILITARY COMMISSION SYSTEM.

It is the sense of Congress that—

(1) the fairness and effectiveness of the military commissions system under chapter 47A of title 10, United States Code (as amended by section 1802), will depend to a significant degree on the adequacy of defense counsel and associated resources for individuals accused, particularly in the case of capital cases, under such chapter 47A; and (2) defense counsel in military commission cases, particularly in capital cases, under such chapter 47A of title 10, United States Code (as so amended), should be fully resourced as provided in such chapter 47A.

SECTION 552 OF TITLE 5, UNITED STATES CODE (THE "FREEDOM OF INFORMATION ACT")

SECTION 552. PUBLIC INFORMATION; AGENCY RULES, OPINIONS, ORDERS, RECORDS, AND PROCEEDINGS.

(a) Each agency shall make available to the public information as follows:

(1) Each agency shall separately state and currently publish in the Federal Register for the guidance of the public—

(A) descriptions of its central and field organization and the established places at which, the employees (and in the case of a uniformed service, the members) from whom, and the methods whereby, the public may obtain information, make submittals or requests, or obtain decisions;

(B) statements of the general course and method by which its functions are channeled and determined, including the nature and requirements of all formal and informal procedures available;

(C) rules of procedure, descriptions of forms available or the places at which forms may be obtained, and instructions as to the scope and contents of all papers, reports, or examinations;

(D) substantive rules of general applicability adopted as authorized by law, and statements of general policy or interpretations of general applicability formulated and adopted by the agency; and

(E) each amendment, revision, or repeal of the foregoing. Except to the extent that a person has actual and timely notice of the terms thereof, a person may not in any manner be required to resort to, or be adversely affected by, a matter required to be published in the Federal Register and not so published. For the purpose of this paragraph, matter reasonably available to the class of persons affected thereby is deemed published in the Federal Register when incorporated by reference therein with the approval of the Director of the Federal Register.

(2) Each agency, in accordance with published rules, shall make available for public inspection and copying—

(A) final opinions, including concurring and dissenting opinions, as well as orders, made in the adjudication of cases;

(B) those statements of policy and interpretations which have been adopted by the agency and are not published in the Federal Register;

(C) administrative staff manuals and instructions to staff that affect a member of the public;

643

(D) copies of all records, regardless of form or format, which have been released to any person under paragraph (3) and which, because of the nature of their subject matter, the agency determines have become or are likely to become the subject of subsequent requests for substantially the same records; and (E) a general index of the records referred to under subparagraph (D); unless the materials are promptly published and copies offered for sale. For records created on or after November 1, 1996, within one year after such date, each agency shall make such records available, including by computer telecommunications or, if computer telecommunications means have not been established by the agency, by other electronic means. To the extent required to prevent a clearly unwarranted invasion of personal privacy, an agency may delete identifying details when it makes available or publishes an opinion, statement of policy, interpretation, staff manual, instruction, or copies of records referred to in subparagraph (D). However, in each case the justification for the deletion shall be explained fully in writing, and the extent of such deletion shall be indicated on the portion of the record which is made available or published, unless including that indication would harm an interest protected by the exemption in subsection (b) under which the deletion is made. If technically feasible, the extent of the deletion shall be indicated at the place in the record where the deletion was made. Each agency shall also maintain and make available for public inspection and copying current indexes providing identifying information for the public as to any matter issued, adopted, or promulgated after July 4, 1967, and required by this paragraph to be made available or published. Each agency shall promptly publish, quarterly or more frequently, and distribute (by sale or otherwise) copies of each index or supplements thereto unless it determines by order published in the Federal Register that the publication would be unnecessary and impracticable, in which case the agency shall nonetheless provide copies of such index on request at a cost not to exceed the direct cost of duplication. Each agency shall make the index referred to in subparagraph (E) available by computer telecommunications by December 31, 1999. A final order, opinion, statement of policy, interpretation, or staff manual or instruction that affects a member of the public may be relied on, used, or cited as precedent by an agency against a party other than an agency only if—

(i) it has been indexed and either made available or published as provided by this paragraph; or

(ii) the party has actual and timely notice of the terms thereof.

(3) (A) Except with respect to the records made available under paragraphs (1) and (2) of this subsection, and except as provided in subparagraph (E), each agency, upon any request for records which

(i) reasonably describes such records and

(ii) is made in accordance with published rules stating the time, place, fees (if any), and procedures to be followed, shall make the records promptly available to any person.

(B) In making any record available to a person under this paragraph, an agency shall provide the record in any form or format requested by the person if the record is readily reproducible by the agency in that form or format. Each agency shall make reasonable efforts to maintain its records in forms or formats that are reproducible for purposes of this section.

(C) In responding under this paragraph to a request for records, an agency shall make reasonable efforts to search for the records in electronic form or format, except when such efforts would significantly interfere with the operation of the agency's automated information system.

(D) For purposes of this paragraph, the term "search" means to review, manually or by automated means, agency records for the purpose of locating those records which are responsive to a request.

(E) An agency, or part of an agency, that is an element of the intelligence community (as that term is defined in section 3(4) of the National Security Act of 1947 (50 U.S.C. §401a (4))) shall not make any record available under this paragraph to—

(i) any government entity, other than a State, territory, commonwealth, or district of the United States, or any subdivision thereof; or

(ii) a representative of a government entity described in clause (i).

(4) (A) (i) In order to carry out the provisions of this section, each agency shall promulgate regulations, pursuant to notice and receipt of public comment, specifying the schedule of fees applicable to the processing of requests under this section and establishing procedures and guidelines for determining when such fees should be waived or reduced. Such schedule shall conform to the guidelines which shall be

promulgated, pursuant to notice and receipt of public comment, by the Director of the Office of Management and Budget and which shall provide for a uniform schedule of fees for all agencies.

(ii) Such agency regulations shall provide that—

(I) fees shall be limited to reasonable standard charges for document search, duplication, and review, when records are requested for commercial use;

(II) fees shall be limited to reasonable standard charges for document duplication when records are not sought for commercial use and the request is made by an educational or noncommercial scientific institution, whose purpose is scholarly or scientific research; or a representative of the news media; and

(III) for any request not described in (I) or (II), fees shall be limited to reasonable standard charges for document search and duplication.

In this clause, the term 'a representative of the news media' means any person or entity that gathers information of potential interest to a segment of the public, uses its editorial skills to turn the raw materials into a distinct work, and distributes that work to an audience. In this clause, the term 'news' means information that is about current events or that would be of current interest to the public. Examples of news-media entities are television or radio stations broadcasting to the public at large and publishers of periodicals (but only if such entities qualify as disseminators of 'news') who make their products available for purchase by or subscription by or free distribution to the general public. These examples are not all-inclusive. Moreover, as methods of news delivery evolve (for example, the adoption of the electronic dissemination of newspapers through telecommunications services), such alternative media shall be considered to be news-media entities. A freelance journalist shall be regarded as working for a newsmedia entity if the journalist can demonstrate a solid basis for expecting publication through that entity, whether or not the journalist is actually employed by the entity. A publication contract would present a solid basis for such an expectation; the Government may also consider the past publication record of the requester in making such a determination.

(iii) Documents shall be furnished without any charge or at a charge reduced below the fees established under clause (ii) if disclosure of the information is in the public interest because it is likely to contribute significantly to public understanding of the operations or activities of the government and is not primarily in the commercial interest of the requester.

(iv) Fee schedules shall provide for the recovery of only the direct costs of search, duplication, or review. Review costs shall include only the direct costs incurred during the initial examination of a document for the purposes of determining whether the documents must be disclosed under this section and for the purposes of withholding any portions exempt from disclosure under this section. Review costs may not include any costs incurred in resolving issues of law or policy that may be raised in the course of processing a request under this section. No fee may be charged by any agency under this section—

(I) if the costs of routine collection and processing of the fee are likely to equal or exceed the amount of the fee; or

(II) for any request described in clause (ii) (II) or (III) of this subparagraph for the first two hours of search time or for the first one hundred pages of duplication.

(v) No agency may require advance payment of any fee unless the requester has previously failed to pay fees in a timely fashion, or the agency has determined that the fee will exceed $250.

(vi) Nothing in this subparagraph shall supersede fees chargeable under a statute specifically providing for setting the level of fees for particular types of records.

(vii) In any action by a requester regarding the waiver of fees under this section, the court shall determine the matter de novo: Provided, That the court's review of the matter shall be limited to the record before the agency.

(viii) An agency shall not assess search fees (or in the case of a requester described under clause (ii)(II), duplication fees) under this subparagraph if the agency fails to comply with any time limit under paragraph (6), if no unusual or exceptional circumstances (as those terms are defined for purposes of paragraphs (6)(B) and (C), respectively) apply to the processing of the request.

(B) On complaint, the district court of the United States in the district in which the complainant resides, or has his principal place of business, or in which the agency records are situated, or in the District of Columbia, has jurisdiction to enjoin the agency from withholding agency records and to order the production of any agency records improperly withheld from the complainant. In such a case the court shall determine the matter de novo, and may examine the contents of such agency records in camera to determine whether such records or any part thereof shall be withheld under any of the exemptions set forth in subsection (b) of this section, and the burden is on the agency to sustain its action. In addition to any other matters to which a court accords substantial weight, a court shall accord substantial weight to an affidavit of an agency concerning the agency's determination as to technical feasibility under paragraph (2)(C) and subsection (b) and reproducibility under paragraph (3)(B).

(C) Notwithstanding any other provision of law, the defendant shall serve an answer or otherwise plead to any complaint made under this subsection within thirty days after service upon the defendant of the pleading in which such complaint is made, unless the court otherwise directs for good cause shown.

(D) Repealed. Pub. L. 98–620, title IV, §402(2), Nov. 8, 1984, 98 Stat. 3357.

(E) (i) The court may assess against the United States reasonable attorney fees and other litigation costs reasonably incurred in any case under this section in which the complainant has substantially prevailed.

(ii) For purposes of this subparagraph, a complainant has substantially prevailed if the complainant has obtained relief through either—

(I) a judicial order, or an enforceable written agreement or consent decree; or

(II) a voluntary or unilateral change in position by the agency, if the complainant's claim is not insubstantial.

(F) (i) Whenever the court orders the production of any agency records improperly withheld from the complainant and assesses against the United States reasonable attorney fees and other litigation costs, and the court additionally issues a written finding that the circumstances surrounding the withholding raise questions whether agency personnel acted arbitrarily or capriciously with respect to the withholding, the Special Counsel shall promptly initiate a proceeding to determine whether disciplinary action is warranted against the officer or employee who was primarily responsible for the withholding. The Special Counsel, after investigation and consideration of the evidence submitted, shall submit his findings and recommendations to the administrative authority of the agency concerned and shall send copies of the findings and recommendations to the officer or employee or his representative. The administrative authority shall take the corrective action that the Special Counsel recommends.

(ii) The Attorney General shall—

(I) notify the Special Counsel of each civil action described under the first sentence of clause (i); and

(II) annually submit a report to Congress on the number of such civil actions in the preceding year.

(iii) The Special Counsel shall annually submit a report to Congress on the actions taken by the Special Counsel under clause (i).

(G) In the event of noncompliance with the order of the court, the district court may punish for contempt the responsible employee, and in the case of a uniformed service, the responsible member.

(5) Each agency having more than one member shall maintain and make available for public inspection a record of the final votes of each member in every agency proceeding.

(6) (A) Each agency, upon any request for records made under paragraph (1), (2), or (3) of this subsection, shall—

(i) determine within 20 days (excepting Saturdays, Sundays, and legal public holidays) after the receipt of any such request whether to comply with such request and shall immediately notify the person making such request of such determination and the reasons therefor, and of the right of such person to appeal to the head of the agency any adverse determination; and

(ii) make a determination with respect to any appeal within twenty days (excepting Saturdays, Sundays, and legal public holidays) after the receipt of such appeal. If on appeal the denial of the request for records is in whole or in part upheld, the agency shall notify the person making such request of the provisions for judicial review of that determination under paragraph (4) of this subsection. The 20-day period under clause (i) shall commence on the date on which the request is first received by the appropriate component of the agency, but in any event not later than ten days after the request is first received by any component of the agency that is designated in the agency's regulations under this section to receive requests under this section. The 20-day period shall not be tolled by the agency except—

>   (I) that the agency may make one request to the requester for information and toll the 20-day period while it is awaiting such information that it has reasonably requested from the requester under this section; or
>
>   (II) if necessary to clarify with the requester issues regarding fee assessment. In either case, the agency's receipt of the requester's response to the agency's request for information or clarification ends the tolling period.

(B) (i) In unusual circumstances as specified in this subparagraph, the time limits prescribed in either clause (i) or clause (ii) of subparagraph (A) may be extended by written notice to the person making such request setting forth the unusual circumstances for such extension and the date on which a determination is expected to be dispatched. No such notice shall specify a date that would result in an extension for more than ten working days, except as provided in clause (ii) of this subparagraph.

>   (ii) With respect to a request for which a written notice under clause (i) extends the time limits prescribed under clause (i) of subparagraph (A), the agency shall notify the person making the request if the request cannot be processed within the time limit specified in that clause and shall provide the person an opportunity to limit the scope of the request so that it may be processed within that time limit or an opportunity to arrange with the agency an alternative time frame for processing the request or a modified request. To aid the requester, each

agency shall make available its FOIA Public Liaison, who shall assist in the resolution of any disputes between the requester and the agency. Refusal by the person to reasonably modify the request or arrange such an alternative time frame shall be considered as a factor in determining whether exceptional circumstances exist for purposes of subparagraph (C).

(iii) As used in this subparagraph, "unusual circumstances" means, but only to the extent reasonably necessary to the proper processing of the particular requests—

> (I) the need to search for and collect the requested records from field facilities or other establishments that are separate from the office processing the request;
>
> (II) the need to search for, collect, and appropriately examine a voluminous amount of separate and distinct records which are demanded in a single request; or
>
> (III) the need for consultation, which shall be conducted with all practicable speed, with another agency having a substantial interest in the determination of the request or among two or more components of the agency having substantial subject-matter interest therein.
>
> (iv) Each agency may promulgate regulations, pursuant to notice and receipt of public comment, providing for the aggregation of certain requests by the same requestor, or by a group of requestors acting in concert, if the agency reasonably believes that such requests actually constitute a single request, which would otherwise satisfy the unusual circumstances specified in this subparagraph, and the requests involve clearly related matters. Multiple requests involving unrelated matters shall not be aggregated.

(C) (i) Any person making a request to any agency for records under paragraph (1), (2), or (3) of this subsection shall be deemed to have exhausted his administrative remedies with respect to such request if the agency fails to comply with the applicable time limit provisions of this paragraph. If the

Government can show exceptional circumstances exist and that the agency is exercising due diligence in responding to the request, the court may retain jurisdiction and allow the agency additional time to complete its review of the records. Upon any determination by an agency to comply with a request for records, the records shall be made promptly available to such person making such request. Any notification of denial of any request for records under this subsection shall set forth the names and titles or positions of each person responsible for the denial of such request.

(ii) For purposes of this subparagraph, the term "exceptional circumstances" does not include a delay that results from a predictable agency workload of requests under this section, unless the agency demonstrates reasonable progress in reducing its backlog of pending requests.

(iii) Refusal by a person to reasonably modify the scope of a request or arrange an alternative time frame for processing a request (or a modified request) under clause (ii) after being given an opportunity to do so by the agency to whom the person made the request shall be considered as a factor in determining whether exceptional circumstances exist for purposes of this subparagraph.

(D) (i) Each agency may promulgate regulations, pursuant to notice and receipt of public comment, providing for multitrack processing of requests for records based on the amount of work or time (or both) involved in processing requests.

(ii) Regulations under this subparagraph may provide a person making a request that does not qualify for the fastest multitrack processing an opportunity to limit the scope of the request in order to qualify for faster processing.

(iii) This subparagraph shall not be considered to affect the requirement under subparagraph (C) to exercise due diligence.

(E) (i) Each agency shall promulgate regulations, pursuant to notice and receipt of public comment, providing for expedited processing of requests for records—

(I) in cases in which the person requesting the records demonstrates a compelling need; and

(II) in other cases determined by the agency.

652

(ii) Notwithstanding clause (i), regulations under this subparagraph must ensure—

> (I) that a determination of whether to provide expedited processing shall be made, and notice of the determination shall be provided to the person making the request, within 10 days after the date of the request; and
>
> (II) expeditious consideration of administrative appeals of such determinations of whether to provide expedited processing.

(iii) An agency shall process as soon as practicable any request for records to which the agency has granted expedited processing under this subparagraph. Agency action to deny or affirm denial of a request for expedited processing pursuant to this subparagraph, and failure by an agency to respond in a timely manner to such a request shall be subject to judicial review under paragraph (4), except that the judicial review shall be based on the record before the agency at the time of the determination.

(iv) A district court of the United States shall not have jurisdiction to review an agency denial of expedited processing of a request for records after the agency has provided a complete response to the request.

(v) For purposes of this subparagraph, the term "compelling need" means—

> (I) that a failure to obtain requested records on an expedited basis under this paragraph could reasonably be expected to pose an imminent threat to the life or physical safety of an individual; or
>
> (II) with respect to a request made by a person primarily engaged in disseminating information, urgency to inform the public concerning actual or alleged Federal Government activity.

(vi) A demonstration of a compelling need by a person making a request for expedited processing shall be made by a statement certified by such person to be true and correct to the best of such person's knowledge and belief.

(F) In denying a request for records, in whole or in part, an agency shall make a reasonable effort to estimate the volume of any requested matter the provision of which is denied, and shall provide any such estimate to the person making the request, unless providing such estimate would harm an interest protected by the exemption in subsection (b) pursuant to which the denial is made.

(7) Each agency shall—

(A) establish a system to assign an individualized tracking number for each request received that will take longer than ten days to process and provide to each person making a request the tracking number assigned to the request; and

(B) establish a telephone line or Internet service that provides information about the status of a request to the person making the request using the assigned tracking number, including—

(i) the date on which the agency originally received the request; and

(ii) an estimated date on which the agency will complete action on the request.

(b) This section does not apply to matters that are—

(1) (A) specifically authorized under criteria established by an Executive order to be kept secret in the interest of national defense or foreign policy and

(B) are in fact properly classified pursuant to such Executive order;

(2) related solely to the internal personnel rules and practices of an agency;

(3) specifically exempted from disclosure by statute (other than section 552b of this title), provided that such statute

(A)(i) requires that the matters be withheld from the public in such a manner as to leave no discretion on the issue, or

(ii) establishes particular criteria for withholding or refers to particular types of matters to be withheld; and

(B) if enacted after the date of enactment of the OPEN FOIA Act of 2009, specifically cites to this paragraph.

(4) trade secrets and commercial or financial information obtained from a person and privileged or confidential;

(5) inter-agency or intra-agency memorandums or letters which would not be available by law to a party other than an agency in litigation with the agency;

(6) personnel and medical files and similar files the disclosure of which would constitute a clearly unwarranted invasion of personal privacy;

(7) records or information compiled for law enforcement purposes, but only to the extent that the production of such law enforcement records or information

    (A) could reasonably be expected to interfere with enforcement proceedings,

    (B) would deprive a person of a right to a fair trial or an impartial adjudication,

    (C) could reasonably be expected to constitute an unwarranted invasion of personal privacy,

    (D) could reasonably be expected to disclose the identity of a confidential source, including a State, local, or foreign agency or authority or any private institution which furnished information on a confidential basis, and, in the case of a record or information compiled by criminal law enforcement authority in the course of a criminal investigation or by an agency conducting a lawful national security intelligence investigation, information furnished by a confidential source,

    (E) would disclose techniques and procedures for law enforcement investigations or prosecutions, or would disclose guidelines for law enforcement investigations or prosecutions if such disclosure could reasonably be expected to risk circumvention of the law, or

    (F) could reasonably be expected to endanger the life or physical safety of any individual;

(8) contained in or related to examination, operating, or condition reports prepared by, on behalf of, or for the use of an agency responsible for the regulation or supervision of financial institutions; or

(9) geological and geophysical information and data, including maps, concerning wells.

Any reasonably segregable portion of a record shall be provided to any person requesting such record after deletion of the portions which are exempt under this subsection. The amount of information deleted, and the exemption under which the deletion is made, shall be indicated on the released portion of the record, unless including that indication would harm an interest protected by the exemption in this subsection under which the deletion is made. If technically feasible, the amount of the information deleted, and the exemption under which the deletion is made, shall be indicated at the place in the record where such deletion is made.

(c) (1) Whenever a request is made which involves access to records described in subsection (b)(7)(A) and—

(A) the investigation or proceeding involves a possible violation of criminal law; and

(B) there is reason to believe that

(i) the subject of the investigation or proceeding is not aware of its pendency, and

(ii) disclosure of the existence of the records could reasonably be expected to interfere with enforcement proceedings, the agency may, during only such time as that circumstance continues, treat the records as not subject to the requirements of this section.

(2) Whenever informant records maintained by a criminal law enforcement agency under an informant's name or personal identifier are requested by a third party according to the informant's name or personal identifier, the agency may treat the records as not subject to the requirements of this section unless the informant's status as an informant has been officially confirmed.

(3) Whenever a request is made which involves access to records maintained by the Federal Bureau of Investigation pertaining to foreign intelligence or counterintelligence, or international terrorism, and the existence of the records is classified information as provided in subsection (b)(1), the Bureau may, as long as the existence of the records remains classified information, treat the records as not subject to the requirements of this section.

(d) This section does not authorize withholding of information or limit the availability of records to the public, except as specifically stated in this section. This section is not authority to withhold information from Congress.

(e) (1) On or before February 1 of each year, each agency shall submit to the Attorney General of the United States a report which shall cover the preceding fiscal year and which shall include—

(A) the number of determinations made by the agency not to comply with requests for records made to such agency under subsection (a) and the reasons for each such determination;

(B) (i) the number of appeals made by persons under subsection (a)(6), the result of such appeals, and the reason for the action upon each appeal that results in a denial of information; and

(ii) a complete list of all statutes that the agency relies upon to authorize the agency to withhold information under subsection (b)(3), the number of occasions on which each statute was relied upon, a description of whether a court has upheld the decision of the agency to withhold information under each such statute, and a concise description of the scope of any information withheld;

(C) the number of requests for records pending before the agency as of September 30 of the preceding year, and the median and average number of days that such requests had been pending before the agency as of that date;

(D) the number of requests for records received by the agency and the number of requests which the agency processed;

(E) the median number of days taken by the agency to process different types of requests, based on the date on which the requests were received by the agency;

(F) the average number of days for the agency to respond to a request beginning on the date on which the request was received by the agency, the median number of days for the agency to respond to such requests, and the range in number of days for the agency to respond to such requests;

(G) based on the number of business days that have elapsed since each request was originally received by the agency—

    (i) the number of requests for records to which the agency has responded with a determination within a period up to and including 20 days, and in 20- day increments up to and including 200 days;

    (ii) the number of requests for records to which the agency has responded with a determination within a period greater than 200 days and less than 301 days;

    (iii) the number of requests for records to which the agency has responded with a determination within a period greater than 300 days and less than 401 days; and

    (iv) the number of requests for records to which the agency has responded with a determination within a period greater than 400 days;

(H) the average number of days for the agency to provide the granted information beginning on the date on which the request was originally filed, the median number of days for the agency to provide the granted information, and the range in number of days for the agency to provide the granted information;

(I) the median and average number of days for the agency to respond to administrative appeals based on the date on which the appeals originally were received by the agency, the highest number of business days taken by the agency to respond to an administrative appeal, and the lowest number of business days taken by the agency to respond to an administrative appeal;

(J) data on the 10 active requests with the earliest filing dates pending at each agency, including the amount of time that has elapsed since each request was originally received by the agency;

(K) data on the 10 active administrative appeals with the earliest filing dates pending before the agency as of September 30 of the preceding year, including the number of business days that have elapsed since the requests were originally received by the agency;

(L) the number of expedited review requests that are granted and denied, the average and median number of days for adjudicating expedited review requests, and the number adjudicated within the required 10 days;

(M) the number of fee waiver requests that are granted and denied, and the average and median number of days for adjudicating fee waiver determinations;

(N) the total amount of fees collected by the agency for processing requests; and

(O) the number of full-time staff of the agency devoted to processing requests for records under this section, and the total amount expended by the agency for processing such requests.

(2) Information in each report submitted under paragraph (1) shall be expressed in terms of each principal component of the agency and for the agency overall.

(3) Each agency shall make each such report available to the public including by computer telecommunications, or if computer telecommunications means have not been established by the agency, by other electronic means. In addition, each agency shall make the raw statistical data used in its reports available electronically to the public upon request.

(4) The Attorney General of the United States shall make each report which has been made available by electronic means available at a single electronic access point. The Attorney General of the United States shall notify the Chairman and ranking minority member of the Committee on Government Reform and Oversight of the House of Representatives and the Chairman and ranking minority member of the Committees on Governmental Affairs and the Judiciary of the Senate, no later than April 1 of the year in which each such report is issued, that such reports are available by electronic means.

(5) The Attorney General of the United States, in consultation with the Director of the Office of Management and Budget, shall develop reporting and performance guidelines in connection with reports required

by this subsection by October 1, 1997, and may establish additional requirements for such reports as the Attorney General determines may be useful.

(6) The Attorney General of the United States shall submit an annual report on or before April 1 of each calendar year which shall include for the prior calendar year a listing of the number of cases arising under this section, the exemption involved in each case, the disposition of such case, and the cost, fees, and penalties assessed under subparagraphs (E), (F), and (G) of subsection (a)(4). Such report shall also include a description of the efforts undertaken by the Department of Justice to encourage agency compliance with this section.

(f) For purposes of this section, the term—

(1) "agency" as defined in section 551 (1) of this title includes any executive department, military department, Government corporation, Government controlled corporation, or other establishment in the executive branch of the Government (including the Executive Office of the President), or any independent regulatory agency; and

(2) 'record' and any other term used in this section in reference to information includes—

(A) any information that would be an agency record subject to the requirements of this section when maintained by an agency in any format, including an electronic format; and

(B) any information described under subparagraph (A) that is maintained for an agency by an entity under Government contract, for the purposes of records management.

(g) The head of each agency shall prepare and make publicly available upon request, reference material or a guide for requesting records or information from the agency, subject to the exemptions in subsection (b), including—

(1) an index of all major information systems of the agency;

(2) a description of major information and record locator systems maintained by the agency; and

(3) a handbook for obtaining various types and categories of public information from the agency pursuant to chapter 35 of title 44, and under this section.

(h)(1) There is established the Office of Government Information Services within the National Archives and Records Administration.

(2) The Office of Government Information Services shall—

(A) review policies and procedures of administrative agencies under this section;

(B) review compliance with this section by administrative agencies; and

(C) recommend policy changes to Congress and the President to improve the administration of this section.

(3) The Office of Government Information Services shall offer mediation services to resolve disputes between persons making requests under this section and administrative agencies as a nonexclusive alternative to litigation and, at the discretion of the Office, may issue advisory opinions if mediation has not resolved the dispute.

(i) The Government Accountability Office shall conduct audits of administrative agencies on the implementation of this section and issue reports detailing the results of such audits.

(j) Each agency shall designate a Chief FOIA Officer who shall be a senior official of such agency (at the Assistant Secretary or equivalent level).

(k) The Chief FOIA Officer of each agency shall, subject to the authority of the head of the agency—

(1) have agency-wide responsibility for efficient and appropriate compliance with this section;

(2) monitor implementation of this section throughout the agency and keep the head of the agency, the chief legal officer of the agency, and the Attorney General appropriately informed of the agency's performance in implementing this section;

(3) recommend to the head of the agency such adjustments to agency practices, policies, personnel, and funding as may be necessary to improve its implementation of this section;

(4) review and report to the Attorney General, through the head of the agency, at such times and in such formats as the Attorney General may direct, on the agency's performance in implementing this section;

(5) facilitate public understanding of the purposes of the statutory exemptions of this section by including concise descriptions of the exemptions in both the agency's handbook issued under subsection (g), and the agency's annual report on this section, and by providing an overview, where appropriate, of certain general categories of agency records to which those exemptions apply; and

(6) designate one or more FOIA Public Liaisons.

(l) FOIA Public Liaisons shall report to the agency Chief FOIA Officer and shall serve as supervisory officials to whom a requester under this section can raise concerns about the service the requester has received from the FOIA Requester Center, following an initial response from the FOIA Requester Center Staff. FOIA Public Liaisons shall be responsible for assisting in reducing delays, increasing transparency and understanding of the status of requests, and assisting in the resolution of disputes.

SECTION 552A OF TITLE 5, UNITED STATES CODE (THE "PRIVACY ACT")

SECTION 552a. RECORDS MAINTAINED ON INDIVIDUALS

(a) DEFINITIONS.—For purposes of this section—

(1) the term "agency" means agency as defined in section 552(e) of this title;

(2) the term "individual" means a citizen of the United States or an alien lawfully admitted for permanent residence;

(3) the term "maintain" includes maintain, collect, use, or disseminate;

(4) the term "record" means any item, collection, or grouping of information about an individual that is maintained by an agency, including, but not limited to, his education, financial transactions, medical history, and criminal or employment history and that contains his name, or the identifying number, symbol, or other identifying particular assigned to the individual, such as a finger or voice print or a photograph;

(5) the term "system of records" means a group of any records under the control of any agency from which information is retrieved by the name of the individual or by some identifying number, symbol, or other identifying particular assigned to the individual;

(6) the term "statistical record" means a record in a system of records maintained for statistical research or reporting purposes only and not used in whole or in part in making any determination about an identifiable individual, except as provided by section 8 of title 13;

(7) the term "routine use" means, with respect to the disclosure of a record, the use of such record for a purpose which is compatible with the purpose for which it was collected;

(8) the term "matching program"—

(A) means any computerized comparison of—

(i) two or more automated systems of records or a system of records with non-Federal records for the purpose of—

(I) establishing or verifying the eligibility of, or continuing compliance with statutory and regulatory requirements by, applicants for, recipients or beneficiaries of, participants in, or providers of services with respect to, cash or in-kind assistance or payments under Federal benefit programs, or

(II) recouping payments or delinquent debts under such Federal benefit programs, or

(ii) two or more automated Federal personnel or payroll systems of records or a system of Federal personnel or payroll records with non-Federal records,

(B) but does not include—

(i) matches performed to produce aggregate statistical data without any personal identifiers;

(ii) matches performed to support any research or statistical project, the specific data of which may not be used to make decisions concerning the rights, benefits, or privileges of specific individuals;

(iii) matches performed, by an agency (or component thereof) which performs as its principal function any activity pertaining to the enforcement of criminal laws, subsequent to the initiation of a specific criminal or civil law enforcement investigation of a named person or persons for the purpose of gathering evidence against such person or persons;

(iv) matches of tax information

(I)   pursuant to section 6103(d) of the Internal Revenue Code of 1986,

(II)   for purposes of tax administration as defined in section 6103(b)(4) of such Code,

(III)   for the purpose of intercepting a tax refund due an individual under authority granted by section 404(e), 464, or 1137 of the Social Security Act; or

(IV)   for the purpose of intercepting a tax refund due an individual under any other tax refund intercept program authorized by statute which has been determined by the Director of the Office of Management and Budget to contain verification, notice, and hearing requirements that are substantially similar to the procedures in section 1137 of the Social Security Act;

(v) matches—

(I) using records predominantly relating to Federal personnel, that are performed for routine administrative purposes (subject to guidance provided by the Director of the Office of

Management and Budget pursuant to subsection (v)); or

(II) conducted by an agency using only records from systems of records maintained by that agency;

if the purpose of the match is not to take any adverse financial, personnel, disciplinary, or other adverse action against Federal personnel;

(vi) matches performed for foreign counterintelligence purposes or to produce background checks for security clearances of Federal personnel or Federal contractor personnel;

(vii) matches performed incident to a levy described in section 6103(k)(8) of the Internal Revenue Code of 1986;

(viii) matches performed pursuant to section 202(x)(3) or 1611(e)(1) of the Social Security Act (42 U.S.C. §402(x)(3), 1382(e)(1)); or

(ix) matches performed by the Secretary of Health and Human Services or the Inspector General of the Department of Health and Human Services with respect to potential fraud, waste, and abuse, including matches of a system of records with non-Federal records;

(9) the term "recipient agency" means any agency, or contractor thereof, receiving records contained in a system of records from a source agency for use in a matching program;

(10) the term "non-Federal agency" means any State or local government, or agency thereof, which receives records contained in a system of records from a source agency for use in a matching program;

(11) the term "source agency" means any agency which discloses records contained in a system of records to be used in a matching program, or any State or local government, or agency thereof, which discloses records to be used in a matching program;

(12) the term "Federal benefit program" means any program administered or funded by the Federal Government, or by any agent or State on behalf of the Federal Government, providing cash or in-kind assistance in the form of payments, grants, loans, or loan guarantees to individuals; and

(13) the term "Federal personnel" means officers and employees of the Government of the United States, members of the uniformed services (including members of the Reserve Components), individuals entitled to receive immediate or deferred retirement benefits under any retirement

program of the Government of the United States (including survivor benefits).

(b) CONDITIONS OF DISCLOSURE.—No agency shall disclose any record which is contained in a system of records by any means of communication to any person, or to another agency, except pursuant to a written request by, or with the prior written consent of, the individual to whom the record pertains, unless disclosure of the record would be—

(1) to those officers and employees of the agency which maintains the record who have a need for the record in the performance of their duties;

(2) required under section 552 of this title;

(3) for a routine use as defined in subsection (a)(7) of this section and described under subsection (e)(4)(D) of this section;

(4) to the Bureau of the Census for purposes of planning or carrying out a census or survey or related activity pursuant to the provisions of title 13;

(5) to a recipient who has provided the agency with advance adequate written assurance that the record will be used solely as a statistical research or reporting record, and the record is to be transferred in a form that is not individually identifiable;

(6) to the National Archives and Records Administration as a record which has sufficient historical or other value to warrant its continued preservation by the United States Government, or for evaluation by the Archivist of the United States or the designee of the Archivist to determine whether the record has such value;

(7) to another agency or to an instrumentality of any governmental jurisdiction within or under the control of the United States for a civil or criminal law enforcement activity if the activity is authorized by law, and if the head of the agency or instrumentality has made a written request to the agency which maintains the record specifying the particular portion desired and the law enforcement activity for which the record is sought;

(8) to a person pursuant to a showing of compelling circumstances affecting the health or safety of an individual if upon such disclosure notification is transmitted to the last known address of such individual;

(9) to either House of Congress, or, to the extent of matter within its jurisdiction, any committee or subcommittee thereof, any joint committee of Congress or subcommittee of any such joint committee;

(10) to the Comptroller General, or any of his authorized representatives, in the course of the performance of the duties of the Government Accountability Office;

(11) pursuant to the order of a court of competent jurisdiction; or

(12) to a consumer reporting agency in accordance with section 3711(e) of title 31.

(c) ACCOUNTING OF CERTAIN DISCLOSURES.—Each agency, with respect to each system of records under its control, shall—

    (1) except for disclosures made under subsections (b)(1) or (b)(2) of this section, keep an accurate accounting of—

        (A) the date, nature, and purpose of each disclosure of a record to any person or to another agency made under subsection (b) of this section; and

        (B) the name and address of the person or agency to whom the disclosure is made;

    (2) retain the accounting made under paragraph (1) of this subsection for at least five years or the life of the record, whichever is longer, after the disclosure for which the accounting is made;

    (3) except for disclosures made under subsection (b)(7) of this section, make the accounting made under paragraph (1) of this subsection available to the individual named in the record at his request; and

    (4) inform any person or other agency about any correction or notation of dispute made by the agency in accordance with subsection (d) of this section of any record that has been disclosed to the person or agency if an accounting of the disclosure was made.

(d) ACCESS TO RECORDS.—Each agency that maintains a system of records shall—

    (1) upon request by any individual to gain access to his record or to any information pertaining to him which is contained in the system, permit him and upon his request, a person of his own choosing to accompany him, to review the record and have a copy made of all or any portion thereof in a form comprehensible to him, except that the agency may require the individual to furnish a written statement authorizing discussion of that individual's record in the accompanying person's presence;

    (2) permit the individual to request amendment of a record pertaining to him and—

        (A) not later than 10 days (excluding Saturdays, Sundays, and legal public holidays) after the date of receipt of such request, acknowledge in writing such receipt; and

        (B) promptly, either—

            (i) make any correction of any portion thereof which the individual believes is not accurate, relevant, timely, or complete; or

            (ii) inform the individual of its refusal to amend the record in accordance with his request, the reason for the refusal, the procedures established by the agency for the individual to request a review of that refusal by the head of the agency or an officer designated by the head of the agency, and the name and business address of that official;

(3) permit the individual who disagrees with the refusal of the agency to amend his record to request a review of such refusal, and not later than 30 days (excluding Saturdays, Sundays, and legal public holidays) from the date on which the individual requests such review, complete such review and make a final determination unless, for good cause shown, the head of the agency extends such 30-day period; and if, after his review, the reviewing official also refuses to amend the record in accordance with the request, permit the individual to file with the agency a concise statement setting forth the reasons for his disagreement with the refusal of the agency, and notify the individual of the provisions for judicial review of the reviewing official's determination under subsection (g)(1)(A) of this section;

(4) in any disclosure, containing information about which the individual has filed a statement of disagreement, occurring after the filing of the statement under paragraph (3) of this subsection, clearly note any portion of the record which is disputed and provide copies of the statement and, if the agency deems it appropriate, copies of a concise statement of the reasons of the agency for not making the amendments requested, to persons or other agencies to whom the disputed record has been disclosed; and

(5) nothing in this section shall allow an individual access to any information compiled in reasonable anticipation of a civil action or proceeding.

(e) AGENCY REQUIREMENTS.—Each agency that maintains a system of records shall—

(1) maintain in its records only such information about an individual as is relevant and necessary to accomplish a purpose of the agency required to be accomplished by statute or by executive order of the President;

(2) collect information to the greatest extent practicable directly from the subject individual when the information may result in adverse determinations about an individual's rights, benefits, and privileges under Federal programs;

(3) inform each individual whom it asks to supply information, on the form which it uses to collect the information or on a separate form that can be retained by the individual—

(A) the authority (whether granted by statute, or by executive order of the President) which authorizes the solicitation of the information and whether disclosure of such information is mandatory or voluntary;

(B) the principal purpose or purposes for which the information is intended to be used;

(C) the routine uses which may be made of the information, as published pursuant to paragraph (4)(D) of this subsection; and

(D) the effects on him, if any, of not providing all or any part of the requested information;

(4) subject to the provisions of paragraph (11) of this subsection, publish in the Federal Register upon establishment or revision a notice of the existence and character of the system of records, which notice shall include—

(A) the name and location of the system;

(B) the categories of individuals on whom records are maintained in the system;

(C) the categories of records maintained in the system;

(D) each routine use of the records contained in the system, including the categories of users and the purpose of such use;

(E) the policies and practices of the agency regarding storage, retrievability, access controls, retention, and disposal of the records;

(F) the title and business address of the agency official who is responsible for the system of records;

(G) the agency procedures whereby an individual can be notified at his request if the system of records contains a record pertaining to him;

(H) the agency procedures whereby an individual can be notified at his request how he can gain access to any record pertaining to him contained in the system of records, and how he can contest its content; and

(I) the categories of sources of records in the system;

(5) maintain all records which are used by the agency in making any determination about any individual with such accuracy, relevance, timeliness, and completeness as is reasonably necessary to assure fairness to the individual in the determination;

(6) prior to disseminating any record about an individual to any person other than an agency, unless the dissemination is made pursuant to subsection (b)(2) of this section, make reasonable efforts to assure that such records are accurate, complete, timely, and relevant for agency purposes;

(7) maintain no record describing how any individual exercises rights guaranteed by the First Amendment unless expressly authorized by statute or by the individual about whom the record is maintained or

unless pertinent to and within the scope of an authorized law enforcement activity;

(8) make reasonable efforts to serve notice on an individual when any record on such individual is made available to any person under compulsory legal process when such process becomes a matter of public record;

(9) establish rules of conduct for persons involved in the design, development, operation, or maintenance of any system of records, or in maintaining any record, and instruct each such person with respect to such rules and the requirements of this section, including any other rules and procedures adopted pursuant to this section and the penalties for noncompliance;

(10) establish appropriate administrative, technical, and physical safeguards to insure the security and confidentiality of records and to protect against any anticipated threats or hazards to their security or integrity which could result in substantial harm, embarrassment, inconvenience, or unfairness to any individual on whom information is maintained;

(11) at least 30 days prior to publication of information under paragraph (4)(D) of this subsection, publish in the Federal Register notice of any new use or intended use of the information in the system, and provide an opportunity for interested persons to submit written data, views, or arguments to the agency; and

(12) if such agency is a recipient agency or a source agency in a matching program with a non-Federal agency, with respect to any establishment or revision of a matching program, at least 30 days prior to conducting such program, publish in the Federal Register notice of such establishment or revision.

(f) AGENCY RULES.—In order to carry out the provisions of this section, each agency that maintains a system of records shall promulgate rules, in accordance with the requirements (including general notice) of section 553 of this title, which shall—

(1) establish procedures whereby an individual can be notified in response to his request if any system of records named by the individual contains a record pertaining to him;

(2) define reasonable times, places, and requirements for identifying an individual who requests his record or information pertaining to him before the agency shall make the record or information available to the individual;

(3) establish procedures for the disclosure to an individual upon his request of his record or information pertaining to him, including special

procedure, if deemed necessary, for the disclosure to an individual of medical records, including psychological records, pertaining to him;

(4) establish procedures for reviewing a request from an individual concerning the amendment of any record or information pertaining to the individual, for making a determination on the request, for an appeal within the agency of an initial adverse agency determination, and for whatever additional means may be necessary for each individual to be able to exercise fully his rights under this section; and

(5) establish fees to be charged, if any, to any individual for making copies of his record, excluding the cost of any search for and review of the record.

The Office of the Federal Register shall biennially compile and publish the rules promulgated under this subsection and agency notices published under subsection (e)(4) of this section in a form available to the public at low cost.

(g)(1) CIVIL REMEDIES.—Whenever any agency

(A) makes a determination under subsection (d)(3) of this section not to amend an individual's record in accordance with his request, or fails to make such review in conformity with that subsection;

(B) refuses to comply with an individual request under subsection (d)(1) of this section;

(C) fails to maintain any record concerning any individual with such accuracy, relevance, timeliness, and completeness as is necessary to assure fairness in any determination relating to the qualifications, character, rights, or opportunities of, or benefits to the individual that may be made on the basis of such record, and consequently a determination is made which is adverse to the individual; or

(D) fails to comply with any other provision of this section, or any rule promulgated thereunder, in such a way as to have an adverse effect on an individual,

the individual may bring a civil action against the agency, and the district courts of the United States shall have jurisdiction in the matters under the provisions of this subsection.

(2)(A) In any suit brought under the provisions of subsection (g)(1)(A) of this section, the court may order the agency to amend the individual's record in accordance with his request or in such other way as the court may direct. In such a case the court shall determine the matter de novo.

(B) The court may assess against the United States reasonable attorney fees and other litigation costs reasonably incurred in any case under this paragraph in which the complainant has substantially prevailed.

(3)(A) In any suit brought under the provisions of subsection (g)(1)(B) of this section, the court may enjoin the agency from withholding the records and order the production to the complainant of any agency records improperly withheld from him. In such a case the court shall determine the matter de novo, and may examine the contents of any agency records in camera to determine whether the records or any portion thereof may be withheld under any of the exemptions set forth in subsection (k) of this section, and the burden is on the agency to sustain its action.

(B) The court may assess against the United States reasonable attorney fees and other litigation costs reasonably incurred in any case under this paragraph in which the complainant has substantially prevailed.

(4) In any suit brought under the provisions of subsection (g)(1)(C) or (D) of this section in which the court determines that the agency acted in a manner which was intentional or willful, the United States shall be liable to the individual in an amount equal to the sum of—

(A) actual damages sustained by the individual as a result of the refusal or failure, but in no case shall a person entitled to recovery receive less than the sum of $1,000; and

(B) the costs of the action together with reasonable attorney fees as determined by the court.

(5) An action to enforce any liability created under this section may be brought in the district court of the United States in the district in which the complainant resides, or has his principal place of business, or in which the agency records are situated, or in the District of Columbia, without regard to the amount in controversy, within two years from the date on which the cause of action arises, except that where an agency has materially and willfully misrepresented any information required under this section to be disclosed to an individual and the information so misrepresented is material to establishment of the liability of the agency to the individual under this section, the action may be brought at any time within two years after discovery by the individual of the misrepresentation. Nothing in this section shall be construed to authorize any civil action by reason of any injury sustained as the result of a disclosure of a record prior to September 27, 1975.

(h) RIGHTS OF LEGAL GUARDIANS.—For the purposes of this section, the parent of any minor, or the legal guardian of any individual who has been declared to be incompetent due to physical or mental incapacity or age by a court of competent jurisdiction, may act on behalf of the individual.

(i)(1) CRIMINAL PENALTIES.—Any officer or employee of an agency, who by virtue of his employment or official position, has possession of, or access to, agency records which contain individually identifiable information the disclosure of which is prohibited by this section or by rules or regulations established thereunder, and who knowing that disclosure of the specific material is so prohibited, willfully discloses the material in any manner to any person or agency not entitled to receive it, shall be guilty of a misdemeanor and fined not more than $5,000.

(2) Any officer or employee of any agency who willfully maintains a system of records without meeting the notice requirements of subsection (e)(4) of this section shall be guilty of a misdemeanor and fined not more than $5,000.

(3) Any person who knowingly and willfully requests or obtains any record concerning an individual from an agency under false pretenses shall be guilty of a misdemeanor and fined not more than $5,000.

(j) GENERAL EXEMPTIONS.—The head of any agency may promulgate rules, in accordance with the requirements (including general notice) of sections 553(b)(1), (2), and (3), (c), and (e) of this title, to exempt any system of records within the agency from any part of this section except subsections (b), (c)(1) and (2), (e)(4)(A) through (F), (e)(6), (7), (9), (10), and (11), and (i) if the system of records is—

(1) maintained by the Central Intelligence Agency; or

(2) maintained by an agency or component thereof which performs as its principal function any activity pertaining to the enforcement of criminal laws, including police efforts to prevent, control, or reduce crime or to apprehend criminals, and the activities of prosecutors, courts, correctional, probation, pardon, or parole authorities, and which consists of (A) information compiled for the purpose of identifying individual criminal offenders and alleged offenders and consisting only of identifying data and notations of arrests, the nature and disposition of criminal charges, sentencing, confinement, release, and parole and probation status; (B) information compiled for the purpose of a criminal investigation, including reports of informants and investigators, and associated with an identifiable individual; or (C) reports identifiable to an individual compiled at any stage of the process of enforcement of the criminal laws from arrest or indictment through release from supervision.

At the time rules are adopted under this subsection, the agency shall include in the statement required under section 553(c) of this title, the reasons why the system of records is to be exempted from a provision of this section.

(k) SPECIFIC EXEMPTIONS.—The head of any agency may promulgate rules, in accordance with the requirements (including general notice) of sections 553(b)(1), (2), and (3), (c), and (e) of this title, to exempt any system of records within the agency from subsections (c)(3), (d), (e)(1), (e)(4)(G), (H), and (I) and (f) of this section if the system of records is—

(1) subject to the provisions of section 552(b)(1) of this title;

(2) investigatory material compiled for law enforcement purposes, other than material within the scope of subsection (j)(2) of this section: Provided, however, That if any individual is denied any right, privilege, or benefit that he would otherwise be entitled by Federal law, or for which he would otherwise be eligible, as a result of the maintenance of such material, such material shall be provided to such individual, except to the extent that the disclosure of such material would reveal the identity of a source who furnished information to the Government under an express promise that the identity of the source would be held in confidence, or, prior to the effective date of this section, under an implied promise that the identity of the source would be held in confidence;

(3) maintained in connection with providing protective services to the President of the United States or other individuals pursuant to section 3056 of title 18;

(4) required by statute to be maintained and used solely as statistical records;

(5) investigatory material compiled solely for the purpose of determining suitability, eligibility, or qualifications for Federal civilian employment, military service, Federal contracts, or access to classified information, but only to the extent that the disclosure of such material would reveal the identity of a source who furnished information to the Government under an express promise that the identity of the source would be held in confidence, or, prior to the effective date of this section, under an implied promise that the identity of the source would be held in confidence;

(6) testing or examination material used solely to determine individual qualifications for appointment or promotion in the Federal service the disclosure of which would compromise the objectivity or fairness of the testing or examination process; or

(7) evaluation material used to determine potential for promotion in the armed services, but only to the extent that the disclosure of such material would reveal the identity of a source who furnished information to the Government under an express promise that the identity of the source would be held in confidence, or, prior to the effective date of this section, under an implied promise that the identity of the source would be held in confidence.

At the time rules are adopted under this subsection, the agency shall include in the statement required under section 553(c) of this title, the reasons why the system of records is to be exempted from a provision of this section.

(l)(1) ARCHIVAL RECORDS.—Each agency record which is accepted by the Archivist of the United States for storage, processing, and servicing in accordance with section 3103 of title 44 shall, for the purposes of this section, be considered to be maintained by the agency which deposited the record and shall be subject to the provisions of this section. The Archivist of the United States shall not disclose the record except to the agency which maintains the record, or under rules established by that agency which are not inconsistent with the provisions of this section.

> (2) Each agency record pertaining to an identifiable individual which was transferred to the National Archives of the United States as a record which has sufficient historical or other value to warrant its continued preservation by the United States Government, prior to the effective date of this section, shall, for the purposes of this section, be considered to be maintained by the National Archives and shall not be subject to the provisions of this section, except that a statement generally describing such records (modeled after the requirements relating to records subject to subsections (e)(4)(A) through (G) of this section) shall be published in the Federal Register.

> (3) Each agency record pertaining to an identifiable individual which is transferred to the National Archives of the United States as a record which has sufficient historical or other value to warrant its continued preservation by the United States Government, on or after the effective date of this section, shall, for the purposes of this section, be considered to be maintained by the National Archives and shall be exempt from the requirements of this section except subsections (e)(4)(A) through (G) and (e)(9) of this section.

(m)(1) GOVERNMENT CONTRACTORS.—When an agency provides by a contract for the operation by or on behalf of the agency of a system of records to accomplish an agency function, the agency shall, consistent with its authority, cause the requirements of this section to be applied to such system. For purposes of subsection (i) of this section any such contractor and any employee of such contractor, if such contract is agreed to on or after the effective date of this section, shall be considered to be an employee of an agency.

> (2) A consumer reporting agency to which a record is disclosed under section 3711(e) of title 31 shall not be considered a contractor for the purposes of this section.

(n) MAILING LISTS.—An individual's name and address may not be sold or rented by an agency unless such action is specifically authorized by law. This provision shall not be construed to require the withholding of names and addresses otherwise permitted to be made public.

(o) MATCHING AGREEMENTS.—

(1) No record which is contained in a system of records may be disclosed to a recipient agency or non-Federal agency for use in a computer matching program except pursuant to a written agreement between the source agency and the recipient agency or non-Federal agency specifying—

(A) the purpose and legal authority for conducting the program;

(B) the justification for the program and the anticipated results, including a specific estimate of any savings;

(C) a description of the records that will be matched, including each data element that will be used, the approximate number of records that will be matched, and the projected starting and completion dates of the matching program;

(D) procedures for providing individualized notice at the time of application, and notice periodically thereafter as directed by the Data Integrity Board of such agency (subject to guidance provided by the Director of the Office of Management and Budget pursuant to subsection (v)), to—

(i) applicants for and recipients of financial assistance or payments under Federal benefit programs, and

(ii) applicants for and holders of positions as Federal personnel,

that any information provided by such applicants, recipients, holders, and individuals may be subject to verification through matching programs;

(E) procedures for verifying information produced in such matching program as required by subsection (p);

(F) procedures for the retention and timely destruction of identifiable records created by a recipient agency or non-Federal agency in such matching program;

(G) procedures for ensuring the administrative, technical, and physical security of the records matched and the results of such programs;

(H) prohibitions on duplication and redisclosure of records provided by the source agency within or outside the recipient agency or the non-Federal agency, except where required by law or essential to the conduct of the matching program;

(I) procedures governing the use by a recipient agency or non-Federal agency of records provided in a matching program by a source agency, including procedures governing return of the records to the source agency or destruction of records used in such program;

(J) information on assessments that have been made on the accuracy of the records that will be used in such matching program; and

(K) that the Comptroller General may have access to all records of a recipient agency or a non-Federal agency that the Comptroller General deems necessary in order to monitor or verify compliance with the agreement.

(2)(A) A copy of each agreement entered into pursuant to paragraph (1) shall—

(i) be transmitted to the Committee on Governmental Affairs of the Senate and the Committee on Government Operations of the House of Representatives; and

(ii) be available upon request to the public.

(B) No such agreement shall be effective until 30 days after the date on which such a copy is transmitted pursuant to subparagraph (A)(i).

(C) Such an agreement shall remain in effect only for such period, not to exceed 18 months, as the Data Integrity Board of the agency determines is appropriate in light of the purposes, and length of time necessary for the conduct, of the matching program.

(D) Within 3 months prior to the expiration of such an agreement pursuant to subparagraph (C), the Data Integrity Board of the agency may, without additional review, renew the matching agreement for a current, ongoing matching program for not more than one additional year if—

(i) such program will be conducted without any change; and

(ii) each party to the agreement certifies to the Board in writing that the program has been conducted in compliance with the agreement.

(p) VERIFICATION AND OPPORTUNITY TO CONTEST FINDINGS.—

(1) In order to protect any individual whose records are used in a matching program, no recipient agency, non-Federal agency, or source agency may suspend, terminate, reduce, or make a final denial of any financial assistance or payment under a Federal benefit program to such individual, or take other adverse action against such individual, as a result of information produced by such matching program, until—

(A)(i) the agency has independently verified the information; or

(ii) the Data Integrity Board of the agency, or in the case of a non-Federal agency the Data Integrity Board of the source agency, determines in accordance with guidance issued by the Director of the Office of Management and Budget that—

(I) the information is limited to identification and amount of benefits paid by the source agency under a Federal benefit program; and

(II) there is a high degree of confidence that the information provided to the recipient agency is accurate;

(B) the individual receives a notice from the agency containing a statement of its findings and informing the individual of the opportunity to contest such findings; and

(C)(i) the expiration of any time period established for the program by statute or regulation for the individual to respond to that notice; or

(ii) in the case of a program for which no such period is established, the end of the 30-day period beginning on the date on which notice under subparagraph (B) is mailed or otherwise provided to the individual.

(2) Independent verification referred to in paragraph (1) requires investigation and confirmation of specific information relating to an individual that is used as a basis for an adverse action against the individual, including where applicable investigation and confirmation of—

(A) the amount of any asset or income involved;

(B) whether such individual actually has or had access to such asset or income for such individual's own use; and

(C) the period or periods when the individual actually had such asset or income.

(3) Notwithstanding paragraph (1), an agency may take any appropriate action otherwise prohibited by such paragraph if the agency determines that the public health or public safety may be adversely affected or significantly threatened during any notice period required by such paragraph.

(q) SANCTIONS.—

(1) Notwithstanding any other provision of law, no source agency may disclose any record which is contained in a system of records to a recipient agency or non-Federal agency for a matching program if such source agency has reason to believe that the requirements of subsection (p), or any matching agreement entered into pursuant to subsection (o), or both, are not being met by such recipient agency.

(2) No source agency may renew a matching agreement unless—

(A) the recipient agency or non-Federal agency has certified that it has complied with the provisions of that agreement; and

(B) the source agency has no reason to believe that the certification is inaccurate.

(r) REPORT ON NEW SYSTEMS AND MATCHING PROGRAMS.—Each agency that proposes to establish or make a significant change in a system of records or a matching program shall provide adequate advance notice of any such proposal (in duplicate) to the Committee on Government Operations of the House of Representatives, the Committee on Governmental Affairs of the Senate, and the Office of Management and Budget in order to permit an evaluation of the probable or potential effect of such proposal on the privacy or other rights of individuals.

(s) BIENNIAL REPORT.—The President shall biennially submit to the Speaker of the House of Representatives and the President pro tempore of the Senate a report—

(1) describing the actions of the Director of the Office of Management and Budget pursuant to section 6 of the Privacy Act of 1974 during the preceding 2 years;

(2) describing the exercise of individual rights of access and amendment under this section during such years;

(3) identifying changes in or additions to systems of records;

(4) containing such other information concerning administration of this section as may be necessary or useful to the Congress in reviewing the effectiveness of this section in carrying out the purposes of the Privacy Act of 1974.

(t)(1) EFFECT OF OTHER LAWS.—No agency shall rely on any exemption contained in section 552 of this title to withhold from an individual any record which is otherwise accessible to such individual under the provisions of this section.

(2) No agency shall rely on any exemption in this section to withhold from an individual any record which is otherwise accessible to such individual under the provisions of section 552 of this title.

(u) DATA INTEGRITY BOARDS.—

(1) Every agency conducting or participating in a matching program shall establish a Data Integrity Board to oversee and coordinate among the various components of such agency the agency's implementation of this section.

(2) Each Data Integrity Board shall consist of senior officials designated by the head of the agency, and shall include any senior official designated by the head of the agency as responsible for implementation of this section, and the inspector general of the agency, if any. The inspector general shall not serve as chairman of the Data Integrity Board.

677

(3) Each Data Integrity Board—
    (A) shall review, approve, and maintain all written agreements for receipt or disclosure of agency records for matching programs to ensure compliance with subsection (o), and all relevant statutes, regulations, and guidelines;
    (B) shall review all matching programs in which the agency has participated during the year, either as a source agency or recipient agency, determine compliance with applicable laws, regulations, guidelines, and agency agreements, and assess the costs and benefits of such programs;
    (C) shall review all recurring matching programs in which the agency has participated during the year, either as a source agency or recipient agency, for continued justification for such disclosures;
    (D) shall compile an annual report, which shall be submitted to the head of the agency and the Office of Management and Budget and made available to the public on request, describing the matching activities of the agency, including—
        (i) matching programs in which the agency has participated as a source agency or recipient agency;
        (ii) matching agreements proposed under subsection (o) that were disapproved by the Board;
        (iii) any changes in membership or structure of the Board in the preceding year;
        (iv) the reasons for any waiver of the requirement in paragraph (4) of this section for completion and submission of a cost-benefit analysis prior to the approval of a matching program;
        (v) any violations of matching agreements that have been alleged or identified and any corrective action taken; and
        (vi) any other information required by the Director of the Office of Management and Budget to be included in such report;
    (E) shall serve as a clearinghouse for receiving and providing information on the accuracy, completeness, and reliability of records used in matching programs;
    (F) shall provide interpretation and guidance to agency components and personnel on the requirements of this section for matching programs;

(G) shall review agency recordkeeping and disposal policies and practices for matching programs to assure compliance with this section; and

(H) may review and report on any agency matching activities that are not matching programs.

(4)(A) Except as provided in subparagraphs (B) and (C), a Data Integrity Board shall not approve any written agreement for a matching program unless the agency has completed and submitted to such Board a cost-benefit analysis of the proposed program and such analysis demonstrates that the program is likely to be cost effective.

(B) The Board may waive the requirements of subparagraph (A) of this paragraph if it determines in writing, in accordance with guidelines prescribed by the Director of the Office of Management and Budget, that a cost-benefit analysis is not required.

(C) A cost-benefit analysis shall not be required under subparagraph (A) prior to the initial approval of a written agreement for a matching program that is specifically required by statute. Any subsequent written agreement for such a program shall not be approved by the Data Integrity Board unless the agency has submitted a cost-benefit analysis of the program as conducted under the preceding approval of such agreement.

(5)(A) If a matching agreement is disapproved by a Data Integrity Board, any party to such agreement may appeal the disapproval to the Director of the Office of Management and Budget. Timely notice of the filing of such an appeal shall be provided by the Director of the Office of Management and Budget to the Committee on Governmental Affairs of the Senate and the Committee on Government Operations of the House of Representatives.

(B) The Director of the Office of Management and Budget may approve a matching agreement notwithstanding the disapproval of a Data Integrity Board if the Director determines that—

(i) the matching program will be consistent with all applicable legal, regulatory, and policy requirements;

(ii) there is adequate evidence that the matching agreement will be cost-effective; and

(iii) the matching program is in the public interest.

(C) The decision of the Director to approve a matching agreement shall not take effect until 30 days after it is reported to committees described in subparagraph (A).

(D) If the Data Integrity Board and the Director of the Office of Management and Budget disapprove a matching program proposed by the inspector general of an agency, the inspector general may report the disapproval to the head of the agency and to the Congress.

(6) In the reports required by paragraph (3)(D), agency matching activities that are not matching programs may be reported on an aggregate basis, if and to the extent necessary to protect ongoing law enforcement or counterintelligence investigations.

(v) OFFICE OF MANAGEMENT AND BUDGET RESPONSIBILITIES.—The Director of the Office of Management and Budget shall—

(1) develop and, after notice and opportunity for public comment, prescribe guidelines and regulations for the use of agencies in implementing the provisions of this section; and

(2) provide continuing assistance to and oversight of the implementation of this section by agencies.

(w) APPLICABILITY TO BUREAU OF CONSUMER FINANCIAL PROTECTION.— Except as provided in the Consumer Financial Protection Act of 2010, this section shall apply with respect to the Bureau of Consumer Financial Protection.

FEDERAL INFORMATION SECURITY MANAGEMENT ACT

(Public Law 107-347; 116 Stat. 2899; November 25, 2002. FISMA amends chapter 35 of Title 44 United States Code; Section 11331 of Title 40 United States Code; and Sections 20 and 21 of the National Institute of Standards and Technology Act (15 U.S.C. §278-g3 and 278-g4))

AMENDMENTS TO:
TITLE 44 UNITED STATES CODE

CHAPTER 35 – COORDINATION OF FEDERAL INFORMATION POLICY
SUBCHAPTER II – INFORMATION SECURITY

SECTION. 3541. PURPOSES
The purposes of this subchapter are to—

(1) provide a comprehensive framework for ensuring the effectiveness of information security controls over information resources that support Federal operations and assets;

(2) recognize the highly networked nature of the current Federal computing environment and provide effective Government-wide management and oversight of the related information security risks, including coordination of information security efforts throughout the civilian, national security, and law enforcement communities;

(3) provide for development and maintenance of minimum controls required to protect Federal information and information systems;

(4) provide a mechanism for improved oversight of Federal agency information security programs;

(5) acknowledge that commercially developed information security products offer advanced, dynamic, robust, and effective information security solutions, reflecting market solutions for the protection of critical information infrastructures important to the national defense and economic security of the nation that are designed, built, and operated by the private sector; and

(6) recognize that the selection of specific technical hardware and software information security solutions should be left to individual agencies from among commercially developed products.

SEC. 3542. DEFINITIONS
(a) IN GENERAL.—Except as provided under subsection (b), the definitions under section 3502 shall apply to this subchapter.

(b) ADDITIONAL DEFINITIONS.—As used in this subchapter:

681

(1) The term "information security" means protecting information and information systems from unauthorized access, use, disclosure, disruption, modification, or destruction in order to provide—

    (A) integrity, which means guarding against improper information modification or destruction, and includes ensuring information non-repudiation and authenticity;

    (B) confidentiality, which means preserving authorized restrictions on access and disclosure, including means for protecting personal privacy and proprietary information; and

    (C) availability, which means ensuring timely and reliable access to and use of information.

(2)(A) The term "national security system" means any information system (including any telecommunications system) used or operated by an agency or by a contractor of an agency, or other organization on behalf of an agency—

    (i) the function, operation, or use of which—

        (I) involves intelligence activities;

        (II) involves cryptologic activities related to national security;

        (III) involves command and control of military forces;

        (IV) involves equipment that is an integral part of a weapon or weapons system; or

        (V) subject to subparagraph (B), is critical to the direct fulfillment of military or intelligence missions; or

    (ii) is protected at all times by procedures established for information that have been specifically authorized under criteria established by an Executive order or an Act of Congress to be kept classified in the interest of national defense or foreign policy.

    (B) Subparagraph (A)(i)(V) does not include a system that is to be used for routine administrative and business applications (including payroll, finance, logistics, and personnel management applications).

(3) The term "information technology" has the meaning given that term in section 11101 of title 40.

SEC. 3543. AUTHORITY AND FUNCTIONS OF THE DIRECTOR.

(a) IN GENERAL.—The Director shall oversee agency information security policies and practices, including—

(1) developing and overseeing the implementation of policies, principles, standards, and guidelines on information security, including through ensuring timely agency adoption of and compliance with standards promulgated under section 11331 of title 40;

(2) requiring agencies, consistent with the standards promulgated under such section 11331 and the requirements of this subchapter, to identify and provide information security protections commensurate with the risk and magnitude of the harm resulting from the unauthorized access, use, disclosure, disruption, modification, or destruction of—

    (A) information collected or maintained by or on behalf of an agency; or

    (B) information systems used or operated by an agency or by a contractor of an agency or other organization on behalf of an agency;

(3) coordinating the development of standards and guidelines under section 20 of the National Institute of Standards and Technology Act (15 U.S.C. §§278g-3) with agencies and offices operating or exercising control of national security systems (including the National Security Agency) to assure, to the maximum extent feasible, that such standards and guidelines are complementary with standards and guidelines developed for national security systems;

(4) overseeing agency compliance with the requirements of this subchapter, including through any authorized action under section 11303 of title 40, to enforce accountability for compliance with such requirements;

(5) reviewing at least annually, and approving or disapproving, agency information security programs required under section 3544(b);

(6) coordinating information security policies and procedures with related information resources management policies and procedures;

(7) overseeing the operation of the Federal information security incident center required under section 3546; and

(8) reporting to Congress no later than March 1 of each year on agency compliance with the requirements of this subchapter, including—

    (A) a summary of the findings of evaluations required by section 3545;

    (B) an assessment of the development, promulgation, and adoption of, and compliance with, standards developed under section 20 of the National Institute of Standards and Technology Act (15 U.S.C. §§278g-3) and promulgated under section 11331 of title 40;

    (C) significant deficiencies in agency information security practices;

(D) planned remedial action to address such deficiencies; and

(E) a summary of, and the views of the Director on, the report prepared by the National Institute of Standards and Technology under section 20(d)(10) of the National Institute of Standards and Technology Act (15 U.S.C. §§278g-3).

(b) NATIONAL SECURITY SYSTEMS.—Except for the authorities described in paragraphs (4) and (8) of subsection (a), the authorities of the Director under this section shall not apply to national security systems.

(c) DEPARTMENT OF DEFENSE AND CENTRAL INTELLIGENCE AGENCY SYSTEMS. –

(1) The authorities of the Director described in paragraphs (1) and (2) of subsection (a) shall be delegated to the Secretary of Defense in the case of systems described in paragraph (2) and to the Director of Central Intelligence in the case of systems described in paragraph (3).

(2) The systems described in this paragraph are systems that are operated by the Department of Defense, a contractor of the Department of Defense, or another entity on behalf of the Department of Defense that processes any information the unauthorized access, use, disclosure, disruption, modification, or destruction of which would have a debilitating impact on the mission of the Department of Defense.

(3) The systems described in this paragraph are systems that are operated by the Central Intelligence Agency, a contractor of the Central Intelligence Agency, or another entity on behalf of the Central Intelligence Agency that processes any information the unauthorized access, use, disclosure, disruption, modification, or destruction of which would have a debilitating impact on the mission of the Central Intelligence Agency.

SEC. 3544. FEDERAL AGENCY RESPONSIBILITIES.

(a) IN GENERAL.—The head of each agency shall—

(1) be responsible for—

(A) providing information security protections commensurate with the risk and magnitude of the harm resulting from unauthorized access, use, disclosure, disruption, modification, or destruction of—

(i) information collected or maintained by or on behalf of the agency; and

(ii) information systems used or operated by an agency or by a contractor of an agency or other organization on behalf of an agency;

(B) complying with the requirements of this subchapter and related policies, procedures, standards, and guidelines, including—

(i) information security standards promulgated under section 11331 of title 40; and

(ii) information security standards and guidelines for national security systems issued in accordance with law and as directed by the President; and

(C) ensuring that information security management processes are integrated with agency strategic and operational planning processes;

(2) ensure that senior agency officials provide information security for the information and information systems that support the operations and assets under their control, including through

(A) assessing the risk and magnitude of the harm that could result from the unauthorized access, use, disclosure, disruption, modification, or destruction of such information or information systems;

(B) determining the levels of information security appropriate to protect such information and information systems in accordance with standards promulgated under section 11331 of title 40, for information security classifications and related requirements;

(C) implementing policies and procedures to cost-effectively reduce risks to an acceptable level; and

(D) periodically testing and evaluating information security controls and techniques to ensure that they are effectively implemented;

(3) delegate to the agency Chief Information Officer established under section 3506 (or comparable official in an agency not covered by such section) the authority to ensure compliance with the requirements imposed on the agency under this subchapter, including—

(A) designating a senior agency information security officer who shall—

(i) carry out the Chief Information Officer's responsibilities under this section;

(ii) possess professional qualifications, including training and experience, required to administer the functions described under this section;

(iii) have information security duties as that official's primary duty; and

(iv) head an office with the mission and resources to assist in ensuring agency compliance with this section;

(B) developing and maintaining an agency wide information security program as required by subsection (b);

(C) developing and maintaining information security policies, procedures, and control techniques to address all applicable requirements, including those issued under section 3543 of this title, and section 11331 of title 40;

(D) training and overseeing personnel with significant responsibilities for information security with respect to such responsibilities; and

(E) assisting senior agency officials concerning their responsibilities under paragraph (2);

(4) ensure that the agency has trained personnel sufficient to assist the agency in complying with the requirements of this subchapter and related policies, procedures, standards, and guidelines; and

(5) ensure that the agency Chief Information Officer, in coordination with other senior agency officials, reports annually to the agency head on the effectiveness of the agency information security program, including progress of remedial actions.

(b) AGENCY PROGRAM.—Each agency shall develop, document, and implement an agency-wide information security program, approved by the Director under section 3543(a)(5), to provide information security for the information and information systems that support the operations and assets of the agency, including those provided or managed by another agency, contractor, or other source, that includes—

(1) periodic assessments of the risk and magnitude of the harm that could result from the unauthorized access, use, disclosure, disruption, modification, or destruction of information and information systems that support the operations and assets of the agency;

(2) policies and procedures that—

(A) are based on the risk assessments required by paragraph (1);

(B) cost-effectively reduce information security risks to an acceptable level;

(C) ensure that information security is addressed throughout the life cycle of each agency information system; and

(D) ensure compliance with—

(i) the requirements of this subchapter;

(ii) policies and procedures as may be prescribed by the Director, and information security standards promulgated under section 11331 of title 40;

(iii) minimally acceptable system configuration requirements, as determined by the agency; and

      (iv) any other applicable requirements, including standards and guidelines for national security systems issued in accordance with law and as directed by the President;

(3) subordinate plans for providing adequate information security for networks, facilities, and systems or groups of information systems, as appropriate;

(4) security awareness training to inform personnel, including contractors and other users of information systems that support the operations and assets of the agency, of—

      (A) information security risks associated with their activities; and

      (B) their responsibilities in complying with agency policies and procedures designed to reduce these risks;

(5) periodic testing and evaluation of the effectiveness of information security policies, procedures, and practices, to be performed with a frequency depending on risk, but no less than annually, of which such testing—

      (A) shall include testing of management, operational, and technical controls of every information system identified in the inventory required under section 3505(c); and

      (B) may include testing relied on in a evaluation under section 3545;

(6) a process for planning, implementing, evaluating, and documenting remedial action to address any deficiencies in the information security policies, procedures, and practices of the agency;

(7) procedures for detecting, reporting, and responding to security incidents, consistent with standards and guidelines issued pursuant to section 3546(b), including—

      (A) mitigating risks associated with such incidents before substantial damage is done;

      (B) notifying and consulting with the Federal information security incident center referred to in section 3546; and

      (C) notifying and consulting with, as appropriate—

            (i) law enforcement agencies and relevant Offices of Inspector General;

            (ii) an office designated by the President for any incident involving a national security system; and

            (iii) any other agency or office, in accordance with law or as directed by the President; and

(8) plans and procedures to ensure continuity of operations for information systems that support the operations and assets of the agency.

(c) AGENCY REPORTING.—Each agency shall—

    (1) report annually to the Director, the Committees on Government Reform and Science of the House of Representatives, the Committees on Governmental Affairs and Commerce , Science, and Transportation of the Senate, the appropriate authorization and appropriations committees of Congress, and the Comptroller General on the adequacy and effectiveness of information security policies, procedures, and practices, and compliance with the requirements of this subchapter, including compliance with each requirement of subsection (b);

    (2) address the adequacy and effectiveness of information security policies, procedures, and practices in plans and reports relating to—

        (A) annual agency budgets;

        (B) information resources management under subchapter 1 of this chapter;

        (C) information technology management under subtitle III of title 40;

        (D) program performance under sections 1105 and 1115 through 1119 of title 31, and sections 2801 and 2805 of title 39;

        (E) financial management under chapter 9 of title 31, and the Chief Financial Officers Act of 1990 (31 U.S.C. §501 note; Public Law 101-576) (and the amendments made by that Act);

        (F) financial management systems under the Federal Financial Management Improvement Act (31 U.S.C. §3512 note); and

        (G) internal accounting and administrative controls under section 3512 of title 31, (known as the "Federal Managers Financial Integrity Act"); and

    (3) report any significant deficiency in a policy, procedure, or practice identified under paragraph (1) or (2)—

        (A) as a material weakness in reporting under section 3512 of title 31; and

        (B) if relating to financial management systems, as an instance of a lack of substantial compliance under the Federal Financial Management Improvement Act (31 U.S.C. §3512 note).

(d) PERFORMANCE PLAN.—

    (1) In addition to the requirements of subsection (c), each agency, in consultation with the Director, shall include as part of the performance plan required under section 1115 of title 31 a description of—

        (A) the time periods, and

        (B) the resources, including budget, staffing, and training, that are necessary to implement the program required under subsection (b).

(2) The description under paragraph (1) shall be based on the risk assessments required under subsection (b)(2)(1).

(e) PUBLIC NOTICE AND COMMENT.—Each agency shall provide the public with timely notice and opportunities for comment on proposed information security policies and procedures to the extent that such policies and procedures affect communication with the public.

SEC. 3545. ANNUAL INDEPENDENT EVALUATION.

(a) IN GENERAL.—

> (1) Each year each agency shall have performed an independent evaluation of the information security program and practices of that agency to determine the effectiveness of such program and practices.
>
> (2) Each evaluation under this section shall include—
>
>> (A) testing of the effectiveness of information security policies, procedures, and practices of a representative subset of the agency's information systems;
>>
>> (B) an assessment (made on the basis of the results of the testing) of compliance with—
>>
>>> (i) the requirements of this subchapter; and
>>>
>>> (ii) related information security policies, procedures, standards, and guidelines; and
>>
>> (C) separate presentations, as appropriate, regarding information security relating to national security systems.

(b) INDEPENDENT AUDITOR.—Subject to subsection (c)—

> (1) for each agency with an Inspector General appointed under the Inspector General Act of 1978 or any other law, the annual evaluation required by this section shall be performed by the Inspector General or by an independent external auditor, as determined by the Inspector General of the agency; and
>
> (2) for each agency to which paragraph (1) does not apply, the head of the agency shall engage an independent external auditor to perform the evaluation.

(c) NATIONAL SECURITY SYSTEMS.—For each agency operating or exercising control of a national security system, that portion of the evaluation required by this section directly relating to a national security system shall be performed—

> (1) only by an entity designated by the agency head; and
>
> (2) in such a manner as to ensure appropriate protection for information associated with any information security vulnerability in such system commensurate with the risk and in accordance with all applicable laws.

(d) EXISTING EVALUATIONS.—The evaluation required by this section may be based in whole or in part on an audit, evaluation, or report relating to programs or practices of the applicable agency.

(e) AGENCY REPORTING.—

(1) Each year, not later than such date established by the Director, the head of each agency shall submit to the Director the results of the evaluation required under this section.

(2) To the extent an evaluation required under this section directly relates to a national security system, the evaluation results submitted to the Director shall contain only a summary and assessment of that portion of the evaluation directly relating to a national security system.

(f) PROTECTION OF INFORMATION.—Agencies and evaluators shall take appropriate steps to ensure the protection of information which, if disclosed, may adversely affect information security. Such protections shall be commensurate with the risk and comply with all applicable laws and regulations.

(g) OMB REPORTS TO CONGRESS.—

(1) The Director shall summarize the results of the evaluations conducted under this section in the report to Congress required under section 3543(a)(8).

(2) The Director's report to Congress under this subsection shall summarize information regarding information security relating to national security systems in such a manner as to ensure appropriate protection for information associated with any information security vulnerability in such system commensurate with the risk and in accordance with all applicable laws.

(3) Evaluations and any other descriptions of information systems under the authority and control of the Director of Central Intelligence or of National Foreign Intelligence Programs systems under the authority and control of the Secretary of Defense shall be made available to Congress only through the appropriate oversight committees of Congress, in accordance with applicable laws.

(h) COMPTROLLER GENERAL.—The Comptroller General shall periodically evaluate and report to Congress on—

(1) the adequacy and effectiveness of agency information security policies and practices; and

(2) implementation of the requirements of this subchapter.

SEC. 3546. FEDERAL INFORMATION SECURITY INCIDENT CENTER.

(a) IN GENERAL.—The Director shall ensure the operation of a central Federal information security incident center to—

(1) provide timely technical assistance to operators of agency information systems regarding security incidents, including guidance on detecting and handling information security incidents;

(2) compile and analyze information about incidents that threaten information security;

(3) inform operators of agency information systems about current and potential information security threats, and vulnerabilities; and

(4) consult with the National Institute of Standards and Technology, agencies or offices operating or exercising control of national security systems (including the National Security Agency), and such other agencies or offices in accordance with law and as directed by the President regarding information security incidents and related matters.

(b) NATIONAL SECURITY SYSTEMS.—Each agency operating or exercising control of a national security system shall share information about information security incidents, threats, and vulnerabilities with the Federal information security incident center to the extent consistent with standards and guidelines for national security systems, issued in accordance with law and as directed by the President.

SEC. 3547. NATIONAL SECURITY SYSTEMS.

The head of each agency operating or exercising control of a national security system shall be responsible for ensuring that the agency—

(1) provides information security protections commensurate with the risk and magnitude of the harm resulting from the unauthorized access, use, disclosure, disruption, modification, or destruction of the information contained in such system;

(2) implements information security policies and practices as required by standards and guidelines for national security systems, issued in accordance with law and as directed by the President; and

(3) complies with the requirements of this subchapter.

SEC. 3548. AUTHORIZATION OF APPROPRIATIONS.

There are authorized to be appropriated to carry out the provisions of this subchapter such sums as may be necessary for each of fiscal years 2003 through 2007.

SEC. 3549. EFFECT ON EXISTING LAW.

Nothing in this subchapter, section 11331 of title 40, or section 20 of the National Standards and Technology Act (15 U.S.C. §278g-3) may be construed as affecting the authority of the President, the Office of Management and Budget or the Director thereof, the National Institute of Standards and Technology, or the head of any agency, with respect to the authorized use or disclosure of information, including with regard to the protection of personal privacy under section 552a of title 5, the disclosure of information under section 552 of title 5, the management and disposition of records under chapters 29, 31, or 33 of title

44, the management of information resources under subchapter I of chapter 35 of this title, or the disclosure of information to the Congress or the Comptroller General of the United States. While this subchapter is in effect, subchapter II of this chapter shall not apply.

AMENDMENTS TO:

TITLE 40 UNITED STATES CODE
CHAPTER 113–RESPONSIBILITY FOR ACQUISITIONS
OF INFORMATION TECHNOLOGY
SUBCHAPTER III–OTHER RESPONSIBILITIES

SEC. 11331. RESPONSIBILITIES FOR FEDERAL INFORMATION SYSTEMS STANDARDS.

(a) DEFINITION.—In this section, the term "information security" has the meaning given that term in section 3532(b)(1) of title 44

(b) REQUIREMENT TO PRESCRIBE STANDARDS.

    (1)IN GENERAL.—

        (A) REQUIREMENT.—Except as provided under paragraph (2), the Director of the Office of Management and Budget shall, on the basis of proposed standards developed by the National Institute of Standards and Technology pursuant to paragraphs (2) and (3) of section 20(a) of the National Institute of Standards and Technology Act (15 U.S.C. 278g-3(a)) and in consultation with the Secretary of Homeland Security, promulgate information security standards pertaining to Federal information systems.

        (B) REQUIRED STANDARDS.—Standards promulgated under subparagraph (A) shall include—

            (i) standards that provide minimum information security requirements as determined under section 20(b) of the National Institute of Standards and Technology Act (15 U.S.C. 278g-3(b)); and

            (ii) such standards that are otherwise necessary to improve the efficiency of operation or security of Federal information systems.

(c)APPLICATION OF MORE STRINGENT STANDARDS.—The head of an agency may employ standards for the cost-effective information security for all operations and assets within or under the supervision of that agency that are more stringent than the standards promulgated by the Director under this section, if such standards—

(1) contain, at a minimum, the provisions of those applicable standards made compulsory and binding by the Director; and

(2) are otherwise consistent with policies and guidelines issued under section 3533 of title 44.

(d)REQUIREMENTS REGARDING DECISIONS BY DIRECTOR.—

(1) DEADLINE. —The decision regarding the promulgation of any standard by the Director under subsection (b) shall occur not later than 6 months after the submission of the proposed standard to the Director by the National Institute of Standards and Technology, as provided under section 20 of the National Institute of Standards and Technology Act (15 U.S.C. 278g-3).

(2) NOTICE AND COMMENT. —A decision by the Director to significantly modify, or not promulgate a proposed standard submitted to the Director by the National Institute of Standards and Technology, as provided under section 20 of the National Institute of Standards and Technology Act (15 U.S.C. 278g-3), shall be made after the public is given an opportunity to comment on the Director's proposed decision.

AMENDMENTS TO:
NATIONAL INSTITUTE OF STANDARDS AND TECHNOLOGY ACT
SECTIONS 20 AND 21

COMPUTER STANDARDS PROGRAM

SECTION 20 [15 U.S.C. §278g-3].

(a) IN GENERAL. The Institute shall—

(1) have the mission of developing standards, guidelines, and associated methods and techniques for information systems;

(2) develop standards and guidelines, including minimum requirements, for information systems used or operated by an agency or by a contractor of an agency or other organization on behalf of an agency, other than national security systems (as defined in section 3532(b)(2) of title 44);

(3) develop standards and guidelines, including minimum requirements, for providing adequate information security for all agency operations and assets, but such standards and guidelines shall not apply to national security systems; and

(4) carry out the responsibilities described in paragraph (3) through the Computer Security Division.

(b) MINIMUM REQUIREMENTS FOR STANDARDS AND GUIDELINES.—The standards and guidelines required by subsection (a) of this section shall include, at a minimum—

(1)

(A) standards to be used by all agencies to categorize all information and information

systems collected or maintained by or on behalf of each agency based on the objectives

of providing appropriate levels of information security according to a range of risk levels;

(B) guidelines recommending the types of information and information systems to be included in each such category; and

(C) minimum information security requirements for information and information systems in each such category;

(2) a definition of and guidelines concerning detection and handling of information security incidents; and

(3) guidelines developed in coordination with the National Security Agency for identifying an information system as a national security system consistent with applicable requirements for national security systems, issued in accordance with law and as directed by the President.

(c) DEVELOPMENT OF STANDARDS AND GUIDELINES.—In developing standards and guidelines required by subsections (a) and (b) of this section, the Institute shall—

(1) consult with other agencies and offices (including, but not limited to, the Director of the Office of Management and Budget, the Departments of Defense and Energy, the National Security Agency, the Government Accountability Office, and the Secretary of Homeland Security) to assure—

(A) use of appropriate information security policies, procedures, and techniques, in order to improve information security and avoid unnecessary and costly duplication of effort; and

(B) that such standards and guidelines are complementary with standards and guidelines employed for the protection of national security systems and information contained in such systems;

(2) provide the public with an opportunity to comment on proposed standards and guidelines;

(3) submit to the Director of the Office of Management and Budget for promulgation under section 11331 of title 40—

(A) standards, as required under subsection (b)(1)(A) of this section, no later than 12 months after November 25, 2002; and

   (B) minimum information security requirements for each
   category, as required under subsection (b)(1)(C) of this section,
   no later than 36 months after November 25, 2002;
  (4) issue guidelines as required under subsection (b)(1)(B) of this
  section, no later than 18 months after November 25, 2002;
  (5) ensure that such standards and guidelines do not require specific
  technological solutions or products, including any specific hardware or
  software security solutions;
  (6) ensure that such standards and guidelines provide for sufficient
  flexibility to permit alternative solutions to provide equivalent levels of
  protection for identified information security risks; and
  (7) use flexible, performance-based standards and guidelines that, to the
  greatest extent possible, permit the use of off-the-shelf commercially
  developed information security products.
 (d) INFORMATION SECURITY FUNCTIONS. The Institute shall—
  (1) submit standards developed pursuant to subsection (a) of this section,
  along with recommendations as to the extent to which these should be
  made compulsory and binding, to the Director of the Office of
  Management and Budget for promulgation under section 11331 of title
  40;
  (2) provide assistance to agencies regarding—
   (A) compliance with the standards and guidelines developed
   under subsection (a) of this section;
   (B) detecting and handling information security incidents; and
   (C) information security policies, procedures, and practices;
  (3) conduct research, as needed, to determine the nature and extent of
  information security vulnerabilities and techniques for providing cost-
  effective information security;
  (4) develop and periodically revise performance indicators and measures
  for agency information security policies and practices;
  (5) evaluate private sector information security policies and practices and
  commercially available information technologies to assess potential
  application by agencies to strengthen information security;
  (6) evaluate security policies and practices developed for national
  security systems to assess potential application by agencies to strengthen
  information security;
  (7) periodically assess the effectiveness of standards and guidelines
  developed under this section and undertake revisions as appropriate;
  (8) solicit and consider the recommendations of the Information Security
  and Privacy Advisory Board, established by section 278g-4 of this title,
  regarding standards and guidelines developed under subsection (a) of this
  section and submit such recommendations to the Director of the Office

of Management and Budget with such standards submitted to the Director; and

(9) prepare an annual public report on activities undertaken in the previous year, and planned for the coming year, to carry out responsibilities under this section.

(e) DEFINITIONS.—As used in this section—

(1) the term "agency" has the same meaning as provided in section 3502(1) of title 44;

(2) the term "information security" has the same meaning as provided in section 3532(1) of such title;

(3) the term "information system" has the same meaning as provided in section 3502(8) of such title;

(4) the term "information technology" has the same meaning as provided in section 11101 of title 40; and

(5) the term "national security system" has the same meaning as provided in section 3532(b)(2) of such title.

INFORMATION SECURITY AND PRIVACY ADVISORY BOARD

SEC. 21. [15 U.S.C. §278g-4].

(a) ESTABLISHMENT AND COMPOSITION.—There is hereby established an Information Security and Privacy Advisory Board within the Department of Commerce. The Secretary of Commerce shall appoint the chairman of the Board. The Board shall be composed of twelve additional members appointed by the Secretary of Commerce as follows:

(1) four members from outside the Federal Government who are eminent in the information technology industry, at least one of whom is representative of small or medium sized companies in such industries;

(2) four members from outside the Federal Government who are eminent in the fields of information technology, or related disciplines, but who are not employed by or representative of a producer of information technology; and

(3) four members from the Federal Government who have information system management experience, including experience in information security and privacy, at least one of whom shall be from the National Security Agency.

(b) DUTIES.—The duties of the Board shall be—

(1) to identify emerging managerial, technical, administrative, and physical safeguard issues relative to information security and privacy;

(2) to advise the Institute, the Secretary of Commerce, and the Director of the Office of Management and Budget on information security and privacy issues pertaining to Federal Government information systems,

696

including through review of proposed standards and guidelines developed under section 278g-3 of this title; and

(3) to report annually its findings to the Secretary of Commerce, the Director of the Office of Management and Budget, the Director of the National Security Agency, and the appropriate committees of the Congress.

(c) TERM OF OFFICE.—The term of office of each member of the Board shall be four years, except that—

(1) of the initial members, three shall be appointed for terms of one year, three shall be appointed for terms of two years, three shall be appointed for terms of three years, and three shall be appointed for terms of four years; and

(2) any member appointed to fill a vacancy in the Board shall serve for the remainder of the term for which his predecessor was appointed.

(d) QUORUM.—The Board shall not act in the absence of a quorum, which shall consist of seven members.

(e) ALLOWANCE FOR TRAVEL EXPENSES.—Members of the Board, other than full-time employees of the Federal Government, while attending meetings of such committees or while otherwise performing duties at the request of the Board Chairman while away from their homes or a regular place of business, may be allowed travel expenses in accordance with subchapter I of chapter 57 of title 5.

(f) MEETINGS. —The Board shall hold meetings at such locations and at such time and place as determined by a majority of the Board.

(g) STAFF SERVICES AND UTILIZATION OF FEDERAL PERSONNEL.—To provide the staff services necessary to assist the Board in carrying out its functions, the Board may utilize personnel from the Institute or any other agency of the Federal Government with the consent of the head of the agency.

(h) DEFINITIONS.—As used in this section, the terms "information system" and "information technology" have the meanings given in section 278g-3 of this title.

WAR CRIMES ACT OF 1996

SHORT TITLE.

SECTION 1. This Act may be cited as the `War Crimes Act of 1996'.

CRIMINAL PENALTIES FOR CERTAIN WAR CRIMES.

SEC. 2.

(a) IN GENERAL—Title 18, United States Code, is amended by inserting after chapter 117 the following:

(a) OFFENSE.—Whoever, whether inside or outside the United States, commits a war crime, in any of the circumstances described in subsection (b), shall be fined under this title or imprisoned for life or any term of years, or both, and if death results to the victim, shall also be subject to the penalty of death.

(b) CIRCUMSTANCES.—The circumstances referred to in subsection (a) are that the person committing such war crime or the victim of such war crime is a member of the Armed Forces of the United States or a national of the United States (as defined in section 101 of the Immigration and Nationality Act).

(c) DEFINITION.—As used in this section the term "war crime" means any conduct—

> (1) defined as a grave breach in any of the international conventions signed at Geneva 12 August 1949, or any protocol to such convention to which the United States is a party;
>
> (2) prohibited by Article 23, 25, 27, or 28 of the Annex to the Hague Convention IV, Respecting the Laws and Customs of War on Land, signed 18 October 1907;
>
> (3) which constitutes a grave breach of common Article 3 (as defined in subsection (d)) when committed in the context of and in association with an armed conflict not of an international character; or
>
> (4) of a person who, in relation to an armed conflict and contrary to the provisions of the Protocol on Prohibitions or Restrictions on the Use of Mines, Booby-Traps and Other Devices as amended at Geneva on 3 May 1996 (Protocol II as amended on 3 May 1996), when the United States is a party to such Protocol, willfully kills or causes serious injury to civilians.

(d) COMMON ARTICLE 3 VIOLATIONS.—

> (1) PROHIBITED CONDUCT.—In subsection (c)(3), the term "grave breach of common Article 3" means any conduct (such conduct constituting a grave breach of common Article 3 of the international conventions done at Geneva August 12, 1949), as follows:

(A) TORTURE.—The act of a person who commits, or conspires or attempts to commit, an act specifically intended to inflict severe physical or mental pain or suffering (other than pain or suffering incidental to lawful sanctions) upon another person within his custody or physical control for the purpose of obtaining information or a confession, punishment, intimidation, coercion, or any reason based on discrimination of any kind.

(B) CRUEL OR INHUMAN TREATMENT.—The act of a person who commits, or conspires or attempts to commit, an act intended to inflict severe or serious physical or mental pain or suffering (other than pain or suffering incidental to lawful sanctions), including serious physical abuse, upon another within his custody or control.

(C) PERFORMING BIOLOGICAL EXPERIMENTS.—The act of a person who subjects, or conspires or attempts to subject, one or more persons within his custody or physical control to biological experiments without a legitimate medical or dental purpose and in so doing endangers the body or health of such person or persons.

(D) MURDER.—The act of a person who intentionally kills, or conspires or attempts to kill, or kills whether intentionally or unintentionally in the course of committing any other offense under this subsection, one or more persons taking no active part in the hostilities, including those placed out of combat by sickness, wounds, detention, or any other cause.

(E) MUTILATION OR MAIMING.—The act of a person who intentionally injures, or conspires or attempts to injure, or injures whether intentionally or unintentionally in the course of committing any other offense under this subsection, one or more persons taking no active part in the hostilities, including those placed out of combat by sickness, wounds, detention, or any other cause, by disfiguring the person or persons by any mutilation thereof or by permanently disabling any member, limb, or organ of his body, without any legitimate medical or dental purpose.

(F) INTENTIONALLY CAUSING SERIOUS BODILY INJURY.—The act of a person who intentionally causes, or conspires or attempts to cause, serious bodily injury to one or more persons, including lawful combatants, in violation of the law of war.

(G) RAPE.—The act of a person who forcibly or with coercion or threat of force wrongfully invades, or conspires or attempts to invade, the body of a person by penetrating, however slightly, the anal or genital opening of the victim with any part of the body of the accused, or with any foreign object.

(H) SEXUAL ASSAULT OR ABUSE.—The act of a person who forcibly or with coercion or threat of force engages, or conspires or attempts to engage, in sexual contact with one or more persons, or causes, or conspires or attempts to cause, one or more persons to engage in sexual contact.

(I) TAKING HOSTAGES.—The act of a person who, having knowingly seized or detained one or more persons, threatens to kill, injure, or continue to detain such person or persons with the intent of compelling any nation, person other than the hostage, or group of persons to act or refrain from acting as an explicit or implicit condition for the safety or release of such person or persons.

(2) DEFINITIONS.—In the case of an offense under subsection (a) by reason of subsection (c)(3)—

(A) the term "severe mental pain or suffering" shall be applied for purposes of paragraphs (1)(A) and (1)(B) in accordance with the meaning given that term in section 2340(2) of this title;

(B) the term "serious bodily injury" shall be applied for purposes of paragraph (1)(F) in accordance with the meaning given that term in section 113(b)(2) of this title;

(C) the term "sexual contact" shall be applied for purposes of paragraph (1)(G) in accordance with the meaning given that term in section 2246(3) of this title;

(D) the term "serious physical pain or suffering" shall be applied for purposes of paragraph (1)(B) as meaning bodily injury that involves—

(i) a substantial risk of death;

(ii) extreme physical pain;

(iii) a burn or physical disfigurement of a serious nature (other than cuts, abrasions, or bruises); or

(iv) significant loss or impairment of the function of a bodily member, organ, or mental faculty; and

(E) the term "serious mental pain or suffering" shall be applied for purposes of paragraph (1)(B) in accordance with the meaning given the term "severe mental pain or suffering" (as defined in section 2340(2) of this title), except that—

(i) the term "serious" shall replace the term "severe" where it appears; and

(ii) as to conduct occurring after the date of the enactment of the Military Commissions Act of 2006, the

701

term "serious and non-transitory mental harm (which need not be prolonged)" shall replace the term "prolonged mental harm" where it appears.

(3) INAPPLICABILITY OF CERTAIN PROVISIONS WITH RESPECT TO COLLATERAL DAMAGE OR INCIDENT OF LAWFUL ATTACK.—The intent specified for the conduct stated in subparagraphs (D), (E), and (F) or paragraph (1) precludes the applicability of those subparagraphs to an offense under subsection (a) by reasons of subsection (c)(3) with respect to—

    (A) collateral damage; or

    (B) death, damage, or injury incident to a lawful attack.

(4) INAPPLICABILITY OF TAKING HOSTAGES TO PRISONER EXCHANGE.— Paragraph (1)(I) does not apply to an offense under subsection (a) by reason of subsection (c)(3) in the case of a prisoner exchange during wartime.

(5) DEFINITION OF GRAVE BREACHES.—The definitions in this subsection are intended only to define the grave breaches of common Article 3 and not the full scope of United States obligations under that Article."

WIRE AND ELECTRONIC COMMUNICATIONS INTERCEPTION AND INTERCEPTION OF ORAL COMMUNICATIONS

CHAPTER 119 OF TITLE 18, UNITED STATES CODE

Interception and Disclosure of Wire, Oral or Electronic Communications Prohibited

SECTION. 2511.

(1) Except as otherwise specifically provided in this chapter any person who—

(a) intentionally intercepts, endeavors to intercept, or procures any other person to intercept or endeavor to intercept, any wire, oral, or electronic communication;

(b) intentionally uses, endeavors to use, or procures any other person to use or endeavor to use any electronic, mechanical, or other device to intercept any oral communication when—

(i) such device is affixed to, or otherwise transmits a signal through, a wire, cable, or other like connection used in wire communication; or

(ii) such device transmits communications by radio, or interferes with the transmission of such communication; or

(iii) such person knows, or has reason to know, that such device or any component thereof has been sent through the mail or transported in interstate or foreign commerce; or

(iv) such use or endeavor to use (A) takes place on the premises of any business or other commercial establishment the operations of which affect interstate or foreign commerce; or (B) obtains or is for the purpose of obtaining information relating to the operations of any business or other commercial establishment the operations of which affect interstate or foreign commerce; or

(v) such person acts in the District of Columbia, the Commonwealth of Puerto Rico, or any territory or possession of the United States;

(c) intentionally discloses, or endeavors to disclose, to any other person the contents of any wire, oral, or electronic communication, knowing or having reason to know that the information was obtained through the interception of a wire, oral, or electronic communication in violation of this subsection;

(d) intentionally uses, or endeavors to use, the contents of any wire, oral, or electronic communication, knowing or having reason to know that the information was obtained through the interception of a wire, oral, or electronic communication in violation of this subsection; or

(e)(i) intentionally discloses, or endeavors to disclose, to any other person the contents of any wire, oral, or electronic communication, intercepted by

703

means authorized by sections 2511 (2)(a)(ii), 2511 (2)(b)–(c), 2511(2)(e), 2516, and 2518 of this chapter,

(ii) knowing or having reason to know that the information was obtained through the interception of such a communication in connection with a criminal investigation,

(iii) having obtained or received the information in connection with a criminal investigation, and

(iv) with intent to improperly obstruct, impede, or interfere with a duly authorized criminal investigation,

shall be punished as provided in subsection (4) or shall be subject to suit as provided in subsection (5).

(2)(a)(i) It shall not be unlawful under this chapter for an operator of a switchboard, or an officer, employee, or agent of a provider of wire or electronic communication service, whose facilities are used in the transmission of a wire or electronic communication, to intercept, disclose, or use that communication in the normal course of his employment while engaged in any activity which is a necessary incident to the rendition of his service or to the protection of the rights or property of the provider of that service, except that a provider of wire communication service to the public shall not utilize service observing or random monitoring except for mechanical or service quality control checks.

(ii) Notwithstanding any other law, providers of wire or electronic communication service, their officers, employees, and agents, landlords, custodians, or other persons, are authorized to provide information, facilities, or technical assistance to persons authorized by law to intercept wire, oral, or electronic communications or to conduct electronic surveillance, as defined in section 101 of the Foreign Intelligence Surveillance Act of 1978, if such provider, its officers, employees, or agents, landlord, custodian, or other specified person, has been provided with—

(A) a court order directing such assistance or a court order pursuant to section 704 of the Foreign Intelligence Surveillance Act of 1978 signed by the authorizing judge, or

(B) a certification in writing by a person specified in section 2518 (7) of this title or the Attorney General of the United States that no warrant or court order is required by law, that all statutory requirements have been met, and that the specified assistance is required, setting forth the period of time during which the provision of the information, facilities, or technical assistance is authorized and specifying the information, facilities, or technical assistance required. No provider of wire or electronic communication service, officer, employee, or agent thereof, or landlord, custodian, or other specified person shall disclose the existence of any interception or surveillance or the device used to accomplish the interception or surveillance with respect to which the person has been furnished a court order or certification under this chapter, except as may otherwise be required by legal process and then only after prior notification to the Attorney General or to the principal prosecuting attorney of a State or any political subdivision of a State, as may be appropriate. Any such disclosure, shall render such person liable for the civil damages provided for in section 2520. No cause of action shall lie in any court against any provider of wire or electronic communication service, its officers, employees, or agents, landlord, custodian, or other specified person for providing information, facilities, or assistance in accordance with the terms of a court order, statutory authorization, or certification under this chapter.

'(iii) If a certification under subparagraph (ii)(B) for assistance to obtain foreign intelligence information is based on statutory authority, the certification shall identify the specific statutory provision and shall certify that the statutory requirements have been met.

(b) It shall not be unlawful under this chapter for an officer, employee, or agent of the Federal Communications Commission, in the normal course of his employment and in discharge of the monitoring responsibilities exercised by the Commission in the enforcement of chapter 5 of title 47 of the United States Code, to intercept a wire or electronic communication, or oral communication transmitted by radio, or to disclose or use the information thereby obtained.

(c) It shall not be unlawful under this chapter for a person acting under color of law to intercept a wire, oral, or electronic communication, where such person is a party to the communication or one of the parties to the communication has given prior consent to such interception.

(d) It shall not be unlawful under this chapter for a person not acting under color of law to intercept a wire, oral, or electronic communication where such person is a party to the communication or where one of the parties to the communication has given prior consent to such interception unless such communication is intercepted for the purpose of committing any criminal or tortious act in violation of the Constitution or laws of the United States or of any State.

(e) Notwithstanding any other provision of this title or section 705 or 706 of the Communications Act of 1934, it shall not be unlawful for an officer, employee, or agent of the United States in the normal course of his official duty to conduct electronic surveillance, as defined in section 101 of the Foreign Intelligence Surveillance Act of 1978, as authorized by that Act.

(f) Nothing contained in this chapter or chapter 121 or 206 of this title, or section 705 of the Communications Act of 1934, shall be deemed to affect

705

the acquisition by the United States Government of foreign intelligence information from international or foreign communications, or foreign intelligence activities conducted in accordance with otherwise applicable Federal law involving a foreign electronic communications system, utilizing a means other than electronic surveillance as defined in section 101 of the Foreign Intelligence Surveillance Act of 1978, and procedures in this chapter or chapter 121 and the Foreign Intelligence Surveillance Act of 1978 shall be the exclusive means by which electronic surveillance, as defined in section 101 of such Act, and the interception of domestic wire, oral, and electronic communications may be conducted.

(g) It shall not be unlawful under this chapter or chapter 121 of this title for any person—

    (i) to intercept or access an electronic communication made through an electronic communication system that is configured so that such electronic communication is readily accessible to the general public;

    (ii) to intercept any radio communication which is transmitted—

        (I) by any station for the use of the general public, or that relates to ships, aircraft, vehicles, or persons in distress;

        (II) by any governmental, law enforcement, civil defense, private land mobile, or public safety communications system, including police and fire, readily accessible to the general public;

        (III) by a station operating on an authorized frequency within the bands allocated to the amateur, citizens band, or general mobile radio services; or

        (IV) by any marine or aeronautical communications system;

    (iii) to engage in any conduct which—

        (I) is prohibited by section 633 of the Communications Act of 1934; or

        (II) is excepted from the application of section 705(a) of the Communications Act of 1934 by section 705(b) of that Act;

    (iv) to intercept any wire or electronic communication the transmission of which is causing harmful interference to any lawfully operating station or consumer electronic equipment, to the extent necessary to identify the source of such interference; or

    (v) for other users of the same frequency to intercept any radio communication made through a system that utilizes frequencies monitored by individuals engaged in the provision or the use of such system, if such communication is not scrambled or encrypted.

(h) It shall not be unlawful under this chapter—

    (i) to use a pen register or a trap and trace device (as those terms are defined for the purposes of chapter 206 (relating to pen registers and trap and trace devices) of this title); or

(ii) for a provider of electronic communication service to record the fact that a wire or electronic communication was initiated or completed in order to protect such provider, another provider furnishing service toward the completion of the wire or electronic communication, or a user of that service, from fraudulent, unlawful or abusive use of such service.

(i) It shall not be unlawful under this chapter for a person acting under color of law to intercept the wire or electronic communications of a computer trespasser transmitted to, through, or from the protected computer, if—

(I) the owner or operator of the protected computer authorizes the interception of the computer trespasser's communications on the protected computer;

(II) the person acting under color of law is lawfully engaged in an investigation;

(III) the person acting under color of law has reasonable grounds to believe that the contents of the computer trespasser's communications will be relevant to the investigation; and

(IV) such interception does not acquire communications other than those transmitted to or from the computer trespasser.

(3)(a) Except as provided in paragraph (b) of this subsection, a person or entity providing an electronic communication service to the public shall not intentionally divulge the contents of any communication (other than one to such person or entity, or an agent thereof) while in transmission on that service to any person or entity other than an addressee or intended recipient of such communication or an agent of such addressee or intended recipient.

(b) A person or entity providing electronic communication service to the public may divulge the contents of any such communication—

(i) as otherwise authorized in section 2511 (2)(a) or 2517 of this title;

(ii) with the lawful consent of the originator or any addressee or intended recipient of such communication;

(iii) to a person employed or authorized, or whose facilities are used, to forward such communication to its destination; or

(iv) which were inadvertently obtained by the service provider and which appear to pertain to the commission of a crime, if such divulgence is made to a law enforcement agency.

(4)(a) Except as provided in paragraph (b) of this subsection or in subsection (5), whoever violates subsection (1) of this section shall be fined under this title or imprisoned not more than five years, or both.

(b) Conduct otherwise an offense under this subsection that consists of or relates to the interception of a satellite transmission that is not encrypted or scrambled and that is transmitted—

(i) to a broadcasting station for purposes of retransmission to the general public; or

(ii) as an audio subcarrier intended for redistribution to facilities open to the public, but not including data transmissions or telephone calls,

is not an offense under this subsection unless the conduct is for the purposes of direct or indirect commercial advantage or private financial gain.

(5)(a)(i) If the communication is—

(A) a private satellite video communication that is not scrambled or encrypted and the conduct in violation of this chapter is the private viewing of that communication and is not for a tortious or illegal purpose or for purposes of direct or indirect commercial advantage or private commercial gain; or

(B) a radio communication that is transmitted on frequencies allocated under subpart D of part 74 of the rules of the Federal Communications Commission that is not scrambled or encrypted and the conduct in violation of this chapter is not for a tortious or illegal purpose or for purposes of direct or indirect commercial advantage or private commercial gain,

then the person who engages in such conduct shall be subject to suit by the Federal Government in a court of competent jurisdiction.

(ii) In an action under this subsection—

(A) if the violation of this chapter is a first offense for the person under paragraph (a) of subsection (4) and such person has not been found liable in a civil action under section 2520 of this title, the Federal Government shall be entitled to appropriate injunctive relief; and

(B) if the violation of this chapter is a second or subsequent offense under paragraph (a) of subsection (4) or such person has been found liable in any prior civil action under section 2520, the person shall be subject to a mandatory $500 civil fine.

(b) The court may use any means within its authority to enforce an injunction issued under paragraph (ii)(A), and shall impose a civil fine of not less than $500 for each violation of such an injunction.

IMPLEMENTING RECOMMENDATIONS OF THE 9/11 COMMISSION ACT OF 2007

(Public Law 110-53 of August 3, 2007)

AN ACT To provide for the implementation of the recommendations of the National Commission on Terrorist Attacks Upon the United States.

Be it enacted by the Senate and House of Representatives of the United States of America in Congress assembled

SHORT TITLE; TABLE OF CONTENTS

SECTION 1.

(a) SHORT TITLE—This Act may be cited as the `Implementing Recommendations of the 9/11 Commission Act of 2007'.

(b) TABLE OF CONTENTS—The table of contents for this Act is as follows:

TITLE V—IMPROVING INTELLIGENCE AND INFORMATION SHARING WITHIN THE FEDERAL GOVERNMENT AND WITH STATE, LOCAL, AND TRIBAL GOVERNMENTS

[Amendments omitted here – see the Intelligence Reform and Terrorism Prevention Act and Homeland Security Act in this book]

TITLE VI—CONGRESSIONAL OVERSIGHT OF INTELLIGENCE

AVAILABILITY TO PUBLIC OF CERTAIN INTELLIGENCE FUNDING INFORMATION.

SEC. 601.

(a) Amounts Appropriated Each Fiscal Year—Not later than 30 days after the end of each fiscal year beginning with fiscal year 2007, the Director of National Intelligence shall disclose to the public the aggregate amount of funds appropriated by Congress for the National Intelligence Program for such fiscal year.

(b) Waiver—Beginning with fiscal year 2009, the President may waive or postpone the disclosure required by subsection (a) for any fiscal year by, not later than 30 days after the end of such fiscal year, submitting to the Select Committee on Intelligence of the Senate and Permanent Select Committee on Intelligence of the House of Representatives—

(1) a statement, in unclassified form, that the disclosure required in subsection (a) for that fiscal year would damage national security; and

718

(2) a statement detailing the reasons for the waiver or postponement, which may be submitted in classified form.

(c) Definition—As used in this section, the term `National Intelligence Program' has the meaning given the term in section 3(6) of the National Security Act of 1947 (50 U.S.C. 401a(6)).

SEC. 602. [Omitted.]

SENSE OF THE SENATE REGARDING A REPORT ON THE 9/11 COMMISSION RECOMMENDATIONS WITH RESPECT TO INTELLIGENCE REFORM AND CONGRESSIONAL INTELLIGENCE OVERSIGHT REFORM.

SEC. 603.

(a) Findings—Congress makes the following findings:

(1) The National Commission on Terrorist Attacks Upon the United States (referred to in this section as the `9/11 Commission') conducted a lengthy review of the facts and circumstances relating to the terrorist attacks of September 11, 2001, including those relating to the intelligence community, law enforcement agencies, and the role of congressional oversight and resource allocation.

(2) In its final report, the 9/11 Commission found that—

(A) congressional oversight of the intelligence activities of the United States is dysfunctional;

(B) under the rules of the Senate and the House of Representatives in effect at the time the report was completed, the committees of Congress charged with oversight of the intelligence activities lacked the power, influence, and sustained capability to meet the daunting challenges faced by the intelligence community of the United States;

(C) as long as such oversight is governed by such rules of the Senate and the House of Representatives, the people of the United States will not get the security they want and need;

(D) a strong, stable, and capable congressional committee structure is needed to give the intelligence community of the United States appropriate oversight, support, and leadership; and

(E) the reforms recommended by the 9/11 Commission in its final report will not succeed if congressional oversight of the intelligence community in the United States is not changed.

(3) The 9/11 Commission recommended structural changes to Congress to improve the oversight of intelligence activities.

(4) Congress has enacted some of the recommendations made by the 9/11 Commission and is considering implementing additional recommendations of the 9/11 Commission.

719

(5) The Senate adopted Senate Resolution 445 in the 108th Congress to address some of the intelligence oversight recommendations of the 9/11 Commission by abolishing term limits for the members of the Select Committee on Intelligence, clarifying jurisdiction for intelligence-related nominations, and streamlining procedures for the referral of intelligence-related legislation, but other aspects of the 9/11 Commission recommendations regarding intelligence oversight have not been implemented.

(b) Sense of the Senate—It is the sense of the Senate that the Committee on Homeland Security and Governmental Affairs and the Select Committee on Intelligence of the Senate each, or jointly, should—

(1) undertake a review of the recommendations made in the final report of the 9/11 Commission with respect to intelligence reform and congressional intelligence oversight reform;

(2) review and consider any other suggestions, options, or recommendations for improving intelligence oversight; and

(3) not later than December 21, 2007, submit to the Senate a report that includes the recommendations of the committees, if any, for carrying out such reforms.

SEC. 604. [Omitted.]

AVAILABILITY OF THE EXECUTIVE SUMMARY OF THE REPORT ON CENTRAL INTELLIGENCE AGENCY ACCOUNTABILITY REGARDING THE TERRORIST ATTACKS OF SEPTEMBER 11, 2001.

SEC. 605.

(a) Public Availability—Not later than 30 days after the date of the enactment of this Act, the Director of the Central Intelligence Agency shall prepare and make available to the public a version of the Executive Summary of the report entitled the 'Office of Inspector General Report on Central Intelligence Agency Accountability Regarding Findings and Conclusions of the Joint Inquiry into Intelligence Community Activities Before and After the Terrorist Attacks of September 11, 2001' issued in June 2005 that is declassified to the maximum extent possible, consistent with national security.

(b) Report to Congress—The Director of the Central Intelligence Agency shall submit to Congress a classified annex to the redacted Executive Summary made available under subsection (a) that explains the reason that any redacted material in the Executive Summary was withheld from the public.

TITLE VIII—PRIVACY AND CIVIL LIBERTIES

MODIFICATION OF AUTHORITIES RELATING TO PRIVACY AND CIVIL LIBERTIES OVERSIGHT BOARD.

SEC. 801.

(a) [Omitted. See the Intelligence Reform and Terrorism Prevention Act and Homeland Security Act in this book]

(b) Security Rules and Procedures—The Privacy and Civil Liberties Oversight Board shall promptly adopt the security rules and procedures required under section 1061(k)(2) of the National Security Intelligence Reform Act of 2004 (as added by subsection (a) of this section).

(c) Transition Provisions—

(1) TREATMENT OF INCUMBENT MEMBERS OF THE PRIVACY AND CIVIL LIBERTIES OVERSIGHT BOARD—

(A) CONTINUATION OF SERVICE—Any individual who is a member of the Privacy and Civil Liberties Oversight Board on the date of enactment of this Act may continue to serve on the Board until 180 days after the date of enactment of this Act.

(B) TERMINATION OF TERMS—The term of any individual who is a member of the Privacy and Civil Liberties Oversight Board on the date of enactment of this Act shall terminate 180 days after the date of enactment of this Act.

(2) APPOINTMENTS—

(A) IN GENERAL—The President and the Senate shall take such actions as necessary for the President, by and with the advice and consent of the Senate, to appoint members to the Privacy and Civil Liberties Oversight Board as constituted under the amendments made by subsection (a) in a timely manner to provide for the continuing operation of the Board and orderly implementation of this section.

(B) DESIGNATIONS—In making the appointments described under subparagraph (A) of the first members of the Privacy and Civil Liberties Oversight Board as constituted under the amendments made by subsection (a), the President shall provide for the members to serve terms of 2, 3, 4, 5, and 6 years beginning on the effective date described under subsection (d)(1), with the term of each such member to be designated by the President.

(d) Effective Date—

(1) IN GENERAL—The amendments made by subsection (a) and subsection (b) shall take effect 180 days after the date of enactment of this Act.

(2) TRANSITION PROVISIONS—Subsection (c) shall take effect on the date of enactment of this Act.

SEC. 802. [Omitted.]

SEC. 803. [Omitted. See the Intelligence Reform and Terrorism Prevention Act and Homeland Security Act in this book]

FEDERAL AGENCY DATA MINING REPORTING ACT OF 2007.

SEC. 804.

(a) Short Title—This section may be cited as the `Federal Agency Data Mining Reporting Act of 2007'.

(b) Definitions—In this section:

(1) DATA MINING—The term `data mining' means a program involving pattern-based queries, searches, or other analyses of 1 or more electronic databases, where—

(A) a department or agency of the Federal Government, or a non-Federal entity acting on behalf of the Federal Government, is conducting the queries, searches, or other analyses to discover or locate a predictive pattern or anomaly indicative of terrorist or criminal activity on the part of any individual or individuals;

(B) the queries, searches, or other analyses are not subject-based and do not use personal identifiers of a specific individual, or inputs associated with a specific individual or group of individuals, to retrieve information from the database or databases; and

(C) the purpose of the queries, searches, or other analyses is not solely—

(i) the detection of fraud, waste, or abuse in a Government agency or program; or

(ii) the security of a Government computer system.

(2) DATABASE—The term `database' does not include telephone directories, news reporting, information publicly available to any member of the public without payment of a fee, or databases of judicial and administrative opinions or other legal research sources.

(c) Reports on Data Mining Activities by Federal Agencies—

(1) REQUIREMENT FOR REPORT—The head of each department or agency of the Federal Government that is engaged in any activity to use or develop data mining shall submit a report to Congress on all such activities of the department or agency under the jurisdiction of that official. The report shall be produced in coordination with the privacy officer of that department or agency, if applicable, and shall be made available to the public, except for an annex described in subparagraph (C).

(2) CONTENT OF REPORT—Each report submitted under subparagraph (A) shall include, for each activity to use or develop data mining, the following information:

(A) A thorough description of the data mining activity, its goals, and, where appropriate, the target dates for the deployment of the data mining activity.

(B) A thorough description of the data mining technology that is being used or will be used, including the basis for determining whether a particular pattern or anomaly is indicative of terrorist or criminal activity.

(C) A thorough description of the data sources that are being or will be used.

(D) An assessment of the efficacy or likely efficacy of the data mining activity in providing accurate information consistent with and valuable to the stated goals and plans for the use or development of the data mining activity.

(E) An assessment of the impact or likely impact of the implementation of the data mining activity on the privacy and civil liberties of individuals, including a thorough description of the actions that are being taken or will be taken with regard to the property, privacy, or other rights or privileges of any individual or individuals as a result of the implementation of the data mining activity.

(F) A list and analysis of the laws and regulations that govern the information being or to be collected, reviewed, gathered, analyzed, or used in conjunction with the data mining activity, to the extent applicable in the context of the data mining activity.

(G) A thorough discussion of the policies, procedures, and guidelines that are in place or that are to be developed and applied in the use of such data mining activity in order to—

(i) protect the privacy and due process rights of individuals, such as redress procedures; and

(ii) ensure that only accurate and complete information is collected, reviewed, gathered, analyzed, or used, and guard against any harmful consequences of potential inaccuracies.

(3) ANNEX—

(A) IN GENERAL—A report under subparagraph (A) shall include in an annex any necessary—

(i) classified information;

(ii) law enforcement sensitive information;

(iii) proprietary business information; or

(iv) trade secrets (as that term is defined in section 1839 of title 18, United States Code).

(B) AVAILABILITY—Any annex described in clause (i)—

(i) shall be available, as appropriate, and consistent with the National Security Act of 1947 (50 U.S.C. 401 et seq.), to the Committee on Homeland Security and Governmental Affairs, the Committee on the

Judiciary, the Select Committee on Intelligence, the Committee on Appropriations, and the Committee on Banking, Housing, and Urban Affairs of the Senate and the Committee on Homeland Security, the Committee on the Judiciary, the Permanent Select Committee on Intelligence, the Committee on Appropriations, and the Committee on Financial Services of the House of Representatives; and

(ii) shall not be made available to the public.

(4) TIME FOR REPORT—Each report required under subparagraph (A) shall be—

(A) submitted not later than 180 days after the date of enactment of this Act; and

(B) updated not less frequently than annually thereafter, to include any activity to use or develop data mining engaged in after the date of the prior report submitted under subparagraph (A).

EXECUTIVE ORDER 12139:
EXERCISE OF CERTAIN AUTHORITY
RESPECTING ELECTRONIC SURVEILLANCE

(Federal Register Vol. 60, No. 103 (May 25, 1979),
amended by EO 12333 (1981), EO 13383 (2005), and EO 13475 (2008))

By the authority vested in me as President by Sections 102 and 104 of the Foreign Intelligence Surveillance Act of 1978 (50 U.S.C. 1802 and 1804), in order to provide as set forth in that Act (this chapter) for the authorization of electronic surveillance for foreign intelligence purposes, it is hereby ordered as follows:

1-101. Pursuant to Section 102(a)(1) of the Foreign Intelligence Surveillance Act of 1978 (50 U.S.C. 1802(a)), the Attorney General is authorized to approve electronic surveillance to acquire foreign intelligence information without a court order, but only if the Attorney General makes the certifications required by that Section.

1-102. Pursuant to Section 102(b) of the Foreign Intelligence Act of 1978 (50 U.S.C. 1802(b)), the Attorney General is authorized to approve applications to the court having jurisdiction under Section 103 of that Act (50 U.S.C. 1803) to obtain orders for electronic surveillance for the purpose of obtaining foreign intelligence information.

1-103. Pursuant to Section 104(a)(6) of the Foreign Intelligence Surveillance Act of 1978 (50 U.S.C. 1804(a)(6)), the following officials, each of whom is employed in the area of national security or defense, is designated to make the certifications required by Section 104(a)(6) of the Act in support of applications to conduct electronic surveillance:

(a) Secretary of State.
(b) Secretary of Defense.
(c) Director of National Intelligence.
(d) Director of the Federal Bureau of Investigation.
(e) Deputy Secretary of State.
(f) Deputy Secretary of Defense.
(g) Director of the Central Intelligence Agency
(h) Principal Deputy Director of National Intelligence; and
(i) Deputy Director of the Federal Bureau of Investigation.

None of the above officials, nor anyone officially acting in that capacity, may exercise the authority to make the above certifications, unless that official has been appointed by the President with the advice and consent of the Senate. The requirement of the preceding sentence that the named official must be appointed by the President with the advice and consent of the Senate does not apply to the Deputy Director of the Federal Bureau of Investigation.

1-104. Section 2-202 of Executive Order No. 12036 (set out under section 401 of this title) is amended by inserting the following at the end of that section: "Any electronic surveillance, as defined in the Foreign Intelligence Surveillance Act of 1978, shall be conducted in accordance with that Act as well as this Order.".

1-105. Section 2-203 of Executive Order No. 12036 (set out under section 401 of this title) is amended by inserting the following at the end of that section: "Any monitoring which constitutes   electronic surveillance as defined in the Foreign Intelligence Surveillance Act of 1978 shall be conducted in accordance with that Act as well as this Order.".

-/S/- Jimmy Carter.
THE WHITE HOUSE,
May 23, 1979.

EXECUTIVE ORDER 12333:
UNITED STATES INTELLIGENCE ACTIVITIES

(Federal Register Vol. 40, No. 235 (December 8, 1981),
amended by EO 13284 (2003), EO 13355 (2004), and EO 13470 (2008))

PREAMBLE

Timely, accurate, and insightful information about the activities, capabilities, plans, and intentions of foreign powers, organizations, and persons, and their agents, is essential to the national security of the United States. All reasonable and lawful means must be used to ensure that the United States will receive the best intelligence possible. For that purpose, by virtue of the authority vested in me by the Constitution and the laws of the United States of America, including the National Security Act of 1947, as amended, (Act) and as President of the United States of America, in order to provide for the effective conduct of United States intelligence activities and the protection of constitutional rights, it is hereby ordered as follows:

PART 1 – GOALS, DIRECTIONS, DUTIES, AND RESPONSIBILITIES WITH RESPECT TO UNITED STATES INTELLIGENCE EFFORTS

SECTION 1.1 GOALS. The United States intelligence effort shall provide the President, the National Security Council, and the Homeland Security Council with the necessary information on which to base decisions concerning the development and conduct of foreign, defense, and economic policies, and the protection of United States national interests from foreign security threats. All departments and agencies shall cooperate fully to fulfill this goal.

(a) All means, consistent with applicable Federal law and this order, and with full consideration of the rights of United States persons, shall be used to obtain reliable intelligence information to protect the United States and its interests.

(b) The United States Government has a solemn obligation, and shall continue in the conduct of intelligence activities under this order, to protect fully the legal rights of all United States persons, including freedoms, civil liberties, and privacy rights guaranteed by Federal law.

(c) Intelligence collection under this order should be guided by the need for information to respond to intelligence priorities set by the President.

(d) Special emphasis should be given to detecting and countering:

(1) Espionage and other threats and activities directed by foreign powers or their intelligence services against the United States and its interests;

(2) Threats to the United States and its interests from terrorism; and

(3) Threats to the United States and its interests from the development, possession, proliferation, or use of weapons of mass destruction.

(e) Special emphasis shall be given to the production of timely, accurate, and insightful reports, responsive to decisionmakers in the executive branch, that draw on all appropriate sources of information, including open source information, meet rigorous analytic standards, consider diverse analytic viewpoints, and accurately represent appropriate alternative views.

(f) State, local, and tribal governments are critical partners in securing and defending the United States from terrorism and other threats to the United States and its interests. Our national intelligence effort should take into account the responsibilities and requirements of State, local, and tribal governments and, as appropriate, private sector entities, when undertaking the collection and dissemination of information and intelligence to protect the United States.

(g) All departments and agencies have a responsibility to prepare and to provide intelligence in a manner that allows the full and free exchange of information, consistent with applicable law and presidential guidance.

SEC. 1.2 THE NATIONAL SECURITY COUNCIL.

(a) PURPOSE. The National Security Council (NSC) shall act as the highest ranking executive branch entity that provides support to the President for review of, guidance for, and direction to the conduct of all foreign intelligence, counterintelligence, and covert action, and attendant policies and programs.

(b) COVERT ACTION AND OTHER SENSITIVE INTELLIGENCE OPERATIONS. The NSC shall consider and submit to the President a policy recommendation, including all dissents, on each proposed covert action and conduct a periodic review of ongoing covert action activities, including an evaluation of the effectiveness and consistency with current national policy of such activities and consistency with applicable legal requirements. The NSC shall perform such other functions related to covert action as the President may direct, but shall not undertake the conduct of covert actions. The NSC shall also review proposals for other sensitive intelligence operations.

SEC. 1.3 DIRECTOR OF NATIONAL INTELLIGENCE. Subject to the authority, direction, and control of the President, the Director of National Intelligence (Director) shall serve as the head of the Intelligence Community, act as the principal adviser to the President, to the NSC, and to the Homeland Security Council for intelligence matters related to national security, and shall oversee and direct the implementation of the National Intelligence Program and execution of the National Intelligence Program budget. The Director will lead a unified, coordinated, and effective intelligence effort. In addition, the Director shall, in carrying out the duties and responsibilities under this section, take into account the views of the heads of departments containing an element of the Intelligence Community and of the Director of the Central Intelligence Agency.

(a) Except as otherwise directed by the President or prohibited by law, the Director shall have access to all information and intelligence described in section 1.5(a) of this order. For the purpose of access to and sharing of information and intelligence, the Director:

(1) Is hereby assigned the function under section 3(5) of the Act, to determine that intelligence, regardless of the source from which derived and including information gathered within or outside the United States, pertains to more than one United States Government agency; and

(2) Shall develop guidelines for how information or intelligence is provided to or accessed by the Intelligence Community in accordance with section 1.5(a) of this order, and for how the information or intelligence may be used and shared by the Intelligence Community. All guidelines developed in accordance with this section shall be approved by the Attorney General and, where applicable, shall be consistent with guidelines issued pursuant to section 1016 of the Intelligence Reform and Terrorism Protection Act of 2004 (Public Law 108-458) (IRTPA).

(b) In addition to fulfilling the obligations and responsibilities prescribed by the Act, the Director:

(1) Shall establish objectives, priorities, and guidance for the Intelligence Community to ensure timely and effective collection, processing, analysis, and dissemination of intelligence, of whatever nature and from whatever source derived;

(2) May designate, in consultation with affected heads of departments or Intelligence Community elements, one or more Intelligence Community elements to develop and to maintain services of common concern on behalf of the Intelligence Community if the Director determines such services can be more efficiently or effectively accomplished in a consolidated manner;

(3) Shall oversee and provide advice to the President and the NSC with respect to all ongoing and proposed covert action programs;

(4) In regard to the establishment and conduct of intelligence arrangements and agreements with foreign governments and international organizations:

(A) May enter into intelligence and counterintelligence arrangements and agreements with foreign governments and international organizations;

(B) Shall formulate policies concerning intelligence and counterintelligence arrangements and agreements with foreign governments and international organizations; and

(C) Shall align and synchronize intelligence and counterintelligence foreign relationships among the elements of the Intelligence Community to further United States national security, policy, and intelligence objectives;

(5) Shall participate in the development of procedures approved by the Attorney General governing criminal drug intelligence activities abroad to ensure that these activities are consistent with foreign intelligence programs;

(6) Shall establish common security and access standards for managing and handling intelligence systems, information, and products, with special emphasis on facilitating:

(A) The fullest and most prompt access to and dissemination of information and intelligence practicable, assigning the highest priority to detecting, preventing, preempting, and disrupting terrorist threats and activities against the United States, its interests, and allies; and

(B) The establishment of standards for an interoperable information sharing enterprise that facilitates the sharing of intelligence information among elements of the Intelligence Community;

(7) Shall ensure that appropriate departments and agencies have access to intelligence and receive the support needed to perform independent analysis;

(8) Shall protect, and ensure that programs are developed to protect, intelligence sources, methods, and activities from unauthorized disclosure;

(9) Shall, after consultation with the heads of affected departments and agencies, establish guidelines for Intelligence Community elements for:

(A) Classification and declassification of all intelligence and intelligence-related information classified under the authority of the Director or the authority of the head of a department or Intelligence Community element; and

(B) Access to and dissemination of all intelligence and intelligence-related information, both in its final form and in the form when initially gathered, to include intelligence originally classified by the head of a department or Intelligence Community element, except that access to and dissemination of information concerning United States persons shall be governed by procedures developed in accordance with Part 2 of this order;

(10) May, only with respect to Intelligence Community elements, and after consultation with the head of the originating Intelligence Community element or the head of the originating department, declassify, or direct the declassification of, information or intelligence relating to intelligence sources, methods, and activities. The Director

may only delegate this authority to the Principal Deputy Director of National Intelligence;

(11) May establish, operate, and direct one or more national intelligence centers to address intelligence priorities;

(12) May establish Functional Managers and Mission Managers, and designate officers or employees of the United States to serve in these positions.

> (A) Functional Managers shall report to the Director concerning the execution of their duties as Functional Managers, and may be charged with developing and implementing strategic guidance, policies, and procedures for activities related to a specific intelligence discipline or set of intelligence activities; set training and tradecraft standards; and ensure coordination within and across intelligence disciplines and Intelligence Community elements and with related non-intelligence activities. Functional Managers may also advise the Director on: the management of resources; policies and procedures; collection capabilities and gaps; processing and dissemination of intelligence; technical architectures; and other issues or activities determined by the Director.
>
> > (i) The Director of the National Security Agency is designated the Functional Manager for signals intelligence;
> >
> > (ii) The Director of the Central Intelligence Agency is designated the Functional Manager for human intelligence; and
> >
> > (iii) The Director of the National Geospatial-Intelligence Agency is designated the Functional Manager for geospatial intelligence.
>
> (B) Mission Managers shall serve as principal substantive advisors on all or specified aspects of intelligence related to designated countries, regions, topics, or functional issues;

(13) Shall establish uniform criteria for the determination of relative priorities for the transmission of critical foreign intelligence, and advise the Secretary of Defense concerning the communications requirements of the Intelligence Community for the transmission of such communications;

(14) Shall have ultimate responsibility for production and dissemination of intelligence produced by the Intelligence Community and authority to levy analytic tasks on intelligence production organizations within the Intelligence Community, in consultation with the heads of the Intelligence Community elements concerned;

(15) May establish advisory groups for the purpose of obtaining advice from within the Intelligence Community to carry out the Director's responsibilities, to include Intelligence Community executive management committees composed of senior Intelligence Community leaders. Advisory groups shall consist of representatives from elements of the Intelligence Community, as designated by the Director, or other executive branch departments, agencies, and offices, as appropriate;

(16) Shall ensure the timely exploitation and dissemination of data gathered by national intelligence collection means, and ensure that the resulting intelligence is disseminated immediately to appropriate government elements, including military commands;

(17) Shall determine requirements and priorities for, and manage and direct the tasking, collection, analysis, production, and dissemination of, national intelligence by elements of the Intelligence Community, including approving requirements for collection and analysis and resolving conflicts in collection requirements and in the tasking of national collection assets of Intelligence Community elements (except when otherwise directed by the President or when the Secretary of Defense exercises collection tasking authority under plans and arrangements approved by the Secretary of Defense and the Director);

(18) May provide advisory tasking concerning collection and analysis of information or intelligence relevant to national intelligence or national security to departments, agencies, and establishments of the United States Government that are not elements of the Intelligence Community; and shall establish procedures, in consultation with affected heads of departments or agencies and subject to approval by the Attorney General, to implement this authority and to monitor or evaluate the responsiveness of United States Government departments, agencies, and other establishments;

(19) Shall fulfill the responsibilities in section 1.3(b)(17) and (18) of this order, consistent with applicable law and with full consideration of the rights of United States persons, whether information is to be collected inside or outside the United States;

(20) Shall ensure, through appropriate policies and procedures, the deconfliction, coordination, and integration of all intelligence activities conducted by an Intelligence Community element or funded by the National Intelligence Program. In accordance with these policies and procedures:

    (A) The Director of the Federal Bureau of Investigation shall coordinate the clandestine collection of foreign intelligence collected through human sources or through human-enabled means and counterintelligence activities inside the United States;

(B) The Director of the Central Intelligence Agency shall coordinate the clandestine collection of foreign intelligence collected through human sources or through human-enabled means and counterintelligence activities outside the United States;

(C) All policies and procedures for the coordination of counterintelligence activities and the clandestine collection of foreign intelligence inside the United States shall be subject to the approval of the Attorney General; and

(D) All policies and procedures developed under this section shall be coordinated with the heads of affected departments and Intelligence Community elements;

(21) Shall, with the concurrence of the heads of affected departments and agencies, establish joint procedures to deconflict, coordinate, and synchronize intelligence activities conducted by an Intelligence Community element or funded by the National Intelligence Program, with intelligence activities, activities that involve foreign intelligence and security services, or activities that involve the use of clandestine methods, conducted by other United States Government departments, agencies, and establishments;

(22) Shall, in coordination with the heads of departments containing elements of the Intelligence Community, develop procedures to govern major system acquisitions funded in whole or in majority part by the National Intelligence Program;

(23) Shall seek advice from the Secretary of State to ensure that the foreign policy implications of proposed intelligence activities are considered, and shall ensure, through appropriate policies and procedures, that intelligence activities are conducted in a manner consistent with the responsibilities pursuant to law and presidential direction of Chiefs of United States Missions; and

(24) Shall facilitate the use of Intelligence Community products by the Congress in a secure manner.

(c) The Director's exercise of authorities in the Act and this order shall not abrogate the statutory or other responsibilities of the heads of departments of the United States Government or the Director of the Central Intelligence Agency. Directives issued and actions taken by the Director in the exercise of the Director's authorities and responsibilities to integrate, coordinate, and make the Intelligence Community more effective in providing intelligence related to national security shall be implemented by the elements of the Intelligence Community, provided that any department head whose department contains an element of the Intelligence Community and who believes that a directive or action of the Director violates the requirements of section 1018 of the IRTPA or this subsection shall bring the issue to the attention of the Director, the NSC, or the President for resolution in a manner that respects and does not abrogate the statutory responsibilities of the heads of the departments.

(d) Appointments to certain positions.

(1) The relevant department or bureau head shall provide recommendations and obtain the concurrence of the Director for the selection of: the Director of the National Security Agency, the Director of the National Reconnaissance Office, the Director of the National Geospatial-Intelligence Agency, the Under Secretary of Homeland Security for Intelligence and Analysis, the Assistant Secretary of State for Intelligence and Research, the Director of the Office of Intelligence and Counterintelligence of the Department of Energy, the Assistant Secretary for Intelligence and Analysis of the Department of the Treasury, and the Executive Assistant Director for the National Security Branch of the Federal Bureau of Investigation. If the Director does not concur in the recommendation, the department head may not fill the vacancy or make the recommendation to the President, as the case may be. If the department head and the Director do not reach an agreement on the selection or recommendation, the Director and the department head concerned may advise the President directly of the Director's intention to withhold concurrence.

(2) The relevant department head shall consult with the Director before appointing an individual to fill a vacancy or recommending to the President an individual be nominated to fill a vacancy in any of the following positions: the Under Secretary of Defense for Intelligence; the Director of the Defense Intelligence Agency; uniformed heads of the intelligence elements of the Army, the Navy, the Air Force, and the Marine Corps above the rank of Major General or Rear Admiral; the Assistant Commandant of the Coast Guard for Intelligence; and the Assistant Attorney General for National Security.

(e) Removal from certain positions.

(1) Except for the Director of the Central Intelligence Agency, whose removal the Director may recommend to the President, the Director and the relevant department head shall consult on the removal, or recommendation to the President for removal, as the case may be, of: the Director of the National Security Agency, the Director of the National Geospatial-Intelligence Agency, the Director of the Defense Intelligence Agency, the Under Secretary of Homeland Security for Intelligence and Analysis, the Assistant Secretary of State for Intelligence and Research, and the Assistant Secretary for Intelligence and Analysis of the Department of the Treasury. If the Director and the department head do

not agree on removal, or recommendation for removal, either may make a recommendation to the President for the removal of the individual.

(2) The Director and the relevant department or bureau head shall consult on the removal of: the Executive Assistant Director for the National Security Branch of the Federal Bureau of Investigation, the Director of the Office of Intelligence and Counterintelligence of the Department of Energy, the Director of the National Reconnaissance Office, the Assistant Commandant of the Coast Guard for Intelligence, and the Under Secretary of Defense for Intelligence. With respect to an individual appointed by a department head, the department head may remove the individual upon the request of the Director; if the department head chooses not to remove the individual, either the Director or the department head may advise the President of the department head's intention to retain the individual. In the case of the Under Secretary of Defense for Intelligence, the Secretary of Defense may recommend to the President either the removal or the retention of the individual. For uniformed heads of the intelligence elements of the Army, the Navy, the Air Force, and the Marine Corps, the Director may make a recommendation for removal to the Secretary of Defense.

(3) Nothing in this subsection shall be construed to limit or otherwise affect the authority of the President to nominate, appoint, assign, or terminate the appointment or assignment of any individual, with or without a consultation, recommendation, or concurrence.

SEC. 1.4 THE INTELLIGENCE COMMUNITY. Consistent with applicable Federal law and with the other provisions of this order, and under the leadership of the Director, as specified in such law and this order, the Intelligence Community shall:

(a) Collect and provide information needed by the President and, in the performance of executive functions, the Vice President, the NSC, the Homeland Security Council, the Chairman of the Joint Chiefs of Staff, senior military commanders, and other executive branch officials and, as appropriate, the Congress of the United States;

(b) In accordance with priorities set by the President, collect information concerning, and conduct activities to protect against, international terrorism, proliferation of weapons of mass destruction, intelligence activities directed against the United States, international criminal drug activities, and other hostile activities directed against the United States by foreign powers, organizations, persons, and their agents;

(c) Analyze, produce, and disseminate intelligence;

(d) Conduct administrative, technical, and other support activities within the United States and abroad necessary for the performance of authorized activities, to include providing services of common concern for the Intelligence Community as designated by the Director in accordance with this order;

(e) Conduct research, development, and procurement of technical systems and devices relating to authorized functions and missions or the provision of services of common concern for the Intelligence Community;

(f) Protect the security of intelligence related activities, information, installations, property, and employees by appropriate means, including such investigations of applicants, employees, contractors, and other persons with similar associations with the Intelligence Community elements as are necessary;

(g) Take into account State, local, and tribal governments' and, as appropriate, private sector entities' information needs relating to national and homeland security;

(h) Deconflict, coordinate, and integrate all intelligence activities and other information gathering in accordance with section 1.3(b)(20) of this order; and

(i) Perform such other functions and duties related to intelligence activities as the President may direct.

SEC. 1.5 DUTIES AND RESPONSIBILITIES OF THE HEADS OF EXECUTIVE BRANCH DEPARTMENTS AND AGENCIES. The heads of all departments and agencies shall:

(a) Provide the Director access to all information and intelligence relevant to the national security or that otherwise is required for the performance of the Director's duties, to include administrative and other appropriate management information, except such information excluded by law, by the President, or by the Attorney General acting under this order at the direction of the President;

(b) Provide all programmatic and budgetary information necessary to support the Director in developing the National Intelligence Program;

(c) Coordinate development and implementation of intelligence systems and architectures and, as appropriate, operational systems and architectures of their departments, agencies, and other elements with the Director to respond to national intelligence requirements and all applicable information sharing and security guidelines, information privacy, and other legal requirements;

(d) Provide, to the maximum extent permitted by law, subject to the availability of appropriations and not inconsistent with the mission of the department or agency, such further support to the Director as the Director may request, after consultation with the head of the department or agency, for the performance of the Director's functions;

(e) Respond to advisory tasking from the Director under section 1.3(b)(18) of this order to the greatest extent possible, in accordance with applicable policies established by the head of the responding department or agency;

(f) Ensure that all elements within the department or agency comply with the provisions of Part 2 of this order, regardless of Intelligence Community affiliation, when performing foreign intelligence and counterintelligence functions;

(g) Deconflict, coordinate, and integrate all intelligence activities in accordance with section 1.3(b)(20), and intelligence and other activities in accordance with section 1.3(b)(21) of this order;

(h) Inform the Attorney General, either directly or through the Federal Bureau of Investigation, and the Director of clandestine collection of foreign intelligence and counterintelligence activities inside the United States not coordinated with the Federal Bureau of Investigation;

(i) Pursuant to arrangements developed by the head of the department or agency and the Director of the Central Intelligence Agency and approved by the Director, inform the Director and the Director of the Central Intelligence Agency, either directly or through his designee serving outside the United States, as appropriate, of clandestine collection of foreign intelligence collected through human sources or through human-enabled means outside the United States that has not been coordinated with the Central Intelligence Agency; and

(j) Inform the Secretary of Defense, either directly or through his designee, as appropriate, of clandestine collection of foreign intelligence outside the United States in a region of combat or contingency military operations designated by the Secretary of Defense, for purposes of this paragraph, after consultation with the Director of National Intelligence.

SEC. 1.6 HEADS OF ELEMENTS OF THE INTELLIGENCE COMMUNITY. The heads of elements of the Intelligence Community shall:

(a) Provide the Director access to all information and intelligence relevant to the national security or that otherwise is required for the performance of the Director's duties, to include administrative and other appropriate management information, except such information excluded by law, by the President, or by the Attorney General acting under this order at the direction of the President;

(b) Report to the Attorney General possible violations of Federal criminal laws by employees and of specified Federal criminal laws by any other person as provided in procedures agreed upon by the Attorney General and the head of the department, agency, or establishment concerned, in a manner consistent with the protection of intelligence sources and methods, as specified in those procedures;

(c) Report to the Intelligence Oversight Board, consistent with Executive Order 13462 of February 29, 2008, and provide copies of all such reports to the Director, concerning any intelligence activities of their elements that they have reason to believe may be unlawful or contrary to executive order or presidential directive;

(d) Protect intelligence and intelligence sources, methods, and activities from unauthorized disclosure in accordance with guidance from the Director;

(e) Facilitate, as appropriate, the sharing of information or intelligence, as directed by law or the President, to State, local, tribal, and private sector entities;

(f) Disseminate information or intelligence to foreign governments and international organizations under intelligence or counterintelligence arrangements or agreements established in accordance with section 1.3(b)(4) of this order;

(g) Participate in the development of procedures approved by the Attorney General governing production and dissemination of information or intelligence resulting from criminal drug intelligence activities abroad if they have intelligence responsibilities for foreign or domestic criminal drug production and trafficking; and

(h) Ensure that the inspectors general, general counsels, and agency officials responsible for privacy or civil liberties protection for their respective organizations have access to any information or intelligence necessary to perform their official duties.

SEC. 1.7 INTELLIGENCE COMMUNITY ELEMENTS. Each element of the Intelligence Community shall have the duties and responsibilities specified below, in addition to those specified by law or elsewhere in this order. Intelligence Community elements within executive departments shall serve the information and intelligence needs of their respective heads of departments and also shall operate as part of an integrated Intelligence Community, as provided in law or this order.

(a) THE CENTRAL INTELLIGENCE AGENCY. The Director of the Central Intelligence Agency shall:

(1) Collect (including through clandestine means), analyze, produce, and disseminate foreign intelligence and counterintelligence;

(2) Conduct counterintelligence activities without assuming or performing any internal security functions within the United States;

(3) Conduct administrative and technical support activities within and outside the United States as necessary for cover and proprietary arrangements;

(4) Conduct covert action activities approved by the President. No agency except the Central Intelligence Agency (or the Armed Forces of the United States in time of war declared by the Congress or during any period covered by a report from the President to the Congress consistent with the War Powers Resolution, Public Law 93-148) may conduct any covert action activity unless the President determines that another agency is more likely to achieve a particular objective;

(5) Conduct foreign intelligence liaison relationships with intelligence or security services of foreign governments or international organizations consistent with section 1.3(b)(4) of this order;

(6) Under the direction and guidance of the Director, and in accordance with section 1.3(b)(4) of this order, coordinate the implementation of intelligence and counterintelligence relationships between elements of the Intelligence Community and the intelligence or security services of foreign governments or international organizations; and

(7) Perform such other functions and duties related to intelligence as the Director may direct.

(b) THE DEFENSE INTELLIGENCE AGENCY. The Director of the Defense Intelligence Agency shall:

(1) Collect (including through clandestine means), analyze, produce, and disseminate foreign intelligence and counterintelligence to support national and departmental missions;

(2) Collect, analyze, produce, or, through tasking and coordination, provide defense and defense-related intelligence for the Secretary of Defense, the Chairman of the Joint Chiefs of Staff, combatant commanders, other Defense components, and non-Defense agencies;

(3) Conduct counterintelligence activities;

(4) Conduct administrative and technical support activities within and outside the United States as necessary for cover and proprietary arrangements;

(5) Conduct foreign defense intelligence liaison relationships and defense intelligence exchange programs with foreign defense establishments, intelligence or security services of foreign governments, and international organizations in accordance with sections 1.3(b)(4), 1.7(a)(6), and 1.10(i) of this order;

(6) Manage and coordinate all matters related to the Defense Attaché system; and

(7) Provide foreign intelligence and counterintelligence staff support as directed by the Secretary of Defense.

(c) THE NATIONAL SECURITY AGENCY. The Director of the National Security Agency shall:

(1) Collect (including through clandestine means), process, analyze, produce, and disseminate signals intelligence information and data for foreign intelligence and counterintelligence purposes to support national and departmental missions;

(2) Establish and operate an effective unified organization for signals intelligence activities, except for the delegation of operational control over certain operations that are conducted through other elements of the Intelligence Community. No other department or agency may engage in signals intelligence activities except pursuant to a delegation by the Secretary of Defense, after coordination with the Director;

(3) Control signals intelligence collection and processing activities, including assignment of resources to an appropriate agent for such periods and tasks as required for the direct support of military commanders;

(4) Conduct administrative and technical support activities within and outside the United States as necessary for cover arrangements;

(5) Provide signals intelligence support for national and departmental requirements and for the conduct of military operations;

(6) Act as the National Manager for National Security Systems as established in law and policy, and in this capacity be responsible to the Secretary of Defense and to the Director;

(7) Prescribe, consistent with section 102A(g) of the Act, within its field of authorized operations, security regulations covering operating practices, including the transmission, handling, and distribution of signals intelligence and communications security material within and among the elements under control of the Director of the National Security Agency, and exercise the necessary supervisory control to ensure compliance with the regulations; and

(8) Conduct foreign cryptologic liaison relationships in accordance with sections 1.3(b)(4), 1.7(a)(6), and 1.10(i) of this order.

(d) THE NATIONAL RECONNAISSANCE OFFICE. The Director of the National Reconnaissance Office shall:

(1) Be responsible for research and development, acquisition, launch, deployment, and operation of overhead systems and related data processing facilities to collect intelligence and information to support national and departmental missions and other United States Government needs; and

(2) Conduct foreign liaison relationships relating to the above missions, in accordance with sections 1.3(b)(4), 1.7(a)(6), and 1.10(i) of this order.

(e) THE NATIONAL GEOSPATIAL-INTELLIGENCE AGENCY. The Director of the National Geospatial-Intelligence Agency shall:

(1) Collect, process, analyze, produce, and disseminate geospatial intelligence information and data for foreign intelligence and counterintelligence purposes to support national and departmental missions;

(2) Provide geospatial intelligence support for national and departmental requirements and for the conduct of military operations;

(3) Conduct administrative and technical support activities within and outside the United States as necessary for cover arrangements; and

(4) Conduct foreign geospatial intelligence liaison relationships, in accordance with sections 1.3(b)(4), 1.7(a)(6), and 1.10(i) of this order.

(f) THE INTELLIGENCE AND COUNTERINTELLIGENCE ELEMENTS OF THE ARMY, NAVY, AIR FORCE, AND MARINE CORPS. The Commanders and heads of the intelligence and counterintelligence elements of the Army, Navy, Air Force, and Marine Corps shall:

(1) Collect (including through clandestine means), produce, analyze, and disseminate defense and defense-related intelligence and counterintelligence to support departmental requirements, and, as appropriate, national requirements;

(2) Conduct counterintelligence activities;

(3) Monitor the development, procurement, and management of tactical intelligence systems and equipment and conduct related research, development, and test and evaluation activities; and

(4) Conduct military intelligence liaison relationships and military intelligence exchange programs with selected cooperative foreign defense establishments and international organizations in accordance with sections 1.3(b)(4), 1.7(a)(6), and 1.10(i) of this order.

(g) INTELLIGENCE ELEMENTS OF THE FEDERAL BUREAU OF INVESTIGATION. Under the supervision of the Attorney General and pursuant to such regulations as the Attorney General may establish, the intelligence elements of the Federal Bureau of Investigation shall:

(1) Collect (including through clandestine means), analyze, produce, and disseminate foreign intelligence and counterintelligence to support national and departmental missions, in accordance with procedural guidelines approved by the Attorney General, after consultation with the Director;

(2) Conduct counterintelligence activities; and

(3) Conduct foreign intelligence and counterintelligence liaison relationships with intelligence, security, and law enforcement services of foreign governments or international organizations in accordance with sections 1.3(b)(4) and 1.7(a)(6) of this order.

(h) THE INTELLIGENCE AND COUNTERINTELLIGENCE ELEMENTS OF THE COAST GUARD. The Commandant of the Coast Guard shall:

(1) Collect (including through clandestine means), analyze, produce, and disseminate foreign intelligence and counterintelligence including defense and defense-related information and intelligence to support national and departmental missions;

(2) Conduct counterintelligence activities;

(3) Monitor the development, procurement, and management of tactical intelligence systems and equipment and conduct related research, development, and test and evaluation activities; and

(4) Conduct foreign intelligence liaison relationships and intelligence exchange programs with foreign intelligence services, security services

or international organizations in accordance with sections 1.3(b)(4), 1.7(a)(6), and, when operating as part of the Department of Defense, 1.10(i) of this order.

(i) THE BUREAU OF INTELLIGENCE AND RESEARCH, DEPARTMENT OF STATE; THE OFFICE OF INTELLIGENCE AND ANALYSIS, DEPARTMENT OF THE TREASURY; THE OFFICE OF NATIONAL SECURITY INTELLIGENCE, DRUG ENFORCEMENT ADMINISTRATION; THE OFFICE OF INTELLIGENCE AND ANALYSIS, DEPARTMENT OF HOMELAND SECURITY; AND THE OFFICE OF INTELLIGENCE AND COUNTERINTELLIGENCE, DEPARTMENT OF ENERGY. The heads of the Bureau of Intelligence and Research, Department of State; the Office of Intelligence and Analysis, Department of the Treasury; the Office of National Security Intelligence, Drug Enforcement Administration; the Office of Intelligence and Analysis, Department of Homeland Security; and the Office of Intelligence and Counterintelligence, Department of Energy shall:

(1) Collect (overtly or through publicly available sources), analyze, produce, and disseminate information, intelligence, and counterintelligence to support national and departmental missions; and

(2) Conduct and participate in analytic or information exchanges with foreign partners and international organizations in accordance with sections 1.3(b)(4) and 1.7(a)(6) of this order.

(j) THE OFFICE OF THE DIRECTOR OF NATIONAL INTELLIGENCE. The Director shall collect (overtly or through publicly available sources), analyze, produce, and disseminate information, intelligence, and counterintelligence to support the missions of the Office of the Director of National Intelligence, including the National Counterterrorism Center, and to support other national missions.

SEC. 1.8 THE DEPARTMENT OF STATE. In addition to the authorities exercised by the Bureau of Intelligence and Research under sections 1.4 and 1.7(i) of this order, the Secretary of State shall:

(a) Collect (overtly or through publicly available sources) information relevant to United States foreign policy and national security concerns;

(b) Disseminate, to the maximum extent possible, reports received from United States diplomatic and consular posts;

(c) Transmit reporting requirements and advisory taskings of the Intelligence Community to the Chiefs of United States Missions abroad; and

(d) Support Chiefs of United States Missions in discharging their responsibilities pursuant to law and presidential direction.

SEC. 1.9 THE DEPARTMENT OF THE TREASURY. In addition to the authorities exercised by the Office of Intelligence and Analysis of the Department of the

Treasury under sections 1.4 and 1.7(i) of this order the Secretary of the Treasury shall collect (overtly or through publicly available sources) foreign financial information and, in consultation with the Department of State, foreign economic information.

SEC. 1.10 THE DEPARTMENT OF DEFENSE. The Secretary of Defense shall:

(a) Collect (including through clandestine means), analyze, produce, and disseminate information and intelligence and be responsive to collection tasking and advisory tasking by the Director;

(b) Collect (including through clandestine means), analyze, produce, and disseminate defense and defense-related intelligence and counterintelligence, as required for execution of the Secretary's responsibilities;

(c) Conduct programs and missions necessary to fulfill national, departmental, and tactical intelligence requirements;

(d) Conduct counterintelligence activities in support of Department of Defense components and coordinate counterintelligence activities in accordance with section 1.3(b)(20) and (21) of this order;

(e) Act, in coordination with the Director, as the executive agent of the United States Government for signals intelligence activities;

(f) Provide for the timely transmission of critical intelligence, as defined by the Director, within the United States Government;

(g) Carry out or contract for research, development, and procurement of technical systems and devices relating to authorized intelligence functions;

(h) Protect the security of Department of Defense installations, activities, information, property, and employees by appropriate means, including such investigations of applicants, employees, contractors, and other persons with similar associations with the Department of Defense as are necessary;

(i) Establish and maintain defense intelligence relationships and defense intelligence exchange programs with selected cooperative foreign defense establishments, intelligence or security services of foreign governments, and international organizations, and ensure that such relationships and programs are in accordance with sections 1.3(b)(4), 1.3(b)(21) and 1.7(a)(6) of this order;

(j) Conduct such administrative and technical support activities within and outside the United States as are necessary to provide for cover and proprietary arrangements, to perform the functions described in sections (a) though (i) above, and to support the Intelligence Community elements of the Department of Defense; and

(k) Use the Intelligence Community elements within the Department of Defense identified in section 1.7(b) through (f) and, when the Coast Guard is operating as part of the Department of Defense, (h) above to carry out the Secretary of Defense's responsibilities assigned in this section or other departments, agencies, or offices within the Department of Defense, as appropriate, to conduct the intelligence missions and responsibilities assigned to the Secretary of Defense.

SEC. 1.11 THE DEPARTMENT OF HOMELAND SECURITY. In addition to the authorities exercised by the Office of Intelligence and Analysis of the Department of Homeland Security under sections 1.4 and 1.7(i) of this order, the Secretary of Homeland Security shall conduct, through the United States Secret Service, activities to determine the existence and capability of surveillance equipment being used against the President or the Vice President of the United States, the Executive Office of the President, and, as authorized by the Secretary of Homeland Security or the President, other Secret Service protectees and United States officials. No information shall be acquired intentionally through such activities except to protect against use of such surveillance equipment, and those activities shall be conducted pursuant to procedures agreed upon by the Secretary of Homeland Security and the Attorney General.

SEC. 1.12 The Department of Energy. In addition to the authorities exercised by the Office of Intelligence and Counterintelligence of the Department of Energy under sections 1.4 and 1.7(i) of this order, the Secretary of Energy shall:
(a) Provide expert scientific, technical, analytic, and research capabilities to other agencies within the Intelligence Community, as appropriate;
(b) Participate in formulating intelligence collection and analysis requirements where the special expert capability of the Department can contribute; and
(c) Participate with the Department of State in overtly collecting information with respect to foreign energy matters.

SEC. 1.13 THE FEDERAL BUREAU OF INVESTIGATION. In addition to the authorities exercised by the intelligence elements of the Federal Bureau of Investigation of the Department of Justice under sections 1.4 and 1.7(g) of this order and under the supervision of the Attorney General and pursuant to such regulations as the Attorney General may establish, the Director of the Federal Bureau of Investigation shall provide technical assistance, within or outside the United States, to foreign intelligence and law enforcement services, consistent with section 1.3(b)(20) and (21) of this order, as may be necessary to support national or departmental missions.

PART 2 – CONDUCT OF INTELLIGENCE ACTIVITIES

SECTION. 2.1 NEED. Timely, accurate, and insightful information about the activities, capabilities, plans, and intentions of foreign powers, organizations, and persons, and their agents, is essential to informed decisionmaking in the areas of national security, national defense, and foreign relations. Collection of such information is a priority objective and will be pursued in a vigorous, innovative, and responsible manner that is consistent with the Constitution and applicable law and respectful of the principles upon which the United States was founded.

SEC. 2.2 PURPOSE. This Order is intended to enhance human and technical collection techniques, especially those undertaken abroad, and the acquisition of significant foreign intelligence, as well as the detection and countering of international terrorist activities, the spread of weapons of mass destruction, and espionage conducted by foreign powers. Set forth below are certain general principles that, in addition to and consistent with applicable laws, are intended to achieve the proper balance between the acquisition of essential information and protection of individual interests. Nothing in this Order shall be construed to apply to or interfere with any authorized civil or criminal law enforcement responsibility of any department or agency.

SEC. 2.3 COLLECTION OF INFORMATION. Elements of the Intelligence Community are authorized to collect, retain, or disseminate information concerning United States persons only in accordance with procedures established by the head of the Intelligence Community element concerned or by the head of a department containing such element and approved by the Attorney General, consistent with the authorities provided by Part 1 of this Order, after consultation with the Director. Those procedures shall permit collection, retention, and dissemination of the following types of information:

(a) Information that is publicly available or collected with the consent of the person concerned;

(b) Information constituting foreign intelligence or counterintelligence, including such information concerning corporations or other commercial organizations. Collection within the United States of foreign intelligence not otherwise obtainable shall be undertaken by the Federal Bureau of Investigation (FBI) or, when significant foreign intelligence is sought, by other authorized elements of the Intelligence Community, provided that no foreign intelligence collection by such elements may be undertaken for the purpose of acquiring information concerning the domestic activities of United States persons;

(c) Information obtained in the course of a lawful foreign intelligence, counterintelligence, international drug or international terrorism investigation;

(d) Information needed to protect the safety of any persons or organizations, including those who are targets, victims, or hostages of international terrorist organizations;

(e) Information needed to protect foreign intelligence or counterintelligence sources, methods, and activities from unauthorized disclosure. Collection within the United States shall be undertaken by the FBI except that other elements of the Intelligence Community may also collect such information concerning present or former employees, present or former intelligence element contractors or their present or former employees, or applicants for such employment or contracting;

(f) Information concerning persons who are reasonably believed to be potential sources or contacts for the purpose of determining their suitability or credibility;

(g) Information arising out of a lawful personnel, physical, or communications security investigation;

(h) Information acquired by overhead reconnaissance not directed at specific United States persons;

(i) Incidentally obtained information that may indicate involvement in activities that may violate Federal, state, local, or foreign laws; and

(j) Information necessary for administrative purposes.

In addition, elements of the Intelligence Community may disseminate information to each appropriate element within the Intelligence Community for purposes of allowing the recipient element to determine whether the information is relevant to its responsibilities and can be retained by it, except that information derived from signals intelligence may only be disseminated or made available to Intelligence Community elements in accordance with procedures established by the Director in coordination with the Secretary of Defense and approved by the Attorney General.

SEC. 2.4 COLLECTION TECHNIQUES. Elements of the Intelligence Community shall use the least intrusive collection techniques feasible within the United States or directed against United States persons abroad. Elements of the Intelligence Community are not authorized to use such techniques as electronic surveillance, unconsented physical searches, mail surveillance, physical surveillance, or monitoring devices unless they are in accordance with procedures established by the head of the Intelligence Community element concerned or the head of a department containing such element and approved by the Attorney General, after consultation with the Director. Such procedures shall protect constitutional and other legal rights and limit use of such information to lawful governmental purposes. These procedures shall not authorize:

(a) The Central Intelligence Agency (CIA) to engage in electronic surveillance within the United States except for the purpose of training, testing, or conducting countermeasures to hostile electronic surveillance;

(b) Unconsented physical searches in the United States by elements of the Intelligence Community other than the FBI, except for:

> (1) Searches by counterintelligence elements of the military services directed against military personnel within the United States or abroad for intelligence purposes, when authorized by a military commander empowered to approve physical searches for law enforcement purposes,

based upon a finding of probable cause to believe that such persons are acting as agents of foreign powers; and

(2) Searches by CIA of personal property of non-United States persons lawfully in its possession;

(c) Physical surveillance of a United States person in the United States by elements of the Intelligence Community other than the FBI, except for:

(1) Physical surveillance of present or former employees, present or former intelligence element contractors or their present or former employees, or applicants for any such employment or contracting; and

(2) Physical surveillance of a military person employed by a non-intelligence element of a military service; and

(d) Physical surveillance of a United States person abroad to collect foreign intelligence, except to obtain significant information that cannot reasonably be acquired by other means.

SEC. 2.5 ATTORNEY GENERAL APPROVAL. The Attorney General hereby is delegated the power to approve the use for intelligence purposes, within the United States or against a United States person abroad, of any technique for which a warrant would be required if undertaken for law enforcement purposes, provided that such techniques shall not be undertaken unless the Attorney General has determined in each case that there is probable cause to believe that the technique is directed against a foreign power or an agent of a foreign power. The authority delegated pursuant to this paragraph, including the authority to approve the use of electronic surveillance as defined in the Foreign Intelligence Surveillance Act of 1978, as amended, shall be exercised in accordance with that Act.

SEC. 2.6 ASSISTANCE TO LAW ENFORCEMENT AND OTHER CIVIL AUTHORITIES. Elements of the Intelligence Community are authorized to:

(a) Cooperate with appropriate law enforcement agencies for the purpose of protecting the employees, information, property, and facilities of any element of the Intelligence Community;

(b) Unless otherwise precluded by law or this Order, participate in law enforcement activities to investigate or prevent clandestine intelligence activities by foreign powers, or international terrorist or narcotics activities;

(c) Provide specialized equipment, technical knowledge, or assistance of expert personnel for use by any department or agency, or when lives are endangered, to support local law enforcement agencies. Provision of assistance by expert personnel shall be approved in each case by the general counsel of the providing element or department; and

(d) Render any other assistance and cooperation to law enforcement or other civil authorities not precluded by applicable law.

SEC. 2.7 CONTRACTING. Elements of the Intelligence Community are authorized to enter into contracts or arrangements for the provision of goods or services with private companies or institutions in the United States and need not reveal the sponsorship of such contracts or arrangements for authorized intelligence purposes. Contracts or arrangements with academic institutions may be undertaken only with the consent of appropriate officials of the institution.

SEC. 2.8 CONSISTENCY WITH OTHER LAWS. Nothing in this Order shall be construed to authorize any activity in violation of the Constitution or statutes of the United States.

SEC. 2.9 UNDISCLOSED PARTICIPATION IN ORGANIZATIONS WITHIN THE UNITED STATES. No one acting on behalf of elements of the Intelligence Community may join or otherwise participate in any organization in the United States on behalf of any element of the Intelligence Community without disclosing such person's intelligence affiliation to appropriate officials of the organization, except in accordance with procedures established by the head of the Intelligence Community element concerned or the head of a department containing such element and approved by the Attorney General, after consultation with the Director. Such participation shall be authorized only if it is essential to achieving lawful purposes as determined by the Intelligence Community element head or designee. No such participation may be undertaken for the purpose of influencing the activity of the organization or its members except in cases where:
(a) The participation is undertaken on behalf of the FBI in the course of a lawful investigation; or
(b) The organization concerned is composed primarily of individuals who are not United States persons and is reasonably believed to be acting on behalf of a foreign power.

SEC. 2.10 HUMAN EXPERIMENTATION. No element of the Intelligence Community shall sponsor, contract for, or conduct research on human subjects except in accordance with guidelines issued by the Department of Health and Human Services. The subject's informed consent shall be documented as required by those guidelines.

SEC. 2.11 PROHIBITION ON ASSASSINATION. No person employed by or acting on behalf of the United States Government shall engage in or conspire to engage in assassination.

SEC. 2.12 INDIRECT PARTICIPATION. No element of the Intelligence Community shall participate in or request any person to undertake activities forbidden by this Order.

SEC. 2.13 LIMITATION ON COVERT ACTION. No covert action may be conducted which is intended to influence United States political processes, public opinion, policies, or media.

PART 3 – GENERAL PROVISIONS

SECTION. 3.1 CONGRESSIONAL OVERSIGHT. The duties and responsibilities of the Director and the heads of other departments, agencies, elements, and entities engaged in intelligence activities to cooperate with the Congress in the conduct of its responsibilities for oversight of intelligence activities shall be implemented in accordance with applicable law, including title V of the Act. The requirements of applicable law, including title V of the Act, shall apply to all covert action activities as defined in this Order.

SEC. 3.2 IMPLEMENTATION. The President, supported by the NSC, and the Director shall issue such appropriate directives, procedures, and guidance as are necessary to implement this order. Heads of elements within the Intelligence Community shall issue appropriate procedures and supplementary directives consistent with this order. No procedures to implement Part 2 of this order shall be issued without the Attorney General's approval, after consultation with the Director. The Attorney General shall provide a statement of reasons for not approving any procedures established by the head of an element in the Intelligence Community (or the head of the department containing such element) other than the FBI. In instances where the element head or department head and the Attorney General are unable to reach agreements on other than constitutional or other legal grounds, the Attorney General, the head of department concerned, or the Director shall refer the matter to the NSC.

SEC. 3.3 PROCEDURES. The activities herein authorized that require procedures shall be conducted in accordance with existing procedures or requirements established under Executive Order 12333. New procedures, as required by Executive Order 12333, as further amended, shall be established as expeditiously as possible. All new procedures promulgated pursuant to Executive Order 12333, as amended, shall be made available to the Select Committee on Intelligence of the Senate and the Permanent Select Committee on Intelligence of the House of Representatives.

SEC. 3.4 REFERENCES AND TRANSITION. References to "Senior Officials of the Intelligence Community" or "SOICs" in executive orders or other Presidential guidance, shall be deemed references to the heads of elements in the Intelligence Community, unless the President otherwise directs; references in Intelligence Community or Intelligence Community element policies or guidance, shall be deemed to be references to the heads of elements of the Intelligence Community, unless the President or the Director otherwise directs.

SEC. 3.5 DEFINITIONS. For the purposes of this Order, the following terms shall have these meanings:

(a) Counterintelligence means information gathered and activities conducted to identify, deceive, exploit, disrupt, or protect against espionage, other intelligence activities, sabotage, or assassinations conducted for or on behalf of foreign powers, organizations, or persons, or their agents, or international terrorist organizations or activities.

(b) Covert action means an activity or activities of the United States Government to influence political, economic, or military conditions abroad, where it is intended that the role of the United States Government will not be apparent or acknowledged publicly, but does not include:

> (1) Activities the primary purpose of which is to acquire intelligence, traditional counterintelligence activities, traditional activities to improve or maintain the operational security of United States Government programs, or administrative activities;

> (2) Traditional diplomatic or military activities or routine support to such activities;

> (3) Traditional law enforcement activities conducted by United States Government law enforcement agencies or routine support to such activities; or

> (4) Activities to provide routine support to the overt activities (other than activities described in paragraph (1), (2), or (3)) of other United States Government agencies abroad.

(c) Electronic surveillance means acquisition of a nonpublic communication by electronic means without the consent of a person who is a party to an electronic communication or, in the case of a nonelectronic communication, without the consent of a person who is visibly present at the place of communication, but not including the use of radio direction-finding equipment solely to determine the location of a transmitter.

(d) Employee means a person employed by, assigned or detailed to, or acting for an element within the Intelligence Community.

(e) Foreign intelligence means information relating to the capabilities, intentions, or activities of foreign governments or elements thereof, foreign organizations, foreign persons, or international terrorists.

(f) Intelligence includes foreign intelligence and counterintelligence.

(g) Intelligence activities means all activities that elements of the Intelligence Community are authorized to conduct pursuant to this order.

(h) Intelligence Community and elements of the Intelligence Community refers to:

(1) The Office of the Director of National Intelligence;

(2) The Central Intelligence Agency;

(3) The National Security Agency;

(4) The Defense Intelligence Agency;

(5) The National Geospatial-Intelligence Agency;

(6) The National Reconnaissance Office;

(7) The other offices within the Department of Defense for the collection of specialized national foreign intelligence through reconnaissance programs;

(8) The intelligence and counterintelligence elements of the Army, the Navy, the Air Force, and the Marine Corps;

(9) The intelligence elements of the Federal Bureau of Investigation;

(10) The Office of National Security Intelligence of the Drug Enforcement Administration;

(11) The Office of Intelligence and Counterintelligence of the Department of Energy;

(12) The Bureau of Intelligence and Research of the Department of State;

(13) The Office of Intelligence and Analysis of the Department of the Treasury;

(14) The Office of Intelligence and Analysis of the Department of Homeland Security;

(15) The intelligence and counterintelligence elements of the Coast Guard; and

(16) Such other elements of any department or agency as may be designated by the President, or designated jointly by the Director and the head of the department or agency concerned, as an element of the Intelligence Community.

(i) National Intelligence and Intelligence Related to National Security means all intelligence, regardless of the source from which derived and including information gathered within or outside the United States, that pertains, as determined consistent with any guidance issued by the President, or that is determined for the purpose of access to information by the Director in accordance with section 1.3(a)(1) of this order, to pertain to more than one United States Government agency; and that involves threats to the United States, its people, property, or interests; the development, proliferation, or use of weapons of mass destruction; or any other matter bearing on United States national or homeland security.

(j) The National Intelligence Program means all programs, projects, and activities of the Intelligence Community, as well as any other programs of the Intelligence Community designated jointly by the Director and the head of a United States department or agency or by the President. Such term does not include programs, projects, or activities of the military departments to acquire intelligence solely for the planning and conduct of tactical military operations by United States Armed Forces.

(k) United States person means a United States citizen, an alien known by the intelligence element concerned to be a permanent resident alien, an unincorporated association substantially composed of United States citizens or permanent resident aliens, or a corporation incorporated in the United States, except for a corporation directed and controlled by a foreign government or governments.

SEC. 3.6 REVOCATION. Executive Orders 13354 and 13355 of August 27, 2004, are revoked; and paragraphs 1.3(b)(9) and (10) of Part 1 supersede provisions within Executive Order 12958, as amended, to the extent such provisions in Executive Order 12958, as amended, are inconsistent with this Order.

SEC. 3.7 GENERAL PROVISIONS.

(a) Consistent with section 1.3(c) of this order, nothing in this order shall be construed to impair or otherwise affect:

> (1) Authority granted by law to a department or agency, or the head thereof; or
>
> (2) Functions of the Director of the Office of Management and Budget relating to budget, administrative, or legislative proposals.

(b) This order shall be implemented consistent with applicable law and subject to the availability of appropriations.

(c) This order is intended only to improve the internal management of the executive branch and is not intended to, and does not, create any right or benefit, substantive or procedural, enforceable at law or in equity, by any party against the United States, its departments, agencies or entities, its officers, employees, or agents, or any other person.

-/S/- Ronald Reagan
THE WHITE HOUSE,
December 4, 1981.

EXECUTIVE ORDER 12949:
FOREIGN INTELLIGENCE PHYSICAL SEARCHES

(Federal Register Vol. 60, No. 29 (Feb. 13, 1995),
amended by EO 13475 (2008))

By the authority vested in me as President by the Constitution and the laws of the United States, including sections 302 and 303 of the Foreign Intelligence Surveillance Act of 1978 (''Act'') (50 U.S.C. 1801, *et seq.*), as amended by Public Law 103–359, and in order to provide for the authorization of physical searches for foreign intelligence purposes as set forth in the Act, it is hereby ordered as follows:

Section 1. Pursuant to section 302(a)(1) of the Act, the Attorney General is authorized to approve physical searches, without a court order, to acquire foreign intelligence information for periods of up to one year, if the Attorney General makes the certifications required by that section.

Sec. 2. Pursuant to section 302(b) of the Act, the Attorney General is authorized to approve applications to the Foreign Intelligence Surveillance Court under section 303 of the Act to obtain orders for physical searches for the purpose of collecting foreign intelligence information.

Sec. 3. Pursuant to section 303(a)(6) of the Act, the following officials, each of whom is employed in the area of national security or defense, is designated to make the certifications required by section 303(a)(6) of the Act in support of applications to conduct physical searches:

(a) Secretary of State;
(b) Secretary of Defense;
(c) Director of National Intelligence;
(d) Director of the Federal Bureau of Investigation;
(e) Deputy Secretary of State;
(f) Deputy Secretary of Defense;
(g) Director of the Central Intelligence Agency
(h) Principal Deputy Director of National Intelligence; and
(i) Deputy Director of the Federal Bureau of Investigation.

None of the above officials, nor anyone officially acting in that capacity, may exercise the authority to make the above certifications, unless that official has been appointed by the President, by and with the advice and consent of the Senate. The requirement of the preceding sentence that the named official must be appointed by the President with the advice and consent of the Senate does not apply to the Deputy Director of the Federal Bureau of Investigation."

-/S/- William J. Clinton
THE WHITE HOUSE,
February 9, 1995.

EXECUTIVE ORDER 12968:
ACCESS TO CLASSIFIED INFORMATION

(Federal Register Vol. 60, No. 151 (August 7, 1995),
as amended by EO 13467 (2008))

The national interest requires that certain information be maintained in confidence through a system of classification in order to protect our citizens, our democratic institutions, and our participation within the community of nations. The unauthorized disclosure of information classified in the national interest can cause irreparable damage to the national security and loss of human life.

Security policies designed to protect classified information must ensure consistent, cost effective, and efficient protection of our Nation's classified information, while providing fair and equitable treatment to those Americans upon whom we rely to guard our national security.

This order establishes a uniform Federal personnel security program for employees who will be considered for initial or continued access to classified information.

NOW, THEREFORE, by the authority vested in me as President by the Constitution and the laws of the United States of America, it is hereby ordered as follows:

PART 1—DEFINITIONS, ACCESS TO CLASSIFIED INFORMATION, FINANCIAL DISCLOSURE, AND OTHER ITEMS

SECTION 1.1. DEFINITIONS. For the purposes of this order:
(a) "Agency" means any "Executive agency," as defined in 5 U.S.C. §105, the "military departments," as defined in 5 U.S.C. §102, and any other entity within the executive branch that comes into the possession of classified information, including the Defense Intelligence Agency, National Security Agency, and the National Reconnaissance Office.
(b) "Applicant" means a person other than an employee who has received an authorized conditional offer of employment for a position that requires access to classified information.
(c) "Authorized investigative agency" means an agency authorized by law or regulation to conduct a counterintelligence investigation or investigation of persons who are proposed for access to classified information to ascertain whether such persons satisfy the criteria for obtaining and retaining access to such information.

(d) "Classified information" means information that has been determined pursuant to Executive Order No. 12958, or any successor order, Executive Order No. 12951, or any successor order, or the Atomic Energy Act of 1954 (42 U.S.C. §2011), to require protection against unauthorized disclosure.

(e) "Employee" means a person, other than the President and Vice President, employed by, detailed or assigned to, an agency, including members of the Armed Forces; an expert or consultant to an agency; an industrial or commercial contractor, licensee, certificate holder, or grantee of an agency, including all subcontractors; a personal services contractor; or any other category of person who acts for or on behalf of an agency as determined by the appropriate agency head.

(f) "Foreign power" and "agent of a foreign power" have the meaning provided in 50 U.S.C. §1801.

(g) "Need for access" means a determination that an employee requires access to a particular level of classified information in order to perform or assist in a lawful and authorized governmental function.

(h) "Need-to-know" means a determination made by an authorized holder of classified information that a prospective recipient requires access to specific classified information in order to perform or assist in a lawful and authorized governmental function.

(i) "Overseas Security Executive Agent" means the Security Executive Agent established by the President to consider, develop, coordinate and promote policies, standards and agreements on overseas security operations, programs and projects that affect all United States Government agencies under the authority of a Chief of Mission.

(j) "Security Executive Agent" means the Board established by the President to consider, coordinate, and recommend policy directives for U.S. security policies, procedures, and practices.

(k) "Special access program" has the meaning provided in section 4.1 of Executive Order No. 12958, or any successor order.

SEC. 1.2. ACCESS TO CLASSIFIED INFORMATION.

(a) No employee shall be granted access to classified information unless that employee has been determined to be eligible in accordance with this order and to possess a need-to-know.

(b) Agency heads shall be responsible for establishing and maintaining an effective program to ensure that access to classified information by each employee is clearly consistent with the interests of the national security.

(c) Employees shall not be granted access to classified information unless they:

    (1) have been determined to be eligible for access under section 3.1 of this order by agency heads or designated officials based upon a favorable

adjudication of an appropriate investigation of the employee's background;

(2) have a demonstrated need-to-know; and

(3) have signed an approved nondisclosure agreement.

(d) All employees shall be subject to investigation by an appropriate government authority prior to being granted access to classified information and at any time during the period of access to ascertain whether they continue to meet the requirements for access.

(e)(1) All employees granted access to classified information shall be required as a condition of such access to provide to the employing agency written consent permitting access by an authorized investigative agency, for such time as access to classified information is maintained and for a period of 3 years thereafter, to:

(A) relevant financial records that are maintained by a financial institution as defined in 31 U.S.C. §5312(a) or by a holding company as defined in section 1101(6) of the Right to Financial Privacy Act of 1978 (12 U.S.C. §3401);

(B) consumer reports pertaining to the employee under the Fair Credit Reporting Act (15 U.S.C. §1681a); and

(C) records maintained by commercial entities within the United States pertaining to any travel by the employee outside the United States.

(2) Information may be requested pursuant to employee consent under this section where:

(A) there are reasonable grounds to believe, based on credible information, that the employee or former employee is, or may be, disclosing classified information in an unauthorized manner to a foreign power or agent of a foreign power;

(B) information the employing agency deems credible indicates the employee or former employee has incurred excessive indebtedness or has acquired a level of affluence that cannot be explained by other information; or

(C) circumstances indicate the employee or former employee had the capability and opportunity to disclose classified information that is known to have been lost or compromised to a foreign power or an agent of a foreign power.

(3) Nothing in this section shall be construed to affect the authority of an investigating agency to obtain information pursuant to the Right to Financial Privacy Act, the Fair Credit Reporting Act or any other applicable law.

SEC. 1.3. FINANCIAL DISCLOSURE.

(a) Not later than 180 days after the effective date of this order, the head of each agency that originates, handles, transmits, or possesses classified information shall designate each employee, by position or category where possible, who has a regular need for access to classified information that, in the discretion of the agency head, would reveal:

> (1) the identity of covert agents as defined in the Intelligence Identities Protection Act of 1982 (50 U.S.C. §421);
>
> (2) technical or specialized national intelligence collection and processing systems that, if disclosed in an unauthorized manner, would substantially negate or impair the effectiveness of the system;
>
> (3) the details of:
>
>> (A) the nature, contents, algorithm, preparation, or use of any code, cipher, or cryptographic system or;
>>
>> (B) the design, construction, functioning, maintenance, or repair of any cryptographic equipment; but not including information concerning the use of cryptographic equipment and services;
>
> (4) particularly sensitive special access programs, the disclosure of which would substantially negate or impair the effectiveness of the information or activity involved; or
>
> (5) especially sensitive nuclear weapons design information (but only for those positions that have been certified as being of a high degree of importance or sensitivity, as described in section 145(f) of the Atomic Energy Act of 1954, as amended).

(b) An employee may not be granted access, or hold a position designated as requiring access, to information described in subsection (a) unless, as a condition of access to such information, the employee:

> (1) files with the head of the agency a financial disclosure report, including information with respect to the spouse and dependent children of the employee, as part of all background investigations or reinvestigations;
>
> (2) is subject to annual financial disclosure requirements, if selected by the agency head; and
>
> (3) files relevant information concerning foreign travel, as determined by the Security Executive Agent.

(c) Not later than 180 days after the effective date of this order, the Security Executive Agent shall develop procedures for the implementation of this section, including a standard financial disclosure form for use by employees under subsection (b) of this section, and agency heads shall identify certain employees, by position or category, who are subject to annual financial disclosure.

SEC. 1.4. USE OF AUTOMATED FINANCIAL RECORD DATA BASES. As part of all investigations and reinvestigations described in section 1.2(d) of this order, agencies may request the Department of the Treasury, under terms and conditions prescribed by the Secretary of the Treasury, to search automated data bases consisting of reports of currency transactions by financial institutions, international transportation of currency or monetary instruments, foreign bank and financial accounts, transactions under $10,000 that are reported as possible money laundering violations, and records of foreign travel.

SEC. 1.5. EMPLOYEE EDUCATION AND ASSISTANCE. The head of each agency that grants access to classified information shall establish a program for employees with access to classified information to:
(a) educate employees about individual responsibilities under this order; and
(b) inform employees about guidance and assistance available concerning issues that may affect their eligibility for access to classified information, including sources of assistance for employees who have questions or concerns about financial matters, mental health, or substance abuse.

PART 2—ACCESS ELIGIBILITY POLICY AND PROCEDURE

SEC. 2.1. ELIGIBILITY DETERMINATIONS.
(a) Determinations of eligibility for access to classified information shall be based on criteria established under this order. Such determinations are separate from suitability determinations with respect to the hiring or retention of persons for employment by the government or any other personnel actions.
(b) The number of employees that each agency determines are eligible for access to classified information shall be kept to the minimum required for the conduct of agency functions.
> (1) Eligibility for access to classified information shall not be requested or granted solely to permit entry to, or ease of movement within, controlled areas when the employee has no need for access and access to classified information may reasonably be prevented. Where circumstances indicate employees may be inadvertently exposed to classified information in the course of their duties, agencies are authorized to grant or deny, in their discretion, facility access approvals to such employees based on an appropriate level of investigation as determined by each agency.
> (2) Except in agencies where eligibility for access is a mandatory condition of employment, eligibility for access to classified information shall only be requested or granted based on a demonstrated, foreseeable need for access. Requesting or approving eligibility in excess of actual requirements is prohibited.

759

(3) Eligibility for access to classified information may be granted where there is a temporary need for access, such as one-time participation in a classified project, provided the investigative standards established under this order have been satisfied. In such cases, a fixed date or event for expiration shall be identified and access to classified information shall be limited to information related to the particular project or assignment.

(4) Access to classified information shall be terminated when an employee no longer has a need for access.

SEC. 2.2. LEVEL OF ACCESS APPROVAL.

(a) The level at which an access approval is granted for an employee shall be limited, and relate directly, to the level of classified information for which there is a need for access. Eligibility for access to a higher level of classified information includes eligibility for access to information classified at a lower level.

(b) Access to classified information relating to a special access program shall be granted in accordance with procedures established by the head of the agency that created the program or, for programs pertaining to intelligence activities (including special activities but not including military operational, strategic, and tactical programs) or intelligence sources and methods, by the Director of Central Intelligence. To the extent possible and consistent with the national security interests of the United States, such procedures shall be consistent with the standards and procedures established by and under this order.

SEC. 2.3 TEMPORARY ACCESS TO HIGHER LEVELS.

(a) An employee who has been determined to be eligible for access to classified information based on favorable adjudication of a completed investigation may be granted temporary access to a higher level where security personnel authorized by the agency head to make access eligibility determinations find that such access:

>(1) is necessary to meet operational or contractual exigencies not expected to be of a recurring nature;
>(2) will not exceed 180 days; and
>(3) is limited to specific, identifiable information that is made the subject of a written access record.

(b) Where the access granted under subsection (a) of this section involves another agency's classified information, that agency must concur before access to its information is granted.

SEC. 2.4. RECIPROCAL ACCEPTANCE OF ACCESS ELIGIBILITY DETERMINATIONS.

(a) Except when an agency has substantial information indicating that an employee may not satisfy the standards in section 3.1 of this order, background investigations and eligibility determinations conducted under this order shall be mutually and reciprocally accepted by all agencies.

(b) Except where there is substantial information indicating that the employee may not satisfy the standards in section 3.1 of this order, an employee with existing access to a special access program shall not be denied eligibility for access to another special access program at the same sensitivity level as determined personally by the agency head or deputy agency head, or have an existing access eligibility readjudicated, so long as the employee has a need for access to the information involved.

(c) This section shall not preclude agency heads from establishing additional, but not duplicative, investigative or adjudicative procedures for a special access program or for candidates for detail or assignment to their agencies, where such procedures are required in exceptional circumstances to protect the national security.

(d) Where temporary eligibility for access is granted under sections 2.3 or 3.3 of this order or where the determination of eligibility for access is conditional, the fact of such temporary or conditional access shall be conveyed to any other agency that considers affording the employee access to its information.

SEC. 2.5. SPECIFIC ACCESS REQUIREMENT.

(a) Employees who have been determined to be eligible for access to classified information shall be given access to classified information only where there is a need-to-know that information.

(b) It is the responsibility of employees who are authorized holders of classified information to verify that a prospective recipient's eligibility for access has been granted by an authorized agency official and to ensure that a need-to-know exists prior to allowing such access, and to challenge requests for access that do not appear well-founded.

SEC. 2.6. ACCESS BY NON-UNITED STATES CITIZENS.

(a) Where there are compelling reasons in furtherance of an agency mission, immigrant alien and foreign national employees who possess a special expertise may, in the discretion of the agency, be granted limited access to classified information only for specific programs, projects, contracts, licenses, certificates, or grants for which there is a need for access. Such individuals shall not be eligible for access to any greater level of classified information than the United States Government has determined may be releasable to the country of which the subject is currently a citizen, and such limited access may be approved only if the prior 10 years of the subject's life can be appropriately investigated. If there are any doubts concerning granting access, additional lawful investigative procedures shall be fully pursued.

(b) Exceptions to these requirements may be permitted only by the agency head or the senior agency official designated under section 6.1 of this order to further substantial national security interests.

PART 3—ACCESS ELIGIBILITY STANDARDS

SEC. 3.1. STANDARDS.

(a) No employee shall be deemed to be eligible for access to classified information merely by reason of Federal service or contracting, licensee, certificate holder, or grantee status, or as a matter of right or privilege, or as a result of any particular title, rank, position, or affiliation.

(b) Except as provided in sections 2.6 and 3.3 of this order, eligibility for access to classified information shall be granted only to employees who are United States citizens for whom an appropriate investigation has been completed and whose personal and professional history affirmatively indicates loyalty to the United States, strength of character, trustworthiness, honesty, reliability, discretion, and sound judgment, as well as freedom from conflicting allegiances and potential for coercion, and willingness and ability to abide by regulations governing the use, handling, and protection of classified information. A determination of eligibility for access to such information is a discretionary security decision based on judgments by appropriately trained adjudicative personnel or appropriate automated procedures. Eligibility shall be granted only where facts and circumstances indicate access to classified information is clearly consistent with the national security interests of the United States, and any doubt shall be resolved in favor of the national security.

(c) The United States Government does not discriminate on the basis of race, color, religion, sex, national origin, disability, or sexual orientation in granting access to classified information.

(d) In determining eligibility for access under this order, agencies may investigate and consider any matter that relates to the determination of whether access is clearly consistent with the interests of national security. No inference concerning the standards in this section may be raised solely on the basis of the sexual orientation of the employee.

(e) No negative inference concerning the standards in this section may be raised solely on the basis of mental health counseling. Such counseling can be a positive factor in eligibility determinations. However, mental health counseling, where relevant to the adjudication of access to classified information, may justify further inquiry to determine whether the standards of subsection (b) of this section are satisfied, and mental health may be considered where it directly relates to those standards.

(f) Not later than 180 days after the effective date of this order, the Security Executive Agent shall develop a common set of adjudicative guidelines for determining eligibility for access to classified information, including access to special access programs.

SEC. 3.2. BASIS FOR ELIGIBILITY APPROVAL.

(a) Eligibility determinations for access to classified information shall be based on information concerning the applicant or employee that is acquired through the investigation conducted pursuant to this order or otherwise available to security officials and shall be made part of the applicant's or employee's security record. Applicants or employees shall be required to provide relevant information pertaining to their background and character for use in investigating and adjudicating their eligibility for access.

(b) Not later than 180 days after the effective date of this order, the Security Executive Agent shall develop a common set of investigative standards for background investigations for access to classified information. These standards may vary for the various levels of access.

(c) Nothing in this order shall prohibit an agency from utilizing any lawful investigative procedure in addition to the investigative requirements set forth in this order and its implementing regulations to resolve issues that may arise during the course of a background investigation or reinvestigation.

SEC. 3.3. SPECIAL CIRCUMSTANCES.

(a) In exceptional circumstances where official functions must be performed prior to the completion of the investigative and adjudication process, temporary eligibility for access to classified information may be granted to an employee while the initial investigation is underway. When such eligibility is granted, the initial investigation shall be expedited.

(1) Temporary eligibility for access under this section shall include a justification, and the employee must be notified in writing that further access is expressly conditioned on the favorable completion of the investigation and issuance of an access eligibility approval. Access will be immediately terminated, along with any assignment requiring an access eligibility approval, if such approval is not granted.

(2) Temporary eligibility for access may be granted only by security personnel authorized by the agency head to make access eligibility determinations and shall be based on minimum investigative standards developed by the Security Executive Agent not later than 180 days after the effective date of this order.

(3) Temporary eligibility for access may be granted only to particular, identified categories of classified information necessary to perform the lawful and authorized functions that are the basis for the granting of temporary access.

(b) Nothing in subsection (a) shall be construed as altering the authority of an agency head to waive requirements for granting access to classified information pursuant to statutory authority.

(c) Where access has been terminated under section 2.1(b)(4) of this order and a new need for access arises, access eligibility up to the same level shall be reapproved without further investigation as to employees who were determined to be eligible based on a favorable adjudication of an investigation completed within the prior 5 years, provided they have remained employed by the same employer during the period in question, the employee certifies in writing that there has been no change in the relevant information provided by the employee for the last background investigation, and there is no information that would tend to indicate the employee may no longer satisfy the standards established by this order for access to classified information.

(d) Access eligibility shall be reapproved for individuals who were determined to be eligible based on a favorable adjudication of an investigation completed within the prior 5 years and who have been retired or otherwise separated from United States Government employment for not more than 2 years; provided there is no indication the individual may no longer satisfy the standards of this order, the individual certifies in writing that there has been no change in the relevant information provided by the individual for the last background investigation, and an appropriate record check reveals no unfavorable information.

SEC. 3.4. REINVESTIGATION REQUIREMENTS.

(a) Because circumstances and characteristics may change dramatically over time and thereby alter the eligibility of employees for continued access to classified information, reinvestigations shall be conducted with the same priority and care as initial investigations.

(b) Employees who are eligible for access to classified information shall be the subject of periodic reinvestigations and may also be reinvestigated if, at any time, there is reason to believe that they may no longer meet the standards for access established in this order.

(c) Not later than 180 days after the effective date of this order, the Security Executive Agent shall develop a common set of reinvestigative standards, including the frequency of reinvestigations.

SEC. 3.5. CONTINUOUS EVALUATION. An individual who has been determined to be eligible for or who currently has access to classified information shall be subject to continuous evaluation under standards (including, but not limited to, the frequency of such evaluation) as determined by the Director of National Intelligence.

PART 4—INVESTIGATIONS FOR FOREIGN GOVERNMENTS

SEC. 4. AUTHORITY.

Agencies that conduct background investigations, including the Federal Bureau of Investigation and the Department of State, are authorized to conduct personnel security investigations in the United States when requested by a foreign government as part of its own personnel security program and with the consent of the individual.

PART 5—REVIEW OF ACCESS DETERMINATIONS

SEC. 5.1. DETERMINATIONS OF NEED FOR ACCESS.

A determination under section 2.1(b)(4) of this order that an employee does not have, or no longer has, a need for access is a discretionary determination and shall be conclusive.

SEC. 5.2. Review Proceedings for Denials or Revocations of Eligibility for Access.

(a) Applicants and employees who are determined to not meet the standards for access to classified information established in section 3.1 of this order shall be:

> (1) provided as comprehensive and detailed a written explanation of the basis for that conclusion as the national security interests of the United States and other applicable law permit;
>
> (2) provided within 30 days, upon request and to the extent the documents would be provided if requested under the Freedom of Information Act (5 U.S.C. §552) or the Privacy Act (3 U.S.C. §552a), as applicable, any documents, records, and reports upon which a denial or revocation is based;
>
> (3) informed of their right to be represented by counsel or other representative at their own expense; to request any documents, records, and reports as described in section 5.2(a)(2) upon which a denial or revocation is based; and to request the entire investigative file, as permitted by the national security and other applicable law, which, if requested, shall be promptly provided prior to the time set for a written reply;
>
> (4) provided a reasonable opportunity to reply in writing to, and to request a review of, the determination;
>
> (5) provided written notice of and reasons for the results of the review, the identity of the deciding authority, and written notice of the right to appeal;
>
> (6) provided an opportunity to appeal in writing to a high level panel, appointed by the agency head, which shall be comprised of at least three

members, two of whom shall be selected from outside the security field. Decisions of the panel shall be in writing, and final except as provided in subsection (b) of this section; and

(7) provided an opportunity to appear personally and to present relevant documents, materials, and information at some point in the process before an adjudicative or other authority, other than the investigating entity, as determined by the agency head. A written summary or recording of such appearance shall be made part of the applicant's or employee's security record, unless such appearance occurs in the presence of the appeals panel described in subsection (a)(6) of this section.

(b) Nothing in this section shall prohibit an agency head from personally exercising the appeal authority in subsection (a)(6) of this section based upon recommendations from an appeals panel. In such case, the decision of the agency head shall be final.

(c) Agency heads shall promulgate regulations to implement this section and, at their sole discretion and as resources and national security considerations permit, may provide additional review proceedings beyond those required by subsection (a) of this section. This section does not require additional proceedings, however, and creates no procedural or substantive rights.

(d) When the head of an agency or principal deputy personally certifies that a procedure set forth in this section cannot be made available in a particular case without damaging the national security interests of the United States by revealing classified information, the particular procedure shall not be made available. This certification shall be conclusive.

(e) This section shall not be deemed to limit or affect the responsibility and power of an agency head pursuant to any law or other Executive order to deny or terminate access to classified information in the interests of national security. The power and responsibility to deny or terminate access to classified information pursuant to any law or other Executive order may be exercised only where the agency head determines that the procedures prescribed in subsection (a) of this section cannot be invoked in a manner that is consistent with national security. This determination shall be conclusive.

(f)(1) This section shall not be deemed to limit or affect the responsibility and power of an agency head to make determinations of suitability for employment.

(2) Nothing in this section shall require that an agency provide the procedures prescribed in subsection (a) of this section to an applicant where a conditional offer of employment is withdrawn for reasons of suitability or any other reason other than denial of eligibility for access to classified information.

(3) A suitability determination shall not be used for the purpose of denying an applicant or employee the review proceedings of this section

where there has been a denial or revocation of eligibility for access to classified information.

PART 6—IMPLEMENTATION

SEC. 6.1. AGENCY IMPLEMENTING RESPONSIBILITIES. Heads of agencies that grant employees access to classified information shall:

(a) designate a senior agency official to direct and administer the agency's personnel security program established by this order. All such programs shall include active oversight and continuing security education and awareness programs to ensure effective implementation of this order;

(b) cooperate, under the guidance of the Security Executive Agent, with other agencies to achieve practical, consistent, and effective adjudicative training and guidelines; and

(c) conduct periodic evaluations of the agency's implementation and administration of this order, including the implementation of section 1.3(a) of this order. Copies of each report shall be provided to the Security Executive Agent.

SEC. 6.2. EMPLOYEE RESPONSIBILITIES.

(a) Employees who are granted eligibility for access to classified information shall:

   (1) protect classified information in their custody from unauthorized disclosure;

   (2) report all contacts with persons, including foreign nationals, who seek in any way to obtain unauthorized access to classified information;

   (3) report all violations of security regulations to the appropriate security officials; and

   (4) comply with all other security requirements set forth in this order and its implementing regulations.

(b) Employees are encouraged and expected to report any information that raises doubts as to whether another employee's continued eligibility for access to classified information is clearly consistent with the national security.

SEC. 6.3. SECURITY EXECUTIVE AGENT RESPONSIBILITIES AND IMPLEMENTATION.

(a) With respect to actions taken by the Security Executive Agent pursuant to sections 1.3(c), 3.1(f), 3.2(b), 3.3(a)(2), and 3.4(c) of this order, the Director of National Intelligence shall serve as the final authority for implementation.

(b) Any guidelines, standards, or procedures developed by the Security Executive Agent pursuant to this order shall be consistent with those guidelines issued by the Federal Bureau of Investigation in March 1994 on Background Investigations Policy/Guidelines Regarding Sexual Orientation.

(c) In carrying out its responsibilities under this order, the Security Executive Agent shall consult where appropriate with the Overseas Security Executive Agent. In carrying out its responsibilities under section 1.3(c) of this order, the Security Executive Agent shall obtain the concurrence of the Director of the Office of Management and Budget.

SEC. 6.4. SANCTIONS. Employees shall be subject to appropriate sanctions if they knowingly and willfully grant eligibility for, or allow access to, classified information in violation of this order or its implementing regulations. Sanctions may include reprimand, suspension without pay, removal, and other actions in accordance with applicable law and agency regulations.

PART 7—GENERAL PROVISIONS

SEC. 7.1. CLASSIFIED INFORMATION PROCEDURES ACT. Nothing in this order is intended to alter the procedures established under the Classified Information Procedures Act (18 U.S.C. App. §1).

SEC. 7.2. GENERAL.

(a) Information obtained by an agency under sections 1.2(e) or 1.3 of this order may not be disseminated outside the agency, except to:

> (1) the agency employing the employee who is the subject of the records or information;
>
> (2) the Department of Justice for law enforcement or counterintelligence purposes; or
>
> (3) any agency if such information is clearly relevant to the authorized responsibilities of such agency.

(b) The Attorney General, at the request of the head of an agency, shall render an interpretation of this order with respect to any question arising in the course of its administration.

(c) No prior Executive orders are repealed by this order. To the extent that this order is inconsistent with any provision of any prior Executive order, this order shall control, except that this order shall not diminish or otherwise affect the requirements of Executive Order No. 10450, the denial and revocation procedures provided to individuals covered by Executive Order No. 10865, as amended, or access by historical researchers and former presidential appointees under Executive Order No. 12958 or any successor order.

(d) If any provision of this order or the application of such provision is held to be invalid, the remainder of this order shall not be affected.

(e) This Executive order is intended only to improve the internal management of the executive branch and is not intended to, and does not, create any right to administrative or judicial review, or any other right or benefit or trust responsibility, substantive or procedural, enforceable by a party against the United States, its agencies or instrumentalities, its officers or employees, or any other person.

(f) This order is effective immediately.

-/S/-William J. Clinton
THE WHITE HOUSE,
August 2, 1995.

EXECUTIVE ORDER 13388:
FURTHER STRENGTHENING THE SHARING OF
TERRORISM INFORMATION TO PROTECT AMERICANS

(Federal Register Vol. 70, No. 207 (October 27, 2005))

By the authority vested in me as President by the Constitution and the laws of the United States of America, including section 1016 of the Intelligence Reform and Terrorism Prevention Act of 2004 (Public Law 108– 458), and in order to further strengthen the effective conduct of United States counterterrorism activities and protect the territory, people, and interests of the United States of America, including against terrorist attacks, it is hereby ordered as follows:

SECTION 1. POLICY. To the maximum extent consistent with applicable law, agencies shall, in the design and use of information systems and in the dissemination of information among agencies:
(a) give the highest priority to
> (1) the detection, prevention, disruption, preemption, and mitigation of the effects of terrorist activities against the territory, people, and interests of the United States of America;
> (2) the interchange of terrorism information among agencies;
> (3) the interchange of terrorism information between agencies and appropriate authorities of State, local, and tribal governments, and between agencies and appropriate private sector entities; and
> (4) the protection of the ability of agencies to acquire additional such information; and

(b) protect the freedom, information privacy, and other legal rights of Americans in the conduct of activities implementing subsection (a).

SEC. 2. DUTIES OF HEADS OF AGENCIES POSSESSING OR ACQUIRING TERRORISM INFORMATION. To implement the policy set forth in section 1 of this order, the head of each agency that possesses or acquires terrorism information:
(a) shall promptly give access to the terrorism information to the head of each other agency that has counterterrorism functions, and provide the terrorism information to each such agency, unless otherwise directed by the President, and consistent with
> (1) the statutory responsibilities of the agencies providing and receiving the information;
> (2) any guidance issued by the Attorney General to fulfill the policy set forth in subsection 1(b) of this order; and
> (3) other applicable law, including sections 102A(g) and (i) of the National Security Act of 1947, section 1016 of the Intelligence Reform

and Terrorism Prevention Act of 2004 (including any policies, procedures, guidelines, rules, and standards issued pursuant thereto), sections 202 and 892 of the Homeland Security Act of 2002, Executive Order 12958 of April 17, 1995, as amended, and Executive Order 13311 of July 29, 2003; and

(b) shall cooperate in and facilitate production of reports based on terrorism information with contents and formats that permit dissemination that maximizes the utility of the information in protecting the territory, people, and interests of the United States.

SEC. 3. PREPARING TERRORISM INFORMATION FOR MAXIMUM DISTRIBUTION. To assist in expeditious and effective implementation by agencies of the policy set forth in section 1 of this order, the common standards for the sharing of terrorism information established pursuant to section 3 of Executive Order 13356 of August 27, 2004, shall be used, as appropriate, in carrying out section 1016 of the Intelligence Reform and Terrorism Prevention Act of 2004.

SEC. 4. REQUIREMENTS FOR COLLECTION OF TERRORISM INFORMATION INSIDE THE UNITED STATES. To assist in expeditious and effective implementation by agencies of the policy set forth in section 1 of this order, the recommendations regarding the establishment of executive branch-wide collection and sharing requirements, procedures, and guidelines for terrorism information collected within the United States made pursuant to section 4 of Executive Order 13356 shall be used, as appropriate, in carrying out section 1016 of the Intelligence Reform and Terrorism Prevention Act of 2004.

SEC. 5. ESTABLISHMENT AND FUNCTIONS OF INFORMATION SHARING COUNCIL. (a) Consistent with section 1016(g) of the Intelligence Reform and Terrorism Prevention Act of 2004, there is hereby established an Information Sharing Council (Council), chaired by the Program Manager to whom section 1016 of such Act refers, and composed exclusively of designees of: the Secretaries of State, the Treasury, Defense, Commerce, Energy, and Homeland Security; the Attorney General; the Director of National Intelligence; the Director of the Central Intelligence Agency; the Director of the Office of Management and Budget; the Director of the Federal Bureau of Investigation; the Director of the National Counterterrorism Center; and such other heads of departments or agencies as the Director of National Intelligence may designate.

(b) The mission of the Council is to

(1) provide advice and information concerning the establishment of an interoperable terrorism information sharing environment to facilitate automated sharing of terrorism information among appropriate agencies to implement the policy set forth in section 1 of this order; and

(2) perform the duties set forth in section 1016(g) of the Intelligence Reform and Terrorism Prevention Act of 2004.

(c) To assist in expeditious and effective implementation by agencies of the policy set forth in section 1 of this order, the plan for establishment of a proposed interoperable terrorism information sharing environment reported under section 5(c) of Executive Order 13356 shall be used, as appropriate, in carrying out section 1016 of the Intelligence Reform and Terrorism Prevention Act of 2004.

SEC. 6. DEFINITIONS. As used in this order:

(a) the term "agency" has the meaning set forth for the term "executive agency" in section 105 of title 5, United States Code, together with the Department of Homeland Security, but includes the Postal Rate Commission and the United States Postal Service and excludes the Government Accountability Office; and

(b) the term "terrorism information" has the meaning set forth for such term in section 1016(a)(4) of the Intelligence Reform and Terrorism Prevention Act of 2004.

SEC. 7. GENERAL PROVISIONS.

(a) This order:
>(1) shall be implemented in a manner consistent with applicable law, including Federal law protecting the information privacy and other legal rights of Americans, and subject to the availability of appropriations;
>(2) shall be implemented in a manner consistent with the authority of the principal officers of agencies as heads of their respective agencies, including under section 199 of the Revised Statutes (22 U.S.C. §2651), section 201 of the Department of Energy Organization Act (42 U.S.C. §7131), section 103 of the National Security Act of 1947 (50 U.S.C. §403–3), section 102(a) of the Homeland Security Act of 2002 (6 U.S.C. §112(a)), and sections 301 of title 5, 113(b) and 162(b) of title 10, 1501 of title 15, 503 of title 28, and 301(b) of title 31, United States Code;
>(3) shall be implemented consistent with the Presidential Memorandum of June 2, 2005, on "Strengthening Information Sharing, Access, and Integration—Organizational, Management, and Policy Development Structures for Creating the Terrorism Information Sharing Environment;"
>(4) shall not be construed to impair or otherwise affect the functions of the Director of the Office of Management and Budget relating to budget,
>(5) shall be implemented in a manner consistent with section 102A of the National Security Act of 1947.

(b) This order is intended only to improve the internal management of the Federal Government and is not intended to, and does not, create any rights or benefits, substantive or procedural, enforceable at law or in equity by a party against the United States, its departments, agencies, instrumentalities, or entities, its officers, employees, or agents, or any other person.

SEC. 8. AMENDMENTS AND REVOCATION.
(a) Executive Order 13311 of July 29, 2003, is amended:
>   (1) by striking "Director of Central Intelligence" each place it appears and inserting in lieu thereof in each such place "Director of National Intelligence"; and
>   (2) by striking "103(c)(7)" and inserting in lieu thereof "102A(i)(1)".
(b) Executive Order 13356 of August 27, 2004, is hereby revoked.

-/S/-George W. Bush
THE WHITE HOUSE,
October 25, 2005.

EXECUTIVE ORDER 13462:
PRESIDENT'S INTELLIGENCE ADVISORY BOARD AND
INTELLIGENCE OVERSIGHT BOARD

(Federal Register Vol. 73, No. 43 (March 4, 2008),
amended by EO 13516 (2009))

By the authority vested in me as President by the Constitution and the laws of the
United States of America, it is hereby ordered as follows:

SECTION 1. POLICY.
It is the policy of the United States to ensure that the President and other officers
of the United States with responsibility for the security of the Nation and the
advancement of its interests have access to accurate, insightful, objective, and
timely information concerning the capabilities, intentions, and activities of
foreign powers.

SEC. 2. DEFINITIONS. As used in this order:
(a) "department concerned" means an executive department listed in section 101
of title 5, United States Code, that contains an organization listed in or designated
pursuant to section 3(4) of the National Security Act of 1947, as amended (50
U.S.C. 401a(4));
(b) "intelligence activities" has the meaning specified in section 3.5 of Executive
Order 12333 of December 4, 1981, as amended; and
(c) "intelligence community" means the organizations listed in or designated
pursuant to section 3(4) of the National Security Act of 1947, as amended.

SEC. 3. ESTABLISHMENT OF THE PRESIDENT'S INTELLIGENCE ADVISORY BOARD.
(a) There is hereby established, within the Executive Office of the President and
exclusively to advise and assist the President as set forth in this order, the
President's Intelligence Advisory Board (PIAB).
(b) The PIAB shall consist of not more than 16 members appointed by the
President from among individuals who are not full-time employees of the Federal
Government.
(c) The President shall designate a Chair or Co-Chairs from among the members
of the PIAB, who shall convene and preside at meetings of the PIAB, determine
its agenda, and direct its work.
(d) Members of the PIAB and the Intelligence Oversight Board (IOB) established
in section 5 of this order:
> (i) shall serve without any compensation for their work on the PIAB or
> the IOB; and

(ii) while engaged in the work of the PIAB or the IOB, may be allowed travel expenses, including per diem in lieu of subsistence, as authorized by law for persons serving intermittently in the Government (5 U.S.C. 5701-5707).

(e) The PIAB shall utilize such full-time professional and administrative staff as authorized by the Chair and approved by the President or the President's designee. Such staff shall be supervised by an Executive Director of the PIAB, appointed by the President, whom the President may designate to serve also as the Executive Director of the IOB.

SEC. 4. FUNCTIONS OF THE PIAB. Consistent with the policy set forth in section 1 of this order, the PIAB shall have the authority to, as the PIAB determines appropriate, or shall, when directed by the President:

(a) assess the quality, quantity, and adequacy of intelligence collection, of analysis and estimates, and of counterintelligence and other intelligence activities, assess the adequacy of management, personnel and organization in the intelligence community, and review the performance of all agencies of the Federal Government that are engaged in the collection, evaluation, or production of intelligence or the execution of intelligence policy and report the results of such assessments or reviews:

(i) to the President, as necessary but not less than twice each year; and

(ii) to the Director of National Intelligence (DNI) and the heads of departments concerned when the PIAB determines appropriate; and

(b) consider and make appropriate recommendations to the President, the DNI, or the head of the department concerned with respect to matters identified to the PIAB by the DNI or the head of a department concerned.

SEC. 5. ESTABLISHMENT OF INTELLIGENCE OVERSIGHT BOARD.

(a) There is hereby established a committee of the PIAB to be known as the Intelligence Oversight Board.

(b) The IOB shall consist of not more than five members of the PIAB who are designated by the President from among members of the PIAB to serve on the IOB. The IOB shall utilize such full-time professional and administrative staff as authorized by the Chair and approved by the President or the President's designee. Such staff shall be supervised by an Executive Director of the IOB, appointed by the President, whom the President may designate to serve also as the Executive Director of the PIAB.

(c) The President shall designate a Chair from among the members of the IOB, who shall convene and preside at meetings of the IOB, determine its agenda, and direct its work.

SEC. 6. FUNCTIONS OF THE IOB. Consistent with the policy set forth in section 1 of this order, the IOB shall:

(a) issue criteria on the thresholds for reporting matters to the IOB, to the extent consistent with section 1.6(c) of Executive Order 12333 or the corresponding provision of any successor order;

(b) inform the President of intelligence activities that the IOB believes:

(i)(A) may be unlawful or contrary to Executive Order or presidential directive; and

(B) are not being adequately addressed by the Attorney General, the DNI, or the head of the department concerned; or

(ii) should be immediately reported to the President.

(c) forward to the Attorney General information concerning intelligence activities that involve possible violations of Federal criminal law or otherwise implicate the authority of the Attorney General;

(d) review and assess the effectiveness, efficiency, and sufficiency of the processes by which the DNI and the heads of departments concerned perform their respective functions under this order and report thereon as necessary, together with any recommendations, to the President and, as appropriate, the DNI and the head of the department concerned;

(e) receive and review information submitted by the DNI under subsection 7(c) of this order and make recommendations thereon, including for any needed corrective action, with respect to such information, and the intelligence activities to which the information relates, as necessary, but not less than twice each year, to the President, the DNI, and the head of the department concerned; and

(f) conduct, or request that the DNI or the head of the department concerned, as appropriate, carry out and report to the IOB the results of, investigations of intelligence activities that the IOB determines are necessary to enable the IOB to carry out its functions under this order.

SEC. 7. FUNCTIONS OF THE DIRECTOR OF NATIONAL INTELLIGENCE. Consistent with the policy set forth in section 1 of this order, the DNI shall:

(a) with respect to guidelines applicable to organizations within the intelligence community that concern reporting of intelligence activities described in subsection 6(b)(i)(A) of this order:

(i) review and ensure that such guidelines are consistent with section 1.6(c) of Executive Order 12333, or a corresponding provision of any successor order, and this order; and

(ii) issue for incorporation in such guidelines instructions relating to the format and schedule of such reporting as necessary to implement this order;

(b) with respect to intelligence activities described in subsection 6(b)(i)(A) of this order:

(i) receive reports submitted to the IOB pursuant to section 1.6(c) of Executive Order 12333, or a corresponding provision of any successor order;

(ii) forward to the Attorney General information in such reports relating to such intelligence activities to the extent that such activities involve possible violations of Federal criminal laws or implicate the authority of the Attorney General unless the DNI or the head of the department concerned has previously provided such information to the Attorney General; and

(iii) monitor the intelligence community to ensure that the head of the department concerned has directed needed corrective actions and that such actions have been taken and report to the IOB and the head of the department concerned, and as appropriate the President, when such actions have not been timely taken; and

(c) submit to the IOB as necessary and no less than twice each year:

(i) an analysis of the reports received under subsection (b)(i) of this section, including an assessment of the gravity, frequency, trends, and patterns of occurrences of intelligence activities described in subsection 6(b)(i)(A) of this order;

(ii) a summary of direction under subsection (b)(iii) of this section and any related recommendations; and

(iii) an assessment of the effectiveness of corrective action taken by the DNI or the head of the department concerned with respect to intelligence activities described in subsection 6(b)(i)(A) of this order.

SEC. 8. FUNCTIONS OF HEADS OF DEPARTMENTS CONCERNED AND ADDITIONAL FUNCTIONS OF THE DIRECTOR OF NATIONAL INTELLIGENCE.

(a) To the extent permitted by law, the DNI and the heads of departments concerned shall provide such information and assistance as the PIAB and the IOB determine is needed to perform their functions under this order.

(b) The heads of departments concerned shall:

(i) ensure that the DNI receives:

(A) copies of reports submitted to the IOB pursuant to section 1.6(c) of Executive Order 12333, or a corresponding provision of any successor order; and

(B) such information and assistance as the DNI may need to perform functions under this order; and

(ii) designate the offices within their respective organizations that shall submit reports to the IOB required by Executive Order and inform the DNI and the IOB of such designations; and

(iii) ensure that departments concerned comply with instructions issued by the DNI under subsection 7(a)(ii) of this order.

(c) The head of a department concerned who does not implement a recommendation to that head of department from the PIAB under subsection 4(b) of this order or from the IOB under subsections 6(c) or 6(d) of this order shall promptly report through the DNI to the Board that made the recommendation, or to the President, the reasons for not implementing the recommendation.

(d) The DNI shall ensure that the Director of the Central Intelligence Agency performs the functions with respect to the Central Intelligence Agency under this order that a head of a department concerned performs with respect to organizations within the intelligence community that are part of that department.

SEC. 9. REFERENCES AND TRANSITION.

(a) References in Executive Orders other than this order, or in any other presidential guidance, to the "President's Foreign Intelligence Advisory Board" shall be deemed to be references to the President's Intelligence Advisory Board established by this order.

(b) Individuals who are members of the President's Foreign Intelligence Advisory Board under Executive Order 12863 of September 13, 1993, as amended, immediately prior to the signing of this order shall be members of the President's Intelligence Advisory Board immediately upon the signing of this order, to serve as such consistent with this order until the date that is 15 months following the date of this order.

(c) Individuals who are members of the Intelligence Oversight Board under Executive Order 12863 immediately prior to the signing of this order shall be members of the Intelligence Oversight Board under this order, to serve as such consistent with this order until the date that is 15 months following the date of this order.

(d) The individual serving as Executive Director of the President's Foreign Intelligence Advisory Board immediately prior to the signing of this order shall serve as the Executive Director of the PIAB until such person resigns, dies, or is removed, or upon appointment of a successor under this order and shall serve as the Executive Director of the IOB until an Executive Director of the IOB is appointed or designated under this order.

SEC. 10. REVOCATION. Executive Order 12863 is revoked.

SEC. 11. GENERAL PROVISIONS.

(a) Nothing in this order shall be construed to impair or otherwise affect:

    (i) authority granted by law to a department or agency, or the head thereof; or

    (ii) functions of the Director of the Office of Management and Budget relating to budget, administrative, or legislative proposals.

(b) Any person who is a member of the PIAB or IOB, or who is granted access to classified national security information in relation to the activities of the PIAB or the IOB, as a condition of access to such information, shall sign and comply with appropriate agreements to protect such information from unauthorized disclosure. This order shall be implemented in a manner consistent with Executive Order 12958 of April 17, 1995, as amended, and Executive Order 12968 of August 2, 1995, as amended.

(c) This order shall be implemented consistent with applicable law and subject to the availability of appropriations.

(d) This order is intended only to improve the internal management of the executive branch and is not intended to, and does not, create any right or benefit, substantive or procedural, enforceable at law or in equity, by any party against the United States, its departments, agencies or entities, its officers, employees, or agents, or any other person.

-/S/- George W. Bush
THE WHITE HOUSE,
February 29, 2008.

EXECUTIVE ORDER 13467:
REFORMING PROCESSES RELATED TO SUITABILITY FOR GOVERNMENT EMPLOYMENT, FITNESS FOR CONTRACTOR EMPLOYEES, AND ELIGIBILITY FOR ACCESS TO CLASSIFIED NATIONAL SECURITY INFORMATION

(Federal Register Vol. 73, No. 128 (July 2, 2008))

By the authority vested in me as President by the Constitution and the laws of the United States of America, and in order to ensure an efficient, practical, reciprocal, and aligned system for investigating and determining suitability for Government employment, contractor employee fitness, and eligibility for access to classified information, while taking appropriate account of title III of Public Law 108-458, it is hereby ordered as follows:

PART 1 —POLICY, APPLICABILITY, AND DEFINITIONS

SECTION 1.1. POLICY. Executive branch policies and procedures relating to suitability, contractor employee fitness, eligibility to hold a sensitive position, access to federally controlled facilities and information systems, and eligibility for access to classified information shall be aligned using consistent standards to the extent possible, provide for reciprocal recognition, and shall ensure cost-effective, timely, and efficient protection of the national interest, while providing fair treatment to those upon whom the Federal Government relies to conduct our Nation's business and protect national security.

SEC. 1.2. APPLICABILITY.
(a) This order applies to all covered individuals as defined in section 1.3(g), except that:
>   (i) the provisions regarding eligibility for physical access to federally controlled facilities and logical access to federally controlled information systems do not apply to individuals exempted in accordance with guidance pursuant to the Federal Information Security Management Act (title III of Public Law 107-347) and Homeland Security Presidential Directive 12; and
>   (ii) the qualification standards for enlistment, appointment, and induction into the Armed Forces pursuant to title 10, United States Code, are unaffected by this order.

(b) This order also applies to investigations and determinations of eligibility for access to classified information for employees of agencies working in or for the legislative or judicial branches when those investigations or determinations are conducted by the executive branch.

SEC. 1.3. DEFINITIONS. For the purpose of this order:

(a) "Adjudication" means the evaluation of pertinent data in a background investigation, as well as any other available information that is relevant and reliable, to determine whether a covered individual is:

    (i) suitable for Government employment;

    (ii) eligible for logical and physical access;

    (iii) eligible for access to classified information;

    (iv) eligible to hold a sensitive position; or

    (v) fit to perform work for or on behalf of the Government as a contractor employee.

(b) "Agency" means any "Executive agency" as defined in section 105 of title 5, United States Code, including the "military departments," as defined in section 102 of title 5, United States Code, and any other entity within the executive branch that comes into possession of classified information or has designated positions as sensitive, except such an entity headed by an officer who is not a covered individual.

(c) "Classified information" means information that has been determined pursuant to Executive Order 12958 of April 17, 1995, as amended, or a successor or predecessor order, or the Atomic Energy Act of 1954 (42 U.S.C. 2011 *et seq.*) to require protection against unauthorized disclosure.

(d) "Continuous evaluation" means reviewing the background of an individual who has been determined to be eligible for access to classified information (including additional or new checks of commercial databases, Government databases, and other information lawfully available to security officials) at any time during the period of eligibility to determine whether that individual continues to meet the requirements for eligibility for access to classified information.

(e) "Contractor" means an expert or consultant (not appointed under section 3109 of title 5, United States Code) to an agency; an industrial or commercial contractor, licensee, certificate holder, or grantee of any agency, including all subcontractors; a personal services contractor; or any other category of person who performs work for or on behalf of an agency (but not a Federal employee).

(f) "Contractor employee fitness" means fitness based on character and conduct for work for or on behalf of the Government as a contractor employee.

(g) "Covered individual" means a person who performs work for or on behalf of the executive branch, or who seeks to perform work for or on behalf of the executive branch, but does not include:

    (i) the President or (except to the extent otherwise directed by the President) employees of the President under section 105 or 107 of title 3, United States Code; or

(ii) the Vice President or (except to the extent otherwise directed by the Vice President) employees of the Vice President under section 106 of title 3 or annual legislative branch appropriations acts.

(h) "End-to-end automation" means an executive branch-wide federated system that uses automation to manage and monitor cases and maintain relevant documentation of the application (but not an employment application), investigation, adjudication, and continuous evaluation processes.

(i) "Federally controlled facilities" and "federally controlled information systems" have the meanings prescribed in guidance pursuant to the Federal Information Security Management Act (title III of Public Law 107-347) and Homeland Security Presidential Directive 12.

(j) "Logical and physical access" means access other than occasional or intermittent access to federally controlled facilities or information systems.

(k) "Sensitive position" means any position so designated under Executive Order 10450 of April 27, 1953, as amended.

(l) "Suitability" has the meaning and coverage provided in 5 CFR Part 731.

PART 2 —ALIGNMENT, RECIPROCITY, AND GOVERNANCE

SEC. 2.1. ALIGNED SYSTEM.

(a) Investigations and adjudications of covered individuals who require a determination of suitability, eligibility for logical and physical access, eligibility to hold a sensitive position, eligibility for access to classified information, and, as appropriate, contractor employee fitness, shall be aligned using consistent standards to the extent possible. Each successively higher level of investigation and adjudication shall build upon, but not duplicate, the ones below it.

(b) The aligned system shall employ updated and consistent standards and methods, enable innovations with enterprise information technology capabilities and end-to-end automation to the extent practicable, and ensure that relevant information maintained by agencies can be accessed and shared rapidly across the executive branch, while protecting national security, protecting privacy-related information, ensuring resulting decisions are in the national interest, and providing the Federal Government with an effective workforce.

(c) Except as otherwise authorized by law, background investigations and adjudications shall be mutually and reciprocally accepted by all agencies. An agency may not establish additional investigative or adjudicative requirements (other than requirements for the conduct of a polygraph examination consistent with law, directive, or regulation) that exceed the requirements for suitability, contractor employee fitness, eligibility for logical or physical access, eligibility to hold a sensitive position, or eligibility for access to classified information without the approval of the Suitability Executive Agent or Security Executive Agent, as appropriate, and provided that approval to establish additional requirements shall be limited to circumstances where additional requirements are necessary to address significant needs unique to the agency involved or to protect national security.

SEC. 2.2. ESTABLISHMENT AND FUNCTIONS OF PERFORMANCE ACCOUNTABILITY COUNCIL.

(a) There is hereby established a Suitability and Security Clearance Performance Accountability Council (Council).

(b) The Deputy Director for Management, Office of Management and Budget, shall serve as Chair of the Council and shall have authority, direction, and control over the Council's functions. Membership on the Council shall include the Suitability Executive Agent and the Security Executive Agent. The Chair shall select a Vice Chair to act in the Chair's absence. The Chair shall have authority to designate officials from additional agencies who shall serve as members of the Council. Council membership shall be limited to Federal Government employees and shall include suitability and security professionals.

(c) The Council shall be accountable to the President to achieve, consistent with this order, the goals of reform, and is responsible for driving implementation of the reform effort, ensuring accountability by agencies, ensuring the Suitability Executive Agent and the Security Executive Agent align their respective processes, and sustaining reform momentum.

(d) The Council shall:

> (i) ensure alignment of suitability, security, and, as appropriate, contractor employee fitness investigative and adjudicative processes;
> (ii) hold agencies accountable for the implementation of suitability, security, and, as appropriate, contractor employee fitness processes and procedures;
> (iii) establish requirements for enterprise information technology;
> (iv) establish annual goals and progress metrics and prepare annual reports on results;
> (v) ensure and oversee the development of tools and techniques for enhancing background investigations and the making of eligibility determinations;
> (vi) arbitrate disparities in procedures between the Suitability Executive Agent and the Security Executive Agent;
> (vii) ensure sharing of best practices; and
> (viii) advise the Suitability Executive Agent and the Security Executive Agent on policies affecting the alignment of investigations and adjudications.

(e) The Chair may, to ensure the effective implementation of the policy set forth in section 1.1 of this order and to the extent consistent with law, assign, in whole or in part, to the head of any agency (solely or jointly) any function within the

Council's responsibility relating to alignment and improvement of investigations and determinations of suitability, contractor employee fitness, eligibility for logical and physical access, eligibility for access to classified information, or eligibility to hold a sensitive position.

SEC. 2.3. ESTABLISHMENT, DESIGNATION, AND FUNCTIONS OF EXECUTIVE AGENTS.

(a) There is hereby established a Suitability Executive Agent and a Security Executive Agent.

(b) The Director of the Office of Personnel Management shall serve as the Suitability Executive Agent. As the Suitability Executive Agent, the Director of the Office of Personnel Management will continue to be responsible for developing and implementing uniform and consistent policies and procedures to ensure the effective, efficient, and timely completion of investigations and adjudications relating to determinations of suitability and eligibility for logical and physical access.

(c) The Director of National Intelligence shall serve as the Security Executive Agent. The Security Executive Agent:

    (i) shall direct the oversight of investigations and determinations of eligibility for access to classified information or eligibility to hold a sensitive position made by any agency;

    (ii) shall be responsible for developing uniform and consistent policies and procedures to ensure the effective, efficient, and timely completion of investigations and adjudications relating to determinations of eligibility for access to classified information or eligibility to hold a sensitive position;

    (iii) may issue guidelines and instructions to the heads of agencies to ensure appropriate uniformity, centralization, efficiency, effectiveness, and timeliness in processes relating to determinations by agencies of eligibility for access to classified information or eligibility to hold a sensitive position;

    (iv) shall serve as the final authority to designate an agency or agencies to conduct investigations of persons who are proposed for access to classified information to ascertain whether such persons satisfy the criteria for obtaining and retaining access to classified information or eligibility to hold a sensitive position;

    (v) shall serve as the final authority to designate an agency or agencies to determine eligibility for access to classified information in accordance with Executive Order 12968 of August 2, 1995;

    (vi) shall ensure reciprocal recognition of eligibility for access to classified information among the agencies, including acting as the final authority to arbitrate and resolve disputes among the agencies involving the reciprocity of investigations and determinations of eligibility for access to classified information or eligibility to hold a sensitive position; and

(vii) may assign, in whole or in part, to the head of any agency (solely or jointly) any of the functions detailed in (i) through (vi), above, with the agency's exercise of such assigned functions to be subject to the Security Executive Agent's oversight and with such terms and conditions (including approval by the Security Executive Agent) as the Security Executive Agent determines appropriate.

(d) Nothing in this order shall be construed in a manner that would limit the authorities of the Director of the Office of Personnel Management or the Director of National Intelligence under law.

SEC. 2.4. ADDITIONAL FUNCTIONS.

(a) The duties assigned to the Security Policy Board by Executive Order 12968 of August 2, 1995, to consider, coordinate, and recommend policy directives for executive branch security policies, procedures, and practices are reassigned to the Security Executive Agent.

(b) Heads of agencies shall:

(i) carry out any function assigned to the agency head by the Chair, and shall assist the Chair, the Council, the Suitability Executive Agent, and the Security Executive Agent in carrying out any function under sections 2.2 and 2.3 of this order;

(ii) implement any policy or procedure developed pursuant to this order;

(iii) to the extent permitted by law, make available to the Performance Accountability Council, the Suitability Executive Agent, or the Security Executive Agent such information as may be requested to implement this order;

(iv) ensure that all actions taken under this order take account of the counterintelligence interests of the United States, as appropriate; and

(v) ensure that actions taken under this order are consistent with the President's constitutional authority to:

(A) conduct the foreign affairs of the United States;

(B) withhold information the disclosure of which could impair the foreign relations, the national security, the deliberative processes of the Executive, or the performance of the Executive's constitutional duties;

(C) recommend for congressional consideration such measures as the President may judge necessary or expedient; and

(D) supervise the unitary executive branch.

PART 3 – MISCELLANEOUS

SEC. 3. GENERAL PROVISIONS.

(a) Executive Order 13381 of June 27, 2005, as amended, is revoked. Nothing in this order shall:

(i) supersede, impede, or otherwise affect:

(A) Executive Order 10450 of April 27, 1953, as amended;

(B) Executive Order 10577 of November 23, 1954, as amended;

(C) Executive Order 12333 of December 4, 1981, as amended;

(D) Executive Order 12829 of January 6, 1993, as amended; or

(E) Executive Order 12958 of April 17, 1995, as amended; nor

(ii) diminish or otherwise affect the denial and revocation procedures provided to individuals covered by Executive Order 10865 of February 20, 1960, as amended.

(b) Executive Order 12968 of August 2, 1995 is amended:

(i) by inserting: "Sec. 3.5. Continuous Evaluation. An individual who has been determined to be eligible for or who currently has access to classified information shall be subject to continuous evaluation under standards (including, but not limited to, the frequency of such evaluation) as determined by the Director of National Intelligence."; and

(ii) by striking "the Security Policy Board shall make recommendations to the President through the Assistant to the President for National Security Affairs" in section 6.3(a) and inserting in lieu thereof "the Director of National Intelligence shall serve as the final authority";

(iii) by striking "Security Policy Board" and inserting in lieu thereof "Security Executive Agent" in each instance;

(iv) by striking "the Board" in section 1.1(j) and inserting in lieu thereof "the Security Executive Agent"; and

(v) by inserting "or appropriate automated procedures" in section 3.1(b) after "by appropriately trained adjudicative personnel".

(c) Nothing in this order shall supersede, impede, or otherwise affect the remainder of Executive Order 12968 of August 2, 1995, as amended.

(d) Executive Order 12171 of November 19, 1979, as amended, is further amended by striking "The Center for Federal Investigative Services" in section 1-216 and inserting in lieu thereof "The Federal Investigative Services Division."

(e) Nothing in this order shall be construed to impair or otherwise affect the:

(i) authority granted by law to a department or agency, or the head thereof; or

(ii) functions of the Director of the Office of Management and Budget relating to budget, administrative, or legislative proposals.

(f) This order shall be implemented consistent with applicable law and subject to the availability of appropriations.

(g) Existing delegations of authority made pursuant to Executive Order 13381 of June 27, 2005, as amended, to any agency relating to granting eligibility for access to classified information and conducting investigations shall remain in effect, subject to the exercise of authorities pursuant to this order to revise or revoke such delegation.

(h) If any provision of this order or the application of such provision is held to be invalid, the remainder of this order shall not be affected.

(i) This order is intended only to improve the internal management of the executive branch and is not intended to, and does not, create any right or benefit, substantive or procedural, enforceable at law or in equity, by any party against the United States, its agencies, instrumentalities, or entities, its officers or employees, or any other person.

-/S/- George W. Bush
THE WHITE HOUSE,
June 30, 2008.

EXECUTIVE ORDER 13491:
ENSURING LAWFUL INTERROGATION

(Federal Register Vol. 74, No. 16 (January 27, 2009))

By the authority vested in me by the Constitution and the laws of the United States of America, in order to improve the effectiveness of human intelligence gathering, to promote the safe, lawful, and humane treatment of individuals in United States custody and of United States personnel who are detained in armed conflicts, to ensure compliance with the treaty obligations of the United States, including the Geneva Conventions, and to take care that the laws of the United States are faithfully executed, I hereby order as follows:

SECTION 1. REVOCATION. Executive Order 13440 of July 20, 2007, is revoked. All executive directives, orders, and regulations inconsistent with this order, including but not limited to those issued to or by the Central Intelligence Agency (CIA) from September 11, 2001, to January 20, 2009, concerning detention or the interrogation of detained individuals, are revoked to the extent of their inconsistency with this order. Heads of departments and agencies shall take all necessary steps to ensure that all directives, orders, and regulations of their respective departments or agencies are consistent with this order. Upon request, the Attorney General shall provide guidance about which directives, orders, and regulations are inconsistent with this order.

SEC. 2. DEFINITIONS. As used in this order:
(a) "Army Field Manual 2 22.3" means FM 2-22.3, Human Intelligence Collector Operations, issued by the Department of the Army on September 6, 2006.
(b) "Army Field Manual 34-52" means FM 34 52, Intelligence Interrogation, issued by the Department of the Army on May 8, 1987.
(c) "Common Article 3" means Article 3 of each of the Geneva Conventions.
(d) "Convention Against Torture" means the Convention Against Torture and Other Cruel, Inhuman or Degrading Treatment or Punishment, December 10, 1984, 1465 U.N.T.S. 85, S. Treaty Doc. No. 100 20 (1988).
(e) "Geneva Conventions" means:
   (i)   the Convention for the Amelioration of the Condition of the Wounded and Sick in Armed Forces in the Field, August 12, 1949 (6 UST 3114);
   (ii) the Convention for the Amelioration of the Condition of Wounded, Sick and Shipwrecked Members of Armed Forces at Sea, August 12, 1949 (6 UST 3217);
   (iii) the Convention Relative to the Treatment of Prisoners of War, August 12, 1949 (6 UST 3316); and

(iv)   the Convention Relative to the Protection of Civilian Persons in Time of War, August 12, 1949 (6 UST 3516).

(f) "Treated humanely," "violence to life and person," "murder of all kinds," "mutilation," "cruel treatment," "torture," "outrages upon personal dignity," and "humiliating and degrading treatment" refer to, and have the same meaning as, those same terms in Common Article 3.

(g) The terms "detention facilities" and "detention facility" in section 4(a) of this order do not refer to facilities used only to hold people on a short-term, transitory basis.

SEC. 3. STANDARDS AND PRACTICES FOR INTERROGATION OF INDIVIDUALS IN THE CUSTODY OR CONTROL OF THE UNITED STATES IN ARMED CONFLICTS.

(a) Common Article 3 Standards as a Minimum Baseline. Consistent with the requirements of the Federal torture statute, 18 U.S.C. 2340 2340A, section 1003 of the Detainee Treatment Act of 2005, 42 U.S.C. 2000dd, the Convention Against Torture, Common Article 3, and other laws regulating the treatment and interrogation of individuals detained in any armed conflict, such persons shall in all circumstances be treated humanely and shall not be subjected to violence to life and person (including murder of all kinds, mutilation, cruel treatment, and torture), nor to outrages upon personal dignity (including humiliating and degrading treatment), whenever such individuals are in the custody or under the effective control of an officer, employee, or other agent of the United States Government or detained within a facility owned, operated, or controlled by a department or agency of the United States.

(b) Interrogation Techniques and Interrogation-Related Treatment. Effective immediately, an individual in the custody or under the effective control of an officer, employee, or other agent of the United States Government, or detained within a facility owned, operated, or controlled by a department or agency of the United States, in any armed conflict, shall not be subjected to any interrogation technique or approach, or any treatment related to interrogation, that is not authorized by and listed in Army Field Manual 2-22.3 (Manual). Interrogation techniques, approaches, and treatments described in the Manual shall be implemented strictly in accord with the principles, processes, conditions, and limitations the Manual prescribes. Where processes required by the Manual, such as a requirement of approval by specified Department of Defense officials, are inapposite to a department or an agency other than the Department of Defense, such a department or agency shall use processes that are substantially equivalent to the processes the Manual prescribes for the Department of Defense. Nothing in this section shall preclude the Federal Bureau of Investigation, or other Federal law enforcement agencies, from continuing to use authorized, non-coercive techniques of interrogation that are designed to elicit voluntary statements and do not involve the use of force, threats, or promises.

(c) Interpretations of Common Article 3 and the Army Field Manual. From this day forward, unless the Attorney General with appropriate consultation provides further guidance, officers, employees, and other agents of the United States Government may, in conducting interrogations, act in reliance upon Army Field Manual 2-22.3, but may not, in conducting interrogations, rely upon any interpretation of the law governing interrogation —including interpretations of Federal criminal laws, the Convention Against Torture, Common Article 3, Army Field Manual 2-22.3, and its predecessor document, Army Field Manual 34-52 – issued by the Department of Justice between September 11, 2001, and January 20, 2009.

SEC. 4. PROHIBITION OF CERTAIN DETENTION FACILITIES, AND RED CROSS ACCESS TO DETAINED INDIVIDUALS.
(a) CIA Detention. The CIA shall close as expeditiously as possible any detention facilities that it currently operates and shall not operate any such detention facility in the future.
(b) International Committee of the Red Cross Access to Detained Individuals. All departments and agencies of the Federal Government shall provide the International Committee of the Red Cross with notification of, and timely access to, any individual detained in any armed conflict in the custody or under the effective control of an officer, employee, or other agent of the United States Government or detained within a facility owned, operated, or controlled by a department or agency of the United States Government, consistent with Department of Defense regulations and policies.

SEC. 5. SPECIAL INTERAGENCY TASK FORCE ON INTERROGATION AND TRANSFER POLICIES.
(a) Establishment of Special Interagency Task Force. There shall be established a Special Task Force on Interrogation and Transfer Policies (Special Task Force) to review interrogation and transfer policies.
(b) Membership. The Special Task Force shall consist of the following members, or their designees:
    (i)   the Attorney General, who shall serve as Chair;
    (ii)   the Director of National Intelligence, who shall serve as Co-Vice-Chair;
    (iii) the Secretary of Defense, who shall serve as Co-Vice-Chair;
    (iv) the Secretary of State;
    (v)   the Secretary of Homeland Security;
    (vi) the Director of the Central Intelligence Agency;
    (vii) the Chairman of the Joint Chiefs of Staff; and
    (viii) other officers or full-time or permanent part time employees of the United States, as determined by the Chair, with the concurrence of the head of the department or agency concerned.

(c) Staff. The Chair may designate officers and employees within the Department of Justice to serve as staff to support the Special Task Force. At the request of the Chair, officers and employees from other departments or agencies may serve on the Special Task Force with the concurrence of the head of the department or agency that employ such individuals. Such staff must be officers or full-time or permanent part-time employees of the United States. The Chair shall designate an officer or employee of the Department of Justice to serve as the Executive Secretary of the Special Task Force.

(d) Operation. The Chair shall convene meetings of the Special Task Force, determine its agenda, and direct its work. The Chair may establish and direct subgroups of the Special Task Force, consisting exclusively of members of the Special Task Force, to deal with particular subjects.

(e) Mission. The mission of the Special Task Force shall be:

   (i) to study and evaluate whether the interrogation practices and techniques in Army Field Manual 2 22.3, when employed by departments or agencies outside the military, provide an appropriate means of acquiring the intelligence necessary to protect the Nation, and, if warranted, to recommend any additional or different guidance for other departments or agencies; and

   (ii) to study and evaluate the practices of transferring individuals to other nations in order to ensure that such practices comply with the domestic laws, international obligations, and policies of the United States and do not result in the transfer of individuals to other nations to face torture or otherwise for the purpose, or with the effect, of undermining or circumventing the commitments or obligations of the United States to ensure the humane treatment of individuals in its custody or control.

(f) Administration. The Special Task Force shall be established for administrative purposes within the Department of Justice and the Department of Justice shall, to

the extent permitted by law and subject to the availability of appropriations, provide administrative support and funding for the Special Task Force.

(g) Recommendations. The Special Task Force shall provide a report to the President, through the Assistant to the President for National Security Affairs and the Counsel to the President, on the matters set forth in subsection (d) within 180 days of the date of this order, unless the Chair determines that an extension is necessary.

(h) Termination. The Chair shall terminate the Special Task Force upon the completion of its duties.

SEC. 6. CONSTRUCTION WITH OTHER LAWS. Nothing in this order shall be construed to affect the obligations of officers, employees, and other agents of the United States Government to comply with all pertinent laws and treaties of the United States governing detention and interrogation, including but not limited to:

the Fifth and Eighth Amendments to the United States Constitution; the Federal torture statute, 18 U.S.C. 2340 2340A; the War Crimes Act, 18 U.S.C. 2441; the Federal assault statute, 18 U.S.C. 113; the Federal maiming statute, 18 U.S.C. 114; the Federal "stalking" statute, 18 U.S.C. 2261A; articles 93, 124, 128, and 134 of the Uniform Code of Military Justice, 10 U.S.C. 893, 924, 928, and 934; section 1003 of the Detainee Treatment Act of 2005, 42 U.S.C. 2000dd; section 6(c) of the Military Commissions Act of 2006, Public Law 109 366; the Geneva Conventions; and the Convention Against Torture. Nothing in this order shall be construed to diminish any rights that any individual may have under these or other laws and treaties. This order is not intended to, and does not, create any right or benefit, substantive or procedural, enforceable at law or in equity against the United States, its departments, agencies, or other entities, its officers or employees, or any other person.

-/S/- Barack Obama
THE WHITE HOUSE,
January 22, 2009

EXECUTIVE ORDER 13526: CLASSIFIED NATIONAL SECURITY INFORMATION

(Federal Register Vol. 75, No. 2 (January 5, 2010))

This order prescribes a uniform system for classifying, safeguarding, and declassifying national security information, including information relating to defense against transnational terrorism. Our democratic principles require that the American people be informed of the activities of their Government. Also, our Nation's progress depends on the free flow of information both within the Government and to the American people. Nevertheless, throughout our history, the national defense has required that certain information be maintained in confidence in order to protect our citizens, our democratic institutions, our homeland security, and our interactions with foreign nations. Protecting information critical to our Nation's security and demonstrating our commitment to open Government through accurate and accountable application of classification standards and routine, secure, and effective declassification are equally important priorities.

NOW, THEREFORE, I, BARACK OBAMA, by the authority vested in me as President by the Constitution and the laws of the United States of America, it is hereby ordered as follows:

PART 1—ORIGINAL CLASSIFICATION

SECTION 1.1. CLASSIFICATION STANDARDS.
(a) Information may be originally classified under the terms of this order only if all of the following conditions are met:
(1) an original classification authority is classifying the information;
(2) the information is owned by, produced by or for, or is under the control of the United States Government;
(3) the information falls within one or more of the categories of information listed in section 1.4 of this order; and
(4) the original classification authority determines that the unauthorized disclosure of the information reasonably could be expected to result in damage to the national security, which includes defense against transnational terrorism, and the original classification authority is able to identify or describe the damage.
(b) If there is significant doubt about the need to classify information, it shall not be classified. This provision does not:
(1) amplify or modify the substantive criteria or procedures for classification; or
(2) create any substantive or procedural rights subject to judicial review.

(c) Classified information shall not be declassified automatically as a result of any unauthorized disclosure of identical or similar information.
(d) The unauthorized disclosure of foreign government information is presumed to cause damage to the national security.

SEC. 1.2. CLASSIFICATION LEVELS.
(a) Information may be classified at one of the following three levels:
(1) ''Top Secret'' shall be applied to information, the unauthorized disclosure of which reasonably could be expected to cause exceptionally grave damage to the national security that the original classification authority is able to identify or describe.
(2) ''Secret'' shall be applied to information, the unauthorized disclosure of which reasonably could be expected to cause serious damage to the national security that the original classification authority is able to identify or describe.
(3) ''Confidential'' shall be applied to information, the unauthorized disclosure of which reasonably could be expected to cause damage to the national security that the original classification authority is able to identify or describe.
(b) Except as otherwise provided by statute, no other terms shall be used to identify United States classified information.
(c) If there is significant doubt about the appropriate level of classification, it shall be classified at the lower level.

SEC. 1.3. CLASSIFICATION AUTHORITY.
(a) The authority to classify information originally may be exercised only by:
(1) the President and the Vice President;
(2) agency heads and officials designated by the President; and
(3) United States Government officials delegated this authority pursuant to paragraph (c) of this section.
(b) Officials authorized to classify information at a specified level are also authorized to classify information at a lower level.
(c) Delegation of original classification authority.
(1) Delegations of original classification authority shall be limited to the minimum required to administer this order. Agency heads are responsible for ensuring that designated subordinate officials have a demonstrable and continuing need to exercise this authority.
(2) ''Top Secret'' original classification authority may be delegated only by the President, the Vice President, or an agency head or official designated pursuant to paragraph (a)(2) of this section.
(3) ''Secret'' or ''Confidential'' original classification authority may be delegated only by the President, the Vice President, an agency head or official designated pursuant to paragraph (a)(2) of this section, or the senior agency official designated under section 5.4(d) of this order, provided that official has

been delegated "Top Secret" original classification authority by the agency head.

(4) Each delegation of original classification authority shall be in writing and the authority shall not be redelegated except as provided in this order. Each delegation shall identify the official by name or position.

(5) Delegations of original classification authority shall be reported or made available by name or position to the Director of the Information Security Oversight Office.

(d) All original classification authorities must receive training in proper classification (including the avoidance of over-classification) and declassification as provided in this order and its implementing directives at least once a calendar year. Such training must include instruction on the proper safeguarding of classified information and on the sanctions in section 5.5 of this order that may be brought against an individual who fails to classify information properly or protect classified information from unauthorized disclosure. Original classification authorities who do not receive such mandatory training at least once within a calendar year shall have their classification authority suspended by the agency head or the senior agency official designated under section 5.4(d) of this order until such training has taken place. A waiver may be granted by the agency head, the deputy agency head, or the senior agency official if an individual is unable to receive such training due to unavoidable circumstances. Whenever a waiver is granted, the individual shall receive such training as soon as practicable.

(e) Exceptional cases. When an employee, government contractor, licensee, certificate holder, or grantee of an agency who does not have original classification authority originates information believed by that person to require classification, the information shall be protected in a manner consistent with this order and its implementing directives. The information shall be transmitted promptly as provided under this order or its implementing directives to the agency that has appropriate subject matter interest and classification authority with respect to this information. That agency shall decide within 30 days whether to classify this information.

SEC. 1.4. CLASSIFICATION CATEGORIES.

Information shall not be considered for classification unless its unauthorized disclosure could reasonably be expected to cause identifiable or describable damage to the national security in accordance with section 1.2 of this order, and it pertains to one or more of the following:

(a) military plans, weapons systems, or operations;

(b) foreign government information;

(c) intelligence activities (including covert action), intelligence sources or methods, or cryptology;

(d) foreign relations or foreign activities of the United States, including confidential sources;

(e) scientific, technological, or economic matters relating to the national security;

(f) United States Government programs for safeguarding nuclear materials or facilities;

(g) vulnerabilities or capabilities of systems, installations, infrastructures, projects, plans, or protection services relating to the national security; or

(h) the development, production, or use of weapons of mass destruction.

SEC. 1.5. DURATION OF CLASSIFICATION.

(a) At the time of original classification, the original classification authority shall establish a specific date or event for declassification based on the duration of the national security sensitivity of the information. Upon reaching the date or event, the information shall be automatically declassified. Except for information that should clearly and demonstrably be expected to reveal the identity of a confidential human source or a human intelligence source or key design concepts of weapons of mass destruction, the date or event shall not exceed the time frame established in paragraph (b) of this section.

(b) If the original classification authority cannot determine an earlier specific date or event for declassification, information shall be marked for declassification 10 years from the date of the original decision, unless the original classification authority otherwise determines that the sensitivity of the information requires that it be marked for declassification for up to 25 years from the date of the original decision.

(c) An original classification authority may extend the duration of classification up to 25 years from the date of origin of the document, change the level of classification, or reclassify specific information only when the standards and procedures for classifying information under this order are followed.

(d) No information may remain classified indefinitely. Information marked for an indefinite duration of classification under predecessor orders, for example, marked as "Originating Agency's Determination Required," or classified information that contains incomplete declassification instructions or lacks declassification instructions shall be declassified in accordance with part 3 of this order.

SEC. 1.6. IDENTIFICATION AND MARKINGS.

(a) At the time of original classification, the following shall be indicated in a manner that is immediately apparent:

(1) one of the three classification levels defined in section 1.2 of this order;

(2) the identity, by name and position, or by personal identifier, of the original classification authority;

(3) the agency and office of origin, if not otherwise evident;

(4) declassification instructions, which shall indicate one of the following:

(A) the date or event for declassification, as prescribed in section 1.5(a);

(B) the date that is 10 years from the date of original classification, as prescribed in section 1.5(b);

(C) the date that is up to 25 years from the date of original classification, as prescribed in
section 1.5(b); or

(D) in the case of information that should clearly and demonstrably be expected to reveal the identity of a confidential human source or a human intelligence source or key design concepts of weapons of mass destruction, the marking prescribed in implementing directives issued pursuant to this order; and

(5) a concise reason for classification that, at a minimum, cites the applicable classification categories in section 1.4 of this order.

(b) Specific information required in paragraph (a) of this section may be excluded if it would reveal additional classified information.

(c) With respect to each classified document, the agency originating the document shall, by marking or other means, indicate which portions are classified, with the applicable classification level, and which portions are unclassified. In accordance with standards prescribed in directives issued under this order, the Director of the Information Security Oversight Office may grant and revoke temporary waivers of this requirement. The Director shall revoke any waiver upon a finding of abuse.

(d) Markings or other indicia implementing the provisions of this order, including abbreviations and requirements to safeguard classified working papers, shall conform to the standards prescribed in implementing directives issued pursuant to this order.

(e) Foreign government information shall retain its original classification markings or shall be assigned a U.S. classification that provides a degree of protection at least equivalent to that required by the entity that furnished the information. Foreign government information retaining its original classification markings need not be assigned a U.S. classification marking provided that the responsible agency determines that the foreign government markings are adequate to meet the purposes served by U.S. classification markings.

(f) Information assigned a level of classification under this or predecessor orders shall be considered as classified at that level of classification despite the omission of other required markings. Whenever such information is used in the derivative classification process or is reviewed for possible declassification, holders of such information shall coordinate with an appropriate classification authority for the application of omitted markings.

(g) The classification authority shall, whenever practicable, use a classified addendum whenever classified information constitutes a small portion of an otherwise unclassified document or prepare a product to allow for dissemination at the lowest level of classification possible or in unclassified form.

(h) Prior to public release, all declassified records shall be appropriately marked to reflect their declassification.

SEC. 1.7. CLASSIFICATION PROHIBITIONS AND LIMITATIONS.

(a) In no case shall information be classified, continue to be maintained as classified, or fail
to be declassified in order to:

(1) conceal violations of law, inefficiency, or administrative error;

(2) prevent embarrassment to a person, organization, or agency;

(3) restrain competition; or

(4) prevent or delay the release of information that does not require protection in the interest of the national security.

(b) Basic scientific research information not clearly related to the national security shall not be classified.

(c) Information may not be reclassified after declassification and release to the public under proper authority unless: (1) the reclassification is personally approved in writing by the agency head based on a document-by-document determination by the agency that reclassification is required to prevent significant and demonstrable damage to the national security;

(2) the information may be reasonably recovered without bringing undue attention to the information;

(3) the reclassification action is reported promptly to the Assistant to the President for National Security Affairs (National Security Advisor) and the Director of the Information Security Oversight Office; and

(4) for documents in the physical and legal custody of the National Archives and Records Administration (National Archives) that have been available for public use, the agency head has, after making the determinations required by this paragraph, notified the Archivist of the United States (Archivist), who shall suspend public access pending approval of the reclassification action by the Director of the Information Security Oversight Office. Any such decision by the Director may be appealed
by the agency head to the President through the National Security Advisor. Public access shall remain suspended pending a prompt decision on the appeal.

(d) Information that has not previously been disclosed to the public under proper authority may be classified or reclassified after an agency has received a request for it under the Freedom of Information Act (5 U.S.C. 552), the Presidential Records Act, 44 U.S.C. 2204(c)(1), the Privacy Act of 1974
(5 U.S.C. 552a), or the mandatory review provisions of section 3.5 of this order only if such classification meets the requirements of this order and is accomplished on a document-by-document basis with the personal participation

or under the direction of the agency head, the deputy agency head, or the senior agency official designated under section 5.4 of this order. The requirements in this paragraph also apply to those situations in which information has been declassified in accordance with a specific date or

event determined by an original classification authority in accordance with section 1.5 of this order.

(e) Compilations of items of information that are individually unclassified may be classified if the compiled information reveals an additional association or relationship that:

(1) meets the standards for classification under this order; and

(2) is not otherwise revealed in the individual items of information.

SEC. 1.8. CLASSIFICATION CHALLENGES.

(a) Authorized holders of information who, in good faith, believe that its classification status is improper are encouraged and expected to challenge the classification status of the information in accordance with agency procedures established under paragraph (b) of this section.

(b) In accordance with implementing directives issued pursuant to this order, an agency head or senior agency official shall establish procedures under which authorized holders of information, including authorized holders outside the classifying agency, are encouraged and expected to challenge

the classification of information that they believe is improperly classified or unclassified. These procedures shall ensure that:

(1) individuals are not subject to retribution for bringing such actions;

(2) an opportunity is provided for review by an impartial official or panel; and

(3) individuals are advised of their right to appeal agency decisions to the Interagency Security Classification Appeals Panel (Panel) established by section 5.3 of this order.

(c) Documents required to be submitted for prepublication review or other administrative process pursuant to an approved nondisclosure agreement are not covered by this section.

SEC. 1.9. FUNDAMENTAL CLASSIFICATION GUIDANCE REVIEW.

(a) Agency heads shall complete on a periodic basis a comprehensive review of the agency's classification guidance, particularly classification guides, to ensure the guidance reflects current circumstances and to identify classified information that no longer requires protection and can be declassified. The initial fundamental classification guidance review shall be completed within 2 years

of the effective date of this order.

(b) The classification guidance review shall include an evaluation of classified information to determine if it meets the standards for classification under section

1.4 of this order, taking into account an up-to-date assessment of likely damage as described under section 1.2 of this order.

(c) The classification guidance review shall include original classification authorities and agency subject matter experts to ensure a broad range of perspectives.

(d) Agency heads shall provide a report summarizing the results of the classification guidance review to the Director of the Information Security Oversight Office and shall release an unclassified version of this report to the public.

PART 2—DERIVATIVE CLASSIFICATION

SEC. 2.1. USE OF DERIVATIVE CLASSIFICATION.

(a) Persons who reproduce, extract, or summarize classified information, or who apply classification markings derived from source material or as directed by a classification guide, need not possess original classification authority.

(b) Persons who apply derivative classification markings shall:

(1) be identified by name and position, or by personal identifier, in a manner that is immediately apparent for each derivative classification action;

(2) observe and respect original classification decisions; and

(3) carry forward to any newly created documents the pertinent classification markings. For information derivatively classified based on multiple sources, the derivative classifier shall carry forward:

(A) the date or event for declassification that corresponds to the longest period of classification among the sources, or the marking established pursuant to section 1.6(a)(4)(D) of this order; and

(B) a listing of the source materials.

(c) Derivative classifiers shall, whenever practicable, use a classified addendum whenever classified information constitutes a small portion of an otherwise unclassified document or prepare a product to allow for dissemination at the lowest level of classification possible or in unclassified form.

(d) Persons who apply derivative classification markings shall receive training in the proper application of the derivative classification principles of the order, with an emphasis on avoiding over-classification, at least once every 2 years. Derivative classifiers who do not receive such training at least once every 2 years shall have their authority to apply derivative classification markings suspended until they have received such training. A waiver may be granted by the agency head, the deputy agency head, or the senior agency official if an individual is unable to receive such training due to unavoidable circumstances. Whenever a waiver is granted, the individual shall receive such training as soon as practicable.

SEC. 2.2. CLASSIFICATION GUIDES.

(a) Agencies with original classification authority shall prepare classification guides to facilitate the proper and uniform derivative classification of information. These guides shall conform to standards contained in directives issued under this order.

(b) Each guide shall be approved personally and in writing by an official who:

(1) has program or supervisory responsibility over the information or is the senior agency official; and

(2) is authorized to classify information originally at the highest level of classification prescribed in the guide.

(c) Agencies shall establish procedures to ensure that classification guides are reviewed and updated as provided in directives issued under this order.

(d) Agencies shall incorporate original classification decisions into classification guides on a timely basis and in accordance with directives issued under this order.

(e) Agencies may incorporate exemptions from automatic declassification approved pursuant to section 3.3(j) of this order into classification guides, provided that the Panel is notified of the intent to take such action for specific information in advance of approval and the information remains in active use.

(f) The duration of classification of a document classified by a derivative classifier using a classification guide shall not exceed 25 years from the date of the origin of the document, except for:

(1) information that should clearly and demonstrably be expected to reveal the identity of a confidential human source or a human intelligence source or key design concepts of weapons of mass destruction; and

(2) specific information incorporated into classification guides in accordance with section 2.2(e) of this order.

PART 3—DECLASSIFICATION AND DOWNGRADING

SEC. 3.1. AUTHORITY FOR DECLASSIFICATION.

(a) Information shall be declassified as soon as it no longer meets the standards for classification under this order.

(b) Information shall be declassified or downgraded by:

(1) the official who authorized the original classification, if that official is still serving in the same position and has original classification authority;

(2) the originator's current successor in function, if that individual has original classification authority;

(3) a supervisory official of either the originator or his or her successor in function, if the supervisory official has original classification authority; or

(4) officials delegated declassification authority in writing by the agency head or the senior agency official of the originating agency.

(c) The Director of National Intelligence (or, if delegated by the Director of National Intelligence, the Principal Deputy Director of National Intelligence) may, with respect to the Intelligence Community, after consultation with the head of the originating Intelligence Community element or department, declassify, downgrade, or direct the declassification or downgrading of information or intelligence relating to intelligence sources, methods, or activities.

(d) It is presumed that information that continues to meet the classification requirements under this order requires continued protection. In some exceptional cases, however, the need to protect such information may be outweighed by the public interest in disclosure of the information, and in these cases the information should be declassified. When such questions arise, they shall be referred to the agency head or the senior agency official. That official will determine, as an exercise of discretion, whether the public interest in disclosure outweighs the damage to the national security that might reasonably be expected from disclosure. This provision does not:

(1) amplify or modify the substantive criteria or procedures for classification; or

(2) create any substantive or procedural rights subject to judicial review.

(e) If the Director of the Information Security Oversight Office determines that information is classified in violation of this order, the Director may require the information to be declassified by the agency that originated the classification. Any such decision by the Director may be appealed to the President through the National Security Advisor. The information shall remain classified pending a prompt decision on the appeal.

(f) The provisions of this section shall also apply to agencies that, under the terms of this order, do not have original classification authority, but had such authority under predecessor orders.

(g) No information may be excluded from declassification under section 3.3 of this order based solely on the type of document or record in which it is found. Rather, the classified information must be considered on the basis of its content.

(h) Classified nonrecord materials, including artifacts, shall be declassified as soon as they no longer meet the standards for classification under this order.

(i) When making decisions under sections 3.3, 3.4, and 3.5 of this order, agencies shall consider the final decisions of the Panel.

SEC. 3.2. TRANSFERRED RECORDS.

(a) In the case of classified records transferred in conjunction with a transfer of functions, and not merely for storage purposes, the receiving agency shall be deemed to be the originating agency for purposes of this order.

(b) In the case of classified records that are not officially transferred as described in paragraph (a) of this section, but that originated in an agency that has ceased to exist and for which there is no successor agency, each agency in possession of such records shall be deemed to be the originating agency for purposes of this order. Such records may be declassified or downgraded by the agency in possession of the records after consultation with any other agency that has an interest in the subject matter of the records.

(c) Classified records accessioned into the National Archives shall be declassified or downgraded by the Archivist in accordance with this order, the directives issued pursuant to this order, agency declassification guides, and any existing procedural agreement between the Archivist and the relevant agency head.

(d) The originating agency shall take all reasonable steps to declassify classified information contained in records determined to have permanent historical value before they are accessioned into the National Archives. However, the Archivist may require that classified records be accessioned into the National Archives when necessary to comply with the provisions of the Federal Records Act. This provision does not apply to records transferred to the Archivist pursuant to section 2203 of title 44, United States Code, or records for which the National Archives serves as the custodian of the records of an agency or organization that has gone out of existence.

(e) To the extent practicable, agencies shall adopt a system of records management that will facilitate the public release of documents at the time such documents are declassified pursuant to the provisions for automatic declassification in section 3.3 of this order.

SEC. 3.3. AUTOMATIC DECLASSIFICATION.

(a) Subject to paragraphs (b)–(d) and (g)–(j) of this section, all classified records that (1) are more than 25 years old and (2) have been determined to have permanent historical value under title 44, United States Code, shall be automatically declassified whether or not the records have been reviewed. All classified records shall be automatically declassified on December 31 of the year that is 25 years from the date of origin, except as provided in paragraphs (b)–(d) and (g)–(j) of this section. If the date of origin of an individual record cannot be readily determined, the date of original classification shall be used instead.

(b) An agency head may exempt from automatic declassification under paragraph (a) of this section specific information, the release of which should clearly and demonstrably be expected to:

(1) reveal the identity of a confidential human source, a human intelligence source, a relationship with an intelligence or security service of a foreign government or international organization, or a nonhuman intelligence source; or impair the effectiveness of an intelligence method currently in use, available for use, or under development;

(2) reveal information that would assist in the development, production, or use of weapons of mass destruction;

(3) reveal information that would impair U.S. cryptologic systems or activities;

(4) reveal information that would impair the application of state-of-theart technology within a U.S. weapon system;

(5) reveal formally named or numbered U.S. military war plans that remain in effect, or reveal operational or tactical elements of prior plans that are contained in such active plans;

(6) reveal information, including foreign government information, that would cause serious harm to relations between the United States and a foreign government, or to ongoing diplomatic activities of the United States;

(7) reveal information that would impair the current ability of United States Government officials to protect the President, Vice President, and other protectees for whom protection services, in the interest of the national security, are authorized;

(8) reveal information that would seriously impair current national security emergency preparedness plans or reveal current vulnerabilities of systems, installations, or infrastructures relating to the national security; or

(9) violate a statute, treaty, or international agreement that does not permit the automatic or unilateral declassification of information at 25 years.

(c)(1) An agency head shall notify the Panel of any specific file series of records for which a review or assessment has determined that the information within that file series almost invariably falls within one or more of the exemption categories listed in paragraph (b) of this section and that the agency proposes to exempt from automatic declassification at 25 years.

(2) The notification shall include:

(A) a description of the file series;

(B) an explanation of why the information within the file series is almost invariably exempt from automatic declassification and why the information must remain classified for a longer period of time; and

(C) except when the information within the file series almost invariably identifies a confidential human source or a human intelligence source or key design concepts of weapons of mass destruction, a specific date or event for declassification of the information, not to exceed December 31 of the year that is 50 years from the date of origin of the records.

(3) The Panel may direct the agency not to exempt a designated file series or to declassify the information within that series at an earlier date than recommended. The agency head may appeal such a decision to the President through the National Security Advisor.

(4) File series exemptions approved by the President prior to December 31, 2008, shall remain valid without any additional agency action pending Panel review by

the later of December 31, 2010, or December 31 of the year that is 10 years from the date of previous approval.

(d) The following provisions shall apply to the onset of automatic declassification:

(1) Classified records within an integral file block, as defined in this order, that are otherwise subject to automatic declassification under this section shall not be automatically declassified until December 31 of the year that is 25 years from the date of the most recent record within the file block.

(2) After consultation with the Director of the National Declassification Center (the Center) established by section 3.7 of this order and before the records are subject to automatic declassification, an agency head or senior agency official may delay automatic declassification for up to five additional years for classified information contained in media that make a review for possible declassification exemptions more difficult or costly.

(3) Other than for records that are properly exempted from automatic declassification, records containing classified information that originated with other agencies or the disclosure of which would affect the interests or activities of other agencies with respect to the classified information and could reasonably be expected to fall under one or more of the exemptions in paragraph (b) of this section shall be identified prior to the onset of automatic declassification for later referral to those agencies.

(A) The information of concern shall be referred by the Center established by section 3.7 of this order, or by the centralized facilities referred to in section 3.7(e) of this order, in a prioritized and scheduled manner determined by the Center.

(B) If an agency fails to provide a final determination on a referral made by the Center within 1 year of referral, or by the centralized facilities referred to in section 3.7(e) of this order within 3 years of referral, its equities in the referred records shall be automatically declassified.

(C) If any disagreement arises between affected agencies and the Center regarding the referral review period, the Director of the Information Security Oversight Office shall determine the appropriate period of review of referred records.

(D) Referrals identified prior to the establishment of the Center by section 3.7 of this order shall be subject to automatic declassification only in accordance with subparagraphs (d)(3)(A)–(C) of this section.

(4) After consultation with the Director of the Information Security Oversight Office, an agency head may delay automatic declassification for up to 3 years from the date of discovery of classified records that were inadvertently not reviewed prior to the effective date of automatic declassification.

(e) Information exempted from automatic declassification under this section shall remain subject to the mandatory and systematic declassification review provisions of this order.

(f) The Secretary of State shall determine when the United States should commence negotiations with the appropriate officials of a foreign government or international organization of governments to modify any treaty or international agreement that requires the classification of information contained in records affected by this section for a period longer than 25 years from the date of its creation, unless the treaty or international agreement pertains to information that may otherwise remain classified beyond 25 years under this section.

(g) The Secretary of Energy shall determine when information concerning foreign nuclear programs that was removed from the Restricted Data category in order to carry out provisions of the National Security Act of 1947, as amended, may be declassified. Unless otherwise determined, such information shall be declassified when comparable information concerning the United States nuclear program is declassified.

(h) Not later than 3 years from the effective date of this order, all records exempted from automatic declassification under paragraphs (b) and (c) of this section shall be automatically declassified on December 31 of a year that is no more than 50 years from the date of origin, subject to the following:

(1) Records that contain information the release of which should clearly and demonstrably be expected to reveal the following are exempt from automatic declassification at 50 years:

(A) the identity of a confidential human source or a human intelligence source; or

(B) key design concepts of weapons of mass destruction.

(2) In extraordinary cases, agency heads may, within 5 years of the onset of automatic declassification, propose to exempt additional specific information from declassification at 50 years.

(3) Records exempted from automatic declassification under this paragraph shall be automatically declassified on December 31 of a year that is no more than 75 years from the date of origin unless an agency head, within 5 years of that date, proposes to exempt specific information from declassification at 75 years and the proposal is formally approved by the Panel.

(i) Specific records exempted from automatic declassification prior to the establishment of the Center described in section 3.7 of this order shall be subject to the provisions of paragraph (h) of this section in a scheduled and prioritized manner determined by the Center.

(j) At least 1 year before information is subject to automatic declassification under this section, an agency head or senior agency official shall notify the Director of the Information Security Oversight Office, serving as Executive Secretary of the Panel, of any specific information that the agency proposes to exempt from automatic declassification under paragraphs (b) and (h) of this section.

(1) The notification shall include:

(A) a detailed description of the information, either by reference to information in specific records or in the form of a declassification guide;

(B) an explanation of why the information should be exempt from automatic declassification and must remain classified for a longer period of time; and

(C) a specific date or a specific and independently verifiable event for automatic declassification of specific records that contain the information proposed for exemption.

(2) The Panel may direct the agency not to exempt the information or to declassify it at an earlier date than recommended. An agency head may appeal such a decision to the President through the National Security Advisor. The information will remain classified while such an appeal is pending.

(k) For information in a file series of records determined not to have permanent historical value, the duration of classification beyond 25 years shall be the same as the disposition (destruction) date of those records in each Agency Records Control Schedule or General Records Schedule, although the duration of classification shall be extended if the record has been retained for business reasons beyond the scheduled disposition date.

SEC. 3.4. SYSTEMATIC DECLASSIFICATION REVIEW.

(a) Each agency that has originated classified information under this order or its predecessors shall establish and conduct a program for systematic declassification review for records of permanent historical value exempted from automatic declassification under section 3.3 of this order. Agencies shall prioritize their review of such records in accordance with priorities established by the Center.

(b) The Archivist shall conduct a systematic declassification review program for classified records:

(1) accessioned into the National Archives; (2) transferred to the Archivist pursuant to 44 U.S.C. 2203; and (3) for which the National Archives serves as the custodian for an agency or organization that has gone out of existence.

SEC. 3.5. MANDATORY DECLASSIFICATION REVIEW.

(a) Except as provided in paragraph (b) of this section, all information classified under this order or predecessor orders shall be subject to a review for declassification by the originating agency if:

(1) the request for a review describes the document or material containing the information with sufficient specificity to enable the agency to locate it with a reasonable amount of effort;

(2) the document or material containing the information responsive to the request is not contained within an operational file exempted from search and review, publication, and disclosure under 5 U.S.C. 552 in accordance with law; and

(3) the information is not the subject of pending litigation.

(b) Information originated by the incumbent President or the incumbent Vice President; the incumbent President's White House Staff or the incumbent Vice President's Staff; committees, commissions, or boards appointed by the incumbent President; or other entities within the Executive Office of the President that solely advise and assist the incumbent President is exempted from the provisions of paragraph (a) of this section. However, the Archivist shall have the authority to review, downgrade, and declassify papers or records of former Presidents and Vice Presidents under the control of the Archivist pursuant to 44 U.S.C. 2107, 2111, 2111 note, or 2203. Review procedures developed by the Archivist shall provide for consultation with agencies having primary subject matter interest and shall be consistent with the provisions of applicable laws or lawful agreements that pertain to the respective Presidential papers or records. Agencies with primary subject matter interest shall be notified promptly of the archivist's decision. Any final decision by the Archivist may be appealed by the requester or an agency to the Panel. The information shall remain classified pending a prompt decision on the appeal.

(c) Agencies conducting a mandatory review for declassification shall declassify information that no longer meets the standards for classification under this order. They shall release this information unless withholding is otherwise authorized and warranted under applicable law.

(d) If an agency has reviewed the requested information for declassification within the past 2 years, the agency need not conduct another review and may instead inform the requester of this fact and the prior review decision and advise the requester of appeal rights provided under subsection (e) of this section.

(e) In accordance with directives issued pursuant to this order, agency heads shall develop procedures to process requests for the mandatory review of classified information. These procedures shall apply to information classified under this or predecessor orders. They also shall provide a means for administratively appealing a denial of a mandatory review request, and for notifying the requester of the right to appeal a final agency decision to the Panel.

(f) After consultation with affected agencies, the Secretary of Defense shall develop special procedures for the review of cryptologic information; the Director of National Intelligence shall develop special procedures for the review of information pertaining to intelligence sources, methods, and activities; and the

Archivist shall develop special procedures for the review of information accessioned into the National Archives.

(g) Documents required to be submitted for prepublication review or other administrative process pursuant to an approved nondisclosure agreement are not covered by this section.

(h) This section shall not apply to any request for a review made to an element of the Intelligence Community that is made by a person other than an individual as that term is defined by 5 U.S.C. 552a(a)(2), or by a foreign government entity or any representative thereof.

SEC. 3.6. PROCESSING REQUESTS AND REVIEWS.

Notwithstanding section 4.1(i) of this order, in response to a request for information under the Freedom
of Information Act, the Presidential Records Act, the Privacy Act of 1974, or the mandatory review provisions of this order:

(a) An agency may refuse to confirm or deny the existence or nonexistence of requested records whenever the fact of their existence or nonexistence is itself classified under this order or its predecessors.

(b) When an agency receives any request for documents in its custody that contain classified information that originated with other agencies or the disclosure of which would affect the interests or activities of other agencies with respect to the classified information, or identifies such documents in the process of implementing sections 3.3 or 3.4 of this order, it shall refer copies of any request and the pertinent documents to the originating agency for processing and may, after consultation with the originating
agency, inform any requester of the referral unless such association is itself classified under this order or its predecessors. In cases in which the originating agency determines in writing that a response under paragraph
(a) of this section is required, the referring agency shall respond to the requester in accordance with that paragraph.

(c) Agencies may extend the classification of information in records determined not to have permanent historical value or nonrecord materials, including artifacts, beyond the time frames established in sections 1.5(b) and 2.2(f) of this order, provided:

(1) the specific information has been approved pursuant to section 3.3(j) of this order for exemption from automatic declassification; and

(2) the extension does not exceed the date established in section 3.3(j) of this order.

SEC. 3.7. NATIONAL DECLASSIFICATION CENTER.

(a) There is established within

811

the National Archives a National Declassification Center to streamline declassification processes, facilitate quality-assurance measures, and implement standardized training regarding the declassification of records determined to have permanent historical value. There shall be a Director of the Center who shall be appointed or removed by the Archivist in consultation with the Secretaries of State, Defense, Energy, and Homeland Security, the Attorney General, and the Director of National Intelligence.

(b) Under the administration of the Director, the Center shall coordinate:

(1) timely and appropriate processing of referrals in accordance with section 3.3(d)(3) of this order for accessioned Federal records and transferred presidential records.

(2) general interagency declassification activities necessary to fulfill the requirements of sections 3.3 and 3.4 of this order;

(3) the exchange among agencies of detailed declassification guidance to enable the referral of records in accordance with section 3.3(d)(3) of this order;

(4) the development of effective, transparent, and standard declassification work processes, training, and quality assurance measures;

(5) the development of solutions to declassification challenges posed by electronic records, special media, and emerging technologies;

(6) the linkage and effective utilization of existing agency databases and the use of new technologies to document and make public declassification review decisions and support declassification activities under the purview of the Center; and

(7) storage and related services, on a reimbursable basis, for Federal records containing classified national security information.

(c) Agency heads shall fully cooperate with the Archivist in the activities of the Center and shall:

(1) provide the Director with adequate and current declassification guidance to enable the referral of records in accordance with section 3.3(d)(3) of this order; and

(2) upon request of the Archivist, assign agency personnel to the Center who shall be delegated authority by the agency head to review and exempt or declassify information originated by their agency contained in records accessioned into the National Archives, after consultation with subjectmatter experts as necessary.

(d) The Archivist, in consultation with representatives of the participants in the Center and after input from the general public, shall develop priorities for declassification activities under the purview of the Center that take into account the degree of researcher interest and the likelihood of declassification.

(e) Agency heads may establish such centralized facilities and internal operations to conduct internal declassification reviews as appropriate to achieve optimized records management and declassification business processes. Once established, all referral processing of accessioned records shall take place at the Center, and such agency facilities and operations shall be coordinated with the Center to ensure the maximum degree of consistency in policies and procedures that relate to records determined to have permanent historical value.

(f) Agency heads may exempt from automatic declassification or continue the classification of their own originally classified information under section 3.3(a) of this order except that in the case of the Director of National Intelligence, the Director shall also retain such authority with respect to the Intelligence Community.

(g) The Archivist shall, in consultation with the Secretaries of State, Defense, Energy, and Homeland Security, the Attorney General, the Director of National Intelligence, the Director of the Central Intelligence Agency, and the Director of the Information Security Oversight Office, provide the National Security Advisor with a detailed concept of operations for the Center and a proposed implementing directive under section 5.1 of this order that reflects the coordinated views of the aforementioned agencies.

PART 4—SAFEGUARDING

SEC. 4.1. GENERAL RESTRICTIONS ON ACCESS.

(a) A person may have access to classified information provided that:

(1) a favorable determination of eligibility for access has been made by an agency head or the agency head's designee;

(2) the person has signed an approved nondisclosure agreement; and

(3) the person has a need-to-know the information.

(b) Every person who has met the standards for access to classified information in paragraph (a) of this section shall receive contemporaneous training on the proper safeguarding of classified information and on the criminal, civil, and administrative sanctions that may be imposed on an individual who fails to protect classified information from unauthorized disclosure.

(c) An official or employee leaving agency service may not remove classified information from the agency's control or direct that information be declassified in order to remove it from agency control.

(d) Classified information may not be removed from official premises without proper authorization.

(e) Persons authorized to disseminate classified information outside the executive branch shall ensure the protection of the information in a manner equivalent to that provided within the executive branch.

(f) Consistent with law, executive orders, directives, and regulations, an agency head or senior agency official or, with respect to the Intelligence Community, the Director of National Intelligence, shall establish uniform procedures to ensure that automated information systems, including networks and telecommunications systems, that collect, create, communicate, compute, disseminate, process, or store classified information:

(1) prevent access by unauthorized persons;

(2) ensure the integrity of the information; and

(3) to the maximum extent practicable, use:

(A) common information technology standards, protocols, and interfaces that maximize the availability of, and access to, the information in a form and manner that facilitates its authorized use; and

(B) standardized electronic formats to maximize the accessibility of information to persons who meet the criteria set forth in section 4.1(a) of this order.

(g) Consistent with law, executive orders, directives, and regulations, each agency head or senior agency official, or with respect to the Intelligence Community, the Director of National Intelligence, shall establish controls to ensure that classified information is used, processed, stored, reproduced, transmitted, and destroyed under conditions that provide adequate protection and prevent access by unauthorized persons.

(h) Consistent with directives issued pursuant to this order, an agency shall safeguard foreign government information under standards that provide a degree of protection at least equivalent to that required by the government or international organization of governments that furnished the information. When adequate to achieve equivalency, these standards may be less restrictive than the safeguarding standards that ordinarily apply to U.S. ''Confidential'' information, including modified handling and transmission and allowing access to individuals with a need-to-know who have not otherwise been cleared for access to classified information or executed an approved nondisclosure agreement.

(i)(1) Classified information originating in one agency may be disseminated to another agency or U.S. entity by any agency to which it has been made available without the consent of the originating agency, as long as the criteria for access under section 4.1(a) of this order are met, unless the originating agency has determined that prior authorization is required for such dissemination and has marked or indicated such requirement on the medium containing the classified information in accordance with implementing directives issued pursuant to this order.

(2) Classified information originating in one agency may be disseminated by any other agency to which it has been made available to a foreign government in accordance with statute, this order, directives implementing this order, direction of the President, or with the consent of the originating agency. For the purposes of this section, ''foreign government'' includes any element of a foreign government, or an international organization of governments, or any element thereof.

(3) Documents created prior to the effective date of this order shall not be disseminated outside any other agency to which they have been made available

without the consent of the originating agency. An agency head or senior agency official may waive this requirement for specific information that originated within that agency.

(4) For purposes of this section, the Department of Defense shall be considered one agency, except that any dissemination of information regarding intelligence sources, methods, or activities shall be consistent with directives issued pursuant to section 6.2(b) of this order.

(5) Prior consent of the originating agency is not required when referring records for declassification review that contain information originating in more than one agency.

SEC. 4.2. DISTRIBUTION CONTROLS.

(a) The head of each agency shall establish procedures in accordance with applicable law and consistent with directives issued pursuant to this order to ensure that classified information is accessible to the maximum extent possible by individuals who meet the criteria set forth in section 4.1(a) of this order.

(b) In an emergency, when necessary to respond to an imminent threat to life or in defense of the homeland, the agency head or any designee may authorize the disclosure of classified information (including information marked pursuant to section 4.1(i)(1) of this order) to an individual or individuals who are otherwise not eligible for access. Such actions shall be taken only in accordance with directives implementing this order and any procedure issued by agencies governing the classified information, which shall be designed to minimize the classified information that is disclosed under these circumstances and the number of individuals who receive it. Information disclosed under this provision or implementing directives and procedures shall not be deemed declassified as a result of such disclosure or subsequent use by a recipient. Such disclosures shall be reported promptly to the originator of the classified information. For purposes of this section, the Director of National Intelligence may issue an implementing directive governing the emergency disclosure of classified intelligence information.

(c) Each agency shall update, at least annually, the automatic, routine, or recurring distribution mechanism for classified information that it distributes. Recipients shall cooperate fully with distributors who are updating distribution lists and shall notify distributors whenever a relevant change in status occurs.

SEC. 4.3. SPECIAL ACCESS PROGRAMS.

(a) Establishment of special access programs. Unless otherwise authorized by the President, only the Secretaries of State, Defense, Energy, and Homeland Security, the Attorney General, and the Director of National Intelligence, or the principal deputy of each, may create a special access program. For special access

programs pertaining to intelligence sources, methods, and activities (but not including military
operational, strategic, and tactical programs), this function shall be exercised by the Director of National Intelligence. These officials shall keep the number of these programs at an absolute minimum, and shall establish them only when the program is required by statute or upon a specific finding that:

(1) the vulnerability of, or threat to, specific information is exceptional; and

(2) the normal criteria for determining eligibility for access applicable to information classified at the same level are not deemed sufficient to protect the information from unauthorized disclosure.

(b) Requirements and limitations.

(1) Special access programs shall be limited to programs in which the number of persons who ordinarily will have access will be reasonably small and commensurate with the objective of providing enhanced protection for the information involved.

(2) Each agency head shall establish and maintain a system of accounting for special access programs consistent with directives issued pursuant to this order.

(3) Special access programs shall be subject to the oversight program established under section 5.4(d) of this order. In addition, the Director of the Information Security Oversight Office shall be afforded access to these programs, in accordance with the security requirements of each program, in order to perform the functions assigned to the Information Security Oversight Office under this order. An agency head may limit access to a special access program to the Director of the Information Security Oversight Office and no more than one other employee of the Information Security Oversight Office or, for special access programs that are extraordinarily sensitive and vulnerable, to the Director only.

(4) The agency head or principal deputy shall review annually each special access program to determine whether it continues to meet the requirements of this order.

(5) Upon request, an agency head shall brief the National Security Advisor, or a designee, on any or all of the agency's special access programs.

(6) For the purposes of this section, the term ''agency head'' refers only to the Secretaries of State, Defense, Energy, and Homeland Security, the Attorney General, and the Director of National Intelligence, or the principal deputy of each.

(c) Nothing in this order shall supersede any requirement made by or under 10 U.S.C. 119.

SEC. 4.4. ACCESS BY HISTORICAL RESEARCHERS AND CERTAIN FORMER GOVERNMENT PERSONNEL.

(a) The requirement in section 4.1(a)(3) of this order that access to classified information may be granted only to individuals who have a need-to-know the information may be waived for persons who:
(1) are engaged in historical research projects;
(2) previously have occupied senior policy-making positions to which they were appointed or designated by the President or the Vice President; or
(3) served as President or Vice President.
(b) Waivers under this section may be granted only if the agency head or senior agency official of the originating agency:
(1) determines in writing that access is consistent with the interest of the national security;
(2) takes appropriate steps to protect classified information from unauthorized disclosure or compromise, and ensures that the information is safeguarded in a manner consistent with this order; and
(3) limits the access granted to former Presidential appointees or designees and Vice Presidential appointees or designees to items that the person originated, reviewed, signed, or received while serving as a Presidential or Vice Presidential appointee or designee.

PART 5—IMPLEMENTATION AND REVIEW

SEC. 5.1. PROGRAM DIRECTION.
(a) The Director of the Information Security Oversight Office, under the direction of the Archivist and in consultation with the National Security Advisor, shall issue such directives as are necessary to implement this order. These directives shall be binding on the agencies. Directives issued by the Director of the Information Security Oversight Office shall establish standards for:
(1) classification, declassification, and marking principles;
(2) safeguarding classified information, which shall pertain to the handling, storage, distribution, transmittal, and destruction of and accounting for classified information;
(3) agency security education and training programs;
(4) agency self-inspection programs; and
(5) classification and declassification guides.
(b) The Archivist shall delegate the implementation and monitoring functions of this program to the Director of the Information Security Oversight Office.
(c) The Director of National Intelligence, after consultation with the heads of affected agencies and the Director of the Information Security Oversight Office, may issue directives to implement this order with respect to the protection of intelligence sources, methods, and activities. Such directives shall be consistent with this order and directives issued under paragraph (a) of this section.

SEC. 5.2. INFORMATION SECURITY OVERSIGHT OFFICE.
(a) There is established within the National Archives an Information Security Oversight Office. The Archivist shall appoint the Director of the Information Security Oversight Office, subject to the approval of the President.
(b) Under the direction of the Archivist, acting in consultation with the National Security Advisor, the Director of the Information Security Oversight Office shall:
(1) develop directives for the implementation of this order;
(2) oversee agency actions to ensure compliance with this order and its implementing directives;
(3) review and approve agency implementing regulations prior to their issuance to ensure their consistency with this order and directives issued under section 5.1(a) of this order;
(4) have the authority to conduct on-site reviews of each agency's program established under this order, and to require of each agency those reports and information and other cooperation that may be necessary to fulfill its responsibilities. If granting access to specific categories of classified information would pose an exceptional national security risk, the affected agency head or the senior agency official shall submit a written justification recommending the denial of access to the President through the National Security Advisor within 60 days of the request for access. Access shall be denied pending the response;
(5) review requests for original classification authority from agencies or officials not granted original classification authority and, if deemed appropriate, recommend Presidential approval through the National Security Advisor;
(6) consider and take action on complaints and suggestions from persons within or outside the Government with respect to the administration of the program established under this order;
(7) have the authority to prescribe, after consultation with affected agencies, standardization of forms or procedures that will promote the implementation of the program established under this order;
(8) report at least annually to the President on the implementation of this order; and
(9) convene and chair interagency meetings to discuss matters pertaining to the program established by this order.
SEC. 5.3. INTERAGENCY SECURITY CLASSIFICATION APPEALS PANEL.
(a) Establishment and administration.
(1) There is established an Interagency Security Classification Appeals Panel. The Departments of State, Defense, and Justice, the National Archives, the Office of the Director of National Intelligence, and the National Security Advisor shall each be represented by a senior-level representative who is a full-time or permanent part-time Federal officer or employee designated to serve as a member of the Panel by the respective agency head. The President shall designate a Chair from among the members of the Panel.

(2) Additionally, the Director of the Central Intelligence Agency may appoint a temporary representative who meets the criteria in paragraph (a)(1) of this section to participate as a voting member in all Panel deliberations and associated support activities concerning classified information originated by the Central Intelligence Agency.

(3) A vacancy on the Panel shall be filled as quickly as possible as provided in paragraph (a)(1) of this section.

(4) The Director of the Information Security Oversight Office shall serve as the Executive Secretary of the Panel. The staff of the Information Security Oversight Office shall provide program and administrative support for the Panel.

(5) The members and staff of the Panel shall be required to meet eligibility for access standards in order to fulfill the Panel's functions.

(6) The Panel shall meet at the call of the Chair. The Chair shall schedule meetings as may be necessary for the Panel to fulfill its functions in a timely manner.

(7) The Information Security Oversight Office shall include in its reports to the President a summary of the Panel's activities.

(b) Functions. The Panel shall:

(1) decide on appeals by persons who have filed classification challenges under section 1.8 of this order;

(2) approve, deny, or amend agency exemptions from automatic declassification as provided in section 3.3 of this order;

(3) decide on appeals by persons or entities who have filed requests for mandatory declassification review under section 3.5 of this order; and

(4) appropriately inform senior agency officials and the public of final Panel decisions on appeals under sections 1.8 and 3.5 of this order.

(c) Rules and procedures. The Panel shall issue bylaws, which shall be published in the *Federal Register*. The bylaws shall establish the rules and procedures that the Panel will follow in accepting, considering, and issuing decisions on appeals. The rules and procedures of the Panel shall provide that the Panel will consider appeals only on actions in which:

(1) the appellant has exhausted his or her administrative remedies within the responsible agency;

(2) there is no current action pending on the issue within the Federal courts; and

(3) the information has not been the subject of review by the Federal courts or the Panel within the past 2 years.

(d) Agency heads shall cooperate fully with the Panel so that it can fulfill its functions in a timely and fully informed manner. The Panel shall report to the President through the National Security Advisor any instance in which it believes that an agency head is not cooperating fully with the Panel.

(e) The Panel is established for the sole purpose of advising and assisting the President in the discharge of his constitutional and discretionary authority to protect the national security of the United States. Panel decisions are committed to the discretion of the Panel, unless changed by the President.

(f) An agency head may appeal a decision of the Panel to the President through the National Security Advisor. The information shall remain classified pending a decision on the appeal.

SEC. 5.4. GENERAL RESPONSIBILITIES.

Heads of agencies that originate or handle classified information shall:

(a) demonstrate personal commitment and commit senior management to the successful implementation of the program established under this order;

(b) commit necessary resources to the effective implementation of the program established under this order;

(c) ensure that agency records systems are designed and maintained to optimize the appropriate sharing and safeguarding of classified information, and to facilitate its declassification under the terms of this order when it no longer meets the standards for continued classification; and

(d) designate a senior agency official to direct and administer the program, whose responsibilities shall include:

(1) overseeing the agency's program established under this order, provided an agency head may designate a separate official to oversee special access programs authorized under this order. This official shall provide a full accounting of the agency's special access programs at least annually;

(2) promulgating implementing regulations, which shall be published in the *Federal Register* to the extent that they affect members of the public;

(3) establishing and maintaining security education and training programs;

(4) establishing and maintaining an ongoing self-inspection program, which shall include the regular reviews of representative samples of the agency's original and derivative classification actions, and shall authorize appropriate agency officials to correct misclassification actions not covered by sections 1.7(c) and 1.7(d) of this order; and reporting annually to the Director of the Information Security Oversight Office on the agency's self-inspection program;

(5) establishing procedures consistent with directives issued pursuant to this order to prevent unnecessary access to classified information, including procedures that:

(A) require that a need for access to classified information be established before initiating administrative clearance procedures; and

(B) ensure that the number of persons granted access to classified information meets the mission needs of the agency while also satisfying operational and security requirements and needs;

(6) developing special contingency plans for the safeguarding of classified information used in or near hostile or potentially hostile areas;

(7) ensuring that the performance contract or other system used to rate civilian or military personnel performance includes the designation and management of classified information as a critical element or item to be evaluated in the rating of:

(A) original classification authorities;

(B) security managers or security specialists; and

(C) all other personnel whose duties significantly involve the creation or handling of classified information, including personnel who regularly apply derivative classification markings;

(8) accounting for the costs associated with the implementation of this order, which shall be reported to the Director of the Information Security Oversight Office for publication;

(9) assigning in a prompt manner agency personnel to respond to any request, appeal, challenge, complaint, or suggestion arising out of this order that pertains to classified information that originated in a component of the agency that no longer exists and for which there is no clear successor in function; and

(10) establishing a secure capability to receive information, allegations, or complaints regarding over-classification or incorrect classification within the agency and to provide guidance to personnel on proper classification as needed.

SEC. 5.5. SANCTIONS.

(a) If the Director of the Information Security Oversight Office finds that a violation of this order or its implementing directives has occurred, the Director shall make a report to the head of the agency or to the senior agency official so that corrective steps, if appropriate, may be taken.

(b) Officers and employees of the United States Government, and its contractors, licensees, certificate holders, and grantees shall be subject to appropriate sanctions if they knowingly, willfully, or negligently:

(1) disclose to unauthorized persons information properly classified under this order or predecessor orders;

(2) classify or continue the classification of information in violation of this order or any implementing directive;

(3) create or continue a special access program contrary to the requirements of this order; or

(4) contravene any other provision of this order or its implementing directives.

(c) Sanctions may include reprimand, suspension without pay, removal, termination of classification authority, loss or denial of access to classified information, or other sanctions in accordance with applicable law and agency regulation.

(d) The agency head, senior agency official, or other supervisory official shall, at a minimum, promptly remove the classification authority of any individual who demonstrates reckless disregard or a pattern of error in applying the classification standards of this order.

(e) The agency head or senior agency official shall:

(1) take appropriate and prompt corrective action when a violation or infraction under paragraph (b) of this section occurs; and

(2) notify the Director of the Information Security Oversight Office when a violation under paragraph (b)(1), (2), or (3) of this section occurs.

PART 6—GENERAL PROVISIONS

SEC. 6.1. DEFINITIONS.

For purposes of this order:

(a) "Access" means the ability or opportunity to gain knowledge of classified information.

(b) "Agency" means any "Executive agency," as defined in 5 U.S.C. 105; any "Military department" as defined in 5 U.S.C. 102; and any other entity within the executive branch that comes into the possession of classified information.

(c) "Authorized holder" of classified information means anyone who satisfies the conditions for access stated in section 4.1(a) of this order.

(d) "Automated information system" means an assembly of computer hardware, software, or firmware configured to collect, create, communicate, compute, disseminate, process, store, or control data or information.

(e) "Automatic declassification" means the declassification of information based solely upon:

(1) the occurrence of a specific date or event as determined by the original classification authority; or

(2) the expiration of a maximum time frame for duration of classification established under this order.

(f) "Classification" means the act or process by which information is determined to be classified information.

(g) "Classification guidance" means any instruction or source that prescribes the classification of specific information.

(h) "Classification guide" means a documentary form of classification guidance issued by an original classification authority that identifies the elements of information regarding a specific subject that must be classified and establishes the level and duration of classification for each such element.

(i) "Classified national security information" or "classified information" means information that has been determined pursuant to this order or any predecessor order to require protection against unauthorized disclosure and is marked to indicate its classified status when in documentary form.

(j) "Compilation" means an aggregation of preexisting unclassified items of information.

(k) ''Confidential source'' means any individual or organization that has provided, or that may reasonably be expected to provide, information to the United States on matters pertaining to the national security with the expectation that the information or relationship, or both, are to be held in confidence.

(l) ''Damage to the national security'' means harm to the national defense or foreign relations of the United States from the unauthorized disclosure of information, taking into consideration such aspects of the information as the sensitivity, value, utility, and provenance of that information.

(m) ''Declassification'' means the authorized change in the status of information from classified information to unclassified information.

(n) ''Declassification guide'' means written instructions issued by a declassification authority that describes the elements of information regarding a specific subject that may be declassified and the elements that must remain classified.

(o) ''Derivative classification'' means the incorporating, paraphrasing, restating, or generating in new form information that is already classified, and marking the newly developed material consistent with the classification markings that apply to the source information. Derivative classification includes the classification of information based on classification guidance. The duplication or reproduction of existing classified information is not derivative classification.

(p) ''Document'' means any recorded information, regardless of the nature of the medium or the method or circumstances of recording.

(q) ''Downgrading'' means a determination by a declassification authority that information classified and safeguarded at a specified level shall be classified and safeguarded at a lower level.

(r) ''File series'' means file units or documents arranged according to a filing system or kept together because they relate to a particular subject or function, result from the same activity, document a specific kind of transaction, take a particular physical form, or have some other relationship arising out of their creation, receipt, or use, such as restrictions on access or use.

(s) ''Foreign government information'' means:

(1) information provided to the United States Government by a foreign government or governments, an international organization of governments, or any element thereof, with the expectation that the information, the source of the information, or both, are to be held in confidence;

(2) information produced by the United States Government pursuant to or as a result of a joint arrangement with a foreign government or governments, or an international organization of governments, or any element thereof, requiring that the information, the arrangement, or both, are to be held in confidence; or

(3) information received and treated as ''foreign government information'' under the terms of a predecessor order.

(t) "Information" means any knowledge that can be communicated or documentary material, regardless of its physical form or characteristics, that is owned by, is produced by or for, or is under the control of the United States Government.

(u) "Infraction" means any knowing, willful, or negligent action contrary to the requirements of this order or its implementing directives that does not constitute a "violation," as defined below.

(v) "Integral file block" means a distinct component of a file series, as defined in this section, that should be maintained as a separate unit in order to ensure the integrity of the records. An integral file block may consist of a set of records covering either a specific topic or a range of time, such as a Presidential administration or a 5-year retirement schedule within a specific file series that is retired from active use as a group. For purposes of automatic declassification, integral file blocks shall contain only records dated within 10 years of the oldest record in the file block.

(w) "Integrity" means the state that exists when information is unchanged from its source and has not been accidentally or intentionally modified, altered, or destroyed.

(x) "Intelligence" includes foreign intelligence and counterintelligence as defined by Executive Order 12333 of December 4, 1981, as amended, or by a successor order.

(y) "Intelligence activities" means all activities that elements of the Intelligence Community are authorized to conduct pursuant to law or Executive Order 12333, as amended, or a successor order.

(z) "Intelligence Community" means an element or agency of the U.S. Government identified in or designated pursuant to section 3(4) of the National Security Act of 1947, as amended, or section 3.5(h) of Executive Order 12333, as amended.

(aa) "Mandatory declassification review" means the review for declassification of classified information in response to a request for declassification that meets the requirements under section 3.5 of this order.

(bb) "Multiple sources" means two or more source documents, classification guides, or a combination of both.

(cc) "National security" means the national defense or foreign relations of the United States.

(dd) "Need-to-know" means a determination within the executive branch in accordance with directives issued pursuant to this order that a prospective recipient requires access to specific classified information in order to perform or assist in a lawful and authorized governmental function.

(ee) "Network" means a system of two or more computers that can exchange data or information.

(ff) "Original classification" means an initial determination that information requires, in the interest of the national security, protection against unauthorized disclosure.

(gg) "Original classification authority" means an individual authorized in writing, either by the President, the Vice President, or by agency heads or other officials designated by the President, to classify information in the first instance.

(hh) "Records" means the records of an agency and Presidential papers or Presidential records, as those terms are defined in title 44, United States Code, including those created or maintained by a government contractor, licensee, certificate holder, or grantee that are subject to the sponsoring agency's control under the terms of the contract, license, certificate, or grant.

(ii) "Records having permanent historical value" means Presidential papers or Presidential records and the records of an agency that the Archivist has determined should be maintained permanently in accordance with title 44, United States Code.

(jj) "Records management" means the planning, controlling, directing, organizing, training, promoting, and other managerial activities involved with respect to records creation, records maintenance and use, and records disposition in order to achieve adequate and proper documentation of the policies and transactions of the Federal Government and effective and economical management of agency operations.

(kk) "Safeguarding" means measures and controls that are prescribed to protect classified information.

(ll) "Self-inspection" means the internal review and evaluation of individual agency activities and the agency as a whole with respect to the implementation of the program established under this order and its implementing directives.

(mm) "Senior agency official" means the official designated by the agency head under section 5.4(d) of this order to direct and administer the agency's program under which information is classified, safeguarded, and declassified.

(nn) "Source document" means an existing document that contains classified information that is incorporated, paraphrased, restated, or generated in new form into a new document.

(oo) "Special access program" means a program established for a specific class of classified information that imposes safeguarding and access requirements that exceed those normally required for information at the same classification level.

(pp) "Systematic declassification review" means the review for declassification of classified information contained in records that have been determined by the Archivist to have permanent historical value in accordance with title 44, United States Code.

(qq) "Telecommunications" means the preparation, transmission, or communication of information by electronic means.

(rr) "Unauthorized disclosure" means a communication or physical transfer of classified information to an unauthorized recipient.

(ss) "U.S. entity" includes:

(1) State, local, or tribal governments;

(2) State, local, and tribal law enforcement and firefighting entities;

(3) public health and medical entities;

(4) regional, state, local, and tribal emergency management entities, including State Adjutants General and other appropriate public safety entities; or

(5) private sector entities serving as part of the nation's Critical Infrastructure/Key Resources.

(tt) "Violation" means:

(1) any knowing, willful, or negligent action that could reasonably be expected to result in an unauthorized disclosure of classified information;

(2) any knowing, willful, or negligent action to classify or continue the classification of information contrary to the requirements of this order or its implementing directives; or

(3) any knowing, willful, or negligent action to create or continue a special access program contrary to the requirements of this order.

(uu) "Weapons of mass destruction" means any weapon of mass destruction as defined in 50 U.S.C. 1801(p).

SEC. 6.2. GENERAL PROVISIONS

(a) Nothing in this order shall supersede any requirement made by or under the Atomic Energy Act of 1954, as amended, or the National Security Act of 1947, as amended. "Restricted Data" and "Formerly Restricted Data" shall be handled, protected, classified, downgraded, and declassified in conformity with the provisions of the Atomic Energy Act of 1954, as amended, and regulations issued under that Act.

(b) The Director of National Intelligence may, with respect to the Intelligence Community and after consultation with the heads of affected departments and agencies, issue such policy directives and guidelines as the Director of National Intelligence deems necessary to implement this order with respect to the classification and declassification of all intelligence and intelligence-related information, and for access to and dissemination of all intelligence and intelligence-related information, both in its final form
and in the form when initially gathered. Procedures or other guidance issued by Intelligence Community element heads shall be in accordance with such policy directives or guidelines issued by the Director of National Intelligence. Any such policy directives or guidelines issued by the Director of National Intelligence shall be in accordance with directives issued by the Director of the Information Security Oversight Office under section 5.1(a) of this order.

(c) The Attorney General, upon request by the head of an agency or the Director of the Information Security Oversight Office, shall render an interpretation of this order with respect to any question arising in the course of its administration.

(d) Nothing in this order limits the protection afforded any information by other provisions of law, including the Constitution, Freedom of Information Act exemptions, the Privacy Act of 1974, and the National Security Act of 1947, as amended. This order is not intended to and does not create any right or benefit, substantive or procedural, enforceable at law by a party against the United States, its departments, agencies, or entities, its officers, employees, or agents, or any other person. The foregoing is in addition to the specific provisos set forth in sections 1.1(b), 3.1(c) and 5.3(e) of this order.

(e) Nothing in this order shall be construed to obligate action or otherwise affect functions by the Director of the Office of Management and Budget relating to budgetary, administrative, or legislative proposals.

(f) This order shall be implemented subject to the availability of appropriations.

(g) Executive Order 12958 of April 17, 1995, and amendments thereto, including Executive Order 13292 of March 25, 2003, are hereby revoked as of the effective date of this order.

SEC. 6.3. EFFECTIVE DATE.

This order is effective 180 days from the date of this order, except for sections 1.7, 3.3, and 3.7, which are effective immediately.

SEC. 6.4. PUBLICATION.

The Archivist of the United States shall publish this Executive Order in the *Federal Register*.

-/S/- Barack Obama
THE WHITE HOUSE,
December 29, 2009.

EXECUTIVE ORDER 13587:
STRUCTURAL REFORMS TO IMPROVE THE SECURITY OF CLASSIFIED NETWORKS AND THE RESPONSIBLE SHARING AND SAFEGUARDING OF CLASSIFIED INFORMATION

(Federal Register Vol. 76, No. 198 (October 13, 2011))

By the authority vested in me as President by the Constitution and the laws of the United States of America and in order to ensure the responsible sharing and safeguarding of classified national security information (classified information) on computer networks, it is hereby ordered as follows:

SECTION 1. POLICY.
Our Nation's security requires classified information to be shared immediately with authorized users around the world but also requires sophisticated and vigilant means to ensure it is shared securely. Computer networks have individual and common vulnerabilities that require coordinated decisions on risk management.

This order directs structural reforms to ensure responsible sharing and safeguarding of classified information on computer networks that shall be consistent with appropriate protections for privacy and civil liberties. Agencies bear the primary responsibility for meeting these twin goals. These structural reforms will ensure coordinated interagency development and reliable implementation of policies and minimum standards regarding information security, personnel security, and systems security; address both internal and external security threats and vulnerabilities; and provide policies and minimum standards for sharing classified information both within and outside the Federal Government. These policies and minimum standards will address all agencies that operate or access classified computer networks, all users of classified computer networks (including contractors and others who operate or access classified computer networks controlled by the Federal Government), and all classified information on those networks.

SEC. 2. GENERAL RESPONSIBILITIES OF AGENCIES.

SEC. 2.1.
The heads of agencies that operate or access classified computer networks shall have responsibility for appropriately sharing and safeguarding classified information on computer networks. As part of this responsibility, they shall:
(a) designate a senior official to be charged with overseeing classified

829

information sharing and safeguarding efforts for the agency;

(b) implement an insider threat detection and prevention program consistent with guidance and standards developed by the Insider Threat Task Force established in section 6 of this order;

(c) perform self-assessments of compliance with policies and standards issued pursuant to sections 3.3, 5.2, and 6.3 of this order, as well as other applicable policies and standards, the results of which shall be reported annually to the Senior Information Sharing and Safeguarding Steering Committee established in section 3 of this order;

(d) provide information and access, as warranted and consistent with law and section 7(d) of this order, to enable independent assessments by the Executive Agent for Safeguarding Classified Information on Computer Networks and the Insider Threat Task Force of compliance with relevant established policies and standards; and

(e) detail or assign staff as appropriate and necessary to the Classified Information Sharing and Safeguarding Office and the Insider Threat Task Force on an ongoing basis.

SEC. 3. SENIOR INFORMATION SHARING AND SAFEGUARDING STEERING COMMITTEE.

SEC. 3.1.
 There is established a Senior Information Sharing and Safeguarding Steering Committee (Steering Committee) to exercise overall responsibility and ensure senior-level accountability for the coordinated interagency development and implementation of policies and standards regarding the sharing and safeguarding of classified information on computer networks.

SEC. 3.2.
The Steering Committee shall be co-chaired by senior representatives of the Office of Management and Budget and the National Security Staff. Members of the committee shall be officers of the United States as designated by the heads of the Departments of State, Defense, Justice, Energy, and Homeland Security, the Office of the Director of National Intelligence, the Central Intelligence Agency, and the Information Security Oversight Office within the National Archives and Records Administration (ISOO), as well as such additional agencies as the co-chairs of the Steering Committee may designate.

SEC. 3.3.
The responsibilities of the Steering Committee shall include:

(a) establishing Government-wide classified information sharing and safeguarding
goals and annually reviewing executive branch successes and shortcomings in achieving those goals;

(b) preparing within 90 days of the date of this order and at least annually thereafter, a report for the President assessing the executive branch's successes and shortcomings in sharing and safeguarding classified information on computer networks and discussing potential future vulnerabilities;

(c) developing program and budget recommendations to achieve Government-wide classified information sharing and safeguarding goals;

(d) coordinating the interagency development and implementation of priorities, policies, and standards for sharing and safeguarding classified information on computer networks;

(e) recommending overarching policies, when appropriate, for promulgation by the Office of Management and Budget or the ISOO;

(f) coordinating efforts by agencies, the Executive Agent, and the Task Force to assess compliance with established policies and standards and recommending corrective actions needed to ensure compliance;

(g) providing overall mission guidance for the Program Manager-Information Sharing Environment (PM–ISE) with respect to the functions to be performed by the Classified Information Sharing and Safeguarding Office established in section 4 of this order; and

(h) referring policy and compliance issues that cannot be resolved by the Steering Committee to the Deputies Committee of the National Security Council in accordance with Presidential Policy Directive/PPD–1 of February 13, 2009 (Organization of the National Security Council System).

SEC. 4. CLASSIFIED INFORMATION SHARING AND SAFEGUARDING OFFICE.

SEC. 4.1.
There shall be established a Classified Information Sharing and Safeguarding Office (CISSO) within and subordinate to the office of the PM–ISE to provide expert, full-time, sustained focus on responsible sharing and safeguarding of classified information on computer networks. Staff of the CISSO shall include detailees, as needed and appropriate, from agencies represented on the Steering Committee.

SEC. 4.2.
The responsibilities of CISSO shall include:
(a) providing staff support for the Steering Committee;
(b) advising the Executive Agent for Safeguarding Classified Information on Computer Networks and the Insider Threat Task Force on the development

of an effective program to monitor compliance with established policies and standards needed to achieve classified information sharing and safeguarding goals; and

(c) consulting with the Departments of State, Defense, and Homeland Security, the ISOO, the Office of the Director of National Intelligence, and others, as appropriate, to ensure consistency with policies and standards under Executive Order 13526 of December 29, 2009, Executive Order 12829 of January 6, 1993, as amended, Executive Order 13549 of August 18, 2010, and Executive Order 13556 of November 4, 2010.

SEC. 5. EXECUTIVE AGENT FOR SAFEGUARDING CLASSIFIED INFORMATION ON COMPUTER NETWORKS.

SEC. 5.1.

The Secretary of Defense and the Director, National Security Agency, shall jointly act as the Executive Agent for Safeguarding Classified Information on Computer Networks (the "Executive Agent"), exercising the existing authorities of the Executive Agent and National Manager for national security systems, respectively, under National Security Directive/NSD–42 of July 5, 1990, as supplemented by and subject to this order.

SEC. 5.2.

The Executive Agent's responsibilities, in addition to those specified by NSD–42, shall include the following:

(a) developing effective technical safeguarding policies and standards in coordination with the Committee on National Security Systems (CNSS), as re-designated by Executive Orders 13286 of February 28, 2003, and 13231 of October 16, 2001, that address the safeguarding of classified information within national security systems, as well as the safeguarding of national security systems themselves;

(b) referring to the Steering Committee for resolution any unresolved issues delaying the Executive Agent's timely development and issuance of technical policies and standards;

(c) reporting at least annually to the Steering Committee on the work of CNSS, including recommendations for any changes needed to improve the timeliness and effectiveness of that work; and

(d) conducting independent assessments of agency compliance with established safeguarding policies and standards, and reporting the results of such assessments to the Steering Committee.

SEC. 6. INSIDER THREAT TASK FORCE.

SEC. 6.1.
There is established an interagency Insider Threat Task Force
that shall develop a Government-wide program (insider threat program) for
deterring, detecting, and mitigating insider threats, including the safeguarding
of classified information from exploitation, compromise, or other unauthorized
disclosure, taking into account risk levels, as well as the distinct needs,
missions, and systems of individual agencies. This program shall include
development of policies, objectives, and priorities for establishing and integrating
security, counterintelligence, user audits and monitoring, and other
safeguarding capabilities and practices within agencies.

SEC. 6.2.
The Task Force shall be co-chaired by the Attorney General and
the Director of National Intelligence, or their designees. Membership on
the Task Force shall be composed of officers of the United States from,
and designated by the heads of, the Departments of State, Defense, Justice,
Energy, and Homeland Security, the Office of the Director of National
Intelligence, the Central Intelligence Agency, and the ISOO, as well as such
additional agencies as the co-chairs of the Task Force may designate. It
shall be staffed by personnel from the Federal Bureau of Investigation and
the Office of the National Counterintelligence Executive (ONCIX), and other
agencies, as determined by the co-chairs for their respective agencies and
to the extent permitted by law. Such personnel must be officers or fulltime
or permanent part-time employees of the United States. To the extent
permitted by law, ONCIX shall provide an appropriate work site and
administrative support for the Task Force.

SEC. 6.3.
The Task Force's responsibilities shall include the following:
(a) developing, in coordination with the Executive Agent, a Government-wide
policy for the deterrence, detection, and mitigation of insider threats,
which shall be submitted to the Steering Committee for appropriate review;
(b) in coordination with appropriate agencies, developing minimum standards
and guidance for implementation of the insider threat program's Government-
wide policy and, within 1 year of the date of this order, issuing
those minimum standards and guidance, which shall be binding on the
executive branch;
(c) if sufficient appropriations or authorizations are obtained, continuing
in coordination with appropriate agencies after 1 year from the date of
this order to add to or modify those minimum standards and guidance,
as appropriate;
(d) if sufficient appropriations or authorizations are not obtained, recommending

for promulgation by the Office of Management and Budget or
the ISOO any additional or modified minimum standards and guidance
developed more than 1 year after the date of this order;
(e) referring to the Steering Committee for resolution any unresolved issues
delaying the timely development and issuance of minimum standards;
(f) conducting, in accordance with procedures to be developed by the
Task Force, independent assessments of the adequacy of agency programs
to implement established policies and minimum standards, and reporting
the results of such assessments to the Steering Committee;
(g) providing assistance to agencies, as requested, including through the
dissemination of best practices; and
(h) providing analysis of new and continuing insider threat challenges
facing the United States Government.

SEC. 7. GENERAL PROVISIONS.
 (a) For the purposes of this order, the word "agencies" shall have the meaning
set forth in section 6.1(b) of Executive Order 13526 of December 29, 2009.
(b) Nothing in this order shall be construed to change the requirements
of Executive Orders 12333 of December 4, 1981, 12829 of January 6, 1993,
12968 of August 2, 1995, 13388 of October 25, 2005, 13467 of June 30,
2008, 13526 of December 29, 2009, 13549 of August 18, 2010, and their
successor orders and directives.
(c) Nothing in this order shall be construed to supersede or change the
authorities of the Secretary of Energy or the Nuclear Regulatory Commission
under the Atomic Energy Act of 1954, as amended; the Secretary of Defense
under Executive Order 12829, as amended; the Secretary of Homeland Security
under Executive Order 13549; the Secretary of State under title 22,
United States Code, and the Omnibus Diplomatic Security and Antiterrorism
Act of 1986; the Director of ISOO under Executive Orders 13526 and 12829,
as amended; the PM–ISE under Executive Order 13388 or the Intelligence
Reform and Terrorism Prevention Act of 2004, as amended; the Director,
Central Intelligence Agency under NSD–42 and Executive Order 13286, as
amended; the National Counterintelligence Executive, under the
Counterintelligence Enhancement Act of 2002; or the Director of National
Intelligence under the National Security Act of 1947, as amended, the
Intelligence Reform and Terrorism Prevention Act of 2004, as amended, NSD–
42, and Executive Orders 12333, as amended, 12968, as amended, 13286, as
amended, 13467, and 13526.
(d) Nothing in this order shall authorize the Steering Committee, CISSO,
CNSS, or the Task Force to examine the facilities or systems of other agencies,
without advance consultation with the head of such agency, nor to collect
information for any purpose not provided herein.

(e) The entities created and the activities directed by this order shall not seek to deter, detect, or mitigate disclosures of information by Government employees or contractors that are lawful under and protected by the Intelligence Community Whistleblower Protection Act of 1998, Whistleblower Protection Act of 1989, Inspector General Act of 1978, or similar statutes, regulations, or policies.

(f) With respect to the Intelligence Community, the Director of National Intelligence, after consultation with the heads of affected agencies, may issue such policy directives and guidance as the Director of National Intelligence deems necessary to implement this order.

(g) Nothing in this order shall be construed to impair or otherwise affect:

(1) the authority granted by law to an agency, or the head thereof; or

(2) the functions of the Director of the Office of Management and Budget relating to budgetary, administrative, or legislative proposals.

(h) This order shall be implemented consistent with applicable law and appropriate protections for privacy and civil liberties, and subject to the availability of appropriations.

(i) This order is not intended to, and does not, create any right or benefit, substantive or procedural, enforceable at law or in equity by any party against the United States, its departments, agencies, or entities, its officers, employees, or agents, or any other person.

-/S/- Barack Obama
THE WHITE HOUSE,
October 7, 2011.

INTELLIGENCE SHARING PROCEDURES FOR FOREIGN INTELLIGENCE AND FOREIGN COUNTERINTELLIGENCE INVESTIGATIONS CONDUCTED BY THE FEDERAL BUREAU OF INVESTIGATION

OFFICE OF THE ATTORNEY GENERAL
WASHINGTON, D.C. 20530

March 6, 2002

MEMORANDUM

TO: Director, FBI
                Assistant Attorney General, Criminal Division
                Counsel for Intelligence Policy
                United States Attorneys

FROM: The Attorney General -/S/-John Ashcroft

SUBJECT: Intelligence Sharing Procedures for Foreign Intelligence and Foreign Counterintelligence Investigations Conducted by the FBI

I.   INTRODUCTION AND STATEMENT OF GENERAL PRINCIPLES

Unless otherwise specified by the Attorney General, these procedures apply to foreign intelligence (FI) and foreign counterintelligence (FCI) investigations conducted by the Federal Bureau of Investigations (FBI). They are designed to ensure that FI and FCI investigations are conducted lawfully, particularly in light of requirements imposed by the Foreign Intelligence Surveillance Act (FISA), and to promote the effective coordination and performance of the criminal and counterintelligence functions of the Department of Justice (DOJ). These procedures supersede the procedures adopted by the Attorney General on July 19, 1995 (including the annex concerning the Southern District of New York), the interim measures approved by the Attorney General on January 21, 2000, and the memorandum issued by the Deputy Attorney General on August 6, 2001. Terms used in these procedures shall be interpreted in keeping with definitions contained in FISA. References in these procedures to particular positions or components within the Department of Justice shall apply to any successor position or component.

Prior to the USA Patriot Act, FISA could be used only for "primary purpose" of obtaining "foreign intelligence information." The term "foreign intelligence information" was and is defined to include information that is necessary, or relevant, to the ability of the United Sates to protect against foreign threats to national security, such as attack, sabotage, terrorism, or clandestine intelligence activities. See 50 U.S.C. §1801(e)(1). Under the primary purpose standard, the government could have a significant law enforcement purpose for using FISA, but only if it was subordinate to the primary foreign intelligence purpose. The USA PATRIOT Act allows FISA to be used for "a significant purpose," rather than the primary purpose, of obtaining foreign intelligence information. Thus, it allows FISA to be used primarily for a law enforcement purpose, as long as a significant foreign intelligence purpose remains. See U.S.C. §1804 (a)(7)(B), 1823 (a)(7)(B).

The Act also expressly authorizes intelligence officers who are using FISA to "consult" with federal law enforcement officers to "coordinate efforts to investigate or protect against" foreign threats to national security. Under this authority, intelligence and law enforcement officers may exchange a full range of information and advice concerning such efforts in FI or FCI investigation, including information and advice designed to preserve or enhance the possibility of a criminal prosecution. The USA Patriot Act provides that such consultation intelligence and law enforcement officers "shall not" preclude the government's certification of a significant foreign intelligence purpose or the issuance of a FISA warrant. See 50 U.S.C. §§1806 (k), 1825 (k).

Consistent with the USA Patriot Act and with standards of effective management, all relevant DOJ components, including the Criminal Division, the relevant United States Attorney's Offices (USAOs), and the Office of Intelligence Policy and Review (OIPR), must be fully informed about the nature, scope, and conduct of all full field FI and FCI investigations, whether or not those investigations involve the use of FISA. Correspondingly, the Attorney General can most effectively direct and control such FI and FCI investigation only if all relevant DOJ components are free to offer advice and make recommendations, both strategic and tactical, about the conduct and goals of the investigations. The overriding need to protect the national security from foreign threats compels a full and free exchange of information and ideas.

II.   INTELLIGENCE SHARING PROCEDURES CONCERNING THE CRIMINAL DIVISION

A.   Disseminating Information.

The Criminal Division and OIPR shall have access to all information developed in full field FI and FCI investigations except as limited by orders issued by the Foreign Intelligence Surveillance Court, controls imposed by the originator of sensitive material, and restrictions established by the Attorney General or the Deputy Attorney General in particular cases. See 50 U.S.C §§1801 (h), 1806 (a), 1825 (a).

The FBI shall keep the Criminal Division and OIPR apprised of all information developed in full field FI and FCI investigations that is necessary to the ability of the United States to investigate or protect against foreign attack, sabotage, terrorism, and clandestine intelligence activities, subject to the limits set forth above. Relevant information includes both foreign intelligence information and information concerning a crime which has been, is being, or is about to be committed. The Criminal Division and OIPR must have access to this information to ensure the ability of the United States to coordinate efforts to investigate and protect against foreign threats to national security, including protection against such threats through criminal investigation and prosecution, and in keeping with the need of the United States to obtain, produce, and disseminate foreign intelligence information. See 50 U.S.C. §§1801(h)(1), 1806(k), 1825(k).

The FBI shall also keep the Criminal Division and OIPR apprised of information developed in full field FI and FCI investigations that concerns any crime which has been, is being, or is about to be committed. See U.S.C §1801(h)(3).

As part of its responsibility under the preceding paragraphs, the FBI shall provide to the Criminal Division and OIPR copies of annual Letterhead Memoranda (or successor summary documents) in all full field FI and FCI investigation, and shall make available to the Criminal Division and OIPR relevant information from investigative files, as appropriate. The Criminal Division shall adhere to any reasonable conditions on the storage and disclosure of such documents and information that the FBI or OIPR may require.

All information acquired pursuant to a FISA electronic surveillance or physical search that is disseminate to the Criminal Division shall be accompanied by a statement that such information, or any information derived therefrom, may only be used in any criminal proceeding (including search and arrest warrant affidavits and grand jury subpoenas and proceedings) with the advance authorization of the Attorney General. See 50 U.S.C. §§1806(b), 1825(c).

B. Providing Advice.

The FBI, the Criminal Division, and OIPR shall consult with one another concerning full field FI and FCI investigations except as limited by these procedures, orders issued by the Foreign Intelligence Surveillance Court, and restrictions established by the Attorney General or the Deputy Attorney General in particular cases.

Consultations may include the exchange of advice and recommendations on all issues necessary to the ability of the United States to investigate or protect against foreign attack, sabotage, terrorism, and clandestine intelligence activities, including protection against the foregoing through criminal investigations and prosecution, subject to the limits set forth above. Relevant issues include, but are not limited to, the strategy and goals for the investigation; the law enforcement and intelligence methods to be used in conducting the investigation; the interaction between intelligence and law enforcement components as part of the investigation; and the initiation, operation, continuation, or expansion of FISA searches or surveillance. Such consultations are necessary to the ability of the United States to coordinate efforts to investigate and protect against foreign threats to national security as set forth in 50 U.S.C. §§1806(k), 1825(k).

The FBI, the Criminal Division, and OIPR shall meet regularly to conduct consultations. Consultations may also be conducted directly between two or more components at any time. Disagreements arising from consultations may be presented to the Deputy Attorney General or the Attorney General for resolution.

III. INTELLIGENCE SHARING PROCEDURES CONCERNING A USAO

With respect to FI or FCI investigation involving international terrorism, the relevant USAOs shall receive information and engage in consultations to the same extent as the Criminal Division under Parts II.A and II.B of these procedures. Thus, the relevant USAOs shall have access to information developed in full field investigations, shall be kept apprised of information necessary to protect national security, shall be kept apprised of information concerning crimes, shall receive copies of LHMs or successor summary documents, and shall have access to the FBI files to the same extent as the Criminal Division. The relevant USAOs shall receive such information and access from the FBI field offices. The relevant USAOs also may and shall engage in regular consultations with the FBI and OIPR to the same extent as the Criminal Division.

With respect to FI or FCI investigations involving espionage, the Criminal Division shall, as appropriate, authorize the dissemination of information to a USAO, and shall also, as appropriate, authorize consultations between the FBI and a USAO, subject to the limits set forth in Parts II.A and II.B of these procedures. In an emergency, the FBI may disseminate information t, and consult with, a United States Attorney's Office concerning an espionage investigation without the approval of the Criminal Division, but shall notify the Criminal Division as soon as possible after the fact.

All information disseminated to a USAO pursuant to these procedures, whether or not the information is derived from FISA and whether or not it concerns a terrorism or espionage investigation, shall be disseminated only to the United States Attorney (USA) and/or any Assistant United States Attorneys (AUSUAs) designated to the Department of Justice by the USA as points of contact to receive such information. The USAs and the designated AUSAs shall have appropriate security clearances and shall receive training in the handling of classified information and information derived from FISA, including training concerning restrictions on the use and dissemination of such information.

Except in an emergency, where circumstances preclude the opportunity of consultation, the USAOs shall take no action on the information disseminated pursuant to these procedures without consulting with the Criminal Division and OIPR. The term "action" is defined to include the use of such information in any criminal proceeding (including search and arrest warrant affidavits and grand jury subpoenas and proceedings), and the disclosure of such information to a court or to any non-government personnel. See also U.S. Attorney's Manual §§9-2.136, 9-90.020. Disagreements arising from consultations pursuant to this paragraph may be presented to the Deputy Attorney General or the Attorney General for resolution.

All information acquired pursuant to a FISA electronic surveillance or physical search that is disseminated to a USAO shall be accompanied by a statement that such information, or any information derived therefrom, may only be used in any criminal proceeding (including search and arrest warrant affidavits and grand jury subpoenas and proceedings) with the advance authorization of the

Attorney General. See 50 U.S.C. §§1806(b), 1835(c). Whenever a USAO requests authority from Attorney General to use such information in a criminal proceeding, it shall simultaneously notify the Criminal Division.

GUIDELINES FOR DISCLOSURE OF GRAND JURY AND ELECTRONIC, WIRE, AND ORAL INTERCEPTION INFORMATION IDENTIFYING UNITED STATES PERSONS

OFFICE OF THE ATTORNEY GENERAL

WASHINGTON, DC 20530

September 23, 2002

MEMORANDUM FOR HEADS OF DEPARTMENT COMPONENTS

FROM   THE ATTORNEY General -/S/-John Ashcroft

Subject   Guidelines for Disclosure of Grand Jury and Electronic, Wire, and
              Oral Interception Information Identifying United States Persons

The prevention of terrorist activity is the overriding priority of the Department of Justice and improved information sharing among federal agencies is a critical component of our overall strategy to protect the security of America and the safety of her people.

Section 203 of the Uniting and Strengthening America by Providing Appropriate Tools Required to Intercept and Obstruct Terrorism (USA PATRIOT) Act of 2001, Pub. L. 107-56, 115 Stat. 272,278-81, authorizes the sharing of foreign intelligence, counterintelligence, and foreign intelligence information obtained through grand jury proceedings and electronic, wire, and oral interception, with relevant Federal officials to assist in the performance of their duties. This authorization greatly enhances the capacity of law enforcement to share information and coordinate activities with other federal officials in our common effort to prevent and disrupt terrorist activities.

At the same time, the law places special restrictions on the handling of intelligence information concerning United States persons ("U.S. person information"). Executive Order 12333,46 FR 59941 (Dec. 8, 1981) ("EO 12333"), for example, restricts the type of U.S. person information that agencies within the intelligence community may collect, and requires that the collection, retention, and dissemination of such information must conform with procedures established by the head of the agency concerned and approved by the Attorney General. Section 203(c) of the USA PATRIOT Act, likewise, directs the

Attorney General to establish procedures for the disclosure of grand jury and electronic, wire, and oral interception information "that identifies a United States person, as that term is defined in section 101 of the Foreign Intelligence Surveillance Act of 1978(50 U.S.C. §1801)."

Pursuant to section 203(c), this memorandum specifies the procedures for labeling information that identifies U .S. persons. Information identifying U.S. persons disseminated pursuant to section 203 must be marked to identify that it contains such identifying information prior to disclosure.

Section 101 of the Foreign Intelligence Surveillance Act of 1978 (50 U.S.C. §1801) provides:

"United States person" means a citizen of the United States, an alien lawfully admitted for permanent residence (as defined in section 1101 (a)(20) of Title 8), an unincorporated association a substantial number of members of which are citizens of the United States or aliens lawfully admitted for permanent residence, or a corporation which is incorporated in the United States, but does not include a corporation or an association which is a foreign power, as defined in subsection (a)(1), (2), or (3) of this section.

Information should be marked as containing U.S. person information if the information identifies any U.S. person. The U.S. person need not be the target or subject of the grand jury investigation or electronic, wire, and oral surveillance; the U.S. person need only be mentioned in the information to be disclosed. However, t he U.S. person must be "identified." That is, the grand jury or electronic, wire, and oral interception information must discuss or refer to the U.S person by name (or nickname or alias), rather than merely including potentially identifying information such as an address or telephone number that requires additional investigation to associate with a particular person.

Determining whether grand jury or electronic, wire, and oral interception information identifies a U. S. person may not always be easy. Grand jury and electronic, wire, and oral interception information standing alone will usually not establish unequivocally that an identified individual or entity is a U.S. person. In most instances, it will be necessary to use the context and circumstances of the information pertaining to the individual in question to determine whether the individual is a U.S. person. If the person is known to be located in the U.S., or if the location is unknown, he or she should be treated as a U.S. person unless the individual is identified as an alien who has not been admitted for permanent residence or circumstances give rise to the reasonable belief that the individual is not a U.S. person. Similarly, if the individual identified is known or believed to be located outside the U.S., he or she should be treated as a non-U.S. person unless the individual is identified as a U.S. person or circumstances give rise to the reasonable belief that the individual is a U.S. person.

Grand jury and electronic, wire, and oral interception information disclosed under section 203 should be received in the recipient agency by an individual who is designated to be a point of contact for such information for that agency. Grand jury and electronic, wire, and oral interception information identifying U.S. persons is subject to section 2.3 of EO 12333 and the procedures of each intelligence agency implementing EO 12333, each of which place important limitations on the types of U.S. person information that may be retained and disseminated by the United States intelligence community. These provisions require that information identifying a U.S. person be deleted from intelligence information except in limited circumstances. An intelligence agency that, pursuant to section 203, receives from the Department of Justice(or another Federal law enforcement agency) information acquired by electronic, wire, and oral interception techniques should handle such information in accordance with its own procedures implementing EO 12333 that are applicable to information acquired by the agency through such techniques.

In addition, the Justice Department will disclose grand jury and electronic, w ire, and oral interception information subject to use restrictions necessary to comply with notice and record keeping requirements and as necessary to protect sensitive law enforcement sources and ongoing criminal investigations. When imposed, use restrictions shall be no more restrictive than necessary to accomplish the desired effect.

These procedures are intended to be simple and minimally burdensome so that information sharing will not be unnecessarily impeded. Nevertheless, where warranted by exigent or unusual circumstances, the procedures may be modified in particular cases by memorandum of the Attorney General, Deputy Attorney General, or their designees, with notification to the Director of Central Intelligence or his designee. These procedures are not intended to and do not create any rights, privileges, or benefits, substantive or procedural, enforceable by any party against the United States, its departments, agencies, or other entities, its officers or employees or any other person.

The guidelines in this memorandum shall be effective immediately.

GUIDELINES REGARDING DISCLOSURE TO THE DIRECTOR OF CENTRAL INTELLIGENCE AND HOMELAND SECURITY OFFICIALS OF FOREIGN INTELLIGENCE ACQUIRED IN THE COURSE OF A CRIMINAL INVESTIGATION

OFFICE OF THE ATTORNEY GENERAL

WASHINGTON, DC 20530

September 23, 2002

MEMORANDUM FOR HEADS OF DEPARTMENT OF JUSTICE COMPONENTS AND HEADS OF FEDERAL DEPARTMENTS AND AGENCIES WITH LAW ENFORCEMENT RESPONSIBILITIES

FROM THE ATTORNEY GENERAL -/S/-John Ashcroft

SUBJECT: Guidelines Regarding Disclosure to the Director of Central Intelligence and Homeland Security Officials of Foreign Intelligence Acquired in the course of a Criminal Investigation

Background

The Uniting and Strengthening America by Providing Appropriate Tools Required to Intercept and Obstruct Terrorism (USA PATRIOT) Act of 2001, Pub. L. 107-56, 115 Stat. 272, 389, enacted into law certain requirements for the sharing of information by Federal Law enforcement agencies with the intelligence community. Specifically, section 905(a) of the USA PATRIOT Act provides that "the Attorney General, or the head of any other department or agency of the Federal Government with law enforcement responsibilities, shall expeditiously disclose to the Director of Central Intelligence, pursuant to guidelines developed by the Attorney General in consultation with the Director, foreign intelligence acquired by an element of the Department of Justice or an element of such department or agency, as the case may be, in the course of a criminal investigation."

Since the enactment of the USA PATRIOT Act, federal law enforcement agencies have taken steps to improve existing channels of communication with the intelligence community and certain offices relating to homeland security (collectively, "Receiving Agencies") in order to share foreign intelligence acquired in the course of criminal investigations. The purpose of these guidelines is to formalize a framework pursuant to section 905(a) of the USA

PATRIOT Act that will facilitate and increase to the fullest extent possible the continued expeditious sharing of such information. The procedures established by these guidelines for the sharing of information between components of the Department of Justice or other departments and agencies having law enforcement responsibilities with Recipients (as defined below) are not, however, intended to replace or supersede existing operational or information sharing mechanisms between Federal law enforcement agencies and Receiving Agencies. As appropriate, those relationships should continue to be used to the fullest extent possible.

Heads of Department of Justice components and heads of other departments and agencies of the Federal government having law enforcement responsibility shall distribute these guidelines within their respective departments, components and agencies, as appropriate, to ensure prompt and effective implementation of section 905(a) and these guidelines.

Guidelines for Section 905(a) Information Sharing

1   Scope of Application. These guidelines apply to all elements of the Department of Justice having criminal investigative or prosecutorial responsibilities and to all other departments and agencies of the Federal government having law enforcement responsibilities (herinafter, collectively, "Federal Law Enforcement Agencies"). These guidelines do not apply to agencies that provide support to criminal investigations, but that do not themselves conduct criminal investigations (e.g., the Department of Treasury's Office of Foreign Assets Control and Financial Crimes Enforcement Network).

2   Law Enforcement Information Subject to Mandatory Disclosure. Subject to any exceptions established by the Attorney General in consultation with the Director of Central Intelligence (the "Director") and Assistant to the President for Homeland Security, section 905(a) and these guidelines require expeditious disclosure to the Director, the Assistant to the President for Homeland Security or other members of the U.S. intelligence community or homeland security agencies as are designated under paragraph 4, *infra*, of foreign intelligence acquired in the course of a criminal investigation conducted by Federal Law Enforcement Agencies.

      a.   As used herein, the term "foreign intelligence" is defined in section 3 of the National Security Act of 1947 (50 U.S.C. §401a) as: "information relating to the capabilities, intentions, or activities of foreign governments or elements thereof, foreign organizations, or foreign persons, or international terrorist activities."

b. The term "section 905(a) information" means foreign intelligence acquired in the course of a criminal investigation.

c. Section 203(d) of the USA PATRIOT Act, provides that: "Notwithstanding any other law, it shall be lawful for foreign intelligence or counterintelligence (as defined in section 3 of the National Security Act of 1947 (50 U.S.C §401a)) or foreign intelligence information obtained as part of a criminal investigation to be disclosed to any Federal law enforcement, intelligence, protective, immigration, national defense, or national security official in order to assist the official receiving that information in the performance of his official duties." Thus, no other Federal or state law operates to prevent the sharing of such information so long as disclosure of such information will assist the Director and the Assistant to the President for Homeland Security in the performance of their official duties, and Federal Law Enforcement Agencies shall, notwithstanding any other law, expeditiously disclose to the Recipients (as defined below) section 905(a) information.

3   Training. Pursuant to section 908 of the USA PATRIOT Act, the department of Justice, in consultation with the Director, the Assistant to the President for Homeland Security, and other Federal Law Enforcement Agencies, will develop a training curriculum and program to ensure that law enforcement officials receive sufficient training to identify foreign intelligence subject to the disclosure requirements under these guidelines.

4   Entities to Whom Disclosure Shall Be Made. The Director, in consultation with the Assistant to the President for Homeland Security, shall promptly advise the Attorney General of his designations of appropriate offices, entities and/or officials of Receiving Agencies to receive the disclosure of section 905(a) information not covered by an established operational or information sharing mechanism. Said designees, together with the Director and the Assistant to the President for Homeland Security and all offices, entities, or individuals covered by such an established mechanism,

are collectively referred to herein as the "Recipients." The Director, in consultation with the Assistant to the President for Homeland Security, shall ensure that sufficient Recipients are identified to facilitate expeditious sharing and handling of section 905(a) information.

5 Methods for Disclosure of Section 905(a) Information. Subject only to any exceptions that may be established pursuant to paragraph 9(a), *infra,* all section 905(a) information shall be shared as expeditiously as possible with one or more of the Recipients. The procedures established in this paragraph may be supplemented by more detailed definitions and protocols disseminated to appropriate law enforcement, intelligence, and homeland security officials in classified or confidential form.

 a. Terrorism or Weapons of Mass Destruction (WMD) Information. Federal law enforcement officials shall disclose immediately to one or more Recipients information which they reasonably believe relates to a potential terrorism or WMD threat to the United States homeland, its critical infrastructure, key resources (whether physical or electronic), or to United States persons or interests worldwide. Other terrorism or WMD information, as defined by section 5(a)(i) and (ii), shall be disclosed to one or more Recipients as expeditiously as possible. In all cases, the official shall disclose such information with the understood priorities of disrupting terrorist plans, preventing terrorists' attacks, and preserving the lives of United States persons. Disclosure may be made through one or more of the following: existing field-level operational or information sharing mechanisms, including a Joint Terrorism Task Force (JTTF); existing headquarters operational or information sharing mechanisms; or when the officer reasonably believes that time does not permit the use of any such established mechanisms, any other field level or other mechanism intended to facilitate immediate action, response or other efforts to address such threats.

 As soon as possible after any disclosure under the preceding paragraph, the disclosing official shall notify the relevant JTTF of the disclosure. The JTTF shall, as appropriate, keep the relevant Anti-Terrorism Task Force (ATTF) apprised of the nature of the information disclosed. The relevant ATTF shall, in turn, apprise the Department of Justice Criminal Division's Terrorism and Violent Crime Section (TVCS). Where information is disclosed by the headquarters of the relevant Federal Law Enforcement Agency, the headquarters shall, as soon as practicable and to the extent reasonable, notify TVCS of all disclosures. Federal agencies may require additional notification procedures where appropriate.

For purposes of these guidelines, "terrorism information" and "weapons of mass destruction information" are defined as follows:

> Terrorism Information: All information relating to the existence, organization, capabilities, plans, intentions, vulnerabilities, means of finance or material support, or activities of foreign or international terrorist groups or individuals or threats posed by such groups or individuals to the United States, United States persons, or United States interests, or to those of other nations, or to communications between such groups or individuals, or information relating to groups or individuals reasonably believed to be assisting or associated with them.

> Weapons of Mass Destruction (WMD) Information: All information relating to conventional explosive weapons and non-conventional weapons capable of causing mass casualties and damage, including chemical, biological, radiological and nuclear agents and weapons and the means of delivery of such weapons.

b. All Other Section 905(a) Information. In consultation with the Department of Justice and the Director, Federal Law Enforcement Agencies shall develop (or continue to follow existing) protocols (which may be classified or confidential) to provide for the expeditious sharing of section 905(a) information concerning all other subjects.

c. Consultation With Respect to Title III and Grand Jury Materials. Except as to section 905(a) information related to a potential terrorism or WMD threat, disclosure of 905(a) information will be accomplished in consultation with the prosecuting official assigned to the case if: (i) the information was developed through investigatory activities occurring after a particular investigation has been referred formally to the Department of Justice for prosecution; and (ii) the information was produced by an electronic, wire, or oral interception or solely as a result of a grand jury subpoena or testimony occurring before a grand jury receiving information concerning the particular investigation. This consultation may be the basis for identifying appropriate use restrictions or for seeking an exception to the section 905(a) disclosure requirements as set forth in paragraph 9, *infra*. Consultation shall be accomplished expeditiously, and any resulting disclosure shall occur no later than 48 hours after the prosecutor is initially notified. Section 905(a) information that a Federal law enforcement official reasonably believes is related to a potential terrorism or WMD threat, including information received from an electronic, wire, or oral interception or as a result of a grand jury subpoena or testimony occurring before a grand jury, shall be immediately disclosed by the Federal law enforcement official using the mechanisms described in paragraph 5(a), *supra*, and without need for advance consultation with the prosecuting official responsible for the case. Contemporaneously or as soon after making the disclosure as possible, the Federal law enforcement official shall notify the prosecuting official responsible for the case in order to facilitate notice to the court, if necessary or appropriate.

6   Requests for Additional Information and Amplification on Initial Disclosure.

a. Initial disclosure of section 905(a) information to Recipients shall be accomplished automatically and without specific prior request to the disclosing department, component, or agency.

b. Requests by any Recipient for additional information or for clarification or amplification related to the initial disclosure should be coordinated, as applicable, through the component that provided the initial information or the designated headquarters office of the relevant Federal law enforcement agency.

7   Disclosure of Grand Jury and Electronic, Wire, and Oral Interception
       Information.

    a.   Sections 203(a) and (b) of the USA PATRIOT Act permit the
       disclosure of federal grand jury information and electronic, wire
       and oral interception information to specified recipients for
       specified purposes (hereinafter "section 203 information").

    b.   Where section 203 information is shared pursuant to Paragraph
       5, notice of such disclosures shall be promptly provided to the
       Office of Enforcement Operations (OEO) of the Department of
       Justice, Criminal Division. OEO shall establish appropriate
       record keeping procedures to ensure compliance with notice
       requirements related to the disclosure of grand jury information
       pursuant to section 203.

    c.   The USA PATRIOT Act requires special procedures for the
       disclosure of section 203 information that identifies United
       States persons. The Federal law enforcement agency disclosing
       section 203 information pursuant to these guidelines shall
       observe the procedures established by the Attorney General for
       disclosing such information that identifies a United States
       person. A copy of the section 203 United States person
       information procedures is attached as Appendix B.

    d.   By these guidelines the special procedures that were established
       pursuant to section 203(c) are made applicable to all section
       905(a) disclosures of information that identify a United States
       person.

8.   Information Use Restrictions.

    a.   In the absence of any significant law enforcement interests, as
       identified below in paragraph 8(b), necessitating the imposition
       of use restrictions, Federal Law Enforcement Agencies shall
       disclose section 905(a) information to Recipients pursuant to
       these guidelines free of any originator controls or information
       use restrictions.

    b.   The originator of the section 905(a) information may impose
       appropriate use restrictions necessary to protect sensitive law
       enforcement sources and ongoing criminal investigations and

prosecutions. The scope and duration of such restrictions, including caveats restricting use of the disclosed information to a particular level or element of the intelligence community, will be tailored to address the particular situation or subject matter involved.

    i.   When imposed, use restrictions shall be no more restrictive than necessary to accomplish the desired effect.

    ii.   Once imposed, use restrictions shall be reviewed periodically by the originator to determine whether they can be narrowed or lifted at the request of Recipients.

c.   Section 203 information shall be disclosed subject to any use restrictions necessary to comply with notice and record keeping requirements and to protect sensitive law enforcement sources and ongoing criminal investigations and prosecutions.

9.   **Attorney General Exceptions to Mandatory Disclosure of Section 905 Information.**

a.   Section 905(a) expressly authorizes the Attorney General, in consultation with the Director, to exempt by regulation from the mandatory disclosure obligation one or more classes of foreign intelligence or foreign intelligence related to one or more targets or matters.

b.   Pending the development of appropriate permanent exceptions, exemptions from the mandatory disclosure obligation will be determined by the Attorney General in consultation with the Director and the Assistant to the President for Homeland Security on a case-by-case basis.

c.   Requests for an Attorney General exception to mandatory disclosure of section 905(a) information must be submitted by the department, component or agency head in writing with a complete description of the facts and circumstances giving rise to the need for an exception and why lesser measures such as use restrictions are not adequate.

10. <u>Administering Agent.</u> The Assistant Attorney General of the Criminal Division, in consultation with affected Agencies, Offices and Divisions of the Department of Justice, will act as executive agent for the Attorney General in administering these guidelines and providing advice and assistance to Federal law enforcement regarding the implementation of sections 203 and 905.

11. <u>No Private Rights Created</u>. These procedures are not intended to and do not create and rights, privileges, or benefits, substantive or procedural, enforceable by any party against the United States, its departments, agencies, or other entities, its officers or employees, or any other person

12. <u>Effective Immediately</u>. The guidelines in this memorandum shall be effective immediately.

APPENDICES:

A. Extract Copy of Section 905
Procedures for Marking, Handling and Disclosing Information that Identifies a United States Person.

GUIDELINES REGARDING PROMPT HANDLING OF REPORTS OF POSSIBLE CRIMINAL ACTIVITY INVOLVING FOREIGN INTELLIGENCE SOURCES

OFFICE OF THE ATTORNEY GENERAL

WASHINGTON, DC 20530

September 23, 2002

MEMORANDUM FOR HEADS OF DEPARTMENT COMPONENTS

FROM THE ATTORNEY GENERAL -/S/-John Ashcroft

SUBJECT: Guidelines Regarding Prompt Handling of Reports of Possible Criminal Activity Involving Foreign Intelligence Sources

Section 905(b) of the Uniting and Strengthening America by Providing Appropriate Tools Required to Intercept and Obstruct Terrorism (USA PATRIOT) Act of 2001, Pub. L. 107-56, 115 Stat. 272,389, requires the Attorney General to develop guidelines to ensure that the Department of Justice responds within a reasonable period of time to reports from the intelligence community of possible criminal activity involving foreign intelligence sources or potential foreign intelligence sources. See 50 U.S.C. §403-5b(b). This memorandum establishes procedures to administer the requirement so f section 905 (b).

Pursuant to section 1.7(a) of Executive Order 12333; 28 U.S.C. §535(b); and the *1995 Memorandum of Understanding: Reporting of Information Concerning Federal Crimes* ("1995 MOU") between the Department of Justice and members of the intelligence community (Attachment A hereto), the intelligence community is required, inter alia, to report to the Assistant Attorney General or a designated Deputy Assistant Attorney General of the Criminal Division information that it has collected in the performance of its intelligence activities concerning possible federal crimes by employees of an intelligence agency and violations of specified federal criminal laws by any other person. This reporting requirement extends to matters in which the intelligence community agency determines that investigation or prosecution of the matter "may result in a public disclosure of classified information or intelligence sources or methods or would jeopardize the security of ongoing intelligence operations." 1995 MOU at 9

Upon receipt of a report of possible criminal activity pursuant to the 1995 MOU, the designated Deputy Assistant Attorney General shall refer the possible crime report to the appropriate component within the Department of Justice for review, including a determination of whether to commence or decline to commence a criminal investigation.

Section 905(b) reflects a recognition that when the possible criminal activities involve a foreign intelligence source or potential foreign intelligence source, the referring intelligence community agency may have a strong interest in knowing on an expedited basis whether the Department of Justice intends to investigate potential crimes.

Accordingly, I hereby direct that, when an intelligence community agency making such a possible crime report (all of which fall within the scope of and therefore should be made pursuant to the 1995 MOU) to the Criminal Division of the Department:

(1) notifies the Assistant Attorney General or designated Deputy Assistant Attorney General[1] that the possible crime report involves activity of a foreign intelligence source or potential foreign intelligence source; and

(2) requests an expedited determination of the Department of Justice's intent to commence or decline to commence a criminal investigation,

the designated Deputy Assistant Attorney General and/or another attorney within the Criminal Division or other relevant component of the Department shall expeditiously confer with the referring intelligence community agency about the possible criminal activity, the reasons for the time sensitivity, and the nature and extent of the intelligence equities that may be affected by a decision to commence or decline to commence a criminal investigation of the reported activity. Upon receipt of the report, the designated Deputy Assistant Attorney General shall determine whether immediate contact with the referring agency is necessary. If a need for immediate contact is not established, an appropriate Department attorney will be made available for an initial contact with the referring intelligence community agency within seven days of the receipt of the report requesting an expedited determination.

---

[1] The notification should be documented in writing, consistent with the procedures set forth in the 1995 Memorandum of Understanding governing the reporting by the intelligence community of possible criminal activity to the Department of Justice.

After conferencing with the referencing agency, receiving any necessary additional information, and consulting with other appropriate Department components, the Assistant Attorney General or the designated Deputy Assistant Attorney General of the Criminal Division or another appropriate Department attorney shall inform the referring agency within a reasonable period of time whether the Department intends to commence or decline t o commence a criminal investigation of the conduct described in the crime report. In all cases, Department attorneys shall take into account any special time urgency associated with the intelligence community agency's intelligence equities or the possible criminal activity and, if necessary, provide notice of the prosecutorial decision on a highly expedited basis. Except in extraordinary circumstances, the referencing agency should be informed within 30 days. Extraordinary circumstances requiring more than 30 days may include situations where the case is of unusual complexity or where information necessary for a prosecutorial decision is unavailable.

These procedures are not intended to and do not create any rights, privileges, or benefits, substantive or procedural, enforceable by any party against the United State, its departments, agencies, or other entities, its officers or employees, or any other person.

The guidelines in this memorandum shall be effective immediately.

THE ATTORNEY GENERAL'S GUIDELINES
FOR DOMESTIC FBI OPERATIONS

OFFICE OF THE ATTORNEY GENERAL

WASHINGTON, DC 20530

SEPTEMBER 29, 2008

PREAMBLE

These Guidelines are issued under the authority of the Attorney General as provided in sections 509, 510, 533, and 534 of title 28, United States Code, and Executive Order 12333. They apply to domestic investigative activities of the Federal Bureau of Investigation (FBI) and other activities as provided herein.

TABLE OF CONTENTS

861

IV. INTELLIGENCE ANALYSIS AND PLANNING
    A.   STRATEGIC INTELLIGENCE ANALYSIS
    B.   REPORTS AND ASSESSMENTS GENERALLY
    C.   INTELLIGENCE SYSTEMS

V. AUTHORIZED METHODS
    A.   PARTICULAR METHODS
    B.   SPECIAL REQUIREMENTS
    C.   OTHERWISE ILLEGAL ACTIVITY

VI. RETENTION AND SHARING OF INFORMATION
    A.   RETENTION OF INFORMATION
    B.   INFORMATION SHARING GENERALLY
    C.   INFORMATION RELATING TO CRIMINAL MATTERS
    D.   INFORMATION RELATING TO NATIONAL SECURITY AND
        FOREIGN INTELLIGENCE MATTERS

VII. DEFINITIONS

INTRODUCTION

As the primary investigative agency of the federal government, the Federal Bureau of Investigation (FBI) has the authority and responsibility to investigate all violations of federal law that are not exclusively assigned to another federal agency. The FBI is further vested by law and by Presidential directives with the primary role in carrying out investigations within the United States of threats to the national security. This includes the lead domestic role in investigating international terrorist threats to the United States, and in conducting counterintelligence activities to meet foreign entities' espionage and intelligence efforts directed against the United States. The FBI is also vested with important functions in collecting foreign intelligence as a member agency of the U.S. Intelligence Community. The FBI accordingly plays crucial roles in the enforcement of federal law and the proper administration of justice in the United States, in the protection of the national security, and in obtaining information needed by the United States for the conduct of its foreign affairs. These roles reflect the wide range of the FBI's current responsibilities and obligations, which require the FBI to be both an agency that effectively detects, investigates, and prevents crimes, and an agency that effectively protects the national security and collects intelligence.

The general objective of these Guidelines is the full utilization of all authorities and investigative methods, consistent with the Constitution and laws of the United States, to protect the United States and its people from terrorism and other threats to the national security, to protect the United States and its people from victimization by all crimes in violation of federal law, and to further the foreign intelligence objectives of the United States. At the same time, it is axiomatic that the FBI must conduct its investigations and other activities in a lawful and reasonable manner that respects liberty and privacy and avoids unnecessary intrusions into the lives of law-abiding people. The purpose of these Guidelines, therefore, is to establish consistent policy in such matters. They will enable the FBI to perform its duties with effectiveness, certainty, and confidence, and will provide the American people with a firm assurance that the FBI is acting properly under the law.

The issuance of these Guidelines represents the culmination of the historical evolution of the FBI and the policies governing its domestic operations subsequent to the September 11, 2001, terrorist attacks on the United States. Reflecting decisions and directives of the President and the Attorney General, inquiries and enactments of Congress, and the conclusions of national commissions, it was recognized that the FBI's functions needed to be expanded and better integrated to meet contemporary realities:

> [C]ontinuing coordination . . . is necessary to optimize the FBI's performance in both national security and criminal investigations . . . . [The] new reality requires first that the FBI and other agencies do a better job of gathering intelligence inside the United States, and second that we eliminate the remnants of the old "wall" between foreign intelligence and domestic law enforcement. Both tasks must be accomplished without sacrificing our domestic liberties and the rule of law, and both depend on building a very different FBI from the one we had on September 10, 2001. (Report of the Commission on the Intelligence Capabilities of the United States Regarding Weapons of Mass Destruction 466, 452 (2005).)

In line with these objectives, the FBI has reorganized and reoriented its programs and missions, and the guidelines issued by the Attorney General for FBI operations have been extensively revised over the past several years. Nevertheless, the principal directives of the Attorney General governing the FBI's conduct of criminal investigations, national security investigations, and foreign intelligence collection have persisted as separate documents involving different standards and procedures for comparable activities. These Guidelines effect a more complete integration and harmonization of standards, thereby providing the FBI and other affected Justice Department components with clearer, more consistent, and more accessible guidance for their activities, and making available to the public in a single document the basic body of rules for the FBI's domestic operations.

These Guidelines also incorporate effective oversight measures involving many Department of Justice and FBI components, which have been adopted to ensure that all FBI activities are conducted in a manner consistent with law and policy.

The broad operational areas addressed by these Guidelines are the FBI's conduct of investigative and intelligence gathering activities, including cooperation and coordination with other components and agencies in such activities, and the intelligence analysis and planning functions of the FBI.

A. FBI RESPONSIBILITIES – FEDERAL CRIMES, THREATS TO THE NATIONAL SECURITY, FOREIGN INTELLIGENCE

Part II of these Guidelines authorizes the FBI to carry out investigations to detect, obtain information about, or prevent or protect against federal crimes or threats to the national security or to collect foreign intelligence. The major subject areas of information gathering activities under these Guidelines – federal crimes, threats to the national security, and foreign intelligence – are not distinct, but rather overlap extensively. For example, an investigation relating to international terrorism will invariably crosscut these areas because international terrorism is included under these Guidelines' definition of "threat to the national security," because international terrorism subject to investigation within the United States usually involves criminal acts that violate federal law, and because information relating to international terrorism also falls within the definition of "foreign intelligence." Likewise, counterintelligence activities relating to espionage are likely to concern matters that constitute threats to the national security, that implicate violations or potential violations of federal espionage laws, and that involve information falling under the definition of "foreign intelligence."

While some distinctions in the requirements and procedures for investigations are necessary in different subject areas, the general design of these Guidelines is to take a uniform approach wherever possible, thereby promoting certainty and consistency regarding the applicable standards and facilitating compliance with those standards. Hence, these Guidelines do not require that the FBI's information gathering activities be differentially labeled as "criminal investigations," "national security investigations," or "foreign intelligence collections," or that the categories of FBI personnel who carry out investigations be segregated from each other based on the subject areas in which they operate. Rather, all of the FBI's legal authorities are available for deployment in all cases to which they apply to protect the public from crimes and threats to the national security and to further the United States' foreign intelligence objectives. In many cases, a single investigation will be supportable as an exercise of a number of these authorities – i.e., as an investigation of a federal crime or crimes, as an investigation of a threat to the national security, and/or as a collection of foreign intelligence.

1. Federal Crimes

The FBI has the authority to investigate all federal crimes that are not exclusively assigned to other agencies. In most ordinary criminal investigations, the immediate objectives include such matters as: determining whether a federal crime has occurred or is occurring, or if planning or preparation for such a crime is taking place; identifying, locating, and apprehending the perpetrators; and obtaining the evidence needed for prosecution. Hence, close cooperation and coordination with federal prosecutors in the United States Attorneys' Offices and the Justice Department litigating divisions are essential both to ensure that agents have the investigative tools and legal advice at their disposal for which prosecutorial assistance or approval is needed, and to ensure that investigations are conducted in a manner that will lead to successful prosecution. Provisions in many parts of these Guidelines establish procedures and requirements for such coordination.

2. Threats to the National Security

The FBI's authority to investigate threats to the national security derives from the executive order concerning U.S. intelligence activities, from delegations of functions by the Attorney General, and from various statutory sources. See, e.g., E.O. 12333; 50 U.S.C. 401 et seq.; 50 U.S.C. 1801 et seq. These Guidelines (Part VII.S) specifically define threats to the national security to mean: international terrorism; espionage and other intelligence activities, sabotage, and assassination, conducted by, for, or on behalf of foreign powers, organizations, or persons; foreign computer intrusion; and other matters determined by the Attorney General, consistent with Executive Order 12333 or any successor order.

Activities within the definition of "threat to the national security" that are subject to investigation under these Guidelines commonly involve violations (or potential violations) of federal criminal laws. Hence, investigations of such threats may constitute an exercise both of the FBI's criminal investigation authority and of the FBI's authority to investigate threats to the national security. As with criminal investigations generally, detecting and solving the crimes, and eventually arresting and prosecuting the perpetrators, are likely to be among the objectives of investigations relating to threats to the national security. But these investigations also often serve important purposes outside the ambit of normal criminal investigation and prosecution, by providing the basis for, and informing decisions concerning, other measures needed to protect the national security. These measures may include, for example: excluding or removing persons involved in terrorism or espionage from the United States; recruitment of double agents; freezing assets of organizations that engage in or support terrorism; securing targets of terrorism or espionage; providing threat information and warnings to other federal, state, local, and private agencies and entities; diplomatic or military actions; and actions by other intelligence agencies to counter international terrorism or other national security threats.

In line with this broad range of purposes, investigations of threats to the national security present special needs to coordinate with other Justice Department components, including particularly the Justice Department's National Security Division, and to share information and cooperate with other agencies with national security responsibilities, including other agencies of the U.S. Intelligence Community, the Department of Homeland Security, and relevant White House (including National Security Council and Homeland Security Council) agencies and entities. Various provisions in these Guidelines establish procedures and requirements to facilitate such coordination.

3. Foreign Intelligence

As with the investigation of threats to the national security, the FBI's authority to collect foreign intelligence derives from a mixture of administrative and statutory sources. See, e.g., E.O. 12333; 50 U.S.C. 401 et seq.; 50 U.S.C. 1801 et seq.; 28 U.S.C. 532 note (incorporating P.L. 108-458 §§ 2001-2003). These Guidelines (Part VII.E) define foreign intelligence to mean "information relating to the capabilities, intentions, or activities of foreign governments or elements thereof, foreign organizations or foreign persons, or international terrorists."

The FBI's foreign intelligence collection activities have been expanded by legislative and administrative reforms subsequent to the September 11, 2001, terrorist attacks, reflecting the FBI's role as the primary collector of foreign intelligence within the United States, and the recognized imperative that the United States' foreign intelligence collection activities become more flexible, more proactive, and more efficient in order to protect the homeland and adequately inform the United States' crucial decisions in its dealings with the rest of the world:

> The collection of information is the foundation of everything that the Intelligence Community does. While successful collection cannot ensure a good analytical product, the failure to collect information . . . turns analysis into guesswork. And as our review demonstrates, the Intelligence Community's human and technical intelligence collection agencies have collected far too little information on many of the issues we care about most. (Report of the Commission on the Intelligence Capabilities of the United States Regarding Weapons of Mass Destruction 351 (2005).)

These Guidelines accordingly provide standards and procedures for the FBI's foreign intelligence collection activities that meet current needs and realities and optimize the FBI's ability to discharge its foreign intelligence collection functions.

The authority to collect foreign intelligence extends the sphere of the FBI's information gathering activities beyond federal crimes and threats to the national security, and permits the FBI to seek information regarding a broader range of matters relating to foreign powers, organizations, or persons that may be of interest to the conduct of the United States' foreign affairs. The FBI's role is central to the effective collection of foreign intelligence within the United States because the authorized domestic activities of other intelligence agencies are more constrained than those of the FBI under applicable statutes and Executive Order 12333. In collecting foreign intelligence, the FBI will generally be guided by nationally-determined intelligence requirements, including the National Intelligence Priorities Framework and the National HUMINT Collection Directives, or any successor directives issued under the authority of the Director of National Intelligence (DNI). As provided in Part VII.F of these Guidelines, foreign intelligence requirements may also be established by the President or Intelligence Community officials designated by the President, and by the Attorney General, the Deputy Attorney General, or an official designated by the Attorney General.

The general guidance of the FBI's foreign intelligence collection activities by DNI-authorized requirements does not, however, limit the FBI's authority to conduct investigations supportable on the basis of its other authorities – to investigate federal crimes and threats to the national security – in areas in which the information sought also falls under the definition of foreign intelligence. The FBI conducts investigations of federal crimes and threats to the national security based on priorities and strategic objectives set by the Department of Justice and the FBI, independent of DNI-established foreign intelligence collection requirements.

Since the authority to collect foreign intelligence enables the FBI to obtain information pertinent to the United States' conduct of its foreign affairs, even if that information is not related to criminal activity or threats to the national security, the information so gathered may concern lawful activities. The FBI should accordingly operate openly and consensually with U.S. persons to the extent practicable when collecting foreign intelligence that does not concern criminal activities or threats to the national security.

B. THE FBI AS AN INTELLIGENCE AGENCY

The FBI is an intelligence agency as well as a law enforcement agency. Its basic functions accordingly extend beyond limited investigations of discrete matters, and include broader analytic and planning functions. The FBI's responsibilities in this area derive from various administrative and statutory sources. See, e.g., E.O. 12333; 28 U.S.C. 532 note (incorporating P.L. 108-458 §§ 2001-2003) and 534 note (incorporating P.L. 109-162 § 1107).

Enhancement of the FBI's intelligence analysis capabilities and functions has consistently been recognized as a key priority in the legislative and administrative reform efforts following the September 11, 2001, terrorist attacks:

> [Counterterrorism] strategy should . . . encompass specific efforts to . . . enhance the depth and quality of domestic intelligence collection and analysis . . . . [T]he FBI should strengthen and improve its domestic [intelligence] capability as fully and expeditiously as possible by immediately instituting measures to . . . significantly improve strategic analytical capabilities . . . . (Joint Inquiry into Intelligence Community Activities Before and After the Terrorist Attacks of September 11, 2001, S. Rep. No. 351 & H.R. Rep. No. 792, 107th Cong., 2d Sess. 4-7 (2002) (errata print).)

> A "smart" government would *integrate* all sources of information to see the enemy as a whole. Integrated all-source analysis should also inform and shape strategies to collect more intelligence. . . . The importance of integrated, all-source analysis cannot be overstated. Without it, it is not possible to "connect the dots." (Final Report of the National Commission on Terrorist Attacks Upon the United States 401, 408 (2004).)

Part IV of these Guidelines accordingly authorizes the FBI to engage in intelligence analysis and planning, drawing on all lawful sources of information.

The functions authorized under that Part include: (i) development of overviews and analyses concerning threats to and vulnerabilities of the United States and its interests, (ii) research and analysis to produce reports and assessments concerning matters relevant to investigative activities or other authorized FBI activities, and (iii) the operation of intelligence systems that facilitate and support investigations through the compilation and analysis of data and information on an ongoing basis.

C. OVERSIGHT

The activities authorized by these Guidelines must be conducted in a manner consistent with all applicable laws, regulations, and policies, including those protecting privacy and civil liberties. The Justice Department's National Security Division and the FBI's Inspection Division, Office of General Counsel, and Office of Integrity and Compliance, along with other components, share the responsibility to ensure that the Department meets these goals with respect to national security and foreign intelligence matters. In particular, the National Security Division's Oversight Section, in conjunction with the FBI's Office of General Counsel, is responsible for conducting regular reviews of all aspects of FBI national security and foreign intelligence activities. These reviews, conducted at FBI field offices and headquarter units, broadly examine such activities for compliance with these Guidelines and other applicable requirements.

Various features of these Guidelines facilitate the National Security Division's oversight functions. Relevant requirements and provisions include: (i) required notification by the FBI to the National Security Division concerning full investigations that involve foreign intelligence collection or investigation of United States persons in relation to threats of the national security, (ii) annual reports by the FBI to the National Security Division concerning the FBI's foreign intelligence collection program, including information on the scope and nature of foreign intelligence collection activities in each FBI field office, and (iii) access by the National Security Division to information obtained by the FBI through national security or foreign intelligence activities and general authority for the Assistant Attorney General for National Security to obtain reports from the FBI concerning these activities.

Pursuant to these Guidelines, other Attorney General guidelines, and institutional assignments of responsibility within the Justice Department, additional Department components – including the Criminal Division, the United States Attorneys' Offices, and the Office of Privacy and Civil Liberties – are involved in the common endeavor with the FBI of ensuring that the activities of all Department components are lawful, appropriate, and ethical as well as effective. Examples include the involvement of both FBI and prosecutorial personnel in the review of undercover operations involving sensitive circumstances, notice requirements for investigations involving sensitive investigative matters (as defined in Part VII.N of these Guidelines), and notice and oversight provisions for enterprise investigations, which may involve a broad examination of groups implicated in the gravest criminal and national security threats. These requirements and procedures help to ensure that the rule of law is respected in the Department's activities and that public confidence is maintained in these activities.

I. GENERAL AUTHORITIES AND PRINCIPLES

A. SCOPE

These Guidelines apply to investigative activities conducted by the FBI within the United States or outside the territories of all countries. They do not apply to investigative activities of the FBI in foreign countries, which are governed by the Attorney General's Guidelines for Extraterritorial FBI Operations.

B. GENERAL AUTHORITIES

1. The FBI is authorized to conduct investigations to detect, obtain information about, and prevent and protect against federal crimes and threats to the national security and to collect foreign intelligence, as provided in Part II of these Guidelines.
2. The FBI is authorized to provide investigative assistance to other federal agencies, state, local, or tribal agencies, and foreign agencies as provided in Part III of these Guidelines.
3. The FBI is authorized to conduct intelligence analysis and planning as provided in Part IV of these Guidelines.
4. The FBI is authorized to retain and share information obtained pursuant to these Guidelines as provided in Part VI of these Guidelines.

C. USE OF AUTHORITIES AND METHODS

1. **Protection of the United States and Its People**
   The FBI shall fully utilize the authorities provided and the methods authorized by these Guidelines to protect the United States and its people from crimes in violation of federal law and threats to the national security, and to further the foreign intelligence objectives of the United States.

2. Choice of Methods

a. The conduct of investigations and other activities authorized by these Guidelines may present choices between the use of different investigative methods that are each operationally sound and effective, but that are more or less intrusive, considering such factors as the effect on the privacy and civil liberties of individuals and potential damage to reputation. The least intrusive method feasible is to be used in such situations. It is recognized, however, that the choice of methods is a matter of judgment. The FBI shall not hesitate to use any lawful method consistent with these Guidelines, even if intrusive, where the degree of intrusiveness is warranted in light of the seriousness of a criminal or national security threat or the strength of the information indicating its existence, or in light of the importance of foreign intelligence sought to the United States' interests. This point is to be particularly observed in investigations relating to terrorism.

b. United States persons shall be dealt with openly and consensually to the extent practicable when collecting foreign intelligence that does not concern criminal activities or threats to the national security.

3. Respect for Legal Rights

All activities under these Guidelines must have a valid purpose consistent with these Guidelines, and must be carried out in conformity with the Constitution and all applicable statutes, executive orders, Department of Justice regulations and policies, and Attorney General guidelines. These Guidelines do not authorize investigating or collecting or maintaining information on United States persons solely for the purpose of monitoring activities protected by the First Amendment or the lawful exercise of other rights secured by the Constitution or laws of the United States. These Guidelines also do not authorize any conduct prohibited by the Guidance Regarding the Use of Race by Federal Law Enforcement Agencies.

4. Undisclosed Participation in Organizations

Undisclosed participation in organizations in activities under these Guidelines shall be conducted in accordance with FBI policy approved by the Attorney General.

5. Maintenance of Records under the Privacy Act

The Privacy Act restricts the maintenance of records relating to certain activities of individuals who are United States persons, with exceptions for circumstances in which the collection of such information is pertinent to and within the scope of an authorized law enforcement activity or is otherwise authorized by statute. 5 U.S.C. 552a(e)(7). Activities authorized by these Guidelines are authorized law enforcement activities or activities for which there is otherwise statutory authority for purposes of the Privacy Act. These Guidelines, however, do not provide an exhaustive enumeration of authorized FBI law enforcement activities or FBI activities for which there is otherwise statutory authority, and no restriction is implied with respect to such activities carried out by the FBI pursuant to other authorities. Further questions about the application of the Privacy Act to authorized activities of the FBI should be addressed to the FBI Office of the General Counsel, the FBI Privacy and Civil Liberties Unit, or the Department of Justice Office of Privacy and Civil Liberties.

D. NATURE AND APPLICATION OF THE GUIDELINES

1. Repealers

These Guidelines supersede the following guidelines, which are hereby repealed:

a. The Attorney General's Guidelines on General Crimes, Racketeering Enterprise and Terrorism Enterprise Investigations (May 30, 2002) and all predecessor guidelines thereto.

b. The Attorney General's Guidelines for FBI National Security Investigations and Foreign Intelligence Collection (October 31, 2003) and all predecessor guidelines thereto.

c. The Attorney General's Supplemental Guidelines for Collection, Retention, and Dissemination of Foreign Intelligence (November 29, 2006).

d. The Attorney General Procedure for Reporting and Use of Information Concerning Violations of Law and Authorization for Participation in Otherwise Illegal Activity in FBI Foreign Intelligence, Counterintelligence or International Terrorism Intelligence Investigations (August 8, 1988).

e. The Attorney General's Guidelines for Reporting on Civil Disorders and Demonstrations Involving a Federal Interest (April 5, 1976).

2. Status as Internal Guidance

These Guidelines are set forth solely for the purpose of internal Department of Justice guidance. They are not intended to, do not, and may not be relied upon to create any rights, substantive or procedural, enforceable by law by any party in any matter, civil or criminal, nor do they place any limitation on otherwise lawful investigative and litigative prerogatives of the Department of Justice.

3. **Departures from the Guidelines**

Departures from these Guidelines must be approved by the Director of the FBI, by the Deputy Director of the FBI, or by an Executive Assistant Director designated by the Director. If a departure is necessary without such prior approval because of the immediacy or gravity of a threat to the safety of persons or property or to the national security, the Director, the Deputy Director, or a designated Executive Assistant Director shall be notified as soon thereafter as practicable. The FBI shall provide timely written notice of departures from these Guidelines to the Criminal Division and the National Security Division, and those divisions shall notify the Attorney General and the Deputy Attorney General. Notwithstanding this paragraph, all activities in all circumstances must be carried out in a manner consistent with the Constitution and laws of the United States.

4. **Other Activities Not Limited**

These Guidelines apply to FBI activities as provided herein and do not limit other authorized activities of the FBI, such as the FBI's responsibilities to conduct background checks and inquiries concerning applicants and employees under federal personnel security programs, the FBI's maintenance and operation of national criminal records systems and preparation of national crime statistics, and the forensic assistance and administration functions of the FBI Laboratory.

II.   INVESTIGATIONS AND INTELLIGENCE GATHERING

This Part of the Guidelines authorizes the FBI to conduct investigations to detect, obtain information about, and prevent and protect against federal crimes and threats to the national security and to collect foreign intelligence.

When an authorized purpose exists, the focus of activities authorized by this Part may be whatever the circumstances warrant. The subject of such an activity may be, for example, a particular crime or threatened crime; conduct constituting a threat to the national security; an individual, group, or organization that may be involved in criminal or national security-threatening conduct; or a topical matter of foreign intelligence interest.

Investigations may also be undertaken for protective purposes in relation to individuals, groups, or other entities that may be targeted for criminal victimization or acquisition, or for terrorist attack or other depredations by the enemies of the United States. For example, the participation of the FBI in special events management, in relation to public events or other activities whose character may make them attractive targets for terrorist attack, is an authorized exercise of the authorities conveyed by these Guidelines. Likewise, FBI counterintelligence activities directed to identifying and securing facilities, personnel, or information that may be targeted for infiltration, recruitment, or acquisition by foreign intelligence services are authorized exercises of the authorities conveyed by these Guidelines.

The identification and recruitment of human sources – who may be able to provide or obtain information relating to criminal activities, information relating to terrorism, espionage, or other threats to the national security, or information relating to matters of foreign intelligence interest – is also critical to the effectiveness of the FBI's law enforcement, national security, and intelligence programs, and activities undertaken for this purpose are authorized and encouraged.

The scope of authorized activities under this Part is not limited to "investigation" in a narrow sense, such as solving particular cases or obtaining evidence for use in particular criminal prosecutions. Rather, these activities also provide critical information needed for broader analytic and intelligence purposes to facilitate the solution and prevention of crime, protect the national security, and further foreign intelligence objectives. These purposes include use of the information in intelligence analysis and planning under Part IV, and dissemination of the information to other law enforcement, Intelligence Community, and White House agencies under Part VI. Information obtained at all stages of investigative activity is accordingly to be retained and disseminated for these purposes as provided in these Guidelines, or in FBI policy consistent with these Guidelines, regardless of whether it furthers investigative objectives in a narrower or more immediate sense.

In the course of activities under these Guidelines, the FBI may incidentally obtain information relating to matters outside of its areas of primary investigative responsibility. For example, information relating to violations of state or local law or foreign law may be incidentally obtained in the course of investigating federal crimes or threats to the national security or in collecting foreign intelligence. These Guidelines do not bar the acquisition of such information in the course of authorized investigative activities, the retention of such information, or its dissemination as appropriate to the responsible authorities in other agencies or jurisdictions. Part VI of these Guidelines includes specific authorizations and requirements for sharing such information with relevant agencies and officials.

This Part authorizes different levels of information gathering activity, which afford the FBI flexibility, under appropriate standards and procedures, to adapt the methods utilized and the information sought to the nature of the matter under investigation and the character of the information supporting the need for investigation.

Assessments, authorized by Subpart A of this Part, require an authorized purpose but not any particular factual predication. For example, to carry out its central mission of preventing the commission of terrorist acts against the United States and its people, the FBI must proactively draw on available sources of information to identify terrorist threats and activities. It cannot be content to wait for leads to come in through the actions of others, but rather must be vigilant in detecting terrorist activities to the full extent permitted by law, with an eye towards early intervention and prevention of acts of terrorism before they occur. Likewise, in the exercise of its protective functions, the FBI is not constrained to wait until information is received indicating that a particular event, activity, or facility has drawn the attention of those who would threaten the national security. Rather, the FBI must take the initiative to secure and protect activities and entities whose character may make them attractive targets for terrorism or espionage. The proactive investigative authority conveyed in assessments is designed for, and may be utilized by, the FBI in the discharge of these responsibilities. For example, assessments may be conducted as part of the FBI's special events management activities.

More broadly, detecting and interrupting criminal activities at their early stages, and preventing crimes from occurring in the first place, is preferable to allowing criminal plots and activities to come to fruition. Hence, assessments may be undertaken proactively with such objectives as detecting criminal activities; obtaining information on individuals, groups, or organizations of possible investigative interest, either because they may be involved in criminal or national security-threatening activities or because they may be targeted for attack or victimization by such activities; and identifying and assessing individuals who may have value as human sources. For example, assessment activities may involve proactively surfing the Internet to find publicly accessible websites and services through which recruitment by terrorist organizations and promotion of terrorist crimes is openly taking place; through which child pornography is advertised and traded; through which efforts are made by sexual predators to lure children for purposes of sexual abuse; or through which fraudulent schemes are perpetrated against the public.

The methods authorized in assessments are generally those of relatively low intrusiveness, such as obtaining publicly available information, checking government records, and requesting information from members of the public. These Guidelines do not impose supervisory approval requirements in assessments, given the types of techniques that are authorized at this stage (e.g., perusing the Internet for publicly available information). However, FBI policy will prescribe supervisory approval requirements for certain assessments, considering such matters as the purpose of the assessment and the methods being utilized.

Beyond the proactive information gathering functions described above, assessments may be used when allegations or other information concerning crimes or threats to the national security is received or obtained, and the matter can be checked out or resolved through the relatively non-intrusive methods authorized in assessments. The checking of investigative leads in this manner can avoid the need to proceed to more formal levels of investigative activity, if the results of an assessment indicate that further investigation is not warranted.

Subpart B of this Part authorizes a second level of investigative activity, predicated investigations. The purposes or objectives of predicated investigations are essentially the same as those of assessments, but predication as provided in these Guidelines is needed – generally, allegations, reports, facts or circumstances indicative of possible criminal or national security-threatening activity, or the potential for acquiring information responsive to foreign intelligence requirements – and supervisory approval must be obtained, to initiate predicated investigations. Corresponding to the stronger predication and approval requirements, all lawful methods may be used in predicated investigations. A classified directive provides further specification concerning circumstances supporting certain predicated investigations.

Predicated investigations that concern federal crimes or threats to the national security are subdivided into preliminary investigations and full investigations. Preliminary investigations may be initiated on the basis of any allegation or information indicative of possible criminal or national security-threatening activity, but more substantial factual predication is required for full investigations. While time limits are set for the completion of preliminary investigations, full investigations may be pursued without preset limits on their duration.

The final investigative category under this Part of the Guidelines is enterprise investigations, authorized by Subpart C, which permit a general examination of the structure, scope, and nature of certain groups and organizations. Enterprise investigations are a type of full investigations. Hence, they are subject to the purpose, approval, and predication requirements that apply to full investigations, and all lawful methods may be used in carrying them out. The distinctive characteristic of enterprise investigations is that they concern groups or organizations that may be involved in the most serious criminal or national security threats to the public – generally, patterns of racketeering activity, terrorism or other threats to the national security, or the commission of offenses characteristically involved in terrorism as described in 18 U.S.C. 2332b(g)(5)(B). A broad examination of the characteristics of groups satisfying these criteria is authorized in enterprise investigations, including any relationship of the group to a foreign power, its size and composition, its geographic dimensions and finances, its past acts and goals, and its capacity for harm.

A. ASSESSMENTS

1. Purposes
Assessments may be carried out to detect, obtain information about, or prevent or protect against federal crimes or threats to the national security or to collect foreign intelligence.

2. Approval
The conduct of assessments is subject to any supervisory approval requirements prescribed by FBI policy.

3. Authorized Activities
Activities that may be carried out for the purposes described in paragraph 1. in an assessment include:

    a. seeking information, proactively or in response to investigative leads, relating to:

        i. activities constituting violations of federal criminal law or threats to the national security,

        ii. the involvement or role of individuals, groups, or organizations in such activities; or

        iii. matters of foreign intelligence interest responsive to foreign intelligence requirements;

    b. identifying and obtaining information about potential targets of or vulnerabilities to criminal activities in violation of federal law or threats to the national security;

    c. seeking information to identify potential human sources, assess the suitability, credibility, or value of individuals as human sources, validate human sources, or maintain the cover or credibility of human sources, who may be able to provide or obtain information relating to criminal activities in violation of federal law, threats to the national security, or matters of foreign intelligence interest; and

    d. obtaining information to inform or facilitate intelligence analysis and planning as described in Part IV of these Guidelines.

4. Authorized Methods

Only the following methods may be used in assessments:

    a. Obtain publicly available information.

    b. Access and examine FBI and other Department of Justice records, and obtain information from any FBI or other Department of Justice personnel.

    c. Access and examine records maintained by, and request information from, other federal, state, local, or tribal, or foreign governmental entities or agencies.

    d. Use online services and resources (whether nonprofit or commercial).

    e. Use and recruit human sources in conformity with the Attorney General's Guidelines Regarding the Use of FBI Confidential Human Sources.

    f. Interview or request information from members of the public and private entities.

    g. Accept information voluntarily provided by governmental or private entities.

    h. Engage in observation or surveillance not requiring a court order.

    i. Grand jury subpoenas for telephone or electronic mail subscriber information.

B. PREDICATED INVESTIGATIONS

1. Purposes

Predicated investigations may be carried out to detect, obtain information about, or prevent or protect against federal crimes or threats to the national security or to collect foreign intelligence.

2. Approval

The initiation of a predicated investigation requires supervisory approval at a level or levels specified by FBI policy. A predicated investigation based on paragraph 3.c. (relating to foreign intelligence) must be approved by a Special Agent in Charge or by an FBI Headquarters official as provided in such policy.

3. **Circumstances Warranting Investigation**

A predicated investigation may be initiated on the basis of any of the following circumstances:

a. An activity constituting a federal crime or a threat to the national security has or may have occurred, is or may be occurring, or will or may occur and the investigation may obtain information relating to the activity or the involvement or role of an individual, group, or organization in such activity.

b. An individual, group, organization, entity, information, property, or activity is or may be a target of attack, victimization, acquisition, infiltration, or recruitment in connection with criminal activity in violation of federal law or a threat to the national security and the investigation may obtain information that would help to protect against such activity or threat.

c. The investigation may obtain foreign intelligence that is responsive to a foreign intelligence requirement.

4. **Preliminary and Full Investigations**

A predicated investigation relating to a federal crime or threat to the national security may be conducted as a preliminary investigation or a full investigation. A predicated investigation that is based solely on the authority to collect foreign intelligence may be conducted only as a full investigation.

a. **Preliminary investigations**

i. **Predication Required for Preliminary Investigations**

A preliminary investigation may be initiated on the basis of information or an allegation indicating the existence of a circumstance described in paragraph 3.a.-.b.

ii. **Duration of Preliminary Investigations**

A preliminary investigation must be concluded within six months of its initiation, which may be extended by up to six months by the Special Agent in Charge. Extensions of preliminary investigations beyond a year must be approved by FBI Headquarters.

iii. **Methods Allowed in Preliminary Investigations**

All lawful methods may be used in a preliminary investigation except for methods within the scope of Part V.A.11.-.13. of these Guidelines.

b. Full Investigations

i. Predication Required for Full Investigations

A full investigation may be initiated if there is an articulable factual basis for the investigation that reasonably indicates that a circumstance described in paragraph 3.a.-.b. exists or if a circumstance described in paragraph 3.c. exists.

ii. Methods Allowed in Full Investigations

All lawful methods may be used in a full investigation.

5. Notice Requirements

a. An FBI field office shall notify FBI Headquarters and the United States Attorney or other appropriate Department of Justice official of the initiation by the field office of a predicated investigation involving a sensitive investigative matter. If the investigation is initiated by FBI Headquarters, FBI Headquarters shall notify the United States Attorney or other appropriate Department of Justice official of the initiation of such an investigation. If the investigation concerns a threat to the national security, an official of the National Security Division must be notified. The notice shall identify all sensitive investigative matters involved in the investigation.

b. The FBI shall notify the National Security Division of:

   i. the initiation of any full investigation of a United States person relating to a threat to the national security; and

   ii. the initiation of any full investigation that is based on paragraph 3.c. (relating to foreign intelligence).

c. The notifications under subparagraphs a. and b. shall be made as soon as practicable, but no later than 30 days after the initiation of an investigation.

d. The FBI shall notify the Deputy Attorney General if FBI Headquarters disapproves a field office's initiation of a predicated investigation relating to a threat to the national security on the ground that the predication for the investigation is insufficient.

C. ENTERPRISE INVESTIGATIONS

1. **Definition**

   A full investigation of a group or organization may be initiated as an enterprise investigation if there is an articulable factual basis for the investigation that reasonably indicates that the group or organization may have engaged or may be engaged in, or may have or may be engaged in planning or preparation or provision of support for:

   a. a pattern of racketeering activity as defined in 18 U.S.C. 1961(5);
   b. international terrorism or other threat to the national security;
   c. domestic terrorism as defined in 18 U.S.C. 2331(5) involving a violation of federal criminal law;
   d. furthering political or social goals wholly or in part through activities that involve force or violence and a violation of federal criminal law; or
   e. an offense described in 18 U.S.C. 2332b(g)(5)(B) or 18 U.S.C. 43.

2. **Scope**

   The information sought in an enterprise investigation may include a general examination of the structure, scope, and nature of the group or organization including: its relationship, if any, to a foreign power; the identity and relationship of its members, employees, or other persons who may be acting in furtherance of its objectives; its finances and resources; its geographical dimensions; and its past and future activities and goals.

3. **Notice and Reporting Requirements**

   a. The responsible Department of Justice component for the purpose of notification and reports in enterprise investigations is the National Security Division, except that, for the purpose of notifications and reports in an enterprise investigation relating to a pattern of racketeering activity that does not involve an offense or offenses described in 18 U.S.C. 2332b(g)(5)(B), the responsible Department of Justice component is the Organized Crime and Racketeering Section of the Criminal Division.
   b. An FBI field office shall notify FBI Headquarters of the initiation by the field office of an enterprise investigation.
   c. The FBI shall notify the National Security Division or the Organized Crime and Racketeering Section of the initiation of an enterprise investigation, whether by a field office or by FBI Headquarters, and the component so notified shall notify the Attorney General and the Deputy Attorney General. The

FBI shall also notify any relevant United States Attorney's Office, except that any investigation within the scope of Part VI.D.1.d of these Guidelines (relating to counterintelligence investigations) is to be treated as provided in that provision. Notifications by the FBI under this subparagraph shall be provided as soon as practicable, but no later than 30 days after the initiation of the investigation.

d. The Assistant Attorney General for National Security or the Chief of the Organized Crime and Racketeering Section, as appropriate, may at any time request the FBI to provide a report on the status of an enterprise investigation and the FBI will provide such reports as requested.

III.   ASSISTANCE TO OTHER AGENCIES

The FBI is authorized to provide investigative assistance to other federal, state, local, or tribal, or foreign agencies as provided in this Part.

The investigative assistance authorized by this Part is often concerned with the same objectives as those identified in Part II of these Guidelines – investigating federal crimes and threats to the national security, and collecting foreign intelligence. In some cases, however, investigative assistance to other agencies is legally authorized for purposes other than those identified in Part II, such as assistance in certain contexts to state or local agencies in the investigation of crimes under state or local law, see 28 U.S.C. 540, 540A, 540B, and assistance to foreign agencies in the investigation of foreign law violations pursuant to international agreements. Investigative assistance for such legally authorized purposes is permitted under this Part, even if it is not for purposes identified as grounds for investigation under Part II.

The authorities provided by this Part are cumulative to Part II and do not limit the FBI's investigative activities under Part II. For example, Subpart B.2 in this Part authorizes investigative activities by the FBI in certain circumstances to inform decisions by the President concerning the deployment of troops to deal with civil disorders, and Subpart B.3 authorizes investigative activities to facilitate demonstrations and related public health and safety measures. The requirements and limitations in these provisions for conducting investigations for the specified purposes do not limit the FBI's authority under Part II to investigate federal crimes or threats to the national security that occur in the context of or in connection with civil disorders or demonstrations.

A. THE INTELLIGENCE COMMUNITY

The FBI may provide investigative assistance (including operational support) to authorized intelligence activities of other Intelligence Community agencies.

B. FEDERAL AGENCIES GENERALLY

1. In General

The FBI may provide assistance to any federal agency in the investigation of federal crimes or threats to the national security or in the collection of foreign intelligence, and investigative assistance to any federal agency for any other purpose that may be legally authorized, including investigative assistance to the Secret Service in support of its protective responsibilities.

2. The President in Relation to Civil Disorders

a. At the direction of the Attorney General, the Deputy Attorney General, or the Assistant Attorney General for the Criminal Division, the FBI shall collect information relating to actual or threatened civil disorders to assist the President in determining (pursuant to the authority of the President under 10 U.S.C. 331-33) whether use of the armed forces or militia is required and how a decision to commit troops should be implemented. The information sought shall concern such matters as:

    i. The size of the actual or threatened disorder, both in number of people involved or affected and in geographic area.

    ii. The potential for violence.

    iii. The potential for expansion of the disorder in light of community conditions and underlying causes of the disorder.

    iv. The relationship of the actual or threatened disorder to the enforcement of federal law or court orders and the likelihood that state or local authorities will assist in enforcing those laws or orders.

    v. The extent of state or local resources available to handle the disorder.

b. Investigations under this paragraph will be authorized only for a period of 30 days, but the authorization may be renewed for subsequent 30 day periods.

c. Notwithstanding Subpart E.2 of this Part, the methods that may be used in an investigation under this paragraph are those described in subparagraphs a.-d., subparagraph f. (other than pretext interviews or requests), or subparagraph g. of Part II.A.4 of these Guidelines. The Attorney General, the Deputy Attorney General, or the Assistant Attorney General for the Criminal Division may also authorize the use of other methods described in Part II.A.4.

3. **Public Health and Safety Authorities in Relation to Demonstrations**

   a. At the direction of the Attorney General, the Deputy Attorney General, or the Assistant Attorney General for the Criminal Division, the FBI shall collect information relating to demonstration activities that are likely to require the federal government to take action to facilitate the activities and provide public health and safety measures with respect to those activities. The information sought in such an investigation shall be that needed to facilitate an adequate federal response to ensure public health and safety and to protect the exercise of First Amendment rights, such as:

      i. The time, place, and type of activities planned.

      ii. The number of persons expected to participate.

      iii. The expected means and routes of travel for participants and expected time of arrival.

      iv. Any plans for lodging or housing of participants in connection with the demonstration.

   b. Notwithstanding Subpart E.2 of this Part, the methods that may be used in an investigation under this paragraph are those described in subparagraphs a.-.d., subparagraph f. (other than pretext interviews or requests), or subparagraph g. of Part II.A.4 of these Guidelines. The Attorney General, the Deputy Attorney General, or the Assistant Attorney General for the Criminal Division may also authorize the use of other methods described in Part II.A.4.

C. STATE, LOCAL, OR TRIBAL AGENCIES

The FBI may provide investigative assistance to state, local, or tribal agencies in the investigation of matters that may involve federal crimes or threats to the national security, or for such other purposes as may be legally authorized.

D. FOREIGN AGENCIES

1. At the request of foreign law enforcement, intelligence, or security agencies, the FBI may conduct investigations or provide assistance to investigations by such agencies, consistent with the interests of the United States (including national security interests) and with due consideration of the effect on any United States person.

Investigations or assistance under this paragraph must be approved as provided by FBI policy. The FBI shall notify the National Security Division concerning investigation or assistance under this paragraph where: (i) FBI Headquarters approval for the activity is required pursuant to the approval policy adopted by the FBI for purposes of this paragraph, and (ii) the activity relates to a threat to the national security. Notification to the National Security Division shall be made as soon as practicable but no later than 30 days after the approval. Provisions regarding notification to or coordination with the Central Intelligence Agency by the FBI in memoranda of understanding or agreements with the Central Intelligence Agency may also apply to activities under this paragraph.

2. The FBI may not provide assistance to foreign law enforcement, intelligence, or security officers conducting investigations within the United States unless such officers have provided prior notification to the Attorney General as required by 18 U.S.C. 951.

3. The FBI may conduct background inquiries concerning consenting individuals when requested by foreign government agencies.

4. The FBI may provide other material and technical assistance to foreign governments to the extent not otherwise prohibited by law.

E. APPLICABLE STANDARDS AND PROCEDURES

1. Authorized investigative assistance by the FBI to other agencies under this Part includes joint operations and activities with such agencies.

2. All lawful methods may be used in investigative assistance activities under this Part.

3. Where the methods used in investigative assistance activities under this Part go beyond the methods authorized in assessments under Part II.A.4 of these Guidelines, the following apply:

    a. Supervisory approval must be obtained for the activity at a level or levels specified in FBI policy.

    b. Notice must be provided concerning sensitive investigative matters in the manner described in Part II.B.5.

    c. A database or records system must be maintained that permits, with respect to each such activity, the prompt retrieval of the status of the activity (open or closed), the dates of opening and closing, and the basis for the activity. This database or records system may be combined with the database or records system for predicated investigations required by Part VI.A.2.

IV.   INTELLIGENCE ANALYSIS AND PLANNING

The FBI is authorized to engage in analysis and planning. The FBI's analytic activities enable the FBI to identify and understand trends, causes, and potential indicia of criminal activity and other threats to the United States that would not be apparent from the investigation of discrete matters alone. By means of intelligence analysis and strategic planning, the FBI can more effectively discover crimes, threats to the national security, and other matters of national intelligence interest and can provide the critical support needed for the effective discharge of its investigative responsibilities and other authorized activities. For example, analysis of threats in the context of special events management, concerning public events or activities that may be targeted for terrorist attack, is an authorized activity under this Part.

In carrying out its intelligence functions under this Part, the FBI is authorized to draw on all lawful sources of information, including but not limited to the results of investigative activities under these Guidelines. Investigative activities under these Guidelines and other legally authorized activities through which the FBI acquires information, data, or intelligence may properly be utilized, structured, and prioritized so as to support and effectuate the FBI's intelligence mission. The remainder of this Part provides further specification concerning activities and functions authorized as part of that mission.

A. STRATEGIC INTELLIGENCE ANALYSIS

The FBI is authorized to develop overviews and analyses of threats to and vulnerabilities of the United States and its interests in areas related to the FBI's responsibilities, including domestic and international criminal threats and activities; domestic and international activities, circumstances, and developments affecting the national security; and matters relevant to the conduct of the United States' foreign affairs. The overviews and analyses prepared under this Subpart may encompass present, emergent, and potential threats and vulnerabilities, their contexts and causes, and identification and analysis of means of responding to them.

B. REPORTS AND ASSESSMENTS GENERALLY

The FBI is authorized to conduct research, analyze information, and prepare reports and assessments concerning matters relevant to authorized FBI activities, such as reports and assessments concerning: types of criminals or criminal activities; organized crime groups; terrorism, espionage, or other threats to the national security; foreign intelligence matters; or the scope and nature of criminal activity in particular geographic areas or sectors of the economy.

C. INTELLIGENCE SYSTEMS

The FBI is authorized to operate intelligence, identification, tracking, and information systems in support of authorized investigative activities, or for such other or additional purposes as may be legally authorized, such as intelligence and tracking systems relating to terrorists, gangs, or organized crime groups.

V. AUTHORIZED METHODS

A. PARTICULAR METHODS

All lawful investigative methods may be used in activities under these Guidelines as authorized by these Guidelines. Authorized methods include, but are not limited to, those identified in the following list. The methods identified in the list are in some instances subject to special restrictions or review or approval requirements as noted:

1. The methods described in Part II.A.4 of these Guidelines.
2. Mail covers.
3. Physical searches of personal or real property where a warrant or court order is not legally required because there is no reasonable expectation of privacy (e.g., trash covers).
4. Consensual monitoring of communications, including consensual computer monitoring, subject to legal review by the Chief Division Counsel or the FBI Office of the General Counsel. Where a sensitive monitoring circumstance is involved, the monitoring must be approved by the Criminal Division or, if the investigation concerns a threat to the national security or foreign intelligence, by the National Security Division.
5. Use of closed-circuit television, direction finders, and other monitoring devices, subject to legal review by the Chief Division Counsel or the FBI Office of the General Counsel. (The methods described in this paragraph usually do not require court orders or warrants unless they involve physical trespass or non-consensual monitoring of communications, but legal review is necessary to ensure compliance with all applicable legal requirements.)
6. Polygraph examinations.
7. Undercover operations. In investigations relating to activities in violation of federal criminal law that do not concern threats to the national security or foreign intelligence, undercover operations must be carried out in conformity with the Attorney General's Guidelines on Federal Bureau of Investigation Undercover Operations. In

investigations that are not subject to the preceding sentence because they concern threats to the national security or foreign intelligence, undercover operations involving religious or political organizations must be reviewed and approved by FBI Headquarters, with participation by the National Security Division in the review process.

8. Compulsory process as authorized by law, including grand jury subpoenas and other subpoenas, National Security Letters (15 U.S.C. 1681u, 1681v; 18 U.S.C. 2709; 12 U.S.C. 3414(a)(5)(A); 50 U.S.C. 436), and Foreign Intelligence Surveillance Act orders for the production of tangible things (50 U.S.C. 1861-63).

9. Accessing stored wire and electronic communications and transactional records in conformity with chapter 121 of title 18, United States Code (18 U.S.C. 2701– 2712).

10. Use of pen registers and trap and trace devices in conformity with chapter 206 of title 18, United States Code (18 U.S.C. 3121-3127), or the Foreign Intelligence Surveillance Act (50 U.S.C. 1841-1846).

11. Electronic surveillance in conformity with chapter 119 of title 18, United States Code (18 U.S.C. 2510-2522), the Foreign Intelligence Surveillance Act, or Executive Order 12333 § 2.5.

12. Physical searches, including mail openings, in conformity with Rule 41 of the Federal Rules of Criminal Procedure, the Foreign Intelligence Surveillance Act, or Executive Order 12333 § 2.5. A classified directive provides additional limitation on certain searches.

13. Acquisition of foreign intelligence information in conformity with title VII of the Foreign Intelligence Surveillance Act.

B. SPECIAL REQUIREMENTS

Beyond the limitations noted in the list above relating to particular investigative methods, the following requirements are to be observed:

1. Contacts with Represented Persons

   Contact with represented persons may implicate legal restrictions and affect the admissibility of resulting evidence. Hence, if an individual is known to be represented by counsel in a particular matter, the FBI will follow applicable law and Department procedure concerning contact with represented individuals in the absence of prior notice to counsel. The Special Agent in Charge and the United States Attorney or their designees shall consult periodically on applicable law and Department procedure. Where issues arise concerning the consistency of contacts with represented persons with applicable attorney conduct rules, the United States Attorney's

Office should consult with the Professional Responsibility Advisory Office.

2. Use of Classified Investigative Technologies

   Inappropriate use of classified investigative technologies may risk the compromise of such technologies. Hence, in an investigation relating to activities in violation of federal criminal law that does not concern a threat to the national security or foreign intelligence, the use of such technologies must be in conformity with the Procedures for the Use of Classified Investigative Technologies in Criminal Cases.

C. OTHERWISE ILLEGAL ACTIVITY

1. Otherwise illegal activity by an FBI agent or employee in an undercover operation relating to activity in violation of federal criminal law that does not concern a threat to the national security or foreign intelligence must be approved in conformity with the Attorney General's Guidelines on Federal Bureau of Investigation Undercover Operations. Approval of otherwise illegal activity in conformity with those guidelines is sufficient and satisfies any approval requirement that would otherwise apply under these Guidelines.

2. Otherwise illegal activity by a human source must be approved in conformity with the Attorney General's Guidelines Regarding the Use of FBI Confidential Human Sources.

3. Otherwise illegal activity by an FBI agent or employee that is not within the scope of paragraph 1. must be approved by a United States Attorney's Office or a Department of Justice Division, except that a Special Agent in Charge may authorize the following:

   a. otherwise illegal activity that would not be a felony under federal, state, local, or tribal law;

   b. consensual monitoring of communications, even if a crime under state, local, or tribal law;

   c. the controlled purchase, receipt, delivery, or sale of drugs, stolen property, or other contraband;

   d. the payment of bribes;

   e. the making of false representations in concealment of personal identity or the true ownership of a proprietary; and

   f. conducting a money laundering transaction or transactions involving an aggregate amount not exceeding $1 million.

   However, in an investigation relating to a threat to the national security or foreign intelligence collection, a Special Agent in

Charge may not authorize an activity that may constitute a violation of export control laws or laws that concern the proliferation of weapons of mass destruction. In such an investigation, a Special Agent in Charge may authorize an activity that may otherwise violate prohibitions of material support to terrorism only in accordance with standards established by the Director of the FBI and agreed to by the Assistant Attorney General for National Security.

4. The following activities may not be authorized:
   a. Acts of violence.
   b. Activities whose authorization is prohibited by law, including unlawful investigative methods, such as illegal electronic surveillance or illegal searches.

   Subparagraph a., however, does not limit the right of FBI agents or employees to engage in any lawful use of force, including the use of force in self-defense or defense of others or otherwise in the lawful discharge of their duties.

5. An agent or employee may engage in otherwise illegal activity that could be authorized under this Subpart without the authorization required by paragraph 3. if necessary to meet an immediate threat to the safety of persons or property or to the national security, or to prevent the compromise of an investigation or the loss of a significant investigative opportunity. In such a case, prior to engaging in the otherwise illegal activity, every effort should be made by the agent or employee to consult with the Special Agent in Charge, and by the Special Agent in Charge to consult with the United States Attorney's Office or appropriate Department of Justice Division where the authorization of that office or division would be required under paragraph 3., unless the circumstances preclude such consultation. Cases in which otherwise illegal activity occurs pursuant to this paragraph without the authorization required by paragraph 3. shall be reported as soon as possible to the Special Agent in Charge, and by the Special Agent in Charge to FBI Headquarters and to the United States Attorney's Office or appropriate Department of Justice Division.

6. In an investigation relating to a threat to the national security or foreign intelligence collection, the National Security Division is the approving component for otherwise illegal activity for which paragraph 3. requires approval beyond internal FBI approval. However, officials in other components may approve otherwise illegal activity in such investigations as authorized by the Assistant Attorney General for National Security.

VI.   RETENTION AND SHARING OF INFORMATION

A. RETENTION OF INFORMATION

1. The FBI shall retain records relating to activities under these Guidelines in accordance with a records retention plan approved by the National Archives and Records Administration.
2. The FBI shall maintain a database or records system that permits, with respect to each predicated investigation, the prompt retrieval of the status of the investigation (open or closed), the dates of opening and closing, and the basis for the investigation.

B. INFORMATION SHARING GENERALLY

1. Permissive Sharing

Consistent with law and with any applicable agreements or understandings with other agencies concerning the dissemination of information they have provided, the FBI may disseminate information obtained or produced through activities under these Guidelines:

    a.   within the FBI and to other components of the Department of Justice;

    b.   to other federal, state, local, or tribal agencies if related to their responsibilities and, in relation to other Intelligence Community agencies, the determination whether the information is related to the recipient's responsibilities may be left to the recipient;

    c.   to congressional committees as authorized by the Department of Justice Office of Legislative Affairs;

    d.   to foreign agencies if the information is related to their responsibilities and the dissemination is consistent with the interests of the United States (including national security interests) and the FBI has considered the effect such dissemination may reasonably be expected to have on any identifiable United States person;

    e.   if the information is publicly available, does not identify United States persons, or is disseminated with the consent of the person whom it concerns;

    f.   if the dissemination is necessary to protect the safety or security of persons or property, to protect against or prevent a crime or threat to the national security, or to obtain information for the conduct of an authorized FBI investigation; or

g. if dissemination of the information is otherwise permitted by the Privacy Act (5 U.S.C. 552a).

2. Required Sharing

The FBI shall share and disseminate information as required by statutes, treaties, Executive Orders, Presidential directives, National Security Council directives, Homeland Security Council directives, and Attorney General-approved policies, memoranda of understanding, or agreements.

C. INFORMATION RELATING TO CRIMINAL MATTERS

1. Coordination with Prosecutors

In an investigation relating to possible criminal activity in violation of federal law, the agent conducting the investigation shall maintain periodic written or oral contact with the appropriate federal prosecutor, as circumstances warrant and as requested by the prosecutor. When, during such an investigation, a matter appears arguably to warrant prosecution, the agent shall present the relevant facts to the appropriate federal prosecutor. Information on investigations that have been closed shall be available on request to a United States Attorney or his or her designee or an appropriate Department of Justice official.

2. Criminal Matters Outside FBI Jurisdiction

When credible information is received by an FBI field office concerning serious criminal activity not within the FBI's investigative jurisdiction, the field office shall promptly transmit the information or refer the complainant to a law enforcement agency having jurisdiction, except where disclosure would jeopardize an ongoing investigation, endanger the safety of an individual, disclose the identity of a human source, interfere with a human source's cooperation, or reveal legally privileged information. If full disclosure is not made for the reasons indicated, then, whenever feasible, the FBI field office shall make at least limited disclosure to a law enforcement agency or agencies having jurisdiction, and full disclosure shall be made as soon as the need for restricting disclosure is no longer present. Where full disclosure is not made to the appropriate law enforcement agencies within 180 days, the FBI field office shall promptly notify FBI Headquarters in writing of the facts and circumstances concerning the criminal activity. The FBI shall make periodic reports to the Deputy Attorney General on such nondisclosures and incomplete disclosures, in a form suitable to protect the identity of human sources.

892

3. Reporting of Criminal Activity

a. When it appears that an FBI agent or employee has engaged in criminal activity in the course of an investigation under these Guidelines, the FBI shall notify the United States Attorney's Office or an appropriate Department of Justice Division. When it appears that a human source has engaged in criminal activity in the course of an investigation under these Guidelines, the FBI shall proceed as provided in the Attorney General's Guidelines Regarding the Use of FBI Confidential Human Sources. When information concerning possible criminal activity by any other person appears in the course of an investigation under these Guidelines, the FBI shall initiate an investigation of the criminal activity if warranted, and shall proceed as provided in paragraph 1. or 2.

b. The reporting requirements under this paragraph relating to criminal activity by FBI agents or employees or human sources do not apply to otherwise illegal activity that is authorized in conformity with these Guidelines or other Attorney General guidelines or to minor traffic offenses.

D. INFORMATION RELATING TO NATIONAL SECURITY AND FOREIGN INTELLIGENCE MATTERS

The general principle reflected in current laws and policies is that there is a responsibility to provide information as consistently and fully as possible to agencies with relevant responsibilities to protect the United States and its people from terrorism and other threats to the national security, except as limited by specific constraints on such sharing. The FBI's responsibilities in this area include carrying out the requirements of the Memorandum of Understanding Between the Intelligence Community, Federal Law Enforcement Agencies, and the Department of Homeland Security Concerning Information Sharing (March 4, 2003), or any successor memorandum of understanding or agreement. Specific requirements also exist for internal coordination and consultation with other Department of Justice components, and for provision of national security and foreign intelligence information to White House agencies, as provided in the ensuing paragraphs.

1. Department of Justice

a. The National Security Division shall have access to all information obtained by the FBI through activities relating to threats to the national security or foreign intelligence. The Director of the FBI and the Assistant Attorney General for

National Security shall consult concerning these activities whenever requested by either of them, and the FBI shall provide such reports and information concerning these activities as the Assistant Attorney General for National Security may request. In addition to any reports or information the Assistant Attorney General for National Security may specially request under this subparagraph, the FBI shall provide annual reports to the National Security Division concerning its foreign intelligence collection program, including information concerning the scope and nature of foreign intelligence collection activities in each FBI field office.

b. The FBI shall keep the National Security Division apprised of all information obtained through activities under these Guidelines that is necessary to the ability of the United States to investigate or protect against threats to the national security, which shall include regular consultations between the FBI and the National Security Division to exchange advice and information relevant to addressing such threats through criminal prosecution or other means.

c. Subject to subparagraphs d. and e., relevant United States Attorneys' Offices shall have access to and shall receive information from the FBI relating to threats to the national security, and may engage in consultations with the FBI relating to such threats, to the same extent as the National Security Division. The relevant United States Attorneys' Offices shall receive such access and information from the FBI field offices.

d. In a counterintelligence investigation – i.e., an investigation relating to a matter described in Part VII.S.2 of these Guidelines – the FBI's provision of information to and consultation with a United States Attorney's Office are subject to authorization by the National Security Division. In consultation with the Executive Office for United States Attorneys and the FBI, the National Security Division shall establish policies setting forth circumstances in which the FBI will consult with the National Security Division prior to informing relevant United States Attorneys' Offices about such an investigation. The policies established by the National Security Division under this subparagraph shall (among other things) provide that:

        i.   the National Security Division will, within 30 days, authorize the FBI to share with the United States Attorneys' Offices information relating to certain espionage investigations, as defined by the policies, unless such information is withheld because of substantial national security considerations; and

       ii. the FBI may consult freely with United States Attorneys' Offices concerning investigations within the scope of this subparagraph during an emergency, so long as the National Security Division is notified of such consultation as soon as practical after the consultation.

  e.   Information shared with a United States Attorney's Office pursuant to subparagraph c. or d. shall be disclosed only to the United States Attorney or any Assistant United States Attorneys designated by the United States Attorney as points of contact to receive such information. The United States Attorneys and designated Assistant United States Attorneys shall have appropriate security clearances and shall receive training in the handling of classified information and information derived from the Foreign Intelligence Surveillance Act, including training concerning the secure handling and storage of such information and training concerning requirements and limitations relating to the use, retention, and dissemination of such information.

  f.   The disclosure and sharing of information by the FBI under this paragraph is subject to any limitations required in orders issued by the Foreign Intelligence Surveillance Court, controls imposed by the originators of sensitive material, and restrictions established by the Attorney General or the Deputy Attorney General in particular cases. The disclosure and sharing of information by the FBI under this paragraph that may disclose the identity of human sources is governed by the relevant provisions of the Attorney General's Guidelines Regarding the Use of FBI Confidential Human Sources.

2. White House

In order to carry out their responsibilities, the President, the Vice President, the Assistant to the President for National Security Affairs, the Assistant to the President for Homeland Security Affairs, the National Security Council and its staff, the Homeland Security Council and its staff, and other White House officials and offices require information from all federal agencies, including foreign intelligence, and information relating to international terrorism and other threats to the national security. The FBI accordingly may disseminate to the White House foreign intelligence and national security information obtained through activities under these Guidelines, subject to the following standards and procedures:

a. Requests to the FBI for such information from the White House shall be made through the National Security Council staff or Homeland Security Council staff including, but not limited to, the National Security Council Legal and Intelligence Directorates and Office of Combating Terrorism, or through the President's Intelligence Advisory Board or the Counsel to the President.

b. Compromising information concerning domestic officials or political organizations, or information concerning activities of United States persons intended to affect the political process in the United States, may be disseminated to the White House only with the approval of the Attorney General, based on a determination that such dissemination is needed for foreign intelligence purposes, for the purpose of protecting against international terrorism or other threats to the national security, or for the conduct of foreign affairs. However, such approval is not required for dissemination to the White House of information concerning efforts of foreign intelligence services to penetrate the White House, or concerning contacts by White House personnel with foreign intelligence service personnel.

c. Examples of types of information that are suitable for dissemination to the White House on a routine basis include, but are not limited to:

    i. information concerning international terrorism;

    ii. information concerning activities of foreign intelligence services in the United States;

    iii. information indicative of imminent hostilities involving any foreign power;

    iv. information concerning potential cyber threats to the United States or its allies;

    v. information indicative of policy positions adopted by foreign officials, governments, or powers, or their reactions to United States foreign policy initiatives;

       vi. information relating to possible changes in leadership positions of foreign governments, parties, factions, or powers;

       vii. information concerning foreign economic or foreign political matters that might have national security ramifications; and

       viii. information set forth in regularly published national intelligence requirements.

    d. Communications by the FBI to the White House that relate to a national security matter and concern a litigation issue for a specific pending case must be made known to the Office of the Attorney General, the Office of the Deputy Attorney General, or the Office of the Associate Attorney General. White House policy may specially limit or prescribe the White House personnel who may request information concerning such issues from the FBI.

    e. The limitations on dissemination of information by the FBI to the White House under these Guidelines do not apply to dissemination to the White House of information acquired in the course of an FBI investigation requested by the White House into the background of a potential employee or appointee, or responses to requests from the White House under Executive Order 10450.

3. Special Statutory Requirements

    a. Dissemination of information acquired under the Foreign Intelligence Surveillance Act is, to the extent provided in that Act, subject to minimization procedures and other requirements specified in that Act.

    b. Information obtained through the use of National Security Letters under 15 U.S.C. 1681v may be disseminated in conformity with the general standards of this Part. Information obtained through the use of National Security Letters under other statutes may be disseminated in conformity with the general standards of this Part, subject to any applicable limitations in their governing statutory provisions: 12 U.S.C. 3414(a)(5)(B); 15 U.S.C. 1681u(f); 18 U.S.C. 2709(d); 50 U.S.C. 436(e).

VII.   <u>DEFINITIONS</u>

A. CONSENSUAL MONITORING: monitoring of communications for which a court order or warrant is not legally required because of the consent of a party to the communication.

B. EMPLOYEE: an FBI employee or an employee of another agency working under the direction and control of the FBI.

C. FOR OR ON BEHALF OF A FOREIGN POWER: the determination that activities are for or on behalf of a foreign power shall be based on consideration of the extent to which the foreign power is involved in:
    1. control or policy direction;
    2. financial or material support; or
    3. leadership, assignments, or discipline.

D. FOREIGN COMPUTER INTRUSION: the use or attempted use of any cyber-activity or other means, by, for, or on behalf of a foreign power to scan, probe, or gain unauthorized access into one or more U.S.-based computers.

E. FOREIGN INTELLIGENCE: information relating to the capabilities, intentions, or activities of foreign governments or elements thereof, foreign organizations or foreign persons, or international terrorists.

F. FOREIGN INTELLIGENCE REQUIREMENTS:
    1. national intelligence requirements issued pursuant to authorization by the Director of National Intelligence, including the National Intelligence Priorities Framework and the National HUMINT Collection Directives, or any successor directives thereto;
    2. requests to collect foreign intelligence by the President or by Intelligence Community officials designated by the President; and
    3. directions to collect foreign intelligence by the Attorney General, the Deputy Attorney General, or an official designated by the Attorney General.

G. FOREIGN POWER:
    1. a foreign government or any component thereof, whether or not recognized by the United States;
    2. a faction of a foreign nation or nations, not substantially composed of United States persons;
    3. an entity that is openly acknowledged by a foreign government or governments to be directed and controlled by such foreign government or governments;

4. a group engaged in international terrorism or activities in preparation therefor;

5. a foreign-based political organization, not substantially composed of United States persons; or

6. an entity that is directed or controlled by a foreign government or governments.

H. HUMAN SOURCE: a Confidential Human Source as defined in the Attorney General's Guidelines Regarding the Use of FBI Confidential Human Sources.

I. INTELLIGENCE ACTIVITIES: any activity conducted for intelligence purposes or to affect political or governmental processes by, for, or on behalf of a foreign power.

J. INTERNATIONAL TERRORISM:
Activities that:
1. involve violent acts or acts dangerous to human life that violate federal, state, local, or tribal criminal law or would violate such law if committed within the United States or a state, local, or tribal jurisdiction;

2. appear to be intended:
   i. to intimidate or coerce a civilian population;
   ii. to influence the policy of a government by intimidation or coercion; or
   iii. to affect the conduct of a government by assassination or kidnapping; and

3. occur totally outside the United States, or transcend national boundaries in terms of the means by which they are accomplished, the persons they appear to be intended to coerce or intimidate, or the locale in which their perpetrators operate or seek asylum.

K. PROPRIETARY: a sole proprietorship, partnership, corporation, or other business entity operated on a commercial basis, which is owned, controlled, or operated wholly or in part on behalf of the FBI, and whose relationship with the FBI is concealed from third parties.

L. PUBLICLY AVAILABLE: information that has been published or broadcast for public consumption, is available on request to the public, is accessible on-line or otherwise to the public, is available to the public by subscription or purchase, could be seen or heard by any casual observer, is made available at a meeting open to the public, or is obtained by visiting any place or attending any event that is open to the public.

M. RECORDS: any records, databases, files, indices, information systems, or other retained information.

N. SENSITIVE INVESTIGATIVE MATTER: an investigative matter involving the activities of a domestic public official or political candidate (involving corruption or a threat to the national security), religious or political organization or individual prominent in such an organization, or news media, or any other matter which, in the judgment of the official authorizing an investigation, should be brought to the attention of FBI Headquarters and other Department of Justice officials.

O. SENSITIVE MONITORING CIRCUMSTANCE:
    1. investigation of a member of Congress, a federal judge, a member of the Executive Branch at Executive Level IV or above, or a person who has served in such capacity within the previous two years;
    2. investigation of the Governor, Lieutenant Governor, or Attorney General of any state or territory, or a judge or justice of the highest court of any state or territory, concerning an offense involving bribery, conflict of interest, or extortion related to the performance of official duties;
    3. a party to the communication is in the custody of the Bureau of Prisons or the United States Marshals Service or is being or has been afforded protection in the Witness Security Program; or
    4. the Attorney General, the Deputy Attorney General, or an Assistant Attorney General has requested that the FBI obtain prior approval for the use of consensual monitoring in a specific investigation.

P. SPECIAL AGENT IN CHARGE: the Special Agent in Charge of an FBI field office (including an Acting Special Agent in Charge), except that the functions authorized for Special Agents in Charge by these Guidelines may also be exercised by the Assistant Director in Charge or by any Special Agent in Charge designated by the Assistant Director in Charge in an FBI field office headed by an Assistant Director, and by FBI Headquarters officials designated by the Director of the FBI.

Q. SPECIAL EVENTS MANAGEMENT: planning and conduct of public events or activities whose character may make them attractive targets for terrorist attack.

R. STATE, LOCAL, OR TRIBAL: any state or territory of the United States or political subdivision thereof, the District of Columbia, or Indian tribe.

S. THREAT TO THE NATIONAL SECURITY:
1. international terrorism;
2. espionage and other intelligence activities, sabotage, and assassination, conducted by, for, or on behalf of foreign powers, organizations, or persons;
3. foreign computer intrusion; and
4. other matters determined by the Attorney General, consistent with Executive Order 12333 or a successor order.

T. UNITED STATES: when used in a geographic sense, means all areas under the territorial sovereignty of the United States.

U. UNITED STATES PERSON:
Any of the following, but not including any association or corporation that is a foreign power as defined in Subpart G.1.-.3.:
1. an individual who is a United States citizen or an alien lawfully admitted for permanent residence;
2. an unincorporated association substantially composed of individuals who are United States persons; or
3. a corporation incorporated in the United States.
In applying paragraph 2., if a group or organization in the United States that is affiliated with a foreign-based international organization operates directly under the control of the international organization and has no independent program or activities in the United States, the membership of the entire international organization shall be considered in determining whether it is substantially composed of United States persons. If, however, the U.S.-based group or organization has programs or activities separate from, or in addition to, those directed by the international organization, only its membership in the United States shall be considered in determining whether it is substantially composed of United States persons. A classified directive provides further guidance concerning the determination of United States person status.

V. USE: when used with respect to human sources, means obtaining information from, tasking, or otherwise operating such sources.

GUIDELINES TO ENSURE THAT THE INFORMATION PRIVACY AND OTHER LEGAL RIGHTS OF AMERICANS ARE PROTECTED IN THE DEVELOPMENT AND USE OF THE INFORMATION SHARING ENVIRONMENT

1. BACKGROUND AND APPLICABILITY.

a. BACKGROUND. Section 1016(d) of the Intelligence Reform and Terrorism Prevention Act of 2004 (IRTPA) calls for the issuance of guidelines to protect privacy and civil liberties in the development and use of the "information sharing environment" (ISE). Section 1 of Executive Order 13388, Further Strengthening the Sharing of Terrorism Information to Protect Americans, provides that, "[t]o the maximum extent consistent with applicable law, agencies shall … give the highest priority to … the interchange of terrorism information among agencies … [and shall] protect the freedom, information privacy, and other legal rights of Americans in the conduct of [such] activities …." These Guidelines implement the requirements under the IRTPA and EO 13388 to protect information privacy rights and provide other legal protections relating to civil liberties and the legal rights of Americans in the development and use of the ISE.

b. Applicability. These Guidelines apply to information about United States citizens and lawful permanent residents that is subject to information privacy or other legal protections under the Constitution and Federal laws of the United States ("protected information"). For the intelligence community, protected information includes information about "United States persons" as defined in Executive Order 12333. Protected information may also include other information that the U.S. Government expressly determines by Executive Order, international agreement, or other similar instrument, should be covered by these Guidelines.

2. COMPLIANCE WITH LAWS.

a. General. In the development and use of the ISE, all agencies shall, without exception, comply with the Constitution and all applicable laws and Executive Orders relating to protected information.

b. RULES ASSESSMENT. Each agency shall implement an ongoing process for identifying and assessing the laws, Executive Orders, policies, and procedures that apply to the protected information that it will make available or access through the ISE. Each agency shall identify, document, and comply with any legal restrictions applicable to such information. Each agency shall adopt internal policies and procedures requiring it to:

(i) only seek or retain protected information that is legally permissible for the agency to seek or retain under the laws, regulations, policies, and executive orders applicable to the agency; and

(ii) ensure that the protected information that the agency makes available through the ISE has been lawfully obtained by the agency and may be lawfully made available through the ISE.

c. CHANGES. If, as part of its rules assessment process, an agency:

(i) identifies an issue that poses a significant risk to information privacy rights or other legal protections, it shall as appropriate develop policies and procedures to provide protections that address that issue;

(ii) identifies a restriction on sharing protected information imposed by internal agency policy, that significantly impedes the sharing of terrorism information, homeland security information, or law enforcement information (as defined in Section 13 below) in a manner that does not appear to be required by applicable laws or to protect information privacy rights or provide other legal protections, it shall review the advisability of maintaining such restriction;

(iii) identifies a restriction on sharing protected information, other than one imposed by internal agency policy, that significantly impedes the sharing of information in a manner that does not appear to be required to protect information privacy rights or provide other legal protections, it shall review such restriction with the ISE Privacy Guidelines Committee (described in Section 12 below), and if an appropriate internal resolution cannot be developed, bring such restriction to the attention of the Attorney General and the Director of National Intelligence (DNI). The Attorney General and the DNI shall review any such restriction and jointly submit any recommendations for changes to such restriction to the Assistant to the President for Homeland Security and Counterterrorism, the Assistant to the President for National Security Affairs, and the Director of the Office of Management and Budget for further review.

3. PURPOSE SPECIFICATION.

Protected information should be shared through the ISE only if it is terrorism information, homeland security information, or law enforcement information (as defined in Section 13 below). Each agency shall adopt internal policies and procedures requiring it to ensure that the agency's access to and use of protected information available through the ISE is consistent with the authorized purpose of the ISE.

4. IDENTIFICATION OF PROTECTED INFORMATION TO BE SHARED THROUGH THE ISE.

a. IDENTIFICATION AND PRIOR REVIEW. In order to facilitate compliance with these Guidelines, particularly Section 2 (Compliance with Laws) and Section 3 (Purpose Specification), each agency shall identify its data holdings that contain protected information to be shared through the ISE, and shall put in place such mechanisms as may be reasonably feasible to ensure that protected information has been reviewed pursuant to these Guidelines before it is made available to the ISE.

b. NOTICE MECHANISMS. Consistent with guidance and standards to be issued for the ISE, each agency shall put in place a mechanism for enabling ISE participants to determine the nature of the protected information hat the agency is making available to the ISE, so that such participants can handle the information in accordance with applicable legal requirements.

Specifically, such a mechanism will, to the extent reasonably feasible and consistent with the agency's legal authorities and mission requirements, allow for ISE participants to determine whether:

(i) the information pertains to a United States citizen or lawful permanent resident;

(ii) the information is subject to specific information privacy or other similar restrictions on access, use or disclosure, and if so, the nature of such restrictions; and

(iii) there are limitations on the reliability or accuracy of the information.

5. DATA QUALITY.

a. ACCURACY. Each agency shall adopt and implement procedures, as appropriate, to facilitate the prevention, identification, and correction of any errors in protected information with the objective of ensuring that such information is accurate and has not erroneously been shared through the ISE.

b. NOTICE OF ERRORS. Each agency, consistent with its legal authorities and mission requirements, shall ensure that when it determines that protected information originating from another agency may be erroneous, includes incorrectly merged information, or lacks adequate context such that the rights of the individual may be affected, the potential error or deficiency will be communicated in writing to the other agency's ISE privacy official (the ISE privacy officials are described in section 12 below).

c. PROCEDURES. Each agency, consistent with its legal authorities and mission requirements, shall adopt and implement policies and procedures with respect to the ISE requiring the agency to:

(i) take appropriate steps, when merging protected information about an individual from two or more sources, to ensure that the information is about the same individual;

(ii) investigate in a timely manner alleged errors and deficiencies and correct, delete, or refrain from using protected information found to be erroneous or deficient; and

(iii) retain protected information only so long as it is relevant and timely for appropriate use by the agency, and update, delete, or refrain from using protected information that is outdated or otherwise irrelevant for such use.

6. Data Security.

Each agency shall use appropriate physical, technical, and administrative measures to safeguard protected information shared through the ISE from unauthorized access, disclosure, modification, use, or destruction.

7. Accountability, Enforcement and Audit.

a. PROCEDURES. Each agency shall modify existing policies and procedures or adopt new ones as appropriate, requiring the agency to:

(i) have and enforce policies for reporting, investigating, and responding to violations of agency policies relating to protected information, including taking appropriate action when violations are found;

(ii) provide training to personnel authorized to share protected information through the ISE regarding the agency's requirements an policies for collection, use, and disclosure of protected information, and, as appropriate, for reporting violations of agency privacy protection policies;

(iii) cooperate with audits and reviews by officials with responsibility for providing oversight with respect to the ISE; and

(iv) designate each agency's ISE privacy official to receive reports (or copies thereof if the agency already has a designated recipient of such reports) regarding alleged errors in protected information that originate from that agency.

b. AUDIT. Each agency shall implement adequate review and audit mechanisms to enable the agency's ISE privacy official and other authorized officials to verify that the agency and its personnel are complying with these Guidelines in the development and use of the SE.

8. Redress.

To the extent consistent with its legal authorities and mission requirements, each agency shall, with respect to its participation in the development and use of the ISE, put in place internal procedures to address complaints from persons regarding protected information about them that is under the agency's control.

9. Execution, Training, and Technology.

a. EXECUTION. The ISE privacy official shall be responsible for ensuring that protections are implemented as appropriate through efforts such as training, business process changes, and system designs.

b. TRAINING. Each agency shall develop an ongoing training program in the implementation of these Guidelines, and shall provide such training to agency personnel participating in the development and use of the ISE.

c. TECHNOLOGY. Where reasonably feasible, and consistent with standards and procedures established for the ISE, each agency shall consider and implement, as appropriate, privacy enhancing technologies including, but not limited to, permissioning systems, hashing, data anonymization, immutable audit logs, and authentication.

10. Awareness.

Each agency shall take steps to facilitate appropriate public awareness of its policies and procedures for implementing these Guidelines.

11. Non-Federal Entities.

Consistent with any standards and procedures that may be issued to govern participation in the ISE by State, tribal, and local governments and private sector entities, the agencies and the PM-ISE will work with non-Federal entities seeking to access protected information through the ISE to ensure that such non-Federal entities develop and implement appropriate policies and procedures that provide protections that are at least as comprehensive as those contained in these Guidelines.

12. Governance.

a. ISE PRIVACY OFFICIALS. Each agency's senior official with overall agency-wide responsibility for information privacy issues (as designated by statute or executive order, or as otherwise identified in response to OMB Memorandum M-05-08 dated February 11, 2005), shall directly oversee the agency's implementation of and compliance with these Guidelines (the "ISE privacy official"). If a different official would be better situated to perform this role, he or she may be so designated by the head of the agency. The ISE privacy official role may be delegated to separate components within an agency, such that there could be multiple ISE privacy officials within one executive department. The ISE privacy official shall be responsible for ensuring that (i) the agency's policies, procedures, and systems are appropriately designed and executed in compliance with these Guidelines, and (ii) changes are made as necessary. The ISE privacy official should be familiar with the agency's activities as they relate to the ISE, possess all necessary security clearances, and be granted the authority and resources, as appropriate, to identify and address privacy and other legal issues arising out of the agency's participation in the ISE. Such authority should be exercised in coordination with the agency's senior ISE official.

b. ISE Privacy Guidelines Committee. All agencies will abide by these Guidelines in their participation in the ISE. The PM shall establish a standing "ISE Privacy Guidelines Committee" to provide ongoing guidance on the implementation of these Guidelines, so that, among other things, agencies follow consistent interpretations of applicable legal requirements, avoid duplication of effort, share best practices, and have a forum for resolving issues on an inter-agency basis. The ISE Privacy Guidelines Committee is not intended to replace legal or policy guidance mechanisms established by law, executive order, or as part of the ISE, and will as appropriate work through or in consultation with such other mechanisms. The ISE Privacy Guidelines Committee shall be chaired by the PM or a senior official designated by the PM, and will consist of the ISE privacy officials of each member of the Information Sharing Council. If an issue cannot be resolved by the ISE Privacy Guidelines Committee, the PM will address the issue through the established ISE governance process. The ISE Privacy Guidelines Committee should request legal or policy guidance on questions relating to the implementation of these Guidelines from those agencies having responsibility or authorities for issuing guidance on such questions; any such requested guidance shall be provided promptly by the appropriate agencies. As the ISE governance process evolves, if a different entity is established or identified that could more effectively perform the functions of the ISE Privacy Guidelines Committee, the ISE Privacy Guidelines Committee structure shall be modified by the PM through such consultation and coordination as may b required by the ISE governance process, to ensure the functions and responsibilities of the ISE Privacy Guidelines Committee remain priorities fully integrated into the overall ISE governance process.

c. PRIVACY AND CIVIL LIBERTIES OVERSIGHT BOARD. The Privacy and Civil Liberties Oversight Board (PCLOB) should be consulted for ongoing advice regarding the protection of privacy and civil liberties in agencies' development and us of the ISE. To facilitate the performance of the PCLOB's duties, the ISE Privacy Guidelines Committee will serve as a mechanism for the PCLOB to obtain information from agencies and to provided advice and guidance consistent with the PCLOB's statutory responsibilities. Accordingly, the ISE Privacy Guidelines Committee should work in consultation with the PCLOB, whose members may attend Committee meetings, provide advice, and review and comment on guidance as appropriate.

d. ISE PRIVACY PROTECTION POLICY. Each agency shall develop and implement a written ISE privacy protection policy that sets forth the mechanisms, policies, and procedures its personnel will follow in implementing these Guidelines. Agencies should consult with the ISE

Privacy Guidelines Committee as appropriate in the development and implementation of such policy.

13. General Provisions.

a. DEFINITIONS.

(i) The term "agency" has the meaning set forth for the term "executive agency" in section 105 of title 5, United States Code, but includes the Postal Rate Commission and the United States Postal Service and excludes the Government Accountability Office

(ii) The term "protected information" has the meaning set forth for such term in paragraph 1(b) of these Guidelines.

(iii) The terms "terrorism information," "homeland security information," and "law enforcement information" are defined as follows:

(I)"Terrorism information," consistent with section 1016(a)(4) of IRTPA means all relating to (A) the existence, organization, capabilities, plans, intentions, vulnerabilities, means of finance or material support, or activities of foreign or international terrorist groups or individuals, or of domestic groups or individuals involved in transnational terrorism, (B) threats posed by such groups or individuals to the United States, United States persons, or United States interests, or to those of other nations, (C) communications of or by such groups or individuals, or (D) groups or individuals reasonably believed to be assisting or associated with such groups or individuals.

(II) "Homeland security information," as derived from section 482(f)(1) of the Homeland Security Act of 2002, means any information possessed by a Federal, State, local, or tribal agency that relates to (A) a threat of terrorist activity, (B) the ability to prevent, interdict, or disrupt terrorist activity, (C) the identification or investigation of a suspected terrorist or terrorist organization or any person, group, or entity associated with or assisting a suspected terrorist or terrorist organization, or (D) a planned or actual response to a terrorist act.

(III) "Law enforcement information" for the purposes of the ISE means any information obtained by or of interest to a law enforcement agency or official that is (A) related to terrorism or the security of our homeland and (B) relevant to a law enforcement mission, including but not limited to information pertaining to an actual or potential criminal, civil, or administrative investigation or a foreign intelligence, counterintelligence, or counterterrorism investigation; assessment of or response to criminal threats and vulnerabilities;

909

the existence, organization, capabilities, plans, intentions, vulnerabilities, means, methods, or activities of individuals or groups involved or suspected of involvement in criminal or unlawful conduct or assisting or associated with criminal or unlawful conduct; the existence, identification, detection, prevention, interdiction, or disruption of, or response to, criminal acts and violations of the law; identification, apprehension, prosecution, release, detention, adjudication, supervision, or rehabilitation of accused persons or criminal offenders; and victim/witness assistance.

b. The treatment of information as "protected information" under these Guidelines does not by itself establish that the individual or entity to which such information pertains does in fact have information privacy or other legal rights with respect to such information.

c. Heads of executive departments and agencies shall, to the extent permitted by law and subject to the availability of appropriations, provide the cooperation, assistance, and information necessary for the implementation of these Guidelines.

d. These Guidelines:

(i) shall be implemented in a manner consistent with applicable laws and executive orders, including Federal laws protecting the information privacy rights and other legal rights of Americans, and subject to the availability of appropriations;

(ii) shall be implemented in a manner consistent with the statutory authority of the principal officers of executive departments and agencies as heads of their respective departments or agencies;

(iii) shall not be construed to impair or otherwise affect the functions of the Director of the Office of Management and Budget relating to budget, administrative, and legislative proposals; and

(iv) are intended only to improve the internal management of the Federal Government and are not intended to, and do not, create any rights or benefits, substantive or procedural, enforceable at law or in equity by a party against the United States, its departments, agencies, or entities, its officers, employees, or agencies, or any other person.

CRITERIA ON THRESHOLDS FOR REPORTING INTELLIGENCE OVERSIGHT MATTERS AND INSTRUCTIONS RELATING TO FORMATTING AND SCHEDULING

Intelligence oversight reporting serves as an early warning of intelligence activities of which the President should be informed, through either his Intelligence Oversight Board (IOB) or the Director of National Intelligence (DNI), or both, and provides a means by which the Executive Branch may timely identify and correct any deficiencies in the conduct of its intelligence activities. The following criteria on thresholds for reporting intelligence oversight matters to the Intelligence Oversight Board, and instructions on formatting and scheduling of reports, are issued under the authority of Executive Order 13462.

I. Criteria on Thresholds for Reporting. The heads of departments with organizations in the Intelligence Community (IC), or the heads of such organizations, or their designees, shall:

A. Report to the IOB, with copies to the DNI, any intelligence activity with respect to which there is reason to believe may be unlawful or contrary to executive order (EO) or presidential directive (PD). The following guidance applies to determining whether a particular matter should be reported:

1. "Intelligence activities" are defined in Part 3.4(e) of EO 12333 and, for purposes of these criteria, include, but are not limited to, the acquisition, collection, retention, analysis, and dissemination of intelligence information.

2. Intelligence activities are reportable if a reasonable person would believe they may be unlawful or contrary to EO or PD without waiting for substantiation, investigation, formal adjudication, or resolution of the issue of whether a particular matter is unlawful or contrary to EO or PD.

3. Intelligence activities to be reported under EOs 13462 and 12333 are not limited to those that concern "United States persons," as defined in Part 3.4(i) of EO 12333 or in any successor EO.

4. "Executive order or presidential directive" means, for purposes of implementing these criteria, a document signed by the President of the United States that has the force of law for the Executive Branch or constitutes the exercise by the President of his Executive authority. Reports may include violations of procedures and guidelines that heads of departments of IC components have established to implement EO 12333, or a successor order, provided, however, that such matters are of

potential presidential interest or deemed appropriate for the IOB's review, e.g., because they involve the apparent violation of substantive rights of individuals.

5. Reportable events include the initiation of, and significant developments in, investigations or other inquiries relating to the legality or propriety of intelligence activities.

6. Initial reports made on the basis of incomplete or inaccurate reporting are to be updated as additional information becomes available. Subsequent or updated reports should be identified in such a manner that they can be accurately related to the relevant initial reports.

7. Intelligence activities are reportable to the IOB if such activities are required to be reported or have been reported to the Attorney General as required by law or other directive, including the Memorandum of Understanding on Reporting of Information Concerning Federal Crimes (1995).

8. Any intelligence activity that is to be reported to any congressional committee or member of Congress because it is or may be unlawful or contrary to executive order or otherwise "significant or highly sensitive" (see paragraph B, below) shall also be reported to the IOB and DNI generally before such a congressional report is made. Any report concerning intelligence activities that is submitted to any committee or member of Congress shall also be submitted to the IOB and DNI if the commencement of the investigation or other inquiry regarding such activities was also reportable under these criteria.

B. Report to the DNI, and the IOB as appropriate, significant or highly sensitive matters, whether or not unlawful or contrary to EO or PD.

1. "Significant or highly sensitive matters" are developments or circumstances involving intelligence activities that could impugn the reputation or integrity of the IC, or otherwise call into question the propriety of intelligence activities.

2. Such matters might be manifested in or by:

    a. congressional inquiries or investigations;

    b. adverse media coverage;

    c. impact on foreign relations or foreign partners; or

    d. unauthorized disclosure of protected information.

II. Content of Reports. Intelligence oversight reports should include (to the extent practicable without compromising the timeliness of reporting) the following:

A. A narrative describing each intelligence activity in question.

B. Why the matter is being reported, i.e., it is:

    1. a potential violation of law (cite the relevant law, if a judgment has been made);

    2. potentially contrary to EO or PD (cite the relevant section or part of the EO or PD);

    3. a potential violation of agency procedures implementing EO 12333 (cite the specific rule or procedure, if a judgment has been made);

    4. "'significant' because..."; or

    5. "'highly sensitive' because... ."

C. An explanation and analysis of how or why the incident occurred.

D. An assessment of any impact of the incident on national security or international relations, as well as any mitigation efforts, including success and failures of such efforts.

E. Any remedial action the IC element has taken or is taking to prevent recurrence of the incident being reported.

F. An assessment of any impact the reported intelligence activity may have on civil liberties or protected privacy rights.

G. How the IC element concerned is addressing any information improperly acquired, handled, used, destroyed, etc., as a consequence of the mater being reported.

H. A summary of the gravity, frequency, trends, and patterns of matters reported for the quarter.

I. Any additional information that the reporting official considers relevant for purposes of fully and completely informing the IOB and the DNI on intelligence oversight matters.

III. Formatting of Reports. Reports may be formatted in accordance with departmental or agency policies, provided all the substantive information described above is included in each report.

IV. Schedule for Reporting.

    A. Significant or highly sensitive matters must be reported immediately.

        1. Significant or highly sensitive matters may be reported orally, if necessary, and followed up with a written report as soon as possible thereafter. The preference is for written reports.

        2. Significant or highly sensitive matters that may be unlawful of contrary to EO or PD shall be reported to the DNI and IOB.

        3. Significant or highly sensitive matters that are NOT unlawful or contrary to EO or PD shall be reported to the DNI.

B. Routine reports shall be submitted on a quarterly basis. The first report for the calendar year shall cover 1 January through 31 March, and so on for each quarter of the year.

C. Quarterly reports are due the last day of the month following the end of the quarter. For example, a report for the first quarter of the calendar year is due 30 April.

D. All IC elements must submit reports at least quarterly, even if a component has not been made aware of any reportable matter during the reporting period.

Questions concerning the implementation of EO 13462, or intelligence oversight reporting in general, may be submitted to the IOB's General Counsel by calling 202-456-2352, or to the ODNI IOB Team by calling 703-482-6304 (ODNI/OIG) or 703-275-2523 (ODNI/OGC).

MEMORANDUM OF UNDERSTANDING: REPORTING OF INFORMATION CONCERNING FEDERAL CRIMES

I. Introduction

Section 1.7 (a) of Executive Order (E.O.) 12333 requires senior officials of the Intelligence Community to—

> report to the Attorney General possible violations of the federal criminal laws by employees and of specified federal criminal laws by any other person as provided in procedures agreed upon by the Attorney General and the head of the department or agency concerned, in a manner consistent with the protection of intelligence sources and Methods, as specified in those procedures.

Title 28, Unites States Code, Section 535 (b) requires that—

> [a]ny information, allegation, or complaint received in a department or agency of the executive branch of government relating to violations of title 18 involving Government officers and employees shall be expeditiously reported to the Attorney General by the head of the department or agency, unless—
> (1) the responsibility to perform an investigation with respect thereto is specifically assigned otherwise by another provision of law; or
> (2) as to any department or agency of the Government, the Attorney General directors otherwise with respect to a specified class of information, allegation, or complaint.

This Memorandum of Understanding (MOU) sets forth the procedures by which each agency and organization within the Intelligence Community shall report to the Attorney General and to federal investigative agencies information concerning possible federal crimes by employees of an intelligence agency or organization, or violations of specified federal criminal laws by any other person, which information was collected by it during the performance of its designated intelligence activities, as those activities are defines in E.O. 12333, §§1.8-1.13.

II. Definitions

   A. "Agency," as that term is used herein, refers to those agencies and organizations within the Intelligence Community as defined in E.O. 12333, §3.4(f), but excluding the intelligence elements of the Federal Bureau of Investigation and the Department of Treasury.

   B. "Employee," as that term is used herein, means:

1. a staff employee, contract employee, asset, or other person or entity providing service to or acting on behalf of any agency within the intelligence community;

2. a former officer or employee of any agency within the intelligence community for purposes of an offense committed during such person's employment, and for purposes of an offense involving a violation of 18 U.S.C. §207 (Conflict of interest); and

3. any other Government employee on detail to the Agency.

C. "General Counsel" means the general counsel of the Agency or of the Department of which it is a component or an oversight person designated by such person to act on his/her behalf, and for purposes of these procedures may include an Inspector General or equivalent official if agency or departmental procedures so require or if designated by the agency or department head.

D. "Inspector General" or "IG" means the inspector general of the Agency or of the department of which the Agency is a component.

E. "Reasonable basis" exists when there are facts and circumstances, either personally known or of which knowledge is acquired from a source believed to be reasonably trustworthy, that would cause a person of reasonable caution to believe that a crime has been, is being, or will be committed. The question of which federal law enforcement or judicial entity has jurisdiction over the alleged criminal acts shall have no bearing upon the issue of whether a reasonable basis exists.

III. Scope

A. This MOU shall not be construed to authorize or require the Agency, or any person or entity acting on behalf of the Agency, to conduct any investigation not otherwise authorized by law, or to collect any information in a manner not authorized by law.

B. This MOU ordinarily does not require an intelligence agency or organization to report crimes information that was collected and disseminated to it by another department, agency, or organization. Where, however, the receiving agency is the primary or sole recipient of that information, or if analysis by the receiving agency reveals additional crimes information, the receiving agency shall be responsible for reporting all such crimes information in accordance with the provisions of this MOU.

C. This MOU does not in any way alter or supersede the obligation of an employee of an intelligence agency to report potential criminal behavior by other employees of that agency to an IG, as required either by statute or by agency regulations, nor affect any protections afforded any persons reporting such behavior to an IG. Nor does this MOU affect any crimes reporting procedures between the IG Offices and the Department of Justice.

D. This MOU does not in any way alter or supersede any obligation of a department or agency to report to the Attorney General criminal behavior by Government employees not employed by the intelligence community, as required by 28 U.S.C. §535.

E. This MOU does not affect the obligation to report to the Federal Bureau of Investigation alleged or suspected espionage activities as required under Section 811(c) of the Intelligence Authorization Act of 1995.

F. The following crimes information is exempted from the application of this memorandum if the specified conditions are met:

1. Crimes information that has been reported to an IG;[1]

2. Crimes information received by a Department of Defense intelligence component concerning a Defense intelligence component employee who either is subject to the Uniform Code of Military Justice or is a civilian and has been accused of criminal behavior related to his/her assigned duties or position, if (a) the information is submitted to and investigated by the appropriate Defense Criminal Investigative Organization, and (b) in cases involving crimes committed during the performance of intelligence activities, the General Counsel provides to the Department of Justice a report reflecting the nature of the charges and the disposition thereof;

3. Information regarding non-employee crimes listed in Section VII that is collected by the intelligence component of a Department also having within it a law enforcement organization where (a) the crime is of the type that the Department's law enforcement organization has jurisdiction to investigate; and (b) the Department's intelligence organization submits that crimes information to the Department's law enforcement organization for investigation and further handling in accordance with Department policies and procedures;[2]

4. Crimes information regarding persons who are not employees of the Agency, as those terms are defined in Section II, that involve crimes against property in an amount of $1,000 or less, or, in the case of

---

[1] If, however, the IG determines that the reported information is not properly subject to that office's jurisdiction, but that such information may be reportable pursuant to this MOU, the IG may forward the information to the DOJ in compliance with these procedures. Alternatively, the IG may transmit the information to the Agency's General Counsel for a determination of what response, if any, is required by this MOU.

[2] This MOU does not affect the crimes reporting obligations of any law enforcement and other non-intelligence components of a department, agency, or organization.

Agency employees, crimes against property in an amount of $500 or less. As to other relatively minor offenses to which this MOU would ordinarily apply, but which, in the General Counsel's opinion, do not warrant reporting pursuant to this MOU, the General Counsel may orally contact the Assistant Attorney General, Criminal Division,[*] or his/her designee. If the Department of Justice concurs with that opinion, no further reporting under these procedures is required. The General Counsel shall maintain an appropriate record of such contacts with the Department. If deemed appropriate by the General Counsel, he/she may take necessary steps to pass such information to the appropriate law enforcement authorities; or

5. Information, other than that relating to homicide or espionage, regarding crimes that were completed more than ten years prior to the date such allegations became known to the agency. If, however, the Agency has a reasonable basis to believe that the alleged criminal activities occurring ten or more years previously relate to, or are a part of, a pattern of criminal activities that continued within that ten year interval, the reporting procedures herein will apply to those activities.

G. The Procedures set forth herein are not intended to affect whether an intelligence agency reports to state or local authorities activity that appears to constitute a crime under state law. In the event that an intelligence agency considers it appropriate to report to state or local authorities possible criminal activity that may implicate classified information or intelligence sources or methods, it should inform the AAG, or the designated Deputy AAG, Criminal Division, in accordance with paragraph VIII.C, below; the Criminal Division will consult with the intelligence agency regarding appropriate methods for conveying the information to state or local authorities. In the event that an intelligence agency considers it appropriate to report to state or local authorities possible criminal activity that is not expected to implicate classified information or intelligence sources or methods, it should nevertheless provide a copy of such report to the AAG, or to the designated Deputy AAG, Criminal Division.

---

[*] [Pursuant to Attorney General Alberto Gonzales's letter of September 14, 2007 to Director of National Intelligence J. Michael McConnell, within this Memorandum of Understanding all referenced functions of the Assistant Attorney General for the Criminal Division or of the Criminal Division, generally, shall be read to refer to the Assistant Attorney General for National Security and the National Security Division, respectively.]

IV. General Considerations: Allegations of Criminal Acts Committed By Agency Employees

A. This Agreement requires each employee of the Agency to report to the General Counsel or IG facts or circumstances that reasonably indicate to the employee that an employee of an intelligence agency has committed, is committing, or will commit a violation of federal criminal law.[3]

B. Except as exempted in Section III, when the General Counsel has received allegations, complaints or information (hereinafter allegations) that an employee of the Agency may have violated, may be violating, or may violate a federal criminal statue, that General Counsel should within a reasonable period of time determine whether there is a reasonable basis to believe that a federal crime has been, is being, or will be committed and that it is a crime which, under this memorandum, must be reported. The General Counsel may, as set forth in Section V, below, conduct a preliminary inquiry for this purpose. If a preliminary inquiry reveals that there is a reasonable basis for the allegations, the General Counsel will follow the reporting procedures set forth in Section VIII, below. If a preliminary inquiry reveals that the allegations are without a reasonable basis, the General Counsel will make a record, as appropriate, of that finding and no reporting under these procedures is required.

V. Preliminary Inquiry Into Allegations Against An Agency Employee

A. The General Counsel's preliminary inquiry regarding allegations against an Agency employee will ordinarily be limited to the following:
1. review of materials submitted in support of the allegations;
2. review of Agency indices, records, documents, and files;
3. examination of premises occupied by the Agency;
4. examination of publicly available federal, state, and local government records and other publicly available records and information;
5. interview of the complainant; and
6. interview of any Agency employee, other than the accused, who, in the opinion of the General Counsel, may be able to corroborate or refute the allegations.

---

[3] When a General Counsel or IG has received information concerning alleged violations of federal law by an employee of another intelligence community agency, and those violations are not exempted under section III. E. 4, hereof, the General Counsel shall notify in writing the General Counsel of the accused employee's agency. The latter General Counsel must then determine whether this MOU requires the allegations to be reported to the Department of Justice.

B. Where criminal allegations against an Agency employee are subject to this MOU, an interview of that employee may only be undertaken in compliance with the following conditions:

1. Where the crime alleged against an Agency employee does not pertain to a serious felony offense,[4] a responsible Agency official may interview the accused employee; however, such interview shall only be conducted with the approval of the General Counsel, the IG, or, as to Defense and military employees, the responsible military Judge Advocate General or the responsible Defense Criminal Investigative Organization.

2. Where the crime alleged against an Agency employee is a serious felony offense, the Agency shall ordinarily not interview the accused employee, except where, in the opinion of the General Counsel, there are exigent circumstances[5] which require that the employee be interviewed. If such exigent circumstances exist, the General Counsel or other attorney in the General Counsel's office may interview the accused employee to the extent reasonably necessary to eliminate or substantially reduce the exigency.

3. In all other cases of alleged serious felonies, the General Counsel, or the General Counsel's designee, may interview the accused employee only   after consultation with the Agency's IG, a Defense Criminal Investigative Organization (for Defense and military employees), or with the Department of Justice regarding the procedures to be used during an interview with the accused employee.

Any interview of an accused employee that is undertaken shall be conducted in a manner that does not cause the loss, concealment, destruction, damage or alteration of evidence of the alleged crime, nor result in the immunization of any statements made by the accused employee during that interview. The Agency shall not otherwise be limited by this MOU either as to the techniques it is otherwise authorized to use, or as to its responsibility to provide for its security functions pursuant to E.O. 12333.

---

[4] A "serious felony offense" includes any offense listed in Section VII, hereof, violent crimes, and other offenses which, if committed in the presence of a reasonably prudent and law-abiding person, would cause that person immediately to report that conduct directly to the police. For purposes of this MOU, crimes against government property that do not exceed $5,000 and are not part of a pattern of continuing behavior or of a criminal conspiracy shall not be considered serious felony offenses.

[5] "Exigent circumstances" are circumstances requiring prompt action by the Agency in order to protect life or substantial property interests; to apprehend or identify a fleeing offender; or to prevent the compromise, loss, concealment, destruction, or alteration of evidence in a crime.

VI. General Considerations: Allegations Of Criminal Acts Committed by Non-Employees

A. This MOU requires each employee of the Agency to report, to the General Counsel or as otherwise directed by the Department or Agency head, facts or circumstances that reasonably indicate to the employee that a non-employee has committed, is committing, or will commit one or more of the specified crimes in Section VII, below.

B. When an Agency has received information concerning alleged violations of federal law by a person other than an employee of an intelligence agency, and has determined that the reported information provides a reasonable basis to conclude that a violation of one of the specified crimes in Section VII has occurred, is occurring, or may occur, the Agency shall report that information to the Department of Justice in accordance with Sections VIII or IX, below.

VII. Reportable Offenses by Non-Employees

A. Unless exempted under Section III, above, allegations concerning criminal activities by non-employees are reportable if they pertain to one or more of the following specified violations of federal criminal law:

1. Crimes involving intentional infliction or threat of death or serious physical harm. These include but are not limited to homicide, kidnapping, hostage taking, assault (including sexual assault), or threats or attempts to commit such offenses, against any person in the United States or a U.S. national or internationally protected person (as defined in 18 U.S.C. §1116(b)(4)), whether in the United States or abroad.

2. Crimes, including acts of terrorism, that are likely to affect the national security, defense or foreign relations of the United States. These may include but are not limited to:

    a. Espionage; sabotage; unauthorized disclosure of classified information; seditious conspiracies to overthrow the government of the United States; fund transfers violating the International Emergency Economic Powers Act; providing material or financial support to terrorists; unauthorized traffic in controlled munitions or technology; or unauthorized traffic in, use of, or contamination by nuclear materials, chemical or biological weapons, or chemical or biological agents; whether in the United States or abroad;

    b. Fraudulent entry of persons into the United States, the violation of immigration restrictions or the failure to register as a foreign agent or an intelligence trained agent;

    c. Offenses involving interference with foreign governments or interference with the foreign policy of the United States whether occurring in the United States or abroad;

    d. Acts of terrorism anywhere in the world which target the U.S. government or its property, U.S. persons, or any property in the United States, or in which the perpetrator is a U.S. person; aircraft hijacking; attacks on aircraft or international aviation facilities; or maritime piracy;

    e. The unauthorized transportation or use of firearms or explosives in interstate or foreign commerce.

3. Crimes involving foreign interference with the integrity of U.S. governmental institutions or processes. Such crimes may include:

    a. Activities to defraud the U.S. government or any federally protected financial institution, whether occurring in the United States or abroad;

    b. Obstruction of justice or bribery of U.S. officials or witnesses in U.S. proceedings, whether occurring in the United States or abroad;

    c. Interference with U.S. election proceedings or illegal contributions by foreign persons to U.S. candidates or election committees;

    d. Perjury in connection with U.S. proceedings, or false statements made in connection with formal reports or applications to the U.S. government, or in connection with a formal criminal or administrative investigation, whether committed in the United States or abroad;

    e. Counterfeiting U.S. obligations or any other governmental currency, security or identification documents used in the United States, whether committed in the United States or abroad; transactions involving stolen governmental securities or identification documents or stolen or counterfeit non-governmental securities.

4. Crimes related to unauthorized electronic surveillance in the United States or to tampering with, or unauthorized access to, computer systems.

5. Violations of U.S. drug laws including: the cultivation, production, transportation, importation, sale, or possession (other than possession of user quantities) of controlled substances; the production, transportation, importation, and sale of precursor or essential chemicals.

6. The transmittal, investment and/or laundering of the proceeds of any of the unlawful activities listed in this Section, whether committed in the United States or abroad.

B. Any conspiracy or attempt to commit a crime reportable under this section shall be reported if the conspiracy or attempt itself meets the applicable reporting criteria.

C. The Attorney General also encourages the Agency to notify the Department of Justice when the Agency's otherwise routine collection of intelligence in accordance with its authorities results in its acquisition of information about the commission of other serious felony offenses by non-employees, e.g. violations of U.S. environmental laws relating to ocean and inland water discharging or dumping, drinking water contamination, or hazardous waste disposal, and crimes involving interference with the integrity of U.S. governmental institutions or processes that would not otherwise be reportable under section VII.A.3.

VIII. Procedure For Submitting Special Crimes Reports

A. Where the Agency determines that a matter must be the subject of a special report to the Department of Justice, it may, consistent with paragraphs VIII.B and VIII.C, below, make such a report (1) by letter or other, similar communication from the General Counsel, or (2) by electronic or courier dissemination of information from operational or analytical units, provided that in all cases, the subject line and the text of such communication or dissemination clearly reflects that it is a report of possible criminal activity. The Department of Justice shall maintain a record of all special crimes reports received from the Agency.

B. Where the Agency determines that a matter must be the subject of a special report to the Department of Justice; and where the Agency further determines that no public disclosure of classified information or intelligence sources and methods would result from further investigation or prosecution, and the security of ongoing intelligent operations would not be jeopardized thereby, the Agency will report the matter to the federal investigative agency having jurisdiction over the criminal matter. A copy of that report must also be provided to the AAG, or designated Deputy AAG, Criminal Division.

C. Where the Agency determines that further investigation or prosecution of a matter that must be specifically reported may result in a public disclosure of classified information or intelligence sources or methods or would jeopardize the security of ongoing intelligence operations, the Agency shall report the matter to the AAG or designated Deputy AAG, Criminal Division. A copy of that report must also be provided to the Assistant Director, Criminal Investigations or National Security

Divisions, Federal Bureau of Investigation, or in the event that the principal investigative responsibility resides with a different federal investigative agency, to an appropriately cleared person of equivalent position in such agency. The Agency's report should explain the security or operational problems that would or might arise from a criminal investigation or prosecution.

D. Written documents associated with the reports submitted pursuant to this section may refer to persons who are the subjects of the reports by non-identifying terms (such as "John Doe # ____"). The Agency shall advise the Department of Justice or relevant federal investigative agency of the true identities of such persons if so requested.

E. It is agreed that, in acting upon information reported in accordance with these procedures, the Agency, the Department of Justice and the relevant federal investigative agencies will deal with classified information, including sources and methods, in a manner consistent with the provisions of relevant statutes and Executive Orders, including the Classified Information Procedures Act.

IX. When Routine Dissemination May be Used in Lieu Of A Special Crimes Report

A. Except as set forth in IX.B, below, the Agency may report crimes information regarding non-employees to the Department of Justice by routine dissemination, provided that:

1. the crimes information is of the type that is routinely disseminated by the Agency to headquarters elements of cognizant federal investigative agencies;

2. the criminal activity is of a kind that is normally collected and disseminated to law enforcement by the Agency (e.g., drug trafficking, money laundering, terrorism, or sanctions violations); and

3. the persons or entities involved are members of a class that are routinely the targets or objects of such collection and dissemination.

If all three of these conditions are met, the Agency may satisfy its crimes reporting obligation through routine dissemination to the Department of Justice, Criminal Division, and to all cognizant federal law enforcement agencies, which shall retain primary responsibility for review of disseminated information for evidence of criminal activity. In all other cases, the special reporting procedures in Section VIII shall apply. As requested by the Department of Justice, the Agency will coordinate with the Department to facilitate the Department's analytical capabilities as to the Agency's routine dissemination of crimes information in compliance with this MOU.

B. Routine dissemination, as discussed in IX.A, above, may not be used in lieu of the special reporting requirements set forth herein as to the following categories of criminal activities:

1. Certain crimes involving the intentional infliction or threat of death or serious physical harm (VII.A.1, above);
2. Espionage; sabotage; unauthorized disclosure of classified information; and seditious conspiracies to overthrow the government of the United States (VII.A.2.a, above); and
3. Certain crimes involving foreign interference with the integrity of U.S. governmental institutions or processes (VII.A.3.b and c, above).

X. Other Agency Responsibilities

A. The Agency shall develop internal procedures in accordance with the provisions of Sections VIII and IX for the reporting of criminal information by its employees as required under Sections IV.A and VI.A.
B. The Agency shall also establish initial and continuing training to ensure that its employees engaged in the review and analysis of collected intelligence are knowledgeable of and in compliance with the provisions of this MOU.

XI. Relation to Other Procedures and Agreements

A. If the Agency desires, for administrative or security reasons, to conduct a more extensive investigation into the activities of an employee relating to any matter reported pursuant to this MOU, it will inform the Department of Justice and the federal investigative agency to which the matter was reported. The Agency may also take appropriate administrative, disciplinary, or other adverse action at any time against any employee whose activities are reported under these procedures. However, such investigations or adverse actions shall be coordinated with the proper investigative or prosecuting officials to avoid prejudice to any criminal investigation or prosecution.
B. Nothing in these procedures shall be construed to restrict the exchange of information among the Agencies in the Intelligence Community or between those Agencies and law enforcement entities other than the Department of Justice.
C. This MOU supersedes all prior crimes reporting memoranda of understanding executed pursuant to the requirements of E.O. 12333. To the extent that there exist any conflicts between other Agency policies of directives and the provisions herein, such conflicts shall be resolved in accordance with the provisions of this MOU. However, this MOU shall not be construed to modify in any way the August 1984 Memorandum of

Understanding between the Department of Defense and the Department of Justice relating to the investigation and prosecution of certain crimes.

D. The parties understand and agree that nothing herein shall be construed to alter in any way the current routine dissemination by the Agency of intelligence information, including information regarding alleged criminal activities by any person, to the Department of Justice or to federal law enforcement agencies.

XII. Miscellaneous

A. This MOU shall become effective as to each agency below as of the date signed by the listed representative of that agency.

B. The Intelligence-Law Enforcement Policy Board, within one year of the date of the effective date hereof, and as it deems appropriate thereafter, will appoint a working group consisting of an equal number of representatives from the intelligence and law enforcement communities, including the Criminal Division. That working group shall do the following:

1. review the Agency's implementation of Sections III.F and IV.B, hereof;

2. consider whether the crimes reporting requirements of E.O. 12333 and other authorities are being met through the operation of this MOU;

3. review each of the provisions of this MOU and determine what, if any, modifications thereof should be recommended to the Policy Board, or its successor; and

4. issue a report to the Policy Board of its finding and recommendations in each of the foregoing categories.

C. The Policy Board in turn shall make recommendations to the Attorney General, the Director of Central Intelligence, and the heads of the affected agencies concerning any modifications to the MOU that it considers necessary.

-/S/-Janet Reno
Attorney General
Date: August 3, 1995

-/S/-William J. Perry
Secretary of Defense
Date: 11 AUG 1995

-/S/-John Deutch
Director of Central Intelligence
Date: 3 August 1995

-/S/-JM McConnell
Director, National Security Agency
Date: 22 Aug 1995

-/S/-Michael F. Munson
Director, Defense Intelligence
Intelligence Agency
Date: 2 Aug 1995

-/S/-Toby T. Gati
Assistant Secretary of State,
Intelligence and Research
Date: 8/14/95

-/S/-Kenneth E. Baker
Director, Office Of Non-Proliferation
and National Security,
Department of Energy
Date: 15 Aug 95

INTELLIGENCE COMMUNITY AND GOVERNMENT WEBSITES

OFFICE OF THE DIRECTOR OF NATIONAL INTELLIGENCE: www.dni.gov
   NATIONAL COUNTERTERRORISM CENTER: www.nctc.gov
   NATIONAL COUNTER INTELLIGENCE EXECUTIVE: www.ncix.gov
   PROGRAM MANAGER, INFORMATION SHARING ENVIRONMENT: www.ise.gov
   OPEN SOURCE CENTER: www.opensource.gov
   INTELLIGENCE COMMUNITY LEGAL REFERENCE BOOK: www.dni.gov/ogc

CENTRAL INTELLIGENCE AGENCY: www.cia.gov

NATIONAL SECURITY AGENCY: www.nsa.gov

DEFENSE INTELLIGENCE AGENCY: www.dia.mil

NATIONAL GEOSPATIAL-INTELLIGENCE AGENCY: www.nga.mil

NATIONAL RECONNAISSANCE OFFICE: www.nro.gov

DEPARTMENT OF DEFENSE: www.defenselink.mil; www.defense.gov
   ARMY: www.army.mil
      INSCOM: www.inscom.army.mil
   NAVY: www.navy.mil
      ONI: www.nmic.navy.mil
      NCIS: www.ncis.navy.mil
   MARINE CORP: www.marines.mil
      USMC INTELLIGENCE: hqinet001.hqmc.usmc.mil/DirInt/default.html
   AIR FORCE: www.af.mil
      AF ISR AGENCY: www.afisr.af.mil

DEPARTMENT OF JUSTICE: www.usdoj.gov
   FBI: www.fbi.gov
   DEA: www.dea.gov
   OLC: www.usdoj.gov/olc
   NSD: www.usdoj.gov/nsd

DEPARTMENT OF STATE: www.state.gov

DEPARTMENT OF TREASURY: www.ustreas.gov

DEPARTMENT OF HOMELAND SECURITY: www.dhs.gov
    COAST GUARD: www.uscg.mil
    Homeland Security Digital Library: www.hsdl.org

DEPARTMENT OF ENERGY: www.energy.gov

WHITE HOUSE: www.whitehouse.gov

U.S. SENATE: www.senate.gov
    SELECT COMMITTEE ON INTELLIGENCE: intelligence.senate.gov
    JUDICIARY COMMITTEE: judiciary.senate.gov
    ARMED SERVICES COMMITTEE: armed-services.senate.gov
    FOREIGN RELATIONS COMMITTEE: foreign.senate.gov
    HOMELAND SECURITY & GOVERNMENTAL AFFAIRS COMMITTEE:
        hsgac.senate.gov/public

U.S. HOUSE OF REPRESENTATIVES: www.house.gov
    PERMANENT SELECT COMMITTEE ON INTELLIGENCE: intelligence.house.gov
    JUDICIARY COMMITTEE: judiciary.house.gov
    ARMED SERVICES COMMITTEE: armedservices.house.gov
    FOREIGN AFFAIRS: foreignaffairs.house.gov
    HOMELAND SECURITY: homeland.house.gov
    OVERSIGHT & GOVERNMENT REFORM: oversight.house.gov

LIBRARY OF CONGRESS: www.loc.gov
    THOMAS: thomas.loc.gov